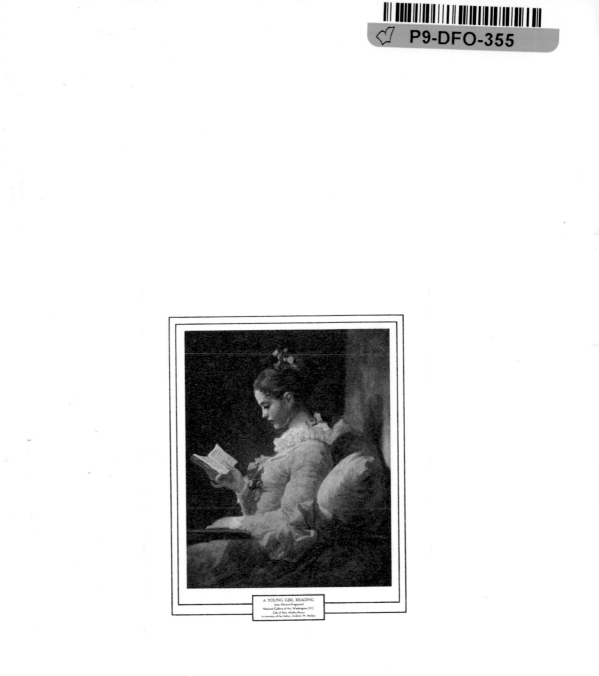

A YOUNG GIRL READING
Jean-Honoré Fragonard
National Gallery of Art, Washington, D.C.
Gift of Mrs. Mellon Bruce
in memory of her father, Andrew W. Mellon

Top Management Planning

STUDIES OF THE MODERN CORPORATION

Columbia University, Graduate School of Business

Francis Joseph Aguilar, *Scanning the Business Environment*

Herman W. Bevis, *Corporate Financial Reporting in a Competitive Economy*

Richard Eells, *The Corporation and the Arts*

Richard Eells and Clarence Walton, *Man in the City of the Future*

Jay W. Lorsch, *Product Innovation and Organization*

Kenneth G. Patrick and Richard Eells, *Education and the Business Dollar*

Irving Pfeffer, *The Financing of Small Business*

George A. Steiner, *Top Management Planning*

George A. Steiner and Warren M. Cannon, *Multinational Corporate Planning*

George A. Steiner and William G. Ryan, *Industrial Project Management*

Gus Tyler, *The Political Imperative*

Clarence Walton and Richard Eells, *The Business System* (3 volumes)

Top Management Planning

by GEORGE A. STEINER

THE MACMILLAN COMPANY
AN ARKVILLE PRESS BOOK

MACMILLAN PUBLISHING CO., INC.
NEW YORK
COLLIER MACMILLAN PUBLISHERS
LONDON

49627

Macmillan Publishing Co., Inc.
866 Third Avenue, New York, New York 10022

Collier-Macmillan Canada Ltd.

Library of Congress Catalog Card Number: 69-17783

printing number
12   13   14   15   16   17   18   19   20

This book is dedicated to
my son
John Frederick Steiner

STUDIES OF THE
MODERN CORPORATION

Columbia University, Graduate School of Business

The Program for Studies of the Modern Corporation is devoted to the advancement and dissemination of knowledge about the corporation. Its publications are designed to stimulate inquiry, research, criticism, and reflection. They fall into four categories: works by outstanding businessmen, scholars, and professional men from a variety of backgrounds and academic disciplines; prizewinning doctoral dissertations relating to the corporation; annotated and edited selections of business literature; and business classics that merit republication. The studies are supported by outside grants from private business, professional, and philanthropic institutions interested in the program's objectives.

Richard Eells

Preface

It is traditional for an author to state at the outset just why he has written his book, especially one as long as this. I have no hesitancy in saying that this book was written because I wanted to write it. In 1954 I had the privilege of participating in the development of a comprehensive corporate planning program at the Lockheed Aircraft Corporation, where I was the Senior Economist. This new type of planning program was to become of ever-increasing importance to the success of business firms in the following decade. I have watched with deep interest and fascination the worldwide sweep of comprehensive corporate planning, and this book is a report of my observations about the past, present, and future of this new phenomenon.

In this book I wish to record my view of the importance of effective and efficient comprehensive corporate planning to business success. Indeed, I feel that the major requisites to successful management are a first-rate planning system, charisma, and a sense of competitive urgency. This is especially true for top management. This book deals principally with the first of these requirements, although it touches on the others and therefore examines a major element in the success of every enterprise.

During the past ten years the rapid expansion of comprehensive corporate planning has been matched only by the great dynamism with which new techniques, methods, and approaches have been injected into it. This still continues. While change is and will be rapid, I think there is a certain amount of stability developing in the subject that makes an assessment timely.

My objectives in making this assessment may justify this book, if any justification is needed, because I have sought to rectify two major deficiencies that seem to me to exist in current books on the subject, as insightful and valuable as many of them are. First, they are not complete. They cover only part of the comprehensive planning discipline. Although the present book does not delve into every nook and cranny of the subject matter, I have tried to be reasonably comprehensive in coverage. Second, most current books on long-range planning do not describe the methodology sufficiently to permit a manager who wants to improve the process in his firm to do so with reasonable ease. One of the reasons for the length of this book grows out of the attempt to meet these two needs.

There are certain other characteristics which I sought for this work that should be mentioned in this prefatory statement. The major focus is from top management's point of view. Although this subject has not been sufficiently explored, we are beginning to understand that there is such a thing as top management work, with its own specification of tasks that are not necessarily the same as those of lower-level managers. Of special concern to top management is the net effect, the overall result, of the business. To achieve the overall desired results requires a special type of knowledge, special information, special skills, and special methods of carrying out decisions. The corporate planning program is a fundamental vehicle for permitting top managers to discharge properly their major responsibility to achieve the desired total effect. Clearly, the planning system embraces every aspect of a business at all levels of management, but the view in this book is from top management down. What is of importance to top management is included; what is of lesser importance, or is unimportant, is treated lightly or excluded. The emphasis, therefore, is on strategic planning and not tactical planning, both for the corporation as a whole as well as in major functional parts.

The focus of attention is on the problems of top managers in developing and maintaining better comprehensive planning systems, and the preferred solutions to these problems. The type of problems in mind are those associated with organization; the use of different techniques for decision-making; the semantics of planning; fitting known principles and practices to particular company characteristics, men, and methods; and assuring maximum benefit from planning with minimum resource input.

I have tried to make it easy for both the busy top executive, as well as the casual reader, to get a quick overview of the contents and essence of this book by presenting at the beginning of each chapter a short introductory statement of content, and at the end a concluding summary and guidelines for action.

A major problem in coming to grips with comprehensive corporate planning is semantic. In 1773 Lord Chief Justice William Mansfield observed, "Most of the disputes in the world arise from words." Granting that this is not entirely true in planning (disputes also arise from other causes), there is no question about the semantic entanglement that exists. I find a great interest in definitions of terms associated with planning both in industry and in educational institutions. The reason is that there is growing recognition of the problems that arise because of differences in definition and usage. In this book we shall look carefully at definitions of elements of the planning process. The purpose is not to seek any final definitions that can be cast in bronze for all to accept. That is impossible. The purpose, rather, is to try to clarify basic meanings so as to give the reader a deeper understanding of the fundamental structure and process of corporate planning. This seems to me to be more important than to try to hawk simple or even complex definitions as final.

This book emphasizes current preferred methods to organize for, and undertake, comprehensive corporate planning. This is not to say that what is being done today is necessarily the best. But a great many current principles and practices have brought business success, and those which appear today to have continuing value are therefore highlighted.

It is my conviction that a manager need not be an expert in every discipline touching upon the planning program. But I do feel that it is incumbent upon each manager to identify those major elements, methods, and practices of disciplines that affect his planning and to have at least a conceptual understanding, as compared with a specialist's knowledge, of them. In this light, the discussion in this book is directed at facilitating a conceptual understanding of the major elements involved in top management planning.

Included with what I hope is an appropriate emphasis are newer quantitative tools for planning, recent conclusions of behavioral scientists applicable to planning, and the profile of future horizons for planning. In planning, as in cookery, the art consists in taking the old, mixing it with the new, and creatively achieving a better product. I have tried to balance the old with the new and the yet-to-be.

To follow the gastronomic analogy, one key to the art of cookery is not to overdo things. This is also true in planning and, although I have had to be complete in my expositions, I do hope I have emphasized enough the need for planning to be flexible, adaptive, and not too finished in all details.

Quite frankly, I have written this book with the hope that it will be valuable to both practitioners and students of planning. Although comprehensive corporate planning has spread very rapidly in the United States, I find in my discussions with executives and their staffs an unease about their planning programs and an intense interest in improving them. Outside the United States I find a situation comparable to that in the United States about a decade ago. More and more businesses seem ready to expand rapidly their formal comprehensive planning. To these practitioners I hope this book is useful.

The field of corporate planning is so broad that no one book is likely to serve as a single text in a course in educational institutions; however, I hope this book may come close to filling this need. At least, I visualize this book as a basic reference that might be combined with selected readings to round out a course of special interest to an instructor and his students.

Part I of the book is concerned with the basic nature of planning, conceptual and operational models of comprehensive corporate planning, the importance of comprehensive planning in a business, and the critically important role of top management in assuring its success.

Part II is concerned with the process of developing plans. Included are detailed discussions of both the process and structure of comprehensive corporate planning. Emphasis is given to the nature and development of objectives and strategies, and the way in which they are translated into current operational plans.

Part III discusses the nature of rational decision-making and describes the basic tools and methods at the disposal of management in making planning decisions. The tools examined range from creativity and innovation to some of the more important newer quantitative tools that are useful in top management planning. An effort is made here to provide a balanced view of both quantitative and qualitative tools and their significance to and usage in the planning process.

Part IV deals with planning in major selected functional areas. Planning subject matter in each of the major functional areas is far wider than can be encompassed in this book. The subject matter, therefore, is highly selective in each case.

Finally, Part IV presents major pitfalls that exist in actual corporate planning, important areas for further research, and trends to be expected in corporate planning.

By presenting a balanced appraisal of what might tentatively be called the state of the art of corporate planning, I hope I have made some contribution to thinking on the subject. Cellist Gregor Piatigorsky tells the story of his great wish when a young man to hear in person the unexcelled Pablo Casals. But, instead of listening, he found himself performing before the master. "Casals asked Rudolf Serkin and me to play a Beethoven sonata," writes Piatigorsky. "Both nervous, we gave a poor performance that ended somewhere in the middle. 'Bravo! Wonderful!' Casals applauded. Then he wanted to hear Schumann and Bach. I never played worse. 'Splendid! *Magnifique!*' said Casals, embracing me.

"Bewildered, I left. I knew how badly I had played. Why did he, the master, have to praise and embrace me?

"A few years later, I met Casals in Paris. We had dinner together and played duets. Spurred by his great warmth, I confessed what I had thought of his praising me. Angry, he rushed to the cello. 'Listen!' he played a phrase from the Beethoven sonata. 'Didn't you play this fingering? It was novel to me —it was good. And here, didn't you attack that passage with up-bow, like this?' He went through Schumann and Bach, emphasizing all he liked that I had done.

"'And for the rest,' he said passionately, 'leave it to the ignorant and stupid, who judge by counting only the faults. I can be grateful, and so must you be, for even one note, one wonderful phrase.'" (Piatigorsky, 1965, p. 128.)

I do not want to imply too much from this charming story. I want only to say that my intention has been to improve the art and science of business planning, and I hope those who have occasion to dip into this book will find in it something that is new and novel to them that will help them in their practice and understanding of the marvelous new discipline of comprehensive corporate planning.

As is usual with a book of this nature, the debts of the author are far beyond the numbers that can be reasonably acknowledged in a prefatory note. But some must be mentioned. It is my pleasure to thank with gratitude the support of the McKinsey Foundation for Management Research, Inc., which has been helpful in the completion of this book. Warren Cannon, its President, has been more encouraging than he knows. A major debt I owe to many friends who are in top management positions or who are corporate planners. All of them have been helpful in different ways. This is in many ways their book. My many colleagues who are scholars of management in general and of planning in particular naturally were of great help to me, a fact which I have tried to recognize in my many references to their writings.

Professor Richard Goodman of UCLA and Professor Jack Hayya of Pennsylvania State College were helpful in the development of Chapter 15. I gladly express my thanks and indebtedness to Misses Marcy Fortier, Marilyn McElroy, and Mary McMurray; Mrs. Joy Hudspeth and Mrs. Annabelle Robbins; Messrs. William James and Henry Rath, for typing and editorial assistance in the preparation of this manuscript. I am obliged, also, to Messrs. Dick Sakahara and Bill Keeney for drafting the many charts for this book. The usual caveat must be added, of course, that shortcomings of and errors in this work are mine alone.

G. A. S.

Los Angeles

Contents—An Overview

Analytical Contents

Top Management Planning

PART I

Nature and Concept of Business Planning

1
The Nature of Business Planning and Plans

1
The Nature
of Business Planning
and Plans

INTRODUCTION

In this introductory chapter the fundamental definitions and concepts of planning and plans are set forth as a basis for all that follows in the remainder of the book. Basic definitions of planning, plans, comprehensive business planning, and some elements of planning, are set forth. To give the reader perspective in dealing with the enormous scope of planning, different dimensions of planning in general, and in business in particular, are identified and discussed. Special attention is given to the time dimension in planning. The basic reasons for the dramatic increase in the use of formal corporate planning in recent years are given. Finally, the dynamic nature of business planning is noted.

AN INTRODUCTORY NOTE ON DEFINITIONS

Confucius is reputed to have said that if he were made ruler of the world the first thing he would do would be to fix the meaning of words, because action follows definitions. It would be helpful to both scholars and practitioners of planning if business planning and plans could be described in a way that would be accepted by everyone. Today, there is no generally accepted meaning of planning and plans. Even if a Confucius were made ruler of the world it is doubtful that he could fix a meaning for these terms that would be received as the one and only definition.

It comes from the Latin *planum*, meaning flat surface. The word planning entered the English language, according to the Oxford Dictionary, sometime in the 17th century and referred principally to drawing a form on a flat surface, such as a map or blueprint. Today, the word planning encompasses such a broad scope of human activity that any simple definition is insufficient to convey its full meaning.

Furthermore, there are important differences of definition in both the technical and popular literature on planning. In this and later chapters attention will be given to some of the more important ones. At the outset, however, it seems more appropriate to present my definition of corporate planning, since this is the subject of this book, than to get entangled in semantic squabbles. Although the definitions and descriptions presented in this chapter will not be universally accepted, I think they represent a rather broad consensus in today's planning literature.

COMPREHENSIVE BUSINESS PLANNING

In recent years the words long-range planning have been used to describe a type of planning characteristically done in more and more companies, and different from that generally practiced before World War II. For a variety of reasons discussed later, the use of the words "long-range planning" to describe this planning is gradually being replaced by such words as corporate planning, total planning, over-all planning, and comprehensive planning. I prefer the latter and define it as follows.

Comprehensive business planning must be considered from four points of view, each and all of which are necessary to a complete understanding of its nature. They are: the basic generic nature of planning, the process, the philosophy, and the structure.

GENERIC NATURE OF PLANNING. The generic nature of planning refers to its general, universal, or common characteristics. Fundamentally, all planning is concerned with the future. This can mean, for instance, that planning deals with the futurity of present decisions. This, in turn, can mean one of two things, or both. Planning examines future alternative courses of action which are open to a company. In choosing from among these courses of action an umbrella, a perspective, a frame of reference is established for current decisions. Also it can mean that planning examines the evolving chains of cause and effect likely to result from current decisions. Planning is reasoning about how a business will get where it wants to go. Indeed, a basic task of comprehensive planning is to visualize the business as the managers wish it to be in the future. Planning inherently involves assessing the future and making provision for it. The essence of planning is to see opportunities and threats in the future and, respectively, exploit or combat them as the case may be.

PROCESS. Planning is a process which begins with objectives; defines strategies, policies, and detailed plans to achieve them; which establishes an organization to implement decisions; and includes a review of performance and feed-back to introduce a new planning cycle. This is close to Secretary of Defense McNamara's definition that planning is simply a systematic appraisal and formulation of your objectives and of the actions that you believe necessary to achieve those objectives. A somewhat different, yet comparable, definition is that of Peter Drucker (1959a, p. 240), who wrote that (long-range) planning ". . . is the continuous process of making present entrepreneurial (risk taking) decisions systematically and with the best possible knowledge of their futurity, organizing systematically the efforts needed to carry out these decisions, and measuring the results of these decisions against the expectations through organized, systematic feed-back." As a process, planning may be defined as deciding in advance what is to be done, when it is to be done, how it is to be done, and who is to do it.

Planning is also a continuous process, because changes in business environment are continuous. This is especially true of strategic planning but applies also to the assurance that plans once made be flexibly administered. The idea here is not that plans must be changed every day but only that thought about planning must be continuous and supported by appropriate action. From another point of view planning must be continuous because commitments once made become liquid over a stream of time. Income from past commitments flows continuously and requires, therefore, constant thought about its employment.

Finally, as Robert McNamara and Peter Drucker pointed out in the above definitions, the process is a systematic one. It is organized and conducted on the basis of an understood regularity.

PHILOSOPHY. Planning is a philosophy, not so much in the literal sense of that word but as an attitude, a way of life. Planning necessitates a dedication to acting on the basis of contemplation of the future, a determination to plan constantly and systematically as an integral part of management. Ralph M. Besse, former Chairman of the Board of the Cleveland Electric Illuminating Company, said (1957, p. 47): "The first step toward adequate planning is the establishment of a planning climate." He meant that throughout the company there had to be an acceptance of ". . . planning, *per se,* and as such . . . an identifiable, controllable function essential to the health of the enterprise."

STRUCTURE. Comprehensive business planning is reflected in a structure of plans. This can be expressed in several different ways. First, it includes a reasonably complete and uniform set of plans for the entire business reaching out over an extended period of time. It is an integrated framework within which each of the functional plans is interlinked and all are tied together into an over-all plan for the entire business. Diagrammatically, it would appear, as Kirby Warren says

(1962, pp. 11-12) ". . . as a vast cobweb of short-term and long-term interrelationships between marketing, production, finance, industrial relations, executive development, and all the rest. All of these plans are built on certain assumptions, and the individual plans in turn become premises and assumptions for each other." But, as I have pointed out elsewhere (1963a, p. 112), "It should be recognized that life is so complicated that it is impossible to tie together all plans into a complete coordinated set of relationships. The further out in time, the less detail is appropriate and the looser are the relationships among parts of the planning program. In developing current operational plans, tighter relationships are possible and desirable."

Viewed in another way, comprehensive business planning is composed of structural blocks of plans. The three principal ones are strategic plans, medium-range programs, and short-range detailed plans and budgets. All these are interrelated and each has characteristics which distinguish it from the others. Most of Chapter 2 is devoted to an examination of both conceptual and operational models incorporating these structural blocks.

PLANNING VERSUS PLANS

While the words are similar and interrelated, there is a fundamental difference between planning and plans. Planning is a basic organic function of management. It is a mental process of thinking through what is desired and how it will be achieved. A plan, noted J. O. McKinsey (1932, p. 9) many years ago, is "the tangible evidence of the thinking of the management." It results from planning. Plans are commitments to specific courses of action growing out of the mental process of planning. The planning process need not necessarily result in written plans; plans can be unwritten or expressed orally.

This distinction may appear pedantic, but it is not. Some managers have gone through the mental process of planning and concluded they were discharging their responsibilities even though no concrete plans resulted. Inherent in the planning process is the rigorous obligation to come to a specific action to be taken today. Planning without plans is a waste of time. Some managers who reject the value of planning have been guilty of precisely this sin.

The process of planning engenders flexibility in the implementation of plans. As Branch (1962, p. 39) puts it: "If a business concern is not mindful of [the difference between planning and plans] . . . it is likely to establish a spurious form of corporate planning which invites disappointment. A one-time, static plan cannot solve continuous planning problems. Some companies have developed plans which defined a sound program for a particular period of time, for certain objectives, or subject to conditions remaining constant. Since time, tide, and specific objectives do not remain constant, these companies are disillusioned when they find themselves in difficulties soon after the effectuation of the plans or even before their completion. What has occurred in each case, of course, is that conditions have changed to such an extent that the plan is no longer relevant and acts as a hindrance rather than a help. Unless the planning process itself is the cardinal emphasis and plans are ancillary to it, the business will derive temporary benefit at best. Corporate planning is therefore never static. It adjusts as need be to changing conditions and goals. Fixed commitments to a given objective, procedure, or over-all blueprint of action for extended periods of time are undertaken only when they have been carefully evaluated as desirable."

So important is the idea examined here that it deserves an additional comment. Paul Pearson, Corporate Planning Director of Celanese, makes the point this way (1966, p. 6): "If we have established realistic long-term objectives and strategy, and have backed them up with well thought out shorter-range plans for implementation, then we have done much to anticipate the unforeseen—and have reduced the potential need for any change in our plans. But since the world we live in is becoming increasingly complex, we must always be prepared to adapt to the unforeseen. This is the essential and basic value of good planning; if we have determined in advance where we want to go, what we want to do and how we are going to do it, then we can more clearly recognize the need for improved tactics if the original plan is not on schedule. And, equally important, we can more readily recognize an unforeseen opportunity for what it is worth in terms of our long-range goals."

Planning not only provides the basis for plans, but the foundation from which plans can be flexibly implemented. Planning improves the thought processes that make flexible implementation easier and better.

THE WORLD OF PLANNING

Before examining different types of business plans and their characteristics it is useful to consider briefly the universe of planning. As shown in Chart 1-1, planning can be considered, at one end of a broad spectrum, as being concerned with nations and systems. At this end one may speak, for example, of national and international political, economic, or social systems planning. The European Common Market Charter signed in Rome in 1958, for example, is an international plan which involves large political, economic, and social systems.

Of lesser scope are plans covering a single nation. In recent years five-year national economic plans have become popular in many countries of the world. National plans may cover the entire country or only segments of it, such as a plan in the U.S. to stimulate economic activity by a tax cut, or a plan to expand medical care to a wider segment of the population, or a plan to eliminate pockets of poverty.

Chart 1-1

The Universe of Planning and Plans

Illustrative Definitions and Plans of Varying Scope

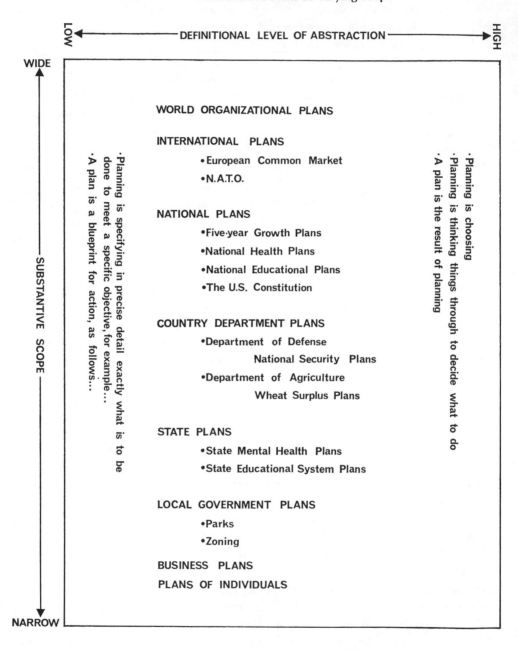

LOW ←——————— DEFINITIONAL LEVEL OF ABSTRACTION ———————→ HIGH

WIDE

SUBSTANTIVE SCOPE

NARROW

·Planning is specifying in precise detail exactly what is to be done to meet a specific objective, for example....

·A plan is a blueprint for action, as follows....

·Planning is choosing
·Planning is thinking things through to decide what to do
·A plan is the result of planning

WORLD ORGANIZATIONAL PLANS

INTERNATIONAL PLANS
- European Common Market
- N.A.T.O.

NATIONAL PLANS
- Five-year Growth Plans
- National Health Plans
- National Educational Plans
- The U.S. Constitution

COUNTRY DEPARTMENT PLANS
- Department of Defense
  National Security Plans
- Department of Agriculture
  Wheat Surplus Plans

STATE PLANS
- State Mental Health Plans
- State Educational System Plans

LOCAL GOVERNMENT PLANS
- Parks
- Zoning

BUSINESS PLANS

PLANS OF INDIVIDUALS

Further to the right on the spectrum are plans of individual departments of government and government subdivisions. Included, for example, would be plans of the Department of Transportation to solve "the transportation problem" in the northeast corridor from Boston to Washington, D.C., or plans of the Department of Interior to reduce water pollution in a specific region. Here, too, are plans of state and local governments, such as a plan of the State of California to build new universities.

Along this spectrum there next might be considered business plans, which will be treated in some detail shortly.

At the far end of the spectrum are plans of individuals. These range from simple plans to do simple things, such as to go downtown, to complex plans concerning a lifetime career.

The universe of planning is an enormous one. One reason for noting this fact here is that frequently the discussion of planning focuses on one segment of this world without specifying it. One result, sometimes, is that confusion arises because what is correct in one type of planning may be incorrect in another. Furthermore, business planning necessarily reflects and often becomes intermixed with other plans outside business.

Chart 1-1 also looks at the universe of planning in terms of level of abstraction. Anything can be described, of course, at different levels of abstraction. The definition of a pencil by a layman is much different from that by a physicist who views it in molecular terms. Much difficulty in the semantics of planning arises from the level of abstraction at which words are defined and used. At a very high level of abstraction, planning can properly be defined as "a process of developing and applying knowledge and intelligence in our affairs" (Barnard 1948, p. 166). At this high level of abstraction planning is "fundamentally choosing," as Billy E. Goetz says (1949, p. 2). Another view at this level is that of Henri Fayol, one of the first to present a broad conception of business planning, who said planning "means both to assess the future and make provision for it. . . ." (1949, p. 43). This is quite similar to the current view that the essence of long-range planning is systematic examination of the future (Schaffir 1963).

At the other end of the abstraction scale are detailed descriptions of planning and plans in operational terms. James Peirce (Lemke and Edwards 1961, p. 8), for example, sees planning as "the construction of an operating program, comprehensive enough to cover all phases of operations, and detailed enough that specific attention may be given to its fulfillment in controllable segments." At this level, for instance, would be a definition of planning framed in terms of the development of a detailed operational plan to market a new product, or schedule a production program, or build a new plant. In between, of course, will be found a wide variety of definitions concerned with all of planning or parts of it.

Chart 1-2

Five Key Dimensions of Business Planning

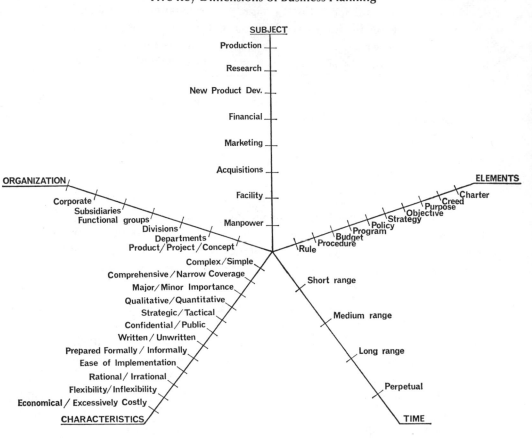

FIVE DIMENSIONS OF PLANNING AND PLANS

In Chart 1-2, five key dimensions of business planning are pictured. The purpose of this chart is to show that planning may be considered from the points of view of the subject of plans, the elements of plans, the time dimension of plans, the organizational unit for which plans are made, and characteristics of plans. Four important observations can be drawn from Chart 1-2.

First, the dimensions classified do not represent an exhaustive list; they are not mutually exclusive, nor are lines of demarcation among them always clear. The distinction, for example, between a short-range and a long-range plan is not always readily apparent. Many problems arise, as will be shown in detail later, in drawing a line of demarcation among some of the elements of planning.

Additions to Chart 1-2 can easily be made not only in terms of items under each of the dimensions presented but also in terms of new dimensions. New dimensions might include size of business, styles of management, management experience with planning, managerial capability, and complexity of product line. Under marketing, further subdivisions might be: market mix, distribution patterns, promotional programs, sales programs, markets for penetration, volume and pricing, customer need fulfillment, and customer service.

Second, the system of business planning and plans is enormously complex. Every one of the dimensions specified in Chart 1-2 is or can be a plan—except possibly the characteristics, which are more traits or qualities of plans. A charter, rule, or procedure, for example, is a plan. A plan can be prepared for a division or a product. A plan can be prepared for total production or for such individual production items as steel forgings. When all the different combinations which are possible from the dimensions presented in Chart 1-2 are considered, it is obvious that the business planning system is indeed intricate and can be considered from many points of view.

Third, when defining or discussing business planning it makes a great deal of difference what dimension of planning and plans is under consideration. What is true about a complex corporate plan for acquiring another company may be untrue for a short-range production rule. Furthermore, the methodology of planning and the techniques used to develop plans in one dimension may be not only inappropriate but actually dangerous when applied to another dimension of planning. To illustrate: top management involvement in the development of a complex corporate plan for acquisition is essential; but, in a medium-size or large corporation the involvement of the chief executive is inappropriate in making a trivial rule involving pennies. Furthermore, a quantitative technique such as a simple dollar alternative cost comparison which could be the sole basis for a minor decision might be dangerous if used as the sole basis for an acquisition.

Finally, it is easy to understand why semantic problems exist in the planning field. As Charts 1-1 and 1-2 are kneaded, a vast range of definitions of planning and plans are moldable. Since definitions of major parts of the planning process will be presented in some detail in later chapters, it is not wise to get further enmeshed in the semantic bramblebush of planning in this introductory chapter.

CAUSES OF EXPANDING
COMPREHENSIVE BUSINESS PLANNING

Men engaged in business have always planned. Throughout history businessmen have been doing both short- and long-range planning. Over the broad sweep of history there have been some dramatic changes in business planning, but none have been more significant than those which have spread through industry during the past fifteen years.

Up to the post-World War II period, business planning in the United States had several characteristics which distinguished it from more recent business planning. The typical manufacturing enterprise was very small compared to today's companies. One hundred years ago, the typical transaction involved very short-range production cycles and very brief time intervals from production planning to actual sale of goods. The average businessman was in a position to react immediately to changing market conditions. Not only could his production swiftly react to changes in demand but his resources were reasonably adaptable to new lines of activity if they seemed more profitable than the one in which he was engaged. Planning was, therefore, largely short-range and geared tightly to current market activities.

When a businessman was engaged in long-range planning, planning probably was intuitive rather than based upon a carefully reasoned and systematic analysis. Although no data exist on the mixture of the two, it is likely that the great bulk of actual planning work was of the short-range operational type.

To be sure, over the past one hundred years companies have grown larger, their fixed capital has been less easy to use for different products, and many did look ahead for long distances. But the theory about and practices of company planning lagged behind developments. Far too many students and practitioners of planning thought in terms of the days of small companies engaged in atomistic competition.

Since the end of World War II, changes in business planning have been as dramatic as any in the entire history of business. They are essentially four in number. First, is the development of comprehensive structured corporate plans, previously defined in this chapter and explained in detail in later chapters. Second, is the widespread creation of planning staffs to help top managers operate formal planning programs. These staffs have been established to help top managers develop comprehensive and well-organized plans on the basis of a specified procedure and produce written plans. The essential characteristics of formal planning are these: plans are prepared on some time cycle on the basis of procedures, are well structured, are comprehensive, are developed by many people in a cooperative effort covering a lengthy time span, and are written. Third, is the development of new and powerful tools and methodological ideas to improve the decision-making process inherent in comprehensive planning. Fourth, is the systematic effort to look much further into the future. The total impact on business life of the meshing of these four forces has been and will continue to be enormous.

Data on formal planning are poor, but there is no doubt about the fact that during the past ten years the growth of planning staffs to help top managers conduct formal planning programs has been nothing short of phenomenal. In 1956 the National Industrial Conference Board reported that only 8 percent of the companies surveyed had one or more persons engaged full time in long-range planning duties. At that time long-range planning was roughly synonymous with the concept of comprehensive planning used here. A few years later *Management*

Methods reported 18 percent of the firms it studied had formulated advanced plans on a formal basis. Another study made in 1962 (Mason, p. 4) reported that less than 20 percent of all U.S. manufacturing companies with annual sales over $10 million had organized planning on a corporate-wide basis. A study made in 1963 (Stanford Research Institute, p. 4) reported that among the 500 largest industrial companies in the U.S., 60 percent had organized, formalized corporate planning programs and another 24 percent intended to develop them. If most of those who said they were going to introduce formal planning actually did so, and I would expect that they did, at least 75 percent of the largest industrial companies in the U.S. today have formally organized comprehensive planning programs. In mid-1966 a survey of 1965 companies revealed that 9 out of 10 said they did long-range planning, as distinguished from annual budgeting (Brown, Sands, and Thompson). A National Planning Association study in 1966 of 420 companies showed that nearly 85 percent said they prepared long-term plans. Half of them prepared plans for only a five-year period, well over half had inaugurated long-term planning since 1960, and about half had planning staffs at top management levels.

A comprehensive and detailed examination of 372 companies in Japan in 1965 (Japan Management Association 1966) showed that 78 percent claimed to have formal, written corporate plans. This percentage, if accurate, as well as that in the U.S., is unquestionably far higher than comparable figures for Western European countries. No surveys have been made to my knowledge of formal planning groups existing in European companies. My own empirical observations, together with discussions with corporate planners and top executives of major companies at a research seminar held at Fontainebleau in 1964, lead me to the conclusion that the very rapid increase during the past two years of seminar discussions, management consulting engagements to introduce formal planning, and articles in European business publications about comprehensive planning, will undoubtedly result in an important growth of comprehensive planning in European companies.

Throughout the world, but particularly in the United States, a number of forces have converged to compel more and more companies to introduce comprehensive corporate planning programs (Steiner 1963b). Some of the major ones are as follows.

First, two formidable restraints on such planning which existed prior to World War II have been removed. A powerful new idea became generally accepted that businesses no longer stood helpless in the face of market forces. A company could, according to this new idea, in the words of Ernest Breech at the time he was Chairman of the Board of the Ford Motor Company, *"make* trends, not . . . follow them."* He went on to say that "With a well-staffed management team in which an aggressive risk-taking spirit is backed up by cool-headed analytical planning, there will be no problem too tough to be solved" (Breech in Bursk and Fenn, Jr., 1956, p. 17*). This is a philosophy that businesses can, to a great degree, determine where they want to go in the future and do things to assure that their objectives are achieved.

The long intellectual heritage that businesses could and should only react to market conditions was buttressed for two centuries before World War II with the certain occurrence of economic booms and busts that came with lamentable unpredictability. The saw-toothed gyrations of economic activity of the past have been replaced in the last 25 years with a remarkable economic stability compared with the past. Although no one is sure this condition will continue into the indefinite future, this experience has created a general impression that with a little luck the U.S. will be able to avoid disastrous fluctuations in the business cycle and commodity prices in the future. A major historical barrier to long-range business planning has thereby been removed.

A second factor is the breath-taking rate of technological change racing throughout all industry. Paracelsus discovered the anesthetic effects of ether, and Valerius Cordus made known the formula for its preparation, but centuries passed before either was used as an anesthetic. In 1714, a patent was granted for a "machine for transcribing and printing letters." The world waited 150 years for Remington, who bought the patents of Latham Scholes, to produce a commercially salable typewriter (Lesher and Howick 1965, p. 47). S. C. Gilfillan (1935, p. 96), after reviewing the life cycles of 19 of the most useful inventions between 1888 and 1913, observed these average intervals: 176 years between conception of invention and patenting of first working machine, 24 more years to the first principal use, 14 more years to commercial success, and 12 more years to important usage. Today's rapid product obsolescence creates a far different cadence for the manager. The Douglas Aircraft Company DC-3, for example, was the leading commercial airliner for about 15 years. The DC-7, a reciprocating engine airplane, and later the Lockheed Aircraft Company's turbo-prop Electra were obsoleted in less than five years by the pure jets—the DC-8 and the Boeing 707. Today, whole new industries are literally being born overnight. The computer and electronics industries are dramatic illustrations.

A third factor is the mounting complexity of the job of managing a business. Businesses are growing in size and diversity. The average sales of the ten largest industrial companies in the U.S. were $3.3 billion in 1954. By 1964 the average was $6.5 billion. The great wave of diversification in recent years has made for a much more heterogenous product mix in American companies. Growth and diversity have taken place in an environment becoming more competitive and complex.

A fourth factor, growing competition, is not easy to quantify and is a matter of controversy which will not be examined here. But the high level of business failures, the speed-up of product obsolescence, and the rapid growth of new industries are conditions which reflect an increase in competition.

A fifth factor is the increasingly complex environment in which business operates. Population changes, rapidly altering consumer tastes, increasingly complex government regulations, labor union activities, and greater community attention to social responsibilities of business are but a few conditions which complicate the managerial job.

A final element may be noted in the lengthening stretch of time which must be examined to make current decisions. Du Pont spent almost $30 million and twelve years' time on the development of nylon before selling one ounce of the fiber at a profit. The airlines today are thinking very carefully about current orders and plans for the use of the supersonic transport; jumbo air transports; and vertical, short take-off, and landing transports which will be available in the next ten to twenty years. They are vitally concerned because, as one airline executive vice president put the matter to me, "We cannot afford to guess wrong. In the past we could miss occasionally on buying the most competitive airplane. But such a large part of our net worth will be committed to the next generation of airplanes that we simply cannot fail to choose the most competitive airplane." Among the most technologically oriented companies today careful thought is being given to the types of technical disciplines which will be needed to keep their product lines competitive ten to fifteen years from now, and how the scientists and engineers needed may be hired and trained.

In sum, what has happened is simply this: for the average company before World War II the development of formal corporate planning was restrained by an intellectual heritage that was at odds with such a concept, and this was buttressed by unpredictable economic change. Since then, various forces not only have facilitated formal planning but have made it mandatory.

WHAT PLANNING IS NOT

Planning is not forecasting. A forecast is a prediction, projection, or estimate of some future event or condition. Forecasts are essential in planning but they are not planning nor plans. For instance, a public utility should make forecasts of population growth in the area it serves. Upon the basis of such forecasts planning can proceed to determine the best alternative courses of action to achieve company objectives. The forecast is a basic premise upon which planning proceeds, but it is not the whole of planning nor is a forecast a plan. To forecast company sales in the future is not to plan. Again, it becomes just one basis for planning. If sales are forecast to be $1 million three years hence, and company objectives are to have sales of $2 million at that time, a problem in planning is apparent.

The one thing that is certain about forecasts for planning is that they will be wrong. In planning, therefore, the effort must be to find the most probable future course of events bearing upon planning and to use that guidance in developing plans. Sophisticated planners know this. They know, too, that the future does not lie somewhere along a straight-line projection.

In actual practice the demarcation between forecasting and planning is sometimes difficult to draw. Take the case in the aerospace industry, for example, where planning is based upon forecasts of future weapons requirements which in turn are based upon, among other things, the technology which a company may be planning to develop. If the company decides it wishes to be in a position to compete favorably for these weapons requirements, and takes current action to get in that position, it is easy to see the intermeshing of forecasting and planning. Their interrelationship, however, must not cloud the fact that they are distinct activities.

Furthermore, as Peter Drucker so well points out (1959a) forecasting attempts to see probable events in the future, but the entrepreneural problem is to innovate and find the unique event that will change the probabilities.

Planning is not making future decisions. Planning is concerned with making current decisions in light of their futurity. Planning is valueless unless it results in current decision. The basic problem of planning is not what should be done in the future but rather what should be done now to make desired things happen in the uncertain future. The problem is, in the words of Peter Drucker (1959a, p. 239), ". . . what futurity do we have to factor into our present thinking and doing, what time spans do we have to consider, and how do we converge them to a simultaneous decision in the present?" Decisions can be made only in the present. Forward planning requires choices among possible events in the future, but decisions made in their light can be made only in the present. Yet, decisions cannot be made only for the present. Once made, the decisions may have long-term irrevocable consequences.

Planning for the future is not an attempt to eliminate risk. This is impossible and to try to do so could be disastrous. The real problem for the manager is to understand the nature of the risks which he faces and then to choose alternative courses of action which will maximize objectives sought, with minimum risk.

Planning is not a blueprint for the future. One of the expressions used as a synonym for comprehensive corporate planning is master planning. This label connotes for business planning the blue-print character of much land development and municipal planning. Business planning should be dominated by a flexibility to alter current decisions over time so as to take advantage of changes in the business and its environment.

Comprehensive corporate planning is not an aggregation of functional plans. It is truly a systems approach to maneuvering the enterprise over time through the uncertain waters of its environment to achieve prescribed aims.

SELECTED CHARACTERISTICS OF
BUSINESS PLANNING

The characteristics of business planning shown in Chart 1-2 should now be discussed. Since most of them will be directly or indirectly elaborated later in this book, the treatment here will be brief.

COMPLEX VERSUS SIMPLE. A plan to replace an obsolete machine with a modern one of the same type, a plan to dispose of obsolete inventory, or a plan to merge two small departments, are simple plans. Complex plans are illustrated by the comprehensive plans of a large corporation where headquarters' strategic plans are used as a basis for the preparation of ten-year divisional plans, and the two are integrated.

COMPREHENSIVE VERSUS NARROW COVERAGE. The broader the coverage of a plan, in terms of organization and subject matter, the more comprehensive it is. A corporate plan for profit growth would be comprehensive whereas a plan to work off a backlog of orders during the next month would not be.

MAJOR VERSUS MINOR IMPORTANCE. This is self-explanatory. A plan to merge with another corporation would be of major importance whereas a plan to hire two new file clerks would not be.

QUALITATIVE VERSUS QUANTITATIVE. An approved formula for replenishing inventory would be completely quantitative. Very few business plans are wholly quantitative. The higher in a business organization plans are prepared, the greater tends to be the significance of qualitative considerations.

STRATEGIC VERSUS TACTICAL. Strategic plans are those having major importance in deploying resources. Tactical plans are made for the minor deployment of resources. These two terms will be given a searching examination in a later chapter.

CONFIDENTIAL VERSUS PUBLIC. A confidential plan would, of course, be proprietary in a company and even within a company might be known to only a few managers. Very few plans of businesses are made public. But company creeds, however, are made public. Indeed, they are often designed to be public relations documents.

WRITTEN VERSUS UNWRITTEN. Actually a large part of planning does not result in written plans. Plans that are written contain only that which is necessary to understand what the plans are. As Chester Barnard (1948, p. 166) observes: "The greater part of a complete plan is unexpressed thought (intention), implied or assumed action not stated, and the materials or 'givens' of the situation to which it relates, much of which is also not made explicit. These are all essential parts of a plan."

PREPARED FORMALLY VERSUS INFORMALLY. Today more than ever before business plans are prepared on the basis of prescribed procedures. Such plans are said to be prepared formally. Informal plans are developed without following such prescribed methodology. As we shall see in a later chapter, strategic plans tend to be prepared more on an informal basis and tactical plans tend to be prepared on a more formal basis. A distinction can be drawn between a formal and an explicit plan. The formal plan can be considered the written plan and the explicit plan can be considered the written plan as well as the unwritten parts of it which are essential to the plan as described above.

EASE OF IMPLEMENTATION. Some plans are easy to implement, such as a decision to build a simple facility. Some plans are difficult to implement, such as those concerning the research and development of a new product. The plan to develop the supersonic transport is a good illustration of one that will be difficult to carry out. Irrespective of ease of implementation, assuming that a plan is a sound one, plans should be as free as possible of ambiguities and should avoid unnecessary complications which make implementation more difficult than necessary.

RATIONAL VERSUS IRRATIONAL. Plans can and should be to the fullest possible extent objective, factual, logical, and realistic in establishing objectives and devising means to attain them. Sewell Avery's plan to husband the cash of Montgomery Ward while awaiting a major economic depression was based upon a very unrealistic appraisal of likely events. As a result Montgomery Ward built up its cash rather than expand and saw its share of the market drop from 40 percent in 1942 to 28 percent in 1952. Managers should try to eliminate distorted biases so as to make plans as unprejudiced as possible. There is no substitute for facts and logic in developing effective plans. But, as will be examined in Chapter 12, what is rational and what is irrational is not always easy to determine, for what is rational to one man may be irrational to another.

FLEXIBILITY VERSUS INFLEXIBILITY. A flexible plan is one that can be adjusted smoothly and quickly to the requirements of changing conditions without serious loss of efficiency or effectiveness. (I use the word efficiency in this context to refer to optimum relationships between input and output, and effectiveness to mean the accomplishment of a specific desired end result.) A comparatively inflexible plan is a fixed rule or procedure. But all business plans should be implemented with flexibility. There are many ways to do this as will be shown in later chapters.

ECONOMICAL VERSUS EXCESSIVELY COSTLY. Unless attention is given to cost, plans can become excessively expensive. There are so many places and occasions in the planning process when costs can exceed benefits that management must constantly be on the alert to see that the expense of planning is exceeded by its benefits. If environmental studies, for example, are not carefully defined in scope their costs can easily outweigh results. Throughout the planning process, management must apply cost-benefit analysis. Overall benefits of planning must also be related to costs. It is more the attention to this concept that is in mind than a rigorous effort to quantify benefits and costs.

There are many other characteristics of planning and plans, as noted above. Except for time, which will now be discussed at some length, the others will be examined at various places throughout the book.

THE TIME DIMENSION IN PLANNING

The lengthening time spans of business resource commitments is one of the more important features of today's society. Weyerhaeuser is planning tree growth from 50 to 75 years in the future. The U.S. Steel Corporation has just completed a survey of how much iron ore it will need in the year 2000. Upon the basis of these projections current commitments having long-range implications will be made.

Two different types of future planning activities must be discerned. First, are long-range projections which become premises in the planning process. Second, are actual plans laid down for specific periods of time. In industry today it is not at all unusual to find long-range projections of economic environment, customer demand for products, or new technology of interest to a company, extending 10 to 20 or more years in the future. Nor is it unusual to find long-range objectives set for 10 years into the future. It is very unusual, however, to find detailed plans extending much beyond five years. To put it another way, it is not exceptional to find strategic plans to achieve specified sales, profits, and market shares, 10 or more years in the future. But operational plans to achieve these objectives are not frequently found for more than five years ahead.

There is great variation in the length of forecasts made for plans not only among different types of decisions but among companies in the same industry. In Table 1-1 Judith Malott (1957) gives a tabulation of forecast periods which company presidents some years ago said were necessary in making plans and decisions in specified areas. It would be a good guess, I think, that in most instances a resurvey of these firms would show that the forecast period has increased in recent years.

A survey of well over 100 companies, conducted in 1965 by the Sales and Marketing Executives Association of Los Angeles, showed that the specified length of planning period was as follows: 8 percent, no definite period; 9 percent, less than 1 year; 37 percent, 1 to 3 years; 41 percent, 3 to 5 years; and 30 percent, 5 or more years.

A more recent survey (National Planning Commission, 1966, p. 29) showed the following distribution of planning periods among 420 companies, in percent of total:

no corporate plan	16
five years only	53
ten years only	11
five and ten years	8
less than 5 years	6
more than 10 years	6

Although companies may have a formal planning period, different types of plans may have varying spans. The Lockheed Aircraft Corportion, for example, asks each of its divisions to develop annually a 10-year plan. But the plans it prepared for the supersonic transport covered 25 years.*

Table 1-1 Planning Decisions and Their Related Forecast Periods*

Responses of company presidents or their representatives to the question: What principal company plans or decisions are you weighing (have you in mind) as you watch forecasts of economic trends; and how far ahead is it important to have an indication of economic conditions for each plan or decision? One respondent may be represented by more than one item.

TYPE OF COMPANY PLANNING OR DECISION	FORECAST PERIOD REPORTED	PRODUCT OR SERVICE OF THE RESPONDENT
Long-range planning for capital improvements	25 years in the case of major improvements	Rail transportation
Acquisition of another company	20 years	Lime and sand
Capital expenditure	10 years	Department store
Increases in capacity	" "	Steel
Expansion, purchase, and construction of plants	" "	Steel
Increase in capacity	" "	Office machines
Expansion of agency organization	" "	Life insurance
Organization of subdivisions in special fields	5 to 10 years	Aircraft
Equipment purchases	10 years	Transportation
Expansion of facilities and development of new products	" "	Electrical equipment
Long-range financial program	" "	Steel products
Equity financing	1 to 10 years	Pumps, tools
Expansion	5 years	Iron castings
Capital expenditures and engineering of new products	" "	Anchors, guying equipment
Plant expansion	" "	Utilities

continued next page

* For a survey of different planning periods see Newell, Jr., 1963.

The above data show that most companies have settled on five years as their long-range planning period. When governments of the world have developed comprehensive plans for their economic systems they have generally adopted five years as the time span. Why five years? Mike Kami, when Director of Planning at International Business Machines, accurately explained the reason in these words (Steiner 1963b, p. 47): ". . . it is because four years seems too short and six years seems too long. This is the main rationale for five years." Businessmen whom I have queried on this subject confirm this view. They say it is just about as far as they can see clearly enough to get involved in any detailed planning.

The question of what is a proper period for planning is not easy to answer. The broad criteria, I think, is well expressed by Koontz and O'Donnell (1964, p. 87†) when they say ". . . since planning and the forecasting that underlies it

Table 1-1   Planning Decisions and Their Related Forecast Periods* (Continued)

TYPE OF COMPANY PLANNING OR DECISION	FORECAST PERIOD REPORTED	PRODUCT OR SERVICE OF THE RESPONDENT
Store leases	" "	Clothing
Investment policy	" "	Life insurance
Cost-reducing improvements	" "	Steel
Capital equipment	" "	Railroad transportation
Plant expansion, equipment purchases, new products, and financial programming	3 to 5 years	Steel products
Expansion of facilities and development of new products	2 to 5 years	Electrical equipment
Refinery expansion, purchase of producing property	4 years	Oil
Acquisition of funds for new construction	3 years	Utilities
Construction program and financing	" "	Telephone service
Production and transmitting facilities planning	" "	Utilities
Increase in engineering personnel	3 years	Aircraft
Capital facilities on ground	6 months to 3 years	Air transportation
Styling new models	2 years	Metal parts
New models	6 months to 2 years	Truck transmission steel
Major plant rearrangement	1½ years	Metal parts
Expanding production facilities	" "	Paper and plastics

* Judith Malott, *Company Organization for Economic Forecasting*, Research Report No. 28 (New York: American Management Association, Inc., 1957), pp. 18-19.

are costly, a company should probably not plan for a longer period than is economically justifiable; yet it is risky to plan for a shorter period. The logical answer as to the right planning period seems to lie in the 'commitment principle,' that planning should encompass the period of time necessary to foresee (through a series of actions) the fulfillment of commitments involved in a decision."

It would seem foolhardy for a manager to make an important capital expenditure decision without a careful examination of the full impact of this expenditure throughout the time needed to recover the cost from income generated. If a new facility costs $10 million, the planning involved in the decision to construct it should look forward to the time required to recoup this initial investment plus all expenses associated with its maintenance, or to that point in time when the sunk costs become unsunk, or that time when full cash recovery is achieved.

But, as Chamberlain (Steiner 1963b*, p. 10) points out: "One of the functions of planners is to keep an eye on those resources which are becoming free or liquid again. . . . The timing of these releases presents the possibility for more decisions. Decisions will have to be made as to how these resources will be committed in the future." So the minimum planning period may properly be expressed as covering the length of commitment plus a little more.

The fixing of the planning period for cash investments is easier than for those which may not directly involve cash, such as a management training and selection plan, retirement plans, or a plan to move from one geographic area to another. Here the "right" planning period is not as clear and must depend upon a manager's judgment about what a sensible planning period may be. What is sensible will usually depend upon his views about a number of considerations.

One consideration clearly involves the need for reliable information concerning the future, how much it costs to get it, and the degree of reliability placed on it when it is acquired. In preparing its supersonic transport plans, the Boeing Company decided it was worth huge expenditures to examine, in detail, airline potential purchases extending through 1990. On the other hand, reliability of data about payoff of basic research is so low that few managers will spend much money trying to relate cost with potential income over any extended period of time.

The time discount of a manager is also important in planning time spans. Because of uncertainties in the future, and because dollars are worth more today than in the future, many managers have a conservative discount rate which they employ. This means they give high value to quick liquidity of investments. For these managers, planning periods are shortened because their liquidity preference is high.

Another consideration is a manager's estimate of his maneuverability in the future to adapt to changing circumstances. For example, if a reasonable estimate is made that it will take 20 years for a new building to recover costs fully, a manager may not feel obliged to study income flows thoroughly over the entire 20 years. To begin with, most of the income may flow in the first 5 to 10 years and because of the low present value of dollars earned from 10 to 20 years ahead the relative importance of being precise about income flows in that time frame is rather low. Furthermore, if the plant is maintained, a manager may reason that at worst he can sell it at a reasonable price, or at best use it to perform different functions, if need be, from those initially planned. The degree of flexibility a manager thinks he will have in resource use in the future will, therefore, influence the period for which detailed plans are prepared.

One final point deserves mention, namely, that for some plans the period covered is virtually infinite. This is true of corporate charters, for example. A long-term objective of maximizing profits also implicitly would stretch over an infinite number of years.

For reasons such as those given here, business plans in most companies cover different time spans, depending upon the subject matter and the other considerations discussed. There is some order in this diversity, however, because for administrative reasons many companies find it desirable to prepare all detailed operational plans for a prescribed and fixed number of years.

PLANNING IS A MAJOR
MANAGEMENT FUNCTION

Managers and students of management have not agreed on the classification of functions of management. The numbers of identifiable functions range up to eight.* But in every listing of functions I have seen planning is included. Although all management functions are performed more or less simultaneously, rather than serially, there is no question but that planning is more dominant than some of the others. One reason for this is that most if not all other functions of management are conducted as a result of or with reference to planning. Marvin Bower (1966, p. 3†) implies this view in his definition of managing, which is: ". . . the activity or task of determining the objectives of an organization and then guiding the people and other resources of the organization in the successful achievement of those objectives."

* Luther Gulick (Gulick and Urwick 1937, p. 13) asks, "What does a chief executive do?" The reply is POSDCORB, or planning, organizing, staffing, directing, co-ordinating, reporting, and budgeting. Other current writers have a different view. Koontz and O'Donnell (1964) would answer: planning, organization, staffing, direction, and control. Newman and Summer (1961) would answer: organizing, planning, leading, measuring and controlling. Dale (1965) would answer: planning, organizing, staffing, direction, control, innovation, representation.

† From *The Will to Manage* by Marvin Bower. Copyright © 1966 by Marvin Bower. Used by permission of McGraw-Hill Book Company.

Chart 1-3
"Ideal" Allocations of Time for Planning
in the "Average" Company

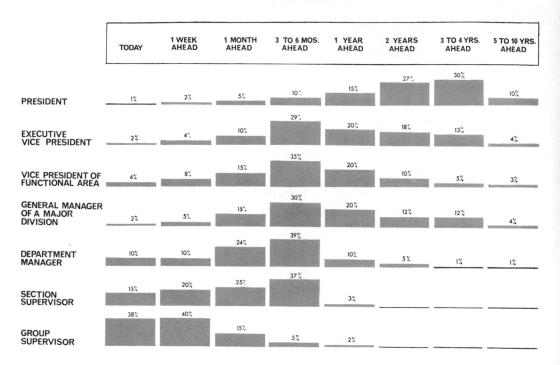

	TODAY	1 WEEK AHEAD	1 MONTH AHEAD	3 TO 6 MOS. AHEAD	1 YEAR AHEAD	2 YEARS AHEAD	3 TO 4 YRS. AHEAD	5 TO 10 YRS. AHEAD
PRESIDENT	1%	2%	5%	10%	15%	27%	30%	10%
EXECUTIVE VICE PRESIDENT	2%	4%	10%	29%	20%	18%	13%	4%
VICE PRESIDENT OF FUNCTIONAL AREA	4%	8%	15%	35%	20%	10%	5%	3%
GENERAL MANAGER OF A MAJOR DIVISION	2%	5%	15%	30%	20%	12%	12%	4%
DEPARTMENT MANAGER	10%	10%	24%	39%	10%	5%	1%	1%
SECTION SUPERVISOR	15%	20%	25%	37%	3%			
GROUP SUPERVISOR	38%	40%	15%	5%	2%			

SOURCE: SUGGESTED BY, BUT NOT THE SAME AS, A CHART APPEARING IN:
RALPH M. BESSE,"COMPANY PLANNING MUST BE PLANNED!" DUN'S REVIEW, APRIL 1957, p.48.

Not only must every manager plan, but it is a primary responsibility of management at all levels in an organization. As the hierarchical ladder is ascended, however, the nature and scope of planning responsibilities will vary. At the highest corporate levels rests the duty of management to establish the fundamental direction of the enterprise and lay out strategies to achieve objectives. At the lowest levels of management practically all planning efforts are very short-range and deal with matters solely under the jurisdiction of the manager. In between these extremes the nature of planning duties changes with level, scope of managerial authority, and company organization.

Chart 1-3 shows suggested "typical" and "ideal" time allocations for executives at various levels. These are, of course, arbitrary and may not fit requirements of different companies. For the average medium-sized company they may be reasonable. For a very large company, however, it is questionable whether the emphasis is great enough for the period beyond five years. This is certainly true for companies involved in commitments beyond five years, such as aerospace companies, airlines, public utilities, and companies heavily involved in advanced technology. On the other hand, a company making women's dresses will find inappropriate the emphasis on the long-range.

For all companies the reality of daily life will undoubtedly not fit the "ideal." If one were to draft a chart as life is, the percentages for the near term would be much higher. The "typical" president, for example, may find it hard to spend less than 25 percent of his time on today's problems. Lower levels may show increasing allocations of time to short-range problems. The group supervisor, at the other extreme, is likely to find it difficult to spend less than 75 percent of his time on today's problems.

DISCIPLINES FOCUSED ON
BUSINESS PLANNING

Eleanor Roosevelt in her last book, *Tomorrow Is Now* (1963), repeatedly counsels that: "The world cannot be understood from a single point of view." So it is with modern business enterprise and its operations. Business planning cannot be understood from the point of view of a single discipline. Many areas of knowledge are required for effective planning. Depending upon the subject of planning the following, among others, may be represented: economics, psychology, behavioral science, mathematics, accounting, political science, sociology, engineering, law, and military science. Modern business planning requires an appropriate blend of these and other areas of modern knowledge. That is what makes it so difficult to grasp and even more difficult to practice. A good bit of literature on business planning looks at the subject from only one area of expertise. This makes discussion easier for the writer, but both students and practitioners of business planning must discount such unperceptive approaches.

THE DYNAMICS OF BUSINESS PLANNING

Business management is a rapidly changing discipline. Anyone at all acquainted with the business world finds the pace of change nothing short of breath-taking. The dynamism of change is reflected in schools of business where, in just about every course of study, last semester's notes can no longer be used without important modification. Research and thinking in some areas in schools of business are ahead of business practice; in other areas business practice is ahead of the scholarly world.

Among all the functions of management, and areas of scholarly thinking about business, none outranks planning in rapidity of change. Over the past ten to fifteen years the nature and practice of business planning has undergone enormous alteration. This short period of time has seen the rise and widespread adoption of a new concept of corporate planning; new powerful tools have been invented and put into practice; and the development and introduction of the computer has brought great changes in business planning.

The trends of the future seem likely to follow the acceleration of the past. By the time this book is published, some of the material will be out of date and some new developments will be unmentioned. Nevertheless, it is my conviction that most of the basic principles and practices presented here will be useful for the foreseeable future.

SUMMARY AND CONCLUSIONS

This introductory chapter sought to lay a basis for subsequent chapters by defining planning, plans, and their major elements; and by discussing a number of basic factors associated with the growth and the future of comprehensive business planning. Some of the major conclusions of the chapter are:

1. The subject matter of planning is enmeshed in semantic entanglement which both practitioners and students must recognize for better understanding.

2. Comprehensive corporate planning can best be understood when it is defined from four points of view: the way planning deals with the futurity of current decisions, the process, its philosophy, and the structure of business plans.

3. Business planning can best be understood within a framework that recognizes the levels of abstraction for definition, the substantive scope of plans, and the major dimensions of business plans. Business planning cannot be understood from the perspective of only one discipline of knowledge. There are many areas of knowledge that enter into the development and implementation of business plans.

4. There are solid reasons for the great expansion of comprehensive corporate planning during the past decade which will assure its continued importance and growth in the future.

5. There are different time dimensions for different plans in the typical company, but more companies have detailed over-all operational plans for a five-year period than for any other time span.

6. Planning is a major function of all managers and is dominant over most other functions. (An "ideal" distribution of time devoted to planning at different levels of management for a "typical" company was suggested.)

7. Comprehensive corporate planning is today a very dynamic process in which major changes are taking place. This phenomenon will continue in the future.

2

A Conceptual
and Operational Model
of Corporate Planning

2

A Conceptual
and Operational Model
of Corporate Planning

INTRODUCTION

In this chapter are presented several basic conceptual and operational models of a comprehensive business planning structure and process. By a conceptual model is meant one that presents an idea of what a thing in general should be, or an image of a thing formed by generalizing from particulars. An operational model, in contrast, is one actually being used by an enterprise. An insightful conceptual model is a powerful tool because it provides proper guidance for practice.

A CONCEPTUAL MODEL FOR
BUSINESS PLANNING

Chart 2-1 sets forth my conceptual model of the structure and process of effective and efficient business planning programs. This model was constructed after studying scores of planning systems. Consequently, it is not at all surprising that a large number of companies have planning systems in operation whose features correspond to it. This model records those plans needed in a typical business, their relationships with one another, and the sequence of actions necessary for proper planning and results. The model, therefore, is a logical expression of a required structure and process of planning and plans.

I have found the model to be flexible and adaptable to almost any size or type of business, style of management, or stage in the development of organized formal planning. These factors in a business can be counted on to cause great

variations in the detailed planning practices of companies. But the strength of
the model is revealed in the fact that when surface differences in planning are
brushed aside, the model can be identified in most companies that have effectively organized comprehensive planning programs. So long as a manager is
interested in undertaking coordinated corporate planning, this conceptual model
can be made operational and adapted to most business environments.

It must be added, however, that although the model in Chart 2-1 is conceptually deceptively simple, it is also deceptively difficult to translate into a first-
rate operational comprehensive planning program. We shall not in this chapter
be concerned with the problems of putting the model into operation. That will
be the subject of future chapters. Our intent here is to present as succinctly as
possible the major features of the model and to compare it with other conceptual
and operational models. A quick glance at Chart 2-1 and the table of contents of
this book will show that various parts of the model will be the subject of future
chapters. In these later discussions there will be presented detailed explanations
and illustrations of each part of the model. The definitions and illustrations in
the following presentation, therefore, can be brief.

BASIC FOUNDATIONS. To the left of Chart 2-1 are three underlying
foundations of any company planning effort: fundamental organizational socio-
economic purposes, values of top managers, and studies of the environment. Each
has a profound and unique contribution to make in planning.

The socio-economic purposes refer to those underlying ends which society
expects of its business institutions if they are to survive. At rock bottom this
means that society demands that businesses utilize the resources at their disposal
to satisfy the wants of society. If this is done, a business will profit and survive.
If it is not done well, a business will make no profits and will die unless society
wishes to subsidize it to assure its survival. It is useful for managers to keep in
mind this underlying reason for the existence of business. It explains why, as
businesses become larger and society becomes more complex, the things society
wants from business, especially large business, become more numerous and sometimes contradictory.

The second fundamental set of foundations for planning are the values, ideas,
and philosophies that managers hold. Each manager has a set of values, code of
ethics, and moral standards which are unique to him. They are basic premises
of planning. Those held by top managers are, of course, most influential in the
overall planning program. Values are injected into all of the important elements
of business planning. They may concern which objectives are to be sought. For
instance, the decision to be the biggest and the technically best company in an
industry, or both, depends upon a chief executive's values. The means chosen
to achieve these ends are influenced by his values. How he wishes to treat employees, customers, competitors, or subcontractors also depends upon his values.

Chart 2-1

Structure and Process of Business Planning

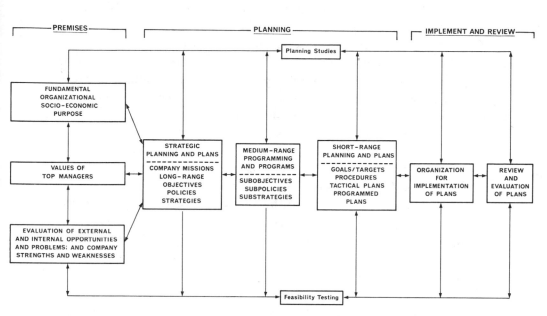

Similar to a diagram in "The Critical Role of Top Management in Long–Range Planning,"
Arizona Review, April 1966, also by George A. Steiner.

Some managers may demand that working conditions for employees be made pleasant; others may not think this important. Some may be ruthless competitors; others may seek to apply a rule of "do unto others as you would have others do unto you." Sometimes, as will be discussed in Chapter 6, the major values of top managers are expressed in written statements. Most values, however, are not. But whether written or not, they are of fundamental significance in the planning process.

A cardinal purpose of planning is to discover future opportunities and make plans to exploit them. Correspondingly, basic to long-range planning is the detection of obstructions that must be removed from the road ahead. The most effective plans are those which exploit opportunities and remove obstacles on the basis of an objective understanding of the strengths and weaknesses of the company. *The New York Times* several years ago saw an opportunity to exploit the Southern California market. The western version of its paper failed because it did not properly assess obstacles and weaknesses in entering this market. Among other things, it failed to see the impact of not having a residential house distribution system. As will be discussed in more detail in Chapter 8, the effort devoted to surveying the future is formidable in large companies, and the reasons are obvious—there is an enormous payoff to the skilled probing of a future and relating it to an unbiased study of a company's strengths and weaknesses.

STRATEGIC PLANNING. The next major structural element in Chart 2-1 is strategic planning. Strategic planning is the process of determining the major objectives of an organization and the policies and strategies that will govern the acquisition, use, and disposition of resources to achieve those objectives. Objectives in the strategic planning process include missions or purposes, if they have not been determined previously, and the specific objectives that are sought by a firm. Although the strategic objectives are usually long-range, they can be short-range. Policies are broad guides to action, and strategies are the means to deploy resources. In this area we are dealing with the major, the most important and basic objectives, policies, and strategies of a company.

Depending upon how one looks at the matter, the basic missions of a company can be included in strategic planning, or placed in the area of fundamental premises to planning. I have chosen to include them in strategic planning.

The basic purposes or missions of the firm are those fundamental ends and lines of business which it wishes to pursue. Basic purposes are fundamental motivations or continuing aims lasting throughout the life of an enterprise, such as the determination to be a highly profitable business. Basic missions are found in corporate charters, but they are often so numerous and permit such a wide diversity of activity that they provide little or no direction for planning. Managers must choose among them those activities to which the firm is to be committed. A selection and statement of missions can make an enormous difference in planning. The Baldwin Locomotive Works might be a profitable company today if its mission had been changed from "making steam locomotives" to "providing motive power for railroads." In recent years more and more companies are coming to understand the power of a simple statement of basic company missions and are drafting such statements for general distribution. It is not necessary to express basic purposes and missions on paper, but as a starting point in planning it is desirable to do so.

The subject matter that may be covered in strategic planning includes every type of activity of concern to an enterprise. Among the areas are profits, capital expenditures, organization, pricing, labor relations, production, marketing, finance, personnel, public relations, advertising, technological capabilities, product improvement, research and development, legal matters, management selection and training, political activities, and so on.

The characteristics of strategic planning differ greatly from those of medium-range programming and short-range planning, differences which will be discussed later in the chapter. At this point it is pertinent to note that strategic planning covers different periods of time for different subjects. For example, a strategic plan may be made to merge with another company within a week. This is clearly short-range as compared with a plan to acquire a major company within a five-year period. Also, strategic plans are not always written; frequently they are found only in the head of the chief executive, who communicates them when he sees fit to do so.

MEDIUM-RANGE PROGRAMMING. Medium-range programming is the process in which detailed, coordinated, and comprehensive plans are made for selected functions of a business to deploy resources to reach objectives by following policies and strategies laid down in the strategic planning process. All medium-range programs and plans for a company cover the same period of time, usually five years. Whatever the period covered, plans are worked out in considerable detail for each year of the planning period. For instance, if a major division of a decentralized company is working out medium-range programs on the basis of objectives, policies, and strategies developed by corporate headquarters in the strategic planning process, it will develop subobjectives, subpolicies, and substrategies for its own operations. It may have a separate set of objectives, policies, and strategies for each of its lines of business. It may develop sets of plans for each product. Or, it may develop only one set of plans for the entire division. But, whatever the breakdown, details are developed for all plans for each of the years included in the planning period.

Detailed plans are most often made in the medium-range programming process for such major functional areas as production, sales, profits, personnel, capital expenditures, finance, and research and development. Usually, *pro forma* balance sheets and profit-and-loss statements are also prepared for each year.

A major characteristic of medium-range programming is thorough coordination throughout the most important functions of the enterprise. At the strategic planning level there is an effort to assure broad general coordination among dominant parts of an enterprise. In the medium-range programming there is a specific and detailed meshing of the parts. For instance, details of research and development are closely related to products that the firm expects to produce and sell in the future, advertising plans are tied to the product, engineers work with production-line managers to design parts in conformance with efficient manufacturing practices, and employee hiring and transfer plans are related to anticipated production schedules. In this planning process an effort is made to have the most important parts of the business system mesh properly.

SHORT-TERM BUDGETS AND DETAILED FUNCTIONAL PLANS. Short-term budgets and detailed functional plans include such matters as short-range targets for salesmen, budgets for material purchases, short-term advertising plans, inventory replenishment, and employment schedules. If the medium-range programs are detailed and the timing of the overall planning cycle coincides with the required dates for budget-making, short-term plans may be the same as the first year of the medium-range programs. The detail of the medium-range programs is not usually deep enough for current operations, hence, a separate set of short-range plans is usually required. For instance, short-term plans may include details on schedules of specific raw materials going through production, into inventory, and out as finished products. Not only may the detail needed for current operations be much greater than required in the medium-range programming process, but it is usually needed on a short-time basis, such as weekly, monthly, or quarterly.

PLANNING STUDIES. At the top of Chart 2-1 recognition is given to planning studies. In mind are studies made especially for the planning process. They may include, for example, analyses of the future markets of a company upon which basis strategic planning proceeds. They may include studies of machinery replacement policy, as the basis for short-term equipment expenditures. These studies are usually basic premises which are of high significance in guiding the planning process. Chapter 8 will deal with them in some detail.

FEASIBILITY TESTING. At all stages in the planning process it is necessary to test the feasibility of aims and means to achieve them. Planning is not well done when ends and means are decided solely by seat-of-the-pants methods. All sorts of conflicts arise in planning which must be reconciled and balances struck. Feasibility tests differ among parts of the planning process, but in general they relate to such questions as the values that managers hold, available facilities, personnel capabilities, timing, cash flows, return on investment, and market penetration.

ORGANIZATION. Plans will not be carried out if suitable organizational arrangements are not made to do so. If plans are made to develop a new product, a suitable organization must be established to carry out those plans. In a company with many new products this may become rather complex. Or, if a set of plans is developed for a new integrated attack to penetrate a new market, there must be a careful organization of effort. These organizational arrangements, of course, should be considered in the planning process. Although they may be planned in the planning process, the organization *per se* assures the carrying out of the plans.

REVIEW AND EVALUATION. An effective planning program needs continuous surveillance as well as periodic review to assure that plans are being carried out and that new plans are devised as required. If events are not in conformance with plans, it then becomes management's responsibility to find out why. It may be that deviation from plans is quite appropriate in light of new considerations. In this event managers implement plans with flexibility and, we shall assume, to the net advantage of the firm. It may also be that plans are not being followed when they should be. In this event it is a function of management to see that plans are followed.

Conceptually, the entire comprehensive planning process should be recycled every year. Naturally, a review and evaluation of past experience should be a major ingredient in the new planning cycle.

FEEDBACK LOOPS. The process of planning is one in which complex feedback loops exist in each part and tie together the different parts. Although obvious, this fact is of high significance. By its coordination, feasibility, and balance, an over-all system optimization can be achieved at a minimum cost of effort and time.

CENTRALIZED VERSUS DECENTRALIZED COMPANIES. In a centralized company, such as Allstate Insurance, the entire process shown in Chart 2-1 is done in the central headquarters of the company. In a decentralized company, such as Celanese, the central headquarters prepares the strategic plans which are then transmitted to the divisions. There, medium-range programming and short-range plans are prepared and then transmitted to headquarters for review and approval. In some companies an over-all medium-range set of plans is prepared for the entire company from the divisional plans. Sometimes this step is omitted.

STRATEGIC VERSUS TACTICAL PLANNING

To comprehend corporate planning it is most important to understand the differences between strategic and tactical planning. At one extreme on a spectrum is strategic planning, as previously defined. At the other end is tactical planning or the detailed deployment of resources to achieve strategic plans. Our interest here is in drawing a line of demarcation between the two extremes to highlight the conceptual distinctions. The following elements are listed in no particular order of importance (Steiner and Cannon 1966, pp. 11-14; Anthony 1904, pp. 18-24; and Anthony 1965).

1. *Level of conduct.* Strategic planning is conducted at the highest levels of management (at headquarters and in major divisions) and relates exclusively to decisions in the province of these levels. Tactical planning is done at and relates to lower management levels.

2. *Regularity.* Strategic planning is both continuous and irregular. The process is continuous but the timing of decision is irregular for it depends upon and is triggered by the appearance of opportunities, new ideas, management initiative, crises, and other nonroutine stimuli. Tactical planning is done for the most part on a periodic cycle that is on a fixed time schedule.

3. *Subjective values.* Strategic planning is more heavily weighted with subjective values of managers than is tactical planning.

4. *Range of alternatives.* The total possible range of alternatives from which a management must choose is far greater, by definition, in strategic than in tactical planning.

5. *Uncertainty.* Again, uncertainty is usually much greater in strategic planning than in tactical planning. Not only is the time dimension much shorter

in tactical than in strategic planning, but risks are much more difficult to assess and are considerably greater in strategic planning.

6. *Nature of problems.* Strategic planning problems are unstructured and tend to be one of a kind. Tactical planning problems are more structured and often repetitive in nature.

7. *Information needs.* Strategic planning requires large amounts of information derived from, and relating to, areas of knowledge outside the corporation. Most of the more relevant data needed relates to the future, is difficult to get with accuracy, and is tailored to each problem. In mind, for example, is information about competitors, future technology, social and political changes affecting corporate decisions, and economic developments altering markets. Tactical informational needs, in contrast, rely more heavily on internally generated data, particularly from accounting systems, and involve a higher proportionate use of historical information. For example, tactical plans to control production rest heavily upon internal historical records of past experience.

8. *Time horizons.* Strategic planning usually covers a long time spectrum but sometimes is very short, and varies from subject to subject. Tactical planning, in contrast, is of shorter duration and more uniform for all parts of the planning program.

9. *Completeness.* Strategic planning conceptually covers the entire scope of an organization. While at any one time only selected areas of business activity may be the subject of strategic planning, no corner of corporate activity is excluded from attention. Tactical planning covers the whole of a suborganizational unit responsible for executing parts of strategic plans. For example, tactical planning may include new product plans, construction, machine replacement, production, and so on, and coordinates these for the whole activity of a subunit.

10. *Reference.* Strategic planning is original in the sense that it is the source or origin for all other planning in an enterprise. In contrast, tactical planning is done within, and in pursuit of, strategic plans.

11. *Detail.* Strategic plans are usually broad and have many fewer details than tactical plans. The further out in time the strategic plans stretch, the fewer still are details. As Anthony (1964, p. 20) notes: "the concept of a master planner who constantly keeps all parts of the organization at some coordinated optimum is a nice concept but an unrealistic one. Life is too complicated for any human, or computer, to do this."

12. *Type of personnel mostly involved.* Strategic planning for the most part is done only by top management and its staff. Included in the concept of staff here would be line managers when acting as staff to top management. The numbers of people involved are comparatively few as contrasted with tactical planning where large numbers of managers and employees usually participate in the process.

13. *Ease of evaluation.* It is usually considerably easier to measure the effectiveness and efficiency of tactical plans than of strategic plans. Results of

strategic planning may become evident only after a number of years. Very frequently it is difficult to disentangle the forces which led to the results. In sharp contrast, tactical planning results are quickly evident and much more easily identified with specific actions.

14. *Development of objectives, policies, and strategies.* The objectives, policies, and strategies developed in strategic planning are new and generally debatable. Experience may be minimal in judging their correctness. At the other extreme, there usually is much experience to guide the development of tactical plans.

15. *Point of view.* Strategic planning is done from a corporate point of view, whereas tactical planning is done principally from a functional point of view.

BLURRING DIFFERENCES. Both conceptually and operationally, the lines of demarcation between strategic and tactical planning are blurred. At the extremes their differences are crystal clear, as in the above comparison. But these distinctions do not always hold. For example, both in theory and practice there is in planning an intricate ends-means chain. Strategy gives rise to tactics, and tactics may be considered a substrategy which in turn employs tactics for execution. What is one manager's strategy is another's tactics, what is one manager's tactics is another's strategy. For example, strategic planning is done at the headquarters of a company. Substrategic planning within this strategic plan may be done in the major divisions of the company. Concretely, the corporation may decide that its strategy is to penetrate the European market by divisional acquisitions of foreign companies. Part of the tactical plan might be for the electronics division to decide to buy a majority interest in a plant in Germany that produces a product similar to one of its own. But this may also be considered a substrategy giving rise to a tactical plan which might be to acquire a minority interest in a specific plant through stock exchange rather than cash.

Differentiation of types of plans within tactical plans is important. At one extreme are tactical plans that have a number of characteristics of strategic plans. At the other extreme are tactical plans that are rather automatic in operation. For example, tactical plans for product improvement involve difficult managerial decisions over design, markets, financing, and pricing. As noted above, such planning in a division of a large company may be said to encompass substrategic planning as well as tactical planning. All depends upon who is looking—top management in central headquarters, or lower management in a division. Also involved in tactical decisions over product improvement are inventory replenishment policy, raw material purchases, machine tool replacement, or handling of new orders. A basic characteristic of such plans is that they are often almost completely automatic. Once management decides on an inventory replacement policy, for example, it automatically operates until management reviews the process and modifies or retains it. Discretion in operation is rather small or nonexistent in this sort of planning.

IMPORTANCE OF DISTINCTIONS. These distinctions are of consequence for many reasons. First of all, a methodology for assuring first-rate strategic planning may be completely inappropriate when applied to tactical planning. Permitting the looseness and intuitive problem-solving techniques to be applied to more or less automatically derived tactical decisions is unwise. On the other hand, a quantitative decision model applicable in tactical planning may not only be inappropriate in strategic planning but may be dangerous. Among the highest requirements for effective strategic planning are imagination, creativity, and a sense of proper timing. Attempts to optimize strategic planning decisions with inappropriate models can weaken rather than strengthen these talents. On the other hand, a proper use of quantitative methods can sharpen the intuition and judgment of managers. (This is an issue to which we shall return in a later chapter.)

Second, the difference between strategic and tactical planning may be the source of conflict in an enterprise. For example, top management may decide as a matter of strategy to grow in sales and profits by shifting its present technological know-how into new products which appear to be more promising than those now being made. This sort of shift will require tactical plans in the functional areas of the company. But, these shifts may serve to reduce the efficiency of the divisions because productivity may actually decline until the shift is made and the product fulfills its promise. The manager of the production division may see his earnings fall off as the transition is made. The head of sales may similarly find costs rising relative to sales as his training expenses mount. Of course, in such situations there may not be open opposition on the part of functional managers, but they can find subtle ways to resist. Resolving such problems demands an understanding of the differences between the two types of planning, how to blend them, and how to manage (Andersen, 1965).

Third, a failure to distinguish between the two types of planning can create problems between line and staff in large enterprises. For example, the staff of a chief executive who is concentrating on the priority strategic directions of his company can easily lose his ear if it gets too deeply enmeshed in tactical planning. In the other direction, a headquarters staff of a company with decentralized authority in division general managers may easily clash with the general managers. This can result, for example, if headquarters staff develops broad objectives and strategies without much clarity as to how the divisions can implement the strategies and achieve the objectives. This is frustrating to division managers especially if they do not readily see how the objectives can be achieved with the strategies devised. On the other hand, if staff develops tactical plans which the division managers do not like there is a tendency for them to say, "You made the plans, now carry them out."

Fourth, strategic planning is usually done at a more leisurely pace than tactical planning. If there is a conflict in schedules, the functional managers may grasp the nettle and do strategic planning. For example, prices may be set without waiting for a general company strategy. Salesmen may be moved about, distribution channels changed, or other major decisions made without waiting to hear from top management.

Finally, there is a tendency for strategic planning and tactical planning to be separated. Although it is important to understand the distinction between strategic and tactical planning, each must be developed with reference to the other.

DISTINCTIONS AMONG MAJOR TYPES
OF PLANNING IN MODEL

These conceptual differences between strategic and tactical planning explain major distinctions among the strategic planning, medium-range programming, and short-range budgeting and detailed functional planning structures given in Chart 2-1. In a general sort of way, the strategic planning in the chart matches the concept in mind in the previous discussion. Although tactical planning is not quite the same thing as short-range planning, for our purposes they can be considered roughly synonymous. In between are the medium-range programs which obviously incorporate both strategic and tactical planning characteristics. So, again, while ·conceptually there are clear distinctions among these three major planning processes, the differences are blurred at the edges of each.

PLANNING VERSUS CONTROL

In most elementary textbooks on management there is a distinction drawn between the management function of planning and that of controlling. To oversimplify, the definition of control is usually given as the process of making sure that performance takes place in conformance with plans. This is in sharp contrast to plans which determine the objectives, means, and standards against which performance is measured. To be sure, the elementary texts underscore the fact that implementation of plans must be done with a flexibility that recognizes the changing circumstances which may make a deviation from the plans not only proper but essential. This sort of determination is a major managerial responsibility. The texts also usually assert that although the basic distinction between planning and control is sharp the two are inseparable. They are inseparable because planning is necessary before controlling can be meaningful, and each must be done in light of the other. I find nothing wrong with these definitions and distinctions except that they do not adequately explain the phenomena.

It is not the purpose of this book to examine management control in detail. But several important considerations are in order to relate the model of Chart

2-1 with management control. First, control is a multidimensional term and should be defined in a manner similar to the treatment of planning in Chapter 1. Control, like planning, has different meanings for its different dimensions.

Second, there is no question about the fact that planning and control, both conceptually (in Chart 2-1) and operationally, are inextricably interwoven. Medium-range programming and short-range budgeting, for example, are a combination of planning and control activities. Each is done in light of the other and a manager mixes both in managing. For example, plans are set, activities then take place, corrections must be made, new plans are prepared to meet the needs for corrections, and so on, for we are dealing here with a continuum. Planning and control are interrelated in another way. In certain instances, people in an enterprise are encouraged and permitted to participate in setting goals and standards for their own achievement. If this is related to efforts to encourage self-control their performance is intermixed with their commitment.*

Third, despite this intermingling, planning and control must be distinguished both conceptually and operationally. Conceptually, for example, the development of plans without proper control of activities taken to carry them out may not only lead to poor results but to developments completely contrary to plans. Planned profits, for example, may turn out to be losses. Perhaps of more realistic consequence is the fact that managerial relationships with people are considerably different as between planning and controlling (McGregor 1967, Chapter 8). Furthermore, the philosophy, attitude, and pursuit of planning and control will differ very much depending on the center of attention. To illustrate, the way in which a manager may go about planning for a new automobile model will vary enormously from the way in which the production line is controlled when the manufacturing process begins. To fail to distinguish between planning and control conceptually and operationally may lead to a misunderstanding not only of the processes themselves but of the ways in which they interrelate. But simple definitions to mark the differences are not too helpful for better understanding.

ANTHONY'S CONCEPTUAL MODEL

In recent years a number of conceptual models of corporate planning have appeared. One that is similar to the model presented above is that of Robert N. Anthony (1965, p. 22).

Anthony's model distinguishes, as shown in Chart 2-2, among strategic

* For example, McGregor (1967, p. 127) says: "The principle is that human beings will direct their effort, exercise self-control and responsibility, use their creativity in the service of goals to which they are committed." The assumption, of course, is that performance is closely related to commitment.

Chart 2-2

Planning and Control Processes in Organization

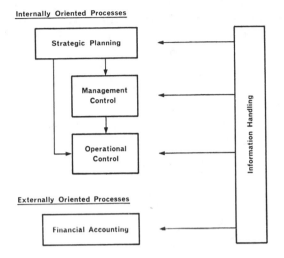

Source: Anthony, Robert N., *Planning and Control Systems: A Frame-work for Analysis* (Boston: Harvard Business School, Division of Research, 1965), p. 22.

planning, management control, and operational control. Strategic planning is defined as in my model. Management control, however, does not quite match my definition of medium-range programming. Anthony (1965, p. 27) defines management control as "the process by which managers assure that resources are obtained and used effectively and efficiently in the accomplishment of the organization's objectives." (Effectiveness and efficiency are defined by Anthony exactly as in Chapter 1.) Anthony draws a sharp distinction between management control and operational control. "Operational control," to him, "is the process of assuring that specific tasks are carried out effectively and efficiently" (1965, p. 69). What he has in mind are controls which are so programmed that rules prescribe actions, such as automated plants, production scheduling, order processing, check handling, and similar activities. His operational control is not synonymous with my short-range budgeting and detailed planning. Only a small part of this process in my model is synonymous with his operational control. Operational control is the same as that part of tactical planning, noted in my model, which is automatic in operation and requires no management attention other than to determine the automatic decision-making process or formula. As it turns out, Anthony's management control would encompass all of my medium-range programming plus a good bit of my short-range budgeting and detailed short-range functional planning.

There are merits in using Anthony's concept of management control because it embraces a combination of planning and control activities which managers actually employ. This is a useful insight, but it also applies to strategic planning at one extreme and to short-range planning at the other. A strategic plan cannot be conceived as being complete without some understanding of the control it exerts over management activities. Similarly, detailed short-range plans are made in the light of previous plans and control changes that may be required in existing plans. Planning and control are inextricably intermeshed in each; only the mix differs. Planning is involved even in automatic controls, such as automatic inventory replenishment, if only in the managerial planning decision to use a certain type of system.

As shown in Chart 2-2, Anthony includes information handling in his model. This is an important element of planning. It is implicit in my model except for the planning studies which are explicitly shown. These studies do not include all the information required in the planning process. They are only one type of planning information.

THE SRI CONCEPTUAL MODEL

Chart 2-3 shows the Stanford Research Institute model of plans. Fundamentally, the aggregations are similar to mine and Anthony's. The strategic plan "outlines in broad, general terms the characteristics and accomplishments that the firm can, and wants to, achieve" (Stewart 1963, p. 7). It includes basic company purpose, selected strategy to accomplish the purpose, specific goals of the strategy, the means for monitoring progress toward goals, and specific conditions (internal and external) which will permit the firm to attain its goals (Stewart, Allen, and Cavender 1963, p. 1). It would appear that this concept of strategic planning would embrace activity which includes all of my foundations for planning to the extreme left of Chart 2-1 plus some, but not all, of my strategic planning.

The SRI strategic plan then leads to a corporate development plan and an operations plan. These in turn lead to further detailed plans. The area covered by these plans presumably would include part of my strategic plan plus all of my medium-range programming plus all of my short-range planning.

THE GILMORE-BRANDENBERG MODEL

The Gilmore-Brandenberg concept was, to my knowledge, the first comprehensive formulation of a corporate planning model. This model breaks down the top-management planning job into four major phases. Furthermore, it identifies key decision or synergistic points in the planning process. These are defined as those where joint performance of several programs may be expected to be greater than the sum of the performance of individual programs before combination.

This model conceptually is quite comparable to the others discussed here.

It is, however, much too detailed to be reproduced here (Gilmore and Branden-berg 1962).

CONCEPTUAL STEPS IN PLANNING

The conceptual steps in planning are essentially those basic problem-solving procedures which must be followed in decision-making. The simplest model includes these elementary steps: (1) determine and define the problem,

Chart 2-3

The System of Plans

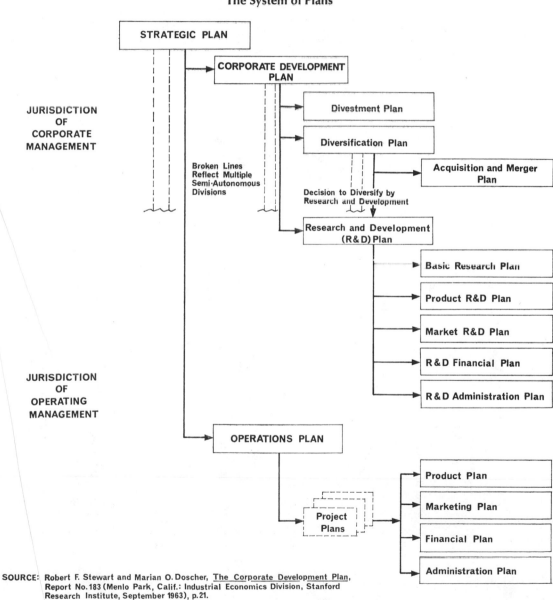

JURISDICTION
OF
CORPORATE
MANAGEMENT

Broken Lines
Reflect Multiple
Semi-Autonomous
Divisions

JURISDICTION
OF
OPERATING
MANAGEMENT

STRATEGIC PLAN

CORPORATE DEVELOPMENT PLAN

Divestment Plan

Diversification Plan

Acquisition and Merger Plan

Decision to Diversify by Research and Development

Research and Development (R&D) Plan

Basic Research Plan

Product R&D Plan

Market R&D Plan

R&D Financial Plan

R&D Administration Plan

OPERATIONS PLAN

Project Plans

Product Plan

Marketing Plan

Financial Plan

Administration Plan

SOURCE: Robert F. Stewart and Marian O. Doscher, <u>The Corporate Development Plan</u>, Report No. 183 (Menlo Park, Calif.: Industrial Economics Division, Stanford Research Institute, September 1963), p. 21.

Table 2-1   Steps in Planning and Problem-Solving*

MAJOR STEPS (A)	MANAGERIAL PLANNING (B)	MILITARY STRATEGY (C)	OPERATIONS RESEARCH (D)	DOD WEAPONS SYSTEMS (E)	SYSTEMS ENGINEERING (F)
1	Plan the plan	—	—	(Strategy & Tactics Analysis)	—
2	Study opportunities, threats, and prepare other premises	Situation observed	—	—	Environmental/ Needs Research
3	—	—	Problem identification	Military need identified	Unsatisfied need identified
4	—	Mission description	Problem formulation	Need specified	Problem definition
5	Set objectives	Situation objectives	Construct model	Objectives defined	Select objective criteria
6	Identify alternative courses of action to achieve objectives	Identify all feasible courses of action	Derive model solution	Concept proposals solicited	System synthesis alternatives
7	Examine alternatives	Analysis of each course	Test model and solution	Conceptual and feasibility studies	Systems analysis
8	Choose alternatives to follow	Compare	—	Cost/effectiveness comparison	Comparison
9	Develop detailed plans	Decision on best	Establish controls	Selection of best	Selection
10	Organize to carry out plans	—	Report results	System Package-Plan defined	Communicating results in prospectus
11	Carry out plans	—	—	—	—
12	Review and evaluate results	Action-plan assembled	—	Action-planning	Action-planning
13	Recycle planning program	—	—	—	—

* Adapted from Donald J. Smalter, "The Influence of D-O-D Practices on Corporate Planning," Management Technology, Vol. 4, No. 2, December 1964, pp. 131-2.

(2) collect all pertinent factors available to solve the problem, and (3) decide which actions to take to solve the problem.

Conceptual sequences for business planning build upon these basic analytical steps in problem-solving. As with conceptual models, there is not one single best series; there are a number of series each of which has its particular value. Fundamentally, however, they all contain the same basic elements.

Table 2-1 presents a comparison of different steps. The managerial planning steps follow the sequences which are found in elementary management textbooks. A little analysis will show that these steps compare with those related to military strategy, operations research, weapons systems analysis, and systems engineering. Each is different, yet each embraces the same fundamental elements. Although the actual step-by-step sequences vary, they show a basic movement from finding out what is to be done, through analysis of ways and means to do it, to laying detailed plans to do it.

A famous series of planning or problem-solving steps is the "Commander's Estimate of the Situation," familiar to military officers. Given in Table 2-2, it has wide applicability in military, business, as well as personal planning.

This by no means exhausts the list of useful conceptual steps in business planning. The steps mentioned apply to planning in a general sort of way. Two conceptual models more applicable to comprehensive corporate planning may be noted. The first is contained in Chart 2-1 and needs no further elaboration. A second is as follows: *

1. Planning the plan
2. Specifying objectives of the enterprise
    * forecasting future prospects
    * measuring the gaps between aspirations and projections
3. Developing strategies
    * to fill the major gaps
4. Developing derivative or detailed plans in major functional areas to fit the strategies
    * research and development
    * production
    * marketing and promotion
    * etc.
5. Carrying out plans
    * starting operations
    * introducing necessary controls
6. Review and recycling

* Adapted from George A. Steiner, 1962, p. 39. For a variety of other approaches specifically designed for small enterprises, see George A. Steiner 1967, pp. 3-16, which appears also as Chapter 7, in Pfeffer 1967.

Table 2-2   Commander's Estimate of Situation

1. MISSION

   A statement of the task and its purpose. If the mission is general in nature, determine by analysis what task must be performed to insure that the mission is accomplished. State multiple tasks in the sequence in which they are to be accomplished.

2. THE SITUATION AND COURSES OF ACTION
   a. Determine all facts or in the absence of facts logical assumptions which have a bearing on the situation and which contribute to or influence the ultimate choice or a course of action. Analyze available facts and/or assumptions and arrive at deduction from these as to their favorable or adverse influence or effect on the accomplishment of the mission.
   b. Determine and list significant difficulties or difficulty patterns which are anticipated and which could adversely affect the accomplishment of the mission.
   c. Determine and list all feasible courses of action which will accomplish the mission if successful.

3. ANALYSIS OF OPPOSING COURSES OF ACTION

   Determine through analysis the probable outcome of each course of action listed in paragraph 2c when opposed by each significant difficulty enumerated in paragraph 2b. This may be done in two steps—

   a. Determine and state those anticipated difficulties or difficulty patterns which have an approximately equal effect on all courses of action.
   b. Analyze each course of action against each significant difficulty or difficulty pattern (except those stated in paragraph 3a above) to determine strength and weakness inherent in each course of action.

4. COMPARISON OF OWN COURSES OF ACTION

   Compare courses of action in terms of significant advantages and disadvantages which emerged during analysis (par. 3 above). Decide which course of action promises to be most successful in accomplishing the mission.

5. DECISION

   Translate the course of action selected into a complete statement, showing *who*, *what*, *when*, *where*, *how*, and *why* as appropriate.

Source: War Department, *Staff Officers' Field Manual*, FM 101-5, U.S. Department of Defense, Washington, U.S. Government Printing Office (1960 edition), page 142.

LENGTH OF PLANNING PERIODS

This subject was treated at some length in Chapter 1 and needs no elaboration here. Conceptually it can be said that statements of purposes and missions are made for all time, until changed. Strategic plans are both of short- and long-range and the timing depends upon subject matter. Medium-range programming should be from at least 2 to 10 years, depending upon the company, with the average company adopting a 5-year span. Short-range plans, of course, are generally for a year or less.

Most firms that have formal planning recycle their planning program once a year. Conceptually, this seems desirable.

OPERATIONAL STRUCTURES AND PROCEDURES

Variations from the above conceptual models in actual operating planning programs are wide. Many factors influence the way planning is done, as noted previously—styles of management, organization and size of the firm, and sophistication of its planning program, to name a few. Most managements also are interested in improving their planning program by changing older ways of doing things and by introducing into the system new techniques and methods. The result is that on the surface actual operating planning systems are not the same as the conceptual models, nor are they the same from one company to another or in the same company from time to time. In one fairly large corporation that I have observed over a long period of time the corporate planning procedures have been different in every year. The structure of plans has been more stable than procedures but it, too, has changed in major ways over a ten-year period.

Despite the detailed operational variations from the conceptual models, the more successful planning programs must reflect to an important degree the conceptual models. The reason is that a violation of the inherent logic in the conceptual models (both structurally and in the sequence of steps) sooner or later will bring about deficiencies in planning. Whatever the actual structural arrangement of plans and the steps in their development, an observer must see behind them the basic elements of the conceptual model structure and planning steps. If this is not possible trouble ahead can be predicted.

It is important to observe that planning should not be conceived as beginning, for example, at the left of Chart 2-1 and proceeding to the right in a sequence that completes one step before moving to the next. Similarly, planning does not conceptually proceed on the basis of the sequences of steps as presented, for example, in Table 2-1. Both conceptually and operationally, planning sequences are iterative. There is much retracing of steps, jumping around from step to step, and tentative trial-and-error decision-making in the process. Very typically, an objective may be set and after examining alternative courses of action to achieve it, or after considering competing objectives, the original mark may be modified. The process may then start all over again until finally an objective is set and current actions are actually taken to achieve it.

KAISER ALUMINUM AND CHEMICAL PLANNING

Chart 2-4 shows the major structural parts and sequential steps taken in the preparation of the comprehensive plans of the Kaiser Aluminum and Chemical Corporation. Comparison of this diagram with Chart 2-1 and column (b) of Table 2-1 shows fundamental similarities but great operational variations.

Chart 2-4

The Planning Process—Flow Chart

(A) Gathering Information

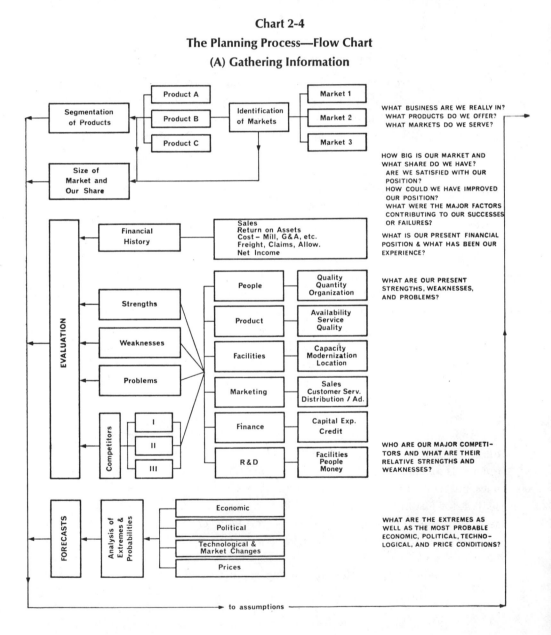

Chart 2-4
The Planning Process—Flow Chart
(B) Assumptions—Establish the Framework
Within Which the Plan is Developed

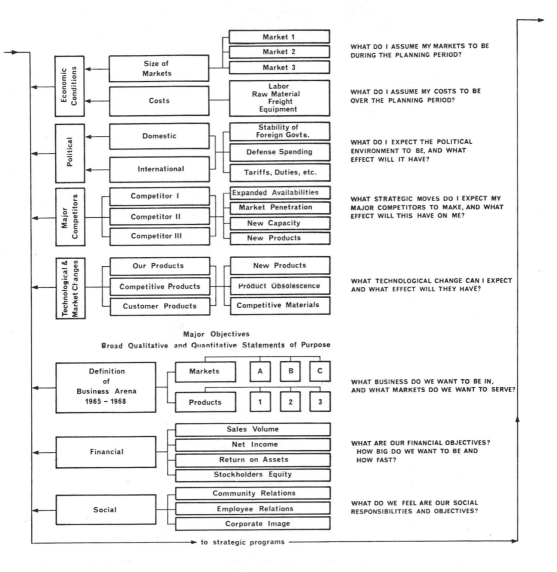

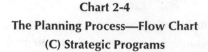

Chart 2-4
The Planning Process—Flow Chart
(C) Strategic Programs

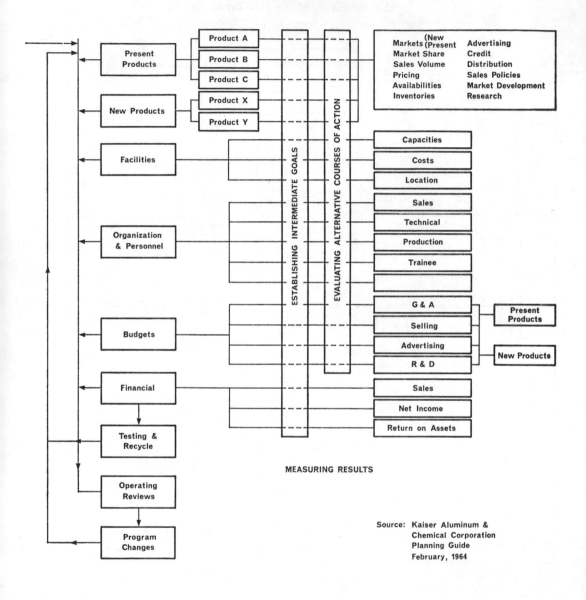

MEASURING RESULTS

Source: Kaiser Aluminum &
         Chemical Corporation
         Planning Guide
         February, 1964

Chart 2-5

Major Steps in Corporate Planning at Allstate Insurance

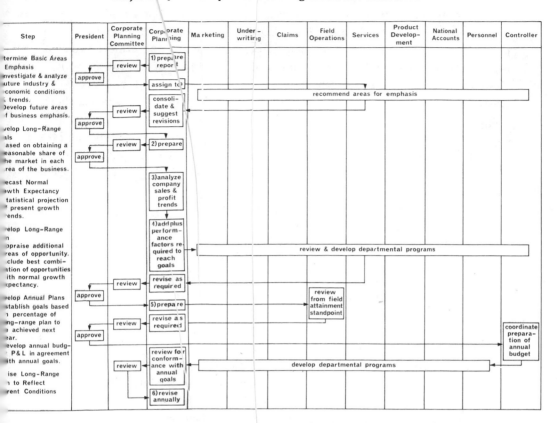

From *Managerial Long-Range Planning*, edited by George A. Steiner. Copyright © 1963 by McGraw-Hill, Inc. Used by permission of McGraw-Hill Book Co.

ALLSTATE INSURANCE COMPANY PLANNING

Chart 2-5 gives the major steps in corporate planning at Allstate Insurance. In this chart there is added to types of plans and sequence of steps, the way in which decisions move among managers. A little of the iterative process of planning is evident in the chart although there is no doubt about the fact that the actual operational flows would show much more retracing of steps than is explicit in the diagram. Here, again, the actual operational model is much different from the conceptual models. But fundamentally their similarity is clear.*

* For descriptions of comprehensive corporate planning programs of many other companies see George A. Steiner 1963b, and Steiner and Cannon 1967.

TABLE OF CONTENTS OF A
CORPORATE PLAN

There is little uniformity in the ways written plans are prepared. A reasonably complete plan would include, following Chart 2-1, a statement of basic purposes and missions as well as some of the major moral and ethical values of top management. Included, too, would be detailed studies of the future outlook of areas of interest to the company. A major section would be devoted to strategic plans, which would be followed by medium-range programs, short-range budgets and plans, and operational instructions.

Actual plans will most likely not fit this pattern but will be prepared with the particular needs and interests of the company in mind. For example, a few years ago the table of contents of the long-range plan of Standard Oil of Ohio was as follows:

    I. Formalized, Written Environmental Forecasts
    II. Summary of Principal Objectives
        1. Corporate Purpose or Function
        2. Overall Corporate Objectives
        3. General Guidelines or Policies Affecting Growth
        4. Abstract of Financial Projections
        5. Key Elements of Competitive Strategy
        6. Individual Growth Program Summaries
    III. Detailed Support for Individual Growth Programs

The following table of contents (Steiner 1967; Pfeffer 1967) is for a written plan developed by a small company having annual sales of about $2 million and 100 employees at the time the plan was drafted. The plan itself was developed by the company president and his four major department heads. Although parts of the plan stretch ahead for ten years, most of the detailed plans cover five years.*

A TABLE OF CONTENTS OF A CORPORATE PLAN
CORPORATE LONG-RANGE PLAN FOR
MAGNETIC DESIGN, INC.

I. Corporate Purposes: the fundamental purposes of **MDI**. Two basic purposes are given, which is about standard. The four modifiers, however, are a little unusual.

    A. Two prime objectives of MDI are:
        • To improve earnings through productive effort primarily applied (but not limited) to the manufacture of magnetic devices and power supply equipment.

---

*For a detailed table of contents of a long-range plan for the Autonetics Division of North American Aviation, Inc., see George A. Steiner 1963b, pp. 151-157.

• To conduct the business in a manner that is constructive, honorable, and mutually profitable for stockholders, employees, customers, suppliers, and the general community.

B. These objectives are amplified further:
  • To earn a reasonable return on investment with due regard to the interests of customers, employees, vendors.
  • To expand sales while increasing profits.
  • To support the military effort of the United States by producing top quality products.
  • To grow at a steady rate.

C. Departmental purposes: Administration, marketing, production and engineering, and finance. It is a little unusual for departmental purposes to be specified at this point in a plan; they are usually blended into specific goals set for their operations. Following are the objectives of the production and engineering department:
  • Manufacture and design quality products with cost and delivery schedules which will be attractive to prospective customers.
  • Stay alert to developments that promise new and improved company products.

II. Basic Corporate Five- and Ten-Year Sales and Profit Objectives:

A. The five-year annual sales and profit objectives are:

	Sales	Pretax Profits	Pretax (%) Profit	Federal Tax	Postax (%) Profit
First year					
Second year					
Third year		[Specified in dollars and percentages.]			
Fourth year					
Fifth year					

B. The ten-year sales and profit objectives are:
  • After taxes, sales will be $5,000,000 and earnings will be $750,000.

III. Basic Premises: forecasts of future markets, technology, competition, and evaluations of internal strengths and weaknesses. A framework of premises, with illustrations from the MDI plan, follows:

A. External projections and forecasts:
  • Survey of general business conditions, including Gross National Product forecast.
  • Survey of the market for company products, based upon general

economic conditions for industrial products and estimates of government spending for company products.

• Forecast of company sales based on the above two forecasts. (MDI made forecasts for each of the next five years. Since the company is in the Midwest, government spending for its products in the Midwest was estimated. Included were the Department of Defense, the National Aeronautics and Space Administration, and the Federal Aviation Agency.)

B. Competition: Because competition is keen for most companies, objective estimates of its strength are important. After looking at what its major competition was likely to do, the firm looked at itself.

• Several advantages have placed MDI several years in advance of competition in the magnetic devices equipment field. These are cryogenic magnets for commercial applications and high reliability power supplies for long-endurance military application.

• However, in order to realize fully the growth commensurate with the above advantages, several weaknesses must be overcome by developing an ability to construct crystals as well as developing more sophisticated test procedures.

C. Internal examination of the past and projections: Analyses of various parts of the enterprise, e.g.

• Product line analysis:

   a. Product (s) performance (i.e., sales volume, profit margin, etc.) .

   b. Customer class served.

   c. Comparison with major competitors' product (s) .

   d. Comparison with substitutes and complementary performance.

   e. Possibilities for product improvement.

   f. Suggestions with regard to new products.

• Market analysis:

   a. Important factors in projected sales changes: product success; marketing organization; advertising; and competitive pressures.

   b. New markets to be penetrated (i.e., geographical areas and customer classes) .

• Financial analysis:

   a. Profit position.

   b. Working capital.

   c. Cash position.

   d. Impact of financial policy on market price per share.

   e. Prospects for future financing.

• Production analysis:

   a. Plant and equipment (maintenance and depreciation) .

    b. Productive capacity and productivity.

    c. Percent of capacity utilized.

    d. Suggestions for: productivity improvements; cost reduction; utilizing excess capacity; and planning expansion.

- Technical analysis:

    a. Research and development performance.

    b. Suggestions for improving research and development effectiveness.

- Employees:

    a. Employment and future needs.

    b. Technical manpower deficiencies.

    c. Appraisal of employee attitudes.

- Facilities:

    a. Evaluation of current facilities to meet new business.

    b. Machine replacement policy and needs.

IV. Basic Objectives, Policies, and Strategies: This covers every important area of the business, but most companies concentrate on A through F of the following:

A. Profits.	G. Research.
B. Sales.	H. Engineering.
C. Finance.	I. Personnel.
D. Marketing.	J. Acquisitions.
E. Capital additions.	K. Organization.
F. Production.	L. Long-range planning.

This list can be expanded. As noted elsewhere, the more concrete the specification here can be, the easier it usually is to implement the plans. It is especially important for a business manager to know precisely what he is seeking and the method to be employed to get there. For example, MDI marketing objectives were set forth as follows:

- Increase sales of magnetic devices 100 percent in the next five years. Increase sales of power supply equipment 200 percent during the next five years.
- Increase the total volume of industrial sales from today's 25 percent to 50 per cent of total sales at the end of five years.
- Penetrate the western market to the point where the company will control 10 percent of it at the end of five years.
- Enter the foreign market within five years by a licensing agreement, a joint venture, or manufacturing facility.

For each of these objectives, the company prepared a detailed series of strategies ranging from a strategy to "sell custom designs directly to prime contractors in geographic regions where their main plants are located" to details such as special services to selected specified customers, training program for employees, and top management meetings with customers.

Further strategies which might be included in this section of the plan, with special regard to marketing, are organization, use of dealers, possibility of distributing products manufactured by others, salesmen's compensation plans, and pricing policy.

Drawing a proper line of demarcation between the strategic plans and the detailed operational plans is difficult. Ideally, the two blend together in a continuous line. This was the case with MDI, where those making the strategic plan also were the ones to implement it.

V. Detailed Medium-Range Plans: more detailed plans growing out of the above. For MDI these plans were developed for each of the succeeding five years:

A. *Pro forma* balance sheet, yearly.
B. Income statement, yearly.
C. Capital expenditure schedule, yearly.
D. Unit production schedule for major products, yearly.
E. Employment schedule, yearly.
F. Detailed schedule to acquire within three years a company with design capability in solid state magnetic devices.

VI. One-Year Plans: the next year's budgets. The first year's budgets for items A through F were, in the aggregate, the same for the first year of the five-year plan, but broken into quarterly time periods. In addition, MDI had other budgets, principally purchasing schedules for major components and raw materials and typical detailed administrative budgets covering such things as travel and telephone.

SOME CHARACTERISTICS OF
CORPORATE PLANS

It will be readily recognized that for a much larger corporation than Magnetic Design, Inc., the documentation of the corporate plan will cover many more categories than noted above and be much more voluminous. For smaller companies the outline will be scantier. But the basic fundamental headings will remain the same for all.

A major problem of each company is to determine what areas shall be covered in a plan, how deeply they shall be studied, and how detailed plans shall be. No company can afford to study in great depth every facet of its business every year. Nor is this sort of examination required. Most companies concentrate their planning on profits, sales, distribution, finance, products, production, and personnel (Newell, Jr., 1963, pp. 100-101; Henry, 1965).

Very few companies prepare periodically or on a selected time basis a comprehensive and integrated strategic plan. Some companies give their divisions general guidance in the planning program upon which basis the divisions develop detailed plans. These are reviewed at the company's headquarters but not aggregated into a single corporate plan. This is the case at Litton Industries. On the other hand, there are companies that do aggregate these plans into a total integrated company plan. Managers are highly pragmatic people and tailor their efforts to fit need. As a result, parts of plans may be written, parts unwritten, and the mix may change from item to item, from time to time, and manager to manager.

Surveys of business plans, together with my empirical observations, lead me to conclude that most companies do not have a complete set of written plans approaching that presented above. The actual plans devised for most firms are a composite of both written and unwritten plans and documentation is made only for selected areas. For example, out of 822 companies recently surveyed (Stewart 1967) only about 40 percent had profit and loss statements and balance sheets extending beyond the current year. About the same percentage had long-range capital budgets. About the same percentage had written profit and sales objectives. When asked whether there were specific plans for future years, written or unwritten, the percentages responding affirmatively for different areas were as follows: between 40 and 49 percent said they had plans for accounting, sales, marketing, corporate management, and planning. Between 31 and 38 percent said they had plans for finance, manufacturing, acquisitions, and product research and development. Future purchasing and industrial relations plans existed for 25 percent, and 22 percent had future public relations plans. Since most companies that plan ahead do so for a 5-year period of time it is a fair presumption that most of these plans covered about the same length of time (Kaiden 1967; Newell, Jr., 1963).

SUMMARY AND CONCLUSIONS

This chapter presented and examined a number of conceptual and operational models of comprehensive corporate planning structures and steps, and compared them. Some of the major conclusions of the chapter are:

1. The author's conceptual model of the structure and process of corporate planning is flexible and adaptable to any size or type of business, style of management, or stage in the development of organized formal planning. Although there are differences with other conceptual models, all the models are fundamentally quite similar.

2. It is of major importance in the development and implementation of comprehensive corporate planning to understand the conceptual distinction be-

tween strategic and tactical planning. The approaches to planning in these two areas differ importantly.

3. Once the distinction between strategic and tactical planning is understood, it is important to see that it is often impossible to draw a line of demarcation between them.

4. While actual operational planning structures and steps may on the surface appear to be rather different from the conceptual models given in this chapter, underneath the conceptual models should be discernible. If not, the planning process is missing some element which eventually will result in poor plans.

5. Planning steps are not sequential but iterative.

6. Planning and control, although considered as separate functions of management, are inextricably interwoven and each is developed and implemented in contemplation of the other. Nevertheless, it is important to distinguish conceptually between the two.

7. While it is desirable to have comprehensive corporate plans written, it is clear that a mass of plans of a company must remain unwritten simply because to record them would result in excessive bulk.

8. The major topics in the table of contents of an "ideal" as well as an acceptable operational plan are reasonably clear, but there is no standard which has received widespread acceptance. (A detailed table of contents of an operational plan was presented in the chapter.)

9. In making corporate plans, it is very important to know how deeply aspects of it should be studied and how detailed parts of it should be in relationship to other parts, and over time.

3

The Importance of
Comprehensive Planning ————

3
The Importance of
Comprehensive Planning

INTRODUCTION

The importance of planning cannot be denied. Yet there are too many managers who are pleased that the future arrives day by day, and who are content to deal with it on that time schedule. They feel that meeting each day's problems is taxing enough without looking very far ahead. They agree with the ditty:

> *Don't worry about the future*
> *The present is all thou hast*
> *The future will soon be present*
> *And the present will soon be past.*

At the other end of the scale are far-sighted managers like Charles Percy, the former President of the Bell & Howell Company, who said that before turning off the lights in his office each evening he looked at a sign on his desk which read: "My job is to build our company's future." Planning ahead was of the highest importance to him.

Among managers one can find all shades of expression about the importance of planning. The scale of skepticism rises the greater the length of time and the wider the subject matter covered in a comprehensive corporate planning program. To organize and maintain an effective planning mechanism is exceedingly difficult in the larger company, and to develop effective plans requires hard and demanding mental work. Some questions about the value of comprehensive planning may well arise from those who either do not know how to get the system started or, having once started it, have problems in making it work effectively.

In the Balkans there is a method of music-making called "singing with book" in which the performer puts a volume on his lap, places a hand over it, and proceeds to sing, totally disregarding the book which he can't read anyway. This analogy cannot be carried too far, but I frequently have found that many who fault comprehensive corporate planning are guilty of not paying attention to what is known about making the process operate effectively.

In this chapter, attention is directed to some of the outstanding reasons why comprehensive planning is so important in a business enterprise.

ESSENTIAL TO DISCHARGING TOP MANAGEMENT RESPONSIBILITY

The type of comprehensive planning discussed in this book is indispensable to a top manager's effectively discharging his responsibilities. The job of a top manager essentially concerns the way in which his total organization reacts to its environment to achieve the objectives set for the organization. His concern is with the totality of the enterprise and how it operates in its environment. Although his attention is on the entire system of his business he must also be concerned with the internal operations of the subsystems.

All top managers, of course, must break down this responsibility into components that will tell them in more concrete terms how to tackle the task. Marvin Bower (1966, pp. 17-18) says there are fourteen basic and well-known managing processes that make up the components from which a management system for any business can be fashioned. He lists them as follows: setting objectives, planning strategy, establishing goals, developing a company philosophy, establishing policies, planning the organization structure, providing personnel, establishing procedures, providing facilities, providing capital, setting standards, establishing management programs and operational plans, providing control information, and activating people.

Charles E. St. Thomas (1965, pp. 20-21) queried a representative group of businessmen who were asked to enumerate the most pressing problems they faced. They were asked to respond not so much in terms of their day-to-day headaches but with respect to longer-range, recurrent problems which did not stay solved despite attempts to settle them. He found a consensus that the five most pressing managerial problems are:

"1. Offering products and services *ahead* of the competition.
2. Locating and retaining capable people.
3. Encouraging managers in lower echelons to accept delegated authority.
4. Really knowing the important things that are going on within the business, particularly in a complex organization.
5. Integrating the work of all functions into a cohesive whole so that the full force of the business can be placed behind its major activities."

These problems, of course, are not unique to a top manager, for they are problems which managers at all levels face. They also are common to all kinds of businesses. Each problem and its significance will vary from business to business, from time to time, and under different circumstances. "But," says St. Thomas (p. 21), "the common thread of the problem—the *principle*—is one which all managers can be relatively certain of facing throughout the greater portion of their business careers."

In another study (Stieglitz and Janger 1965) published by the National Industrial Conference Board, the minimum job of top management in a decentralized company was specified as covering (p. [1]):

"1. Determining corporate objectives—in terms of fields of business—and allocation of resources to these objectives

2. Creating the basic value system—policies and ethical principles—that will govern the conduct of the various parts of the company

3. Determining the organization structure and selecting key personnel to man the structure

4. Evaluating the total enterprise and its components as they move toward established objectives

5. Allocating the proceeds of the company's efforts to the various claimants —stockholders, employees, governments, and the company itself."

The NICB concludes that: "These reserved responsibilities of top management can be summarized as overall planning and control" (p. [199]).

The conclusion so apparent in considering Bower's fourteen requirements in building a management system, St. Thomas' managerial problems, and the NICB's reserved responsibilities is that they cannot be dealt with adequately in the absence of an effective system of planning. No system of planning, no matter how skillfully it is created, will handle all the responsibilities and problems of a top manager. Many will lie outside the planning system. Nor, once planning is perfected and plans put into operation, will the top managerial task be completed. But it is apparent that a very large part of the decision-making that is the direct responsibility of top management can be and is made in a comprehensive planning process.

SIMULATES THE FUTURE

One of the great advantages of comprehensive corporate planning is that it simulates the future—on paper. If the simulation does not result in the desired picture the exercise can be erased and started all over again. Simulation choices are reversible. In keeping with Lord Nelson's famous axiom: "Your drill ground must be your battle ground," planning prepares a business to cope better with the environmental changes of the future.

Simulation has many other advantages. It encourages and permits the manager to see, evaluate, and accept or discard a far greater number of alternative courses of action than he might otherwise consider. Although identification of the "right" course of action is far more significant than generating numbers of alternatives, the fact that more alternatives are brought forth for review may produce ideas that a lesser effort would not uncover.

A comprehensive formal planning program also organizes information flows. The process provides a channel for information flows. Managers are thereby given a much greater capability of handling information. Other things being equal, this should bring to bear more and better factual data at the point of decision.

The fact that simulation allows experimentation without actually committing resources encourages managers to try different courses of action. Computers have and will increasingly facilitate the development of models of the real world and permit managers to experiment with different decisions and possible influences.

Continuous planning should make managers better planners. This is difficult to substantiate quantitatively, but I agree with Piet Hein's (1966) "The Road to Wisdom." The road to wisdom?—well, it's plain and simple to express:

> Err
> and err
> and err again
> but less
> and less
> and less.

APPLIES THE SYSTEMS APPROACH

Comprehensive business planning is the application of the systems approach to management. It does not deal with each separate element of the business alone, by itself, but rather permits the manager to see things as parts of a whole.

The ancient Greeks thought this way and as Edith Hamilton (1963, pp. 284-285) tells us: ". . . this habit of mind is stamped upon everything they did. It is the underlying cause of the difference between their art and ours. Architecture, perhaps, is the clearest illustration. The greatest buildings since Greek days, the cathedrals of the Middle Ages, were built, it would seem, without any regard to their situation, placed haphazard, wherever it was convenient. Almost invariably a cathedral stands low down in the midst of a huddle of little houses, often as old or older, where it is marked by its incongruity with the surroundings. The situation of the building did not enter into the architect's plans. They were concerned only with the cathedral itself. The idea never occurred to them to think of it in relation to what was around it. It was not part of a whole to them; it was the whole. But to the Greek architect the setting of his temple was all-important. He planned it, seeing it in clear outline against sea or sky, determining its size by its situation on plain hilltop or the wide plateau of an acropolis. It dominated the scene, indeed; it became through his genius the most important feature in it, but was always a part of it. He did not think of it in and for itself, as just the building he was making; he conceived of it in relation to the hills and the seas and the arch of the sky.

"To see anything in relation to other things is to see it simplified. A house is a very complicated matter considered by itself: plan, decoration, furnishings; each room, indeed, made up of many things; but, if it is considered as part of a block or part of a city, the details sink out of sight. Just as a city in itself is a mass of complexity but is reduced to a few essentials when it is thought of as belonging to a country. The earth shows an infinite diversity, but in relation to the universe it is a sphere swinging in space, nothing more.

"So the Greek temple, conceived of as a part of its setting, was simplified, the simplest of all the great buildings of the world, and the Gothic cathedral, seen as a complete whole in itself, unrelated to anything beyond itself, was of all buildings the most elaborated in detail."

So it is with business planning. Comprehensive planning permits management to focus attention on the major issues relevant to the successful survival of its enterprise. It provides a mechanism for the interrelated parts to be coordinated, thereby avoiding suboptimization of parts at the expense of the whole. It also provides a structure for avoiding top management's getting bogged down in petty detail.

In contrast to this approach to planning is an informal type which takes place only when a problem arises. This is *ad hoc*. It is *random*. It follows the slogan of the Donnybrook Fair—hit a head when you see it. This is not to imply that no planning is done in this approach. Some planning must take place in the mind of the manager while a problem is being solved. But it is a type activity far removed from the formal comprehensive planning discussed in this book.

This approach has many shortcomings. For example, it may result in decisions which seriously narrow choices available for future action and may, thereby, be very costly. A simple illustration is that of the public utility that constructed an eight-inch water pipeline to accommodate a new suburban development. The utility had no time for long-range forecasts and failed to see (what was readily predictable) that within one year several new plants were to be built close to the older area and the demands for water in that region would be tripled. The old eight-inch pipeline was abandoned and a new twenty-four-inch line constructed. Aside from creating great inconvenience among its customers the failure to plan was costly.

STIMULATES DEVELOPMENT OF AIMS AND ACHIEVEMENT

Planning must be based upon an identification of the basic missions of the business, its long-range objectives, and its short-range goals. The power afforded a company by having this network of aims cannot be overemphasized.

The National Industrial Conference Board (Brown, Dobson, and Thompson 1966, p. 7) surveyed 138 manufacturing companies that grew rapidly from 1960 to 1965. The rate of growth was most impressive for some of the companies: 57 reported an increase of over 50 percent in volume of business during the period; 13 reported more than 100 percent growth; and 5 said sales grew over 200 percent. Only 11 companies reported sales growth under 25 percent. The NICB reported: "Over three-fourths of the survey respondents believe that their expansion from 1960 to 1965 was in large measure the result of deliberate planning for growth, and nearly half gave planning virtually full credit for their increased volume of business."

Another study of the reasons for the success of the thirteen fastest growing companies in the U.S. concluded that six factors were characteristic in all. The first was giving top priority to long-range planning* (Weiner 1964, p. 30).

A penetrating analysis of long-range planning in industrial corporations concluded that: ". . . every business corporation should have a formal long-range planning system to force managers to specify their objectives and how they expect to achieve them. This view is based on the experience and evaluations of formal planning systems by the executives and planners who were interviewed. However, such a system does not need to be complex. A simple set of target goals, operational plans, and financial projections for the next few years would be adequate for many firms" (Henry 1965, p. 189).

The many reasons why a well-developed network of aims is so important will be examined in a later chapter. One concluding observation is in order, however. William Burgess (1965, p. 5) of Electronic Specialty Company asks the question and answers it: "Why do many companies return only a fraction of the possible return on invested capital to their shareholders? The answer is that many companies have not even stated their goals. Most companies operate on a self-restrictive basis that does not permit their managers even to see the goals they could be reaching. A relative few have proved that, although certain ultimate limitations do exist for business growth at any given time in a company's development, these limitations are so far beyond the limitations that most managers place on themselves as to be practically nonexistent."

---

* The other factors cited (pp. 31-32) were: " (2) A truly dynamic corporate structure that enables the company to seize a profit opportunity whenever or wherever one appears. (3) An active, viable program to encourage employee innovation and creativity. (4) An infallible sense of time, of being equally adept at knowing when to launch a new product or close down an old plant. (5) Above-average investment acumen, a particularly challenging capability that few corporations can really master. (6) An integrated product line, with a program of product development and acquisition designed to avoid both risk and merely temporary gain."

REVEALS AND CLARIFIES FUTURE
OPPORTUNITIES AND THREATS

Henrik Ibsen said: "I hold that man is in the right who is most clearly in league with the future." The great value of comprehensive corporate planning is that it helps a manager foresee new opportunities and then permits him to exercise his innovative skills in exploiting them. Conversely, looking ahead reveals threats. Being forewarned, managers are in a much better position to eliminate them or lessen their impact than if they appear unexpectedly. Foreknowledge is power.

Around every company there usually is a word that is used with reverence. At Harris-Intertype Corporation that word is "planning" (*Business Week* 1966c). Planning has helped top management there to see opportunities and exploit them. This company grew during the past twenty years from a family held, loosely run maker of printing presses with $10 million sales in its only product line to a publicly held, tightly managed maker of many products. It has currently the highest sales and earnings in the graphic arts equipment industry. In 1964, to illustrate its perception in taking advantage of opportunities in the future, the company decided (following a study of the money markets) that capital costs would rise sharply. Although it had no need for cash at the time it sold $25 million of debentures at $4\frac{3}{8}$ percent. One year later the rate would probably have been 7 percent.

An outstanding illustration of a company's seeing and grasping an opportunity was Boeing's decision to put millions of dollars of its own funds into the development of the KC 135 tanker. This led to a contract with the Department of Defense for this airplane and a whole new generation of subsonic jets beginning with the Boeing 707.

Business history is filled with sad stories of companies that did not see rocks in the road ahead and tripped over them. A classic story, of course, is that of the railroad industry with which, at the end of the 19th century, no other means of transportation could compete in speed, flexibility, comfort, cost and durability. Within 30 years of their strongest hold on the transportation system of the nation, they were desperately trying to avoid bankruptcy.

The first diesel locomotive was built in 1913 in Sweden. General Electric and Alcoa built diesel-electric switching locomotives for yard work in the U.S. in 1923, and in 1934 the first road diesel was built by General Motors. The Baldwin Locomotive Works, the largest producer of steam locomotives, not only failed to look ahead but did not see what was currently happening to its market. As a result it eventually went bankrupt.

The important point about these last two examples is that in each case the competitive threat which brought or threatened bankruptcy could have been anticipated with just a little thinking about the future. But in each case the threat was not perceived, was ignored, or completely underestimated. Effective corporate planning could have prevented these disasters.

FRAMEWORK FOR DECISION-MAKING
THROUGHOUT COMPANY

The structure of plans needed in an effective corporate planning program has high significance in providing an overall framework for decision-making throughout the company. This will prevent piecemeal decisions and provide a basis for testing value judgments. Each of these aspects is very significant.

One of the more important attributes of an effective planning program is that it gives guidance to managers throughout a business in making decisions which are in line with the aims and strategies of upper management levels. When a company has developed overall objectives, strategies, and policies, managers down the line have a basis for making both major and minor decisions in conformance with top management wishes. No planning program can or should try to foresee all decisions which managers must make in their day-to-day operations. As a result there are thousands of decisions managers make which, individually and cumulatively, have an important impact on both short- and long-range success or failure of a business. Without an organized planning program it is much more difficult for managers to make decisions in a direction determined by top management.

In the study referred to earlier in this chapter which identified the major reasons why the fastest growing companies were so successful, the dominant position of planning was specified. But the nature of this planning is also important. Each of these companies was able to assure management involvement in all levels of planning.

By participating in and making decisions on the basis of an integrated planning framework, managers are better able to use their time on activities that pay off. Their efforts are focused on meaningful actions in line with their own and company interests.

Improved manager motivation and morale should accompany such planning. In participating in their own plans managers have a sense of satisfaction in at least a partial creation of their own destiny. They know what is expected of them which when achieved has its own sense of satisfaction. A feeling of personal security is enhanced and confidence is built.

Not only do those inside but others outside a business benefit from a well-developed plan. Paul Davies, when Chairman of the Board of the Food Machinery Corporation, said that FMC's successful expansion program was due in very large part to the company's long-term plan. "We don't even look at anything that doesn't fit into the plan," he said. "But once a company does fit into it (usually because it possesses a raw-material source, a market position, or similar advantage needed by FMC), FMC does not hesitate to acquire it" (Weiner 1965, p. 27).

Litton's outstanding acquisition program is centered on its long-range plan. "People we talk merger with," says Litton President Roy Ash, "find the plan meaningful, and thus find reasons for being part of it. We've never elbowed our way into a company" (Weiner 1965, p. 27).

Today, only the very smallest companies can operate on the basis of one-man decision-making. Throughout managerial levels in most corporations decisions are made which have important implications for current as well as long-range profits. Knowledge is a resource in business. As such it must be used, and this means that entrepreneurial type decisions are made throughout a business. Knowledge is not something that can be commanded or monopolized. A staff researcher in a laboratory has an opportunity to work on one project as compared with another, or to emphasize one type of development versus another. A marketing economist will make recommendations about which markets to penetrate, and the sales manager to whom the recommendations will be made will in some degree be influenced by this staff work. In all areas of an enterprise decisions will be made having an impact on the direction which the enterprise takes and the success it enjoys. A planning framework provides a powerful guide to decision-making which is integrated and unified behind the aims of top management.

PREVENTS PIECEMEAL DECISIONS

A well-developed long-range planning program prevents piecemeal decisions. One of the reasons for the $425 million loss of General Dynamics due to the low sales of its Convair-880 transport was that decision-making was piecemeal (R. A. Smith 1962). This was probably the largest dollar loss resulting from a product failure in U.S. history. By early 1955 Convair had preliminary designs for two long-range jets, but negotiation problems with Howard Hughes continued while Boeing with its 707 and Douglas with its DC-8 beat Convair to the market. Still interested in jet transport, Convair in 1956 designed a short- to medium-range jet which would have been the only airplane of that type in that market. But as time went by the airplane grew larger and larger and finally found its competition to be the big Boeing and Douglas airplanes. In the meantime the Caravelle and the Lockheed Electra took the short- and medium-range markets. There were many reasons other than piecemeal decision-making for Convair's loss, but poor planning was a major consideration.

With costs of capital expenditures rising and lead times for new product development lengthening, most businesses today simply cannot afford piecemeal decisions. Costs of facilities, personnel development, research and engineering development, and other costs of developing new products are simply too great for a company to plan in short time spans. The best interests of a company are better served by requiring the analytical decisions requisite to a proper planning program instead of permitting opportunistic decision-making.

TESTS VALUE JUDGMENTS

Value judgments of managers differ throughout an organization. One important advantage of a good planning program is that it forces individuals to test their value judgments with others. One of the dangers in planning is that a forceful or powerful individual with a poor value judgment may dominate. Although a comprehensive planning structure will not reduce substantially a stubbornly held value judgment of such a person, it has in it the possibility of reducing the impact or of correcting the judgment. It may well be that among some companies that have not begun formal planning the reason exists in the disinterest of top management in revealing and, on occasion, yielding on its value judgments. Whereas in those companies which are enthusiastic about organized planning the top managers may welcome testing of value judgments in the best interests of the enterprise, knowing, of course, that in the end they can prevail if they choose.

BASIS FOR OTHER MANAGEMENT FUNCTIONS

Planning both precedes and is inextricably intermeshed with other management functions. For example, planning is obviously essential to effective control. If the purpose of organized effort is not specified and understood, how can resources be controlled effectively? Resources are used most effectively when the objective of their use is known. Specification of objectives and courses of action designed to achieve them are essential to an adequate measurement of accomplishment. Clearly, measurement of efficiency with which a production program is conducted depends upon volume, cost, and quality objectives which have been set for it. Measurement of longer-range profit objectives is essential before success of the custodianship of top management can be appraised.

Planning also is closely intertwined with other managerial functions. Certainly, planning is essential for many organizational changes, coordinating the various elements of an enterprise, staffing, leading, innovating, and the other activities which managers undertake. This is not to say that planning always is the first in time or is always dominant. There is no doubt about the fact, for example, that managerial charisma is of outstanding importance in any firm's success. But other managerial functions are more easily and suitably performed if a planning program of proper scope is conducted.

CHANNEL OF COMMUNICATIONS

A well-organized planning program is an extremely useful communications network. The planning process is a means for communications among all levels of management about objectives, strategies, and detailed operational plans. As plans approach completion, common understanding is generated among all levels of management of opportunities and problems important to individual managers and to the company. The choices made in the planning process are discussed in a common language and the issues are understood by all those participating in the decisions. Once plans are completed and written there is a permanent and clear record of decisions made, who is going to implement them, and how they should be carried out. Misunderstanding is thereby minimized. The advantages of this common channel of communications is lost when plans are formulated and carried out in someone's head.

As a planning program is developed over time, it teaches what data are most needed at what points in decision-making, and the best ways to get needed facts. For example, in one company the first effort to forecast the market for its products was most painful. The methodology for making the forecast was not known, sources of information were vague, who was going to collect what information was unclear, and how the data were to be analyzed and used when the forecast was finished was hazy. For example, a major conflict arose over whether the data were to be calculated and used in terms of current or constant prices. The sales department was dead set against using constant prices partly, I suppose, because this showed a much less optimistic sales curve than if inflationary factors were built in the forecast. I am also convinced a major stumbling block was lack of understanding of the significance of using current prices. Over a series of cycles, however, these difficulties were ironed out and the calculation and use of market demand for most products became routine and occupied 1/10 of the resources formerly employed.

David Ewing (1964b) points out a more subtle advantage deriving from the process of organizing and rearranging information in the planning process. He writes (p. 76): "For example, the planning group looks at a hodgepodge of facts about customers, decides to classify them by profitability, and learns to its surprise that 85 percent of the firm's profits come from less than 15 percent of the customers. Or a man assigned to estimate the volume of future new products pores over a maze of past records and estimates, shuffles and reshuffles the data, and suddenly discovers that there has been a fairly consistent relationship over the years between a dollar invested in research one year and a dollar returned in new product sales five years later. In short, the revelation comes not from the facts themselves but from the effort to classify and relate them in meaningful ways, and this effort is a typical step in long-range planning."

HELPS TO MASTER CHANGE

The value of planning in both anticipating and bringing about change has been noted. A few additional comments, however, are of use.

The testimony of Harold Blancke, Chairman of the Celanese Corporation, in the January 1966 issue of the *Celanese World* devoted to planning in that Company, is as follows: "Planning is so important today that it occupies a major part of the time of some of the most respected men in business—and in Celanese. Planning allows us to *master change*. Planning forces us to organize our expectations and develop a program to bring them about. It is a most effective way to draw out the best in all of us—our best thinking, our best interests and aims—and to enable us to develop the most efficient way of achieving our maximum growth.

"Long-range planning enabled Celanese to become the first chemical company to organize its major activities along completely international lines. It enabled us to launch ourselves into three entirely new and yet related fields of business in less than a year, and to increase our 1965 sales to more than $2\frac{1}{2}$ times our 1961 figure.

"Planning is the intellectual arm of organized growth. It is the prologue to tomorrow. And yet it is not the rarefied activity of a few people—it is really the business of all of us . . . If Celanese is to continue to thrive and prosper, our planning activities must continue to lead the way, for careful and thorough planning is one vital key to the future of Celanese."

The planning process also stirs up fresh attitudes and new ways of thinking. David Ewing (1964b, p. 76) thinks long-range planning will find its way further into managerial favor because, in his words: "By definition, long-range planning implies thinking in a time period beyond the pressure of current events. Freed from the immediate demands of operations and intra-office politics, planners can more seriously question various policies that might never otherwise be disputed. For instance, sometimes a policy of promotion only from within or of remaining first in research in the industry can loom so large in the perspective of day-to-day operations that there seems to be no possibility at all of disputing it seriously except in a completely different context."

While planning is an engine of change it does not proceed smoothly without roadblocks of resistance. Most businesses are filled with contradictory pressures for and against change, which will be discussed in a later chapter.

DEVELOPING PLANNING ATTITUDES

It was noted in Chapter 1, but bears repetition here, that a major purpose of comprehensive planning is the development of attitudes, perspective, ways of thinking, decision-making habits, and planning philosophy, which will result in better decisions. The sharper are these managerial characteristics, the better will be plans and the more responsive management will be to making needed changes. Plans can be copied by competitors but not managerial mental talents. The asset is expressed in Kipling's "The 'Mary Gloster'":

> *"And they asked me how I did it,*
> *And I gave 'em the Scripture text,*
> *'You keep your light so shining*

A little in front o' the next!'
They copied all they could follow,
But they couldn't copy my mind,
And I left 'em sweating and stealing
A year and a half behind."

PERFORMANCE MEASUREMENT

The existence of a comprehensive plan provides a basis for measuring performance. Management has standards of both a quantitative and qualitative nature in a comprehensive plan. The performance of a business should not be measured solely in quantitative financial terms, as so many companies try to do. Certainly financial results are of great importance in gauging success or failure, but nonquantitative characteristics of a business are also of high importance. Creativity, innovation, imagination, motivation, knowledge, for example, may reflect in financial results. But if they are not fostered and measured by top management, a current financial success can easily disappear. A well-conceived planning program will not only permit managers at all levels to measure these attributes in managers under their authority, but will also serve as a method for improving them.

RESISTANCE TO PLANNING

The above discussion should leave no doubt that effective comprehensive planning is an exceedingly powerful management tool that all managers everywhere will embrace with enthusiasm. This is not so. There is not universal approval of formal comprehensive planning. What is the case against it?

In investigating planning among small businessmen (Steiner in Pfeffer 1967) the following responses were given to me as to why so little long-range planning was done: "That's for big companies. Not me." "Why should I? I'm doing O.K." "You can't forecast the future, so how can you do long-range planning?" "Long-range planning is too time-consuming for me. I simply do not have the time, even if I wanted to do long-range planning." "I am in a cash squeeze and that's all I can think about now." "It's too complicated." "My business is simple, and I know what the problems are." "My business is too small to formalize planning." "I can do all the planning I need in my head. Anyway, I don't want to discuss my plans with anyone. Why give someone a chance to find out and lose my competitive advantage?"

Some of these observations are made by some managers of larger enterprises. There are also other reasons given by managers in larger firms. In commenting on the lack of formal long-range planning in Great Britain, I. M. Clark, a management consultant, observed (*The Financial Times*, November 16, 1966) that one main reason for the low attention given to long-range planning is ". . . that successive Governments have failed to create a climate in which any but the boldest companies are prepared to 'have a go.'" Thanks to what they regard as government unpredictability, all too many companies lack the confidence to make the substantial investment of one of their scarcest resources—senior management time—which effective long-range planning requires. Many companies in Europe have not developed formal planning in the American style as described in this book because affairs are too closely held by owner-managers.

A case can be made against formal planning. If a company is in a current crisis, for example, it would probably be a waste of managerial resources to engage in comprehensive formal planning. All its efforts should be devoted to getting out of the current hole. If the top management is not mentally attuned to formal planning, it probably should not be undertaken because it will fail. In most instances, failure after trying is probably worse than not trying at all. The reason is that inhibitions to trying again will probably last longer. Companies engaged in a very difficult current competitive race, which is likely to continue, and having limited resources, probably cannot indulge in much long-range thinking. Also, any company that tries to develop accurate and complete detailed plans for the distant future is making a mistake. This type of planning should not be undertaken.

SUCCESS WITHOUT PLANNING

A number of companies without formal planning have been successful because they have been rapidly growing. Whatever the reason for rapid growth of demand for the products of such a company the momentum of growth can, even for a fairly large company, provide elements which normally flow from a planning program. For example, coordination of resources is related to the momentum of growth, and decisions are made on a day-to-day basis by adjusting to that general direction. The roles of individuals are reasonably well defined and often the great success overshadows the tensions and frustrations which accompany lesser successes. The problem of a company such as this is that it can look great one year and be depressed the next. When the rate of expansion levels off or declines, problems mount and coordination is considerably more difficult.

Richard Neuschel (1965, p. 39) examined the profit performance of many companies in four major industries and concluded that ". . . the difference between the top performer and the bottom performer at any given time is usually far greater than the difference between the high point and low point on the industry trend line." In other words, where a company stands in the profit spectrum within its industry is much more significant to it than where the industry stands on the profit trend line.

Neuschel goes on to observe (p. 39) that superior performance of the profit leaders has resulted from a number of different factors. "Sometimes their relatively high profits are the result of good fortune—of being in the right industry at the right time with the right products or processes or distribution facilities. Sometimes outstanding performance is the result of a few brilliant strategic decisions—to expand capacity, to integrate vertically, to merge with or acquire other companies, and so on. Sometimes profit leadership comes because a company has assembled an outstandingly competent management group. And sometimes profits are superior because top management has effectively channeled its company's effort toward substantial, continuing profit improvement." This last factor, he goes on to say, is the only one immediately available to a management that is willing to make the effort. In other words, there can be success without planning, but a planning system is the method which can best be counted on to achieve success.

Charles Sorensen (1956), in his book about Henry Ford, said "planning" was not for Ford. He could not stand the idea of controls imposed from outside his company. Even inside the company he found it impossible to project a program. According to Sorensen, Ford worked in a seemingly wasteful way, scorning elaborate card indexes, going from trial to error and back again. He kept everything in a turmoil. Nevertheless up to the post World War II period his company was remarkably successful.

FAILURE DESPITE PLANNING

The fact that a company plans is not an open door to success. Many things can happen to upset the best laid plans. The sad story of detailed but inept planning bringing about the financial collapse of the proud and venerable Winchester Company is told brilliantly and in detail in Harold F. Williamson's *Winchester: The Gun That Won The West* (1963). With the purchase of eighty shares of stock in the Volcanic Repeating Arms Company, the seeds of a yet to be mighty corporation were planted in 1857. The company had many problems and was plagued by changing fortunes, but by the end of the 19th century it had established itself as a growing, profitable, and highly regarded enterprise with a top quality product. Between 1889 and 1914 the value of its product grew between three and four hundred percent. With sales in 1914 of almost $12 million it had 28 percent of the industry market. Its net worth was almost $17 million. It was a financially healthy, expanding, profitable, and vigorous enterprise. Difficulties incurred during World War I, and subsequent massive miscalculations in its long-range planning program, proved the undoing of the company and brought bankruptcy in 1931.

Prior to U.S. entrance into the war the company had large contracts with allied nations. But its failure to anticipate rising labor and material costs during 1915 and 1916 robbed it of its anticipated profits. In the meantime it was necessary to raise capital for plant expansion. In mid-1917 the net worth of the company had grown to over $19 million, but it also had contracted a debt to an investment house and banks of almost $17 million due in early 1918. The company had made profits during the period but not enough to finance plant expansion. With the U.S. entrance into the war its contracts soared but financial problems mounted. Additional capital expansion loans were made and while the company was profitable it did not spin off enough cash to pay for the expansion. On the eve of the armistice the company had difficult but not insoluble financial problems.

A major miscalculation made during the expansion, however, was to establish the root cause of the company's eventual difficulties. The wartime building program placed new structures among the old buildings because this facilitated expanded war production. But this arrangement made later separation extremely difficult. Although in 1918 the old buildings had been completely depreciated, they remained not only a financial drain in terms of taxes and maintenance but stimulated the company into a bold postwar expansion program.

Little if any long-range planning was considered during the war and contract cancellation left the company with no prepared plans. A postwar financial reorganization in 1919 provided funds to take care of short-term obligations, and the company found itself in a reasonably strong financial position to face postwar expansion.

One must admire the unfettered imagination and cold courage, if not the skill in planning of the top management of the reorganized company. Up to World War I Winchester had been exclusively a producer of small arms and ammunition. During the war it added a few new items, such as bayonets for its guns, but it still remained predominately a producer of small arms and ammunition. The basic objective for the enterprise after the war was set at no less than to make "Winchester the largest single manufacturing institution in the world manufacturing sporting goods, cutlery, tools, and hardware specialties." This objective was forged so as to expand the output of new lines of business enough to absorb the factory space idled by contract cancellations. To do this, incidentally, meant doubling prewar manufacturing output!

Detailed studies were made to determine those products which might appropriately be included in the new line. An expansive new marketing program was devised to match the scope of the production potential. The company had always sold commercially through jobbing or wholesale houses which in turn sold to retailers. Now, it decided to get quicker results by by-passing these middlemen and offering to the ablest and best equipped hardware merchants in every town with 50,000 or less population an exclusive Winchester agencyship and stock ownership in the parent company. The ultimate aim was to sign up almost one-third of the 26,000 retail hardware dealers in the U.S. into this dealer-agency plan. In addition, the company decided to establish its own retail outlets in cities having over 50,000 population. Some 150 of these outlets were envisioned. Finally, the company decided to continue its distribution of products through jobbing houses. The assumption was made, which proved to be false, that the jobbers would continue to handle Winchester products because of the great demand and reputation of Winchester guns and ammunition.

Despite the extraordinary character of the plans no provision was made for a central coordinating planning committee. Lines of communication were strictly from functional managers to the president. This management weakness was accentuated by the appointment of several managers to key posts without any previous experience in the work they were to perform. These managerial problems were bound to cause trouble when it is remembered that this team was to compete with established firms with as much experience in their respective fields as Winchester had in small arms and ammunition. Furthermore, whereas Winchester had great experience in mass production of these items, its plan now required mass production and sale of a wide variety of new products. This gave rise to new production problems and to the need for an intricate marketing and distribution system. There then followed probably the fastest build-up of new products, both by in-house development and by acquisitions, that any company has tried before or since. Within two years the company added 750 individual items to its product line. Between 1923 and 1924 the president boasted that about 1,000 new products had been added with the result that the company had "The most complete line of sporting goods placed on the market by any single manufacturer; also the most complete line of tools and hardware specialties." By July 1924 the catalog of Winchester contained 7,584 separate items distributed among tools, cutlery, flashlights, paint, steel goods, fishing tackle, baseball and football goods, skates, other athletic supplies, rifles, and ammunition.

One major problem after another plagued this extraordinary departure from the Company's past operations, only a few of which can be treated here. The management overestimated its ability to hold down costs. As a result its products were not competitive and despite favored dealer treatment, Winchester sales were never over four percent of total dealer-agency sales. With the exception of flashlights and batteries, none of the new lines ever showed more than negligible profits between 1919 and 1931.

Costs of distribution were also heavily underestimated. Clerks in sporting goods stores were found to require special knowledge which upgraded their salaries. The Company thought it could centralize warehouses but found that wide location of warehouses was necessary to give its dealers services comparable to those provided by jobbers. Insurmountable problems arose in attempts to maintain adequate stocks of some items and to prevent excessive inventories of others.

To solve the difficult balancing of costs, volume of sales, and distribution, the Company merged with the Associated Simmons Hardware Companies of St. Louis in 1922. The merger made it necessary for Winchester dealers to do a mental flip-flop because Simmons had been one of the strongest enemies of the

Winchester distribution system. The salesmen who had heretofore fought Winchester dealers were now extolling the virtues of Winchester products. But this was not enough to correct the basic cost and distribution problems. Accentuating the problem was a decline in sales of guns and ammunition through independent jobbers and dealers who were unhappy with the competition of the Winchester-owned warehouses and other Company-associated outlets.

At no time did the Company-owned retail stores make any operating profits. The Company had patterned its distribution system on that of the successful Liggett plan which set up the United Drug-Rexall organization, but learned too late that desirable locations for sporting goods and hardware stores were not the same as for drugstores.

Fortunately for the Company the management did not neglect its bread and butter products—guns and ammunition. Three new guns were introduced in 1920 that were comparatively inexpensive. Indeed they were low-priced with the hope they could be put into production rapidly, find a wide market, and help use excess plant capacity. Nevertheless, management did not give these products the attention they merited in the fortunes of the Company.

Total sales reached a postwar peak of over $18 million in 1923 and dwindled to $7 million in 1931 when the Company was bought at a receivers' sale by the Olin interests of East Alton, Illinois. Despite the massive addition of new product lines, at no point in postwar history up to receivership were new lines' sales greater than those of the old lines, and generally they were from one-third to a half of old-line product sales. Furthermore, deficiencies of the long-range plan and neglect of the bread-and-butter business resulted in a diminishing share of the arms and ammunition market for Winchester. With 28 percent of the industry in 1914, the share dropped to 20 percent in 1921 and thereafter stabilized at between 16 and 17 percent. Had Winchester been able to maintain its prewar share of the market its sales for arms and ammunition would have been about $18.6 millions in 1923. This was higher than actual total sales for all products in any year. Winchester is now a thriving division of Olin Mathieson, but its traumatic experiences in the 1920's stand as dramatic and specific blueprints of corporate planning failure.

A classic case of failure despite the most sophisticated planning was the Edsel (Brooks 1959; Reynolds 1967). Studies began in 1948 at Ford to look at the wisdom of entering a new different medium-priced car market. There is a well-known practice among lower-income car-owners to "trade-up" to medium-priced cars; and there was a tendency for Ford owners to trade-up, not to the Ford medium-priced Mercury, but to cars of other producers. The Edsel was approved in 1955 to fill this market and placed on sale in 1957; but only about 110,000 were sold throughout the life of the car, and the company reportedly lost $250 million.

Despite the obvious failure of the Edsel, however, the net impact on the

Ford Motor Company was by no means as disastrous as this estimated cost to the Company. In the long run, there are Company officials who think that defeat was turned into victory. One of them was Ernest Breech, who put the story this way:

"The true Edsel story hasn't been told. We turned the Edsel defeat into a great victory because we moved quickly and, had it not been for the machine tools we got in to build the engines, transmissions and presses for stamping projected Edsel production, we'd have been a whole year or more later bringing out the Falcon—which is the one that should have been brought out instead of the Edsel. The pattern was changing in the industry. Imports were nothing when the Edsel was conceived of, but the medium-priced-car field was getting a substantial part of the business. There was a place in Ford for another car. Frankly, had the styling on the Edsel been different, had been a hit, the Edsel would not have been a failure. Just one thing: Someone hopped on that front end and called it a toilet seat, and it was dead from that minute.

"Also, from the time we conceived the Edsel and brought it out, which was three years, the pattern of the industry had changed. The imports had gone from practically nothing to a very substantial figure. All this time we'd been designing small cars, but we hadn't brought them out because there was no market for them in sufficient quantity. Ultimately, they became the Falcon. We got a year, maybe 18 months, that we'd never have gotten that early had it not been for the Edsel machine tools in place, which converted quickly. You couldn't get machine tools then, the industry was loaded. It had been 12 to 18 months getting machine tools alone. But we could convert in six months and we did, brought it out in a hurry and we made more money off the Falcon for that one year of early introduction than we ever lost on the Edsel." (*Forbes* 1967.)

LIMITATIONS OF PLANNING

Planning like other good things has its limitations. It is not the answer to all managerial problems. It does suffer from some shortcomings, the more important ones of which follow.

ENVIRONMENTAL EVENTS CANNOT ALWAYS BE CONTROLLED. Forecasting is not an exact science and plans based upon predictions which prove incorrect may fail. In the Edsel case, for instance, an economic recession coincided with the introduction of the automobile and the disaster was one which even a powerful company such as Ford could not overcome. Unexpected events in government action, such as a contract cancellation, or labor union activities which are unpredictable, all underscore the uncertainties of the future and create a hazard to planning.

INTERNAL RESISTANCE. Within enterprises there are potential areas of resistance which can thwart planning. Individuals tend to resist change, and the changes accompanying planning may be countered by this human inclination. President Kennedy used to say, when asked for approval to do something, "Yes, I approve, but the State Department will not go along." Here is illustrated the well-known problem of many executives in trying to get something done when resistance is encountered in an organization. As one wag put it, it is like trying to push something at the end of a piece of string. In larger organizations, old ways of doing things, old rules, old procedures, old methods can become so entrenched that it is difficult to change them. The larger companies become, the greater the amount of this old debris one finds. Old methods which emphasize short-range profit performance may easily deflect longer-range plans.

PLANNING IS EXPENSIVE. In a typical corporate planning effort of even a medium-sized company an enormous effort is required. The time of many people is occupied and costs are incurred for special studies and information. Planning is expensive and managers throughout the planning process must continuously apply a cost-benefit gauge. It is not possible to apply this equation quantitatively for such a large and long-range effort as a corporate plan, but the idea should be kept in mind for it is not difficult to obligate costs which exceed potential benefits.

CURRENT CRISES. Comprehensive corporate long-range plans are not always helpful in a sudden crisis, as noted previously. The problems of the Douglas Aircraft Company in late 1966 illustrate this. In the third quarter of 1966 the Company incurred a loss of $17 million despite a backlog of orders of about $2 billion. There were many reasons for their problem, but basically the Company had sold too many commercial airplanes with different configurations, found production disrupted by delivery delays of engines and pantries, and had under-priced some of its commercial airplanes. Costs got out of hand. Here was a problem which planning should have prevented but did not. Once the problem arose the solution was not found in long-range planning. It came in a merger; a large new infusion of capital, and efforts to get better control over production schedules and costs.

PLANNING IS DIFFICULT. Planning is hard work. It requires a high level of imagination, analytical ability, creativity, and fortitude to choose and become committed. Management must exert pressure to demand the best efforts in managers and staff. Both the talents required are limited and the maintenance of high quality planning is difficult to achieve. But if both requirements are not met, a plan instead of being a boon will be a boondoggle. As Kirby Warren (1962, p. 11) noted: "If a best effort is made and falls short of perfection, those involved, knowing that their best efforts are expected, will reflect and perhaps be stimulated; but where the best is not demanded and less meaningful efforts are accepted, the first people to realize that 'not much is expected of our plans' are those working on them. This is one of the major reasons for poor planning."

PLANNING DEMANDS APPLICATION OF PRINCIPLES, TECHNIQUES, AND MANAGERIAL TALENTS

Although the process of comprehensive planning cannot be counted upon automatically to bring about achievement of objectives, enough illustrations exist to leave no doubt but that when done well it is a powerful force. The requirements for success are principally the understanding of basic principles which have been learned about the process, an ability to apply appropriately and adroitly the many new techniques which have been developed to facilitate planning, and assurance that the best analytical and innovative talents in the business are used in the process. But above all is the role of the chief executive. If he does not commit himself to the planning program it will not succeed. So important is this conclusion that the next chapter will be devoted to a detailed examination of his role.

SOCIAL IMPLICATIONS OF CORPORATE PLANNING

This chapter should not be concluded without mention of the potential social impact of spreading comprehensive planning. The present economic system is much different from that of 100 or 200 years ago. Today's systematic planning among businesses creates a very different type system than in the days when businesses felt they could only react to market conditions. Business planning may prove to be a major cause not only for stable economic growth but for a growth-rate unprecedented in American history.

In an address before the Annual Dinner of the Financial Analysts Federation in Philadelphia on May 18, 1965, the President of the Chrysler Corporation, Lynn A. Townsend, drew the picture this way: "What we now have is a system in which tens of thousands of private business organizations are undertaking separately to explore all the possibilities of the country's economic future, and laying plans for making that future happen. They have no master plan to guide them. They have only their own individual appraisal of opportunity. And they take their own risks. Some of that private planning will turn out to be right— and some of it wrong. The mistakes will be automatically corrected not by changes in some central plan but by the prompt and effective rebuke of the market. If there is such a thing as a cybernetically sound economy, with built-in feedbacks and corrections, we have it. The emergence of this privately planned economy— in which the businessman is the active agent of growth—may be the real revolution of our century."

It is, of course, too early to gauge the impact which comprehensive corporate planning will have on the American economic system and its growth. That there has been and will continue to be an important impact cannot be denied.

SUMMARY AND CONCLUSIONS

This chapter sought to explain in some detail why comprehensive corporate planning is so important to improving and assuring effective management of business enterprises. (The importance described here attaches also to any other organization of any size, public or private.) Among the major conclusions are the following:

1. Comprehensive corporate planning is indispensable to a top manager's effectively discharging his responsibilities.

2. Planning can simulate the future on paper, a practice that not only is comparatively inexpensive but also permits a company to make better decisions about what to do now about future opportunities and threats than waiting until events just happen. Planning itself clarifies opportunities and threats which lie ahead for a company.

3. Comprehensive corporate planning is an effective way to look at a business as a system and apply the new techniques of the systems approach.

4. Planning stimulates the development of appropriate company aims, which, in turn, are powerful motivators of people.

5. Planning provides a framework for decision-making throughout the entire company and thereby makes it more likely that lower-level managers will make decisions in conformance with top management's desires.

6. Over-all corporate planning prevents piecemeal decisions; it prevents suboptimization of parts of the business system at the expense of over-all optimization.

7. The planning process is a basis for testing value judgments of individuals.

8. Planning is necessary for the better exercise of most other managerial functions.

9. Comprehensive corporate planning is a superb channel of communication by means of which people throughout a company converse in a common language about problems of high importance to them and to the company.

10. Comprehensive planning helps a top manager to bring about and master

those changes which are so important to assuring the vitality and growth of his company.

11. Planning builds, among all levels of management, a capability, an attitude, which facilitates quick and proper response to new events.

12. Planning provides a basis for measuring the performance of the entire company and its major parts.

13. There are limitations to comprehensive planning. It is not very effective, for example, in helping a company to overcome an immediate crisis. Also, it is not being done effectively if the costs of doing it are greater than the net benefits. Planning is expensive, it is difficult, it must overcome natural internal resistances, and environmental events may not always accommodate to plans.

14. Planning will not solve all the problems of a manager. Nor will planning *per se* guarantee business success. For some companies, a continuing flow of imaginative ideas is the only thing that can bring success. For some companies, completely unexpected and unpredictable events will bring failure despite sophisticated corporate planning. Some companies will succeed without planning, largely through a benevolent environment. But what has been said here is that, other things being equal, comprehensive corporate planning will bring much better results than if it is not done. It will provide a useful framework for better innovation, creativity, vision, and decision-making. All things considered, managers will be considerably better off with comprehensive planning than without it.

4
Top Management's Role in Planning

4
Top Management's Role in Planning

INTRODUCTION

There can and will be no effective comprehensive corporate planning in any organization where the chief executive does not give it firm support and make sure that others in the organization understand his depth of commitment. This principle should be obvious but it is not. Even when it is accepted, the role of the chief executive is far from clear. In this chapter the focus of attention is on the responsibility for corporate planning which rests with the chief executive and how his role may be determined.

MEANING OF THE TERM CHIEF EXECUTIVE

The term "chief executive" has come to mean the officer of a company who is accountable for the company's total efforts and total results. This is not a new term but it has found more usage in recent years. Following World War II a growing number of companies have designated the chairman of the board as chief executive. Indeed, a recent survey showed that over 25 percent of the companies listed on the New York Stock Exchange have named the chairman of the board as the chief executive (Stieglitz and Janger 1963, pp. 7-11).

Practice varies widely in the use of this designation. When Alfred Sloan was chairman of the board of General Motors he also was chief executive. When Harlow Curtice was president he also was chief executive, and when Frederic Donner was elevated from the presidency to the chairmanship he became chief executive. When Robert Gross was chairman of the board of the Lockheed Aircraft Corporation he also was chief executive and president. Upon his death the term chief executive was dropped at that corporation. Among smaller corporations the term chief executive is not often used officially.

The exigencies of a situation and the personalities of those at the top are responsible for different uses of this designation. Generally, when the chairman is also chief executive there is clearly identified a "number 2" man who is president. Frequently, the president is the only person reporting to the chairman and chief executive. Very often the arrangement is made to assure management continuity.

In this discussion the term chief executive will be used in a generic sense to mean the authority to manage a business. This authority may rest in more than one individual. It can, as noted above, be invested in a chairman of the board and a president, or it may be in the hands of a president and an executive vice-president. It may be found in the office of the president and include his top staff; in a divisionalized company it may be the general manager, so far as the division is concerned.

THE CHIEF EXECUTIVE'S NEED FOR
PLANNING HELP

In the previous chapter a brief description of some of the major responsibilities of chief executives was presented. It was obvious that planning was of the highest importance in his discharging well these duties. One further step should now be taken to show why it is that chief executives of all but the smallest companies need staff help in doing this planning.

A chief executive's duties are spread over a wide area of substance and, in the larger company, ceremony. He must be a leader of men; a skilled judge of human character, motivation, and capability; a business statesman in dealing with government and community leaders; a thoughtful person who can look ahead and know how to get there; a man of action who can make decisions for prompt compliance; an architect of the company management system; an innovator; and a vigilant seeker of opportunities who is willing to come to grips with and solve problems.

Except in the smallest of enterprises, it is obvious that such a job cannot be done properly by one man. As companies have grown, therefore, means have been devised to reduce the burdens of chief executives. These include splitting tasks at the top (as noted in connection with board chairmen and presidents), delegating authority, wider use of committees, creation of staff groups, and designating individual staff assistants.

As a company grows in size and the complexity of the management task increases, the chief executive's managerial problems and his functioning change. From the one-man executive, the job changes to that of an executive presiding over other executives. Although he is the final arbiter, only certain types of decisions come to him. There is no rule about this but in most companies the pattern of decisions that go to the top becomes developed. R. A. Gordon (1945, p. 80) found that for the large companies he studied "the closest approximation to . . . a rule seems to be that the chief executive tends to be least active in decisions leading to changes in production technique and to short-period fluctuations in output." He cannot get too deeply involved in details but must preserve his capacity to see the business as a whole. He must rely increasingly on team work. This means fewer face-to-face dealings with individuals and more participation with groups. He faces a dilemma, because he must maintain close working relationships with some of these groups but at the same time stand somewhat apart. The chief executive more and more becomes an integrator, a coordinator. In the great majority of corporations, coordination is undertaken in the office of the chief executive and not in that of the board of directors. As Gordon put it (p. 107), no further coordination is usually necessary above the chief executive. The board may share the coordinating job. But in the typical case there is not an active, superior, and independent coordinating body above the chief executive.

The planning role of the chief executive tends to alter as the organization over which he presides grows in size. As it expands, planning tends to be done more in terms of patterns—objectives, policies, strategies, and guidelines—than on an item by item basis. As the organization grows in size, there is a tendency for the chief executive to spend more time on planning. The larger the company, the greater the tendency for this time to be devoted more to long-range planning and the social milieu of the enterprise. More attention is devoted to thinking about the social responsibilities of a company as it becomes larger in size and has an obviously greater impact on the community (Newman and Logan 1955).

CORPORATE PLANNING IS
THE CHIEF EXECUTIVE'S JOB

I have clearly identified the overriding responsibility of the chief executive for corporate planning. But surveys of planning problems that I have seen, as well as my own observations, point to the fact that an insufficient commitment to planning by top management is far too prevalent (Brown, Sands, and Thompson 1966, p. 14).

One competent observer feels that this failure may grow out of a lack of understanding by top management of its responsibilities. Myles Mace (1965, p. 50) says: "Probably the single most important problem in corporate planning derives from the belief of some chief operating executives that corporate planning is not a function with which they should be directly concerned. They regard planning as something to be delegated, which subordinates can do without responsible participation by chief executives. They think the end result of effective planning is the compilation of a 'Plans' book. Such volumes get distributed to key executives, who scan the contents briefly, file them away, breathe a sigh of relief, and observe, 'Thank goodness that is done—now let's get back to work.'"

On the other hand there are many chief executives—but obviously not enough of them—who fully comprehend the primacy of their responsibilities for corporate planning. S. C. Beise (1963), when President of the Bank of America, said: "I think it is demonstrably clear that this job of planning and keeping the organization moving toward its goal is the task of the chief executive. He alone can serve as 'ringmaster' in keeping all the diverse efforts and operations of his company headed in the same direction. He may share the task in some measure and delegate operational problems, but his hands must be on the reins at all times to ensure optimum coordination and continuity.

"This is a grave responsibility and a difficult one. It means that the chief executive must keep abreast of broad economic, social, political, and scientific trends and developments outside his immediate business or industry that may at a future point have great impacts on his company."

In driving his point home, Mr. Beise then went on: "Permit me to cite you an example of what happens when chief executives fail to fully comprehend trends. . . . For many years the major part of the American commercial banking industry did not aggressively seek savings deposits. As a result the industry did not involve itself in an important way in the related field of real estate financing. Most banks made a few loans for building or purchasing homes, but they preferred to finance the traditional types of big business and industry, the proven sound credit risks. Up to and through World War II this philosophy was satisfactory, if imperfect. When American soldiers came home, however, they had grown up. They wanted to strike out on their own, marry, and live in their own homes. Suddenly the United States had a building boom on its hands, and home construction was in itself a big industry. But American commercial banks were slow to see this trend developing, and even slower to see the gigantic trends away from small city apartments to the suburbs. Others, however, saw more clearly, and little financial firms began to grow dramatically in order to fill the home financing need. Today these once-small savings and loan companies constitute a big industry in the United States and have given banks stiff competition for savings funds. The commercial banking industry today has made a strong comeback in the fields of savings and real estate lending, but due to its lack of foresight some 20 years ago, the banking industry gave birth to one of its own biggest competitors."

But even when a chief executive accepts the importance of his role in planning it is not always easy for him to find the time, to do what is required with confidence, or to determine precisely what his role ought to be in the many activities, and with the many individuals and groups concerned with planning. There is no single way to discharge properly his responsibilities in planning. The issues are subtle, complex, and vary much from one company to another, from one man to another, and over time.

TIME, TEMPERAMENT, AND DILEMMAS

Major problems standing in the way of many chief executives' clarification and discharge of their planning role are the shortage of time, lack of proper temperament, and difficulties in resolving the many dilemmas they face. Before examining the many aspects of the chief executive's role in planning, these problems deserve attention.

TIME. One of the paradoxes of modern corporate life is that while increased mechanization has eased the physical burden of work and the average work week has shortened, the burdens and work week of the typical business manager have expanded. A major reason for the heavier executive load is that complications in business management increase at a faster rate than the development and application of tools and techniques to lighten the tasks.

As the many duties mentioned above clamor for attention, a basic problem for every chief executive is that of planning how to allocate his time. Some executives never fully solve this planning problem in a satisfactory way (Dale and Urwick 1960, Chapters 1, 2, 3; Drucker 1954, Chapter 14). "The good executive," says Clarence Randall (1959*), former president of Inland Steel, "has a plan for his day. He knows what things have to be accomplished if the required tempo is to be maintained, and times himself accordingly. With deliberate speed he moves from one task to the next, making his decisions resolutely when he senses the matter has consumed the maximum period that can be allotted to it. There is no outward sign of inner struggle, and the job gets done."

Time is a scarce resource and corporate planning requires the lavish use of it. But shortage of time must not be used as the excuse to neglect planning.

How much time should a chief executive spend on planning? Chart 1-3 in Chapter 1 suggested an "ideal" distribution, but there is no pattern that fits all cases. Stewart's survey among 822 companies showed that top management actually spent time on planning as follows (1967, p. 5):

PERCENT OF TIME DEVOTED TO COMPANY PLANNING	PERCENT OF RESPONDENTS
0 or no answer	8
1 - 5	12
6 - 10	16
11 - 25	32
26 - 50	24
Over 50	8

* From *The Folklore of Management*, copyright © 1959, 1960, 1961, by Clarence B. Randall, with permission of Atlantic-Little, Brown and Company.

Comparable results of time distribution were found in another study of 139 chief executives, with the additional point that there were 44 companies out of the total where the chief executive felt he did not spend sufficient time on long-range planning, even though in some instances it amounted to 30 or 40 percent of his total time (Kaiden 1967).

TEMPERAMENT. Most chief executives rise to the top of their companies through one or several functional areas. Depending upon the man, of course, this may not only give him a bias in favor of his own experience, but he may also find his old patterns of thinking uncongenial to the requirements of overall corporate planning. A man who has spent his life in line action may find uncomfortable the type of thinking required in comprehensive planning. As Mainer (1965, p. 4) says: "The crux of the matter is that the behavioral requirements of planning as a management task are often different from, or in conflict with, the processes and content of management work normally prevalent in the organization. Thus, it is quite possible that an organization optimally geared to the pursuit of established objectives may be less than optimally prepared to work on the evaluation and adoption of new objectives or strategies."

There is some, but in my judgment not complete, truth in an observation made by Senator Henry M. Jackson (1959, p. 159) concerning planning done by top administrators of federal government agencies when he said: "I am convinced that we never will get the kind of policy planning we need if we expect the top-level officers to participate actively in the planning process. They simply do not have the time, and in any event they rarely have the outlook or the talents of the good planner. They cannot explore issues deeply and systematically. They cannot argue the advantages and disadvantages at length in the kind of give-and-take essential if one is to reach a solid understanding with others on points of agreement and disagreement."

It is easy to see how a man who has been concerned with acting decisively on short-range problems and has never really set about formulating broad long-range plans can, upon reaching the chief executive office, fully accept his responsibility for corporate planning but never really fully discharge the task. His temperament may not be well-suited to the planning job and this may be reinforced by his lack of experience in doing it.

Lack of experience with, or unease in conducting, corporate planning should not be an excuse for neglecting the job. There are ways to overcome this problem, not the least of which is to share the work with another line officer, or a staff man, who has the proper credentials and motivation to complement the personality and interests of the chief executive.

MANAGERIAL DILEMMAS. Built into chief executive jobs are many dilemmas that can be barriers to asserting strong leadership and participation in planning. On the one hand the chief executive must guarantee a reasonable degree of stability and routine in his business. A business cannot long endure if standard procedures are absent and instability upsets equanimity. On the other hand, the chief executive must be either the architect or major innovator of change. At the extreme, each of these forces inhibits the other. Seymour Tilles (1964, p. 1) points to five dilemmas that larger corporations face, especially the multidivisional company. They are:

"The need for both individual initiative and group consensus.

"The need for both divisional autonomy and a total corporate entity.

"The need for commitment to but objectivity about goals and objectives.

"The need for vigorous direction of internal operations and external awareness of the outside environment.

"The need for incentives which motivate to success on short-run performance and those which motivate to success on long-range goals."

These all represent difficult problems to resolve but they must not prevent an executive from stepping up to his planning problems. In explaining what happened at General Dynamics in the Convair 880 financial failure, then president Frank Pace said: "When you have a company, employing 106,000 people, made up of nine different divisions, each a corporation really in its own right, most of which were separate enterprises before they joined the organization and headed by men who were presidents of corporations, with their own separate legal staffs, financial staffs, etc., all of these highly competent men—the only way to succeed is to operate on a decentralized basis. Our total central office in New York City was something like 200 people, including stenographers. This group can only lay out broad policy. Your capacity to know specifically what is happening in each division just cannot exist. If you did try to know everything that was happening and controlled your men that tightly, your men would leave you or would lose their initiative which made them effective" (Carter, Weintraub, and Ray 1965, p. 141). Although explaining major dilemmas such reasoning would be rejected by many chief executives. There are ways to find out what is happening and to control events without inhibiting the initiative of people. One outstanding method is to step up to the job of designing and maintaining an effective corporate planning and control system.

THE CHIEF EXECUTIVE MUST BE
COMMITTED TO PLANNING

Of first importance is the fact that for corporate planning to be successful the chief executive must "buy" the idea. He must give the effort more than "lip service." Ralph M. Besse (1957, p. 47), when Executive Vice-President, Cleveland Electric Illuminating Company, said on this point that the proper planning climate is essential for effective planning. "Best results are achieved when this begins with top management—the very top—the chairman of the board, the president, the executive vice-president, and the important vice-presidents. They must buy the proposition that planning, *per se* and as such, is an identifiable, controllable function essential to the health of the enterprise. And they will be completely convinced only if they do a little work on the subject."

Effective planning requires involvement by the chief executive in particular, and top management generally. This in turn will stimulate involvement of all managers throughout an organization. Unfortunately, there is no simple answer to the question: How shall the chief executive participate in planning? For the first planning effort the chief executive must be deeply involved. As experience is acquired and more staff help is available a chief executive will know better where and when to become involved in order to exert his proper influence. The degree of involvement also will be influenced by the style of the chief executive, whether he is a "loner" or a democratic-participative operator. Much will depend upon the size of an enterprise, its problems, personalities, and type of industry.

The chief executive also must not become too involved in planning. If he does, he will neglect some of his other duties and frustrations may sour him on planning. Only the chief executive can determine where the correct balance lies between proper and excessive participation in his company's planning process.

A full examination of appropriate chief executive involvement considering all these variations is not possible here. But a few broad normative guidelines may suggest useful patterns of action.

ORGANIZATION FOR PLANNING

It is the major responsibility of the chief executive to see that the proper planning system for his company is developed and maintained. (Steiner, 1966a, *passim*). In this effort, of course, he will have help from subordinates—both line managers and staffs. But it is his responsibility to make sure that the system is appropriate to his business and that it is done at a cost (using this word broadly) under benefit.

Frederick Kappel (1966, p. 42), when President of AT&T, described this responsibility of the chief executive this way: "I would like to stress the responsibility that rests on the leaders, the people at the apex of a business, the individuals who fall in the category to which we apply the rather dry and impersonal term, 'top management.' . . . top management must take the initiative to establish the environment required for effective planning and action. In our view in the Bell System, the situation calls for a planning organization at the top management level that will mark out directions of activity, stimulate analysis of aims and operations, catalyze and coordinate. Such an organization will spur widespread effort, and at the same time prevent duplication, by making the experience in different areas or parts of the business available to all.

"I do not mean that a planning group can plan for another group. Management at each level, all through the business, must conduct its own self-examination. This cannot be delegated. But a skillful, able, persuasive, forceful planning organization will see that this is done."*

In the next chapter organization for planning will be treated in more detail. The discussion in the present chapter, therefore, will be limited to a few issues for the chief executive which arise in setting up the organization for planning.

The size of the enterprise is a major consideration. In a very small company the chief executive has no choice but to do the planning himself. As a company grows he may use his immediate line officers to help him do the planning. In larger organizations he may decide to establish a separate staff to help his organization do planning. If a staff is created the chief executive must see that it begins with the proper sponsorship.

A typical, bland, innocuous, and abstract letter of introduction, instead of generating a stimulating planning climate, will produce what Kirby Warren calls a "Wait-and-See" attitude. He points out, after examination of many planning systems among large companies, that a typical presidential memorandum phrased as follows will lead the experienced executive to hold the memorandum in his "Wait-and-See" file.

"With the greater complexity of doing business, increased competition, and expansion of our divisions, it is important that the company look ahead with more imagination to new opportunities and threats. To lead in this effort I have appointed Mr. _____ as Director of Long-Range Planning.

"While Mr. _____ will have the chief responsibility for organizing and coordinating our long-range planning, every manager throughout the company is expected to give this matter more attention.

"This new program has my personal strong endorsement and I know that each of you will give Mr. _____ your fullest cooperation." (Paraphrased from Warren, 1966, pp. 50-51.)

On the other hand the right kind of communique can do wonders. Many years ago I had the job of helping an organization develop its first comprehensive planning program. In preparing procedures and suggesting roles of people in the organization I ran into grave difficulties. People were not sure of their responsibilities, or did not want to assume the responsibility I suggested. Different people wanted to do different things that did not necessarily mesh. There were also other points of dispute. To solve the entire problem I prepared a letter for the signature of the chief executive which set forth clearly and in detail the essential elements of the planning program, how it was to be developed, and who was responsible for what. This worked like a charm. From that day to this the top executives of that company have watched over the planning process and it is an outstanding system.

* Reprinted from the Winter 1966 issue of the *Columbia Journal of World Business.* Copyright © 1968 by the Trustees of Columbia University.

This is not meant to imply that chief executives must get enmeshed in all the grubby details of a total planning program. What I do say is that they must see to it that the job of planning the plan is done, that authority is clear, and that the process is put into operation.

It is very important that the chief executive name a staff director of planning (if there is one) who will reflect his determination to have an effective planning program. Or, if authority for helping to lead and do the planning job is given to a functional or line manager, the assignment ought to be made to a person who commands the respect of the organization. If, for example, a person is made director of planning in order to remove him from a line job where he failed, or if the job is filled in such a way that people calculate it to be a demotion, or if a weak and obscure person is given the task, the probability of success is not favorable. If, on the other hand, the planning director is obviously well qualified, well suited for the job, and is given the fullest support by top management, success is much more likely. The same comments apply to a functional officer or an assistant to the chief executive, who might be assigned duties concerning long-range planning.

There are many ways to split planning responsibilities. Whatever they are, the chief executive should at least establish the pattern desired and at most should make sure the system is understood and that the responsibility of each manager is reasonably clear.

Organization for planning is very important, but as Seymour Tilles (1964, p. 10) says: "the formal distribution of planning responsibility is less significant than the degree to which the top executives of the company, and especially the chief executive, see themselves as significant contributors to the planning process."

DEVELOPING PLANS

Issues concerning the role of the chief executive in doing the planning job are subtle and complex. The range of alternatives is very wide. A few of the dimensions follow.

T I M E .   The time a manager devotes to an activity is generally a valid measure of the importance he attaches to it. If a chief executive spends a high proportion of his time working on company plans, this fact will not be lost on subordinate managers. Long-range planning is a difficult task, and tangible measures are not very accurate for evaluating the success of lower-level managerial performance in doing it. There is not, therefore, as much motivation to work on longer-range planning as on shorter-range problems where more concrete measures of performance exist. When a chief executive, however, shows by his devotion of time how important he thinks the effort is, lower-level managers will follow his lead.

Similarly, if top management concentrates attention on short-range plans at the expense of long-range planning, this pattern will be followed by lower-level managers. A general manager of a large division of a major company once told me: "We have ten-year plans in my company and the president likes to talk about looking even further into the future in making our plans. When he and the executive vice-president review our plans, however, they have no interest in anything ten years away, let alone fifteen. They concentrate on the next two years."

The chief executive, by what he does, irrespective of what he says, will determine the planning dimensions in a company—both with respect to the allocation of time for the task and the time horizon used.

CLARIFYING RELATIONSHIPS WITH LINE AND STAFF. One of the most important misunderstandings of the planning process that I have found among some chief executives concerns their relationships with their planning staffs. When a chief executive uses his line officers as staff to help him plan, or hires an assistant to aid him, or creates a planning staff, he is merely extending his reach. These people are helping him to do *his* job. This is a recognition that the world is too large for one man to grasp completely and that to the extent he can get others to help him he will be better able to examine a wider range of threats to and opportunities for his organization.

Although problems arise in defining the relationship between the chief executive and any one person, group, or other organization that helps him, the most complex issues exist between the chief executive and planning staffs in large multidivisional companies. Clarification of roles of participants in the process is important, and a major responsibility for clarification rests with the chief executive.

A staff cannot and should not be asked to make plans for a company. That is clearly a line job. Staffs assist line managers in making plans.

Even though all levels of management participate in making corporate plans, a chief executive cannot delegate the assignment and wait until someone hands him the completed plans. If he delegates the job of making plans to a planning staff he may be left in an untenable position. On the one hand, if he makes many changes he may force a substantial redoing of plans. This is expensive and not likely to produce the sort of enthusiasm in his staff that the best planning requires. On the other hand, if he makes few or no changes he is in danger of being a captive of his staff.

Furthermore, if he takes the latter course, he has not discharged his responsibilities in guiding and directing the forward movement of his company, even though he agrees with his staff. The most important consequence of this, if continued, is a deterioration of planning capability. "The most usable end product of planning is not a paper," says Cleveland (1963, p. 4*) "but a person thoroughly

* From *Foreign Affairs*, Vol. 41, July 1963. Copyright held by Council on Foreign Relations. Used with permission.

immersed in the subject—a person whose mind is trained to act, having taken everything into account, on the spur of the moment. And that is why the ultimate decision-maker must himself participate in the planning exercise. A busy boxer, training for the bout of his life, cannot afford to let his sparring partners do all his daily calisthenics for him."

As previously suggested, how much he should participate in actually making plans is a matter for each chief executive to define. Clearly, in undertaking comprehensive planning for the first time the chief executive should be deeply and continuously involved in sculpturing such major plans as long-range objectives for profits, sales, and markets. Decisions with respect to these and the strategies designed to reach them will have a major impact on how his company behaves and prospers. After a series of annual planning cycles the ideas of the chief executive become much better known and his continuous participation in these areas may properly diminish.

Relationships with line and staff people are also influenced by styles of management. A strong one-man executive may specify long-range objectives and give them to his staff and line managers in the form of an edict. This is not likely to produce the desired results, but it may. Problems can be predicted if a strong executive has objectives but, for reasons of his own, is unwilling to phrase them. This leaves both line and staff with wind but without rudder. A better relationship would be one where setting corporate objectives is a continuous process of the intermingling of top management views, staff recommendations, top management approval and suggestion, new staff work, new approval, and so on.

The relationships between the chief executive and his planning staff encounter many subtle human relations issues that are complicated by the special problems of planning. For example, there is a most sensitive question which arises between a corporate planner and the chief executive with respect to frank and open discussion. The chief executive has the most prestigious position in the company and may frequently act imperiously. He can impose his will whenever he chooses. President Eisenhower said that Sir Winston Churchill often commented in a heated discussion: "Gentlemen, all I want is compliance with my wishes—after reasonable discussion."

The staff planner, in helping the chief executive do his job, feels rightfully the enormous significance of his activities. Yet he cannot speak as freely as if he were on the same level. The best assurance that each is contributing his best to the planning effort is the development of a mutual respect and confidence. This is a two-way street, requiring appropriate efforts on the part of both.

If there is any presumption that planning decisions are made upon the basis of participation in group discussions such as the deliberations of a planning council, subtle problems arise between a chief executive who presides at a council meeting and the members of the group. As one perceptive observer (Daniel, 1965, pp. 19-20) has commented: "His role is delicate and requires great tact and sensitivity, for in many situations the distance from group leader to autocrat of the conference table is dangerously short. In one company seemingly managed by a five-man management team, the group leader—a venerable board chairman who happened to be the company's single largest stockholder—one day invited his attorney, a close personal friend, to attend a meeting of the Executive Office. A proposal to build a new plant was discussed in considerable detail. At length the chairman, as was his custom, called a vote. Finding his four colleagues opposed to the plant and only himself in favor, he declared crisply, 'The ayes have it. We'll proceed with construction,' and adjourned the meeting. After the others had left, his startled counselor asked the old man to explain this extraordinary act. 'Francis,' was the reply, 'some days we count the votes around here, and other days we weigh them. Today we weighed them.'"

There is no question about the fact that planning should not be separated from doing. Upon examination, however, this is not as simple as it sounds. In the strategic planning area, for example, plans may be developed for divisional execution. The divisions may not have much, if any, participation in their preparation. Even with close line and staff interrelations at central office headquarters, staff inevitably will make decisions. The mere choice of alternatives to present to line managers, for example, may implicitly approximate line decision-making by staff. Problems of drawing a line of demarcation between staff and line decision-making, and planning and operations, vary from case to case in the development of plans, and from time to time. There can be no simple formula; but efforts to clarify the staff role can prevent unnecessary conflict.

Even when the staff role is clear, difficult problems of relationships may arise. In larger companies with comprehensive planning programs, corporate functional staffs, including long-range planning staffs, review divisional plans at the request of top management. Plans are submitted up the line, but staffs help line managers review them. In one instance a president asked his director of long-range planning to review the plans of a powerful division manager. The president insisted upon a rigorous examination of the plans because of the substantial capital outlays sought by the divisional manager. The planner did so and provided the rationale for rejecting the plans. He was not very happy about his role. He had been cultivating this divisional manager for a long time in order to develop a better planning program in his division and to arrange better communications to help them both do a better planning job. Now the divisional manager felt he had been betrayed. This corporate planner will have problems in rebuilding his lines of communication with this division.

The planning process is complex. There must be an understanding of authority, responsibility, procedures and timing, and the chief executive is responsible for seeing that this need is met.

CHIEF EXECUTIVES MUST STIMULATE. Another way the chief executive must get involved in planning is to make people aware of the fact that he is interested in seeking new methods, new tools, and new procedures to improve the entire planning process. His is a never-ending quest to prevent the planning process from becoming just another routine activity. In all the companies that have a high quality planning system one finds constant changes and efforts to improve the process. When the process becomes routine and is done about the same way in each cycle, the chief executive should be very suspicious about his getting the best plans his staff is capable of producing within the limitations imposed on them.

EVALUATING DIVISIONAL PLANS

When divisional planning exists there must be a mechanism at corporate headquarters for review and evaluation of the plans. The procedures for the development and transmission of these plans should be set forth clearly, as already indicated in the discussion on organization of the planning program. However, there are other issues which deserve the attention of the chief executive.

A subtle problem arises in the transmission and review of division plans. Line plans should be transmitted through and examined directly by superior line managers. This means a chief executive, with or through his immediate line vice-presidents, should receive, review and evaluate plans. Plans should not come through the corporate planning staff. The corporate planning staff cannot be put in a position of reviewing line managers' operating performance. Corporate staff can and should, however, review the plans as part of top management's reviewing process. This is done as a staff service to the chief executive.

A major problem concerns chief executive attitudes in a case, for example, where short-range performance is excellent but long-range planning is terrible. Another problem will arise when long-range planning is superior but short-range performance is poor. The attitude of the chief executive about this sort of experience will naturally influence the future quality of planning. If the high short-term performer is not made to redo his poor homework on long-range planning, long-range planning in the future will naturally be neglected. The obvious reaction of managers throughout the company, if there is no penalty for poor long-range planning, will be that top management really is interested primarily in today's results. This, then, is where attention will be focused.

The same attitude will result if top management penalizes a manager with poor short-term performance even though his long-range planning effort was superior. Obviously, all managers must be made aware that this manager has the full support of top management in continuing his high-grade long-range planning. At the same time, of course, there must be a full understanding of the causes of the short-term failure and proper redress made. The concentration of the efforts of managers on short-term performance is very understandable. But if top managers do not strike a proper balance between short- and long-range performance in their evaluations of lower-level managers, no one else in the organization can be expected to do so.

There is also the issue of rewards and bonuses for long-range planning. Kirby Warren's research (1966, p. 59) revealed that: "Time and again within the survey companies, cynicism toward the importance of long-range planning was based on what managers saw as repeated evidence that promotions, bonuses, and salary increases were earned almost entirely on the basis of short-term results, despite verbal insistence that long- and short-range efforts were considered. If the results were good, whether they had been achieved because of sound long-range planning or by wild, last-minute scrambling seemed relatively unimportant. Despite the fact that this tended to reduce the time and talent devoted to long-range planning at almost all levels of management, many top officers of the survey companies accepted this as a necessary fact of corporate life. As one executive vice-president put it, 'It has to be *results* that count. It always has been and always will.'"

No question can arise about the importance of results. It is the very difficult problem of the chief executive to look beyond the immediate and appraise the extent to which tomorrow's results will be good or poor, depending upon today's planning. One of the more puzzling questions in looking at this issue is the extent to which experience with the process of planning produces a mental agility and capability in dealing with current issues. The question is not so much the nicety of long-range planning as the extent to which doing it builds more effective managers. However, aside from exceptional luck, as the previous chapter showed, long-range success or failure more frequently than not depends upon effective long-range planning. The chief executive has a heavy responsibility in determining the value of the comprehensive planning program as compared with fluctuating current operating performance. Better tools and methods for measuring and evaluating comprehensive planning efforts would be helpful but, even if available, would not provide an automatic basis for judgment.

DECISIONS MUST BE BASED ON PLANS

Comprehensive planning done with and on behalf of top management should result in operating decisions. Without decisions the planning process is incomplete. Failure to take action on prepared plans, or continuous vacillation, will weaken staff efforts. People simply will not be motivated to exert the energy, develop the creativity and use the imagination needed to make quality plans if top management ignores them or cannot seem to act upon them.

In one company I know, one month after a five-year long-range plan had been developed for the first time and approved by top management, the president announced a flat seven percent budget cut for all division budgets. This was his method to reduce costs. The announced reason was the need to reduce costs to increase return on stockholders' equity. With this announcement, the longer-range projects naturally were abandoned and the benefits of long-range planning cast in grave doubt.

The extent to which divisional line managers make decisions in light of strategic corporate plans raises a different type of problem. In some companies the connection between the corporate strategic plan and the divisional intermediate-range plans is very close. The two may, in effect, be prepared together. In one small company of about five hundred people making a variety of electronics equipment, there was a planning program where strategic plans were developed for the company as a whole and the divisions wove their substrategies and detailed long-range plans clearly and closely into the web of the total corporate plan. These were intermeshed because the two were done by about the same people and at about the same time. In other instances, the corporate strategic plan constitutes an umbrella under which the divisional plans are made but the interrelationship between the two is rather loose.

As noted in previous chapters, one of the major attributes of comprehensive corporate planning is that decisions can be made throughout an organization with a reasonable degree of certainty that they are in line with top management wishes. Naturally, if the decisions put into action are not in conformance with the planning program, planning will disappear.

This, of course, does not mean a blind devotion to a plan. Depending upon circumstances, it may be wise for a manager to make decisions that are different from those planned. Plans ought to be implemented with flexibility. Chief executives have a responsibility to see that decisions are made in light of plans and evolving circumstances—not blindly, not without reference to plans, but related meaningfully within a planning framework.

CONCLUSIONS CONCERNING TOP
MANAGEMENT'S ROLE IN PLANNING

Highlights of this chapter are as follows:

1. Corporate planning will fail in the absence of the chief executive's support, participation, and guidance.

2. Corporate planning is the responsibility of the chief executive and cannot be delegated to a planning staff.

3. The chief executive is responsible for assuring that a proper organization for planning is created, that the manner of its functioning is clear and understood, and that it operates effectively and efficiently.

4. The chief executive must see that all managers understand that planning is a continuous function and not one pursued on an *ad hoc* basis or only during a formal planning cycle.

5. The chief executive should see that all managers recognize that planning means change, and the interaction of plans on people and institutions must be understood and considered.

6. Once plans are prepared, top management must make decisions on the basis of plans.

Someone long ago said that the best fertilizer ever invented was the footsteps of the farmer. Similarly, the best assurance of effective planning in an organization is the active participation of the chief executive in doing it.

PART II

The Process
of Developing Plans

5

Organizing for Corporate Planning

5
Organizing for Corporate Planning

INTRODUCTION

An important responsibility of top management in all but the smallest companies is to plan the organization for company planning. Because all line managers have planning responsibilities, and most staffs also become involved in corporate planning, decisions must be made about which duties should be assigned to which people, what authority each should be given, and when results should be required. In short, comprehensive corporate planning must be organized.

There is no single organizational planning pattern that fits all companies, nor is there a single best organization for planning. Factors influencing planning organization vary much among companies, but there are planning arrangements that are becoming more frequently employed. Important among them is the establishment of a central corporate planning staff and, in divisionalized companies, division planning staffs.

In this chapter will be treated different approaches to organizing for corporate planning. Emphasis will be directed, however, to organizations employing planning staffs.

FACTORS INFLUENCING ORGANIZATION
FOR PLANNING

A brief examination of a few major factors influencing planning organization patterns will amply explain why there is no single universal or best arrangement. Planning is so intimately intertwined with the whole process of management and the entire organizational structure of a business that each organization for planning is tailored to particular circumstances.

The requirements for corporate planning, for example, are much different between General Motors on the one extreme and a small metal stamping firm employing a handful of employees on the other extreme. Arrangements will differ also as between a divisionalized company like Celanese and a centrally controlled and functionally organized company like Continental Oil. The degree of authority enjoyed by decentralized divisions will influence the overall planning program. The nature of the product also affects the planning within an organization. In some companies such as those producing automobiles or aerospace equipment the nature of the technology, heavy capital investment, market structures, and long development cycles, demand integrated operations and examination of distant horizons. The result is a very different need than, say, the planning organization for a women's ready-to-wear clothing manufacturer. Personalities of executives will have much to do with organization. A strong chief executive may wish to do his own planning irrespective of the size of his enterprise. Another executive may find it more to his liking to spread the planning task around. Whether a company is just beginning to do formal planning or has had much experience with the process will also influence its organization. The planning organization will differ as between a company in financial crisis and one enjoying great success as a result of past planning. Factors such as these determine the assignment of planning duties around a company.

FORMS OF PLANNING ORGANIZATIONS

Examination of both national and multinational companies reveals that there are five basic classifications of formal planning organization. From the simplest to the most elaborate they are as follows (Steiner and Cannon, 1966, pp. 50-51).

1. No formal planning exists at all. Planning is done, but it is a part of the duty of each executive and no effort is made to formalize the process. This pattern is typical of many very small companies with few managers.
2. Organized planning is done within a functional area of the business. The area can be finance, marketing, sales, or engineering, to illustrate, where some important element exists which can serve as a common thread for organized planning. For example, planning in a public utility may center in the engineering department because facility expansion is a function about which organized planning for such companies may be developed. Marketing may provide the home center for organized planning in a company where products serve as a single rallying point for planning.
3. A planning executive and organization may exist in the divisions of a company, or operating units in the field, but no planning staff exists at the corporate level. In such cases the chief executive may serve as a central focal point for planning, and his functional officers at headquarters may aid him.

4. A corporate headquarters planning department is created but no planning executives or staffs are established in operating units. In such instances, of course, the planning department usually gets involved in detailed planning. This pattern is more typical of a centrally managed company than a divisionalized and decentrally managed one.

5. In this case a planning executive and staff exists at company headquarters and in each major division or operating unit.

GETTING THE PROCESS STARTED

There are, of course, many different ways to begin a formal corporate planning program. Several "typical" cases follow.

Case A. The Concrete Forms Company has sales of $550,000 a year, employs 50 people, and is managed by the president who is assisted by a chief engineer and director of sales who also serves as accountant. The president decided to develop a formal planning program, but in a comparatively simple fashion. It began, as illustrated in Table 5-1, with setting an objective for sales five years in the future. Setting this objective required the answer to many questions, such as: Can this sales level be reached with present products or must there be product modification? Must new products be developed to get the goal desired? If not, should the goal be reached through penetration of new markets, or joint ventures, or acquisitions, or a combination of all of these routes? Once decisions were made about questions such as these other questions immediately arose. For example, what manpower will be

Table 5-1   Sales Objectives

AREA	FIRST YEAR	SECOND YEAR	THIRD YEAR	FOURTH YEAR	FIFTH YEAR
Product modification					
New products					
Joint ventures					
New markets					
Greater market share					
Acquisition					
TOTALS					BEGIN HERE

needed? What financing will be required? How can profit margins be improved? Must some employees be sent to school for management training?

The plan was developed by the president and a consultant, with the casual and infrequent participation of his two managers. When the plan was developed it was written and became the guide for current decisions. Periodically the president and his outside consultant reviewed the plan to bring it up-to-date. Through the plan the company prospered and grew. With its growth a controller was hired and he, together with the director of sales and the chief engineer (all of whom were made vice-presidents), participated in the planning program.

Case B. This is the case of the Sunny Toy Company, which was prosperous, wanted to continue that way, and thought formal planning would help. The president prepared a few objectives for the entire company and then asked each functional officer and each department to prepare three-year plans to achieve them. These plans were presented by each manager at a two-day meeting away from the city in which the company was located. Many good ideas were presented and examined and the exercise was considered very worthwhile. The individual plans, however, were inconsistent, could not be accumulated into a company consolidated plan, and were of varying grades of quality and completeness. However, in subsequent annual preparations these defects were remedied and the company was able to prepare aggregate plans based upon more imaginative and better coordinated department plans.

Case C. The president of Magnetic Design, Inc., decided it was time for a formal five-year company plan. Sales had risen rapidly during the past three years until currently they were $2 million. There were 100 employees and the company was producing a number of products in the magnetic devices equipment field. The president hired a consultant to lay out with him and his line officers the methodology for developing the plan. He then used his line managers as staff in the development of the plan. He and his four major department heads prepared a written plan, parts of which were presented in Chapter 2.

Case D. The Lockheed Aircraft Corporation established its Development Planning Department in 1954. This Department was created because the President of the Company, Mr. Robert Gross, was farsighted in calculating the great changes that were about to take place in the old-line aircraft companies and that those companies which systematically sought to examine the future would be in the best competitive position. The Department developed a procedure for coordinating the plans of the divisions and the corporate functional offices into what was known at the time as The Lockheed Master Plan.

The Administrative Committee which was composed of the President's immediate staff gave broad guidance to, and supported, the planning effort. Immediately underneath this Committee was a Steering Committee on which the Director of Development Planning served as Chairman and the Controller as Vice Chairman. Other corporate staff served as members of the Committee, including, Director of Sales, Budget Director, Assistant Treasurer, and comparable officers. The Steering Committee provided planning assumptions for the development of divisional plans, coordinated the planning program, evaluated the plans, and made recommendations to top management (Root and Steiner, in Ewing, 1964a, Chapter 24).

Case E. The Martin Implement Company decided to get involved in corporate planning because it faced a tough problem. Its farm equipment business had fallen seriously despite a rise in agricultural income, and the company was able to show a profit only because a recent acquisition of a steel forging plant offset losses in other divisions. The outlook was not bright because its tractor line was obsolete and underpowered, its distribution system needed radical overhauling, and its research program was virtually undirected.

The president established a committee to look into the problems of the company, and make recommendations for their solution. One recommendation was that a more permanent and integrated planning program be established. A planning director was appointed and has helped the chief executive to develop a strong, comprehensive planning program.

THE VERY SMALL BUSINESS. The average very small businessman does too little systematic forward planning. (Steiner, *passim*, Chapter 7 in Pfeffer, 1967.) The small businessman has some characteristics which serve as barriers to his long-range planning. He is pressed for time. He has most of the problems of an executive in a medium-sized company but without the help that can be hired in the larger companies. So, he is constantly fighting "brush fires" and, as anyone who has followed business planning knows, these pressures drive out long-range planning. He is a doer; he is a man of action. There is probably more of an inverse correlation than a positive correlation between successful doers and competent planners. Personally, the small businessman is a "loner." He usually starts alone and has a habit of doing things himself.* Typically, too, the small businessman has kept secret his ideas, plans, and intentions. It is not easy to overcome this history of secrecy and share future plans with others. He also may be reluctant to discuss plans which may not materialize because he does not want to be thought foolish or inept.

These reasons have some substance but they are not an excuse for avoiding systematic planning. But what can a small businessman do?

One approach is to begin to ask some major questions that will stimulate the habit of looking ahead to achieve desired profit and other objectives. Such questions as the following are provocative:

What business am I in?
What is my place in the industry?
What customers am I serving? Where is my market?
What is my company image to my major customers?

* For a profile of successful small businessmen, see Collins, Moore, and Unwalla, 1964.

What business do I want to be in five years from now?
What are my specific goals for profit improvement?
Need I have plans for product improvement? If so, what?
What is my greatest strength? Am I using it well?
What is my greatest problem? How am I to solve it?
What share of the market do I want? Next month? Next year?
Are my personnel policies acceptable to employees?
How can I finance growth?

Another approach for the very small businessman has been suggested by Roger Golde. Table 5-2 shows his planning form which is self-explanatory. A manager-owner can work with this form at odd moments, informally, and with a minimum of outside help. It will stimulate thinking and organize action. Many small businessmen find that dealing with abstract questions is more difficult than focusing upon specific courses of action. This form suits this thinking.

There are also other concrete approaches for the small businessman. The approach in Case A above is applicable. Starting with a break-even analysis, discussed fully in Chapter 11, is another one. Beginning with a simple cash-flow analysis (discussed in Chapter 13) is still another.

OTHER CONSIDERATIONS IN GETTING STARTED. These cases by no means exhaust the more or less typical ways formal planning gets started, for the stimulus may come from many directions. Frequently the initiative arises in a chief executive who sees the need for formal planning or decides to undertake it because his competitors are doing it and he fears they may gain a competitive edge. Sometimes a company has a crisis facing it, such as declining sales, dropping share of market, an annual operating loss, or unexpected product obsolescence, and hopes formal planning will help it solve its problems.

Once the initiative is taken, the patterns of planning evolution can take many forms. Not mentioned in the above cases are these possibilities: appoint an assistant to help a president; ask one of the corporate functional officers, such as the controller, to assume the responsibility; ask the chairman of the board to devote his full time to future planning and place all current operating matters in the hands of the president; give the president the job of planning ahead and let the executive vice-president handle day-to-day operations; or create a planning staff reporting to the president.

Whatever the evolution is, a basic rule must be that each new step should be useful and so conceived by managers, particularly the top management. The planning process must not be allowed to fail. As Aguilar has observed correctly, "To introduce planning and then have it fail is probably far worse than doing

Table 5-2 Hypothetical Completed Master Planning Form

ITEM	CHANGE		COMMENT
	Next Year	Year After Next	
Research & Development	Mm	—S	Start development of new altimeter for executive planes.
Products		Ss	First sales of new altimeter.
Product Mix			
Service		s	Slightly different for private planes.
Supplies		s	Needed for new altimeter.
Suppliers			
Inventory			
Subcontracts		S	Most of subassemblies will be subcontracted.
Storage & Handling			
Quality Control			
Space		S	Little bit of production space for new altimeter.
Leasehold Improvements	M		Need for dust-free area.
Equipment	S		New test equipment.
Employees	S		Couple of technicians for development work.
Fringe Benefits			
Customers		sS	Plan to hit owners of executive planes.
Sales Outlets		Mm	Will need more sales representatives rather than own sales force.
Terms of Sale			
Pricing			
Transportation			
Advertising		—M	Not so effective to private owners.
Promotion		m	Will switch to more demonstrations and trade shows.
Packaging			
Market Research	S		Informal poll of private owners known by company.
Financing	S		Additional working capital for production.
Insurance			
Investments			
Management Reports		1	Need for simple product costing system.
Etc.			Etc.

Instructions: All changes are estimated in relation to the preceding year.
If a quantitative change is anticipated—i.e., change in size or amount—use the following symbols: L = large,

nothing, for it might take years to reestablish a climate favorable for another try" (Steiner and Cannon, 1966, p. 57).

As the planning system evolves, care must be taken to assure that each manager understands his part in the process and accepts it as being important in doing his job. If managers do not see the program as being important to their job the whole process becomes just another exercise in paperwork. On the other hand, it can and should be the basis for better decisions and a sure contribution of each manager to achieving the ends sought for the company.

A few years ago I calculated that for the average medium-sized company a period of at least five years elapsed between the inception of a formal planning program and the development of a sophisticated system and plan (1963b, pp. 19-21). Because so much more is known today about how to do effective planning, the time span between the introduction of the system and the creation of an effective planning program should be much shorter. Even so, it takes time to perfect a sophisticated and useful formal planning program. Managers should not become disenchanted with the process if the first effort is not completely to their satisfaction. It takes time and patience to produce a corporate plan that is worth trying to follow.

There are many reasons for this. A major problem in starting formal planning is sorting out the duties that various managers and staff should have. Also, the many values that enter a planning process are at first vague and may take several cycles to clarify. The real position of management, with respect to diversification by acquisition, illustrates one area where top management values may be of dominant consideration and hard to clarify. Lack of information needed for the process becomes more obvious as the process proceeds to identify opportunities and problems, alternative courses of action, and needed methods for evaluating choices.

One final point seems appropriate in connection with getting the process organized. Organization is very important but not so important as capable people supported by top management. But, all other things being equal, an effective organization for planning should produce better results than a poor

---

M = medium, and S = small. Quantitative changes are assumed to be increases unless preceded by a minus sign. If a qualitative change is anticipated, use the following symbols: l = large, m = medium, s = small.

Note that the notions of small, medium, and large changes are obviously subjective and will vary with the person using the form.

In general, a small change denotes some sort of minimum level of change which is thought important enough to make note of. Most of the expected changes will probably fall in the medium category, indicating significant change of some magnitude. The large category will usually be reserved for unusual changes of striking impact.

The notion of qualitative changes may need some clarification. This category of change would cover such items as a change in customer mix (which might or might not result in an increased number of customers). Using a new source of supply for raw materials and changing the media allocation of the advertising budget would also be examples of qualitative changes.

Source: Roger A. Golde, "Practical Planning for Small Business," *Harvard Business Review*, XXIV: 5 (Sept.-Oct. 1964), pp. 151-152.

organization. A poor organization can produce a poor plan, but with competent personnel it can be reworked to become an acceptable plan.

THE CORPORATE PLANNING STAFF

The formal job description of the Director of Corporate Planning at Merck, Sharp and Dohme International begins with these words (Hannoch and Goldman in Steiner and Cannon, 1966, p. 91): "The President is the architect of the Company's future and the Company's chief planning officer. The Director of Corporate Planning . . . provides staff assistance to the President in this capacity." This statement captures well the essential relationship between the chief executive and his planning director. It is time now to examine in depth the role which a planning staff plays in corporate planning.

It is difficult to draft a "typical" conceptual model of the work of a planning staff. But with all its shortcomings it seems more fruitful to make the attempt than to survey broadly the many possible different uses of such staff.

It seems appropriate to consider the "typical" case as being that of a divisionalized-decentralized company in the medium-sized to large class. Since World War II more and more companies have reached a size and complexity that have led them to organize on a divisionalized-decentralized basis. Among these companies there has been more and more attention paid to top management's disengagement with operations in order to give greater attention to planning and control of change. Among these companies, particularly, we find emerging the corporate planning staff to help the chief executives (Stieglitz and Janger, 1965).

For purposes of our "typical" model, picture a company that has enjoyed profit on investment somewhat above the industry average. Sales amount to about $100 million, some 15,000 people are employed, and the company produces a variety of non-homogeneous products in five product divisions. These divisions are scattered throughout the nation and are semi-autonomous profit-making centers. This means essentially that within broad guidelines established by central headquarters the divisions have much freedom in deciding upon their operations. The headquarters management, however, is continuously in touch with division operations and must approve major decisions about the use of resources to assure that division operations are in conformance with broad strategies and objectives of the company. The president of the company is much interested in the development of formal planning in his company and participates in the process.

In this company the Corporate Planning Department performs functions which can be classified in different ways. Table 5-3 presents my conceptual role for the corporate planning staff in a job-description arrangement. Instead of going through this description line by line, I should like to suggest that the major duties of the staff are seven in number, as follows.

Table 5-3 The Role of the Corporate Planning Staff

BASIC OBJECTIVES:

1. Provide staff services to management in the development of and strategies for achieving the Company's objectives.
2. Coordinate the Corporate Planning effort.
3. Stimulate the effective development of formal planning among the divisions.

CORPORATE STRATEGIC PLAN

1. Periodically prepare, with the cooperation of functional and line officers of the company and divisions, the corporate strategic plan.
   a. Emphasis is placed on corporate objectives and basic strategies and policies to achieve them.

CORPORATE PRODUCT DEVELOPMENT PLANNING

1. Examine future potential product requirements of major customers and recommend to management appropriate actions which the corporation and its divisions should take to acquire new business.
2. Recommend appropriate allocations of corporate resources to support new and continuing programs which promise acceptable returns on investment.
3. Identify new products or new product ideas for corporate exploitation.
4. Assist corporate management in evaluation of new product or market proposals of the divisions.
5. Assist corporate management in the development of new product or market strategies for the divisions.
6. Recommend organizational mechanisms which may be required for improved exploitation of new products and markets or the acquisition of new contracts.

DIVERSIFICATION PLANNING

1. Prepare recommendations for in-house diversification and acquisition to meet company objectives.
2. Identify and evaluate the opportunities for acquisitions and other diversification arrangements.
3. Work with other departments, as appropriate, in completing acquisitions.

OTHER CORPORATE PLANNING

1. Periodically, and as requested or required, recommend plans for actions by corporate or divisional managers in all other areas appropriate for corporate planning.

Table 5-3   The Role of the Corporate Planning Staff (Continued)

2. Maintain experts in major disciplines who can be of service as consultants in planning throughout the company.

CUSTOMER-CORPORATE RELATIONSHIPS

1. Maintain a general awareness of interactions between the company and its customers to insure that all appropriate resources (human, material, financial) are used properly in support of authorized lines of business.
2. Survey changing customer actions, attitudes, and perceptions of the company and recommend actions which will advance the company's ability to win contracts and maximize product and service sales.

PLANNING STUDIES

1. Continuously survey:
   a. evolving trends in major environmental forces which are likely to influence customer product and service needs and ability to buy. Included are trends in economic, political, and social affairs both domestically and in foreign countries.
   b. new product possibilities, new markets, new investment opportunities, important conditions within or surrounding customer operations, or other elements of potential importance to the company in the achievement of its objectives and in pursuit of its strategies, both within as well as outside the corporation.
   c. new developments in science and engineering of possible interests to the company.
   d. new methods, techniques, and procedures which will improve planning within the company, reduce costs, or improve product quality and acceptance.
2. Studies for divisions which will aid them in their planning programs.
3. Study and report on implications of divisional plans for the achievement of corporate goals and effective pursuit of corporate strategies.
4. Forecast the future of the company on the basis of its current momentum.

PLANNING RESULTS

1. Maintain an appropriate follow-up program of progress made on corporate decisions resulting from corporate planning activities.

DIVISIONS

1. Help divisions develop effective long-range planning programs.

Table 5-3   The Role of the Corporate Planning Staff (Continued)

2. Prepare appropriate background information for divisions to help in their planning.
3. When requested, aid divisions in developing plans.

COMPETITORS

1. Continuously survey and report to management developments with respect to competitive position.
2. Encourage divisions to maintain appropriate and perceptive information about current and potential competitors.

CORPORATE COMMITTEES

1. Corporate planning staff participates in different committees, including the Corporate Planning Committee. The Director of Corporate Planning shall serve as Secretary to the Committee.
2. Prepare, for approval of the Corporate Planning Committee, the manual of procedures for the corporate planning effort.

First, the staff helps top management to develop long-range objectives, strategies, and policies to reach them. If the occasion arises for a company to evaluate and perhaps change its basic mission, the planning staff may also help managers in this effort. To start a planning cycle in a divisionalized company, the planning staff may help top management prepare specific objectives for such functions as sales, profits, market share, asset growth, employment, facilities, and capital flows. Very broad strategies may be developed to achieve objectives, such as strategies for acquisition, in-house research and development, or market penetration. Staff may help top management by preparing fundamental studies that may lead to strategy recommendations, by helping top management formulate objectives and strategies, and by evaluating for top management the objectives and strategies top management sets forth.

Second, the planning staff coordinates plans. Within overall company objectives and strategies, divisions may prepare subobjectives, substrategies, and detailed five-year plans. When these are received in the central offices, in some companies the planning staff integrates them into one consolidated set of plans for the company. In other instances there is no effort to consolidate all the details of divisional planning, but there is an effort to aggregate divisional plans so as to compare their total objectives (e.g., sales and profits) with those established for the entire company. The planning staff may serve as a coordinator of plans made by functional officers at headquarters as well as those made by the divisions.

Third, the planning staff gives guidance to the divisions in their planning. The staff gives procedural guidance to assure uniformity in the development of the divisional plans. This may take the form of a manual which sets uniform time schedules, forms for presenting data, rules for preparing data, procedures for presentation of plans to top management, and a preliminary statement of basic objectives and strategies of top management. Substantive guidance is also given to the divisions. This includes basic assumptions needed by the divisions for their planning effort, such as product allocation among the divisions, interdivisional pricing, and plant location. The staff makes forecasts of environmental factors of importance to the divisions for their planning activities. Included are forecasts of major product demand, long-range economic conditions, price trends for selected materials, technological trends, and general industry competitive conditions. The planning staff also stands ready to help the divisions, upon request, with substantive problems and forecasts. Throughout this process there is continuous discussion among the central planning staff and corporate management and staff, and between corporate staff and division staff.

Fourth, the central staff reviews and evaluates plans prepared by the divisions. The presentation of the division plans are made directly to line managers (such as the executive vice-president and president) and not to the staff. The central planning staff reviews these plans, particularly the longer-range plans, at the time of and after presentation to top management. The review is only for major problems, gaps, omissions, conflicts, and inconsistencies. The review includes some aggregations of plans for the entire company to evaluate the extent to which the divisional plans permit the company to move toward overall objectives.

Fifth, the central planning staff helps division managers make long-range plans when they have not had the experience or staff to do the task well. This, of course, is more likely to be done for a new division. Staff may also evaluate prospects for a division as a basis for headquarters management action concerning the division. Such action may take the form of divestment.

Sixth, the staff is responsible for undertaking specific studies and evaluations covering a variety of matters of interest to top management. These cover both short- and long-range matters although the tendency is to emphasize the latter.

Seventh, the planning staff may help management in diversification; new product development; and new programs not covered by current divisional endeavors, such as new markets. Not only may the staff be responsible for basic studies underlying recommended actions in these areas, but in some cases the department may participate actively in completing actions taken. This is particularly so in those instances where the staff has responsibilities concerning expansion through acquisition and merger.

In sum, the planning staff is fundamentally a coordinator, an integrator of the planning effort. But it also instigates planning, stimulates creativity and innovation, is a consultant for others doing planning, and provides studies to facilitate the planning process and to aid management in decision-making. In many planning staffs the majority of time is spent on studies which serve as premises for planning or bases for management decision.

DIFFERING PATTERNS
OF PLANNING ORGANIZATIONS

In the following discussion major patterns of organization, and deviations, will be examined from the point of view of planning staff. The work of the planning staff, as well as other organizational elements involved in corporate planning, will vary much from company to company and within the same company over time. In some areas of activity it is very difficult to detect patterns which actually exist as well as patterns which yield best results. There are many organizational combinations which have yielded high-quality plans. Furthermore, very comparable planning organizations have produced widely differing results in different companies.

DECENTRALIZED VERSUS CENTRALIZED COMPANIES. At Continental Airlines, Allstate Insurance, and American Airlines, the corporate planning department does not have counterparts in the divisions. The central planning department in such companies with a homogeneous product or service, and with functional divisions, integrates plans developed by the corporate headquarters' functional staffs. Among companies with a more heterogeneous product line and profit-center divisions, there is greater need of decentralized planning. In such instances the divisions will have strong planning groups and the central planning department will act much as set forth in Table 5-3. The divisional planning staffs may act for the division in much the same fashion as the planning staff does in the centrally controlled company.

SIZE OF COMPANY. The existence, composition, and functioning of a planning staff will vary much depending upon company size. In a very small company the president must be his own planning staff. As the company grows in size the major line managers may serve as staff with the chief executive to develop comprehensive business plans. In a medium-size company the planning staff may be an assistant to the president or one of the functional officers, such as the controller, who may be used as staff in developing plans. In very large companies the staff will function as previously illustrated. In the largest companies, such as Ford, Standard Oil of New Jersey, and General Motors, no single corporate planning department exists. Rather, one of two patterns seems to exist. A number of central headquarters' functional staffs are responsible for comprehensive planning and their work is supervised by a senior vice-president who, in effect, is the corporate planner for the company. Another pattern is for major parts of the company to develop comprehensive plans for their areas and these are informally integrated at the top levels of the company. This is the pattern at Standard Oil of New Jersey. In such instances, of course, there is no single unified corporate plan covering all major areas.

WHO DIRECTS THE PLANNING STAFF? While the main tendency is for the planning staff to report to the president, there is a growing tendency in larger companies for the planning department's effort to be guided partly by a top-level planning committee. The Lockheed Aircraft Corporation, for example, has a Planning Council for which the Executive Vice-President is Chairman and the Director of Development Planning acts as Secretary. On the Council are major corporate functional officers and group vice-presidents. The Development Planning Department initiates action on behalf of the Council but acts also in conformance with directions of the Council. The Continental Oil Company is another illustration of a business with a top-level planning committee. Olin Mathieson has a business planning committee composed of "top brass," and also a planning and coordinating subcommittee, composed of junior executives, who are responsible for reviewing divisional five-year plans.

Sometimes the president's cabinet, or staff, or committee which deals with all company problems, may be the forum for the director of planning to pursue his functions in organizing company planning. Among some companies the planning department reports to the Executive Vice-President. In some companies, the Kimberly-Clark Corporation, for instance, the corporate planning officer reports to the Chairman of the Board. The major tendency in the larger corporation is for the corporate planning department to report administratively to the president through a senior vice-president. Also, the tendency is for a top-level committee to assume responsibilities for the preparation of the corporate plan. In this respect, a combination of the planning department plus line managers aids the chief executive in discharging his planning duties. This tendency is likely to grow as the top management in larger companies finds increasing pressure to structure itself as a team. In such a case, functional staffs will diminish in importance as the need for overall integration increases. The overall integration can be provided by planning departments which are able to avoid functional prejudices and shape their analyses and recommendations in the same frame of reference as the top management team with which they work (Daniel, 1965, p. 26).

Top-level planning committees symbolize and embody the important idea of a team approach to the planning program. In larger companies a chief executive, in discharging his planning duties, needs the help of his planning department, his other functional staffs, and line managers. It is important that line management be combined with staff for only line managers can make decisions governing their operations. Furthermore, staff alone, even with the chief executive's support, cannot get divisions of a large company to exert the energy and devote the talent needed for quality planning. Only line managers can stimulate such efforts and even they sometimes have great difficulties in getting the needed work done. Consequently, such committees provide the power of line management in getting planning done.

The committee also serves as a forum for thrashing out important questions associated with the allocation of resources. Open conflict at the higher administrative levels can leave scars. A planning committee can prevent many deep wounds from being inflicted simply because it exists as an arena for resolving problems before they break out into the open.

These committees can also help to stimulate creativity, innovation, and imaginative thinking in the divisions. Because members of the committee are also responsible for activities in the divisions, they have a high stake in trying to stimulate first-rate planning.

In smaller companies the director of the planning staff may serve as chairman of the planning committee. Unless the corporate planning officer enjoys great respect throughout the company, and has the unswerving support of top and divisional line management, it is better to have a top executive, such as the executive vice-president or the president, be chairman of the planning committee. Planning is a line function and this arrangement fits better that idea.

The greater the degree of complexity of a plan, the more significant and comprehensive it is; and the longer the time horizon covered, the more likely will be committee action to oversee its development and evaluation. Committee action in such a case will be employed at various stages and levels in the development of the plan. Committee action rather than individual action often may provide the final approval of the plan.

There are many reasons for this. Coordination is needed and can be assured by committees. A committee will be a forum for keeping the members informed about what is going on. Collective judgment may be superior to individual judgments in complex cases. The committee also will provide a method to assure participation. A committee also may be a method to allow a chief executive to delegate authority without giving one executive too much power.

There are, of course, disadvantages to the use of such committees. Committee action may result in compromise decisions. The risks which the company ought to take may not be incorporated in the plans. The committee action may result in a feeling that no one has responsibility for the actions of the group. The committee may be dominated by one person, or a clique, and not create the best plans. Committee action is sometimes slow, and it is often expensive.

Although these disadvantages of committee action are well known, a corporate planning council that works with the chief executive need not suffer any of these defects but may enjoy all the advantages expressed above. If the planning organization is suitable, if the planning program is conducted on the basis of a clear procedure and time table, if the purposes of the committee are understood, and if the chief executive accepts the full degree of his planning responsibility in dealing with the planning committee, the results should be wholly beneficial.

Managing a company is coming to be more and more a team operation. Individualism is still important, but the problem so many chief executives face today is blending individualism with team effort to optimize the values of both approaches. A top-level planning council can be a powerful tool toward achieving this result while at the same time assuring the production of a top-quality corporate planning program.

DIVIDING THE PLANNING DEPARTMENT. Not all of the chief executive's planning is done, of course, in the planning department. He has his other functional officers to help him and, as noted above, the planning department may serve to coordinate their efforts. One of the main functions noted above for the planning department—diversification—is often handled outside the planning department. A few companies have split strategic planning from other formal planning. IBM, for example, has three subsystems in its planning—a strategic planning system, an operational measurement and control system, and a management development system. Each of these has a corporate component and a divisional component. The Corporate Planning and Development group of the International Minerals and Chemical Corporation is divided into four subdivisions, as follows (Smalter, 1964, p. 135):

Environment Analysis
- Assembles and evaluates information for corporate and divisional use.
- Provides basic economic and political "intelligence."
- Provides industry and competitive "intelligence."
- Identifies and measures new opportunities and threats to IMC.
- Provides factual support for new ventures.

Strategic Program Planning
- Provides leadership to FIVE-YEAR PLAN assembly.
- Coordinates and assists in the synthesis of market-mission strategies, citing criteria in "program-packages."
- Establishes project priorities and optimum resource allocations.
- Directs management attention to most important challenges facing IMC.

Venture Development
- Analyzes and develops new ventures to achieve strategic goals.

- Appraises and implements acquisitions.
- Seeks and screens opportunities.
- Plans and implements testing and commercialization of new products.
- Evaluates capital plans.
- Develops programming for approved major projects, and initiates action.

Management Planning
- Conducts optimization studies on new and existing "systems."
- Provides analytical problem-solving skills to other functions: mine planning, logistic analysis, venture analysis, etc.
- Analyzes strategic alternatives and resolves best course of action.
- Studies and recommends management staffing needs.

Whether or not a company should break up the central planning staff into separate subsystems depends, of course, upon the nature of the company and the way the chief executives want to manage. So long as there is effective coordination among the groups, and the net result is not to add unnecessarily to overhead costs, there is no reason why the basic functions specified above for the planning group may not be split.

ROLE OF THE BOARD OF DIRECTORS. Although boards of directors are responsible for the broad direction of their companies, their involvement in corporate planning varies much. In some companies the chairman of the board assumes responsibility for developing long-range strategic plans for the company. Some boards are very active in the operations of their company, such as DuPont de Nemours and General Motors. In such instances the boards are intimately involved in the comprehensive planning of their companies. In the majority of cases, however, boards are involved in the corporate planning process principally as (a) initiators of major policies which serve to direct the planning program and (b) recipients of long-range planning briefings after the company has gone through the exercise.

SCOPE OF ROLE OF PLANNING DEPARTMENT. Although I think that the functions specified above for a corporate planning department are rather typical for a large company, not all staffs assume such responsibilities. Some planning staffs participate actively in the meetings chaired by top executives to review and evaluate division plans; other staffs become only indirectly involved. Some staffs have considerable influence over the establishment of basic objectives and strategies; other staffs are merely errand boys. But, by and large, when a planning staff is created, it tends to exert important influence over executive decision-making.

SHOULD A COMPANY HAVE A
PLANNING DEPARTMENT?

Planning departments are expensive and not without problems. An important question arises, therefore, concerning the desirability of having such departments.

In a larger corporation a separate planning department has many advantages. Any department which can suitably discharge the functions sketched above for a planning group will clearly fill a major need in a larger company. A corporate planning department should be able to fulfill these duties with objective judgment and the application of the latest problem-solving tools. In this fashion, functional biases are submerged and staff work is up-to-date. A great many companies have seen the advantages of a separate planning department.

On the other hand, there are arguments against such departments. A department may not be needed in some companies. Smaller companies cannot afford to hire the talent. There are some larger companies, as noted above, who do not have planning departments. At General Motors, overall corporate planning is part of the regular function of top executives and staff. Through General Motors' Policy Groups, all divisional and functional areas are involved in planning. As one official put the case (Kaiden, 1967, p. 30): "Every staff has the responsibility of looking forward. The annual model change is a prod in this direction." There is no central planning group in Standard Oil of New Jersey. An official of that company explains why (Kaiden, 1967 p. 31): "We are not only highly diversified, but we also have a high degree of decentralization. As a result, a large proportion of our planning activity is conducted within our affiliates. Furthermore, since these affiliates all face different problems, each conducts its planning activities in a different manner." Most public utilities, as noted above, do not have central planning departments but do their long-range planning through engineering departments.

If a planning staff becomes removed from operations or tries to do all the planning, it should not be allowed to exist. If it becomes abstract and abstruse in its thinking and deals in matters unrelated to management problems, it should and will be eliminated.

If the existence of a planning department is used as an excuse for top management to avoid its responsibilities for corporate planning, the department should not have been created in the first place.

CHARACTERISTICS OF THE CORPORATE
PLANNER AND HIS STAFF

The ideal choice for a corporate planner, says Kirby Warren (1966, p. 43): "should be a man who is both philosopher and realist, theoretician and practical politician, soothsayer and salesman and . . . he probably should be able to walk on water."* The impossibility of finding a man who fills fully this definition underscores not only the challenges of the job but the difficulties of discharging it properly.

The director of a corporate planning department may hold any one of a number of different titles—for instance, vice-president-planning, director of planning, director of corporate planning, or assistant to the president for planning. He may have a budget ranging from zero to $1 million, but a budget over $500 thousand is rare. The number of other persons in his department may vary from zero to 100. The largest planning department known to me is that of Philips in Einhoven with about 300 people, but this department has many detailed marketing functions, which accounts for the large number. The majority of planning staffs, however, number five or fewer professional personnel (Stewart, 1966). A smaller sample by Melville Branch (1964, p. 90) showed about half the respondents said their staffs had fewer than five personnel.

A typical long-range planning department in a large technologically oriented company might include a scientist or scientists in fields important to the company, technical engineering product-oriented talents, an economist, and someone with a background in accounting and finance. The variations are many. Operations research experts were found in some planning departments a half dozen years ago. They then dropped out of favor but are now back in favor as "systems analysts" and "management scientists."

A company that enjoys shelter from the hazards of competition may get by with little or minimal planning staff assistance. But where a company faces rapid, important, and great change, its ability to survive and remain profitable depends upon management's heightened sensory perception of what is going on in and outside the company. Staff is a major technique for enlarging this management capability. Marion Folsom (1962, p. 26†), former President of Kodak, underscored the worth of such staff when he wrote: "effective staff work is one of the chief reasons why business management has become . . . a profession as well as an art." In companies that face great change, heavy capital investment, and long development cycles, planning staffs tend to be large.

Branch's sample (1964, p. 93) showed that out of 42 corporate planners 13 had a background of general business management. Six rose through a planning function, six through economics and finance, and the remainder were scattered among engineering, manufacturing, marketing, and other functional fields. Among Stewart's sample of 822 companies, 80 percent of the respondents said they had worked in top management positions, 85 percent had been in middle management positions, and 65 percent said they had been in supervisory positions.

* E. Kirby Warren, *Long-Range Planning: The Executive Viewpoint,* © 1966, Prentice-Hall, Inc., Englewood Cliffs, New Jersey.

† From *Executive Decision-Making* by Marion B. Folsom. Copyright © 1962 by the Trustees of Columbia University. Used by permission of McGraw-Hill Book Company.

Table 5-4 Personnel Specifications
Director—Long-Range Planning

HE SHOULD BE:

1. *Mature in bearing and attitude*
   - Emotionally well adjusted.
   - Commanding in demeanor and actions.
   - Sufficiently self-assured to take strong stands when warranted.

2. *Willing to recommend calculated risks to improve the company*
   - Able to cut new patterns.
   - Willing to break out of conventional methods.
   - Willing to generate innovation in order to depart from conventional ways of doing things.

3. *Highly intelligent and creative*
   - Capable of analyzing complex business and economic problems involving all aspects of the business and arriving at sound conclusions.

4. *Tactful and persuasive*
   - Able to deal effectively with both operating and senior executives.
   - Willing to help operating executives with specific planning problems.

5. *In excellent health*
   - Able and willing to devote his time and energies to the demanding requirements of the position.

HE SHOULD HAVE:

1. Experience in developing, coordinating and executing planning procedures and analysis for expansion and diversification, including the following:
   - developing criteria for expansion
   - seeking out and evaluating new fields of interest
   - participating in negotiations leading to successful acquisition or joint venture arrangements.

2. Experience in establishing long-range corporate objectives.

3. A reputation as an astute businessman with the drive and profit orientation to achieve agreed-upon objectives.

4. Knowledge of economic and governmental trends and their effect on present and future business activities.

5. Potential for continued progression in general management.

Personnel specifications for corporate planners that have come across my desk seek the highest qualities one can find in a staff man and include a range of requirements not found in abundance in many people. One sample is given in Table 5-4. Other requirements frequently found in personal specifications include: general management background not closely identified with a particular management function, imagination, ability to establish rapport and confidence among functional and line officers, ability to get along well with the chief executive, and capacity to undertake the research necessary to underpin the planning process and top management decisions. This list is easily extended. But the point is that companies are looking for a superior person who can get along well with people and perform above average in the research, imagination, and balanced judgment needed to help top managers meet their planning responsibilities.

Critically important, of course, is the way that the corporate planning director relates to the chief executive. There must be mutual confidence and understanding between the two for success. This is built up in different ways by different people. One trend of significance among U.S. companies is the way talents of corporate planning groups have been blended with those of line managers. Where top managers have strong economic and finance backgrounds, the corporate planner may complement them with a deep technical background, and just the other way around. Where the line managers are intuitive and empirical, the corporate planner may be more scholarly and theoretical.

In the absence of research findings, as well as for reasons such as the above, too many generalizations about the characteristics of the corporate planner should be avoided. More need be said, however, about his relationships with other individuals and groups in the company. The way he acts toward and influences others in getting the planning job done is secondary in importance only to the role played by the chief executive.

The corporate planner must seek to demonstrate an accomplishment of real value to the company. Planning success may result from brilliant insights into a new opportunity, a basic research study that helped management solve a tough problem correctly, or his stimulation of planning throughout the company. There is no better way for the corporate planner and his staff to generate respect than to show solid and perceived accomplishment.

He must above all understand that he does not make decisions. He must "sell" his views and not "tell" line managers what to do. For a corporate planner this line of demarcation is not always easy. A persuasive planner may in fact make a decision when a top manager accepts his recommendation. A manager may resist rejecting a recommendation simply because to do so would mean dismissing a large staff effort. Whatever the case, a planner must avoid—indeed he must lean backward—giving an impression that he makes decisions for line action.

He must develop a fine and sensitive understanding for the type of information which managers need to make decisions and which he can and should supply. He must avoid overwhelming managers with information familiar to them especially if he neglects information they need. He must appreciate the limitation of data in making decisions and try to supply facts and opinions that will help managers sharpen their intuition. In providing information he must overcome as much as possible his own biases. Although he must have mastery over new techniques for accumulating and analyzing data, he should avoid dwelling too much on methods that are unfamiliar to top management. He should be able to communicate well both orally and in writing.

A corporate planner usually has a good bit of freedom to choose problems upon which to concentrate his efforts. In allocating his time and that of his staff, he must be imaginative in working on areas that will yield high returns for the company. He should sharpen his ability to choose the "right" issues to study.

The planner and his staff must not become so engrossed in planning to plan, or planning on paper, that decisions to act are delayed or compromised. Planning can be fascinating to an intellectual even though no hard decisions are made. The hard part of planning comes after procedures for planning are prepared. On the other hand, a planner must not become too enamored of too complete a set of plans, or try to perfect with ultimate finesse the intermeshing of plans, particularly those concerned with the far future.

When a planner is a member of a top planning committee he usually must stimulate action by the group. The committee usually is, aside from the chief executive, the top authority for planning in the company and gives the orders. But usually the corporate planner has a heavy responsibility in developing and recommending the methodology for conducting the planning program. Although much of the initiative is in his hands, his approach is to persuade by imagination and quality work rather than to direct.

Within a large organization there is an endless series of interrelationships between the corporate planning staff, functional offices in company headquarters, and divisions or other operating units. The opportunity for conflict among staffs as well as between the planning staff and line management are many. There are certain precautions that can help resolve conflicts. One, of course, is a well-conceived planning program. However, the personality of the corporate planner and his staff are also of great importance. His dealings with divisions, for example, should be suggestive and frequently by invitation. The relationship is rarely functional. He must be persuasive by virtue of his knowledge rather than proximity to top management. He should be flexible in his dealings with others and not dogmatic. In short, he must be able to work well with others, both line and staff. This is a human relations problem with strong overtones of expertise.

The corporate planner needs to be well balanced psychologically and be able to resist becoming too frustrated whether from line inattention, or from the too frequent grappling with human and substantive problems that have no single correct answers.

In choosing a corporate planner it is tempting to turn to the chief accounting officer or controller. This man is master over a large volume of information that is important in planning; he is responsible for the budgeting system that is so important in a comprehensive plan, and he has an understanding of the financial situation and requirements of the company. Granting that he may make important contributions to a comprehensive planning program, there is a serious question whether he should be given the task of organizing and coordinating the planning program unless he has the required outlook and characteristics of a corporate planner. The critical element is not so much what he knows and does as a chief accountant or controller, but whether he has the personal and intellectual characteristics required of the corporate planner. Richard G. Martens, an executive with vast experience, succinctly summarizes the problems of a typical controller in meeting these requirements. He says (in Warren, 1962, pp. 13-14):

"The controller's main job is to see that the resources of the business are conserved and being used efficiently. In accomplishing this task he uses the tools of accounting, auditing, and, more recently, budgeting and forecasting. Because of his interest in conservation and efficiency, the controller normally has a functional bias in the direction of saving rather than spending money. His work is primarily with figures and, of necessity, is oriented toward recording and examining the results of past operations. His task is to measure the results of risks taken by other functions of the business rather than to take risks himself . . . Within such a setting, it is only to be expected that forecasting, as developed by the controller, has tended to be a projection of past trends into the future.

"Long-range planning, on the other hand, must contend with the risks of innovation and deal with the exceptional and improbable future. It must be concerned with risk-taking—spending money to make money. The measure of the effectiveness of long-range planning is not efficiency but how well the course of business has been charted on the sea of future risk. Above all, those entrusted with the responsibility for long-range planning must be oriented toward the future—not the past. They must be able to take risks in their stride—not pass the risk to others or act as a passive observer or measurer. The long-range planner must lead—not follow . . .

"Placing the long-range planning function under the average controller will assure its sterility."

This is not meant to be an indictment of accountants. Rather it emphasizes the fact that a strong background in any functional area does not necessarily produce a first-rate corporate planner. Some of the most highly desired qualities of a corporate planner may not be developed in the functional areas.

In conclusion, much more could be added to this brief description of the nature of a corporate planner and what is required of him for success. The requirements for success depend upon circumstances in each company. Each company's requirements are unique and each company planner is unique in his setting. But each situation must be joined with a thorough understanding of those criteria which are imperative for effective planning and the proper role the corporate planner must play in achieving the best planning program.

PLANNING TIME SCHEDULE

The following is a condensed schedule which is presented here for several reasons. The intricate interrelationships between corporate planning groups and other elements of a corporation are readily apparent from a cursory examination of the schedule. The schedule also points out the long period of time usually taken to produce a corporate plan, even among companies that have been engaged in planning for a long time. Although this schedule is more or less typical, there are so many variations in practice that generalization cannot be carried too far. But the reader will see in this schedule many of the basic functions, their sequence, and the role played by the corporate planning staff in planning. In mind here is the preparation of a five-year plan, which includes next year's budget, and the documentation needed to understand the plan. The final table of contents may be considered to be something like that presented in Chapter 2.

In small companies this timing can be shortened. In Magnetic Design, Inc., a formal corporate plan, referred to earlier, was prepared for the first time in about three months. In large companies, the cycle frequently runs a full year. At Celanese (*Celanese World,* January 1966, pp. 9-10) for example, the first of the planning cycle begins in January and ends in June. During this phase there is a review and modification by corporate management of specific strategic objectives of the company. Reviews of the environment are made and operating divisions begin to establish preliminary objectives for their operations. In June the top management gives approval to the preliminary objectives, and the first phase of the planning cycle ends. The second cycle then begins in July and includes the development of detailed plans. In the third phase, revisions are made to take account of changes in the market and internal operating conditions; the final approval of the Chairman and Board of Directors is given late in December. The cycle then is ready to begin again in January of the next year.

PLANNING VERSUS OPERATIONS

All that has been said up to this point makes it crystal clear that there should be no divorce of planning from operations. Planning and operations are part of the same job. They are not separate. General managers who have no part in planning will not consider themselves bound by it. Furthermore, the more people

Table 5-5   Time Schedule for a Corporate Five-Year Plan

AUGUST

1. Corporate Planning Staff (CPS) meets with corporate officers, and checks with division planning staffs, concerning a timetable for planning.
2. CPS confers with corporate officers concerning changes in basic objectives, strategies, and policies that should serve as new guides for the planning program.
3. Corporate Planning Council (CPC) meets to consider time schedule and discuss suggested changes in corporate objectives, strategies and policies. Committee also reviews strengths and weaknesses in the last planning cycle and discusses changes for the next cycle.
4. CPS intensifies efforts to prepare background studies important for the planning program.
5. CPS prepares procedural manual to guide the development of the planning program.
6. CPC meets to review and approve the planning manual for transmission to all participating corporate offices and divisions.
7. Manual, together with studies useful in planning, is sent to all divisions.

SEPTEMBER

1. Division planning staffs meet with division managers to discuss completing their plans in conformance with CPS manual.
2. Division managers approve detailed procedural steps for their plan.
3. Corporate functional officers meet with CPS to discuss nature and relationship of their plans and division plans.
4. CPS meets with division staffs, as invited, to discuss problems in completing their plans.
5. CPS decides on areas for study to aid in evaluating plans when received, modifying existing strategies, and filling expected gaps that may develop in plans.

OCTOBER

1. CPS transmits to divisions additional planning premises, such as market demand, economic outlook, and possible price changes by competitors.
2. Divisions continue planning.
3. CPC meets to discuss problems which arise in preparation of plans.
4. CPS continues to meet with corporate and division personnel to help clarify procedures and aid in resolving problems.

Table 5-5   Time Schedule for a Corporate Five-Year Plan (Cont'd)

NOVEMBER

1. Divisions complete plans.
2. Plans transmitted to CPC with copy to CPS for aggregation and review.
3. CPC meets to review aggregate plans, to consider match between company objectives and total divisional objectives, to examine weaknesses in division plans, and to make suggestions for changes.
4. If chairman of CPC is not Chief Executive, the chairman and the director of corporate planning discuss major issues with the chief executive.
5. Program for planning conference(s) to be held to discuss plans is prepared by CPS for presentation to CPC.
6. CPC meets to review and approve planning conference program.
7. Agenda for planning conference sent to all managers concerned.
8. CPS prepares materials for the conference, such as aggregate company plan, and additional studies for the conference, such as changes in environment affecting plans.

DECEMBER

1. A two-day planning conference is held off site, attended by top executives of company and each division. Each division presents its plan and its problems, alternatives are discussed, and courses of action are determined. The chief executive is chairman of this conference.
2. At the end of the conference the chief executive, who is the *de facto* conference chairman, decides how each plan is to be modified as a result of the conference proceedings.
3. Divisions modify their plans accordingly.
4. An alternative procedure in many companies is for each division to present plans individually to top executives.
5. Changes are incorporated in a new aggregate company plan.
6. An overview and selected parts of the plan are presented to the board of directors by the corporate planner.
7. Annual budget reviews and approvals for next year's operations are made by the chief executive. This may be done in the above (1 to 4) discussions.

participate in the planning program the more they will consider the plan to be theirs.

Participation in planning embodies more than decision-making in planning. Participation means that managers will discuss various problems in planning with subordinates in such a fashion that a free exchange of ideas takes place among all those importantly involved in implementing the final plan.

Managers obviously have difficult problems in deciding what subjects will be discussed, how deeply they will be discussed, what is an appropriate time for discussing different subjects, and whether discussion will be face-to-face with an individual or in a group.

Many important advantages result from effective participation. Bavelas (1948) observes, for example, that there is a greater readiness to accept changes. This is extremely important because the very essence of planning is to bring about change. Likert (1961, pp. 242-244) says there is substantial evidence to support the view that participation in decision-making will increase employee motivation and productivity, and the greater the participation, the greater the benefit. He notes, however, that there is evidence that participation for good results needs to be geared to the values, expectations, and skills, of the people involved.

Three UCLA professors (Tannenbaum, Weschler, and Massarik 1961, p. 94) point out that effective participation may ease the job of management. Fewer managers may be needed for supervision, for subordinates may have a greater sense of responsibility after having participated in decision-making. Furthermore, group participation in planning decisions may make for better decisions. Even if wide participation may not always produce better quality decisions, the search for new ideas in others may provide more alternatives from which a manager may choose and may produce information that will enable him to do a better job in making choices in developing plans.

In a study William Ryan and I (1968) made of project managers in the aerospace industry, we found that high participation of personnel engaged in a project resulted in high motivation, loyalty, and innovation. In projects that had high participation in planning and decision-making the result was a superior technical product made at a much better than average time and cost to prototype.

No elaboration is needed to understand the importance of managers' having no responsibility for planning outside their own areas of authority. Conversely, a manager should have maximum authority to plan in his own area of responsibility.

But in corporate planning there are dilemmas in working within these criteria. Le Breton points out, for example: "Effective planning requires decentralization. Effective coordination requires action from a central point. This is the organizational dilemma of planning."* Decentralization requires that more decisions be made lower in an organization. Participation in planning requires that line managers get assistance from subordinates, line and staff. There is no participation, of course, if a line manager gets assistance in planning from his staff and, without consulting his subordinates, prepares the plan for his organization.

A dilemma arises in expanding participation in strategic planning as compared with medium-range programming or short-range planning. Widespread participation in the development of basic objectives and strategies may be difficult to arrange in a larger company. Anyway, the more explicit strategies are,

* Preston P. Le Breton and Dale A. Henning, *Planning Theory*, © 1961, Prentice-Hall, Inc., Englewood Cliffs, New Jersey.

the more proprietary they tend to become. There are also strategies, of course, that must be held confidential to all but a handful of people in a company. Although they do bind lower-level managers there frequently must be severe limits placed on their participation in the planning.

In some large companies a sense of participation is created in the following fashion. Objectives and strategies are prepared by top management for the planning process. Divisions and functional areas then prepare subobjectives, substrategies, and detailed plans within this framework. These plans are reviewed by top management and on the basis of them alterations may be made in overall company objectives and strategies.

In smaller companies, executives frequently meet away from headquarters to examine fundamental issues, such as the basic mission of the company, as well as long-range objectives and fundamental company strategies. Upon returning home they then develop detailed plans. Even in rather large companies this type of participation is possible and is employed.

THE CORPORATE PLANNER AND CONTROL

A friend of mine was hired by a medium-sized company to be vice-president in charge of planning and was asked whether this title was acceptable: Vice-President Planning and Control. He instinctively replied that the title was acceptable if the last two words were eliminated. He was very wise, for a corporate planner cannot operate effectively if he also is responsible for controlling the implementation of plans.

The case for using the corporate planner as "an inspector general," has been made on the grounds that he probably is in a better position to perform a control function more subtly and with less offense than any other officer (Hoopes, 1962, pp. 59-68). If the corporate planner is expected to receive periodic reports on performance from line managers, oversee actions taken in conformance with plans, interpret and evaluate performance, and report to top management, the planning function of the corporate planner will wither. General Somervell tried this approach at the Koppers Company in 1946 and it worked for a time but eventually was abandoned (Jerome III, 1961, Chapter 15).

The preceding comments, I think, make amply clear the sensitive role which a long-range planner plays in developing corporate plans. If he is asked to be, in effect, a line manager to see that plans are carried out, he inevitably will generate heated friction with line managers. Once friction develops, for whatever cause, the problems of the planner in getting information from managers in order to discharge his planning responsibilities will mount. It is true that a corporate planner basically is an integrator of plans, but to do this also requires constant communications with managers. No matter how voluminous a written plan is, it cannot contain all that is necessary to understand it. If control is added to planning, the planning will suffer because communication will disappear.

There are, of course, other concepts of control that a corporate planner may legitimately and usefully exercise. A corporate planner may exercise influence because of his expertise. Knowledge is authority. This works in business as anywhere else. A planner can exercise a type of control because he is persuasive. He can, within limits, check on performance for a chief executive. For example, a chief executive may ask a corporate planner to find out what divisions are doing about suggestions he has made in various conferences. But even here dangers exist.

GUIDELINES FOR PLANNING ORGANIZATION

In this concluding section a few of the more significant principles and guidelines for developing and maintaining an effective organization for planning are presented. These are not necessarily in order of importance nor in action sequence.

1. An effective organization can be developed only if there is a clear understanding of the nature of the comprehensive plan to be produced.

2. Management must understand that a comprehensive planning program cannot be introduced into a company overnight and expected to produce immediate miraculous results.

3. Planning will fail if adequate time and resources are not spent on it.

4. An organization for comprehensive planning is part of the whole managerial process, and as such it fits into and is subject to the principles and practices of that process.

5. There must be reasonably clear understanding of the planning organization, including distribution of authority, procedures, and nomenclature of planning.

6. The organization for planning must be used to develop plans that are bases for current decisions. Playing with planning rather than completing the process and reaching conclusions should be avoided.

7. Plans must be written, to the extent considered desirable, and made available to authorized personnel.

8. If a director of corporate planning is appointed he should report to an appropriate executive and at the top levels of the company.

9. As wide a participation as possible should be encouraged, especially among those managers and employees who will implement the plans.

10. In larger divisionalized companies planning staffs should be established in the larger divisions.

11. Planning should not be separated from operations.

12. Organization for planning should encompass adequate machinery for implementing plans, reviewing progress, and evaluating results.

13. The corporate planner and planning staffs should be as capable technically and as suitable personally as company resources can afford.

14. Once a comprehensive planning program is begun it should not be allowed to fail, for the result will be worse than if it was not started in the first place.

6
The Network
of Corporate Aims—I

6

The Network of Corporate Aims—I

INTRODUCTION

It has been only in recent years that much attention has been paid to the nature and structure of business aims. The reason is very simple. Up until a few years ago it was generally conceded, both in business and in the academic world, that there was but one aim in business and that was to maximize profits. In recent years, however, there has been a growing recognition that all but the smallest enterprises have multiple aims.

The difference in perspective between past and current thinking is framed in the following two quotations. The first is that famous passage by Adam Smith which not only captured the philosophy of laissez-faire, but set the cornerstone for the concept that the only objective of business was to maximize profits. Smith said in 1776: "It is not from the benevolence of the butcher, the brewer, or the baker that we expect our dinner, but from their regard of their own self-interest. We address ourselves not to their humanity, but to their self-love, and never talk to them of our own necessities, but of their advantage."

Alexander N. McFarlane, when President of Corn Products Company, voiced a somewhat different philosophy which reflects the view that business management has social responsibilities, a business has multiple objectives, and its actions are determined by these objectives. He said (1965, p. 29): "Thoughtful business leaders are vitally concerned with the purposeful relationships between corporations and the rest of society. They recognize that business has social as well as economic responsibilities—and that these must be acted upon. Business must, therefore, define its purposes to provide for their proper discharge. It is the job of corporate management, then:

- to align its corporate purpose with its social and economic responsibility;
- to make sure each person in the corporation not only understands these purposes, but is willing to be committed to them;

• to see that these purposes are acted upon by people of the corporation."

Except for the smallest enterprises, the profit goal is thus joined by others in modern business. Although still dominant in all but the non-profit corporations, it is only one of a number of aims. For the larger companies Eells (1960, p. 117) expresses the current situation this way: "Not only are their *stated* objectives far more numerous than profit seeking; their implicit *goals* are also far more complex. It is inviting to anthropomorphise 'the corporation' as the rational and calculating man of classical theory; but corporations in action bear little resemblance to the 'economic man,' or even to the reconstructed post-Freudian man of unconscious and irrational, as well as ratiocinating, components. It is a complex association of men whose actions are only to some—and varying—degree polarized around the profit motive."

One of the most important functions of top management is to identify and specify aims for the entire enterprise. This is a first and major step in planning, and without it there can be no effective planning. Within overall business aims each manager must identify and clarify less detailed aims to guide his actions as well as those of managers below him. There is no activity more critical in planning and no function more important to managers.

Both in the literature as well as in the practice of business aims there exists a paradox. On the one hand, there is a recognition of the importance of aims. On the other hand, not many companies have well-structured networks of aims and those that do are generally not satisfied with them. The explanation of this paradox is simple: developing a suitable network of business aims is extremely complex, it is an area where oversimplification has retarded better understanding, and it is somewhat unique for each business since it combines value judgments of managers with other elements of organizational operations.

In Chapter 2 the major components of the business network of aims were identified. This chapter and the next will define, illustrate, and analyze them in detail.

NETWORK OF AIMS STRUCTURES

There is no uniformity in the structure of the network of aims found in industry. What is included, what is excluded, how aims are ordered, and how they relate vary from company to company and from time to time in the same company.

It is convenient to view the network of business aims as a pyramid, as shown in Chart 6-1. The number of statements associated with each segment tends to increase as the pyramid is descended. Thus, statements about basic purpose are normally short. Specification of short-term goals, at the other extreme, tends to be lengthy. For small companies the statements of aims frequently do not exist in written form; when written they tend to be only for short-range goals and

Chart 6-1

Network of Business Aims

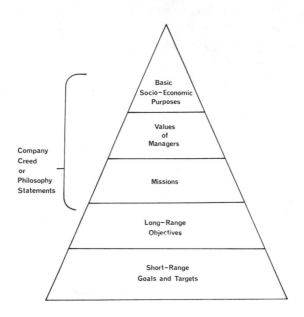

then for but a few—such as cash, production, sales, and employment. As companies grow in size, the list of aims tends to grow.

FUNDAMENTAL SOCIO-ECONOMIC PURPOSES

Enterprises are not isolated from the society of which they are a part. They are creatures of it and are nurtured and supported by it to accomplish specific purposes. They will survive only so long as they satisfy these purposes. One of the major purposes of organized business is to use economic resources efficiently in satisfying consumer wants. Implicit in fulfilling this purpose is the view that the more efficiently a business satisfies consumer wants at the right price, the higher will be the profit. Profit is a powerful motivation in the efficient use of resources. A fundamental purpose, therefore, for any business is to seek profit through effective and efficient use of resources.

MISSIONS. Business firms choose to meet this purpose by pursuing a mission, or line of business. In classical economic theory a firm could easily rearrange its resources to produce something else that consumers wanted in the event that what it was currently producing was not in favor and, therefore, unprofitable. Most companies today do not have such resource flexibility. Furthermore, in today's markets, managers know that specialization gives the advantage to a company that can concentrate its capabilities in selected economic areas. Although corporate charters do restrict business activities of companies, the alternatives are usually too broad to serve as a basis for planning. For these reasons, businesses find it a very important task to specify the basic mission(s) or line(s) of business in which the company will engage.

Companies more and more are thinking seriously about basic mission statements because they do, in fact, direct a company's efforts. A company that says its mission is automobile production is in a much different business than one that says its business is ground transportation. The Cunard Line in 1966 radically changed its line of business when Sir Basil Smallpiece, Chairman of the Board of Cunard Steamship Company, which includes Cunard Line, said: "If we regard the passenger ship no longer simply as a means of transport, but more as a floating resort in which people take a holiday and enjoy themselves, and incidentally get transportation thrown in, then the market outlook is completely changed. We find ourselves in a growth industry, the leisure industry" (*Fortune*, January 1967, p. 58). Rethinking the basic businesses of a company forces a management to ponder some of the profoundest questions that can be asked of it. When a company which has been in the brick-making business, for example, considers getting into the business of producing clay products as its basic mission, or when an old-line farm implement company thinks about changing its mission to earth-moving equipment, major questions arise. What is the nature of the new competitive arena for the company? What strengths of the company will help make the new venture successful? Does the new line of business avoid the company's weaknesses? What are the implications of the new line of business for future growth?

Dealing with such fundamental questions as these is very important for it tells a company, among other things, that being in the business of making toys is far different from being in the business of youth entertainment, or that making and selling typewriters as office machinery is a much different business than making them to be sold to individuals through retail channels.

Changing (or deciding not to change) the basic mission or line(s) of business of a company is one of the most important tasks a chief executive has to perform. If a proper change is not made, stagnation and bankruptcy can result. If a proper change is made, it can open up an entirely new horizon of profitable opportunities, as in the above case of Cunard.

VALUES OF TOP MANAGERS

As noted in Chapter 2, the values of top managers are reflected in the network of aims of an enterprise. Whether written or not, these values have the profoundest impact on the direction in which a firm moves and the way it operates. This is a subject which only recently has attracted the attention of scholars, but from their work it is clear that values can be measured and are partly responsible for the multiplicity of objectives of a business (Guth and Taguiri, 1965; Taguiri, 1965; England, 1967a and 1967b; Clark, 1966).

Value systems of managers are comparatively permanent bases for influencing behavior. They are something like attitudes but are more fixed, ingrained, and stable in nature. Also, values are more general and less tied to specific objects than are attitudes. They are closer to the concept of ideologies and philosophies than to attitudes. As such, they obviously are important in the way a manager perceives situations, solves problems and makes decisions, looks at other individuals and groups, looks at his business, decides where his business should go, determines what is and is not ethical behavior, or accepts organizational behavior (England, 1967a, p. 54).

One manager's value system may lead him to seek rapid growth over profits, another to produce only technically sophisticated products rather than mass-produced items, another to sell only in U.S. markets and not go abroad, another to seek profits over all other considerations, another to stabilize employment at the expense of stockholder dividends, and so on. Values such as these have an obvious relevance to the basic objectives which top managers establish for their enterprises.

WRITTEN CREEDS AND PHILOSOPHIES

During the past fifteen years there has been a rapid increase in publicized statements of company purpose. One study made in 1958 (S. Thompson) concluded that 70 percent of the written creeds found in American business had been prepared in the preceding five years. These documents have been called creeds, philosophies, and, by their more critical observers, public relations beguilements. Although it may be true that many written creeds or philosophies are designed to enhance the public image of a company, they can be, and often are, the cornerstone of a company's direction and method of operation. These creeds frequently express the basic purposes of a company and the beliefs of the chief executives. This includes ethical values as well as philosophies and chosen practices in achieving or adhering to them. The ethical values, of course, refer to personal conduct, moral duty, or an expression of what is right or wrong. Publicized creeds generally include statements associated with the first three tiers in the network of aims shown in Chart 6-1.

Most company creeds tend to be short rather than long, although it seems that more recent additions are expanding. By and large, however, they include one or more of the elements in Table 6-1.

The more concrete, short versions are simple statements, such as: "The purpose of the Martin Steel Company is to make basic fabricated steel shapes and forms at a profit and be a good citizen." Notice the inclusion of three major purposes—line of business, profits, and amity. A bit longer statement including more elements of Table 6-1 is that of the Lockheed Aircraft Corporation, shown in Table 6-2. A much longer statement is shown in Table 6-3. There are some companies that express purpose at a higher level of abstraction and have consciously sought to meet it. A classic illustration is Du Pont's "Better things for better living through chemistry." RCA's is "The most trusted name in electronics," and Union Carbide's is "The discovery company." Celanese has a broad mission, as follows: "To retain our global business leadership through new products and research, supported by aggressive marketing." To be sure, these latter expressions are more slogans or philosophies than basic missions in the sense of a specific line of business. When a company takes such statements seriously, however, it is impossible to exclude them from basic missions or purposes because they become precisely that.

Table 6-1 Brief Resume of Table of Contents of a Company's Creed Statement*

ITEM	PURPOSE OR VALUE STATED OR SOUGHT
Business mission	States area and/or lines of business
Profitability	Dedication to profits
Interests to be satisfied and balanced	Devotion to public interest Devotion to interests of stockholders, employees, suppliers, community
Quality	Seek high quality in products Stimulate high quality in management and employees
Efficiency	Seek low cost, high productivity
Atmosphere of enterprise	Good place for people to work Good company in which to invest Good company from which to buy
Observance of codes of conduct	Honesty Integrity Opportunity Leadership Fairness in all dealings Teamwork Development of employees Open opportunities for employees Preserve private enterprise system Be a good citizen Duty and loyalty Religious devotion

* Suggested by Bertram M. Gross, *The Managing of Organizations* (New York: The Free Press, 1964), p. 488.

A surprising number of company statements of basic purpose do not put profitability first, and some do not mention profits. This is probably not because they think it is subordinate, but because managers feel that a business which achieves its basic social purpose will be profitable. Whether stated first or not at all in written statements, profit is a major purpose of management. The profitability aim when expressed, takes many forms, such as:

- "We believe in generating a proper return on investment through profits adequate to provide security to employees, customers, stockholders, and suppliers."
- ". . . create profits to maintain the health and growth of the company."
- ". . . optimize profits."
- ". . . provide a high and growing record of earnings per share."
- "Net profits after taxes must be sufficient to support normal growth and provide a reasonable return to shareholders."

INTERESTS TO BE SATISFIED AND BALANCED. As statements get longer they tend to include more observations about satisfying various interests. Included are stockholders, employees, customers, suppliers, people in communities in which the business exists, various governments, and other institutions in so-

---

Table 6-2   Statement of Basic Purposes of the Lockheed Aircraft Corporation*

THE BASIC PURPOSES OF LOCKHEED ARE:

1. To be the major company satisfying in the highest technical sense the national security needs of the United States and its allies in space, air, land, and sea.

2. To employ technical resources in meeting the nondefense needs of governments and the requirements of commercial markets.

3. To achieve continuous growth of profits at a rate needed to attract and retain stockholder investment.

4. To recognize and appropriately discharge our responsibilities for the welfare of our employees, the communities in which we do business, and society as a whole.

5. To maintain a large proportion of sales in advanced technical products bearing the Lockheed name.

6. To maintain continuity of the enterprise by holding relatively low rates of change of ownership, management, and employees.

* From the Lockheed Aircraft Corporation; reproduced by special permission.

ciety. Individual businesses take widely varying views about these interests. Illustrative statements are:

- "As a business enterprise operating in the American economy, it is our purpose to satisfy, to the highest possible degree, the interests of stockholders, employees, customers, and the public."
- "This we believe: That a business enterprise does not exist solely for the benefit of any one group, neither customers, nor stockholders, nor

Table 6-3   The Cleveland Electric Illuminating Company Creed

THE COMPANY'S CREED: In order to know the Company, you should know the creed by which it lives:

We Believe the first obligation of the Company and the employees is to supply the public with the best of modern utility service at reasonable rates.

We Believe in keeping the Company a first-class place to work; paying fair and just wages and salaries; providing the employees with such benefits as vacations with pay, sick leave with pay, paid holidays, pensions, and life insurance; and continually endeavoring to maintain good working conditions.

We Believe in the Company doing all it can to assure employees of security, opportunity, and recognition of work well done.

We Believe in the Company and in every employee helping to develop the fullest and finest teamwork.

We Believe in the Company and the employees constantly striving for safety in all operations.

We Believe in safeguarding the investment in the Company, paying a fair return to the investors for the use of their capital, and maintaining a record of earnings which will enable the Company to attract new capital to continue to expand its services.

We Believe the Company has immense opportunity for growth, and that its growth will create new and larger opportunities for the employees.

We Believe in the Company and the employees participating in leadership in community-building.

We Believe in the Company and its employees doing their full part to defend the American way of life from its enemies, and so to preserve freedom and justice.

Source: Stewart Thompson, *Management Creeds and Philosophies,* Research Study No. 32, American Management Association (New York: AMA, 1958), p. 103.

employees, nor public, but that the benefits for all groups must be in balance and that the resulting benefits are the product of a well-run business."

Amity

Businesses live in society and recognize the need to have good relations with their environment. As Eells (1960, p. 130) points out: "The corporation exhibits a need for solidarity with the society in which it operates."

The larger a company, the more importance it attaches to the attitudes of the community toward it and the influence which it may have on the community. There is solid reason for this as will be noted in the next chapter. Some illustrative expressions are:

- "To earn, to deserve, and to retain the favorable regard of its customers, share-owners, employees, suppliers, and the public—providing real leadership in all of its human relations."
- "We believe in being a good corporate citizen."
- "We believe it is our responsibility to be a good neighbor by supporting community projects that will benefit the community."
- "We encourage all employees to take an active part in community life."
- "We will constantly strive for good public relations by assuming our full share of responsibility in the communities in which we operate. It is our duty to conduct our business so that society benefits by our activities."

MANAGEMENT PRACTICES. Clearly reflecting the philosophy and value systems of management is the "style" of management employed, the way "things are done around here," and attitudes with respect to detailed operations. The range of written statements in this classification is wide. Some typical written statements that illustrate this area, are as follows:

General Management.

- "Our philosophy of management is based upon the belief that people, given the opportunity to exercise individual initiative and judgment, will achieve high standards of performance. We also believe that responsibility and authority must be delegated to release the creative energies which make possible their maximum contribution."
- "We believe individuals should be rewarded according to performance and that to the fullest extent possible promotions should be made within the company."
- Quality.

In many statements one finds quality of product, service, technology, and employees as subjects of stated purposes. For example:

". . . maintain the highest technical quality in the industry."

"Our objective is to make products with high and continuous quality of ingredients, packages, and processes."

"Assuring a satisfactory service to our customers is a primary objective of the company."

"Offer products of unexcelled quality at lowest possible prices consistent with an adequate return on investment."

Efficiency, Knowledge, Skill.

- ". . . supply the community with the best possible products at reasonable prices."
- ". . . improve the productivity of employees so that products can be sold at the lowest prices consistent with a reasonable return on investment."
- "We believe that through training and development our employees can lead a better life and contribute to the corporate well-being."
- "Our executives must be persons of talent, education, experience and ability. They must be persons of common sense and full understanding."

OBSERVANCE OF CODES. This is a catch-all classification which encompasses a wide variety of ethical codes of conduct. Some of the subcategories which might be included in this general class are honesty, integrity, leadership, fairness and equity in dealings, opportunities for employees, an appeal to teamwork, duty and loyalty, the preservation of the private enterprise system, and religious devotion. A few illustrations are:

- "We believe our individual and company relationships should be conducted on the basis of the highest standards of conduct and ethics."
- "We believe in the application of the Golden Rule in all our dealings."
- "We believe that professional managers must place the best interests of customers, employees, and the community at large ahead of theirs."
- "We believe the success of our business depends upon the character and integrity of the people working in it."
- "We believe in treating our employees fairly and with dignity. We believe it is important that employees have good working conditions, fair wages, the right to be heard, and that they prosper and lead satisfying lives."
- "It is management's duty to create conditions under which employees will have stable employment, at high wages, and opportunities to advance."

CONCRETENESS. Most business overall statements of purpose are expressed at high levels of abstraction. Vagueness in language at this level is typical and has its virtues. To begin with, a business, particularly a larger one, is a complex system having many aims and many interests to be satisfied. The statements noted above are not designed to express concrete ends but rather to provide motivation, general direction, an image, a tone, and a philosophy to guide the enterprise. To get too specific could detract from the value of these statements in furthering these needs. Precision also might stifle creativity. Much must be left to the continuous planning process.

These statements of purpose are also statements of policy. But not all broad policies of a business are included in them. In considering the basic guidance for the planning program, therefore, the network of policies of a company must be considered. These will be treated in depth in a later chapter.

OBJECTIVES

An objective in our lexicon of business aims refers to a desired or needed result to be achieved by a specific time. It is a value sought by an individual or group. It is a specific category of fundamental purpose. An objective is a desired future state of a business or one of its elements. The time dimension of an objective is long-range, as distinguished from short-range targets and goals.

Objectives may be expressed for every element of an enterprise considered important enough to be the subject of plans. They may be expressed quantitatively or qualitatively, but usually, the more concretely an objective is expressed, the better.

Structures of objectives are almost as diffuse as structures of purpose and philosophies. Here, more than in the overall creeds and philosophies, there is far more concentration on profits and other economic considerations. Again, the number of items included in a company's agenda of long-range objectives varies from a few to many.

Larger enterprises have need for specification of objectives in more areas than do smaller companies. The reason is that more people are involved who need guidance in decision-making, and many interests are concerned about objectives and the way they are to be achieved. But if an overall statement of purpose and philosophy does not exist, or if it is very short, there is no reason why the structure of objectives formulated in the planning process should not include aims which have no terminal point and which are classified as overall missions, creeds or philosophies. Although we can draw conceptually clean-cut distinctions within the network of aims, in practice it is not always necessary or desirable to do so. But the general proposition holds that business objectives as defined here should be as concrete as possible and have a terminal point in time for achievement.

One structure of objectives which covers the essential areas for most companies is as follows:

Profitability

This may be expressed in concrete terms, such as: "Increase profits from $1 million today to $8 million ten years hence." "Increase return on investment to reach 15 percent after taxes by 1978." Profitability can be expressed in share of market, return on assets for the company as a whole as well as major divisions, earnings per share for the entire company, absolute profits by major line of business, or the ratio of profits to sales.

Sales and Markets

Here again there are a number of ways sales objectives may be expressed. To illustrate: "Increase total company sales by 8 percent annually to reach $10 million 10 years from now." "Increase commercial sales so that by 1978 they will be equal to military sales." Sales objectives may, of course, be set for major products, divisions, regions, or nations.

Products

The spectrum of possible product objectives is even wider. Objectives, aside from sales and profitability, may be in terms of product improvement, such as: "By 1978 introduce into the product line a product covering the middle price range." Or, "Begin a research and development program so that within 5 years our first engine line will be completely redesigned and on the market." An objective to phase out a profitless product line may be specified.

Finance

Here would be included objectives concerning cash flow, debt equity ratios, new security issuances, debt retirement, dividend objectives, and comparable financial matters.

Stability

Long-range objectives may be established for stability of sales, profits, and employment. These objectives can be built into the numbers attached to these items so that, for example, sales objectives set for the next 5 years may show stability. The intent to secure stable growth, however, has wide implications in many areas of business activity and may, therefore, properly be a separate objective classification.

Personnel

Depending upon the needs of the business, personnel objectives may be appropriate. They may be useful in terms of new and developing management training and selection programs such as: rotating managers, hiring new managers, training managers and employees, and shifting employees among divisions.

Organization

If organizational changes are contemplated they should, of course, be included. A company may have an objective: "To establish a major division in the western part of the U.S. within 5 years, and a major subsidiary in Europe within 10 years." An objective to alter existing organizations also may be appropriate. Included here also might be managerial techniques, such as: "Install by 1972 a computerized inventory control system." "By 1973 install a real-time production line control system in the assembly division."

Flexibility

An important characteristic of a business is its ability to adapt to changing environment; to do this as quickly as necessary and with a high degree of creativity. While a broad qualitative objective may be expressed about flexibility, there are specific objectives which a company may set that will help to assure it. For example: "Establish a market research group with a full complement of five professionals within three years to assure proper market intelligence." "Increase research and development budgets so that this effort will receive $1 million in 1972." "Undertake a study to be completed in 1971 which will examine thoroughly the world-wide market for new agricultural machines."

Research and Development

Depending upon the research orientation of a company a separate category for this activity may be appropriate. Objectives, aside from dollar statements as noted above, might be: "Within 5 years develop a low cost and palatable protein food supplement from petroleum." "Within 5 years add to the research laboratories' capability in cryogenics and biophysics."

This by no means exhausts the possible major classifications. Standard Pressed Steel has what it calls an objectives index. Its classifications are: nature of the business, markets, marketing products, technology (research and development), industrial relations, public relations, organization, financial, facilities. Under each of these is a detailed breakdown of objectives.

Peter Drucker (1954) suggests another grouping to represent the eight areas where performance and results directly and vitally affect the survival and prosperity of the business (p. 63). The areas are: market standing, innovation, productivity, physical and financial resources, profitability, manager performance and development, worker performance and attitude, public responsibility. This list is much like, but not identical with, the General Electric Company's "Key Result Areas."*

The reader will recall that Kaiser Aluminum, as noted in Chapter 2, has a somewhat different classification. I participated in the development of a comprehensive set of company objectives for one of the largest companies in the U.S. and all objectives included in strategic planning were encompassed in three

---

* General Electric's areas are: profitability, market position, productivity, product leadership, personnel development, employee attitudes, public responsibility, and balance between short-range and long-range goals (Controllership Fdn., Inc., 1955, pp. 30-31).

categories: markets, profits and sales, and company quality and character. In general it seems better to classify objectives in a structure with no more than 8 or 10 categories. Beyond that the system tends to become unwieldy and includes so many items that attention may be diverted from the principal ones.

GOALS

Goals and targets are considered here to be synonymous and refer to short-term and minor aims. Goals are objectives expressed in a specific dimension. They are usually very concrete. Goals may exist for a business as a whole, for major divisions and departments, and for individual performance.

Short-range goals and targets should be established wherever and whenever management wishes to guide activity, set standards for performance, and measure performance. There should be a network of short-range goals covering the entire business at all levels and including individuals. Although for any one subunit in the company, or any individual, the total number of goals may be less than the number of objectives set for the business as a whole, in the aggregate there will be, of course, far more short-range goals than company objectives.

Short-range goals should be as specific as possible to assure action in conformance with them and to facilitate the measurement of results. Short-range goals for the company as a whole may be developed for each of the categories suggested in the above structures. Thus, for example: "Increase sales 5 percent each calendar quarter of the next year." "Raise the per-share earnings to 45 cents for the year." "Hire a new chief economist." "Phase out production of . . ." Similarly, for each division and department there should be goals covering every important activity for which performance should be measured. The further down the line, of course, the narrower is the focus. A sales objective for the company may, for example, narrow down to a short-range goal for the sales department to increase the number of salesmen in the Philadelphia area from 5 to 7 and to give each salesman a specific target for each week for each product.

The bulk of short-range goals are set forth in the budgeting process, which will be examined in detail later. But not all goals, especially of individuals, are developed and quantified in budgets. Individuals have nonquantifiable goals which they themselves may establish or which may be developed for them or in participation with higher-level management. They may, for example, be personal in nature, such as entering a university training program, or improving staff work, or developing better relations with union leaders.

THE TIME SPECTRUM

A major distinction among goals, objectives, and purposes is that they have different time spectrums. Both in theory and practice these points are not fixed and distinctions blur. If the conceptual model in Chart 2-1 is kept in mind, however, the major distinctions are not too difficult to understand in an actual planning operation.

Managements that become preoccupied with either end of the spectrum run grave dangers. If the far distant end is treated without considering the near-term, they are liable to end up doing "blue sky" or "utopian planning." If, on the other hand, they concentrate on the near-term with no more than passing reference to the far-term, they end up doing *ad hoc* planning with a "triumph of technique over purpose" (Sayre, 1943).

WHAT IS BEHIND RECENT EMPHASIS ON AIMS?

During the past ten years business purposes, objectives, and goals have received great attention by businessmen. Furthermore, as noted above this movement has been accompanied by a flood of written purposes which have been made publicly available. Accompanying the development of corporate planning, long-range objectives and goals have been recorded for internal consumption. There are many reasons for these movements, among which the following seem most important.

First, is an acceptance of the philosophy mentioned in Chapter 1 that a business could, within reason, set an objective and pursue a course of action to get there.

Second, is a concomitant philosophy popularized by Peter Drucker (1954) as "management by objectives." At least one book (Odiorne, 1965) now bears this title. Although Drucker popularized management by objective he did not originate it. Harrington Emerson a half century ago wrote with evangelic fervor about the needs for and uses of "ideals," which were to him what we now call goals and objectives. Drucker's view is as follows: "Any business enterprise must build a true team and weld individual efforts into a common effort. Each member of the enterprise contributes something different, but they must all contribute toward a common goal. Their efforts must all pull in the same direction, and their contributions must fit together to produce a whole—without gaps, without friction, without unnecessary duplication of effort.

"Business performance therefore requires that each job be directed toward the objectives of the whole business. And in particular each manager's job must be focused on the success of the whole. The performance that is expected of the manager must be derived from the performance goals of the business, his results must be measured by the contribution they make to the success of the enterprise. The manager must know and understand what the business goals demand of him in terms of performance, and his superior must know what contribution to demand and expect of him—and must judge him accordingly. If these requirements are not met, managers are misdirected. Their efforts are wasted. Instead of teamwork, there is friction, frustration and conflict" (p. 121).

This view clearly is supported by the more recent emphasis upon systems management which can be effective only with a clear specification of aims. A business, of course, is a system in itself and is composed of subsystems. At different levels, therefore, aims must be specified to facilitate systems analysis. Behavioral scientists also have used this concept to develop their theories concerning the interrelationships of people and goals, a subject which will be treated in the next chapter.

Third, larger companies at some point in their growth become quasi-public, a fact recognized by the increasing interest of society in what they do. Fowler McCormick (1953), grandson of the founder of the International Harvester Company, and for several decades the President or Chairman of the Board of the Company, expressed this idea in these words: "Now my thesis contains four propositions: First: Once a business attains a certain size, it becomes a social institution to be operated in the equal interests of stockholders, employees and customers. Secondly: It is the basic responsibility of management to maximize the benefits to the three parties in an equitable manner. (That proposition can be stated in a different form; it is the responsibility of management to fulfill the reasonable expectations of the three parties.) Thirdly: The business should be efficiently, honestly, and fairly managed and operated. Fourthly: The principal objectives of business policies should be to further the long-range welfare of the company, to minimize the need and demand for government regulation of business, to fulfill the reasonable expectation of people within and without the company in regard to the private enterprise system, and to win popular approval of that system."

In recent years large corporations have become concerned about their image to the public because they recognize the interest of the community in what they do. One of the reasons for the wave of publicized company purposes, creeds, and philosophies during the past ten years is the interest of companies in improving their public image. They want to improve their image with all who are concerned with their operations. I think also that many managers want to use these documents to set the tone of operations within their enterprises. Many also want to record what they feel to be their genuine public responsibilities.

Fourth, statements of goals have become popular in the political area, a fact which is reflected in private business. Not only have several recent Presidents of the United States established commissions to forge goals for this nation but they have included national objectives in various statements to the Congress.* Many foreign countries now hammer out with some care five-year objectives for their countries and various sectors in it.

A fifth and final reason is the growing recognition that carefully developed

* See for example *The Report of the President's Commission on National Goals*, New York, Columbia University, The American Assembly, 1961.

networks of aims are helpful, if not absolutely necessary, to the welfare of the enterprise and the people in it. This is a subject which deserves extended examination.

IMPORTANCE OF AIMS

THEY HAVE MOTIVATING POWER. Max Weber (1904) long ago theorized that the society which emphasized individual achievement and effort would progress most. More recently this thesis has been confirmed in a brilliant analysis of growth by David McClelland (1961). In his book he examined many different cultures and rated them according to the extent they emphasized achievement. He then measured their progress and found a positive relationship between their emphasis on achievement and economic growth. This may now appear to be obvious, but it has not always been so. The Florentines, for example, lost their interest in achievement and then lost the thrust of their commercial development. McClelland concluded that: "What each generation wanted above all, it got." He goes on to say: "What saves such a statement from banality is the new fact that the psychologist has now developed tools for finding out what a generation wants, better than it knows itself, and *before* it has had a chance of showing by its actions what it was after. With such knowledge man may be in a better position to shape his destiny" (p. 437). There is little question about the fact that many nations of the world want greater economic development and are achieving their goals accordingly because they have learned this is the first step in getting economic development. This may well turn out to be one of the most significant contributions to economic growth in this century.

In individual enterprises the same importance of setting ends has been found. Luther Gulick (1948) has concluded that: "A clear statement of purpose universally understood is the outstanding guarantee of effective administration." (p. 77) Why this is so and some of the results when done well deserve further comment.

This does not mean, of course, that objectives may be set blindly. As Dean and Smith (1965) persuasively argue, growth objectives of firms should be made in response to real opportunities that are offered by the underlying economies of scale, exploitation of new techniques, penetration of new markets, and other basic considerations. Growth as an objective in itself is not too acceptable.

The General Electric Company undertook a study to determine the effectiveness of the comprehensive performance-appraisal process which it had set up and found a number of things of importance to the discussion here. It discovered that performance improved most when specific objectives and goals were established. It concluded, also, that mutual goal setting produced even greater performance (reported in Meyer, Kay, and French, Jr., 1965).

People cannot perform well if the objectives and goals set for them are vague, unknown, or conflicting. On the other hand the precise motivation which clear and well-conceived aims provide is not easily measured. Motivation of people in organizations is a phenomenon of management which embraces far more than the setting of ends. But, other things being equal, the existence of specific ends to be sought, and the participation of people in establishing them for their own achievement, has great motivational power.

Among managers in profit centers motivation is high when goals are clear. One study (Myers, 1967) of Texas Instruments, which delegates considerable authority to decentralized groups, concluded: "This delegation process requires managers of product-customer centers (and their staff counterparts in the supporting and performance-maximizing centers such as industrial engineering, accounting, and personnel) to establish goals and keep score on themselves in the process of achieving them. Motivation abounds under such circumstances, requiring little stimulation from higher company management. Indeed, management influence under these conditions often must include safeguards against overcommitment or overmotivation, and admonishments to be mindful of home and community responsibilities and the developmental needs of the members of their organizational teams" (p. 66).

Behavioral scientists who have studied worker motivation have come to the conclusion that setting clear goals and permitting employees to participate in their specification is helpful. After reviewing a number of these studies Odiorne (1965), with some restraint, concludes: "There is some evidence . . . that a strong orientation toward goals, coupled with leader enthusiasm, ample rewards for achieving them, and the uniting of people in moving toward them, does have a beneficial effect" (p. 145). This is, of course, what competent managers have known for a long time.

GUIDES TO ACTION. Choices in development of company philosophies and in the managerial style followed are of major significance in directing company efforts. For example, a company may choose to grow rapidly with the thought that profits will follow, or it may adopt a policy of getting profits now and letting tomorrow come as it will. A company may be very aggressive and accept high risks, it may be very cautious and stick to its present products and markets, or it may be moderately venturesome. It may have a vicious competitive philosophy, or it may adopt a "live-and-let-live" philosophy. All sorts of different choices lie in such areas as products, markets, research, management selection, and decision-making, that have the profoundest impact on the life of an enterprise and the people in it.

It is trite to say that management must know what it wants to do before any rational decisions can be taken about what is to be done about it. The whole network of aims is, of course, designed to guide action of people. When General Lucius Clay became President of Continental Can it was two-thirds the size of its major competitor. He decreed that the company was not in the can business but in the packaging business and proceeded to diversify to meet this mission requirement. From this simple statement of business purpose sprang activity which has made the company one of the largest in the industry. Not only will statements of aims guide action but predict it. When North American Aviation merged with Rockwell it was predictable that, when one of the reasons stated for the merger was cross-fertilization of technical know-how, an unusual flood of ideas would be developed in NAA for possible use in Rockwell.

SETS TONE OF BUSINESS. Creeds, philosophies, or statements of beliefs often are prepared by chief executives to set forth those values which guide them and which are expected to guide others in the enterprise. It is often forgotten that a business is not an inanimate institution acting on the basis of cold economic rationality. It is composed of people who have different value systems, the most dominant of which is that of the top management. The company that establishes for itself the image of being "hard-boiled competitively, shrewd, and above all profitable," may wind up with its executives indicted for conspiracy to violate the antitrust price-fixing laws. A company that insists on being "scientifically superior and profitable" is likely to maintain a technical capability which makes it profitable.

Thomas Watson, Jr., Chairman of International Business Machines Corporation, emphasized the importance of company philosophy as follows (1963, p. 3*): "This then is my thesis: I firmly believe that any organization, in order to survive and achieve success, must have a sound set of beliefs on which it premises all its policies and actions.

"Next, I believe that the most important single factor in corporate success is faithful adherence to those beliefs . . .

"In other words, the basic philosophy, spirit, and drive of an organization have far more to do with its relative achievements than do technological or economic resources, organizational structure, innovation and timing. All these things weigh heavily on success. But they are, I think, transcended by how strongly the people in the organization believe in its basic precepts and how faithfully they carry them out."

IMPROVING THE BUSINESS IMAGE. Every company, large or small, has its own personality. This personality consists of the image those inside and outside the business have of that composite body of managerial values, traditions, assumptions about the nature of the business and the way it is run, and all other

* From *A Business and Its Beliefs* by T. J. Watson. Copyright © 1963 by Trustees of Columbia University in the City of New York. Used by permission of McGraw-Hill Book Company.

elements that make up the life of the enterprise. Each company personality is unique. Each has a different atmosphere from any other (Gellerman, 1959).

Images affect the behavior of those in and outside the company. Although modern behavioral psychology lacks the tools to explain and measure the influence the company image has on behavior, the fact of the relationship cannot be denied (Boulding, 1956; Lewin, 1951; Odiorne, 1966). A university has an image of excellence, one business has an image of public responsibility, another has an image of unexcelled management, and another has an image of vigorous and dynamic growth. Litton Industries has gained a reputation for business acumen and growth which in turn has resulted in a price-earnings ratio for its stock much above other companies in the industry. This in turn has given it a lever in acquisitions. The network of business aims cannot alone establish a company image, but it is a major part of it.

PROVIDES BASIS FOR MEASURING PERFORMANCE. Without a network of aims it is impossible to measure the performance of the organization as a whole or the individuals in it. It has been noted previously that with a network of aims and a plan to achieve them a manager has a criterion at hand to measure current performance.

Concepts used in developing aims are quite similar to those employed in analyzing and evaluating performance. For example, by changing a few words each of these points of view can be expressed with the same expression. To illustrate:

Table 6-4   Aim, Performance and Evaluation Concepts*

SUBJECT	AIM	PERFORMANCE	EVALUATION
	We aim to:	We do	You do (not)
Mission	serve customers well		
Production	have high quality products at low prices		
Efficiency	hold costs low		
Growth	increase sales by 10 percent per year		

* Suggested by Bertram M. Gross, *The Managing of Organizations,* New York, The Free Press of Glencoe, 1964, p. 482.

DEVELOPING AND RELATING AIMS

It seems obvious that the network of aims should be integrated; that is, goals and targets should be related to objectives, and objectives to basic purposes and managerial values. In actual operations it is easier to see the direct relationship between a goal and an objective than between an objective and a purpose. This is so because specificity and concreteness increase as one moves from basic purposes and values to short-range goals and targets.

The personality and operation of each enterprise is unique and changes with time, men and circumstances. As a consequence, there is no set of "right" network purposes, objectives, and goals. The development methodology of different parts of a company's network of aims differs as does the timing of the activity. The shorter-range the goal, the greater the frequency with which it must be changed. It follows, too, that the methodology for changing and relating different levels of the network of aims will also vary. Although no single or simple prescription can be used to develop and relate aims, it is possible to illustrate approaches and to set forth some guides which may be applied to the process.

MISSIONS AND CREEDS. It is becoming more popular (which is fortunate) for companies to gather together their top executives and spend a weekend reviewing and, if necessary, revising the scope of their basic line or lines of business. Although on the surface this activity may seem to be easy, it turns out to be one of the most difficult tasks of management. The reason, of course, is that decisions at this level are not obvious, are not made with full knowledge of consequences, and are of the greatest importance to a company.

Preparing a written statement of the ethical and operational philosophy of a company, of course, is a rather personal matter for the chief executives. Staff may help in the formulation but in the end the managers must determine contents. In his study of creeds, Thompson found that among 51 companies studied more than half were initiated by the company president or chairman of the board, but the wording was often first developed by a committee which included top management. Once a draft was prepared, the president usually determined final phraseology (1958, p. 11).

Once these statements are prepared they are not often changed. Perhaps they ought to be reviewed and changed more frequently than they usually are, for they may include company biases, dogmas, blind spots and obsolete standards, which should be eliminated. As Gellerman says (1959, p. 5): "Like an individual without insight, a company whose personality is left unexamined will be likely to keep acting out the same predetermined role, unable to react flexibly to changing conditions."

OBJECTIVES. The principal method for developing long-range objectives is in the comprehensive planning process described in this book. For most companies, objectives are examined and established annually in the planning cycle. It is not possible to recapture the precise way in which objectives are developed. Some represent the snap edict of a chief executive, but the most useful ones grow out of long and intensive analysis by many people in the planning process.

It is not always easy to see the precise connection between objective and basic mission. The fact that the Douglas Aircraft Company has a basic mission to produce commercial aircraft, for example, does not lead directly to any particular aircraft. But given that mission, the competitive situation in the industry, and sufficient resources in the company, the objectives follow of producing the DC-8, DC-9, DC-8-Stretch 61, the DC-10, and so on.

Celanese has four basic purposes:

- "To fulfill human and economic needs through chemistry.
- To maximize earnings on our shareholders' investment.
- To retain our global business leadership through new products and research, supported by aggressive marketing.
- To give Celanese men and women the widest possible latitude to develop their individual resources within the corporation, encouraging their development with full management support, recognition and reward."

These, according to the Company, have resulted in the following basic objectives which have been made public. (These objectives may, as we shall see in later chapters, be defined as strategies or policies. They do not have a fixed time horizon, but it would be easy to insert such a time schedule to make them more nearly fit our definition of objective as expressed above.) Notice the relative looseness with which the objectives are related to basic purposes.

- "To become a major integrated worldwide chemical company through internal growth, joint ventures, and licensing, with a broad line of fibers, chemicals, plastics, coatings, petroleum, forest and allied industrial and consumer products.
- To strengthen our position in Canada, Asia, and Latin America, and to develop a major position in the overall European market.
- To become a major international producer of all significant man-made fibers.
- To expand through growth and diversification into long-term profitable chemical, polymer and plastic markets.
- To become an increasingly profitable worldwide producer and marketer of paints, coatings, resins and specialty chemicals.
- To expand petroleum operations where attractive opportunities exist and build a hydrocarbon-reserve position to improve the competitiveness of Celanese worldwide operations." (*Celanese World*, p. 5.)

Building a network of objectives can and should be rigorous. Top objectives, subobjectives, sub-subobjectives, etc., can and should be closely related. This is so because in the actual operation of an enterprise there is a close interrelationship among the major economic objectives. For instance, an objective to maintain or increase return on investment equal to or above the industry average must be pursued in light of sales objectives, financial objectives, and objectives related to efficient use of resources. One cannot set one without relation to the others. Depending

Table 6-5 Linking Business Objectives

LONG-RANGE OBJECTIVE	SUBOBJECTIVES	SUB-SUBOBJECTIVES SET IN THESE AREAS
Make a Return on Investment of 15% after taxes by end of 5 years (specify for each year)	Increase sales to $10,000,000 in 5 years (specify for each year)	market share advertising expenditures new market penetration redesign of products develop new products for market begin new research and development in selected areas
	Raise gross profits to $2,000,000 in 5 years (specify for each year)	reduce overhead costs by consolidating functions sell obsolete plant and equipment reduce advertising outlays
	Build modern facilities and operate them at capacity over next 5 years (specify construction and rates of capacity for each year)	build new buildings replace tools improve production schedules improve plant utilization rates install better inventory control reduce defective products
	Upgrade and maintain a skilled work force (specify number and skill requirements for each year)	management training programs management additions management hiring schedules skill replacements

upon where one starts, these objectives become subobjectives of each other. This is illustrated in Table 6-5 which shows the dominant objective of return on investment and the way other major objectives, as well as subobjectives, may be related to it. A more extensive "tree" of objectives could easily include other functions the objectives of which must mesh to get a desired return on investment. In relating the network of aims one can start from any one major objective and develop subobjectives from it. However one begins there should be a reasonable meshing of objectives and subobjectives.

Another way of looking at the way in which objectives interlace is shown in Chart 6-2. This illustrates the point that in the hierarchy of objectives there are a number of higher-level objectives that can and should be served by a particular objective. As one multiplies objectives in a larger company, this network can get rather complex.

SHORT-RANGE GOALS. Short-range goals can profitably be set for all levels of management, from the Chairman of the Board to the foreman level. The network of short-range goals and targets is the cutting edge of the objectives and purposes.

Short-range plans have a number of fundamental purposes. First, they make long-range objectives meaningful. Without a direct linkage between long-range objectives and short-range plans the objectives may become idealistic and impracticable. Furthermore, for most managers, interest in planning picks up when the necessity is present for setting short-range goals in order to take specific actions. Also, even though the distance in a large company from top management to the foreman levels is very long, it seems from empirical evidence that, other things being equal, low-level managers perform better when they see the connections between their goals and top objectives. In cutting a stone each sees himself building the cathedral.

Second, short-range goals provide benchmarks for measuring progress towards long-range objectives. All managers can see how step-by-step achievement of short-range targets can lead to achieving ultimate purposes.

Third, they provide a basis for managerial performance appraisal. Not only do they permit managers to see their contribution to corporate objectives, but also provide a standard against which their performance may be measured. Managers are better motivated if they know exactly what contribution they are expected to make and in what areas. If a sales manager knows just what he is to do to increase company return on investment, his contribution is more likely to be made than if his role is vague and unspecified. Company performance must follow from a balancing of activities of all managers. This balance is obviously more likely to be appropriate if each manager understands his own short-range goals which tell him where he has a major responsibility, where his responsibility is minor, and where it is nonexistent.

Chart 6-2
The Interrelationships Among Objectives

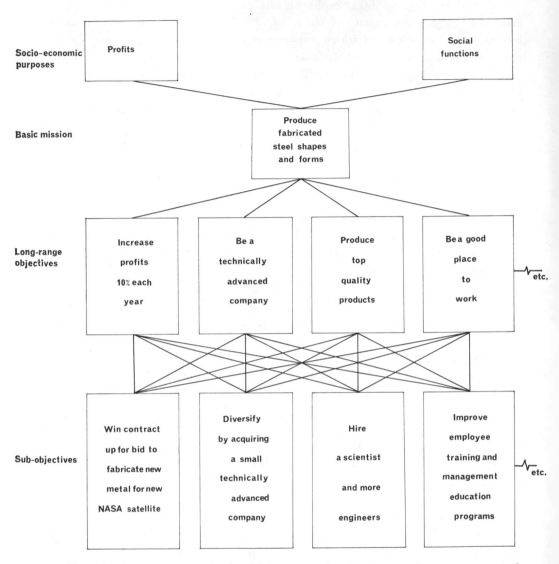

Fourth, short-range goals should have motivating power, for reasons noted previously.

Fifth, if the planning process is conducted with substantial participation by all concerned, the setting of short-range goals should improve subordinate-superior managerial relationships. In a typical planning process, short-range goals are spelled out in the budgeting process which usually evolves with considerable managerial interaction. The budgeting process results in what might be called direct or tangible goals which specifically tie to other goals and objectives. There are also intangible or indirect goals of managers which concern their own behavior, attitudes, skills, and other personal qualities. In many companies, short-range goals for selected factors are set in a discussion with an immediate supervisor. This set of goals will round out those for which each manager is responsible and will provide a comprehensive basis for measuring performance. Every manager should participate in setting the goals which he will be responsible for meeting. In the best run companies, participation is taken seriously and procedures are developed to insure its accomplishment (Miller, 1966; and Valentine, 1966).

KEY RESULT AREAS

The network of short-range goals, if developed rather comprehensively, can result in a large number of targets for which a manager may be responsible. In practically every phase of business life a few phenomena are responsible for the majority of results. As someone has put it, this is the phenomenon of the vital few and the trivial many. For managers to concentrate equally on all the objectives and targets for which they are responsible will obviously diffuse their efforts. For this reason, all managers should choose, from among those aims for which they are responsible, the comparative few that will make the greatest difference in performance.

The higher the level of management, the fewer should these key aims be. For a chief executive they may be but three or four; for a foreman they may be many more. But, at all levels, identification of and concentration on these key aims should be assured.

SUMMARY

This chapter explained in detail why there is not one but many aims of a business firm of any size. There is, indeed, a network of aims composed of the basic socio-economic purposes of the business, its lines of business to be pursued, the value systems of its top managers, its long-range objectives, and its short-term operational goals and targets. Illustrations of their nature and content were given, and the ways in which they are developed and interrelated in a planning process were examined.

The chapter also pointed out that there is an increasing interest in business life in formulating carefully the network of aims and having parts of it available, as appropriate, for external consumption and internal use. Some of the major reasons for this new emphasis is the understanding that there are many aims of a business and they need to be delineated; that a business can set its aims and, by good planning and management, achieve them; that today's businesses are better run by "management by objective"; that large companies at some point in their growth become businesses much affected with a public interest and objectives, especially those for public consumption, should say so; that goal development in the political world is reflected in renewed interest of objectives in the business world; and finally, and of great importance, there is a growing recognition that carefully developed aims have great importance to people in organizations.

A clear and appropriate network of business aims is an indispensable condition for improved business performance and healthy organization. It is a basis for managerial actions which has no substitute. It has great incentive power, stimulates thinking, sets the tone of a business, organizes action within the business, provides a measure of soundness of decisions, predicts behavior, and influences the way those outside the business think and act towards it.

A number of guidelines for the development of business aims were mentioned in this chapter, but they will be incorporated with others presented at the close of the next chapter.

7
The Network of Corporate Aims—II

7

The Network
of Corporate Aims—II

INTRODUCTION

In considering the objectives of an enterprise, there are three controversial issues which are of the greatest importance to individual enterprises, to the individuals in them, and to society as a whole. The first concerns the issue of whether profits are, and should be, the sole objective of a business firm. The second relates to the social responsibilities demanded of, and assumed by, business enterprises. The third relates to conflicts which exist between the goals of individuals within a business firm and the firm's objectives, and what responsibility management has to harmonize them.

These questions are discussed in the world of scholars in a sort of perpetual intellectual hootenanny. However, they are being examined today very seriously by more and more thoughtful business executives. Although the issues may seem remote to many businessmen, they have the profoundest bearing upon the future of business. For these reasons, they will be considered in some detail in this chapter.

THE PROFIT OBJECTIVE

The last chapter showed that as a firm grows larger it develops not one, but a rainbow of aims. There are few responsible business leaders or scholars of business who do not consider profit as the dominant aim in this spectrum. It is clear that a business will not survive in this society without profit, unless, of course, the Government decides to subsidize it. Most people see merit in this ditty:

> *Count that day lost*
> *Whose low descending sun*
> *Sees quotations made at cost*
> *And business done for fun.*

But there are significant questions raised today, both by businessmen and students of business, about the meaning and dominance of the profit objective.

The economist for a long time has insisted that his concept of profit maximization should be considered the sole objective of business enterprises, a view which many businessmen have, or think they have, accepted. It is important to understand what the economist means when he speaks of profit maximization, why the concept has broken down in actual operation, and what the consequences are for the theory of business objectives and management.

Profit maximization means something very specific to the economist. Indeed it can be measured precisely in quantitative terms. Profits are the difference between total cost and total revenue. In the theoretical model of the economist the firm seeks to maximize the difference. So long as the firm adds more to total revenue than to total cost it obviously will pay to increase output. So long as the marginal revenue from the last unit produced is greater than the marginal cost of that unit, there will be a net addition to total profits. When the marginal costs of the last item produced are greater than the marginal revenue brought in, there will be a net reduction of total profits. So, maximum profits are reached when marginal revenue equals marginal costs. This is a theoretical model found in all elementary economics textbooks.

To go one step further, a business firm in theory will try to maximize profits in the long run. The optimum business plan is one which will maximize the present discounted value of net receipts throughout the life of the firm.*

In the economist's model, the owners of the enterprise, or the stockholders, are the same as the managers; and the managers and the firm are considered to be an entity, that is, the two are considered inseparable. Profit maximization, therefore, refers to the practice of a firm's making only those decisions which will maximize returns to stockholders. No possible decision that can be made will yield a higher return.

OPERATIONAL PROBLEMS OF PROFIT MAXIMIZATION. There is recognition of the fact in this theory that, for a businessman to maximize profits in this fashion, it would be necessary that a number of assumptions be correct. For example, the businessman would have to be able to measure accurately all his costs, especially those attributed to the marginal units produced; and he would also have to be able to calculate precisely the revenue received from each additional increment of output. The businessman would have to know exactly what changes in demand would result from alterations in price. He also would have to be able to use the resources at his disposal to produce those items which would serve to maximize his profits. He would need, in short, to have perfect foreknowledge of all consequences of his actions and great flexibility in using his resources.

* For an exposition of the economist's ideal business plan see Hart, 1951.

Although some economists seem to believe that business firms literally strive to operate this way, the majority realize they do not and could not if they chose. There are many reasons why a firm of any size does not try to maximize profits in the above sense. One reason is that the typical multiproduct firm is unable to calculate marginal revenue and marginal cost for different products. Even assuming that he had the data, any businessman trying to adjust price, production, changes in demand, and so on, in order to maximize profits would have his business in a turmoil, and such turmoil in itself would serve to reduce profits. Furthermore, a large company might hesitate to take advantage of a given environment to maximize profit because of possible adverse public reaction. Following World War II, for example, when an enormous pent-up consumer demand was focused on a trickle of new automobiles, the car manufacturers could have reaped very large profits by raising prices had they chosen to do so.

The profit maximization concept, when literally held, does not come to grips with uncertainties in the real world. For example, a firm may wish to be in a rather liquid cash position because of uncertainties. Having a large cash reserve will not serve the maximization principle. (R. A. Gordon [1945, p. 7] says financial expediency outranks profitability in large company decision-making.) Or, take this situation: alternative A can yield profit up to $5 million or a loss of as much as $5 million. Alternative B will yield a certain profit of $1 million. Which should be taken by a businessman? Charles Hitch (Hitch and McKean, 1961) points out with correct insight that firms in the face of great unknowns will suboptimize.

These are but a few of the operational problems a firm would have in seeking to maximize profits in a fashion described in the theoretical economic model of the firm (Anthony, 1960; Margolis, 1958; Nordquist 1965; and Phillips, Jr., 1963). As a result, and because of the rising importance of other objectives of business enterprises, there have grown important challenges to the concept that profit maximization should be the sole aim of a business.

CHALLENGES TO PROFIT MAXIMIZATION. Important challenges to the idea that profit maximization is or should be practiced by a firm have been made by economists, businessmen, and thoughtful persons in other fields of inquiry. A few illustrations may make the point.

Many prominent economists question the singularity of profit maximization as a business objective. For example, Edward Mason (1958) quotes J. M. Keynes as saying "the 'general stability and reputation of the institution' rank above profit maximization in the objectives of management" (p. 6). The late J. M. Clark (1961) pointed out that there are motivations the profit-maximization concept does not serve, such as an interest in survival and growth, or an interest in good management and skill in various parts of the business quite aside from profit (p. 92).

Businessmen also point to other objectives. For example, Harry Klein, former

President of Texaco, said (1952, p. 14): "If we were to try to isolate the one factor, above all others, that transformed the tiny company of 1902 into the industrial giant of 1952, while hundreds of competitors failed and are forgotten, I should say that it has been Texaco's settled policy of thinking first of quality of product and service to the customer, and only second of the size of its profit. To some of you, this may sound somewhat trite. But it is the starkest kind of business realism."* P. F. S. Otten, when President of the Board of Philips Industries of the Netherlands, was even more emphatic in saying: "No longer is it the pursuit of maximum profit that governs our actions; it is the pursuit of continuity. *Continuity* in the conduct of business, which of course creates the necessity for continuity in the rewarding of capital, but also in the opportunities for employment and personal relations, in good contact with customers, etc." (1961).

Others have advanced theories reflecting their own fields of interest. For example, game theorists stress a profit objective which seeks to maximize expected values. Cyberneticists view the firm as a system with interdependent variables and a feedback mechanism for which stability of operations is a dominant objective. Behavioral scientists in increasing numbers are stressing the importance of social objectives. This group looks at a firm as being made up of individuals whose objectives are reflected in the objectives of the firm, and they are not rallied around profit maximization. Indeed, as will be discussed later, harmonizing individual goals with company goals is considered by some behavioral scientists as being a basic requirement for business success.†

USES AND MISUSES OF PROFIT MAXIMIZATION. It is necessary to distinguish two ways in which the term profit maximization is used. First is the technical meaning, that is, its use in the economist's theory of the firm. Second is the general usage which one typically finds in business. It is not at all uncommon for a businessman to say his major objective is to maximize returns to stockholders. This expression is not meant in the technical sense, but rather in the sense of getting as high as possible returns in light of many interests on the business aside from those of stockholders, the state of competition, and market conditions.

Profit maximization in the technical sense is a legitimate goal of the very small business—a job shop, for instance. But even among such firms a dominant objective may be something else—to earn a comfortable living or to do something interesting. In large corporations, there are legitimate efforts to maximize profits in the technical sense in connection with a particular activity, such as the use of a machine tool, deciding inventory levels, or choosing among different means of transport to get goods to customers.

---

* It is recognized, of course, that Mr. Klein is saying that profit will follow if these objectives are met.

† For a brief examination of these different theories, see McGuire, 1961.

For larger firms, and for overall company aims, profit maximization in its technical sense is not a legitimate objective; but profit maximization in the literary sense is.

It should be pointed out that those who persist in considering profit maximization in the technical sense as being the "right" objective of a business are misusing the concept. It was designed not to explain and predict the behavior of a real, going firm, but rather to explain changes taking place within a simplified model of a real firm. As the distinguished economist Fritz Machlup has pointed out (1967, p. 9), to confuse the firm as a theoretical construct with the firm as an empirical concept, to muddle a heuristic fiction with a real, live organization, is to misuse theoretic symbols by attributing to them a direct, observable, and concrete meaning which they do not presume to have.

It should be added hastily, however, that care should be taken not to throw out the baby with the dirty wash water. The technical profit maximization concept is a very useful, and powerful, operational idea if not taken too literally. The principle is extremely important to a businessman in helping him to organize his thinking about how to improve his profit position. Any businessman who does not understand the importance of equating marginal revenue and marginal cost is missing a powerful leverage to improving his profits. But his understanding the concept does not mean that he is a fool not to make it operational in the textbook sense for his entire business. Like so many tools designed to help the businessman, this one is an aid to thinking and not a substitute for it.

WHAT REPLACES PROFIT MAXIMIZATION? As noted above, the general meaning of profit maximization may replace the technical meaning, but this is bound to lead to confusion. If the phrase is to be avoided, what may be used to replace it? Robert Anthony (1960, pp. 126-134) suggests the more usual objective is a satisfactory return on capital employed. Armen Alchian (1950, pp. 211-221) says it is "realized positive profits," which means profits equal to if not a little better than the average for the industry. Herbert Simon (1957b) says it is "satisfactory profits"* (pp. 204-205). These are literary descriptions of the type of quantitative profit objectives businesses set in their planning programs.

In the planning process, as noted in the previous chapter, long-range objectives and short-range goals are determined for profits and are in quantitative terms. These are based upon future expectations tempered by analysis of future events and past experience. The feasibility testing of these quantities involves estimates of costs, sales, price reception, profit margins, competition, and other

---

* See also Simon, 1957a, where he says: "While economic man maximizes—selects the best alternative from among all those available to him; his cousin, whom we shall call administrative man, satisfices—looks for a course of action that is satisfactory or 'good enough.' Examples of satisficing criteria that are familiar enough to businessmen, if unfamiliar to most economists, are 'share of market,' 'adequate profit,' 'fair price' " (p. XXV).

such considerations. The profit results are then often related to investment to get a return on investment. Different companies focus attention on different aspects of this process but generally, especially among the large companies, the objectives and goals are a multiple of interrelated profit aims—absolute profits, return on investment, return on assets, return on equity, profit per share of common stock, and return on sales. The final aims are based upon a multiplicity of balances, trade-offs, and preferences expressed in the planning process. The final overall calculation of the profit aim I call *required profits*, or those needed to satisfy the many claims made on the enterprise, including the level needed to meet the self-satisfaction requirements of top managers.

CORPORATE SOCIAL RESPONSIBILITIES

When profit maximization in the technical sense is eliminated as a sole operating objective of a business, the door is opened for using corporate resources to satisfy other interests than those of stockholders. This raises highly controversial questions of significance to the type of society and enterprise system we wish to preserve.

The question of whether businesses have social responsibilities is not a new one, but it is receiving renewed attention today. The modern corporate form of organization antedates the industrial revolution and, in its older versions, was intimately involved in social as well as governmental functions. For example, the great joint stock trading companies of the early 17th century, such as the East India Company, had economic, military, and political functions (John P. Davis, 1897).

Following the rise of laissez-faire in the latter part of the 18th century, social responsibilities of business were downgraded radically in favor of the economic motive. During the 1930's the issue of corporate social responsibility raised temperatures of both scholars and practitioners.

THE BERLE AND DODD DEBATE.* In the early 1930's, a classic debate concerning corporate objectives was waged between Adolph Berle and E. Merrick Dodd. Berle (1931) started from the position that all corporate powers are powers in trust: "necessarily and at all times exercisable only for the ratable benefit of all the stockholders as their interest appears" (p. 1049). Dodd (1932) agreed that corporate powers were powers in trust but argued that the use of private property was deeply affected with a public interest and the public was becoming more aware of and taking a greater interest in this fact. In this light, Dodd argued, directors of companies should be considered trustees for the whole insti-

* Conveniently summarized and evaluated by Eugene V. Rostow, Chapter 3 in Mason, 1960.

tution and not merely "attorneys for stockholders" (p. 1365). Berle said the idea that the sole purpose of a corporation was to make a profit could not be abandoned until such a time as clear and enforceable rules of social responsibilities could be established. Since there was no such scheme of responsibilities the older rule was the only one to prevent managers from overreaching and self-seeking. Dodd agreed, but thought the rule had lost touch with reality.

In 1954, however, Berle accepted the view of Dodd because, he said, corporations have assumed in appreciable part the role of conscience-carrier of the 20th-century American society, and have done so "without intent to dominate . . ." (p. 182). Berle obviously felt that managers could be trusted to exercise their power in the public interest. In a later book (1959) he spelled out in considerable detail the limitations on and control of economic power wielded by managers of larger corporations.

THE ISSUE TODAY. The issue today is principally how much social responsibility a business will carry. There are a few people, however, who still cling to the earlier Berle thesis. Professor Milton Friedman (1962), for example, is clear in his view that profits should be the only objective and to add others is to endanger the existence of private business. He states his case in the following manner:

> ". . . there is one and only one social responsibility of business—to use its resources and engage in activities designed to increase its profits so long as it stays within the rules of the game, which is to say, engages in open and free competition, without deception or fraud. . . . Few trends could so thoroughly undermine the very foundations of our free society as the acceptance by corporate officials of a social responsibility other than to make as much money for their stockholders as possible. This is a fundamentally subversive doctrine" (p. 133).

While one of the most vocal, Friedman does not stand alone. Professor Theodore Levitt, for example, says (1958, p. 44):

> "But at the rate we are going, there is more than a contingent probability that, with all its resounding good intentions, business statesmanship may create the corporate equivalent of the unitary state. Its proliferating employee welfare programs, its serpentine involvement in community, government, charitable, and educational affairs, its prodigious currying of political and public favor through hundreds of peripheral preoccupations, all these well-intended but insidious contrivances are greasing the rails for our collective descent into a social order that would be as repugnant to the corporations themselves as to their critics. The danger is that all these things will turn the corporation into a twentieth-century equiv-

alent of the medieval Church. The corporation would eventually invest itself with all-embracing duties, obligations, and finally powers—ministering to the whole man and molding him and society in the image of the corporation's narrow ambitions and its essentially unsocial needs."

Levitt's prescription to avoid this calamity is, of course, corporate pursuit of material gains and avoidance of any other social responsibility.

Positions such as these are based upon a number of grounds. Friedman, for example, points out (p. 134) that businessmen have no guides to knowing what their social responsibilities are. If they undertake activities in the public realm and "are civil servants rather than the employees of their stockholders, then in a democracy they will, sooner or later, be chosen by the public techniques of election and appointment." Levitt argues that the end result, and to him a deplorable one, will be that a corporation trying to administer to man and society will mold them in the image of the corporation's narrow ambitions and essentially unsocial needs.

Legally, today, a corporation can use stockholder earnings for social purposes. This was established when the U.S. Supreme Court refused to review a decision of the Supreme Court of New Jersey in the precedent-setting A. P. Smith case in 1953. In 1951 the Board of Directors of the A. P. Smith Company, manufacturers of machinery and equipment for water and gas industries, gave $1,500 to Princeton University as a contribution towards its general maintenance. Questioned by the stockholders, the corporation sought a declaratory judgment asking that its action be sustained. The Supreme Court of New Jersey, in affirming a lower court decision, said:

"It seems to us that just as the conditions prevailing when corporations were originally created required that they serve public as well as private interests, modern conditions require that corporations acknowledge and discharge social as well as private responsibilities as members of the communities within which they operate. Within this broad concept there is no difficulty in sustaining, as incidental to their proper objects and in aid of the public welfare, the power of corporations to contribute corporate funds within reasonable limits in support of academic institutions. But even if we confine ourselves to the terms of the common law rule in its application to current conditions, such expenditures may likewise readily be justified as being for the benefit of the corporation; indeed, if need be the matter may be viewed strictly in terms of actual survival of the corporation in a free enterprise system . . ."*

* *A. P. Smith Manufacturing Company vs. Barlow et al.*, 26 N.J. Super. 106 (1953); affirmed, 98 Atl. (2d) 581; appeal to the U.S. Supreme Court dismissed for want of a substantial federal question, 346 U.S. 861 (1953). For a detailed discussion of this case and its importance, see Eells, 1966.

This important passage makes it clear that corporations legally are assumed to have social responsibilities and that they may engage in a wide range of activities laden with social values because it is to their interests, say the courts, to support free institutions.

The Congress of the U.S. has also recognized the social role of corporations by permitting tax-deductible corporate donations up to 5 percent of net income. Most states also have such legislation. These do not, however, relax the requirement that directors use sound business judgment and act in a fiduciary capacity.

Opposed to the profit-only point of view are the growing interests of both scholars and business leaders in genuinely seeking to understand social responsibilities and the extent to which they should concern themselves and their companies with them. A recent study of the National Industrial Conference Board among over 1,000 companies showed clearly that the vast majority of chief executives felt that public affairs is the primary concern of top management.* The intensity of interest was expressed by the same proportion of managers in small, medium, and large companies. There is no question about the fact that today's managers recognize that the public takes an interest in their affairs and expects them to act in a socially responsible manner (Bowen, 1953; Drucker, 1962). Recent Presidents of the United States have forcefully pointed out this responsibility, for example, in trying to get larger companies to restrain their price increases.† As noted in the last chapter, the growth of company creeds and philosophies is one response to the demands for and recognition of social responsibilities. Although some of the published statements appear to accept very heavy social responsibilities, the great majority of managers hold the profit objective to be overwhelmingly dominant.

In a speech before the Annual Meeting of the Michigan State Chamber of Commerce in Detroit on October 2, 1962, Henry Ford II, Chairman of the Board of The Ford Motor Company, in my judgment has put the two major purposes of an enterprise—economic and social—in proper perspective in these words:

> ". . . America wants business enterprises that are aggressive, that are inventive, that are venturesome, that are profit-oriented and that are, therefore, increasingly efficient. America recognizes that business enterprises are essentially economic tools for achieving the broader objectives of society, and the sharper they are the better they will perform. America also wants enterprises that are rational and responsible citizens, decent in their community relationships, humane in their treatment of

---

* Public affairs in this research effort are related to "what companies are doing about legislative relations, political and economic education, philanthropy and community affairs" (Darling III and Diviney, 1966).

† For the story of the dramatic confrontation between President Kennedy and Roger Blough, Chairman of the Board of U.S. Steel, see Hoopes, 1963.

people. But above all, it must have enterprises that are fundamentally and strongly driven by economic motives. Let me make this clear; I do not mean that a company's motivation is solely economic; I do mean that its specific reason for being is economic rather than social."

David Rockefeller (1964) makes the point in the following quotation* that long-range corporate profits are dependent upon wider understanding of and attention to corporate social responsibilities:

"If a business enterprise is to achieve long-range profitability, it must take account of certain corporate citizenship responsibilities that have no direct bearing on profits. Foremost among these, as Peter Drucker explains, is the responsibility to get across to the layman 'what it is that business does, can do and should do.' Another is to help develop and maintain a favorable economic and political environment in which all businesses can grow and prosper. Still another, to support with financial contributions and personal participation those organizations genuinely concerned with fundamental problems of the community" (p. 23).

"Community problems will never be solved by experts alone, and the experts are the first to acknowledge this. They cannot—indeed, they should not—be relegated exclusively to government. These are the problems calling for action on a broad front and for participation by the entire citizenry. Unless we in the business and banking community are personally concerned and passionately committed to a better life for all, we shall bear witness to a society which falls tragically short of its great promise . . ." (pp. 27-28).

"In terms of management philosophy, it means taking cognizance of the fact that the production of goods and services is simply a means to an end. That end is, immediately, earning a profit which gives the enterprise its driving force; but, ultimately and more importantly, providing opportunity for every individual to live a life of dignity, freedom and fulfillment.

"A growing economy by itself is nothing. What is important is what growth and profit can make possible. Sometimes in the quest for private gain, this point is ignored or forgotten. But the ultimate reality on which business enterprise is based is the conversion of earnings into meaningful human advancement and satisfaction.

"A creative management philosophy must be one which not only seeks through efficient operation to maximize profit, but which also recognizes its responsibility to render economic service—service by private enterprise to the public interest. The British statesman, Lord Halifax, liked to define service as 'the rent we pay for our room on earth.' In the case of business enterprises, this rent comes due not once a month but every day of the year. We can pay it by contributing, through creative management, to economic growth at home and abroad" (pp. 29-30).

Berle (1954*) further underscores the fact that social responsibilities cannot be neglected:

". . . the really great corporation managements have reached a position for the first time in their history in which they must consciously take account of philosophical considerations. They must consider the kind of a community in which they have faith, and which they will serve, and which they intend to help to construct and maintain. In a word, they must consider at least in its more elementary phase the ancient problem of the 'good life,' and how their operations in the community can be adapted to affording or fostering it. They may endeavor to give their views exact statement, or they may merely proceed on undisclosed premises; but explicitly or implicitly, the premises are there" (pp. 166-167).

Criticisms against corporations' acting in any way other than to make as much profit as possible for shareholders have two fundamental shortcomings. First, they overstate the trend and ultimate magnitude of corporate assumption of social responsibilities. Second, they seem to wish corporations not to adapt to changing environment in the face of strong public interest and legal permission to do so.

If managers were to be judged on the basis of criteria applied to public servants, as Friedman fears, the result would be serious indeed. But the real danger, at least in the foreseeable future, is not in the assumption of social responsibilities of businessmen. Rather it is in the chronic practice of businessmen demanding and insisting upon getting government help in the form of subsidies, direct and indirect, or throwing economic grenades at their competitors. No industry has exempted itself from demanding government largesse. It is this, far more than the use of a company's resources to discharge "social responsibility," that blurs the line between public and private enterprise.

The choice is not between pursuit of profits or assumption of social responsibilities. The two are inextricably interwoven whether we like it or not. Nor is business on the way to assuming such a volume of social responsibility, relative

* Reprinted from *The Twentieth Century Capitalist Revolution* by A. A. Berle, Jr., by permission of Harcourt, Brace & World, Inc.

to the aggregate in the society, that the dimension will bring about violent changes in the way people view corporate activity. On the contrary, so many affirmative statements by business executives are made today because many business leaders fear that corporations are not doing enough.

In a thorough study of corporate giving from data published by the Internal Revenue Service, Johnson (1966) concluded there is little evidence that companies wish to exceed the 5 percent limit on deductibility of charitable contributions. For the years between 1936 and 1961 the annual total aggregate contributions as a percent of pretax income was .68 percent (p. 497). A study of 448 companies by the National Industrial Conference Board for 1965 confirmed this figure for that year (Byleveld, 1967, p. 23). Another NICB study concluded that the ratio for Canadian companies was .97 percent. Johnson noted that in only three years in the span he studied were contributions over 1 percent (1945, 1952, 1953) and all these were years of high marginal tax rates on excess profits (p. 492). He also noted that the trend of donations as a percentage of profits was rising.

In a survey of 152 executives, Lorig (1967, pp. 51-54) found that the vast majority feel their chief responsibility is to stockholders as the owners of the business. There was no discernible difference in this view among different-sized corporations. The rankings of all executives of the group to which they felt the chief responsibility were, as a percent of the total: stockholders, 84.2 percent; employees, 11.3 percent; customers, 17.6 percent; creditors, 11.3 percent; and society, 2.4 percent.

In a study of the value systems of over 1,000 managers, England (1967b, p. 108) found that the following were the percentages attributing the highest importance to the goals of business organizations listed: organizational efficiency, 81 percent; high productivity, 80 percent; profit maximization, 72 percent; employee welfare, 65 percent; organizational growth, 60 percent; industrial leadership, 58 percent; organizational stability, 58 percent; and social welfare, 16 percent. While the philosophical basis for social responsibilities is clear, the vast majority of managers obviously do not give this responsibility a high priority in terms of allocation of resources or their concept of their basic responsibility. Nevertheless, corporations are creatures of society and as such have distinct social responsibilities. What they are varies from one age to the next and from one corporation to another. It is easier to describe the range of social responsibilities for corporations generally than to answer the normative question of just what the responsibilities of any one corporation are. We now, nonetheless, should turn to this question.

MEANING OF SOCIAL RESPONSIBILITY. The concept of social responsibility is difficult to state briefly because it is so pervasive in a firm's activities. For convenience, the social responsibilities of a company may be divided into two broad areas: those concerned with internal and those relating to external operations.

Internal matters concern such factors as labor relations (including hiring, promotion, and firing policies), working conditions, safety standards, and comparable matters involving the internal organization and use of resources. The social responsibility implications of such factors may not be as clear for purely domestic companies as for those engaging in international operations. The philosophy a firm expresses about hiring and working conditions in an underdeveloped country, for example, may have enormous social implications, depending upon whether the results upset or fit into the culture of the country.

Externally, of course, social responsibility covers a very broad area. For instance, there may be included consideration of the impact of company action on the community; the impact of product and advertising on social activity; corporate actions relating to health, welfare, or beauty of communities in which it operates; support and research outside the company; philosophies covering actions dealing with the broad environment of society as it affects the corporation; or attitudes towards and support of various social institutions in society.

There is no formula for determining for any corporation what its social responsibilities are and should be. In a real sense, the assumption of social responsibilities implies recognition and understanding of the aspirations of a society and a determination to contribute to its achievement. Also included are actions to strengthen the environmental forces which will serve the long-run interests of the corporation. These two viewpoints are meant to be complementary.

Many managers speak of social responsibility as equal to "good corporate citizenship" (Steiner and Cannon, p. 273). Although this is not a magic formula by means of which social responsibilities for any corporation can be determined easily, it is useful. Being a good corporate citizen in our society, as being a good private citizen, means pursuing one's own self-interests, within a broad framework which channels such pursuit into activities that also foster the collective values esteemed in the society. The pursuit of profit can easily fit this concept. Pursuit of profit in such a way that it conflicts with an important value of society is not in conformance with good corporate citizenship.

While the concept of acting in self-interest in the sense of furthering long run profits is helpful, it does not explain all cases. Being a good citizen may mean, as implied in David Rockefeller's statement, taking action which is mildly detrimental to profits, both in the short and long run. Staying in a less profitable location to avoid bankrupting a town, or keeping old former employees whose usefulness has disappeared, are cases in point. But no corporation, of course, is being a good citizen in a larger sense if such action has more than a minor impact on its profits.

In sum, the major social responsibility of a company is to operate profitably and utilize efficiently the resources at its disposal. Although important, other activities relating to the use of corporate resources to further national goals, employee and community welfare, or other social interests, are today second to this purpose and, except for a limited number of cases (not significant in terms of the whole corporate contribution) are pursued to contribute to achievement of the first purpose in the short and in the long run.

HOW MUCH SOCIAL RESPONSIBILITY? This is a question of importance to an individual corporation as well as to corporations in general. For example, in considering corporations generally, there are a number of dilemmas when the question of social responsibility is imposed. On the one hand, government responds to the social needs of a society. As business develops new technology, which in turn creates social problems, government may step in to help solve the problem (e.g., unemployment insurance and welfare benefits to the needy). The less business is concerned with important social impacts of its actions, the more government interferes in economic life and the more likely are regulations on business. But, the more business becomes concerned with social responsibilities, the less it may be dedicated to the pursuit of high profits. The more this occurs, the less likely society will have the benefit of the most efficient use of resources to produce material wealth. This is a dilemma of the modern affluent and socially conscious society. The problem remains: how much social responsibility is business obligated to carry? But, there is no ready answer.

The key to resolving the problem in an individual company is recognizing, first of all, that there is a problem and then determining to resolve it in a fashion designed to balance the major interests focused in and on the enterprise. This necessarily involves taking the long view, systematically embraced in effective corporate planning. On this basis, suitable guidelines, programs and dollar allocations can be made.

CLASSIFICATION OF SOCIAL RESPONSIBILITY PROGRAMS. One important approach to the problem of determining the scope and direction of social responsibilities is to classify what it is that concerns a company. I should like to suggest, first of all, that there are three major areas of social responsibility that concern larger companies. First is that of corporate philanthropy. Second is developing new concepts which embody socially desirable actions that also directly add to profits. Third are all other actions.

The area of corporate philanthropy may be subdivided as one approach to the examination of preferred directions and magnitudes of effort. As a first formulation of such a classification I suggest the following:

A. Local requests that cannot be turned down by a "good corporate citizen." These are in the nature of "fixed charges." They are gifts to various charities in communities where the company has plants; grants to favored colleges; and gifts to other favored institutions (e.g., art museums).

B. Corporate identification. Here are programs which reflect the major long run self-interests of the company. What programs are included, of course, depend on the definition of the long-range interests of the company, preferences of top management, and a balancing of programs which may have both a direct and indirect potential positive profit impact with those that may be altruistic or have no discernible profit implications. A few subcategories will suggest the type of program in mind.

1. Advancement of education in disciplines of interest to a company.
2. Research concerning causes of and solutions to major environmental problems having a direct or indirect impact on the company.
3. Research in management problems.
4. Research in retraining needs of skilled workmen, engineers, and scientists.
5. Contributions to study the economics of the industry as a path to better understanding of its role.
6. Advancement of education among institutions of interest to the company management.
7. Contributions to help company employees lead richer lives.

The programs delineated here should remain firm over a long period of time. Individual projects within them, of course, will vary considerably from time to time. But the thought is that here is a long-range program tied into the long run interests of a company as the company sees its interest.

C. Temporary and emergency programs. Included in this category are gifts for short periods of time which cannot be foreseen in the development of the longer range program of B above, but which the company wishes to support. Direct support of a program in a university, for example, might be classified here if it does not fit under B.
D. Administration of the program. If a company foundation is established to administer the program, the costs of the personnel are included in this category.

Not much imagination is required to dream up philanthropic projects which will cost far more than any company can afford to spend. Difficult problems of choosing, therefore, will arise.

The second area of socially responsible actions cannot be further classified here because their principal attribute is a new, bright idea. In mind are specific actions which the company can take, or suggest to potential customers, which serve importantly two fundamental objectives: one is to advance some socially desirable objective; the other is to enhance company profits in the short run. Examples of such actions are the establishment of a plant in a distressed area to produce items under contract; training unemployed workers for employment; and development of new programs with educational institutions which aid them and also have a direct payoff (e.g., in terms of acquiring new technical skills for company employees or improving prospects for sale of company educational-type products or services). Another illustration might be the use of a company's skills in furthering the objectives of the U.S. foreign aid program while at the same time earning profits. A systematic effort to correlate problems in the nation's achieving major social objectives, with the preferred profitable applications of a company's resources (managerial and technical) in meeting them, undoubtedly would suggest concrete proposals for programs in this category.

In the third area, these subdivisions suggest themselves:

A. Purely economic actions in the pursuit of profits. The assumption here is that a company normally will not make profits unless it is using its resources in a fashion considered desirable by society. To use resources efficiently, therefore, and thereby make a profit, is to discharge one type of social responsibility.

B. Political activities of various types (e.g., those suggested by David Rockefeller, as noted above).

C. Actions which concern the welfare of employees, communities in which the corporation operates, or governments, but which do not involve major philanthropy such as taking action to prevent the company's polluting streams; actions which seek to contribute to socially identifiable goals but do not involve major philanthropy such as helping NASA in its technology spin-off program even though the firm does not benefit directly; and all other actions of a social, moral, ethical nature which are not classified elsewhere and which do not generally directly contribute to profits but rather may reduce them.

In this category, of course, are an enormous number of specific and concrete actions which the corporation may take. Each of the major categories above, and within each, are subjects which merit analysis. For example, subclass B has many implications for a large company. The answers to the wisdom and propriety of the specific actions of the company or individuals in it in this area are not pat and are important. Many specific cases can be imagined in subclass C, all of which require the elaborate analysis of a major company policy. For example, beautification of company buildings and grounds, developing closer relationships with local educational institutions involving, e.g., classroom appearances of company managers and scientists; helping educational institutions determine future needs for scientists; directing some of the company's own research to social problems, such as air or water pollution, where a future company saleable product does not appear very promising but where there is some possibility; and lending managerial and technical talent to government for short-term tasks. Included here would be the establishment of a plant in an underprivileged area with the specific purpose of providing jobs or training workers even though the costs will be higher than any profits. Also included here would be construction and sale of homes in tenement areas of large cities at cost, or below cost, as a private effort to help reduce inadequate housing.

PRINCIPLES FOR PHILANTHROPIC PROGRAMS. Closely associated with program classification are principles or guidelines for determining the dimensions of a philanthropic program. The following (Eells, 1966, Chapter VII) illustrate the type of guidance in mind:

First, the basic motive for corporate giving is enlightened self-interest of the company. Corporate philanthropy is not almsgiving. Rather, it is to serve the long-range interests of the enterprise within broad social dimensions. It is not a branch of advertising. The aim is to protect the company's autonomy by helping to preserve those conditions in its environment which will ensure its continuity and capability.

Second, there is no fixed formula which can be used to translate the ranges of self-interest of a company into specific programs. Aside from the personal interests of top management, contributions policies and programs should reflect a projection of business needs at least one, and preferably two, decades ahead. As a result of long-range planning, problem areas may be chosen for attention with the likelihood that careful study of them will yield the prospect of benefits to the corporation. For example, the problem of urban development in the U.S. will inevitably bring about a substantial change in the way state and local governments will deal with specific problems alone or in conjunction with the federal government. Contributions to the study of such possibilities in some university in, say, the transportation area, could conceivably be rather important to an aircraft, an automobile, or a railroad company.

Third, continuity in philanthropic programming is necessary to achieve objectives of corporate giving. Continuity does not imply perpetuity in support of any one program. It does mean that when a program is launched there ought to be a reasonable prospect that it will be carried through.

Fourth, the company should participate in both the development of private and public policies regarding the scope and purpose of corporate giving. In mind, of course, is the development of policies associated with the spectrum of programs of the company. Other corporations, foundations, and the federal government are involved in the programs suggested above. There should be some cooperative attention to the programs to assure maximum benefit. Furthermore, a company should be aggressive in stimulating the types of programs which it feels need support. For example, if a corporation thinks research should be undertaken in a particular area it should be prepared to stimulate and promote the accomplishment by competent scholars.

Fifth, to the extent practicable, cost-benefit analysis should be applied to philanthropic programs, especially those for other than charitable purposes. Although convincing quantitative cost-benefit analysis is difficult in this area, there are advantages in using this equation as a basis for decision. It may not be any better than intuitive judgment or executive interest in any one situation. But over time and for a large program, the mere effort to make a cost-benefit analysis should be helpful.

GUIDES FOR SOCIALLY RESPONSIBLE DECISIONS. Problems of social responsibility transcend philanthropy. Managers are faced with conflicts among the objectives of different groups: stockholders want higher dividends; wage earners want higher wages, better working conditions, and greater fringe benefits; customers demand lower prices; the government presses to hold down prices; local communities seek executives who take part in public activities; and customers wish better service. The profit maximization principle resolves these demands quite easily in favor of stockholders. But if social responsibilities are accepted, what principles govern decision-making?

The only response which I can give is to view each issue in light of the self-interests of the enterprise, both in the long- and short-range. But how does this break down in specific cases? Individuals, not companies, make decisions. In the final analysis, decisions must be based upon the collective value judgments of the principal decision-makers. Each manager, therefore, is left with the problem. Each must be his own social philosopher.*

THE MORAL CRISIS OF BUSINESS

The economist's theory of the firm gives the businessman a clear and unequivocal guideline to decision-making which in times past was operable and could be justified morally. The erosion of profit maximization and the rise of social responsibilities as objectives, however, has not resulted in a parallel development of a theory of the firm which specifies for today's world the proper mix for the businessman. There is no simple formula that can be followed to assure a balance between economic and social responsibilities. No one knows what a perfect balance is for any one firm at any one point of time. The result is what some writers call a moral crisis of business. They mean that without the maximization standard the businessman finds it difficult to determine what actions are morally right and what are morally wrong (Petit, 1965a and 1965b).

What is needed, of course, is a philosophy: a theory which gives the businessman firm guidance in solving the problem of balancing the many interests focused on his enterprise. This theory does not now exist. Approaches to the development of a new theory of the firm will be considered in Chapter 12.

It has been demonstrated in many corporations, however, that an aggressive, venturesome, innovating, and tough competitive spirit can exist alongside an assumption of social responsibilities. There is no reason to assume that this type

* For some suggested models, see Petit, 1966.

of balance will not be possible for many well-managed companies while the search for a generally acceptable and clear formula continues.

CONFLICTS AMONG AIMS

In considering fundamental business purposes which are stated in very broad terms, conflicts among purposes are not readily apparent. It is only when these purposes are elaborated in long-range objectives, and further expressed in concrete short-range goals, that conflicts begin to appear.

A major source of conflict results from the degree of priority placed on one or more aims. If return on investment, for example, is given a very high priority it may result in activities which advance short-range profits at the expense of long-range profits. If customers are to be satisfied at all costs, the costs can be heavy in holding unnecessary inventory. If stability of production is a high-priority objective it may be achieved only with lower profits. A high-priority research program may adversely affect short-range earnings per share. The deeper the detail of goals and targets, the more conflicts appear.

Although most conflicts among aims are not serious, there can be conflicts which result in damage to the enterprise, or prevent it from optimizing its objectives. Many small companies have found that their failure to balance growth, short-term working capital, and production costs has been the key factor in their road to bankruptcy.

That there are important conflicts between individuals in enterprise and enterprise goals is not a question of debate. The precise conflict and its importance both to the individual and his enterprise, however, has not been conclusively established by research. The Opinion Research Corporation study in 1959 which attempted to measure friction concluded that 75 percent of the scientific and engineering personnel surveyed felt a discord between their personal goals and the goals of the organization where they worked. In the survey of over 600 scientists and engineers there were 49 percent who felt the conflict was not serious and 26 percent who thought it was serious.

CONFLICTS BETWEEN INDIVIDUALS AND ENTERPRISE AIMS. Until a half dozen years ago both traditional practice and the theory of management were based upon an assumption that human passions and objectives were often in sharp conflict with the interests of enterprises. This was inevitable, it was said, but true. When dissensions came to the surface they were, in this so-called classical view, to be resolved in favor of organizational aim (Fayol, p. 26, and McGregor, 1960, pp. 33-34).

In the pathbreaking studies of Mayo and his colleagues in the Hawthorne Plant of the Western Electric Company in the early 1930's the foundation was laid for a new discipline concerned with the individual in organizations (Mayo,

1945 and 1960, and Roethlisberger and Dickson, 1939). Since then, there has been a flood of literature from a new, young, and immensely important behavioral science discipline about the needs of individuals in organizations as compared with organizational needs. The preponderance of this literature sharply attacks the older view in which individual objectives were generally considered to be secondary to organizational interests when the two were in conflict.

CRITICS OF THE CLASSICAL VIEW. Criticism of the classical view has taken many different directions. At one extreme is Argyris (1957a and 1957b, pp. 1-24) who argues that the needs of the individual and the formal organization are basically incompatible. At the other end of the spectrum are those like Bennis (1966) and McGregor (1960) who feel that the social and psychological needs of individuals can be congruent with organizational goals and effectiveness. Others, such as Tannenbaum, Weschler, and Massarik (1961), agree with this view but argue that changed attitudes are necessary in both workers and managers before serious conflicts can be reconciled. In between are different approaches. Dubin, for example, points out that degrees of conflict between individuals and organizations depend much upon the extent to which they are central life interests. For many people, an organization is expected to fill only a minimal need; for others (Dubin, 1961, pp. 78-81) it must fill a central life interest.

Whyte (1957) has focused attention on the tyranny of organized life over individuals. His thesis is that the modern business, especially the large company, forces individuals to "go-along-with-the-crowd," to conform, to behave as group standards dictate. The result is standardized behavior. He says the manager is becoming an "organization man," at the expense of his individuality, his creativity, and originality. He speaks of the "social ethic" to sum up the behavioral values and guidelines of his organization man. Whyte put his analytical spyglass on business while Reisman (1950) in a best seller focuses on American society in general. He distinguishes between "inner-directed" and "other-directed" men. The first relies on himself and the second on the behavior and thinking of people around him. Reisman contends that society is becoming filled more with "other-directed" people. These are Whyte's organization men in business.

Fundamentally, the critics of classical organization theory say it does not very well fit what is known today about human behavior. Thoughtful behavioral scientists do not advocate complete abandonment of older organization theory but ask that it not be taken too literally. They say it skips over many complexities of human behavior and by so doing makes many assumptions about them which are wrong (Leavitt, 1958, especially Chapter 20).

Although fundamental issues among individual objectives, values, and needs, and organizational aims have been bared for all to see, no one has picked up the broken classical crockery and glued together a new theory that has universal acceptance. Never again will the view be acceptable that human needs must be submerged to serve organization needs. On the other hand, much of the current literature swings to the other extreme in elevating the man over the organization. A balance has not yet been struck. One of the reasons is that we do not know enough about leadership, worker motivation, changing human needs, or management techniques to reconcile conflicts and balance human with organizational requirements. The calculus of values, organizational dynamics, changing circumstances, new managerial methods—all are too complex for easy solutions.

HUMAN MOTIVES AND NEEDS. As McGregor (1960, Chapter 3) pointed out in his Theory X, the older view regarded the individual as disliking work and eager to avoid it if possible. Consequently, personnel had to be coerced with the threat of punishment to put forth effort to achieve organizational objectives (pp. 33-34). This, of course, flies in the face of the puritan ethic, so strong in American life, which emphasizes the need for and satisfaction of work to achieve a viable Christian existence. In place of Theory X, McGregor suggests Theory Y. This theory assumes that work is as natural as play or rest, that man will exercise self-direction and self-control in serving objectives to which he is committed, that commitment to objectives is a function of rewards related to their achievement, that the average human being can learn to accept and seek responsibility, that there is great capacity throughout the population to solve organizational problems, and that the use of the potentialities of the average person is being only partly realized (pp. 47-48).

This latter view, if the assumptions are accepted, creates a challenge for both management and employees in an enterprise. But the problem is even more complicated. Individuals at different times and in different walks of life have different needs that must be met. Maslow (1943) has set forth a theory of motivation which provides insights into the kinds of organizational forces that may motivate behavior and generate conflicts between individual and organization needs. He distinguishes five basic human needs as follows:

1. Physiological needs of hunger, thirst, the activity-sleep cycle, sex, and evacuation.
2. Safety needs for protection against danger, threat, and deprivation.
3. Love needs for satisfactory associations with others, for belonging to groups, and for giving and receiving friendship and affection.
4. Esteem needs for self-respect and the esteem of others, this is often referred to as ego or status needs.
5. Self-realization or self-fulfillment needs to achieve the potential within an individual for self-development, creativity, and self-expression.

Obviously, the intensity of these needs will vary among men and in the same person as his economic status changes and as he grows older. As society becomes more affluent and the lower needs are met, the higher needs become more important, and they are not likely to be satisfied as simply as the lower needs. In a typical cultural lag American management has probably been slow to shift emphasis to meet higher-level social status and self-fulfillment ends. It is likely, too, that the interchangeability of satisfactions has been overemphasized. Study after study has shown, for example, that increasing pay or fringe benefits is not a substitute for social and self-fulfillment needs (Sayles and Strauss).

Although the above hierarchy of needs is useful, it is perhaps more relevant today to consider what factors lead to an improvement in a person's "quality of life" and relate organizational objectives to them. Norm Dalkey of the RAND Corporation (in a private briefing) listed ten factors that are important to an individual in his pursuit of quality of life, as follows: health, status, affluence (income, physical surroundings), activity (meaningful, or self-satisfying work), sociality (degree of interaction with other people), freedom, security, novelty (newness of experiences), aggression (competition), and balance (a meaningful pattern of all the others). This list is given in the descending order of importance which a small sample of RAND employees attributed to each factor.

In looking at American industry today it is undoubtedly true that a better reconciliation of individual and organizational conflicts will follow managerial emphasis on joining organizational objectives with the higher of Maslow's needs.

Professional managers have a desire to harmonize their own needs with company aims. They also feel the pressures from other managers to achieve a concord of interests. Somehow they must balance these pressures while trying to compose them with the objectives of the enterprise and while satisfying their own needs. It has been suggested, and I think it is a useful insight, that: "The basic desire of the professional manager is to maximize his self-interest or lifetime income in monetary and nonmonetary terms" (Monsen, Saxberg, and Sutermeister, 1966, p. 24). This in itself is a formidable puzzle to unravel as anyone can testify who has tried to find out what this means for himself. When the needs and aspirations of others become involved, the problem is terribly complicated.

The difference between levels of management and nonmanagers is substantial in matching individual and firm interests. An owner-manager of a very small enterprise may find a complete congruence between his own personal and his company's aims. Such enterprises have more the characteristics of individuals than of institutions. Heads of very large companies likewise may find a perfect matching of their aims in life with corporate aims.

Lyman Porter (1964) made a study of 2,000 U.S. managers and concluded that higher-level managers fulfill their needs for recognition, autonomy, and self-realization more than do those in lower levels. These findings are the same when the age factor is held constant, so results are not influenced by age. He also concluded that Whyte's "organization man" is much more likely to be found in staff than in line jobs. He also found (p. 45), contrary to Whyte,

". . . the large-company managers generally attach *more* importance to the inner-directed traits than do the small-company managers. Furthermore, this tends to hold for comparisons made at each level of management. Thus our findings—even taken conservatively—raise the question whether large organization size, per se, has as serious a deleterious effect on initiative, ambition, and forceful leadership as has been implied by some others who have not supported their arguments with facts."

The research of Porter also shows that the view of managers about role depends upon where they are looking. Managers feel their superiors should not at all be the "organization type." On the other hand they expect subordinates to be "organization men." They see themselves as somewhere in the middle.

Haire, Ghiselli, and Porter (1966) surveyed over 3,600 managers in 14 different countries to find out how much need fulfillment (using Maslow's definition given above) they were getting out of their job, and the degree to which fulfillment met expectations. They found (p. 80), in response to the first question, that there were rather small differences in the degree of fulfillment from one need to the next. Managers in general regard their job as providing about the same degree of self-actualization needs as, for example, esteem or autonomy needs. Security and social needs are more highly fulfilled. Security, social, and esteem needs, however, are better satisfied in terms of expectations than autonomy and self-actualization needs (p. 108).

Studies such as those of Porter are most helpful in giving us a better understanding of the interrelationships between individual and company interests and of the types of conflicts which actually arise. We need to know much more, however, before we have a really penetrating knowledge of the dimensions of these interrelations and conflicts.

The trend in American industry is clearly in the direction of more permissive and democratic management (Albrook, 1967, pp. 166 ff.), and it is altogether likely that managers will find more agreement between their own and organization objectives. But important conflicts will still remain.

THE CHALLENGE TO MANAGEMENT. McGregor observed (1967, p. 78*) that a person's motivations, potential for development, capacity for assuming responsibility, and readiness to direct behavior toward organization goals are all present. As a consequence, ". . . one of the fundamental characteristics of an appropriate managerial strategy is that of creating conditions which enable the individual to achieve his own goals (including those of self-actualization) best by directing his efforts toward organizational goals."

* From *The Professional Manager* by Warren G. Bennis and Caroline McGregor. Copyright © 1967 by McGraw-Hill, Inc. Used by permission of McGraw-Hill Book Company.

Effective managers and behaviorial scientists are convinced that this observation is true, given certain circumstances. One primary circumstance is the acceptance of the importance of the aims of the enterprise. Each member of the enterprise must feel that the aims are genuinely important to him and that he is making a useful contribution toward achieving them. The individual must have a sense of personal worth and importance.

Likert (1961*) advances a principle of supportive relationships reflecting these conditions. He says (p. 103): "The leadership and other processes of the organization must be such as to ensure a maximum probability that in all interactions and all relationships with the organization each member will, in the light of his background, values, and expectations, view the experience as supportive and one which builds and maintains his sense of personal worth and importance" (italics omitted).

Likert feels that this is a fundamental formula which can be used to tap every basic motive and harness it in each employee to organizational ends. To do so, however, involves a new way of managing in which each person in an organization is a member of one or more work groups, each of which has a high degree of group loyalty, effective skills of interaction, and high performance goals (p. 104).

These are worthwhile objectives for managers, but precisely how management accomplishes such results is not altogether clear. Each situation will vary. Furthermore, there are limitations on the extent to which an organization can satisfy all the wants of individuals in it and still accomplish the basic aims society expects it to achieve. As Kast observes (1961, p. 50): "While the organization is a means for the fulfillment of the individual's needs, it also requires him to subordinate certain wants. Every organization, even the most voluntary social activity, demands that the individual direct his behavior toward the accomplishment of group objectives."

The enterprise must have firm economic and social ends, and it must have discipline in meeting them. One of the major purposes of a comprehensive formal planning program is to assure that, to the extent conditions warrant, the decisions throughout are related to objectives and goals. These ends are predominantly economic and not social. As individuals in an enterprise satisfy their economic needs, the greater are felt social and self-fulfillment needs. To expect business organizations to satisfy all such needs is neither possible nor desirable. There is serious question whether an organization reaching for predominantly economic ends can or should be a means for total satisfaction of individual aims. Managerial efforts to satisfy all needs of an individual should be viewed with alarm for this cannot be done. It should be recognized that some objectives of individuals, perhaps most, must be met outside a business. The management of each enterprise, however, is challenged to find that balance which will properly optimize personal with organizational ends.

NATIONAL INTERESTS AND THE INTERESTS OF A MULTINATIONAL BUSINESS. Another area in which objectives collide concerns multinational (and international) firms and the countries in which they do business. This has always been recognized as a source of friction. But in recent years, with the extraordinary growth of international business operations, the problem has taken on new dimensions (Henry Fowler in Steiner and Cannon, 1966).

It is recognized, of course, that there are many areas of common purpose between a company doing business abroad and its host country. Multinational corporations have brought new technology, higher standards of living, growth, and social progress to the countries where they operate. Multinational corporations are indeed agents capable of great good. As Roger Blough, Chairman of the Board of the U.S. Steel Corporation, says: ". . . the multinational corporation may ultimately prove to be the most productive economic development of the twentieth century for bringing the people of nations together for peaceful purposes to their mutual advantage; and . . . it can thus provide the adhesive which can do more to bind nations together than any other development yet found by man in his pursuit of peace" (Steiner and Cannon, 1966, p. 125).

This may well be the case. But if this estimate is accomplished it will be accompanied by seemingly irreconcilable conflicts between corporate and national interests.

Corporations doing business abroad are faced today with the traditional conflicts of interest—excessive obstruction of tariff barriers and exchange controls, various restrictions on operations and exports in the countries in which they operate, frustrating and uneconomical laws concerning entry, and the necessity for following inefficient local customs and codes. But there is a growing list of other conflicts which become exacerbated as companies become larger. There is the problem, for instance, which a company has in paying higher wages than the norm to attract skilled workers and/or in giving employees a higher standard of living but which, if done, upsets wage and social structures of the country. There is the problem of a company with headquarters in the U.S. whose subsidiary in Canada receives an order for equipment from a communist-block country. The shipment can legally be made by the subsidiary but it would be illegal for an American-based company to make it. What interest will be satisfied? U.S. antitrust laws create special problems for American companies doing business abroad. Extraterritorial application of U.S. antitrust laws may bring an American-based company into conflict with national sovereignties that have a different antitrust law under which the subsidiaries of the American company must operate.

It is not the intention to discuss this subject fully here, but rather to make note of it. The actual and potential conflicts of company and national interests in international operations is probably likely to become more serious and difficult in the foreseeable future. One reason is the important growth which has and will continue to take place in multinational companies. This will not be accompanied by any appreciable diminution of nationalistic interests in favor of foreign interests.

SUMMARY, CONCLUSIONS, AND GUIDELINES
FOR DEVELOPING CORPORATE AIMS

This chapter dealt with three major controversial areas concerning a business firm's objectives. The economist's concept of profit maximization (determined at the point where marginal cost equals marginal revenue), which used to be considered the only valid objective of a business firm, was found to be no longer operational in a literal sense. Today's enterprises have many objectives, not just one; and even though the profit objective is still dominant over all others, as it should be, it is modified by other concepts. Among them are, to name two, "satisfactory profits" and "required profits."

If profit is not the sole objective of an enterprise, the door is open for businesses to assume many types of social responsibilities. Various types of social responsibilities were discussed, and the dangers of going too far in assuming them were examined. It was concluded that there is little danger for the foreseeable future that business, collectively, will go too far, but it was also concluded that it is essential that the profit motive be clearly the dominant motive in business.

Conflicts which may exist between the individuals in an enterprise and the goals of the enterprise were discussed in some detail. Older organizational theory held that organizational goals were dominant in any conflict, but newer theory demands high harmony between the two. It was concluded that a suitable balance should be struck, but that there can be no easy formula for managers to follow to determine where and when there is a proper degree of harmony.

In the preceding two chapters many guidelines were set forth for developing and using effectively the network of corporate aims. In this concluding section are presented the more dominant ones.

First, the chief executive must participate in, approve, and manage the enterprise on the basis of a network of aims. He himself must lay down or approve the basic purposes of his company. He must participate in and approve long-range objectives. He may, depending upon company organization, participate in specifying short-range goals and targets. Without his participation in the preparation of the network of aims they will lose their motivating power.

Second, corporate purposes, objectives, and goals should be written for the best calculated impact on decisions. Basic purposes and philosophies should be written and widely distributed in and out of the company. Objectives, and goals, for the most part, should be written and available on a need-to-know basis. Written and carefully defined objectives and goals afford a minimum of misinterpretation.

Third, the need for precision and quantification of aims varies depending upon purpose. Basic purposes and philosophies can and should be broad in scope. They may be a little vague without blunting their impact. Indeed, a bit of vagueness may add to their value for they will then tend to need less frequent change. Objectives and goals, however, generally should be as precisely worded and as quantitative as possible. Results and ends rather than activities should be specified. Objectives and goals should be specified so that measurement of performance in achieving them is possible. Extreme accuracy with broader objectives is not always critical. Although estimates may be acceptable, precision and quantification are generally preferable.

Fourth, the network of aims should not be arrayed indiscriminately. It should be classified in as few groupings as possible and still retain the structure needed for decision-making. A catalog list of objectives and goals fragments the power of an orderly structure. This is particularly true of individual goals. Too many goals for individuals results in indiscrimination among them. A handful of major goals is more desirable.

Fifth, there should be a structure, a network, of aims in an enterprise extending from basic purposes through company-wide objectives which directly relate to suborganizational and individual goals. Every unit in an enterprise and every manager should know what company objectives are when they are supposed to help in achieving them, and also what subobjectives and goals are within these. Each should be able to see clearly how they relate to the larger system objectives. Staff positions as well as line positions should have goals. Each management level must have goals that relate. Subordinates must know exactly the area for which they are accountable.

Sixth, it is not possible to avoid conflicts among goals either in terms of their substantive achievement or in relation to aspirations and needs of managers and employees in a company. Overlapping and conflict is inevitable. As effective a balance as possible, however, should be struck.

Seventh, the principle should be to seek harmony between individual and enterprise objectives and goals by creating conditions under which a maximum of individual objectives and goals can be met when enterprise objectives and goals are met. But enterprise aims should not be set without reference to the more dominant aims of individuals in the enterprise.

Eighth, as a company grows larger its social responsibilities become greater. The network of aims should express these, but the operation of the enterprise must be predominantly economic, and social actions must be properly subordinated to this basic purpose. Corporate giving should be governed by the principle of enlightened self-interest, and, to the extent practicable, a cost-benefit analysis should be applied to such programs.

Ninth, managers throughout the enterprise should participate in the establishment of objectives and goals for their own performance.

Tenth, aims should be realistic, reasonable, and challenging to the people in the enterprise. Unattainable objectives and goals are not helpful. People become frustrated with them and internal drive and coordination erode. Realistic but "pushy" objectives and goals are preferred. Objectives and goals which challenge rather than frustrate individuals are desired.

Tenth, there is no formula for determining the network of aims for a company. It will vary in detail from one company to another and from one time to another in the same company. Experience in developing the network will help in its formulation. A first-rate planning system is a major framework within which the network is most easily constructed.

8
Appraising the Future Environment for Planning _____

8
Appraising
the Future Environment
for Planning

INTRODUCTION

Planning premises are major parts of the planning process. Premises mean literally that which goes before, previously set forth, or stated as introductory, postulated, or implied. They are basic assumptions for and upon which the planning process proceeds. They may range from a simple quickly derived procedure for planning to the results of detailed studies costing hundreds of thousands of dollars.

Assumptions for planning may be prepared before planning begins, as is the case when a sales forecast determines production planning. Or, they may be made in the process of planning, as for example when assumptions are made about the impact of different alternative courses of action.

Planning premises cut through every part of the planning process. In developing them important choices are required in deciding which premises are applicable, which are most important, which should be studied in depth, and how much resource should be used to define them. Selecting and preparing premises, therefore, is a very complex and important part of planning. This chapter will examine the nature of different types of premises and how they are developed and used.

TYPES OF PREMISES

There are many possible ways to classify planning premises. They may, for example, be grouped in terms of certainty versus uncertainty, procedural versus substantive, environmental versus internal, important versus unimportant, controllable versus uncontrollable, or personal versus impersonal. One of the major purposes of premises is to facilitate the planning process by guiding, directing, simplifying, and reducing the degree of uncertainty in it. These purposes can be illustrated, and the network of premises clearly defined, by a five-fold classification: implied, high impact, low impact, analytical, and procedural.

IMPLIED PREMISES. In every planning situation an enormous number of implied premises are present. Indeed, in any planning process the implied premises far outnumber the expressed premises. They have many sources: the many implications and inferences derived from basic business philosophies, former actions of the top management, the way in which the business is perceived by those doing planning, the way in which the environment is perceived, and the network of intricate interrelationships of people in and outside the business. As planning proceeds one often hears such statements as: "The boss would not like this," or "We cannot operate this way," or "It is not our style," or "This is an action the government would not sanction." Such statements are implied premises.

HIGH IMPACT PREMISES. Critically important premises are those that have a major impact on planning. These can cover any number of possible developments in the firm's environment or outside of it. Of great significance are values, ideas, conclusions and policies which top management has expressed. For example, in one company with which I am familiar the chief executive made a clear-cut decision to diversify by going into different businesses, but he had some definite expressed prejudices about lines of business in which he had no interest. These, of course, became major and critical premises in planning.

The world is so complex that problems to a company may arise from the most unexpected sources. Several years ago chicken growers in the U.S. were adversely affected when a concession was made in connection with negotiations for tariff reductions. An unexpected defense contract cancellation of a prime contract can bankrupt a subcontractor. An unforeseen economic depression can wreck healthy companies. (A business recession was the nemesis of the Edsel automobile.) Environment must be scanned and premises about such forces as these must be prepared for planning.

Some years ago I was asked by an aerospace company to forecast the dispersal policy of the federal government. Following World War II the federal government had a policy that determined geographic areas within which the government would help a company finance facility construction through favorable tax amortization. At the time, the prevailing policy was not to give such tax help for construction within approximately 10 miles of ground zero, or the center of a possible target in the event of nuclear war. The company in question was constructing a plant within 10 miles of ground zero and was told it would have to stop construction if it wanted government help and contracts. The question then, of course, was where to locate? In light of the dispersal policy, suggestions were made to build the plant deep in the desert, high in the mountains, and far away from population centers. Such remote locations, however, were not attractive because the plant was to make highly advanced equipment. In order to attract the scientific talent needed it was felt that some proximity to a large university was necessary, and such universities are generally located in populous areas. There were also other reasons why location in or near a large urban center was compelling. My forecast was that dispersal policy in the near term would tighten, that is the area from ground zero would increase, and after a year or so the policy would disappear because it was not a sensible one. This forecast became the determining factor in the decision to relocate the plant close to a population center.

LOW IMPACT PREMISES. Many premises have a low potential impact, irrespective of the degree of uncertainty surrounding them. Yet they should be recognized. Low-impact assumptions for a company are made without much study or are derived from generally available sources.

Low-impact premises, of course, will vary depending upon the company. To a candy manufacturer, for example, long-range GNP growth may be recognized in planning but not be accorded more than low possible impact, at least so long as economists are predicting real growth as being reasonably stable at rates around 4 percent per annum. He may also recognize but give low impact value to such factors as changing population, the wholesale commodity price index, agricultural income, or labor union turbulence.

Low-impact assumptions are incorporated in premises that are derived from major study efforts. Projecting political changes in a Middle Eastern country is rather important to a large oil company with huge capital investments in that country. In coming to major conclusions about such political trends, of course, many low-impact value premises or assumptions must be made. If they turn out to be high-impact premises they, in turn, become the subject of more intensified study.

ANALYTICAL PREMISES. In the planning process alternative courses of action are constantly being evaluated and choices made from among them. Premises may be thought of as statements about both the wanted and unwanted consequences resulting from choosing one course of action over another. For example, a planner might observe: "If we choose to use stainless steel in our low-priced valves, costs will increase and it is doubtful that we can raise the price to pay for the additional cost." Such premises, of course, can be the subject of penetrating study. All depends upon the importance of the premise to the final decision, what information about it is available, and who is expressing a judgment.

PROCEDURAL PREMISES. Planning programs, particularly among larger companies, must be conducted upon the basis of some standardized procedures, and these become basic premises for planning. For example, procedures may specify that: no division shall engage in the line of business of another division; divisions shall not plan overseas diversification for any products other than those which have been produced profitably at home; and divisional plans must be based upon interdivisional transfer prices which are not in excess of competitive prices. These are assumptions which may be deep matters of company policy, or they may be made merely to facilitate the planning process. Other procedural premises may concern the way plans are put together. For example, the use of uniform price inflation figures to be used by all divisions in future sales estimates and costs of production may be specified as a basic premise. Or, a basic premise may be that all plans will be made in constant prices.

FORECASTING AND PREMISES

All of the above premises are concerned with the future if for no other reason than that planning, for which premises are prepared, deals with the future. Not all the premises, however, involve forecasting. Some are no more than rules to get on with the planning job, but for most of the major premises forecasting the future is basic.

Forecasting, as noted in Chapter 1, is concerned with predicting or foretelling some future event. However, there are different characteristics of forecasts. A forecast may be very precise, specific, and quantitative about the occurrence of a future event. Some people think of this as a prediction or a prophecy. A forecast may also take the form of a likely event which occurs, given certain assumptions. Thus, the forecaster simply says that given certain assumptions about major inputs his GNP estimate will be $950 billion. Some people have called this a projection (Siegel, 1953). Forecasts also may be conjecture or speculation.

Generally speaking, the more accurate the forecasts made for planning the more useful they will be, but precision is not always of paramount importance. If a company is basing its three-month production schedules on a forecast of sales it is obvious that the more accurate the forecast the better the results will likely be. On the other hand, precision in forecasting company sales ten years from now is not necessary. Furthermore, the expense of trying to get such precision would not likely be worth the result. Here, the general direction, the probable range, the trend, is appropriate.

Forecasting is an occupation which is becoming increasingly widespread. During the past few years the market has been flooded with books, articles, and research reports forecasting the future in many fields. As this book is being written a ground swell can be seen of forecasts looking into the 21st century. In the U.S. and Europe, institutes and research centers are springing up to study forecasting, or to make forecasts, or both.

There are many reasons for this explosion in forecasting. One is that both public and private institutions are discovering that by forecasting they are in a much better position to take advantage of events, to change them, or to avoid them. Was it Confucius who said, "If a man take no thought about what is distant, he will find sorrow near at hand"? Also, forecasting tools are getting better even though for most areas they are still inadequate to the task. Another reason is that as planning becomes more widespread there is more need for forecasts as planning premises, and finally, is the need of both public and private institutions to try to penetrate the future, to make the invisible more visible, so as to lessen the uncertainty about the future in the face of certain spectacular, powerful, and rapid environmental changes. There seems little question about the fact that we live in a world with more rapid changes in all areas of life than have occurred since the Industrial Revolution.

No businessman can be spared the need for making forecasts. Even though he may not consciously look ahead, he still forecasts. For example, if he makes a snap decision not to replace a worn-out piece of equipment he implicitly is forecasting that his profits will be higher than if he replaced the machine. The shorter the forecast the more consensus can be found for its importance. But the necessity of longer-range forecasts to company survival is growing rapidly in managerial acceptance. To consider the importance of looking far ahead it is useful to think back but a scant twenty years. There were no electronic computers, no coast-to-coast television programs, no nuclear submarines, no thermonuclear bombs, no modern tranquilizers, no artificial hearts, no PERT, no coast-to-coast nonstop airplanes, no satellites, and no important wars. However dramatic was the changing environment of business in the past two decades, it seems a certainty that it will be even more spectacular in the next two decades.

RANGE OF BUSINESS FORECASTS

Chart 8-1 attempts to illustrate the vast complexity of the environment in which each business operates and to show how many different forces can affect a variety of areas of a business's operations. John Muir once said: "When we try to pick out anything by itself, we find it hitched to everything else in the universe." So it is with a business. Any force which affects it turns out to have roots extending over a wide area.

In the political area, for example, such environmental forces as these are potentially very important to many businesses: problems in aiding underdeveloped countries; new Federal, State, or local governmental regulations; changes in political parties; wars and the threat of wars; Department of Defense procurement volume and policy; and the way in which laws will be administered. Chang-

Chart 8-1
Environmental Impacts on Company Planning

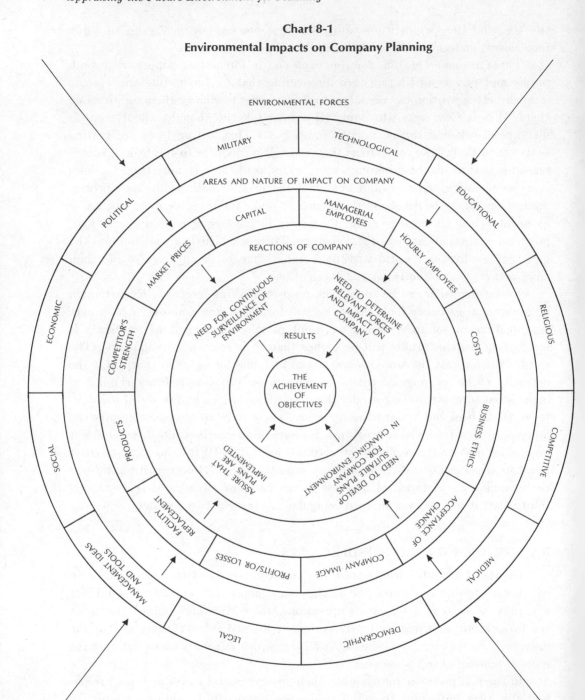

ing styles are important for many businesses, e.g., clothing, automobiles, housing, and furniture. Forecasts can be made of such intangibles as fashion and design acceptability (Dwight Robinson, 1958).

Among all the possible forces in an environment and in internal business operations that can affect a business, the ones really significant to each business must be identified. Once that is decided, the question arises about how much time and energy should be devoted to examining them.

These are important questions because as future change takes place there are golden opportunities that will arise, and serious threats which also will appear. The total possible number of forces, both internal and external, that can be exploited to the advantage of a business or can wreck it, boggle the mind.

There is no formula to tell a manager which forces to forecast or how much time and money to devote to forecasting. A public utility, for example, will devote major attention to population growth in its own geographic area, construction costs, costs of operation, and public utility commission policy. An aerospace company will pay high attention to forecasting the military and space demand for specific products. An automobile company will commit important resources to studying future consumer income, changing style tastes, and public attitudes towards passenger car safety and air pollution. The National Planning Association (1966, p. 8) in a recent survey found that firms serving principally consumer markets make relatively great use of population, labor force, personal income, and regional economic projections. The larger ones also have as much interest in future government policies as firms selling primarily to government. A commodity producing firm makes relatively great use of industry sales and price projections, and relatively modest use of the more aggregate economic indicators. Such firms are more likely to apply projections to production and inventory decisions. Most companies forecast their own sales which in turn forces them to focus attention on the major determinants of their sales. Companies with little staff and a shortage of funds must use their funds sparingly for planning studies. Even though, for example, the near-term economic outlook for their industry may be critical to their plans they will have to make arbitrary assumptions about it, or depend upon trade sources, simply because they cannot afford to make the study themselves.

It would seem valuable for every company, large and small, to determine systematically which forces, external as well as internal, have a high probability of high impact, good or bad, on the company. This need not be an elaborate survey. But the mere idea of attempting to do it should constitute an advantage. One simple and systematic scheme would be to list the more important possibly beneficial and threatening events in each area of Chart 8-1. Beside each listing a simple notation of the degree of possible importance to both the industry and firm should be stated as high, medium, low, or none. Observations about the implications of these events for the achievements of company objectives should

Table 8-1   Developments of Competition to Watch

Developments	IMPORTANCE FOR INDUSTRY			IMPORTANCE FOR COMPANY			COMMENTS
	High	Medium	Low	High	Medium	Low	
Ease of entry into business							
Availability of capital							
Growth of automation							
Quality control							
Technical capability							
Supply of raw materials							
Import and export trends							
How "hungry" is competition?							
Growth of research and development expenditures							
New products possibilities							
Competitors' pricing							
Share of market							

then be prepared. Once a table such as this is made it is easy to review it periodically and with a minimum amount of time. This little exercise will identify major evolving events to be watched carefully as well as those which should receive little or no attention.

Table 8-1 illustrates this technique for competition. It will be noted that some trends are industry wide and others of specific and direct concern to an individual business.

The range of methods for making forecasts is very wide, running from the intuitive to the highly mathematical. Applications of different techniques vary, of course, depending upon subject matter. Forecasting a change in policy of a public utility commission may be done only on a purely subjective basis, whereas a forecast of how a competitor can be expected to shave costs may be quantitative as derived from his financial need for the business. In recent years, despite the mystery that cloaks much forecasting, and aside from the subjective evaluations which exist in practically all forecasts of importance, surprising strides have been made in developing effective methods of prediction. Much remains to be done, but one thing is clear: the area of unpredictable events is rapidly narrowing.

Although the forecasts that may be important to a particular business may range across any discipline, most business forecasts are economic. For this reason, most of the remainder of this chapter will be devoted to economic forecasts with particular reference to sales forecasting. But there is a growing interest in technological forecasting; a subject that will be discussed in detail in Chapter 22.

ECONOMIC FORECASTING

Economic forecasting in business has to be as old as business itself. In recent years economic forecasting has moved an important distance beyond the necromancy of medieval seers, but it is still far from the certainty of the physical sciences. Today the forecaster of economic events is equipped with a wide range of tools, relationships, and data that make his projections more reliable. He is relying increasingly on the concepts and methods of statistics and econometrics in his approach to forecasting. Nevertheless, economists have not yet evolved—if they ever will—a technique for making completely accurate forecasts. One of the problems of economic forecasting is that it is always subject to what General Marshall used to call "chronic obscurity." Or, as Solomon Fabricant once said, "Forecasting is the art of drawing useful conclusions from inadequate premises."

Economic forecasts are getting more reliable, but they cannot be made with certainty, and a forecaster who has been consistently right can suddenly fail. The reasons for this lie in the problems of dealing with economic phenomena.

Robinson, Morton and Calderwood have succinctly depicted major pitfalls that frequently creep into ordinary discussion of economic affairs, and they are presented in Table 8-2. Central in this exposition are the identification, measurement, and sequence of cause and effect. These are major problems for forecasters.

For practically any important economic forecast the causative factors are too numerous to study, so identification of key or strategic factors causing a movement is required. Forecasting the demand for air transport is a function of business conditions, price of seats, speed of airplanes, types of airplanes, consumers' disposable income, rate structures, and a thousand and one other factors. The outlook for interest rates is a function of the demand and supply of money, legislation, capital flows, and numerous other factors. In these and problems like them it is difficult but necessary to select those determinants that are most important in the forecast and to focus attention on them.

Once this determination is made the problem of measurement arises. We know that the Department of Defense budget fundamentally is based upon the threat or actuality of war, technology, economic conditions, and political forces. How do these translate into a quantity of budget dollars? We know that the long-range outlook for construction is greatly influenced by population growth and mix. How is this impact measured?

The task of measurement is complicated by the fact that a very large part of the interrelationship are not linear. They are curvilinear and discontinuous. Costs are not generally straight-line relationships with output; the demand for automobiles is not a straight-line relationship with consumer disposable income; and the demand for aluminum is not a constant relationship with the price of steel. Magnitudes affect relationships and so do changes in other related economic factors.

The sequence of cause and effect relationships is not constant and throws another roadblock in the way of the forecaster. Steel sheet output, for example, used to react fairly directly to automobile demand. This has changed greatly as a result of the introduction of the compact automobile, foreign competition, competition with other metals, and changing gauges of automobile body steel. Furthermore, the sequence of cause and effect will vary with changes in the environment. Buying in anticipation of a strike will change the demand for steel even if everything else remains constant. What happens in economic life is influenced by other forces all over the world.

A major problem of the economic forecaster concerns data. On the one hand, he is faced with the problem of digesting masses of information about the past and present. On the other hand he must make up his mind with insufficient facts having insufficient reliability about the future. Kierkegaard observed, "Life can only be understood backward but it must be lived forward." This sage thought will strike a sensitive spot in economic forecasters.

All this means that judgment is a cardinal ingredient in all forecasting. Judgment is essential in interpreting data, in selecting methods of analysis, and in applying them to a specific problem. Bassie goes so far as to say: "It may . . . be stated as a general rule that any attempt to make forecasts mechanically,

Table 8-2   Pitfalls in Thinking About Economic Affairs

THE SOLUTION OF ECONOMIC PROBLEMS REQUIRES ADHERENCE TO PRINCIPLES OF LOGICAL THINKING. These rules cannot be reviewed here in detail as they would be in a book on logic. But warnings can be stated against several types of error that frequently creep into ordinary discussion.

FIRST is the fallacy that if one thing precedes another (or always precedes it), the first is the cause of the second. The error is clearly illustrated in the sequence of day following night. Day does not cause night, or vice versa. Both result from the workings of the solar system.

SECOND is the error of thinking that a single factor causes a given result, when in fact, a combination of factors may be responsible. For example, many people have had the mistaken idea that wage increases were the sole cause of the inflation that followed the second World War. In fact, a variety of influences were involved: the backlog of demand caused by wartime production controls, large savings balances, and easy availability of bank credit, to mention a few.

THIRD is the fallacy of supposing the whole to be like the parts with which one is familiar. For example, it is a common error to suppose that government finance operates on the same principles as household finance whereas government finance is really quite different. The government generally has substantially more ability to fit its income to its expenditures and substantially more power to borrow.

FOURTH is the fallacy that if things have happened in a given sequence in the past, they will happen that way again. This notion led many people to expect a collapse in prices shortly after the second World War.

FIFTH is the error of wishful thinking—seeing what one wants to see and believing what one wants to believe. This was the prevailing mood before the great stock market crash of 1929.

Another fallacy, which is not limited to economics by any means, may be called "personification" of a problem; that is, identifying a very complicated situation with some prominent person. The identification of former President Hoover with the depression of the thirties and of former President Truman with the postwar inflation are examples of such personification. This form of over-simplifying complex economic and political forces is a way of expressing emotions, but it adds little to the understanding of the issues involved.

A REASONED SOLUTION OF PROBLEMS ALSO REQUIRES AN ATTITUDE OF DETACHMENT AND OBJECTIVITY.

Source: An Introduction to Economic Reasoning, 4th ed., Marshall A. Robinson, Herbert C. Morton and James D. Calderwood, (Washington, D.C.: The Brookings Institution, 1967) pp. 9-10.

Chart 8-2

The Planning Gap

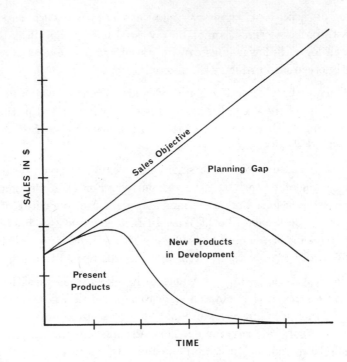

as by projecting cyclical patterns or by relying solely on correlation formulas, must eventually result in failure." (Bassie, 1958, p. 9.) This does not mean that judgment is blind guessing. It is rather the applicability of experience to forecasting. Nor does it mean that forecasting is predominantly subjective. The effort, of course, should be to try to reduce subjective elements to a minimum. But, even when the role of judgment is limited it still is of major importance.

FORECASTING SALES

The great majority of companies forecast sales, and this far surpasses in number any other type forecast made by business. Sord and Welsch (1958, p. 133) found that out of 424 companies surveyed 93 percent develop sales estimates. There can, of course, be no effective planning, either short- or long-range, without estimates of sales.

Chart 8-2 is a simple illustration of the role of sales forecasting in long-range planning. Forecasts of present product sales plus sales of new products usually reveal a planning gap when related to tentative sales objectives. Assuming the accuracy of the sales estimates and the hardness of the sales objective the question for a manager then is how to fill the gap.

The role of sales forecasting for both short- and long-range planning is further illustrated in Chart 8-3. This chart shows that from all pertinent noncontrollable, partially controllable, and controllable environmental factors, sales forecasts are made which provide a basis for plans and operations in all areas of the business. Rational decisions without sales forecasts are impossible. For example, a sales forecast will be the keystone of sales management. With it can be set targets for the sales force, targets for individual salesmen, sales compensation plans, the determining of sales territories and assignments, the emphasis on specific products, advertising, and many other activities under the jurisdiction of the sales department. Sales forecasting is indispensable as a basis for setting production schedules which in turn determine many other operations. It serves as a fundamental integrating and coordinating tool for current operations.

GENERAL ECONOMIC AND
INDUSTRY SALES FORECASTS

A company's sales should be forecast in the light of general economic and industry conditions. As a matter of practice, however, half or less of the companies that forecast their sales do so in light of industry and general economic conditions.

The larger a company grows the more significant general economic conditions are likely to be in its planning, but even small companies should pay attention to general economic conditions. To illustrate, the manager of a small electrical parts company, selling principally but not wholly to commercial construction contractors, tried to keep informed about general business conditions. In late 1965 he foresaw a sharp drop in construction in Los Angeles, which was his principal market. As a result, he tried and was successful in expanding his aerospace sales even though his profits were less than on comparable commercial construction contracts. The construction market did collapse as he predicted. His sales did not fall off, although his profits did slightly. But a number of his competitors incurred net losses and some were forced out of business.

Many large companies make their own general economic forecasts as bases for planning, but many companies, large and small, depend on trade journals and business magazines. There is usually no unanimity among them, however, and the manager who depends upon them is forced to choose from among them. Chart 8-4 illustrates the variations among projections of 35 economists for the year 1963. Although this is not a current illustration it is rather typical of variations from actuality. Sometimes the mass of projections are above what actually happens. The point here is not one of criticism of forecasters but rather caution to users.

Chart 8-3
Role of Sales Forecasting in Planning

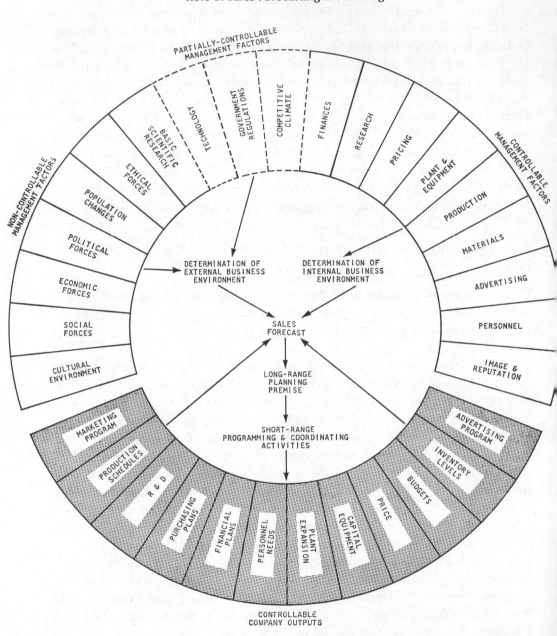

PREPARED BY
GEORGE A. STEINER - 1965

IDEA BASED PARTLY UPON: WILLIAM LAZER, "PERSPECTIVES OF SALES FORECASTING,"
BUSINESS TOPICS, WINTER 1959, p. 43.

Chart 8-4

Gross National Product Forecasts and Actual Developments

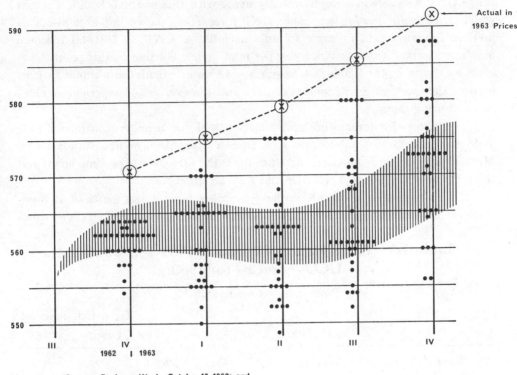

Source: Business Week, October 13, 1962; and
U.S. Department of Commerce Survey of Current Business

The record of general economic forecasts, however, is improving. Each calendar quarter, J. A. Livingston, Financial Editor of the Philadelphia *Bulletin*, sends a questionnaire to 60 professional forecasters for their short-term projection of industrial production. He then prepares a consensus and later compares the prediction with the actual fact. The record was spotty from the end of World War II to 1955. Following 1955 the consensus has been improving but it is not completely accurate.

Space does not permit the presentation of the many methods for making long- and short-range general forecasts of business conditions or major elements of economic activity. However, the methodology for forecasting the Gross National Product, both short- and long-range, is readily available. (Bassie, 1958; Butler and Kavesh, 1966; Lewis, 1959; Moore, 1961, 1966; and Silk, 1963.)

Most Gross National Product (GNP) forecasts are made by projecting individual parts of the national accounts that enter into it. Table 8-3 shows GNP forecasts for 1968 prepared by the U.C.L.A. faculty. The method used was to forecast each major account shown in the table and then to add them. This method has produced surprisingly accurate results over a ten-year period. Long-range GNP forecasts also are frequently made with this method. A different but widely used technique for long-range GNP forecasts is shown in Table 8-4. This method follows a rather simple formula as follows: GNP = f (total national manhours worked times productivity per man hour). Getting to this point, however, as shown in the Table 8-4, requires a series of calculations which in turn involve the examination of masses of data and the exercise of experienced judgment in using them.

Techniques for forecasting major elements of the near-term economic outlook, such as interest rates, prices, wage rates, profits, are not standardized. Methodology depends much upon the subject, the forecaster, the time span, and the purpose of the forecast. (Butler and Kavesh, 1966.)

Once the general economic outlook is forecast, or major parts of it, forecasts for the industry in which a firm operates can then be prepared. Sometimes

Table 8-3   Gross National Product, 1965-1967, and the UCLA Forecast for 1968

(In Billions of Current Dollars)

Line		Actual		Estimated	Forecast
		1965	1966	1967	1968
1	*Personal Consumption Expenditures*	433.1	465.9	492	524
2	Durable Goods	66.0	70.3	72	76
3	Nondurable Goods	191.2	207.5	218	232
4	Services	175.9	188.1	202	216
5	*Gross Private Domestic Investment*	107.4	118.0	111	121
6	Residential Construction	27.0	24.4	24	27
7	Other Construction	25.1	27.9	27	28
8	Producers' Durable Equipment	46.0	52.3	56	60
9	Change in Inventories	9.4	13.4	4	6
10	*Net Exports of Goods & Services*	7.0	5.1	5	4
11	*Gov't Purchases of Goods & Services*	136.4	154.3	177	194
12	Federal	66.8	77.0	91	99
13	(National Defense)	(50.1)	(60.5)	(73.5)	(81)
14	(Other, incl. NASA)	(16.7)	(16.5)	(17.5)	(18)
15	State and Local	69.6	77.2	86	95
16	GROSS NATIONAL PRODUCT	683.9	743.3	785	843
	Increase in GNP from Year Before:				
17	Amount	51.5	59.4	41.7	58
18	Percent	8.1	8.7	5.6	7.4
19	Percent "Real" Increase	6.1	5.8	2.7	4.2
20	Percent Price Increase	2.0	2.9	2.9	3.2

this is not too difficult because consistent correlation may exist between, say, GNP and industry sales, or between consumers' disposable income and industry sales. For many industries, such as steel, automobiles, and heavy machinery, the development of industry forecasts is extremely complex and involves many and sophisticated techniques to get satisfactory results. The many methods to calculate industry sales cannot be presented here, but some of them are much the same as those for forecasting sales of a company and will be presented in the following section.

THE INPUT-OUTPUT GRID

The input of one industry, of course, is the output of another. From this simple proposition, Wassily Leontief before World War II invented a system by means of which it is possible to quantify the impact of one industry on all other industries. In 1966, for the first time, the U.S. Department of Commerce completed an official input-output table for 86 major industries and plans to continue the calculation in the future.

Table 8-5 illustrates the new model for the U.S. economy. When the automobile industry buys $1 billion of goods and services the impact on other industries is shown. It is clear from the table that $85 million is bought from the steel industry. In turn, as illustrated in the table, this amount is redistributed among other industries, and so on.

Table 8-4   Gross National Product Projection for 1975

ITEM	1975
(In 1964 prices)	
Population (000 omitted)	230,415
Labor force (000 omitted)	94,473
Armed forces	2,500
Unemployment	5,737
Civilian employment (000 omitted)	86,236
Average work week hours	35
Average yearly work hours	1,820
Manhours (000 omitted)	156,950
Output per manhour annual percent growth rate	4.0
Output per manhour ($)	6,549
Gross National Product ($ billions)	1,028

In the process of accumulating information for the model it is necessary, of course, to know how the output of one industry is distributed among other industries. An illustration for the chemical industry is shown in Table 8-6.

All this information will be of great use to the development of better industry forecasts. The next step, of course, is to forecast trends in one or more industries which, when plugged into the model, will produce forecasts of what will happen in all other industries. An elaborate effort along these lines is Almon's (1967) work.

One of the major problems with input-output analysis is the development of up-to-date functions, or the impacts which one industry has on others. The American economy is very dynamic with rapidly changing bills of materials, tastes, structures, and output levels. While broad and/or old estimates of input-output relationships may be acceptable for very general conclusions, much more up-to-date and reliable estimates are required for reasonably accurate industry forecasts upon which a firm's plans can be based. Such reliable coefficients are expensive to get but the government is likely to get them and make input-output tables of major use in business sales forecasts.

Table 8-5 Distribution of $1 Billion of Purchases Made by the Automobile Industry Among Other Industries

	Millions of dollars		Thousands of dollars
Glass	$ 10	Stampings, screws, and bolts	$ 510
Metalworking machinery	11	Construction: upkeep and repair	595
Primary nonferrous metals	11	Metalworking machinery	595
Electrical machinery and supplies	15	Machine shop products	595
Transportation and warehousing	20	Finance and insurance	680
Business services	24	Petroleum refining	680
Rubber and plastics	28	Business services	765
Stampings, screws, and bolts	30	Chemicals	850
Wholesale and retail trade		Stone and clay products	1,275
services	31	Primary nonferrous metals	1,360
Other fabricated metal products	35	Other fabricated metal products	1,445
		Electricity, gas, and water	2,040
Steel	85	Coal	2,210
		Wholesale and retail trade services	3,060
Intra-industry purchases	295	Transportation and warehousing	4,505
52 other products		Iron ores	4,590
[less than $1-million each]	92	Intra-industry purchases	19,295
Foreign products [imports]	23	50 other products	
Manpower, rentals, auto profits,		[less than $1/2-million each]	5,355
and interest on money borrowed	290	Foreign products [imports]	1,020
Total	$1-billion	Manpower, rentals, steel profits	
		and interest on money borrowed	33,575
		Total	$85-million

Source: U.S. Department of Commerce

MAKING THE COMPANY SALES FORECAST

The sales forecasters' palette today is rich with techniques but the most commonly used methods are the jury of executive opinion, sales force composite, users' expectation, time-series analysis, statistical correlations, and an eclectic system using many different techniques. On the whole, the methods discussed here are useful for both long- and short-range forecasts, but our treatment will be principally in terms of short-range projections. (Much of the following from NICB, 1963.)

JURY OF EXECUTIVE OPINION. With this method various executives are brought together to make a sales forecast. The actual process can take different forms. Executives from different areas of the company—sales, production, finance, administration—may be brought together to pool their views. Once made, the results can be reviewed by the president, approved, or returned for further evaluation. Information can, of course, be fed to the executives from various sources to help them translate their views into concrete estimates.

An example of this method is that used by the Cooper-Bessemer Corporation, a producer of engines and compressors. The process begins with the sales man-

Table 8-6 Distribution of Purchases by the Chemical Industry from Other Industries

Industry	Percent of sales
Stone and clay products	1.2%
Fabric, yarn and thread mills	1.4
Primary iron and steel mfg.	1.4
Food and kindred products	1.5
Printing and publishing	1.5
Rubber and misc. plastic products	2.5
Paper, except containers	2.8
New construction	3.0
Paints and allied products	3.3
Petroleum refining	3.8
Fabricated textile products	5.1
Agricultural products, except livestock	9.4
Plastic and synthetic materials	9.4
Chemicals and selected products	19.4
State and local government	2.0
Federal government	6.1
Sales to households	1.8
Sales to 36 industries [less than 1% each]	10.6
Sales classified in other industries	8.2
Exports	5.6
Total	100.0%

Source: U.S. Department of Commerce

ager who, drawing on his own experience and knowledge about probable sales, prepares an estimate biannually for the coming year. In making the forecast, data are gathered by the manager of marketing research from a survey of branch manager expectations. He reviews and may modify them before sending them on to the sales manager. The sales manager's forecast, broken down by types and sizes of machines, is given to the controller, who translates the forecast into a profit and loss statement. In making his forecast the controller discusses assumptions—such as plant capacity, costs, and other factors influencing profits—with other managers. His forecast, therefore, reflects a blending of opinions. This preliminary sales forecast and profit and loss statement are submitted to the operating committee of the company. This group, which includes the president and all top executives, reviews this information and prepares a final forecast upon which basis current operations take place.

A new technique called Delphi is much like this one. Although it has been used successfully for GNP forecasts (Campbell, 1966) its principal use has been in technological forecasting. It will, therefore, be discussed in Chapter 22.

SALES FORCE COMPOSITE. This is a so-called grass-roots method in which the forecast is based upon data collected by the sales force. Salesmen are given standard forms to complete which are then discussed with the sales man-

---

Table 8-7   Jury of Executive Opinion: An Evaluation

ADVANTAGES:

1. Can provide forecasts easily and quickly.
2. May not require the preparation of elaborate statistics.
3. Brings a variety of specialized viewpoints together for a pooling of experience and judgment.
4. May be the only feasible means of forecasting, especially in the absence of adequate data.

DISADVANTAGES:

1. Is inferior to a more factual basis of forecasting, since it is based so heavily on opinion.
2. Requires costly executive time.
3. Is not necessarily more accurate because opinion is averaged.
4. Disperses responsibility for accurate forecasting.
5. Presents difficulties in making breakdowns by products, time intervals, or markets for operating purposes.

Source: NICB, *Forecasting Sales,* p. 13.

---

agers. Modifications are made and the results are accumulated and sent to the next tier of management. District and regional estimates are aggregated in the central headquarters. Through this process there is examination and modification depending upon the basis for change at each level. At central headquarters a staff group may make a separate forecast and compare it with that arriving from below. At this level, changes in the forecast may be made as a result of a decision by management to increase or decrease advertising, to modify a particular product, to abandon a product, and so on. Following such a review, the forecast is then completed. This method has merit in that it forces each level to think about its markets, customers, and prospects, and forces different levels to examine their estimates on these fronts. This method, therefore, becomes an important communications network.

The Pennsalt Chemicals Corporation provides field sales personnel with a general economic forecast and asks each person to forecast his product sales to each major customer for the coming year. These forecasts, placed on tabulat-

Table 8-8   Sales Force Composite Method: An Evaluation

ADVANTAGES:

1. Uses specialized knowledge of men closest to the market.
2. Places responsibility for the forecast in the hands of those who must produce the results.
3. Gives sales force greater confidence in quotas developed from forecasts.
4. Tends to give results greater stability because of the magnitude of the sample.
5. Lends itself to the easy development of product, territory, customer, or salesmen breakdowns.

DISADVANTAGES:

1. Salesmen are poor estimators, often being either more optimistic or more pessimistic than conditions warrant.
2. If estimates are used as a basis for setting quotas, salesmen are inclined to understate the demand in order to make the goal easier to achieve.
3. Salesmen are often unaware of the broad economic patterns shaping future sales and are thus incapable of forecasting trends for extended periods.
4. Since sales forecasting is a subsidiary function of the sales force, sufficient time may not be made available for it.
5. Requires an extensive expenditure of time by executives and sales force.
6. Elaborate schemes are sometimes necessary to keep estimates realistic and free from bias.

Source: NICB, Forecasting Sales, p. 21.

ing cards, are reviewed by product managers and by division sales line supervisors. Tabulated runs of the forecasts by product, territory, and any other desired classification are then made. There then follows a formal review of the sales budget in each division. In this review the forecasts are related to the general economic forecast and division general objectives. This then is converted into production requirements, and various budgets for the division are prepared. These forecasts and budgets are then reviewed by top management. The process takes from April to December.

Pennsalt has a number of principles which it uses in adjusting sales forecasts, an important one of which is: sales forecasts should be built from the ground up and submitted figures should be changed by upper-level management only after review with, and agreement from, the responsible operating executives. In this way, of course, operating executives recognize the projections as their own and top management feels it can hold them responsible for meeting the forecasts.

This technique, as shown in Table 8-8, has many advantages including the fact that forecasts are made by those who must meet them. On the other hand, salesmen are notoriously optimistic. But if the numbers are massaged up through

Table 8-9   Users' Expectation Method: An Evaluation

ADVANTAGES:

1. Bases forecast on information obtained direct from product users, whose buying actions will actually determine sales.
2. Gives forecaster a subjective feel of the market and of the thinking behind users' buying intentions.
3. By-passes published or other indirect sources, enabling the inquiring company to obtain its information in the form and detail required.
4. Offers a possible way of making a forecast where other methods may be inadequate or impossible to use—e.g., forecasting demand for a new industrial product for which no previous sales record is available.

DISADVANTAGES:

1. Is difficult to employ in markets where users are numerous or not easily located.
2. Depends on the judgment and cooperation of product users, some of whom may be ill-informed or uncooperative.
3. Bases forecast on expectations, which are subject to subsequent change.
4. Requires considerable expenditure of time and manpower.

Source: NICB, *Forecasting Sales,* p. 31.

the management chain in reasonable collaboration with personnel who must meet goals the results can be accurate and motivating.

USERS' EXPECTATIONS. This approach, as the name implies, is to get information from those who use a product about their expected future purchases. A small company that sells to only one or a few large companies can easily make its forecast if these companies will reveal what they plan to buy from it. Companies who have many customers can also use this method. For example, the National Lead Company has an elaborate and well-developed procedure to find its customer demand. This company produces raw materials purchased by other firms who, in turn, make end products. Since it makes many intermediate products its forecasting problems are formidable, but it has solved them with a detailed interview and questionnaire system. For each large volume product the Company interviews personally about 100 companies, and as many as 500 through a mail questionnaire. Interviews are conducted by marketing research personnel who question three types of executives, in this order: the technical research director (or chief engineer), the sales manager (or director of marketing research), and the director of purchases. These surveys produce an industry sales forecast from which the company forecast is calculated.

Table 8-10 Time-Series Forecasts: An Evaluation

ADVANTAGES:

1. Forces the forecaster to consider the underlying trend, cycle, and seasonal elements in the sales series.
2. Takes into account the particular repetitive or continuing patterns exhibited by the sales in the past.
3. Provides a systematic means of making quantitative projections.

DISADVANTAGES:

1. Assumes the continuation of historical patterns of change in sales components, without considering outside influences that may affect sales in the forecast period.
2. Is often unsatisfactory for short-term forecasting, since, for example, the pinpointing of cyclical turning points by mechanical projections is seldom possible.
3. May be difficult to apply in cases where erratic, irregular forces disrupt or hide the regularity of component patterns within a sales series.
4. Requires technical skill, experience, and judgment.

Source: NICB, *Forecasting Sales,* p. 34.

Chart 8-5

Drug and Proprietary Store Sales, 1961-1967

Source: *Survey of Current Business,* U.S. Department of Commerce.

TIME-SERIES ANALYSIS. It is always helpful to have information about past trends and present movements of a phenomenon under study for with such information a forecaster can then judge the probability that at any point in the future the patterns of the past will continue. Time-series analysis provides a quantitative base for the forecaster to make these judgments better. The analysis can be done by simple inspection or by the use of mathematical techniques.

Chart 8-5 shows past trends of the sales of drug and proprietary stores. It is easy to see in this chart the long-term growth trend. For any time-series where trend growth is fairly constant, and there is no visible reason to think the trend will not continue, this method of projection by inspection can be very useful in making a first approximation of a forecast. Its use, however, is mostly pertinent to long-range projections. It is hazardous to employ this method in making short-term forecasts. To do so automatically is what I call the "mickey finn approach." Events have a habit of changing direction very fast in the short-run and to forget this fact is to court disaster. No mechanical means of forecasting whether for short- or long-range projections, should ever be used without very careful analysis. As Kenneth Boulding once noted: any forecast is useful, even a linear one, providing the forecaster does not believe it.

Sales of most companies are influenced by three basic trends: long-term growth trends, cyclical business fluctuations, and seasonal variations. Time-series analysis is a mathematical method to separate these three trends and to show their interactions in the past as a basis for judgment about the future. Industry sales as well as individual firm product sales generally reveal these trends when data are examined over a long period of time. If patterns of change in an industry are reasonably well defined, and are likely to continue as in the past, mathematically fitted trends can be highly useful in forecasting. Time-series analysis, for example, may be most helpful to a toy manufacturer in telling him what seasonal fluctuations to expect. If past trends are not likely to continue, this method is not apt to be helpful. At any rate, the quantitative techniques involved are rather complex. (Reichard, 1966, Chapters 9 and 10.)

STATISTICAL CORRELATION TECHNIQUES. Correlation analysis measures the relationship between two or more variables. It has been observed, for example, that activity in casinos in Florida increases as the temperature drops and weather becomes more foul in the midwest. The Valhalla of all forecasters is to find a lead series with which they can correlate with certainty the subject of their forecast. Statistical correlation merely establishes a mathematical relationship between sales which is the object of a forecast and some other independent variable. The use of statistical correlation analyses varies from simple scatter diagrams to plot trend (Chart 8-6), to regression and to multiple correlation analysis.

The Eli Lilly Company, for example, has found a correlation between disposable personal income and industry sales of drugs. For every 10 percent change in national disposable income a corresponding change of 5 percent has been found for industry sales. Knowing this correlation exists, and assuming it will hold in the future, the company can make more accurate forecasts by projecting disposable income, calculating the result for industry sales, and then forecasting its own sales by determining the proportion of the market it thinks it will get. The American Radiator Company has found a close correlation between the products of one of its divisions and building permits reported by the F. W. Dodge Corporation.

In using correlation techniques it is of course important to make sure that the relationships are rational, or have a measurable cause and effect. For years some businessmen around Lakes Michigan and Huron forecast the stock market and general business conditions upon the basis of the water level of the two lakes. Historically, the lakes reached a water level peak in 1929 and bottomed out with a low in 1934, corresponding to the great height and bottom of the terrible drop in stock market prices. In 1962 the water levels dropped but the

Chart 8-6

Scatter Diagram of Ajax Company Sales and

Total U.S. Personal Consumption Expenditures

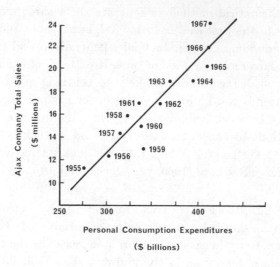

Personal Consumption Expenditures

($ billions)

stock market did not. Since then the accuracy of this correlation has not been well received.

In a simple scatter diagram, as in Chart 8-6, sales of the Ajax Company are related to consumer disposable income. By hand, a trend line can be drawn and upon this basis forecasts of Ajax sales can be readily made if a forecast of consumer disposable income is made. The relationship between Ajax sales and consumer disposable income can be calculated also by a regression equation found in any standard statistics book. This method results in a statistically calculated trend line. The method usually used to calculate the straight line is the least squares method. This is a technique which sets a trend line such that the squares of the deviations about the line are at a minimum. (Reichard, 1966, Chapters 11 and 12.)

When the movement of sales hinges on two or more variables a relationship can be calculated statistically, a trend line drawn, and forecasting simplified. The tire industry, for example, is able to relate the demand for tires to new car production, automobiles in operation, the wearing qualities of tires, and the amount of service they receive. Companies in the industry have been able to make fairly accurate forecasts upon a multiple regression analysis of these factors. The advantages and disadvantages of correlation and mathematical methods are shown in Table 8-11.

COMPUTER SIMULATION ANALYSIS. With the development of the modern computer it is possible to forecast by using highly sophisticated models that, in effect, simulate the future. An illustration of this method is the Airline System Simulation developed by the Lockheed Aircraft Corporation (1966; Gunn and Howard, 1966; and Gunn, 1964, pp. 206-229). This model was developed first to make a forecast of the market for the supersonic transport airplane and has subsequently been used in forecasting the market for various types of commercial transports the company is considering building.

For calculating the market of the supersonic transport the following are grossly simplified steps taken in the simulation:

Table 8-11   Correlation and Mathematical Methods: An Evaluation

ADVANTAGES:

1. Describes in measurable, objective terms the factors and relationship of factors associated with the course of sales.
2. Gives some indication of the expected effect of these relationships and the degree of reliability that can be attached to forecasts.
3. Forces the forecaster to consider the major factors influencing sales.
4. Forces the forecaster to quantify the assumptions underlying his estimates, making it easier for management to check his results.
5. Provides a means of discovering factors associated with sales that intuitive reasoning may not uncover.
6. Enables the forecaster to benefit from the opinions of other forecasters, if sales correlate with a well-known indicator.
7. Enables the forecaster to use current values of an indicator when it has been established that such an indicator leads sales.

DISADVANTAGES:

1. Ties sales forecast to indicators that usually must themselves be forecast, unless sales correlate with leading series.
2. Carries danger of over-reliance on statistical methods.
3. Carries danger of over-reliance on projections of indicators made by other forecasters, when such indicators are used to forecast sales.
4. Carries danger of inaccurate forecasts if the basic relationships previously observed and used in forecasting happen to change.
5. Involves complex statistical methods, which may inhibit management's complete understanding or acceptance of the forecasting process.
6. Requires considerable technical skill, experience, and judgment.

Source: NICB, *Forecasting Sales*, p. 39.

1. Development of Route Interaction. For the entire world, the direct incremental effects, as well as the indirect effects, were determined for different potential aircraft routings among more important terminals. For example, an addition of a nonstop flight from Los Angeles to Pittsburgh will affect the traffic on other one-stop routings such as from Los Angeles to Chicago. Secondary effects of the loss or gain of passengers on these one-stop routings is felt, of course, on other routes that provide passenger service to these legs.

2. Flight Evaluation by Aircraft Type. Flight evaluations were then made on the basis of what would produce the most favorable systems economics. In other words, decisions about routings, flight preferences, frequency of flight, preferred airplane types, and speed preference, were made on the basis of choices which Lockheed considered the affected airline would make to optimize its earnings. To do this, of course, entailed deep and intimate understanding of airline economics, personal preferences, airline schedules, operating expenses, operating revenues, and so on.

3. Flight Assignments. The question was continuously asked, during the first phase of flight assignment: which flight with which aircraft, if added, will produce the maximum increment of earnings to the affected airline? Flights were added until no flight with any aircraft on any route could be added which would increase earnings. In this manner the point of maximum system earnings was determined.

The airlines, however, operate at a much larger scale than necessary to maximize system earnings. They must, of course, maintain larger fleets and make many more flights to accommodate demands for service which must be met even though at less than optimum profit. People in a low-density and short-haul area might get no service at all, and many passengers seeking service in a high-density area at busy traffic hours would not be serviced, if an airline sought and could maximize profits in the technical sense as discussed in Chapter 7. Competition and governmental regulations prevent them from trying even if they wanted to.

Therefore, the second phase of the selection process, which began at the point of maximum systems earnings, asked the question: Which flight with which aircraft, if added, will produce the largest increment of revenue compared to the added increment of cost? Flights were added until some specified level of operations was reached, such as a predetermined rate of return on average total fleet investment, or the assignment of all available aircraft.

4. Forecast. In this final step, the preceding steps continued until a result was reached which produced an acceptable degree of service and profitability. At this point summarization was then completed. The summaries included average airline flight distances, load factors, total passengers, and total passenger miles; airline operating expenses, operating revenues, and system return on investment; and aircraft utilization, flights, and number of each type required.

This model has proven to be very powerful, but it is one that cannot be managed without the modern computer.

OTHER MODELS. The model-building approach, such as indicated in simulation, is an econometric approach and can take many forms in forecasting. What it does (as will be explained in more detail in Chapter 14) is to find the major variables which will be responsible for a future movement and by projecting the variables make a prediction of the item under review. For example, the American Can Company has developed a model to forecast beer sales, which, in turn, of course, is used to determine production of cans for this purpose. The model is based upon the finding that the amount spent on beer tends to rise with family income. (NICB Study 106, 1963, p. 46-47.) Armour and Company has built a complex model to help it estimate the number of cattle which should be slaughtered in the future. Some of the variables in the model are past daily cattle slaughter, range grass conditions, steer-corn price ratio, hog-corn price ratio, cattle sent to feeder lots, and so on. (NICB Study 106, 1963, pp. 87-90.)

THE ECLECTIC APPROACH. Larger firms usually employ many different techniques to forecast sales in an eclectic approach. A typical procedure in a large company for making a short-term sales forecast might be as follows:
1. A projection is made by the company of GNP over the next year, to-

Table 8-12   Computer Simulation: An Evaluation

ADVANTAGES:
1. Can manage masses of data which no other technique can duplicate.
2. Permits speedy summarization on an entire system when detailed adjustments are made in any part of the system.
3. Encourages experimentation with data, and exploration of more alternatives.
4. Permits the development of details not possible with other methods when dealing with a large system.
5. Powerfully sharpens managerial judgment and intuition.

DISADVANTAGES:
1. Is expensive.
2. Must be developed and operated with the service of specialists.
3. Must be carefully watched by management to avoid a tendency to make forecasts by formula without proper injection of judgment.
4. At central headquarters the two estimates are compared and a semifinal forecast is made.
5. This forecast is then modified by top management to reflect internal and external forces over which it has some influence.
6. The final projections are used as a basis for current decisions.

gether with a forecast of economic conditions likely to affect the industry and the company.

2. Various techniques are used by the central headquarters staff to calculate industry sales and sales for each major product of the company.

3. Sales forecasts are built up from sales forces in the sections of the company and modified by managers and staff as they move to central headquarters.

METAMORPHOSIS FROM SALES TO PLANS. Why is it that management does not depend solely upon specialists for sales forecasts? Why does top management get involved? The answer is very simple. Management may get a forecast from a specialist which technically, in consideration of present and future environmental conditions, is perfect. For example, an accurate forecast of demand for fractional horsepower motors for a company may be calculated for next year as 100,000 units. Present capacity, however, may be only 90,000 units. Unless capacity is increased the company could not sell 100,000 units. If the 100,000 unit forecast were used as a basis of next year's plans it would hardly be a firm basis for ordering raw materials, setting production lines, and so on. Management must decide whether the next year's sales goal will be 90,000 or 100,000, or more. Management, for example, may decide that it should build a new plant because sales are going to continue to rise. But, it reasons, it would be uneconomical to build capacity for only 10,000 more units. An economical capacity addition would be at a minimum 20,000 units. Management may then decide to build the new plant but to increase sales to 110,000 by advertising, penetration of new markets, or other means.

In 1962-63 Pendleton shirts were very popular among teen-agers, and the company that produced them faced the question as to whether it should expand capacity to meet a certain next year's higher demand. It decided not to expand because it felt this was only a fad which would disappear and sales would get back to a more normal trend. The management was correct. This is what happened.

Management converts sales forecasts into sales goals for planning purposes. Top management can take into consideration conditions which no one else can and which result in goals and targets sometimes different than specialists' forecasts. It can change production and delivery schedules, alter costs and prices, change promotion and distribution programs, increase capacity, or abandon a product line if sales prospects are poor. Taking a forecast and modifying it to become a goal by considering such matters as these is the essence of planning.

SALES FORECASTING TECHNIQUES IN PRACTICE. Studies about methods actually used to make sales forecasts are not too comprehensive. They do seem to reveal, however, that most companies use sales department estimates, trend extrapolation, and correlations with general economic indicators (Sord and Welsch, 1958). Evidence indicates, too, that judgment alone stands high on the list of techniques used. Even where the most sophisticated tools of forecasting are used, managerial judgment is, or should be exercised throughout the process.

FACTORS IMPORTANT IN DETERMINING RESOURCES DEVOTED TO ECONOMIC FORECASTS

What factors are of importance in deciding how much of a company's resources should be devoted to making economic projections. The following are major criteria (adapted from Mallott, 1957, pp. 24-25):

STABILITY OF MARKETS. Firms which find their markets subject to important cyclical or seasonal variations in demand, or companies which have frequent model changes, generally need specially tailored forecasts. These companies cannot rely on standard forecasts acquired at low cost. Aircraft, steel, automobile, and most consumer durable goods producers, are in this category. Those companies which meet a stable product demand may rely more on standard economic forecasts. In this category are many of the producers of processed foodstuffs.

COMPLEXITY OF MARKETS. Companies which serve one or a few customers and can get a projection of the demand for their product from the customers have a simple forecasting problem. A supplier of a component to an automobile manufacturer might be in this position. Sears Roebuck and Company very frequently makes firm contracts with manufacturers for at least six months so that large production runs can result in lower prices. In contrast are companies serving many customers in many different industries. A producer of lawn mowers, or miscellaneous metal stampings, is in this classification and has a much rougher forecasting problem than manufacturers in the first group.

PRODUCTION SCHEDULES. Firms that produce goods for inventory on a very short time span have a much less complicated forecasting task than a company whose products take a long time to produce, are produced to order, and are subject to consumer deferral. Producers of power plant boilers, like Combustion Engineering, illustrate the latter type. Small machine shops producing standard fittings may illustrate the first.

RELATIONSHIP WITH ULTIMATE CUSTOMER. Companies that can identify one or a few ultimate customers, such as the producer of a special electronic device for a particular airplane, have a comparatively simple forecasting task as compared with a component producer who cannot identify readily his ultimate customers. In the latter category would be producers, for example, of basic fabricated steel shapes and forms, chemicals, or fractional horsepower motors.

AVAILABILITY OF DATA. For some companies the information needed to make good forecasts is not plentiful. If such companies also produce a product subject to great changes in demand, if intense competition prevails in the industry, and if variations in demand can have a profound impact on sales and profits, it is important that significant resources be devoted to economic forecasting. The aerospace and automobile companies, for example, are in this category. It is not at all unusual, therefore, to find sales forecasting absorbing important resources in such companies, and much of the forecasting amounts to original research.

COST AND UTILIZATION. Certainly cost and use is a factor in the determination of the economic forecasts needed by a company. No matter how interesting or useful a forecast might be a firm will not support it if its cost far exceeds its benefit. Cost-utility imbalance can occur also if the forecast is inexpensive but is of no use to the company.

HOW ACCURATE SHOULD SALES FORECASTS BE?

The answer to this question must depend upon the purposes for which the forecast is to be used. The record of forecasting accuracy is blemished and must raise the strongest warning signals about even the specialists' ability to look ahead with 20-20 foresight. One survey of 248 companies showed that the average deviation between the current year's forecast and actual performance was 8 percent. The median deviation was 5 percent, but the range was from 0 to 50 percent (Mallott, 1957, p. 148). Experience will vary over cyclical movements. Another study showed very large errors near cyclical troughs. For example, this study asked companies the percentage by which actual sales varied from forecasted sales which were estimated at the beginning of the accounting year. Variation was requested for the month (or quarter) of each year when sales were highest, and for the month (or quarter) when sales were lowest. The time covered was 1957 to 1961, a period registering an economic recession. For all manufacturing companies, sales forecasts were overestimated by more than 15 percent in 1958. For primary metals the overestimate was 25 percent in 1958 and an underestimate was reported of 25 percent in 1959. Deviations, plus or minus, ranged as high as 28 percent among different industry groups. (Joint Economic Committee, 1962, p. 15.) When aggregates were off as much as 25 percent the chances are that individual products sales are off much more. There is plenty of evidence to show that in periods of rising business activity forecasts of sales tend to be understated, and in periods of declining activity the forecasts are too high. This

certainly is borne out in this study. (Carlson, 1967, pp. 462-481.) It springs from
the fact that the future cannot be foreseen with high accuracy and even the best
forecaster not only is forced to depend heavily on past and current trends but
tends to give them too much weight because of the uncertainties of the future.

Sord and Welsch (1956, p. 137) reported in their study that many executives
said their actual total sales were often only 5 percent off the forecast, but budgeting problems nonetheless were serious because estimates for specific products were
off as much as 25 percent within this aggregate.

The AMA (1956, p. 149) study cited above asked executives what deviations
from forecasts of sales were acceptable. About half reported that 10 percent was
acceptable, but answers ranged from 1 to 25 percent. Service and trade organizations, manufacturers of industrial materials, and miscellaneous suppliers for industry tend to regard 5 percent as the required accuracy for short-range forecasts
of sales.

Short-range forecasting accuracy for sales depends much upon problems of
forecasting. It is much easier to be more accurate in forecasting a service or
product where demand is relatively stable over time, such as electricity and
chewing gum, than a product such as a machine tool with a high unit value, a
deferrable demand, and a long production leadtime.

Accuracy should increase with experience. Accuracy also can be expected to
decrease the longer the time span of the forecast.

In sum, very short-range forecasts for planning purposes of a month or
calendar quarter should seek to be within 2 percent accuracy. For longer periods
of time, up to a year, a 5 percent deviation should be sought. For five years or
more a 10 to 15 percent deviation may be acceptable. These deviations would
also apply to such forecasts as GNP.

SUMMARY AND GUIDELINES FOR DEVELOPING
AND USING PREMISES

This chapter examined the nature of major premises entering into the planning process. Types of premises identified and discussed were: implied, high impact, low impact, analytical, and procedural. It was noted that most, but not
all, premises involve forecasts and the range of forecasts important to a firm is
very wide. This necessitates an important choice by management and staff of
those forecasts to receive attention as well as resources to be devoted to the task.

Because of the high importance to the average firm of economic forecasts,
particularly a firm's sales forecasts, most of the chapter was devoted to this topic.
Factors important in determining resources to be devoted to economic forecasts
were presented. It was noted that managers and staff now have a rich palette
of forecasting methods. Most sales forecasts use a variety of techniques, the most
predominant of which is the jury of executive opinion.

The development of premises is essential to effective planning. In the selection, preparation, and use of premises, management becomes involved with both line and staff. This involvement means that certain types of premises are made principally by management. Certain types of premises are made principally by staff, and management must lay down expectations for their quality and use. A few guidelines for managers in meeting these responsibilities conclude this chapter.

First, management, with the help of staff, must choose those premises of most importance to the company and determine the resources and personnel to be devoted to their preparation. Management should make these decisions on a systematic rather than *ad hoc* basis to the fullest extent possible. A large number of these decisions, to meet this principle, should be made in an organized planning process. Management must determine whether forecasts will be made in the company, outside the company, or a combination of both. Management must also determine which planning premises it alone will make, which premises made by staff it must approve, and which premises made by staff need no management approval.

Second, managers should not take forecasts on faith. They should expect a clear, brief statement of assumptions underlying a forecast and the methods used to make it. All forecasts are based upon assumptions which should be understood by the user. In one case a general manager of a company accepted a forecast of a competitor's price increase, which he promptly followed. He did not know his staff expert had assumed the competitor would advance his price immediately because his costs were rising sharply. This assumption—which the general manager might have questioned had he known about it—was wrong; and because of his price differential, the competitor got enough of an increase in business to spread fixed costs and yield a satisfactory profit at the old price. The general manager eventually had to reduce his price and the experience proved to be rather costly.

When a manager knows the assumptions used in a forecast it will be easier for him to develop mentally a modified forecast if he does not agree with the assumptions. Furthermore, the basic methodology in developing a forecast should be understood by the manager. Forecasts need not, nor should they, be loaded with excessive details about methodology, especially if the details involve a language foreign to the manager. But a manager should know the basic methods used. This will make it easier for him to alter the forecast if he distrusts the methods.

Managers cannot say they are in no position to judge the reasoning underlying a forecast because they do not know the assumptions or understand the methods used. It is their responsibility to know.

Third, managers must expect forecasts that are not too qualified. Most technicians are reluctant to make specific forecasts in time and value. This is understandable because they know what a hazardous occupation economic forecasting really is. As a result, they will qualify if they can so that a wide band of latitude provides them an escape. However, if a forecast is to be used to make decisions upon which basis internal resource allocations are to be made, managers must have forecasts that are precise in time and quantity. On the other hand, a long-range forecast of what competitors are likely to do need not be as precise.

Managers must decide upon their expectations of precision of forecasts. This is an important responsibility that should not be lightly dismissed. Too severe expectations are not likely to be met and may bring about a deterioration of line-staff relationships. On the other hand, too liberal expectations will likely produce the same problem but for different reasons. In the first instance, staff will feel management expects too much; and in the second case, management will feel it is not getting proper forecasts.

Fourth, the system of forecasting and any particular forecast should be economical. Its costs should be less than benefits derived by the company from it. Technicians who make forecasts are often prone to dig deeply into their subject because of their intense interest in protecting themselves with plenty of factual information, as well as in satisfying their intellectual curiosity. One manager who understood this proclivity once told me: "I must watch my economist for he is likely to run off to get information and I won't see him for weeks." Forecasting can be very costly and the cost-benefit equation requires constant attention.

Fifth, managers must understand that a forecasting method which has produced accurate forecasts in the past may suddenly fail. Furthermore, an expert forecaster who has had high marks in accurate forecasting may suddenly produce a very inaccurate forecast. There is no infallible method to project economic conditions into the future. There are few if any coming events that are important to a company, whether internal or external, which can be predicted precisely with an assurance of high accuracy.

It can be said, however, that the more managers and their staffs work on forecasting, the more accurately they will do it. There is no quantitative proof of this assertion, but I have made it a practice to ask those who make forecasts professionally, both in industry and outside it, whether they do become more proficient at forecasting the more they do it. The answer is positive 100 percent of the time!

9
Nature and Development
of Business Strategies

9
Nature and Development
of Business Strategies

INTRODUCTION

Previous chapters noted that business managers are devoting increased attention to strategic planning. This is so because by definition strategic planning is concerned with those basic factors which spell the success or failure of a company. In the strategic planning process the fundamental missions and objectives of an enterprise are set. Here, too, the basic strategies for reaching objectives are determined.

The importance of strategies is framed in a comment made some years ago by General Robert E. Wood of Sears, Roebuck and Company, who was himself a superb strategic planner. He said (Chandler, Jr., 1962, p. 235*): "Business is like war in one respect, if its grand strategy is correct, any number of tactical errors can be made and yet the enterprise proves successful."

Despite the great significance of strategy to a company it has not received the attention in many companies, nor in the scholarly literature, that it deserves. Bruce Henderson ("Preventing Strategy Obsolescence") put his finger on one reason for this shortsightedness in pointing out that the success of any business is dependent upon the superior use of its distinguishing characteristics. There are few companies, however, that systematically examine the strategy that brought them to their present success. Moreover, he says: "success reinforces the organization's belief in the essential correctness of past methods, philosophy, and competitive posture. So long as the underlying competitive conditions and relationships continue to hold, the corporate success may continue also. But in time,

---

* *Strategy and Structure: Chapters in the History of the Industrial Enterprise* by A. D. Chandler, Jr. Copyright © 1962 by The M.I.T. Press, Cambridge, Massachusetts, and used by permission.

these conditions must change. This is why strategies become obsolete and inappropriate in a changing world. It is a matter of common observation that more companies seem to fall prey to creeping decline than to identifiable or specific management mistakes in decision."

Too little attention has been devoted to strategic planning and the development of strategy in the academic world. Not only are the words muzzied in a semantic embranglement but the subject matter is not as easy to master as other areas of business activity and therefore has not received the attention it deserves. The art of strategic planning is barely beginning to take precedence over the more systematic and routine elements of business administration. But because of long neglect, work on strategic planning must expand importantly for a proper balance to be struck between the two. (Cyert and Dill 1964, pp. 226-228.)

In this chapter the definition of strategy will be examined in some detail. This will be followed by an analysis of different types of strategies, how a firm may go about developing them, and some guides for management's developing and appraising strategies.

THE MEANING OF STRATEGY

The word strategy literally means "the art of the general," being derived from the ancient Greek word *strategos* which meant, strictly, a general. Strategy in ancient Greece meant what a general did.

The use of the word strategy extends back to at least 400 B.C. but did not appear in writings until the latter part of the 18th century. Before Napoleon's time, strategy referred to the art and science of directing military forces to defeat an enemy or to mitigate the results of defeat. In Napoleon's day, strategy was extended to include political and economic moves to improve the chances for military victory.

It has only been in the past fifteen years that strategy has found its way into business literature. One major stimulus probably was the development of the theory of games, with its emphasis upon and use of the word strategy. Strategy in game theory is concerned principally with a statistical set of rules for a player in a game to improve the probabilities of a desired payoff.

Although there is considerable confusion today in the uses of the words strategic planning, strategic plan, and strategy, there is a growing consensus. One characteristic of the consensus is the widening of the meaning of the words strategic plan and strategy.

Strategic planning was defined in Chapter 2 as the process of deciding the basic mission of a company, the objectives which it seeks to achieve, and the major strategies and policies governing the use of resources at the disposal of the firm to achieve its objectives. The result of this process, among other things, is a strategic plan. The strategic plan includes, therefore, the missions, objectives, strategies, and policies produced by the strategic planning process.*

Although the above definition of strategic planning does not specifically mention competition, it clearly implies the taking of actions in light of what a competitor might do. But my definition of strategic planning implies much more. Strategic planning can and should deal with anything that is highly important to the success of the company. It includes the adjustment of the organization to the external environment, altering the organization to reflect internal environmental changes, solving basic problems created by competition as well as other environmental forces, coping with limitations, capitalizing on inherent advantages, finding new opportunities, thwarting threats, and so on. Strategic planning can result in a company action to assume certain social responsibilities which will help to improve the environment in which the business operates. It can concern internal moves that may be far removed from the immediate competitive world, such as an action in a management-labor dispute. Although strategic planning may include decisions not directly related to the immediate or long-range competitive environment of a firm, the fact that competition occupies the major attention of management means that the words strategic planning are heavily loaded with competitive connotations.

J. Knight Allen (1965, p. 10) has called strategic planning a common-sense, practical device for assuring that management adopts the so-called systems approach to its work. So it is. Strategic planning is concerned with vitally important plans for dealing with external forces and internal developments that determine the long-range success of a business as an integrated whole.

Strategy means a specific action, usually but not always the deployment of resources, to achieve an objective decided upon in strategic planning. The development of strategy is a part of strategic planning. Strategy can be said to be a plan, but a different type plan than the strategic plan. For example, a strategic plan may set forth the objective of increasing market share for product X in two years by 50 percent. The strategy chosen to do this may be to automate the plant producing the product, in order to reduce unit cost, so that price can be cut while maintaining profit. In this way, market will be captured from competitors who have obsolete plants and cannot cut the price correspondingly without incurring a loss.

Developing a strategy is usually a very difficult and fateful task. It usually means questioning old methods, exploring unfamiliar environmental waters, facing up to an objective evaluation of strengths and weaknesses, forcing important changes on people in the firm and organizational arrangements, and taking high

---

* In a general way this definition is the same as that of a number of distinguished writers in this field. See, for example, Anthony (1965), p. 16; Bower (1966), pp. 47-48; Learned, Christensen, Andrews and Guth (1965), p. 17; Henderson (1964), p. 23; and Tilles (1963a), p. 112.

risks with the firm's capital. This has to be done in a world of rapid change, and it has to be done continuously.

The words strategy, objective, and policy are very different in a fundamental sense. But it is not always easy to distinguish one from the other.

TYPES OF STRATEGIES

There are many different types of strategies in a business. It is useful to consider a few classifications to clarify the dimensions which exist.

First, is a classification based upon scope and importance. This includes what might be called a *master strategy*. Some writers speak of this as embracing the entire pattern of basic company mission and the means to pursue it. (W. Newman, 1967, p. 77.) The master strategy would include any change in mission, plus the objectives, policies, and specific means to deploy resources in order to succeed in the new direction. (This, of course, I have called strategic planning.)

A *pure strategy* is the specific deployment of resources in one area of activity, such as a decision to counteract a price move by a competitor by increasing customer services in a specific way.

A *mixed strategy* involves combining pure strategies and employing them in ways that are somewhat determined by circumstances. Thus, in the above illustration, additional moves might involve raising advertising expenditures if increasing customer services do not achieve the desired results, improving the quality of the product by further expenditures for research and modification, holding price but giving more discounts for volume, or a combination of these moves.

Second, is a classification based on organization. Strategy is something that is of concern, principally, to top management. But in a large company, particularly a multiproduct decentralized one, strategic planning and the development of strategy is conducted at several levels—principally at headquarters and also among the major divisions. As noted elsewhere, however, divisions develop their strategies within those prepared at headquarters. If any demarcation is desired, one may be called "corporate strategy" and the other "divisional strategy," or the overall company strategy may be called "master strategy," or the lower-level strategies can be called "substrategies." Perhaps a new word, such as "stratics" may be useful to delineate the two.

Third, is a classification based upon the quality of the strategy. Patrick Haggerty, now Chairman of the Board of Texas Instruments, says there are many different types of strategies among which he identifies "hold-the-line" strategies, "modest-gain" strategies, and "break-through" strategies. He thinks of those strategies in terms of impact on sales and profits. Each has its proper place in a company.

Fourth, strategies can be concerned with forces external to the firm, internal, or both. External strategy may be determined to reflect a competitor's move, an action by government, or the discovery of a new opportunity. Internal strategy deals with matters inside a firm, such as a reorganization to alter the way management will deal with people. A reorganization, of course, can result from outside forces.

Fifth, strategy can be concerned with material as well as nonmaterial resources at the disposal of the firm. Most strategy deals with physical resources. But strategy can concern the use of managers, scientific personnel, and other employees. Strategy can be concerned with patterns and ways of thinking, such as a company's attitudes towards its social responsibilities.

Sixth, strategies may be classified in terms of personal or business strategies.

Seventh, strategies may be classified by area and function. These last two classifications will be given fuller treatment in the following discussion.

PERSONAL AND BUSINESS STRATEGIES

Because men manage companies, their personal strategies may be distinguished from business strategies. But the two get inextricably mixed and hard to disentangle. These personal strategies of managers are rules of thumb which capture their values, motivations, protections from a hostile environment, methods to change their environment, techniques for dealing with people and getting things done, and ways to maximize their satisfactions and basic needs. As noted in Chapter 7, a manager's personal strategies constitute a fundamental, and generally unwritten, framework within which business strategy is developed.

Classification of personal strategies is a matter of personal choice (Dalton McFarland, 1964, pp. 153-157; and William Newman, 1951, pp. 110-118). Strategies may be aggressive, such as the following: divide and rule, strike while the iron is hot, mass a concentrated offensive, in union there is strength, divide and conquer, and never yield to inferior force. On the other hand, personal strategies may be mild, if not passive. In this area one may find such strategies as: time is a great healer, sow seeds on fertile ground, avoid action until success is certain, avoid decisive engagements when in a weak position, start small, and, things get worse before they get better. Strategies may relate to timing, personal power, dealing with others, and careers, to name a few classifications.

It is sometimes difficult to tell where personal strategies end and purely business strategies begin, if there is a demarcation at all. For example, Karl von Clausewitz said, "The best strategy is always to be very strong, first generally, then at the decisive point." This can, of course, be both a strategy governing personal affairs as well as a military or business strategy. How many times have inappropriate strategies come out acceptably in the end largely because of personal aphorisms of top executives, such as: "Never give up," or "If at first you don't succeed, try, try, and try again." Many business mistakes have been corrected by the tenacity, pressure, and drive of an executive.

An illustration of how personal values may affect a firm's strategy is that of a large research and development company which had most of its work in government contracts and was considering three strategies, as follows: (1) Try to triple sales over the next three to five years by expanding its research base and getting a larger share of growing government contracts; (2) achieve the same sales goal but through production of hardware, on the commercial market, which grows out of its research activity; and (3) aim for a slower growth rate and keep within the same type business.

Three vice presidents of the company had different values which had a bearing on the acceptability of these strategies. One was business-science-oriented and wanted to make as much money as possible while still being part of an intellectually stimulating firm. He wanted profits but from an exclusively research company. Another had the value orientations of a materialist who wanted growth and profitability from widening markets and internal efficiency. He saw that the best path to this goal lay in the commercialization of hardware production. The third was more scientifically oriented. He wanted to continue present research activities and viewed with alarm getting into commercial production.

Taking these motivations and values into consideration, the president felt the best strategy would be to double sales over the next five years by continuing the business along the lines which had brought it to its present position. In this way he felt he was best accommodating the values of his top executives. (Guth and Tagiuri, 1965, pp. 123-124.)

Managers are not always aware of their own values and personal strategies. Furthermore, although they tend to be rather fixed, they do change over time and have different degrees of priority that vary with age and circumstances. Behavioral scientists also conclude that managers are not as perceptive as they should be in sensing the motives and strategies of others. Those who have deep understanding of their own and others' strategies are in a position of advantage.

CHIEF EXECUTIVE IMPACT ON
STRATEGIC PLANNING

All that has been said previously makes it quite clear that the chief executive is the chief strategist of his firm. At this particular point it is useful to classify some of the major ways in which he exercises an impact on strategic planning.

His aspirations about his personal life, the life of his company as an institution, and the lives of those involved in his business, are major determinants of choice of strategy. His mores, habits, and ways of doing things determine how he behaves and decides. His sense of obligation to his company will decide his devotion and choice of subject matter to think about. The rewards system which he is responsible for establishing and maintaining will be significant in how people respond to the strategic planning program. The way the top executive level of the company is organized is his choice and, as noted previously, is vitally important to strategic planning. The time horizon which the chief executive has will obviously impact heavily on planning. These are but a few of the major personal characteristics of the chief executive which must be examined in considering his influence on strategic planning.

FUNCTIONAL STRATEGIES

Strategies can be classified by area and function of a business. Our interest here is not in being definitive but in illustrating. Examples will be given only of overall company, growth, product, market, and financial strategies (for a definitive compilation see Cannon, 1968).

OVERALL COMPANY STRATEGIES. Ralph Cordiner (1960), when Chairman of the Board of General Electric Company, said: "The essence of a sound international business strategy is . . . to integrate the interests of the share owners, their home country, and the host countries. None of these interests can be slighted without weakening the entire structure over the long term." This basic strategy led General Electric to a wide range of substrategies and policies to govern its overseas operations.

Often a major strategic move by a company will give it a new momentum, a new height of achievement—as when IBM decided to produce computers after a near-fatal delay in getting into the business; or when Boeing decided to use its own capital to produce an airplane that eventually became the KC-130 tanker which in turn resulted in the Boeing 707. It is also possible that a mistaken strategy can spell disaster or loss of position that a company finds it hard to recover. When Henry Ford stayed too long with his Model T in the 1930's, he lost a position that took years to regain.

Sears Roebuck has made a number of major strategic decisions over a long period of time that have elevated it to the dominant position in the U.S. in retailing goods. John McDonald (1964, pp. 120 and 123) has identified ten of these as follows:

"The fateful decision in the mid-1920's to add retail stores to the original catalogue business as the farm population came to town in automobiles.

"The decision to centralize merchandising (all buying, promotional, and advertising operations) in Chicago, and to control store operations from territorial headquarters—a unique management structure that forms the warp and woof of Sears today.

"The decision to control the cost, quality, and quantity of Sears' merchandise by having deliveries made to its own specifications. Sears today is responsible for the design details of 95 percent of the goods it sells.

"The sweeping decision after World War II to expand aggressively, to relocate old stores and put new stores in new locations. Thus Sears very early preempted the prize locations as the population went from East to West and from the city to the suburbs.

"The decision in the mid-1950's to expand its sale of soft goods in retail stores, that is, to go to full-line department stores in place of the old hardware sort of stores featuring tools and fishing tackle.

"The more recent decision to play up style and fashion along with economy, a decision that has modernized Sears' image and, incidentally, made it one of the largest mink and diamond merchants in the country.

"The decision to set up a service organization, despite its low or zero profitability, to support the sales of Sears' durable goods.

"The decision to diversify into insurance and other financial services in the Allstate operation, which has possibilities of becoming as big as Sears itself one day. (Right now the corporation is about ready to add a mutual-fund selling operation to Allstate.)

"A series of decisions to invest in supplier corporations, which not only increased Sears' prime strength in distribution but has led to some sizable capital gains.

"Finally, a series of decisions to invest heavily in superior personnel, in part through large-scale training programs (200 to 500 college graduates a year go through these), and related decisions to promote from within, to be generous with profit-sharing, and also to purchase Sears' own stock for the profit-sharing fund, as a result of which the employees today own about 26 percent of the common. The result of such policies has been that Sears has superior management in considerable depth—indeed, it is the target now of management raids by Ward's."

An overall company strategy of the Ford Motor Company, which seems apparent from its actions, is as follows: (1) get as much growth from the U.S. market as possible by capturing small annual increases in market share, (2) achieve a substantial penetration of the faster-growing overseas market, (3) establish a solid position in the defense market, and (4) place abundant Ford capital and management in profitable opportunities here and abroad in the nonautomotive field (Sheehan, 1962).

GROWTH STRATEGIES. Growth is a major objective of most companies; there seems to be a prevailing business philosophy that a firm cannot be healthy if it does not grow. Peter Gutmann (1964, p. 36) examined 53 companies that achieved exceptionally rapid expansion in sales, total profits, and profits per share, and asked what basic strategies they chose. He concluded they were as follows:

"Selection, as the area of business activity, of fast-growth industries and market segments.

"Participation in industries which are still at relatively early phases of industrial growth.

"Expansion into new markets, including foreign markets.

"Adoption of new-product policies.

"Acquisition of other firms."

Texas Instruments is a classic illustration of substantial growth resulting from a decision to get into a fast-growing industry. In 1949, Patrick Haggerty, who was president at that time, decided: "We are a good little company. Now we must become a good *big* company." (McDonald, 1961, p. 123.) Sales of the company were then about $6.4 million, derived from a variety of engineering services and production of highly technically oriented products, including electronics. Haggerty said that "big" to him meant $200 million sales. The objective was a powerful motivator and the management set about to reach this level. After searching around, it decided as a major strategy to enter the semiconductor business. The substrategy or tactic, whichever one prefers, was to develop the silicon transistor, the pocket radio, and a process to make pure silicon. As everyone now knows, production of transistors and small radios turned out to be a major growth industry. This was not clear to everyone at the time. Furthermore, it took great courage for T. I. to risk its capital on mass production in this area when very large competitors had vastly more experience than T. I. But T. I. succeeded and sales rose from $24 million in 1954 to $590 million in 1966!

IBM has grown rapidly because it was in a rapidly growing industry. But choosing an industry that will grow rapidly is only part of the story. Two decades ago there were companies in a stronger position in the office machine market than IBM. In 1951 the company made a major strategic decision. Leaders in the business machine industry had prospered during World War II and several were larger than IBM. During the Korean War, IBM looked ahead and saw tough competition and the obligation to get on top of computer technology. It decided to increase substantially its research expenditures, which already were large, even though the result was a drop in short-range profits. The result is well known. The company produced a superior product which, with additional major strategic moves in resource applications to service and software, has placed it clearly at the top of the industry. IBM now has about 75 percent of the computer market.

Many companies have found a product-mix combination strategy to be the correct road to growth and profits. These combinations are four in number, as shown in the following simple analysis:

PRODUCT \ MARKET	OLD	NEW
OLD		
NEW		

Gutmann (1964) said that 98 percent of the companies he studied chose the sale of old products in old markets as the road to growth. This strategy is only successful, of course, if the old market is growing rapidly. Coca-Cola is a good example of this strategy. Most of its growth has come from aggressive selling of its one product in every corner of the world. However, it has recently begun to diversify.

Gutmann found that 80 percent of the companies he studied chose to sell new products in old markets. No firm can long prosper without changing its product or product line. Minnesota Mining & Manufacturing is an example of a company that has registered rapid growth through new product development. Kellogg has doubled sales in recent years through a continuous introduction of new products for its old markets.

About 40 percent of Gutmann's sample grew through the strategy of developing new products for new markets. DuPont's introduction of nylon illustrates this strategy. Many companies have grown rapidly with this strategy, combined with a strategy of acquisition. W. R. Grace, for example, traditionally is considered as a shipping company operating principally between the U.S. and South America. About fifteen years ago Peter Grace decided he wished to grow faster than this traditional market was likely to permit. He began a large diversification program in the chemicals industry and is now important in this industry. General Motors in the 1930's entered the railroad motive power market with its new diesel engine and in an incredibly short period of time virtually completely eliminated the older steam locomotives.

Some companies have grown fast through the expansion of sales in new markets from their old products. But this is not a typical strategy. Gutmann found only 6 percent of his cases attributed growth to this strategy. A number of architectural and engineering firms have begun overseas operations and shown overall growth as a result.

Burlington Industries, the nation's largest textile firm, shows a different type of growth pattern. Over a forty-year period James Love pursued a large acquisition program by means of which the company became the nation's largest textile firm. When he died in 1962 the company abandoned that strategy and substituted for it a strategy of profit growth through internal expansion and plant improvement. The strategy was to concentrate on profit improvement in areas where the company knew it had strength and forget tackling unknown problems that come with acquisitions. (Freedgood, 1964.)

PRODUCT STRATEGIES. Product strategies may be considered in many categories, among which the following are outstanding and will be used for illustration: nature of the product line; new product development; quality, performance, and obsolescence; dropping old products; and marketing and distribution of products.

The production and sale of a product or service is the reason a business firm exists. Companies must choose the nature of the product line they wish to make and sell and decisions must be made about the mix of products in a line. A classic strategic decision was that of General Motors prior to World War I. Ford was giving the much smaller General Motors stiff competition. It had more than half the market with two cars, the high-volume, low-priced Model T, and the low-volume, high-priced Lincoln. General Motors had about 12 percent of the market. The prevailing view at General Motors at the time was to meet Ford head-on with a revolutionary car design. General Motors then had a line of ten cars, a number of which were in the same price range but none at the low end of a price range. The decision was made to compete over a wide range of price (from $450 to $3,500 in six price classifications), and each car in the line was conceived as having a proper relationship to the others, in an integrated line.

The company then set out on an intricate strategy which was enormously successful. In the words of Alfred Sloan (1964, pp. 67-68), one of the architects of this strategy: "We proposed in general that General Motors should place its cars at the top of each price range and make them of such a quality that they would attract sales from below that price, selling to those customers who might be willing to pay a little more for the additional quality, and attract sales also from above that price, selling to those customers who would see the price advantage in a car of close to the quality of higher-priced competition. This amounted to quality competition against cars below a given price tag, and price competition against cars above that price tag. Of course, a competitor could respond in kind, but where we had little volume we could thereby chip away an increase from above and below, and where we had volume it was up to us to maintain it. Unless the number of models was limited, we said, and unless it was planned that each model should cover its own grade and also overlap into the grades above and below its price, a large volume could not be secured for each car. This large volume, we observed, was necessary to gain the advantages of quantity production, counted on as a most important factor in earning a position of pre-eminence in all the grades."

Ford monopolized the low-price field, but General Motors' strategy was not to meet Ford head-on with the same type and price automobile; rather, the strategy was to produce a better car than Ford and price it at the top end of the low-price field. The price was near that of Ford's, but with the superior car the idea was that demand would be drawn from the Ford grade of car to the slightly higher price in preference to Ford's utility design. This strategy worked and was the basis for the rise of a major corporation. This was a strategy that Ford used after World War II.

New product development raises all sorts of possible strategies, ranging from decisions about research expenditures to the nature, extent, and timing of new product developments. During the past ten years, Pennsalt, a basic chemicals producer, has tripled profits. The reason is that about ten years ago the company decided to concentrate its basic research efforts in six specific channels that appeared to have potential. They were organic sulfur chemicals, organic nitrogen compounds, rubber chemicals, high-energy chemicals, exploratory chemistry, and fluorine chemistry. The decision was right and the Company has prospered. (*Business Week*, 1965c.)

Another product strategy area is that of quality, performance, and obsolescence. The major aerospace companies give high priority to the quality and performance of their products. DuPont has built a widespread reputation for quality products. In a study of the electronics industry, Tilles (undated) concluded that companies which were most successful pursued new product developments in a manner consistent with their distinctive competence.

When two products are considered by consumers to be about equal, the differential advantage of one over the other may be in styling. This sort of situation makes styling of critical importance in sales volume, and leads to a sort of planned obsolescence by means of which firms try to excite consumers to buy new models before the old ones are really worn out. Women's apparel, television sets, and automobiles are industries where this consideration is significant.

There are many other classifications of product strategies. What is said here is only illustrative. More discussion of product strategies will be found in Chapter 18.

MARKET STRATEGIES. Marketing and product strategies are very closely related because they both are developed in response to consumer demands. The scope of possible marketing strategies is wide and would include at least the following areas: distribution channels, marketing services, market research, pricing, selling and advertising, packaging, product brand, and selection of markets. In each of these areas spectrums of choice are open. Selected strategies are illustrated below.

Chas. Pfizer, a major pharmaceutical company, made a major strategic decision in its international business some years ago when it decided to do its own marketing rather than operate through joint ventures or partnerships with foreign nationals. For many years the large chemical companies have been important producers of nitrogenous materials, mainly ammonia. Their strategy in capturing the market for these products has been to acquire fertilizer suppliers, manufacturers, and distributors.

Acme Visible Records, Inc., is a small company in the office equipment industry. In 1965 its volume rose 23 percent as compared with the industry average of 11 percent. Its profits rose 39 percent compared with the average in the industry of 24 percent. This performance was attributed to a strategy which concentrated efforts on highly trained, specialized salesmen who, with the help of home-office engineers, custom-designed systems for most of the company's customers. (*Business Week*, 1967b.)

Pricing strategy is also of great significance. Some companies have or try to give the impression of having a superior product and then price a little bit above the competition. Other companies seek to hold price below that of competitors and thereby increase sales volume. Before pricing an article there should be a strategy. Some of the more commonly considered strategies for pricing new products would include:

"1. Get as much profit as you can, as soon as you can.
2. Set a price that will discourage the advent of competitors.
3. Recover your development costs within a specified period.
4. Set a price that will yield your 'regular' rate of return.
5. Set a price that will win speediest acceptance of the product.
6. Use the product to enhance the sales of the entire line rather than to yield a profit on itself." (Oxenfeldt, 1959, p. 338.)

FINANCIAL STRATEGIES. Financial strategies are vitally important to the survival and growth of a company. Indeed, all strategies are successful or unsuccessful depending upon the extent to which they affect the financial position of a company. This is the ultimate test of a strategy.

Here again, the field of play is enormous. Financial strategies can include such areas as divestment of unwanted assets, extent of customer credit, obtaining funds, financing basic research, and expenditures on major capital facilities. Strategy attaches not only to the decisions made in these areas but between suppliers of capital as well.

Divestment of losing products can be a significant strategic move. When John Connelly headed Crown Cork in 1957 the firm was on the verge of bankruptcy. The world's leading producer of bottle caps was losing money and customers and was heavily in debt. Instead of presiding over a dying enterprise Connelly began a series of moves that reversed the company's fortunes, which involved the disinvestment of unprofitable subsidiaries and product lines. Between 1957 and 1960 he rid the company of more than $20 million of unprofitable business. He sold a tinplate mill and abandoned the production of plastic deodorant containers, icebox trays, copper electronic components, and literally thousands of special-size closures which the company had obligingly supplied to customers who wanted something a little different. (Whalen, 1962, p. 163.)

DEVELOPING STRATEGIES

In my own experience there seem to be two very broad approaches to the development of strategies. On the one hand, the strategy is perfectly obvious. "Our product is obsolete, losing money, and since we cannot modify it easily, we must abandon it and fill the gap in some other way." On the other hand, the solution to the problem is not obvious, and when an executive makes a decision the process by means of which he makes it is not readily identified. In between is a variety of possible approaches.

For decisions as important as strategies the final determination generally rests on intuition, philosophy, and the innovative genius of the executive deciding. The development of strategy alternatives, however, for the most part can and must be based on a methodical, analytical, and rigorous examination of relevant forces. We know rather little about the first process but a good bit about the second. Throughout this process, however—from hard and rigorous analysis wherever that is possible, to the final application of a manager's intuitive decision—emphasis upon the perception, thinking, and creativity in individuals and groups is the proper road to success.

Unfortunately, there are no ready-made formulas, steps, or models to assure that a correct strategy is always chosen. We are not even able to classify strategies comprehensively, let alone display a sure-fire method for making them easily and optimally. However, there are a number of approaches to developing strategies which are highly useful in making the task easier and, if used judiciously, are likely to produce better strategies. The nine approaches presented below are not mutually exclusive; some are intertwined with others. Furthermore, each has its own strength when applied in a way to maximize that strength.

INTEGRATED CORPORATE PLANNING. A major process for developing strategies is through integrated corporate planning. Enough has been said in previous chapters about the uses of this process in developing strategies and the reasons why it is so powerful. Although all of the approaches described below can and usually do form a part of this overall planning process, it is appropriate to identify the entire system as a basic and fundamental approach. Also, the following approaches can be used in cases where a company does not have an integrated formal planning program.

In speaking of approaches to the development of strategies, one certainly should include all the tools and methods that are employed in determining where to look and how to evaluate and decide. For instance, a major new technique which is becoming more widely used in strategic planning is the mixing of probability theory with simulation on computers. These tools will be examined in detail in later chapters. At this point it should only be noted that those which are treated later are subsumed under those presented here.

ADAPTIVE SEARCH. Adaptive search is phraseology which I think Ansoff (1965a, pp. 24-28) first used. He also speaks of it as the "cascade approach," which is perhaps more descriptive. This approach formulates rules in gross terms and then successively refines alternatives through several stages as the generation of a solution proceeds. The method gives the appearance of solving the same problem several times over, but this is not the case. It is a serial solution, each step of which builds upon but does not necessarily duplicate the last. The methodology contrasts, for example, with many operations research solutions, where some objective is to be optimized and a solution is calculated once, as in an inventory replenishment problem.

In adoptive search a major decision is made—for example, whether or not to diversify product line. This is a first step. A second step takes place when a choice is made whether to diversify by investment in a research and development program or by acquiring other companies. A third step takes place in defining the product areas for research, if that is the choice; or deciding in which among the different industries the acquisition search will proceed. Additional steps are obvious in this chain of decision-making. The Ford Motor Company, for example, decided it wanted to get into defense business. It chose to build up a research capability by starting Aeronutronics, in Newport Beach, California. Later it chose also the acquisition route by buying Philco in Philadelphia. Since then it has been making strategic choices with respect to product development in both these firms.

Procedures within each step are similar. A set of objectives is established, the difference between the current position of the firm and the objective is estimated, courses of action are proposed and evaluated, and a final course of action is chosen to meet the objectives or new alternatives are tried. The simplicity of this approach should not lead to an underestimation of its power and efficiency.

INTUITION. By intuition is meant innate or instinctive knowledge, a quick or ready apprehension, without recourse to inference or reasoning. In most major decisions, facts are not complete enough to make the final choice, and a final intuitive judgmental factor is applied from which a decision follows. This does not mean the factual basis is unimportant. On the contrary, the better the factual base for a manager the narrower is the range in applying intuition and the more pertinent it is likely to be.

In 1954 Charles Revson (1964) decided he wanted a refillable lipstick case that was more elegant than the "brass bullets" then on the market. What he wanted was not the usual cosmetic article, but fashion. He said: "I want to see luxury, fashion, expensive jewelry. No more bullets." His strategy was to appeal to the fashion instincts, needs, and desires of women. For a full year he got a constant series of negative responses from his staff, many of whom had been in the business as long as he. Revson persisted and chose the name Futurama for the new product. Expert opinion said this word was too masculine and sounded too much like General Motors who at the time had a motor car display with the same name. Again Revson overrode opposition. The product was produced and became an instant success. Revlon's sales leaped from $34 million in 1954 to $96 million in 1957, which was the peak year for Futurama.

AD HOC, TRIAL AND ERROR. A number of companies have used the *ad hoc* approach in acquisitions with some measure of success. In this approach, for example, a newspaper may acquire a paper mill to assure its supply of raw material. This in turn may lead to purchasing timberland, to finding outlets for the capacity of the mills over that demanded by the newspaper, and so on to other ventures. A not-so-successful trial and error approach was that used by Alcoa following World War II in marketing alloyed aluminum bearings for diesel loco-motives. Alcoa went through nine years of frustration trying a variety of market-ing strategies—large diesel manufacturers, large bearing manufacturers, small bearing manufacturers, and engine users. This particular case showed that inabil-ity to predict the market reception of a new product may leave a company with no other alternative than to try a variety of approaches until one is successful. (Corey, Chap. 38 in Ewing, 1964a.)

INVENTION. The creation of new and better products, services, methods, ideas, and techniques is a very important requirement in the development of strategy. An outstanding strategy of DuPont that has paid off handsomely is investment in basic as well as applied research. More and more American com-panies are emphasizing research as a major strategy to improve their market position by introducing new products as well as to prevent unexpected erosion of the market position of old products.

Prior to World War II DuPont's cellophane was a highly profitable product. Following the war, cellophane began to lose its share of the market as other new products appeared, such as polyethylene film. DuPont then introduced modifica-tions, which included special coatings to reduce winter breakage and add protec-tion, new types to meet a variety of customer needs, and lighter grades of cellophane at prices more competitive with the newer packaging materials. Choices of cellophane types mushroomed from a handful to well over 100 and sales re-versed their trend. Ignoring widespread forecasts of a rapid decline, cellophane sales rose steeply. (Neuschel, 1965.)

There are few if any better strategies than to invent a new product which becomes a generic name for similar products. Among such long-time money-makers are Coca-Cola, Kleenex, Eveready batteries, Hershey's chocolate, Smith Brothers cough drops, Kellogg's corn flakes, and U.S. Borax's 20-mule team soda. Not all such great inventions have been instant successes. For example, it took years for the Gillette razor to catch on.

Another illustration is the difficulty of Chester Carlson. He filed a patent for a process he called electrophotography in 1937, and in the next year he dupli-cated successfully from inked glass an impression on waxed paper. He named the process xerography, from the Greek for "dry writing." For years, however, he had trouble stimulating interest in his machine. More than twenty companies, includ-ing Remington Rand and IBM turned him down. He was finally supported by the Battelle Memorial Institute in 1944, but it was not until 1950 that the first ma-chine was marketed. This machine became the strategic factor in the spectacular growth of the Xerox Corp.

FINDING THE STRATEGIC FACTOR. The concept of the strategic factor has important application throughout the planning process. Chester Barnard (1954, pp. 202-203) borrowed the notion of the "strategic factor" from John R. Commons but elaborated Commons' concept. Says Barnard: "If we take any system, or set of conditions, or conglomeration of circumstances existing at a given time, we recognize that it consists of elements, or parts, or factors, which together make up the whole system, set of conditions, or circumstances. Now, if we approach this system or set of circumstances with a view to the accomplishment of a purpose (and only when we so approach it), the elements or parts become distinguished into two classes: those which if absent or changed would accomplish the desired purpose, provided the others remain unchanged; and these others. The first kind are often called limiting factors, the second, complementary factors . . . The limiting (strategic) factor is the one whose control, in the right form, at the right place and time, will establish a new system or set of conditions which meets the purpose."

If a machine is not operating because a screw is missing, the screw is the strategic (limiting) factor. If an automobile is inoperative because it has no gasoline, then gasoline is the limiting factor. These are simple illustrations, but they embody a major concept. Instead of taking an automobile apart and analyzing each part to find out what is wrong, the more efficient approach is to search for the strategic factor.

There are many applications of this concept to the development of strategy. Every company should ask itself just what are the major strategic factors which must be recognized and perfected to make the company successful. The strategic factor in the success of a toy company may be imaginative creations; for a small component manufacturer for automobiles it may be low cost; for an aerospace company it is scientific and technical perfection; for an automobile company it may be styling; and for a company in trouble it may be a capable chief executive. There are few companies where one strategic factor stands alone as the cause of success or failure. There usually are combinations of strategic factors.

Alan Stoneman explained the decision of Purex to diversify, which resulted in great growth. He reminisced: "We said to ourselves, 'Suppose something should happen that would displace our one big product.'" This led the company to an examination of this strategic factor. The company finally decided that bleach, its product, would not be displaced. They concluded, however, that the multiproduct, national manufacturer of so-called grocery products would enjoy so many economies that they would do much better than smaller competitors. So the company embarked on an acquisition hunt.

Barnard's concept of the strategic factor says to the executive, "look for the critical, the major, the basic element." This counsel can be important in the examination of the strengths and weaknesses of the company. It can be valuable in the identification of the most important elements in the environment that should be studied to find new opportunities and reveal new threats.

STRATEGIC FACTORS FOR BUSINESS SUCCESS. In a recent study (George A. Steiner, 1968) I sought to identify the major strategic factors in the success of U.S. businesses and to measure their importance. The 71 factors listed in Table 9-1 were sent to business executives who were asked to determine their importance by rating them in two ways. First, current performance was determined in terms of how well the executives thought they were doing in meeting the requirement of each factor. Second, each factor was rated in terms of its importance to the success of the company in the next five years. Over 250 responses were received.

The principal conclusions of this study of significance here are as follows. First, it is possible to identify the major strategic factors that businessmen hold to be dominant in the success of their enterprises. About half the total number of responses evaluated sixty of the strategic factors to be either of more than average importance or of the greatest importance. Only 6 percent of the responses evaluated any strategic factor as being of little or no importance. So, throughout industry the strategic factors identified in Table 9-1 are those of importance to business success, as businessmen themselves see the matter.*

Second, different types of business executives held surprisingly similar views about the ten to fifteen factors of the most importance for business success. It is noteworthy, however, that chief executives attributed a higher importance to a far greater number of strategic factors for future business success than did other line and functional officers. All but five of the factors were marked by chief executives as being either of the highest importance or of more than average importance. Also, chief executives were more critical of present business performance than were other managers and staff. They felt that current performance was completely satisfactory with respect only to four factors and gave only satisfactory ratings to a larger number of factors than did other groups. But the differences in grading current performance were not great among the functional groups.

Among all the strategic factors those for which performance was rated to be most satisfactory, in descending order of satisfaction, were:

1. Raising short-term capital (F-18).
2. Raising debt at low cost (F-17a).
3. Raising equity capital at low cost (F-17b).
4. Financing diversification by acquisition (F-23a).
5. Attracting and maintaining high quality top management (F-1).
6. Improving present products (F-58).

* In addition to the original 71 strategic factors in Table 9-1, the respondents suggested 77 more. Most all of these, however, were modifications or subsets of one or more of the original factors. For the most part they represented an effort to emphasize an aspect of an original factor that was of more than average importance to the respondents. Most of the suggested revisions were managerial factors and emphasized study of environmental forces important to the business, communications, and human relations.

Table 9-1 Strategic Factors for Business Success*

A. *GENERAL MANAGERIAL:*

1. Ability to attract and maintain high quality top management

2. Developing future managers for overseas operations

3. Developing future managers for domestic operations

4. Developing a better organizational structure

5. Developing a better long-range planning program

6. Achieving better over-all control of company operations

7. Using more new quantitative tools and techniques in decision-making at:

   (a) Top management levels

   (b) Lower management levels

8. Assuring better judgment, creativity and imagination in decision-making at:

   (a) Top management levels

   (b) Lower management levels

9. Ability to use computers for problem solving and planning

10. Ability to use computers for information handling and financial control

11. Ability to divest nonprofitable enterprises

12. Ability to perceive new needs and opportunities for products

13. Ability to motivate sufficient managerial drive for profits

B. *FINANCIAL:*

17. Ability to raise long-term capital at low cost

    (a) Debt

    (b) Equity

18. Ability to raise short-term capital

19. Ability to maximize value of stockholder investment

20. Ability to provide a competitive return to stockholders

21. Willingness to take risks with commensurate returns in what appear to be excellent new business opportunities in order to achieve growth objectives

22. Ability to apply ROI criteria to R&D investments

23. Ability to finance diversification:

    (a) Through acquisitions

    (b) In-house research and development

C. *MARKETING:*

27. Ability to accumulate better knowledge about markets

28. Establishing a wide customer base

29. Establishing a selective consumer base

30. Establishing an efficient product disbution system

31. Ability to get good business contracts (government and others)

32. Assuring imaginative advertising and sales promotion campaigns

33. Using pricing more effectively (including discounts, customer credit, product service, guarantees, delivery, etc.)

34. Better interrelationships between marketing and new product engineering and production

35. Producing vigor in sales organization

36. Improving service to customers

---

* The break in the continuity of the numbers is due to the fact that blank spaces were provided in the questionnaire for respondents to add their own additional factors.

Table 9-1   Strategic Factors for Business Success   (Continued)

D. *ENGINEERING AND PRODUCTION:*

40. Developing effective machinery and equipment replacement policies

41. Providing more efficient plant layout

42. Developing sufficient capacity for expansion

43. Developing better materials and inventory control

44. Improving product quality control

45. Improving in-house product engineering

46. Improving in-house basic product research capabilities

47. Developing more effective profit improvement (cost reduction) programs

48. Developing better ability to mass produce at low per unit cost

49. Relocating present production facilities

50. Automating production facilities

51. Better management of and better results from research and development expenditures

52. Establishing foreign production facilities

53. Developing more flexibility in using facilities for different products

54. Being on the forefront of technology and being scientifically creative to a very high degree

E. *PRODUCTS:*

58. Improving present products

59. Developing more efficient and effective product-line selection (i.e., adding to or eliminating from present line)

60. Developing new products to replace old ones

61. Developing new products in new markets

62. Developing sales for present products in new markets

63. Diversifying products by acquisition

64. More subcontracting

65. Getting bigger share of market for products

F. *PERSONNEL:*

69. Attracting scientists and highly technically qualified employees

70. Establishing better personnel relations with employees

71. Ability to get along with labor unions

72. Utilizing much better the skills of employees

73. Stimulating more employees at all levels to continue to educate themselves to remain abreast of developments in their fields

74. Ability to level peaks and valleys of employment requirements

75. Ability to stimulate creativity in employees

76. Ability to optimize employee turnover (not too much and not too little)

G. *MATERIALS:*

80. Getting geographically closer to raw material sources

81. Assuring continuity of raw material supplies

82. Finding new sources of raw materials

83. Owning and controlling sources of raw materials

84. Bringing "in-house" presently purchased materials and components

85. Reducing raw material costs

  7. Motivating a managerial drive for profits (F-13).

  8. Improving service to customers (F-36).

  9. Using better judgment, creativity, and imagination in decision-making at top management levels (F-8a).

  10. Establishing better personnel relations with employees (F-70).

The strategic factors rated the most important for the future success of the companies surveyed, in descending order of importance, were:

  1. Attracting and maintaining high quality top management (F-1).

  2. Developing future managers for domestic operations (F-3).

  3. Motivating a sufficient managerial drive for profits (F-13).

  4. Assuring better judgment, creativity, and imagination in decision-making at top management levels (F-8a).

  5. Perceiving new needs and opportunities for profits (F-12).

  6. Developing better long-range planning program (F-5).

  7. Improving service to customers (F-36).

  8. Providing a competitive return to stockholders (F-20).

  9. Maximizing the value of stockholder investment (F-19).

  10. Developing a better willingness to take risks with commensurate returns in what appear to be excellent new business opportunities (F-21).

It is noteworthy that managers feel they have performed best with financial factors, whereas those of most importance to their future are managerial.*

  Third, among industry groups both evaluations of current performance and future importance of strategic factors showed many areas of high agreement and many places where there was sharp disagreement. Practically all industries rated current performance highest, for example, in getting both short-term and long-term capital (F-17 and F-18), attracting high quality top management (F-1), and in motivating the managerial drive for profits (F-13).

  There was considerably more unanimity about the future importance of strategic factors than about current performance ratings. High agreement was found that the following were the most important strategic factors for success in the industries covered: attracting high quality top management (F-1), developing domestic managers (F-3), motivating the managerial drive for profits (F-13), developing better long-range planning (F-5), assuring better judgment and creativity among top managers (F-8a), and perceiving new needs and opportunities for products (F-12). Notice that all these fell in the managerial classification of the questionnaire.

  PICKING PROPITIOUS NICHES. The strategy of picking propitious niches relates to a firm's definition of consumer needs and, by adroit use of its unique resources, making its services distinctive to give it a competitive edge in meeting those needs. This strategy finds a particular spot where the firm can give

---

 * This survey was made before the credit crunch of 1967. A similar survey for 1967 and 1968 might not show such high satisfaction for financial factors.

a customer an irresistible value and do so at relatively low expense. (William H. Newman, 1967, p. 78). In a sense, this is a variation of Barnard's strategic factor. First the strategic factor—the niche—has to be identified and then the strategy is formulated. The toughest part is to identify the niche.

One elementary step in identifying a niche is to analyze the elements of demand for a product or service. How strong is the desire for a product? Is the demand being fully met today? If not, how can it be met? If a strong demand does not now exist, can it be created by changing packaging, advertising, price, quality, or servicing?

A next step must be to analyze present competition in meeting an identified need, as well as competitive possibilities if a decision is made to meet the need. A manager must know the strength, attitude, and flexibility of his competitors. He then must judge what they are likely to do in light of any move he chooses to make. Despite the criticality of this type of "gamesmanship" in business, and the comparative ease in getting legitimately much useful information about competitors, it is astonishing how many businessmen do not give this analysis the attention it deserves.

In each of the above steps a firm must probe on the basis of as objective an analysis as it can make of its own and its competitors' strengths and weaknesses. When a niche is found, a company obviously is more likely to be successful in filling it if it capitalizes on its strengths and takes advantage of the weaknesses of competitors.

A company that knows its strengths and weaknesses will find in this knowledge the basis for initiating strategy as well as for determining it. For example, Time Inc. has been very successful in producing mass-distributed magazines for a general audience. McGraw-Hill Company, Inc., on the other hand, has been very successful in publishing technical and semitechnical magazines to limited audiences in particular fields and industries. This experience suggests that each would look for new profitable opportunities in their areas of strength and avoid their areas of weakness.

After World War II foreign small car manufacturers found a demand which American manufacturers were not meeting. The Ford Motor Company found a demand for an automobile with the characteristics of the Mustang and filled it with great success. Wilkinson found a demand for a longer-lasting razor blade which it filled with great success. The initial competitive edge which it received, however, has been dulled by large competitors such as Gillette.

If the strategy that is chosen has a synergistic effect it is so much the more powerful. Synergy means that the combined effect of two or more strategies will yield a result which is greater than the sum of the strategies chosen. For example, the introduction of a new product in a firm's line, plus widespread advertising, may have a beneficial impact on total sales and profits much greater than would either individually.

A synergistic effect can result, for example, because a strategy may assure that a company will operate much closer to capacity. Sometimes a strategy for one product will produce a demand for other products of a firm. Litton, for example, acquired the Ingalls Shipbuilding Company, in Mississippi, and Hewitt-Robins, Inc., a Connecticut materials handling firm, with the hope that this would help it win the $1 billion competition to produce the Navy's fast deployment logistics ship (FDL). Litton won the competition, but the Congress has withheld funds for the program. When, as, and if the program is funded it will have a synergistic impact not only on these firms but on other companies in the Litton family.

ASKING THE "RIGHT" QUESTIONS. There is no better way to devise effective strategy than to ask the right question. This is an approach the simplicity of which should not be allowed to detract from its very great power. Recall how concentrating on the wrong question led Winchester to disaster. Recall, too, how a simple question which turned out be the right one led Purex to great success.

To ask what is the major characteristic responsible for a company's success is to highlight a source of strength to use in developing and implementing strategy. To ask and answer what critical factor is necessary for success in meeting a new problem is to begin narrowing strategy alternatives. Sometimes a strategy will be obvious if a company asks itself where its greatest vulnerability lies (Drucker, 1964).

Of course, the importance of asking the right question before seeking a solution is obvious, and is inherently necessary for the successful use of any one of the above approaches. It is, however, so often underestimated as a method in itself, and is so often neglected, that there is justification for delineating it here. Other illustrations of this approach will be given in later chapters.

FOLLOWING OTHER COMPANIES. Some companies, particularly in industries dominated by large firms, are content to follow the leader in the industry. They may be protected by the umbrella provided by the leader; they may fear retaliation from the leader; or there may be a sort of collusion with the leader which is inherent in this type organization. For such companies this may not only be an appropriate but the only strategy.

For many companies, for different purposes, a follow-the-leader strategy may be effective. A small company may not have the resources to be a leader in research. It may, therefore, follow the dominant companies in the industry.

TIMING OF STRATEGIC MOVES

Timing a strategic move can be just as important as the move itself. The world was not quite ready for Charles Babbages' computer when he invented it in the early 1800's. Chrysler's airflow automobile of 1934 was ahead of its time, and failed. The Convair 880 airplane was timed poorly in light of Boeing's and Douglas' commanding lead in the large commercial jet transport field.

Sometimes, as in technical industries, timing depends upon the nature of the strategy and technology. Research must precede development, and development must precede production. But, as the aerospace industry has learned, they all can be done somewhat concurrently if the customer is willing to pay the price.

There are no easy guides to assure proper timing, but Newman (1957, p. 85) has a few useful suggestions about selecting a strategic sequence, as follows:

"Resist the temptation to do first what is easiest simply because it requires the least initiative. Each of us typically has a bias for what he does well. A good sequence of activities, however, is more likely to emerge from an objective analysis.

"If a head start is especially valuable on one front, start early there. Sometimes, being the first in the market is particularly desirable (there may be room for only one company). In other cases, the strategic place to begin is the acquiring of key resources; at a later date limited raw materials may already be bought up or the best sites occupied by competitors. The importance of a head start is usually hard to estimate, but probably more money is lost in trying to be first than in catching up with someone else.

"Move into uncertain areas promptly, preferably before making any major commitments. For instance, companies have been so entranced with a desired expansion that they committed substantial funds to new plants before uncertainties regarding the production processes were removed.

"If a particular uncertainty can be investigated quickly and inexpensively, get it out of the way promptly.

"Start early with processes involving long lead-times. For example, if a new synthetic food product must have government approval, the tedious process of testing and reviewing evidence may take a year or two longer than preparation for manufacturing and marketing.

"Delay revealing plans publicly if other companies can easily copy a novel idea. If substantial social readjustment is necessary, however, an early public announcement is often helpful."

STRATEGY AND ORGANIZATION

That the structure of a company and its strategy are closely intertwined is well documented by Chandler (1962) and Penrose (1959). Chandler examined in depth the basic strategies and organizational structures, over their lifetimes, of DuPont, General Motors, Standard Oil of New Jersey, Sears Roebuck and Company, and, less intensively, a number of other companies. He concluded that the basic strategies of these companies grew out of their application of resources to market demand, and that the strategy determined organization structure.

SIMILARITY OF FIRMS' STRATEGIES

What is one firm's successful strategy frequently is another's poison. Some companies, for example, have acquired other companies that were weak and in trouble and, by injecting into them new management talent, have shown profitable growth. Other companies, however, have pursued just the reverse strategy, namely, buying profitable companies with excellent management. The latter companies have felt that the higher price was a bargain because of the acquisition of talented management and a company with powerful momentum. When the acquiring company has a high-earnings ratio the latter course is doubly attractive.

Throughout the range of strategies, what may spell great success for one company at one time may be disastrous for another company. However, there are many similarities among strategic factors necessary for success among companies in the same industry as well as in all companies.

CONCLUSIONS AND GUIDELINES FOR
DEVELOPING STRATEGIES

This chapter defined in depth the meaning of strategy and illustrated the nature of strategies in general, of personal and business strategies, and of strategies in major functional areas. Particular attention was devoted to nine major approaches to the development of strategies in a firm.

Following are guides to the development and implementation of strategies which are summarized from the discussion of this chapter (Tilles, 1963a).

First, a firm's strategy should be identifiable to those in the firm who should know what it is. This does not necessarily mean a strategy should always be spelled out in writing. If a strategy is not in writing, it should be clearly understood through other means of communication.

Second, strategy should be consistent with the environment of the firm. This is an obvious truism because if a strategy is inconsistent with environment it is not likely to succeed. A strategy that flies in the face of a government regulation, an obvious advantage of a competitor, or a hostile labor union, is not consistent with environment and other alternatives should be examined.

Third, strategy should be consistent with internal strengths, objectives, policies, resources, and the personal values of managers and employees.

Fourth, strategy should balance the acceptance of minimum risk with the maximum profit potential consistent with a firm's resources and prospects. A firm with few resources may accept less risk than one better able to stand a loss. There are some risks that not even the largest firms can undertake. A major aim of a strategy is to balance risk and profit in a fashion appropriate to the company.

Fifth, the development of a strategy should result from the process of objective analysis and incorporate maximum application of imagination and creativity in the process. Major attention should be given to defining the problem for which a strategy is devised, because no strategy is worth much which tackles the wrong problem. Major attention should be given to devising and exploring alternatives. Developing imaginative alternatives that have maximum value is a very creative task. It should be understood that there is a need for applying the intuition of the manager in deciding strategies.

Sixth, both managers and staff should understand the many different approaches to developing strategy and know when and how to apply each technique to the problem at hand.

Seventh, strategy should have timing attached to it and not be open ended. An open strategy without action may give competitors time to counteract the strategy, or may result in its erosion in a way that can dilute its success or result in failure.

Eighth, strategies may be forged in the annual planning period as well as at other times. Strategy formulation is a continuous process, not one done on a cyclical time schedule.

Ninth, the best strategies are those tailored to fit a particular situation, company, and management.

Tenth, the larger the company the more strategies are developed throughout the organization. In larger companies one may speak of a chain of strategies ranging from climatic ones at the top of the company to lesser strategies that turn into tactics. This chain may be considered as having sub- or sub-sub-strategy links.

10
Business Policies
and Procedures

10
Business Policies
and Procedures

INTRODUCTION

There exists a great deal of confusion about the nature, use, and formulation of business policies. This confusion is partly semantic because policies are not always clearly delineated from other elements of planning and plans, but there are also other reasons for the confusion. A number of different types of policies exist depending upon how they are classified, and the line of demarcation among them is not always nor easily drawn. Important policies are also frequently developed in the strategic planning process. Since this is not a well understood nor publicized function, it is shrouded in some mystery and hence policy making done in the process takes on some of the mystery. Some policies are considered by managers to be confidential, and there are others, such as those associated with the corporate image, that companies are anxious to publicize.

Despite the confusion surrounding policies they are of major importance in management. This chapter seeks to clarify the nature, significance, and formulation of policies and their derivative procedures and rules.

NATURE OF BUSINESS POLICIES

There is no common meaning in the business world of the world policy. A survey of business firms made by the National Industrial Conference Board concluded the following were some of the definitions used: a broad interest, direction, or philosophy; an expression of the corporation's principles and objectives; guides to thinking and action; general standards not subject to frequent change; and procedures and practices. (Higginson, 1966, p. 15.)

What is a policy is a slippery concept. It has a variety of meanings depending upon its nature and use. Policies have characteristics which distinguish them from other elements of the planning process; but, as noted before and as discussed below, there are times when it is very difficult if not impossible to distinguish policies, say, from strategies and objectives.

Policies are generally considered to be guides to action or channels to thinking. More specifically, policies are guides to carrying out an action. They establish the universe in which action is to be taken. This universe can be very broad if a policy deals, for example, with a general statement of managerial intent, such as "it is our policy to be a good corporate citizen." The universe can be a much more restricted area for action in such directives as, "It is our policy to promote our own managers on the basis of capability, and not seniority, whenever the needed talent is available." Policies may be thought of as codes which state the directions in which action may take place. They set boundaries. Policies stand as ready guides to answering thousands of questions which may arise in the operation of a business.

Policies usually enjoy a long life. As a matter of fact there is too much of a tendency in business for them to live too long without review and revision. At any rate, policies are generally formulated with the long view in mind.

Policies direct action to the achievement of an objective or goal. They explain how aims are to be reached by prescribing guideposts to be followed. They are designed to secure a consistency of purpose and to avoid decisions which are shortsighted and based on expediency.

A business policy can be defined as management's expressed or implied intent to govern action in the achievement of a company's aims.* This definition is at a high level of abstraction. It is necessary, therefore, to dig deeper into the anatomy of a policy to understand its operational character.

THE POLICY PRINCIPLE AND RULE

Ralph Davis (1951, p. 173) points out that policies have two major parts: the principle that governs, and the rule that indicates the general manner of its application. An example is the interdivisional purchasing policy of General Motors. The principle states that unless a true competitive situation is preserved,

---

* Other definitions of policy which are close to the above are: "A business policy, then, is essentially a principle or group of related principles, with their consequent rules of action, that condition and govern the successful achievement of certain business objectives toward which they are directed." (Davis, 1951 p. 173.) "A policy is a definition of common purposes for organization components of the company as a whole in matters where, in the interest of achieving both component and overall company objectives, it is desirable that those responsible for implementation exercise discretion and good judgment in appraising and deciding among alternative courses of action." (General Electric Company, 1953-55, p. 15.) The Policy Manual of one manufacturing company defines policy as follows: "A policy is a statement of management's intent with respect to matters of broad and long-range significance to the company."

as to prices, there is no basis upon which the performance of the divisions can be measured. The rule states that no division is required absolutely to purchase product from another division; it can purchase outside the company if the price is less than at another company division.

Many companies divide their policy statements into parts which differentiate the basic principle from more detailed guidance. Many simply divide the statements into policy, and guidelines. The Marquardt Corporation adds a third—responsibilities. The Lockheed Aircraft Corporation divides each policy statement into: introduction, basic policy, assignment of responsibilities, and interpretation.

This differentiation implies that many policy statements are long documents. They are indeed—often covering several pages of printed matter (Higginson, 1966).

POLICY VERBS

Policies are generally expressed in a qualitative, conditional, and general way. The verbs most often used in stating policies are: to maintain, to continue, to follow, to adhere, to provide, to assist, to assure, to employ, to make, to produce, and to be.

To illustrate: "It is the policy of the Ajax Corporation to control the release to the public, employees, stockholders, and others all information that may disclose company plans, policies, and activities in such a way as to assure a favorable reaction toward the company, its interests, and its products." Or, "It is company policy to protect the assets of the corporation by having an adequate corporate insurance program." Or, "It is the policy of the company to establish and vigorously pursue a program of executive development, recognizing that this starts with the selection and training of supervisory personnel."

POLICIES COMPARED WITH OTHER
TYPES OF PLANS

Policies are often confused with plans, purposes, objectives, goals, procedures, and so on. The word policy frequently is used both in practice and in the scholarly literature to mean these other elements. A policy is indeed a plan—it is a type of plan. While a policy clearly is a guide to action to achieve an objective, the policy itself may become an objective in a sort of ends-means continuum. For example, it is proper to say that "it is our objective to grow (sales) by 10 percent a year." It is also proper to say, "it is our policy to grow through diversification of product by acquisition." This can be considered an objective from a lower level of abstraction. A policy devised to achieve it may be expressed as follows: "It is our policy to acquire companies only by an exchange of stock."

Also, policy and strategy are terms which are synonymous under certain circumstances. It is correct to say, for example: "It is our policy to expand our European market only by acquiring minority positions and hiring nationals to fill top management posts." But it is also proper to call this a strategy when it is a matter of considerable importance. This does not mean that the distinction between strategy and policy is the question of importance. Policies also deal with matters of major importance.

There are two distinctions between strategy and policy. First, strategy as noted in the last chapter is principally reserved only for deployment of resources of major importance to a company. This leads to the second distinction, namely, policies are rather enveloping in a company, whether written or unwritten. They cover the management process like a blanket; they are more diffuse. The word policy draws no line of demarcation between a major policy and a minor one. Of the two words, policy and strategy, policy at once is the larger in scope but also includes details with which a strategy would not consort.

If, after the above argument and that in previous chapters, the reader prefers to use the word policy to include strategy, no harm will be done. But, it does not work the other way around, e.g., one cannot use the word strategy to include policy. Nor can policy be used to mean the same thing as strategic planning. But a strategy may be carried out with the help of policies.

Procedures, standard operating plans, and rules, differ from policies only in degree. All provide guidance about how a particular problem shall be solved.

A procedure is usually considered to be a series of related steps or tasks expressed in chronological order and sequence to achieve a specific purpose. When a sequence of actions becomes well established and is in a sense a basic rule of conduct it is called a standard operating procedure. For instance, a series of steps in filling a customer order, in making a purchase of an office machine, in hiring an employee, or in handling crank letters, becomes a standard operating procedure when it is formalized. Procedures are methods, techniques and detailed ways, by and through which policies are achieved.

Most companies have literally hundreds of standard operating procedures. Depending upon subject matter, of course, there are degrees of leeway in compliance. But most procedures specify patterns and/or steps of action which must be followed with minimum deviation.

Rules are prescribed courses of action which usually are stated in such a way as to leave no doubt about what is to be done. They are specific and permit a minimum of flexibility and freedom of interpretation. "Each operating division will be responsible for the direct export sales of its own products," is a rule. "All quantity discounts must be approved by the Vice-President, Sales," is also a rule. Many times rules are prohibitive and stated negatively, such as "No purchases can be returned." Policies, procedures, and rules are types of standing plans that govern thousands of activities that take place in an enterprise.

The applicability of rules may vary from one division to another, and blind

Chart 10-1

Pyramid of Business Policies

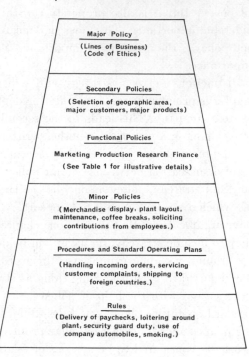

insistence on obeying rules can lead to confusion. Furthermore, rules limit flexibility of managers. Rules cannot substitute for procedures and policies, nor vice versa. All companies, therefore, have the problem of developing a proper blend of policies, procedures, and rules.

THE BUSINESS PYRAMID OF POLICIES

It is clear from the above discussion that in every business there is a pyramid of policies. Chart 10-1 presents a simple illustration of such a pyramid. At the top of the pyramid are very broad fundamental policies concerned with company purpose and ways of doing business. Falling below are policies of lesser scope and importance which shade into procedures and rules.

At lower managerial levels more attention is directed to implementation of higher-level policies and controlling operations, than to making subpolicies. When subpolicies are made the time horizon tends to be shorter and the policy statement tends to get more specific.

Sometimes, as Davis points out, the principle is forgotten at this level and all that remains is the rule. In such cases the principles behind the rule are implied. This may not be desirable because a basic purpose of a policy is to stimulate thinking and to explain the significance of a rule. Acceptance of rules is more likely when there is understanding of the reason for the rule.

While no company can or should have a policy to cover every action and contingency there is a tendency, particularly in the larger companies, to have an organized register of policies. Problems which are unusual in a small company may come frequently enough to be covered by a policy in a larger company. In larger companies there tends to be developed a structure, a comprehensive body, a more-or-less integrated set of policies and their derivatives which becomes something like a legal system for management and other employees. These policies stretch from the highest level of generality in a company to low operating details. They may be broad in specification or specific, concrete or vague, quantitative or qualitative, flexible or inflexible, narrow or long in time.

TYPES OF POLICIES

The foregoing makes clear the need for new words to define elements of planning and plans and to distinguish one part from another. There are, for example, many different types of policies that need to be distinguished. Although there is no need to seek here to settle on a classification, it is useful to suggest some possible groupings if only to further clarify the real nature of policies.

A functional differentiation may be conceptually useful. This would embrace three types of policies: philosophical, resource deployment, and working. The first would include ethical- or moral-type policies. The second would include those concerned with broad allocation of resources, and the third would denote the more or less routine way things are done. Strategy, as discussed in the previous chapter, would be more akin to the second than to the other two.

Another classification of policies could be corporate, divisional, and departmental. At a minimum there should be some distinction between basic and routine policies. The latter classification shades into standard operating procedures and rules. Another is the classification used in Chart 10-1.

Some companies distinguish between corporate, general, and basic policies; and management or directive policies. The former are fundamental to achieving a broad basic objective; the latter are more detailed and apply to more specific actions. General Electric draws the distinction in this way:

"Policies—to achieve company wide unity of purpose and performance, in accord with broad ethical, social, economic principles and efficient business practices.

"Directive policies—to achieve uniformity of detailed performance throughout the company in certain specific functions when it is required for social, economic, or other business reasons or when decentralized discretion is either impossible or contrary to the best interests of the company as a whole." (Higginson, 1966a, p. 60.)

WHAT ARE THE PURPOSES AND FUNCTIONS OF
POLICIES AND OTHER STANDING PLANS?

An answer to this question shows another major difference between policy and strategy. Strategies select a major target and pinpoint a significant approach to it. Strategies are highly selective and generally, but not always, shorter lived. On the other hand, a business of any size, like a society, must have literally thousands of "laws" to govern action of those working in the system.

A web of up-to-date policies and procedures provides a framework within which managerial decision throughout an enterprise can be consistent with the basic purposes and objectives of the firm and the values of top management. The policies, of course, should be in harmony with the network of aims, with other policies, and with strategies, in order to effect the maximum consistency in continuous decision-making. As changes take place in an enterprise, not only in the nature of its work but in managerial shifts of personnel and responsibilities, some comprehensive guidance to action which covers most of the decisions to be made not only is an enormous time saver, but serves to assure consistency. A well-formulated statement of policies permits managers to spend more time on new and urgent problems because they have a ready-made guide to more routine actions.

As organizations grow in size and personnel changes take place there is a tendency for insularity to spread among groups and organizational units. A network of policies provides a basis for communicating among these groups and coordinating their efforts along common lines. Policies are bridges of communications between a central company headquarters and divisions, and among the divisions.

Policies have great importance in predicting action. As organizations grow in size it becomes more important that managers be able to anticipate what others are likely to do. It is difficult enough in large organizations to get people to work together closely and with optimum results, a problem that is compounded when people do not understand what is required of them, or are uncertain about what actions others are likely to take. Appropriate policy guidance enables managers to anticipate and predict action within reasonable margins of error. This permits management by exception and conserves management attention. The more activities in a corporation that are independent one from another, the more important it is to be able to anticipate the actions of others.

Working within suitable policies encourages individual managers to take appropriate initiative. If managers can develop subpolicies within larger policies, they are participating in the operation of the business and, other things being equal, this should encourage their initiative. Also, if they have knowledge of what action is desired of them, and if they know reasonably well what others are likely to do within an understood policy framework, they can act with more assurance. This, too, should foster initiative.

Policies themselves do not produce the above results. Results follow from the actions of managers. In every corporation there are written policies that are not followed and there are accepted practices that contradict written policies. What the above discussion means, of course, is that managers can make sure these values of policies are produced by the way they manage.

All the above relates principally to what is going on inside a company, but policies also concern the environment of a business. Policies may seek to influence the general public's attitudes towards a business or help outside groups and individuals to understand what they can expect from the firm. For example, a company may publicize those policies which attempt to show how it expects to be a good citizen, or which describe the high ethical and moral standards it employs throughout its operations. Policies reflect the thinking of management on a host of relationships with the outside world, and those interested can readily find out what it is. For example, by scanning a firm's policies stockholders may know what to expect by way of dividend payments, maintenance of assets, borrowing on equity, and so on.

POLICY AREAS

It was noted above that there are literally hundreds of areas of a firm's activities for which policies may be appropriate. Table 10-1 presents just a few of the possible areas as an illustration to underscore this point.

Not all company policies are written nor broadly disseminated. Many company policies, especially those that have strategic significance, may be considered proprietary. They may or may not be written. There are also many unwritten company policies which are expressed or implied in words and actions of top managers.

Written policies are not necessarily neatly bundled in one or two manuals. They may appear in annual reports, the company charter, budgets, written plans, employee handbooks, and public relations materials widely distributed to the public. The whole written set of policies and their derivatives are complemented with oral and generally understood but unwritten policies.

It should not be inferred that a company should have policies (or procedures and rules) in all the areas listed in Table 10-1. The principle that should govern written policy development is that policies should be formulated only when they are clearly needed and are likely to assure more than ephemeral guidance to company activities. The attitude of "the fewer, the better" rather than "the more, the merrier" should govern the formulation of written policies. This also applies, of course, to rules and procedures.

Table 10-1   A Classification of Business Policy Areas

I. GENERAL MANAGEMENT:

   A. Divisions and functional staffs

     1. Authority and responsibilities of Divisions concerning pricing, capital authorization, interdivisional transfers, product areas, and authority retained in central headquarters

     2. Functional staff relationships at headquarters and authority in divisions

   B. Growth

     1. Sales rate
     2. Profit rate
     3. Acquisitions

   C. Planning

     1. Budgets
     2. Company basic lines of business
     3. Comprehensive planning
     4. Organization

   D. Policy authority and statements

   E. Miscellaneous

     1. Acceptance of gifts or services by employees
     2. Answering correspondence
     3. Computer procurement
     4. Disaster control
     5. Employment of consultants
     6. Gifts and gratuities to Government and company personnel
     7. Internal auditor reports
     8. Political activities of managers
     9. Records management

II. MARKETING:

   A. Products and services sold

     1. Types
     2. Inventory of parts
     3. Licensing
     4. Modification
     5. Quality
     6. Warranty

   B. Customers

     1. Contract clearance
     2. Export sales
     3. Interdivisional transfers
     4. Market areas
     5. Market channels
     6. Relations with customers, including dealers and distributors
     7. Service for customers
     8. Size of customers

   C. Pricing

     1. Authority to price
     2. Compliance with anti-trust laws
     3. Discounting
     4. Resale price maintenance
     5. Timing of price change

   D. Sales promotion

     1. Advertising media
     2. Product publicity

III. PRODUCTION:

   A. Assignments of products to divisions

   B. Contracting

   C. Manufacturing methods

   D. Production control

   E. Production planning

   F. Quality control

   G. Safety

   H. Shipping

   I. Size of production runs

   J. Stabilization of production

   K. Tooling

IV. PROCUREMENT:

   A. Make-or-buy decisions

   B. Minimum procurement quantities

   C. Purchasing channels

   D. Relations with suppliers

   E. Types of vendors

Table 10-1 A Classification of Business Policy Areas (Continued)

V. RESEARCH:

    A. Allocating funds

    B. Basic research

    C. Evaluating results

    D. Inventions

    E. Patents

    F. Research areas

    G. Research records

    H. Trademarks

VI. FINANCE:

    A. Audit

    B. Budget
        1. Developing
        2. Controlling

    C. Credit
        1. Customers
        2. Employees

    D. Dividend policy
        1. Size relative to profit
        2. Stabilizing

    E. Expenditures
        1. Authority to spend company money
        2. Contributions and donations

    F. Protecting capital
        1. Insurance
        2. Reserves

    G. Structure
        1. Debt rations
        2. Long-term financing
        3. Short-term financing

VII. FACILITIES:

    A. Decision-making process for expenditure

    B. Location

    C. Maintenance

    D. Replacement

VIII. PERSONNEL:

    A. Collective bargaining and union relations

    B. Communications systems

    C. Employment and recruiting

    D. Equal opportunities

    E. Hours of work

    F. Incentives and bonuses

    G. Pensions

    H. Selection

    I. Services
        1. Food service
        2. Health and safety
        3. Insurance
        4. Recreational and educational activities
        5. Retirement
        6. Sick leave
        7. Transportation and parking

    J. Training and education

    K. Wages and salaries

    L. Working conditions

IX. PUBLIC RELATIONS:

    A. Community

    B. Conflict of interests

    C. Contributions

    D. Determining contents of communications

    E. Extent of function

    F. Role of executives

    G. Selecting media for communications

X. LEGAL:

    A. Clearance of contracts

    B. Compliance with law

    C. Patents for employee inventors

    D. Protection of proprietory rights

    E. Reservation of rights and interests

    F. Real property leases

INTERRELATIONSHIP BETWEEN PLANNING
AND POLICY

Business policy, it should be clear by now, is a device which guides the planning program and is also derivative from it. This paradox is explainable, of course, because there are many different types of policies and levels of their application in the affairs of a company.

Policy, for example, can pertain to the entire process of planning. A company may spell out in carefully measured words its policy to conduct annually a planning program with specific dimensions. Or, a company may have an implicit unarticulated policy not to have an organized planning program. The policy guiding a comprehensive planning program may be split into many subjects. It can, for example, establish the policy of having a top management committee in which strategic plans will be formulated. It may deal with the annual budgeting organization and process. Altogether, policy in a larger enterprise will guide the organization for planning, the way in which planning takes place, how people will participate in it, how plans will be put into practice, and how changes in plans will take place.

At the same time, of course, policies are formulated and modified in the planning process. These can range from the most significant policies in directing the affairs of the company to comparatively trivial subpolicies. For example, a company may decide as a matter of policy that it will break out of national boundaries and become a multinational company doing business on all continents. This may be expressed as an objective or as a policy.

Then, of course, once these broad policies are formulated there results in the planning and implementation process a chain reaction in further development of substrategies. A company, for example, may express in its statement of basic purposes that it seeks to be a good corporate citizen. In its strategic planning process it may decide to locate a plant in a minority area or a poverty pocket to do its part in helping the nation to resolve problems associated with each. It may do this not necessarily for altruistic reasons but in its own self-interest in strengthening its environment. As a result of this decision the general manager of a major division may establish a policy that every effort should be made to subcontract work from the plant so long as certain quality and cost standards are met. Department managers might set up policies to determine the quality and costs which are acceptable. Policy with respect to hiring and promoting minority groups then might be constructed. A low-level manager looking at the policy concerning good citizenship might decide he could, within his area of authority, encourage the men working for him to take a more active interest in community affairs. He might also set a new policy that the plant grounds must be kept cleaner and better landscaped so as to add to rather than detract from the beauty of the community.

PRESSURES FOR FORMALIZING POLICY

The same sort of pressures which stimulate more comprehensive and formalized business planning are bringing about more formalization of policy. By formalization of policy is meant a more comprehensive coverage and written promulgation of policy. Many years ago the development and promulgation of policy was a rather informal matter even among the larger companies. Chief executives responded to need as need arose, and generally the totality of written policies was small compared with that of today.

An ever-growing volume of governmental regulations requires more and more internal business policies. A few years ago some high-placed managers of several major companies ran afoul of the antitrust laws concerning price-fixing. This proved to be very embarrassing and costly to both the companies and the managers involved, and it resulted not only in changes in some policies but more vigorous enforcement of policies concerning such actions.

Legal liabilities of product quality have been assessed against more and more companies in recent years. The natural result is more careful specification of policies to minimize such risks.

Codes of morality in business dealings are changing and becoming more stringent. Some years ago a top executive of a major corporation was discovered to have financial interests in a supplier of the company, and the resulting public indignation scarred the image of that company for years. Many larger enterprises having policies relating to the way in which their managers should deal with employees of other companies reviewed them, and others that had no such policies established them.

People in the business world are expecting to have much greater participation than ever before in the affairs of the company for which they work, and more and more employees are seeking to find work which will increase their self-satisfactions far beyond the ranges which heretofore were to be derived from working. They want to be challenged intellectually, they want to be creative, and they want to have a greater sense of accomplishment. More and more firms are responding to this spreading demand, and top management is becoming more permissive and is providing the atmosphere for greater participation. A natural result, of course, is to build up a structure of policies to guide actions of employees within acceptable boundaries.

Union interests have become major matters of concern in American industry over the past thirty years, and a network of interrelationships between unions and business managers has necessitated the development of a large body of company policy. This is often expressed in contracts with the union.

These are but a few of the many impetuses for the formalization of company policies. Most large companies have found that they simply cannot get along without a structure of policies which is formally developed and maintained.

POLICY-MAKING RESPONSIBILITY

The ultimate responsibility for a firm's policy rests in the Board of Directors. But in every company, arrangements of authority and responsibility are worked out over time to settle the locus of authority for policy-making. Most managers of a company have policy-making authority, but the scope of authority differs widely. The policy-making authority in any company will depend upon many characteristics, such as the style of management employed, personalities, organizational arrangements, and types of business.

The Board of Directors of some companies play a very active role in running a business. E. I. Du Pont de Nemours and Company is a classic case of active Board participation in company operations. The organizational plan which Du Pont uses was put into effect in 1921 when Irénée du Pont was President. The Board is composed of 32 members and does much of its work through committees composed of its own members. Of these, the Executive Committee is concerned with the day-to-day management of the company, and the members of this committee have two primary duties. The first is to establish the overall operating policies of the company and to review the activities of the industrial and auxiliary departments of the company (the Treasurer's Department and the Secretary's Department are supervised by the Finance Committee of the Board). The second is to provide technical advice to anyone in the company seeking it. This is done by individuals and not as a Committee function. The Standard Oil Company (New Jersey) and General Motors Corporation are two additional examples of companies whose Board members play an important part in policy-making.

In most companies the Board does not take such an active interest in daily operations. In such cases, the President of the company, or the Chairman of the Board if he is responsible for day-to-day activities, is a focal point of policy-making. He will know when the board should be asked either to make or approve a policy, and he will know those policies which he may determine without direct board approval.

Generally, the chief executive of a firm will assume sole responsibility for major company-wide policies, and this responsibility is often explicitly stated in company policy manuals. Chief executives frequently appoint committees either to help in the formulation of policies or to make them. In many companies the major company-wide policies are formulated in meetings of the President's Staff which is composed of his principal line and staff managers. Standing committees may have authority to determine policy within broad company-wide policies. Such, for example, might be the authority given to a Planning Council, Product Planning Committee, Facilities Committee, Pricing Committee, or Foreign Activities Committee.

All these authorities become generally understood over time. But it is a rare manager who always knows beyond a shadow of a doubt precisely what his policy-making authority is.

MAKING POLICY

Most of the approaches to developing strategy which were discussed in the preceding chapter also are used in developing policies. Policy-making, however, has other approaches the more important additional ones of which are as follows.

First, policy can originate anywhere in a company. New policies may be and often are suggested by a chief executive. Most policies that he makes or approves, however, either originate from lower levels of management or are studied and formulated there. A recent study of policy-making concluded that the following procedure is gaining wider acceptance: a staff executive in charge of policy administration receives a draft of a policy prepared by another functional or line manager. He reviews it in light of other company policies, government regulations, etc., and returns it to the originator. Following his review of suggested changes, it is routed to top management for approval. If it is not approved, it returns to go through the same loop again. If approved, the policy statement is returned to the staff executive for incorporation in the company's policy documentation manuals and dissemination to the appropriate mailing list of company executives. (Higginson, 1966, p. 50.)

Second, policy-making and its derivatives are such an intimate part of management that the process is going on at all times at all levels of management. This means, of course, that participation in policy-making is much wider than that in developing strategy.

Third, policies exist and are applicable because of an implied acceptance; informal arrangements evolve into fixed policies. During World War II, for example, the development of coffee breaks more or less spontaneously evolved in industry, and gradually, over time, company policy covered the practice. Policies may be created by default. If no policy exists concerning customer complaints, for example, action taken by those directly dealing with the matter can result in an entrenched implied policy. Furthermore, policies may exist and be accepted even though they conflict with written policy statements. Company policy may permit a ten-minute coffee break twice a day but a gradual extension of time to fifteen minutes may be the accepted norm despite the written policy.

A CASE STUDY IN POLICY-MAKING

The process of policy-making in larger companies for major policies usually involves rather extensive staff work. The following illustration concerns a major policy of a major corporation with sufficient changes in the facts to hide identity.

The Midwest Conglomerate Company is principally a maker of agricultural implements but has expanded into diversified product lines in electronics, automobile parts, electric motors, material handling equipment, and link belts. It has twelve major semi-autonomous divisions scattered throughout the U.S., and it has had a rapid growth during the past ten years.

Under a policy of encouragement to general managers to grow and increase profit through new and imaginative moves, the company found itself producing tractor parts in Brazil, steel in India, radios in England, and electronic components in Germany. All products produced abroad, while related to products made in the U.S., were really new to the company. Furthermore, it had a variety of equity holdings in different firms in other countries of the world. It seemed that, while the volume of sales of these foreign ventures was high relative to total sales, the current and projected profitability of all but one venture was negative. In short, the foreign investment program had gone sour.

The president of the company asked his long-range planning staff to examine the entire situation and report back to him. This touched off a major study which involved thousands of manhours.

The staff went through a research process which involved, generally, the following steps (many of the steps, of course, were pursued simultaneously):

First, the objectives of the company were reviewed to see whether foreign investment was necessary to reach projected sales and profit aims. The gap between projected objectives and growth from current products was examined to determine whether foreign investment or some other alternative might be a better means to fill the difference.

Second, a thorough examination was made of exactly what the company was doing in foreign countries, what the results were to date, and what the possibilities for the future might be. The staff visited each of the foreign outposts.

Third, the staff examined each of the present and projected product lines of the domestic divisions to see whether they might be sold or produced abroad with profit.

Fourth, an honest examination of the company's strengths and weaknesses in producing new products abroad was made.

Fifth, an exhaustive study was made of economic, political and social conditions in selected countries of the world to determine the climate of investment opportunity for the company. Indeed, this study resulted in a series of research reports of book length and high scholarly caliber.

Sixth, investment strategies were set forth and examined in depth. The strategies considered were: no investment abroad; permit divisions to expand abroad but only produce products sold successfully in the U.S.; permit divisions to produce abroad products complementary to or supporting the present product line; set up an international division to make investments of opportunity; merge with a large company in Western Europe; merge with a company in the U.S. with a strong foreign program; emphasize joint ventures as compared with fixed investment; concentrate in only one or two places in the world; invest all over the world; permit no small investments on the grounds that management does not have the time to devote to them; and concentrate only on big profit possibilities. Each of these strategies was examined on the basis of criteria including company know-how, financial measures, profitability, required flexibility, capability of staff in making acceptable studies, required management attention, sales potential, and general company product strategy.

Seventh, preferred strategies were discussed with all affected managers.

Eighth, all this information was studied and tentative conclusions were drawn.

Ninth, the staff undertook lengthy discussions with top management and other staff groups about the results of the data and implications for policy.

Tenth, the staff formulated a series of recommendations which were presented to top management for approval.

In this particular case, as a result of this substantial research undertaking, the concluding policy was rather simply stated as a prohibition of the divisions of the company from engaging in foreign activities except for products which they have successfully produced and sold at a profit in the U.S.

POLICY DOCUMENTATION

Arguments for recording policies in a policy manual or code book are strong. Executives obviously cannot execute policies to achieve objectives unless they know what the policies are. Without written statements, policy obviously has to be communicated orally. This usually is considerably a poorer means of transmission because of misinterpretation, incompleteness in expressing policy, and other shortcomings of oral communications.

On the other hand, there is a case for not recording policies. When recorded it is difficult to maintain their proprietary nature. Somehow competitors get access to policy manuals. Others who may be in conflict with a company or hostile to its policies may capitalize on written policy statements. In this category may be irate stockholders, disgruntled employees, and labor unions seeking an advantage.

Furthermore, the more specific a policy is the less flexibility it permits. This is, of course, at once an advantage and a disadvantage. Policies are designed to guide action, but they must not stifle initiative in the right direction.

While these arguments against recording may have merit they certainly are not governing. Policies that must be kept classified may be transmitted orally, may be written for only a few to see, or may be included in well-guarded manuals. Even though a company has a code book, it is not necessary that every policy must be written and included in it. In making and disseminating policies, a company must try to achieve a proper balance between guiding action and stifling initiative. This all adds up to the fact that written policies should be prepared but that they should be formulated and disseminated with care.

A number of factors are related to the need for and volume of written policies. They are:

First, the size of a company is important. The larger a company the greater is the need for and volume of written policies.

Second, is the type of industry. Industries that are closely related to government (such as the aerospace industry), those that are considered to be in the regulated industries (such as public utilities), and those that find themselves intimately involved with the public tend to have greater need for and volume of written policies, procedures and rules.

Third, is type of organization. Companies that are highly decentralized have a greater need for and volume of written policies than centralized companies.

Fourth, is type of management. Chief executives that foster participative management have more need for written policies than others.

The volume of policies in specific areas will vary depending upon the nature of the company. Consumer product companies will concentrate on sales policies. International companies will tend to emphasize dealing with foreign national governments and nationals. Defense companies naturally tend to have a large number of policies associated with government regulations and dealings with government.

Responsibility for the mechanics of administration usually is given to the corporate secretary, an assistant to the president, an organization or planning specialist, a systems specialist, a personnel executive, or a public relations executive. (Higginson, 1966, p. 56.)

POLICY REVIEW

Policy review is inherent in the general process of management. In this process, managers must have information about current interpretations which are being made of policies, the obsolescence of policies, the extent to which policies are being followed, and areas where new policies are required.

There are many sources of this sort of information. The planning process is an excellent vehicle for policy review; managers in their day-to-day communications are themselves, of course, major reviewers; and headquarters' staff provide another monitor. Companies with internal auditors also can use them as reviewers of policy. Information from customers, government agencies, banking connections, labor unions, and others interested in the affairs of a company also are sources of information upon which basis policy review is made.

It goes without saying, of course, that policies should be under continuous and purposeful review. This, however, is very difficult. It cannot be the job of one man, but of many. It involves many activities. It requires hard work, especially when a policy needs to be changed. Changing policies also creates uncertainties about impact on activities of the company. In this light it is not at all difficult to understand why policy review is somewhat haphazard in most companies and why policies must often become patently inadequate before they are changed. As one company president said to me, "I will not change or make a policy until I have to." This was a courageous and decisive president, who was merely expressing the hard work and uncertainty associated with policy change.

Because of sluggish policy review and change many corporations have a sort of hardening of their policy arteries. Their policies are out-of-date.

SUMMARY AND GUIDELINES TO DEVELOPING AND USING POLICIES

This chapter explored in some depth the nature of business policies and procedures. The scope of the treatment and the basic conclusions are included in the following principal guidelines (which are derivative from the chapter) for developing and using policies.

RELATING TO ENVIRONMENT AND ORGANIZATION

1. Policies should be in harmony with the economic, political, and social environment of a company. Changes are constantly taking place in the ethical values of society as well as in the laws and regulations of government. To ignore these factors, or to flout them, is to court disaster.
2. Policies must reflect the internal organization of a business. The locus of authority is different in organizations and the requirements for coordination vary from one business to another. Policies clearly should coincide with statements of individual authority and responsibility.
3. Policies predominantly must be based upon and effectively and efficiently guide the organization in achieving its network of aims. Policies should provide the proper coordination among functions, physical factors, personnel factors, and other forces operating in a business, in meeting business aims. Policies must assure consistent action over time.

DEVELOPING POLICIES

4. The locus of authority to make different type policies should be clear. Policies should be prepared whenever there is need to set specific guides or rules to govern a particular activity. In a business, it is obvious that while the chief executive may have the ultimate responsibility for all policies and their derivatives he cannot do all the work in their development. Policies and their derivatives are too important to be left to individual initiative. Therefore, authority and procedure to formulate policies should be clear.
5. Participation in policy-making, as in planning, is likely to produce beneficial results. More and more companies are finding that top

management policies are best prepared in top management committees. Although the chief executive has the final authority to make, and responsibility for, policy he may find it useful to have his principal executives who must execute the policy participate in the formulation of that policy. Of course, this is not an invariable rule and its application will depend much upon managerial style and the nature of the policy being considered.

6. Policies should be developed on the basis of as good a factual analysis as possible. While judgment obviously is a major ingredient in policy-making it is important that, in the analysis of the need for and use to be made of policy, fact be separated from opinion.

7. Policies should be stated as simply and unequivocally as possible and appropriate to the level of policy. Policies should be operational in the sense that they guide and influence specific performance. They should be as clear and understandable as possible to those who will have to operate under them. It takes time to make effective policies, but it may take more time to unravel unhappy events generated by vague policy statements.

8. Policies should complement and supplement one another.

9. A policy should be comprehensive enough to cover a range of actions over a normal span of variations in business activity. If new developments are covered in policy statements there is no need to make policy under pressure. At the same time, comprehensiveness or breadth of coverage should not be built into a policy at the expense of too little clear guidance. There obviously is a balance which must be arranged between breadth and precision. The requirement here, of course, is to apply a principle of flexibility.

THE POLICY STRUCTURE

10. The policy structure should be based upon definitions of terms. The semantics of policy and its derivatives, and the way they relate to other elements of planning, are not likely to be settled soon and unequivocally. To avoid confusion in the development of its policy structure, therefore, a firm should define the meaning of terms to avoid confusion.

11. The policy structure should be reasonably comprehensive and cover major areas of importance to a company. This is an obvious injunction. On the other hand the policy structure need not and should not attempt to cover every policy area such as classified in Table 10-1. Policy-making is expensive and it is obviously a waste of time to make policy for situations that either are unimportant, not likely to arise, or are non-repetitive. Also, the greater the number of policy statements with all the subpolicies, derivatives, procedures, and actions they engender, the

more likely will be confusion and that they will be ignored in practice. The problem for the manager is, therefore, to give careful thought to the policies which are needed, to make those and no others, and to make sure they are followed in practice.

12. The basic policy structure should be reasonably stable. Although changes will take place in individual policies, an effort should be made to formulate policies that are likely to have some stability. Policies associated with fundamental purposes and operational principles of a company should be more stable than those associated with day-to-day operations. But an effort should continuously be made to keep policies in tune with the rapid changes taking place in the company.

DOCUMENTATION

13. Policies should be written and made available to executives who need to know what they are. The practice of writing policies is an exercise in itself which is more likely to inject precision than if policies are communicated orally or not at all. Of course, policies that reflect a major move of some competitive significance should be closely guarded. This does not fracture the principle of the desirability of written policies. Rather, it requires proper dissemination of the written documents.

14. Policy manuals should be separated from management directives and standard operating procedures. If policy statements are kept in the same documents as their derivatives, and papers associated with them, a problem of bulk arises in a larger company. The greater the bulk, the less likely people are to read and understand the basic policy statements. Furthermore, standard operating procedures among different divisions and departments may well be different even though developed from the same basic policy. To include all this in a policy manual for the entire company is to generate unnecessary distribution and bulk. One way to assure that bulk does not inhibit use is to have an easily understood and usable composite index.

POLICY INTERPRETATION AND REVIEW

15. A suitable plan for educating management about the meaning of company policies should be developed. The broader and more comprehensive a policy is, the greater the number of meanings which managers may attribute to it. Policy statements often need not one but constant interpretation. Most of this type activity can take place in the normal process of management, in the planning process, or both. But there are other routine ways in which an educational program can be conducted. Distributing management directives interpreting policy is one such method. Discussions at management club meetings is another.

16. Some procedure for testing compliance with policies should be established. In a very small business this function, of course, can be handled very well by the entrepreneur-owner in the day-to-day process of management. In larger enterprises more system may be appropriate. The official designated to administer the system of policies may check on derivative statements from high-level policies. Internal auditors may help. Most companies have not built any systematic feedback into their communications systems to check on policy compliance. They should.

17. Policies should be reviewed systematically for obsolescence. As important as is the first formulation of a new policy, the reformulation of an obsolete policy may be more important. This is especially so if the old policy is taking the company in the wrong direction. The longer policies are around, the more they are taken for granted and accepted without question. It is not so much that old policies assume narcissistic characteristics but rather that they become accepted without question. Tradition phases into compulsion. Compulsion becomes blind, unthinking acceptance. The old classic gag—"Why do we do things like this around here? There's no reason, it's our policy"—is a sorry truth in too many cases. Rigid adherence to a policy no longer in tune with conditions affecting a company can be ruinous.

11
From Strategic Planning
to Current Action

11

From Strategic Planning
to Current Action

INTRODUCTION

The cutting edge of corporate planning is the making of decisions for current actions. In a company of any size, the line from top corporate strategic planning to current actions taken at the lowest managerial levels and among employees is long and frequently disjointed and broken. In one of his last speeches as Premier of the USSR Khrushchev described his frustrations that grew from the failure of local planners to do what the top Kremlin management wanted. Many presidents of businesses have a similar complaint.

Integrated corporate planning has two important dimensions. First, is the coordination of plans from the top levels of a business down through the organization and among the major components of plans. Second, is the way plans are interrelated in the major planning parts, such as the relationships of functions in medium- and short-range plans.

Although these dimensions have not been neglected in previous chapters, the purpose of the present discussion is to look more deeply into the integration of medium- and short-range plans, and their translation into actions. This chapter is not concerned with details of planning in functional areas, whether long-, medium-, or short-range. They will be treated in Part III of this book.

MEDIUM-RANGE PROGRAMS

As noted previously, there should be no major problem in integrating medium-range programming with strategic planning, on the one hand, and with short-range planning, on the other, when the same group of people do all three. This is the case, of course, in a centrally controlled and operated company. The only issue is how well the plans are integrated.

Chart 11-1

Matrix of Goals, Functions, Product Development Time

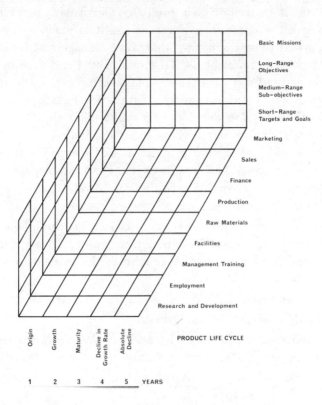

In a decentralized company, however, different managers get involved in different ways in the development of these plans and integration becomes more difficult. Procedural integration can be effected, as noted in previous discussions, by the preparation of manuals to guide operations, by meetings, group discussions, and coordination performed by planning departments.

Substantive coordination among functional plans is a more complex problem, the solution to which involves every tool at the disposal of managers and their staffs. The problem is conceptualized in Chart 11-1 which shows the pieces of a puzzle that must fit together in developing medium-range programs for product development. To visualize the immense complications of the integration problem, consider the details which must be interrelated in each of the functional plans for many products.

Complete planning would require that plans be prepared for every function, both line and staff, and for every product. This would include a much longer list than presented in the table of contents of a corporate plan given in Chapter 5. For example, that table of contents did not include staff plans for accounting, law, or public relations. No company tries to cover everything in comprehensive planning. The principle should be to include only what is necessary and important to concentration on and achievement of a limited number of aims. To try to tie together all the activities of a company, particularly over a long time spectrum, is to seek the impossible. Furthermore, it is unnecessary and costly.

This is not meant to say, of course, that some managers and staff in a company need not make long-range plans. All should. But the degree to which they tie into the main body of a comprehensive planning program will vary. For example, in a large manufacturing company with a legal staff there may be no need for that staff to develop detailed long-range plans that mesh with divisional plans. The relationship may be kept loose and indirect.

The practice is widespread among divisionalized companies for plans to be prepared both quantitatively and qualitatively. For example, the Kaiser Aluminum and Chemical Corp. requests each division to report on standard reporting forms the following information for a five-year period:

1. Assumptions. A qualitative statement concerning the following: pricing; market conditions; costs for labor, transportation, raw materials, machinery and equipment; and other matters determined to be important by the division.

2. Financial summary: a pro forma profit and loss statement.

3. Total market forecast for each product.

4. Sales volume and market share for each product. Included are comments on source of data and significant changes which may affect the numbers.

5. A description of major strengths and weaknesses about competition, facilities, people, distribution, etc.

6. A description of major problems.

7. Major objectives and strategic programs. Included are objectives for such areas as sales, profits, production, and return on investment, for the division as a whole and for major products. (Strategies are the ways resources are to be used in reaching these objectives and are expressed quantitatively and qualitatively.)

8. Major competitors. Competitors are listed and a review is requested of their facilities, marketing, personnel, research, market development, customer relations, products, and general factors. These are compared with the same divisional elements.

9. Research and development. Each project under way and proposed is listed. Comments are asked about such factors as adequacy of facilities for research, research programs the central offices should initiate to help the division, and market or product development programs the central offices should initiate to help the divisions.

10. Production facilities capacity.

11. Unprofitable operations or products. Sales and profits or losses are requested for each item listed.

12. Capital requirements. This is a formidable report requiring a list of projects in various classifications, such as:
    previously authorized projects
    new projects:
        to make better use of previously authorized projects
        to increase capacity, add products, or diversify
        for repair and maintenance
        to reduce costs
        other.
    A description is required for each proposed project.
13. Personnel requirements.
14. Inventory requirements. Requested is the dollar valuation for raw materials, in-process materials, finished goods, and total inventories.

A typical large divisionalized company will ask its divisions to make summaries of plans, usually centered in financial statements, and give supporting details by products and/or product lines. The focal point of Lockheed's divisional planning is a line of business, which is defined as a grouping together of products, services, programs or investments because of their common business requirements in terms of customers, technology, manufacturing techniques, etc. A line of business in this company would be, for example, commercial transports, or large cargo airplane systems, or rigid rotor helicopters. For each line of business, and for each of the next ten years, the divisions are asked to report objectives; current posture assessment (which is defined as the status of strengths and weaknesses relative to the achievement of objectives); an assessment of environmental factors affecting the line of business; the strategy, or deployment of resources, to achieve the objectives; a description of the programs; and events and actions required to bring about the achievement of objectives. Divisions make and aggregate their plans into divisional summaries, and accompany them with divisional plans in major functional areas. All quantitative reporting is put on punch cards for computer aggregation and analysis.

Chart 11-2 is useful in illustrating several important characteristics of the planning process of a large company. It shows the different documents used at different stages in the process, and the time schedule. It also suggests, but does not show, the many interrelationships among different groups in a company in the integration process.

The Westinghouse Electric Corporation has long had a very sophisticated planning program in which current plans are closely related to long-range plans. Table 11-1 shows the type of market information the divisions are asked to provide by product line. Notice that this form requests seven years' historical information, the relationship between previous forecasts for the current year and the current year's approved objective, and information about competitors. Notice, also, that this form is to be completed as a divisional summary and for supporting product lines in the division.

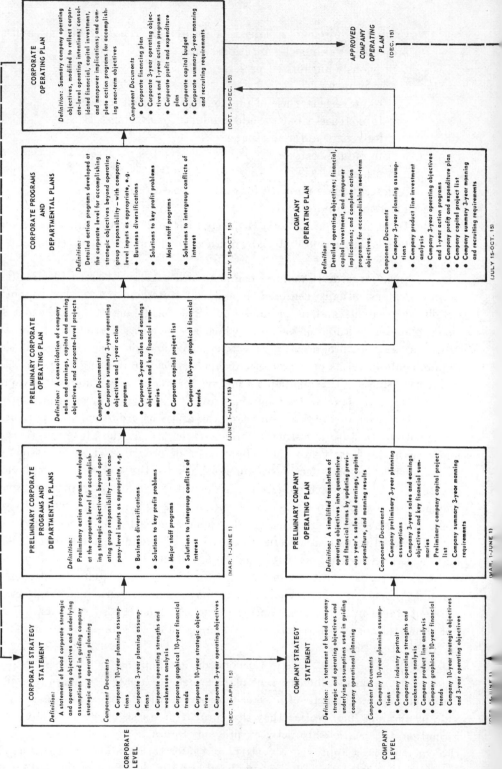

Chart 11-2

Principal Stages of Thinking and Commitment
During the Celanese Strategic and Operational Planning Process

CORPORATE LEVEL

CORPORATE STRATEGY STATEMENT
Definition: A statement of broad corporate strategic and operating objectives and underlying assumptions used in guiding company strategic and operating planning
Component Documents
• Corporate 10-year planning assumptions
• Corporate 3-year planning assumptions
• Corporate operating strengths and weaknesses analysis
• Corporate graphical 10-year financial trends
• Corporate 10-year strategic objectives
• Corporate 3-year operating objectives
(DEC. 15-APR. 15)

PRELIMINARY CORPORATE PROGRAMS AND DEPARTMENTAL PLANS
Definition: Preliminary action programs developed at the corporate level for accomplishing strategic objectives beyond operating group responsibility – with company-level inputs as appropriate, e.g.
• Business diversifications
• Solutions to key profit problems
• Major staff programs
• Solutions to intergroup conflicts of interest
(MAR. 1-JUNE 1)

PRELIMINARY CORPORATE OPERATING PLAN
Definition: A consolidation of company sales and earnings, capital and manning objectives, and corporate-level projects
Component Documents
• Corporate summary 3-year operating objectives and 1-year action programs
• Corporate 3-year sales and earnings objectives and key financial summaries
• Corporate capital project list
• Corporate 10-year graphical financial trends
(JUNE 1-JULY 15)

CORPORATE PROGRAMS AND DEPARTMENTAL PLANS
Definition: Detailed action programs developed at the corporate level for accomplishing strategic objectives beyond operating group responsibility – with company-level inputs as appropriate, e.g.
• Business diversifications
• Solutions to key profit problems
• Major staff programs
• Solutions to intergroup conflicts of interest
(JULY 15-OCT. 15)

CORPORATE OPERATING PLAN
Definition: Summary company operating objectives, modified to reflect corporate-level operating intentions; consolidated financial, capital investment, and manpower implications; and complete action programs for accomplishing near-term objectives
Component Documents
• Corporate financing plan
• Corporate 3-year operating objectives and 1-year action programs
• Corporate profit and expenditure plan
• Corporate capital budget
• Corporate summary 3-year manning and recruiting requirements
(OCT. 15-DEC. 15)

APPROVED COMPANY OPERATING PLAN (DEC. 15)

COMPANY LEVEL

COMPANY STRATEGY STATEMENT
Definition: A statement of broad company strategic and operating objectives and underlying assumptions used in guiding company operational planning
Component Documents
• Company 10-year planning assumptions
• Company industry portrait
• Company operating strengths and weaknesses analysis
• Company product line analysis
• Company graphical 10-year financial trends
• Company 10-year strategic objectives and 3-year operating objectives
(OCT. 15-JUNE 1)

PRELIMINARY COMPANY OPERATING PLAN
Definition: A simplified translation of operating objectives into quantitative and financial terms by updating previous year's sales and earnings, capital expenditure, and manning results
Component Documents
• Company preliminary 3-year planning assumptions
• Company 3-year sales and earnings objectives and key financial summaries
• Preliminary company capital project list
• Company summary 3-year manning requirements
(MAR. 1-JUNE 1)

COMPANY OPERATING PLAN
Definition: Detailed operating objectives; financial, capital investment, and manpower implications; and complete action programs for accomplishing near-term objectives
Component Documents
• Company 3-year planning assumptions
• Company product line investment analysis
• Company 3-year operating objectives and 1-year action programs
• Company profit and expenditure plan
• Company capital project list
• Company summary 3-year manning and recruiting requirements
(JULY 15-OCT. 15)

This form by no means completes the requirements for Westinghouse's divisions. It is shown here only to illustrate one type of detail requested and the requirement to link closely current actions with longer-range plans. Westinghouse, like most companies, asks its divisions for both quantitative and qualitative information.

Some companies—Celanese and Lockheed, for instance—ask their divisions to place probabilities on their future estimates of sales, such as those shown in Chart 11-3. This chart says there is a 50-50 chance that sales of product XYZ will be $5 million and no chance that sales will exceed $10 million. With this sort of information a company can develop Chart 11-4, which shows there is a 50-50 chance total sales of the company will be $150 million ten years hence, a 9-in-10 chance sales will be $100 million, and so on.

Table 11-1 Form for Reporting Basic Market Data
Westinghouse Electric Corporation*

(Dollars in Thousands)

28692 Q · FORM 1

-SION _____ PRODUCT LINES _____ DATE _____

MARKET & WESTINGHOUSE DATA ARE ORDERS ☐ BILLINGS ☐	HISTORY							1967 OBJECTIVE	1967 FORECAST	1968 OBJECTIVE	FORECAST		
	1960	1961	1962	1963	1964	1965	1966				1969 PLAN	1970 PLAN	1973 PLAN
MARKETS (DOMESTIC MFR. & IMPORTS)													
A. DOMESTIC CUSTOMERS (INCL. IMPORTS)													
B1. EXPORTS (WEICO MARKET)													
B2. EXPORTS (OTHER)													
C. INTERUNIT													
C1.													
C2. ADDITIONS TO PRODUCT LINE (AFTER '67)	X X X X X	X X X X X	X X X X X	X X X X X	X X X X X	X X X X X	X X X X X	X X X X X	X X X X X				
D. TOTAL													
WESTINGHOUSE SALES - CURRENT LINE													
A. DOMESTIC CUSTOMERS													
B1. EXPORTS (WEICO MARKET)													
B2. EXPORTS (OTHER)													
C. INTERUNIT													
C1.													
C2. ADDITIONS TO PRODUCT LINE (AFTER '67)	X X X X X	X X X X X	X X X X X	X X X X X	X X X X X	X X X X X	X X X X X	X X X X X	X X X X X				
D. TOTAL													
WESTINGHOUSE % PENETRATION													
A. DOMESTIC CUSTOMERS													
B. EXPORTS (TOTAL)													
C. INTERUNIT													
C1.													
C2. ADDITIONS TO PRODUCT LINE (AFTER '67)	X X X X X	X X X X X	X X X X X	X X X X X	X X X X X	X X X X X	X X X X X	X X X X X	X X X X X				
D. TOTAL													
UNIT VOLUME													
A. U.S. INDUSTRY													
B. WESTINGHOUSE													
C. WESTINGHOUSE % PENETRATION													
PRICE INDEX													
A. ORDERS					100.0								
B. BILLINGS													
WORLDWIDE MARKET													
A. FOREIGN MANUFACTURE (NON-EXPORT)													
B. WORLDWIDE TOTAL (6A + 1D)													
C. WESTINGHOUSE % WORLDWIDE MARKET													
WESTINGHOUSE SALES													

COMPETITION - COMPANIES & %	1962	1963	1964	1965	1966	PRODUCT NAMES & WESTINGHOUSE CODE NUMBERS FOR DATA ON THIS FORM
						SOURCE OF MARKET DATA
						"UNITS" EXPLANATION AND OTHER NOTES

*1968 Planning Procedures, Pittsburgh, Westinghouse Electric Corporation, June 30, 1967.

Chart 11-3
Probability Distribution of Sales for Product XYZ 1968

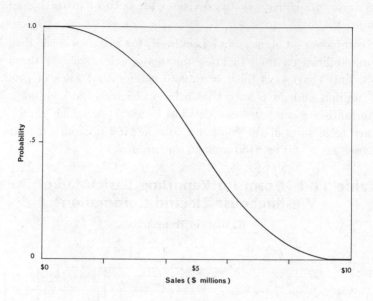

Chart 11-4
Probability Distribution of Sales for Next Ten Years
($ millions)

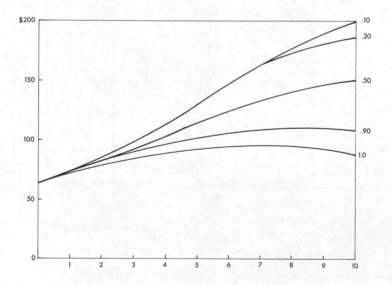

In the actual process of completing forms such as the above there are several interrelated approaches which may be noted to help the reader to get a little better idea of what is actually done.

First, the only way to make the process manageable is to concentrate on plans for major products, functions, and costs. Most companies concentrate on developing financial statements of results of plans which have been built upon the basis of plans for products, which, in turn, are based on marketing forecasts and plans. Facility requirements are, of course, usually closely tied to these plans. Plans for other functional areas are related as appropriate, sometimes closely and sometimes loosely. For example, research and development plans in a highly technically-oriented company must be closely related to future sales. But for a highly market-oriented company this relationship may not be close.

Second, the techniques used in planning extend from intuition at one end of the spectrum to quantitative mathematical formulations at the other. Past ratios are helpful on such matters as employees per dollar of sales, floor space per unit of output, capital requirements per employee, current cash requirement per dollar of accounts receivable, equity to debt, and so on. In some companies, a major oil company for instance, plans for the development of port facilities are based upon a linear programming model which specifies the optimum capacities of contributing facilities (ships, refineries, storage tanks, wharf space, and so on) to permit processing at the lowest cost.

Third, feasibility testing continues throughout the process of developing medium-range plans. These plans, of course, must be tested to see whether they conform to strategic plans. If medium-range plans call for an acquisition of another company and company strategic policy prohibits this sort of action by divisions, the plans are not feasible unless the policy is changed. Feasibility of medium-range plans must be tested in terms of available capital, facilities, technical manpower, and markets; legality; timing of actions; and acceptance by personnel. Sometimes feasibility will turn on the existence of an "advocate," or some manager who is willing to become the leader, the guiding spirit, to get something done. Feasibility testing of plans is not solely a matter of making them as internally consistent as desired, but also must consider practicability of proposed actions.

Fourth, the process is iterative and involves in most companies a complex system of interrelationships among corporate level managers and staff, and between corporate level managers and their staff and divisions or company level managers and staff. This mixture of relationships varies with respect to different parts of the planning structure and process, and from time to time. These relationships are formally prescribed in the planning manual. Many, however, are informal among managers and staff.

Finally, current budgets translate plans into current action.

SHORT-RANGE PLANS

Short-range plans are integrated into medium-range programs and strategic plans in several ways. To begin with, in most companies the figures of the first year of the medium-range programs are the same numbers used in making short-range budgets and detailed derivative plans. The short-range budgets and detailed operational plans are, of course, much more extensive than what is usually found in the first year of the long-range plans. Here again, the spectrum of possible subjects for detailed current plans is wide and management must decide which will be included in budgets, which will be translated into further detailed steps and procedures, and which will be handled automatically.

Feasibility testing is important throughout the process of formulating short-range plans. Plans must be feasible in light of medium-range and strategic plans, and they must also be internally consistent. There is no single or simple formula to guide this testing. A wide range of tools from simple rules-of-thumb to standard financial ratios are in use today, many of which will be discussed in Chapters 13, 14, and 15.

Because budget systems are so important in the translation of plans into action they will be discussed in detail in the following section.

BUDGETING IS A MAJOR INTEGRATING TOOL

Budgeting stands today as a major integrating technique in both business and government planning and control. Its development and wide usage is surprisingly modern. Budgets first appeared in the U.S. in some cities around 1912 in response to demands for civic reforms to prevent misuse of public funds. It was not until 1921, however, that the Budget and Accounting Act entrenched budgeting in the federal government. The use of budgets by American businessmen really began in a serious way, and spread very rapidly, about 1922. The stimulus was the growth of budgeting in governments, plus the publication of a book on budgeting by James McKinsey (1923), the founder of today's McKinsey and Company management consultants.

The word budget is derived from the French *bougette,* meaning a leather bag or briefcase. In the last century the British Chancellor of the Exchequer was in the habit of presenting tax needs for the coming year by opening his briefcase before the House of Commons. About 1870 the word budget attached to the paper he withdrew from his bag.

WHAT IS A BUDGET? The definition of a budget depends much upon the functioning which one sees for it. In a narrow definition, a budget is conceived as a device for comparing what is being done with estimates of what should be done. A behavioral scientist has defined a budget as an accounting technique to control costs through people (Argyris, 1958). Bierman (1959, p.

320) says there are essentially two types of budgets, one is a forecast, which tells a manager where he is likely to be, and the other is a standard, which tells him whether or not the predetermined level of efficiency is being maintained. Some writers look on a budget as a coordinated plan of financial action for an enterprise. A broader definition considers a budget to be a financial plan that serves as a pattern for and a control over future operations, as well as a systematic plan for using manpower, material, or other resources. (Kohler, 1956, p. 67.) Each of these definitions looks at budgets from but one or two of many possible points of view. A more comprehensive definition is needed to reflect today's budgeting practices.

I like the definition of Welsch (1957, p. 1) who says: "A business budget is a plan covering all phases of operations for a definite period in the future. It is a formal expression of policies, plans, objectives, and goals laid down in advance by top management for the concern as a whole and for each subdivision thereof."

BUDGET PROGRAMS. To fit Welsch's definition, a company will have overall budgets for different activities which will be divided into sub-budgets for departments and divisions. These in turn will be subdivided into budgets for smaller units in the organization. The budgets will concern those areas chosen by management for attention.

Components of a comprehensive budgeting system vary among companies. Basically, there are probably four major parts to the system. The first is the planning and budgeting forecasts. The second is the variable expense budget. The third includes supplemental statistics such as break-even analysis and historical growth and cost-volume-profit tables and charts. The fourth includes various budget reports to management which compare the plans and budgets with actual performance, and analyze the differences.

Chart 11-5 pictures a structure of budgets in the first category mentioned above. Variable budgets and break-even analyses may be used in conjunction with those mentioned in the chart, or as separate budgets themselves, as will be noted later. The structure of Chart 11-5 can be used to cover both short and long periods of time.

Larger manufacturing companies tend to have budgeting systems as comprehensive if not more inclusive than suggested in Chart 11-5. Usage varies among companies, however, as a comprehensive study by Sord and Welsch (1958) shows. They investigated 35 companies in depth, and another 386 by questionnaire. The results are summarized in Table 11-2. It should be noted that theirs was a selective sample to represent firms doing a better-than-average job of planning, budgeting, and controlling operations. Companies included were manufacturing, public utilities, transportation, wholesale and retail, finance, and insurance. Their survey reported that in 1958 just about all companies had sales and expense budgets, but not all had other types of budgets. (For much

Chart 11-5

A Simplified Development and Structure of Short-Range Operating Plans

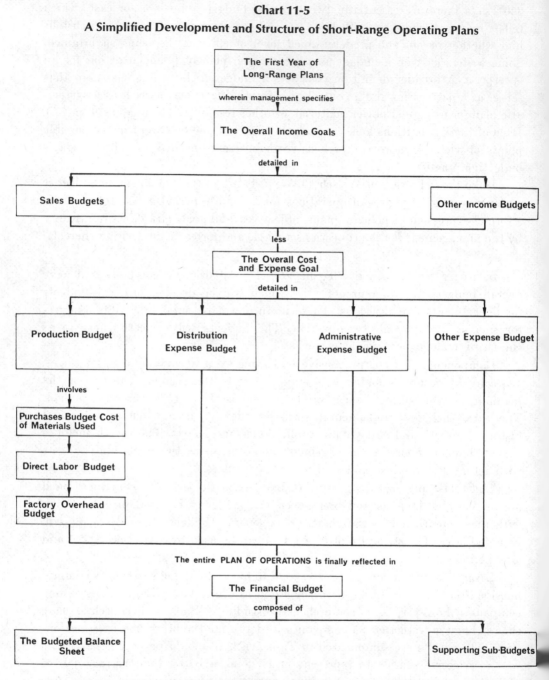

Source: Glenn A. Welsch, *Budgeting Profit Planning and Control,* Second Edition © 1964. Reproduced by permission of Prentice-Hall, Inc., Englewood Cliffs, New Jersey.

the same reasons as given in Chapter 1 for the rapid expansion of planning during the past dozen years, I would expect that a comparable study for 1968 would reveal higher figures in each category listed in Table 11-2.) Other budgets were in use in 1958 by many companies, such as share of the market, return on investment, credit and collections, manpower, and so on, but these were less frequently found than those included in Table 11-2.

Tables 11-3 and 11-4 show typical simplified budget forms. The first is the budget itself, and the second is a report of operations against a budget. They are self-explanatory.

BASIC MANAGERIAL PURPOSES OF BUDGETS. Implicit in the broader definitions of budgets is the existence of a multiplicity of purposes of business budgets. All of them can be encompassed in three overlapping functions: planning, coordinating, and controlling. A well-developed plan naturally lays the basis for coordination, and effective control cannot be assured without planning and coordination. For our purposes here it is useful to discuss these functions individually.

An essential element of planning is the development of detailed budgets covering major activities of the business. An outstanding attribute of a budget, whether long- or short-range, is that it forces managers to direct attention to the formulation of the objectives and goals sought. Since a budget generally is not prepared without a determination of the end sought, and since budgets are usually expressed in quantitative terms, the budgeting process puts pressure

Table 11-2   Percent of Companies Interviewed Having Definite Budget Objectives in Principal Areas

OPERATING AREA	COMPANIES INTERVIEWED (35)	COMPANIES SURVEYED BY MAIL (386)
Sales	100	97
Expenses	100	86
Production	86	78
Capital Expenditures	97	94
Raw Material	80	46
Research	86	74
Advertising	100	93
Cash	94	86

Source: Burnard H. Sord, and Glenn A. Welsch, *Business Budgeting, A Survey of Management Planning and Control Practices* (New York: Controllership Foundation, Inc., 1958), pp. 87-88.

Table 11-3   The ABC Mortgage Co.
Billing Department
Budget for Next Year

	Actual Last Year	Total Year	1st Quarter Jan.	Feb.	March	Total	2nd Qtr.	3rd Qtr.	4th Qtr.
DIRECT HOURS									
OVERTIME HOURS									
VARIABLE EXPENSES:									
HOURLY PAYROLL									
OVERTIME PAY									
EMPLOYEE BENEFITS									
TEMPORARY HELP									
SUPPLIES									
GENERAL EXPENSE									
TOTAL									
FIXED & ALLOCATED EXP.									
SUPERVISORY SALARIES									
EQUIPT. SERV. CONTRACT									
BUILDING COSTS									
DEPRECIATION									
MANAGEMENT FEE									
TOTAL FIXED									
TOTAL EXPENSES									
HOURLY RATE—									

(Header note: BUDGET—NEXT YEAR)

Table 11-4   The ABC Mortgage Co.
Billing Department
Operating Report—March

YEAR TO DATE BETTER OR (WORSE) THAN BUDGET	AMOUNT		THIS MONTH AMOUNT	BETTER OR (WORSE) THAN BUDGET
		CONTROLLABLE (VARIABLE) EXPENSES		
		HOURLY PAYROLL (ACTUAL RATE 1.64)		
		OVERTIME PAY (ACTUAL RATE 2.18)		
		EMPLOYEE BENEFITS		
		TEMPORARY HELP		
		SUPPLIES		
		GENERAL EXPENSE		
		TOTAL		
		FIXED AND ALLOCATED EXPENSES		
		SUPERVISORY SALARIES		
		EQUIPMENT SERVICE CONTRACT COSTS		
		BUILDING COSTS		
		DEPRECIATON		
		MANAGEMENT FEE		
		TOTAL		
		ACTUAL HOURS WORKED—		
		STRAIGHT TIME (BUDGET RATE)		
		OVERTIME (BUDGET RATE)		
		TOTAL		

on managers to express the ends sought in concrete terms. Furthermore, once aims are determined, the budgeting process necessitates development of the specific means to achieve the ends. A budget therefore is a center for focusing attention on plans that result in current actions.

It should not go unnoticed here that the budgeting process in a typical company involves the participation of those who must perform under its terms. If this is done, developing budgets for action should lead to widespread participation in the planning process.

A second major purpose of budgets is to coordinate operations. Smooth current operations depend upon the way various functions are integrated. Forward planning will lay out plans which do indeed determine current actions. But plans laid for the distant future usually only loosely coordinate functional activities. The closer one moves to the present, the more integrated are the functional plans. Table 11-5 illustrates the precision with which coordination can be secured in a budget system. In this table, production, raw material purchases, and direct labor requirements are all coordinated with anticipated sales. In more comprehensive systems there also may be integrated with these budgets, manufacturing expense, inventories, building services, advertising, service and maintenance, cash flow, overhead, and so on.

Third, budgets provide a powerful means for managers to discharge their responsibilities in controlling performance. Budgets themselves do not control anything. They merely set standards against which actions can be measured. But this is very important. Suppose, for example, that sales in Philadelphia for division A were $200,000 last year and selling expenses were $20,000. This past data may or may not be meaningful for current operations. Suppose that in the budgeting process it was determined accurately that sales in Philadelphia next year should be $250,000 but that selling expenses need be no more than $15,000. This budget is a much better standard for measuring performance than historical sales and costs.

Top managers should pay attention only to the unusual or exceptional items that appear in current events and save time for higher priority questions. Reporting systems, evaluation techniques, and performance measures usually associated with budget operations permit managers to do this, or to manage by exception. What is required, of course, are appropriate reports to each level of management concerning what it needs to know in its area of responsibility. The reporting system should not force upon managers routine information, but should get to them quickly news about trouble. Modern electronic systems can be easily programmed to do this.

In sum, budgeting not only facilitates but forces integration of functional elements in both the development of plans and in carrying them out. They force managers to concentrate on quantifying ends to be achieved, they can be used as a vehicle for widespread participation among people in the planning process

Table 11-5   Illustration of Budget Coordination

SALES BUDGET FOR YEAR 196-

Product	Units	Price	Total Sales
1	20,000	$20.00	$ 400,000
2	30,000	30.00	900,000
3	50,000	15.00	750,000
4	5,000	50.00	250,000
	105,000		$2,300,000

PRODUCTION BUDGET

	Products			
Description	1	2	3	4
Quantity	20,000	30,000	50,000	5,000
Ending Inventory	5,000			
Total Required	25,000	etc.		
Less				
Beginning Inventory	3,000			
Required Production	22,000			

RAW MATERIALS UNIT

	Products				
Material	1	2	3	4	Total
St. (lbs.)	10,000	5,000	2,000	1,000	18,000
Cu. (lbs.)					
Al. (lbs.)		etc.			

RAW MATERIALS PURCHASES BUDGET

Material	Prod.	Inv. End.	Total	Less Beg. Inv.	To be Purchased	Price	Cost
St. (lbs.)	18,000	8,000	26,000	6,000	20,000	$150	$3,000,000
Cu. (lbs.)		etc.					
Al. (lbs.)							

DIRECT LABOR BUDGET

Product	Quantity to be Produced	Standard Labor Hours Per Unit	Total Standard Labor	Budget at $5 Per Standard Labor Hour
1	22,000	2	Hours	$220,000
2				
3		etc.		
4				

and thereby promote better understanding and motivation for achievement among managers and employees, and they bridge the gap between strategic planning and current actions.

FLEXIBILITY IN BUDGETING. Jerome (1961, p. 109) correctly says: "To freeze a plan and to put a dollar sign on it is the essence of budgeting. But as soon as plans are frozen, the attitude and behavior of everyone concerned with the plans have a way of freezing too." How can management combat this problem?

There are five principal methods to implement plans in a flexible fashion that not only permits deviations but encourages them when appropriate.

First, is the use of supplemental budgets. This technique is used principally with budgets that establish limits on expenditures. If a capital expenditure budget of a division turns out to be too low, for example, a supplement can be requested and added to the original budget.

Second, is the preparation of alternative budgets. The Clark Equipment Company, Buchanan, Michigan, for example, reportedly made four budgets in 1964. One, the working budget, presumed the then current economic rise would continue into the next year. The other three, just as detailed, assumed the boom would level off and sales would decline. Budgets were prepared for a 10 percent drop, a 15 percent drop, and a 20 percent drop. (*The Wall Street Journal,* November 17, 1964, p. 1.)

Third, is management's acceptance of flexibility. Some large companies prepare highly detailed budgets for each of the divisions for each month of each calendar year, and these budgets are not changed during the year except for major alterations in operations. Top management's review of operations is based less upon the original budget than upon the original budget as it should be modified by actual events. Sometimes performance superior to that originally budgeted turns out to be expected; sometimes lesser performance is accepted without penalty.

Fourth, is to instill flexible thinking in the minds of all managers. This is difficult but derives from effective planning, coupled with top management encouragement and acceptance of deviations from budgets as may be appropriate. This vital force will be discussed later.

Finally, is the use of variable expense budgets. Variable budgets are made to assure proper coordination of activities as changes take place in sales. They are schedules of costs of production that tell managers what levels actually should be as changes occur in sales and output volume. They permit managers to assure a dynamic integration as events require deviations from planned output. Table 11-6 shows a variable budget and what should have happened, as compared with what did happen, when volume changed. Shown in the table is the output and cost budget for the first quarter of the year. Notice how the fixed, semivariable, and variable costs relate to the forecasted output. Effective variable budgeting depends upon identification of these costs and a reasonable understanding of how each changes with different output volumes. In the bottom part of Table 11-6 is shown what actually should have happened when volume dropped 10 percent to 720 units. Variable costs should have dropped 10 percent; semivariable costs, 7 percent; and fixed costs, not at all. Actually, neither the variable nor semivariable costs dropped enough, as shown in the last two columns.

When variable budget schedules are accurate and reports are prompt it is possible for managers to assure a continuous planned integration of operations as changes take place in sales and production volume.

BREAK-EVEN ANALYSIS. Any planning and budgeting system must cope with the intricate interrelationships in the cost-volume-profit-price equation. Break-even analysis is a remarkably simple and effective method to come to grips with enormously complex problems, such as: What happens to profit if volume drops? What happens to profit if price is raised, costs are reduced, and volume declines?

Table 11-6   Illustration of Variable Budgeting in Operation

FIRST QUARTER
OUTPUT AND COST BUDGET

Month	Units	Direct Labor & Materials	Property Taxes	Supervision	Production Total Costs
J	800	$ 640	$100	$280	$1,020
F	1,000	800	100	300	1,200
M	1,200	960	100	320	1,380
Total	3,000	2,400	300	900	3,600

RESUME OF PLANNED AND ACTUAL OPERATIONS FOR JANUARY

Item	Budgeted for Original Program	Budgeted for Actual Volume	Actual Costs at Actual Volume	Variance
Production (Units)	800	720		− 80
Costs:				
Variable	$ 640	$576	$ 630	$ + 54
Taxes	100	100	100	0
Semi-variable	280	260	270	+ 10
Total	1,020	936	1,000	+ 64

Chart 11-6
Methods to Construct Break-Even Charts

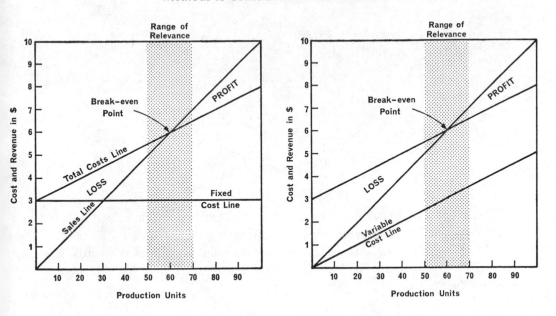

Developed before World War II,* break-even analysis is now widely used in industry. One study showed a majority of companies used the method. (Sord and Welsch, 1958, p. 283.)

Chart 11-6 illustrates two of the more popular ways to draw a break-even chart. The main objective, of course, is to determine the point at which cash income equals cash outgo. To do this it is necessary to know fixed costs, variable costs, sales, the relation of variable costs to volume, volume, and total sales. With these knowns the chart can be drawn and profit and loss quickly determined.

The break-even point can also be derived mathematically when above values identified in Chart 11-6 are known. One formula is:

$$BE = \frac{F_C}{1 - \dfrac{V_C}{S}}$$

Where:

BE = break-even point

F_C = fixed costs

V_C = variable costs

S = corresponding sales

* A pioneering work was Rautenstrauch, 1939, Chapters VI and VII.

To illustrate, if fixed costs are $10,000, unit price is $5, and variable costs are 80 percent of sales price, what is the break-even point?

$$BE = \frac{\$10,000}{1 - \dfrac{\$4}{\$5}}$$

$$BE = \frac{\$10,000}{1 - .80}$$

$$BE = \frac{\$10,000}{.20}$$

$$BE = \frac{\$50,000}{.20)\overline{\$10,000}}$$

$$BE = \$50,000$$

With sales of 10,000 units for a total of $50,000 in revenue, variable and fixed costs will just be covered leaving nothing for profit.

Many different impacts on the break-even point can be conveniently analyzed with this formula. For instance: What will be the impact on a 10 percent increase in fixed costs?

$$BE = \frac{F_C \times 110\%}{1 - \dfrac{V_C}{S}}$$

Identify the impact of a 10 percent decrease in V_C?

$$BE = \frac{F_C}{1 - \dfrac{V_C \times 90\%}{S}}$$

Suppose a 10 percent price increase will reduce units sold by 5 percent, what will be the impact on the break-even point?

$$BE = \frac{F_C}{1 - \dfrac{V_C \times 95\%}{S \times 95\% \times 110\%}}$$

There are a number of basic assumptions that are important in this simple construction. It assumes that costs can be divided between variable and fixed, and that the variability of cost to volume can be calculated and is constant. It assumes a constant selling price, as well as no shift in the general price level. If multiple products are included it assumes the volume mix remains the same. It assumes that productivity is constant, that there is proper synchronization between production and sales, and that it is the same over different volumes and time. It assumes that management efficiency is constant, and that competition is frozen in one pattern.

Seldom, if ever, do these assumptions correspond to fact, and their divergence from reality depends upon many forces. If the divergence is wide and cannot be calculated, the analysis has much less value than where divergence is small and can be corrected. For example, if costs change with volume, and the relationships are known, there is no reason why the varying relationships cannot be put in the chart. The cost curve on Chart 11-6 does not have to be straight. Similarly, if a curved demand function can be calculated for sales there is no reason why it should not replace the straight line. But, generally, to develop such data is expensive and unless it improves the results significantly it will not be done.

For a firm producing products whose material prices fluctuate widely and are a predominant element of costs, whose product-mix changes constantly, whose profit margins vary among products, whose advertising is closely related to sales, and whose technology is rapidly changing, the break-even analysis is of little use without major analysis of these evolving relationships in the future.

The fact of the matter is that for a surprising number of companies the simple relationships projected in Chart 11-6 do hold within a range of relevance shown in the chart. The range of relevance is a well-defined area of activity where operational conditions can be assumed to be predictable on a linear basis. Usually this range of relevance is within the near-future expectations of a company. In such instances the break-even analysis can be an important simple tool in integrating complex components of a budgeting and planning system.

ESSENTIALS FOR EFFECTIVE BUDGETING. Developing and using properly a system of budgets is not an easy job. The basic problems are "people problems." Budgets are effective instruments of internal control and in the process of control many difficulties in dealing with people may arise. Indeed, one can agree with Peirce (1954, p. 58) that, "budgeting rests on principles which have more in common with concepts of human relationship than with rules of accounting; and . . . if these principles are applied, successful practice is inevitable." But there are also important managerial and technical problems that must be avoided in the development of an effective budgeting system. Among many of these, as will be seen in the following requirements for effective budgeting, human relationships are of central importance.

First, there must be top management support. No budgeting system can realize its potential value without the unqualified support of top management. The basic reasons why this is so were examined in Chapter 4, and need no further elaboration here.

Second, there must be a clear-cut organizational structure in the firm. For a budgeting program to be most useful each manager must have a clear-cut understanding of his authority and responsibility, his relationships with superiors and subordinates, and his relationships with other organizational units. This is necessary to make sure a budget does not cover more, nor less, than the legitimate activities of each manager. To do so lessens its value as both a planning and a control tool.

Third, the budget system should be planned, and be a part of an effective company-wide planning program. As with an effective overall planning system, the system of budgets must be planned and integrated with planning. The budget system, as noted above, is the cutting edge of planning. It is part of the planning process, but not all of it. To take long-range plans and translate them into quantitative budgets that assure current coordination among functions, and integration with longer-range programs, is the essence of good business planning. Although it is hard to believe, there are some companies whose planning system and budgeting process are not tied together. This is an error.

Fourth, responsibility for the budgeting system must be fixed and understood. Although the ultimate responsibility is top management's, in all but the smallest companies this task is given to someone else, usually the controller or a budget director. Like the planning and control system of which it is a part, everyone should know what is going on and who is supposed to do what. An important problem in achieving effective budget preparation and control is collecting, organizing, disseminating and evaluating information. In larger companies the procedures for operating the system are usually detailed in a manual of instructions.

Fifth, budgets should not dominate decisions. Budgets are made to guide activities; they must be used not as clubs but as tools to achieve the objectives of the enterprise. This has many important implications. It means, for example, that there must be bred into the system an atmosphere that fosters mutual understanding, trust, and common sense in using budgets. Managers should feel that requests for deviations from budgets to give deserved merit increases, for example, or to take advantage of a new opportunity for improving profits, will be most sympathetically received by top managers. It means that no department will fail to cooperate with another for solely budgetary reasons. It means that there is general understanding that, as events change, more dominant company goals may be thwarted by a rigorous adherence to budgets. All this does not mean, of course, that budgets should not be administered with firmness. Rather, it means that they should be administered in such a way that the larger purposes of a company are served as changes take place or new considerations arise that cannot be accommodated within obsolete budgetary limits.

Sixth, accounting jargon should be held to a minimum. Although budgets are not entirely accounting instruments there is much accounting in the structure. I have seen engineering-oriented managers become completely frustrated in trying to understand budget reports that were loaded with excessive and unnecessary technical accounting language. This does not lend itself to better budgeting.

Seventh, care should be taken to assure that the budgeting system does not become too complex, too cumbersome, and too restrictive. Budgeting is a mechanism for delegating authority, and if budgetary restrictions are too detailed and too confining for the exercise of discretion, it creates at first frustrations, then resentment, and finally inertia. Budgets are tools for management, not management itself.

Eighth, better results are achieved if budgets have clearly stated standards upon which basis performance is to be measured. One of the reasons for quantifying plans into concrete budgets is to establish clear bases for action. This means, among other things, that a manager should have responsibility for achieving a goal in an organization over which he has control. Achievement should not be based on actions over which he has no authority.

Ninth, proper understanding of the purposes and limitations of budgets must be created throughout the firm. Budgets basically are tools to facilitate the achievement of the highest aims of a company. They are not, as some lower level managers sometimes are made to feel, clubs to frustrate people. Budgets basically are tools to assure that actions are taken on the basis of a prepared design, not expediency. They are not pressure devices designed to goad people to higher performance. If a salesman, for instance, is capable of selling 15 units but his supervisor thinks he will sell only 10, the latter should be put in the budget, not 15. The 10 is the number for the budget if for no other reason than it is a better basis for linking production, raw material purchases, etc. If a manager thinks a salesman can sell 5 more, motivation should come through other means than lifting the salesman's budget.

Tenth, some understanding of and attention to budget gamesmanship should ferret out practices that should be much reduced or eliminated. Without detailing these the reader can easily write the lyrics to such song-titles as these: "The Year-end Joyride," "Honest Inflation," "They Are Only Estimates, So Why Worry?" "Onus Without Bonus," "Agony Without Ecstasy," "McQueege's Obsession."

Finally, and of importance, there must be participation in the development and use of budgets. People generally do not like budgets, probably because most people do not like to be controlled. One powerful technique to make the restraints of budgets acceptable is to provide for proper participation of people in making budgets that provide standards for their performance. The amount of participation that is possible and desirable differs among management levels and the individuals involved. At the top management levels one finds in more and more companies today a continuous participation of executives in the decision-making process. At the supervisory level, where operations take place within narrow decision constraints, the opportunities for and value of participation are much more limited. Participation that involves top management and the supervisory level is impossible in a large company and, if tried, may result in chaos.

The actual degree of participation depends much upon the superior and the subordinate. Superiors must not only be trained and willing to deal with subordinates but must provide the opportunity for doing so. The subordinate also must be interested in participation. He must also understand that participation does not transfer the superior's authority to him, but that in the end the superior may be forced to modify, revise, or reject a suggestion of the subordinate. Overall, there must be mutual understanding and trust or participation will not be effective.

If participation between the subordinate and the superior in developing budgets is perfunctory, if subordinate suggestions are not taken seriously, and if the arrangement is an obvious sham, the results will be negative. There is substantial evidence that productive results will be achieved only if the character of participation is related to the values, skills, and expectation of the people involved. (Likert, 1961, p. 242.)

An effective budgeting system requires that plans and budgets be made and reviewed at all levels of management through a superior-subordinate face-to-face relationship. In an effective system there is a blend of guidance from the top and the development of plans and budgets from the bottom. This is a balance between the "top down" and "bottom up" approach to planning and budgeting.

There is ample evidence to support the fact that performance of people is significantly improved when they participate properly in decisions affecting their work. In a survey of 204 lower-level supervisors, 78 percent said they resented plans relating to their department without their participation in making them. (Sord and Welsch, 1964, p. 42.) This survey supports the view also that lower-level supervisors who do not participate in planning feel that plans would be better with their participation. (p. 22.)

The reasons for these conclusions are obvious. Proper participation permits two-way communications that can generate understanding and trust and eliminate fears and uncertainty. Participation can also be a training ground. There is no doubt about the fact that people feel committed to achieving objectives they help to set for themselves. The result also should be one that generates appropriate flexibility in operating under budgetary constraints.

INTEGRATED PLANNING AND CONTROL

Conventional budgeting systems sometimes get too cumbersome and managers devote too much attention to simply filling in spaces on forms. (Tomb, 1962, pp. 57-62.) This sort of budget malaise can stifle creativity and hide opportunities for improving profits. Some companies have found that a job-oriented approach to planning, which concentrates on a limited number of objectives where there is worthwhile payoff, is a valuable supplement to the traditional budget systems.

The approach is simple and requires only three steps:

1. Each manager identifies factors for which he is responsible.

2. Each manager selects from all possibilities those in which significant improvements can be made.

3. For each activity selected a plan is prepared, as illustrated in Table 11-7.

This technique has value in that it makes planning and control an integral part of the daily thinking and acting of each manager. This is accomplished in the description of John Tomb (1962, p. 61), because it:

"Integrates planning with each manager's responsibility by relating his plans to the performance elements in his job.

Table 11-7   Illustration of an Integrated Planning and Control Method

OBJECTIVE

Reduce the frequency and cost of faulty castings received from the XYZ Company.

ACTION PROGRAM

Steps	Responsibility	Timing
Ensure recognition by supplier of problem with "hard spots" in castings	Purchasing Manager Production Manager	Completed
Negotiate price concession on all castings received during weeks when we return more than ten bad castings	Purchasing Manager	January 31, 1962
Step up storage area to accumulate ruined castings	Facilities Manager	January 31, 1962
Establish procedures to record machine downtime and cutter breakage with individual castings	Production Control	February 15, 1962
Submit information weekly to XYZ Company	Purchasing Manager	Begin March 1, 1962

PROFIT IMPACT

		1962 Profit Increase/ (Decrease)
Price concessions		$ 7,000
Effect of improved quality	Scrap	8,500
	Overtime	3,500
	Expense Tools	9,000
	Lost Production	20,000
	Other	12,000
Modifications in storage area		(2,000)
Recording procedures		(1,000)
Other costs		(3,000)
	Total Profit Impact	$54,000

Source: Tomb, *A New Way to Manage,* 1962, p. 60.

"Integrates each manager's planning with the continuing search for ways to improve profits.

"Integrates the objectives that each manager sets with a detailed action program for achieving each one.

"Integrates into each individual's plan a measure of the overall purpose of the enterprise—effect on profits.

"Integrates into each manager's planning a commitment to 'make things happen' regardless of changing conditions."

MANAGEMENT IS THE KEY TO
INTEGRATED PLANNING

It hardly needs saying that management is the fundamental instrument to insure that all plans are integrated in the proper fashion and that plans do result in appropriate current action. This matter has been treated previously, especially with respect to the role of top management in planning. It seems useful at this point, however, to touch upon a few major problems, in the translation of strategic plans into current actions, which require management's attention.

PREVENT EXTRAPOLATIONS. When planning is done on an annual cycle there is a tendency, if not carefully watched, for divisions to extrapolate from last year's plans to get the plan for the year added. For example, if a company makes five-year medium-range programs, there is a tendency for divisions to calculate the new fifth-year plan by extrapolation from the previous year's plans, rather than rethink the entire five-year plan. Planning is difficult, costly, and often frustrating for an executive who wants to get on with today's business. If top management does not guard against extrapolation, it will take place as an easy way to respond to central headquarter's request for medium-range programs.

This malady can afflict plans that are made centrally as well as those prepared decentrally. In both instances the danger of contracting this disease resides in some concepts of profit planning. Profit planning should mean the same things as comprehensive corporate planning with the emphasis placed on the word profit. In some companies, however, profit planning has come to mean a projection into the future of the standard accounting statements of income, expense, profits, facilities, and so on. When such projections become financial guesses rather than the financial results of plans actually made by management and staff, they tend to become extrapolations.

One way to avoid this happening is to have medium-range programming proceed upon the basis of individual products, or lines of business, of a company. Plans are made for products or lines of business, as the case may be, and the results are translated into aggregate balance sheet and income statements. This is a very different process than starting with financial aggregations.

DISTINGUISH BETWEEN COMMITMENTS AND PLANS. One of the reasons for dissatisfaction with formal planning is the failure of managers to distinguish between commitments and plans. A commitment is a decision to act; and if this is confused with planning and the development of plans, trouble is sure to arise. For instance, five-year plans were made in a medium-size electrical component company. It became apparent that to meet objectives the company would have to expand its facilities, increase its product development program, and employ new technical talents. Anxious to get moving, commitments by some executives were made too soon for facilities, equipment, and people. Within a year, circumstances had changed so that a different capital expenditure mix was obvious. Had they waited this could have been incorporated in the next planning cycle and there would have been a much better use of capital. The importance of proper timing in acting on plans has been noted previously. This is an art which can be blunted by failure to distinguish between commitments and plans for the future that are not yet ready to be implemented fully but only in that part pertaining to today's activities.

A medium-range program is designed to lay out steps to achieve objectives in an orderly time sequence. It provides a base for beginning today to get ready to exploit opportunities and stop threats tomorrow. It is a preview of things ahead, but action is taken today only when necessary. Actions that can be delayed until fuller information is available should obviously be avoided.

Whether the planning process is formalized or not, managers must constantly rethink the future. For formalized medium-range programming this means once-a-year revisions, with the watchful eye of management in the meantime reevaluating existing plans. If this is not done, and if plans are once set for five or six years and blindly followed, the result can be unhappy.

ESTABLISH DEGREE OF INTEGRATION AMONG PLANS. Top management must determine the degree of interrelationship to exist between strategic plans and medium-range programs, and between medium-range programs and short-range plans. The relationships can be loose or tight. An advertising program for a nondurable consumer product for five years from today need be specified only in broad terms and related only loosely with sales, engineering, and production. On the other hand, a plan to construct an airplane such as the Boeing SST must be laid out in the greatest detail for perhaps 10 to 15 years ahead. There is no formula to give the proper balance over the planning time horizon between precise detail and close interrelationships, and broad estimates and loose interrelationships.

If planning relationships are too tight, there may be lack of interest in planning and stifling of creativity among lower-level managers. On the other hand, if the relationship is too loose the results may be much the same because lower-level managers will not be sure they are performing in conformance with the wishes of top management. Striking the right balance is a matter of managerial style, the nature of the subject of planning, and the structure of the business.

ASSURE ACTIONS RESULT FROM PLANS. Management must insist, of course, that plans are translated into concrete terms for current actions. Vague guesses about what ought to be done in the future without relating them to current actions are not too helpful. When plans are prepared for current action they must be actionable, that is, they must be capable of being implemented. Furthermore, top managers must review the performance of lower-level managers in terms that will stimulate better planning and adherence to plans. If a general manager of a division, for example, is measured principally or solely upon the basis of the current return on investment of his division, he will seek to optimize that measure without much reference to the future. If a manager's return on investment is reviewed in light of his future plans and the future consequences of his current actions, this will not happen. Anyway, better current decisions will follow a balanced review of performance without undue concentration on any one measure. This will be examined in detail in Chapter 13.

THE ACCEPTANCE OF CHANGE. Most people have a resistance to change, especially great change. But business planning is designed to bring about change, often very great change. One major integrating force from strategic plans to action is creating in an organization an adaptability to and an acceptance of change. This is a major responsibility of top management.

Following the classic book of Berle and Means (1933), which popularized the understanding of how business managers of the largest corporations controlled these enterprises even though they did not own them, there were those who felt that the result would be something less than aggressive management. Nothing of the sort happened. On the contrary, the managers of large and small enterprises in the U.S. have set for themselves aggressive objectives that could not be achieved without making major changes in their companies. A driving entrepreneurial and innovative spirit among U.S. managers is probably greater today than at any time in the last three decades. Nevertheless, there is a growing trend in the opposite direction, particularly as corporations grow larger and become more successful. Among such companies the vigor of youth often gives way to the tiredness of old age, complacency replaces aggressiveness, and change becomes something to be avoided. It is avoided because of the attitude, "things are going so well, why change?" This attitude can stiffen into stubborn if not fearful resistance to change.

Comprehensive corporate planning has been described as being at one and the same time the engine for discovering what major changes should take place, and a mechanism by means of which people through participation more readily accept the results of the change process. But there is much more than that to developing acceptance of change. There is a growing trend for leadership patterns and management methods to give greater individual freedom and initiative in the work of business. This, of course, alters expectations of the way people feel they should be treated. It also makes them more adaptable to changes. (Bennis, 1966 and McGregor, 1967.)

This trend is growing for a variety of reasons. The educational level of workers throughout business is rising, and throughout our society there is increasing concern about the growth of individuals and their ability to lead satisfying lives. President Johnson (1964), in his famous speech about the Great Society, said, "The purpose of protecting the life of our nation and preserving the liberty of our citizens is to pursue the happiness of our people." In another passage, he said, "The challenge of the next half century is whether we have the wisdom to use [our] wealth to enrich and elevate our national life . . . and to advance the quality of American civilization." This is a view that the Great Society must build for each person a richer life of mind and spirit. The spirit of this speech, which in the long run will crystallize into national goals, will more and more affect the way people work in organizations.

The growing complexity of business operations demands the increasing use of specialists from many disciplines, and complex decision-making throughout organizations increasingly requires the participation of these specialists. The rise in this type activity is breaking down the old barriers of rigid and detailed management control methods.

Bennis (1966, p. 19*) has observed that, "Democracy becomes a functional necessity whenever a social system is competing for survival under conditions of chronic change." The term "democracy" he says, is not permissiveness or laissez-faire but rather a system of values, a climate of beliefs governing behavior which people accept and put into practice. They include:

"1. Full and free communication, regardless of rank and power.

2. A reliance on consensus, rather than on the more customary forms of coercion or compromise, to manage conflict.

3. The idea that influence is based on technical competence and knowledge rather than on the vagaries of personal whims or prerogatives of power.

4. An atmosphere that permits and even encourages emotional expression as well as task-oriented acts.

5. A basically human bias, one which accepts the inevitability of conflict between the organization and the individual but which is willing to cope with and mediate this conflict on rational grounds." (pp. 18-19.)

There are today very few companies that operate on the basis of all of these acts of beliefs but as was said above the direction is toward this end. An organization operating with these beliefs as guides will be one in which the acceptance of change will be very high.

It is not necessary to reorganize completely to Bennis' model to improve the acceptance of change. Many things can be done, and are being done, in present organizations to facilitate the change process. It is too much of a generalization to say that people resist all change for most people welcome certain types of change. It is the function of management, therefore, to make proposed changes acceptable to people who are affected by them, if that is at all possible. One chief executive who is highly successful in doing this has set forth the following ten guides growing from his experience:

"Change is more acceptable when it is understood than when it is not.

"Change is more acceptable when it does not threaten security than when it does.

"Change is more acceptable when those affected have helped to create it than when it has been externally imposed.

"Change is more acceptable when it results from an application of previously established impersonal principles than it is when it is dictated by personal order.

"Change is more acceptable when it follows a series of successful changes than it is when it follows a series of failures.

"Change is more acceptable when it is inaugurated after prior change has been assimilated than when it is inaugurated during the confusion of other major change.

"Change is more acceptable if it has been planned than it is if it is experimental.

"Change is more acceptable to people new on the job than to people old on the job.

"Change is more acceptable to people who share in the benefits of change than to those who do not.

"Change is more acceptable if the organization has been trained to plan for improvement than it is if the organization is accustomed to static procedures." (Besse, 1957, pp. 62-63.)

To follow these fundamentals, and to move toward the "democracy" of the behavioral scientists to the extent and to the degree practicable, is to assure much closer and integrated linkage between strategic planning and actions.

GUIDES TO INTEGRATING PLANS

This chapter examined some of the major problems of, and methods for, integrating plans. The cutting edge of planning is making sure that current actions take place in light of longer-range plans. This requires, therefore, not only an interrelationship among strategic, medium-range, and short-range plans, but integration of these plans at different levels and over different time periods. A resumé of guides to integrated planning from this chapter follows.

First, the degree of interrelationship among plans must vary among companies, styles of managements, and other considerations. Each management must determine for itself how loose or how tight the relationship should be. If it is too loose, or too tight, it tends to bring about a sort of planning fatigue which lowers the enthusiasm, interest, and effectiveness of lower-level planning.

Second, efforts to coordinate completely all functions in a planning program, particularly in distant future periods of time, is ill-advised. In most companies, only the major functions are coordinated with any degree of precision. The further out in time, the more precise integration fades into trends and patterns.

Third, integration of plans is facilitated by developing both quantitative and qualitative plans. Many major elements of plans cannot be reduced to quantitative terms and still convey the essential or required meaning. A mixture of quantitative and qualitative plans is helpful in permitting cross-references among functions, interrelating levels of planning, and providing cross-checks for evaluations.

Fourth, methods to integrate plans are numerous but the most universally used basis for translating strategic plans into actions is a budget system. Budgets can be and are made for long periods of time, but the current short-range budgets are the ones which bring action in light of higher-level and longer-range plans. Current budgets are major devices to express planned intentions in quantitative terms, to coordinate different functional operations of the firm, and to provide a means for measuring performance and permitting proper control of operations.

Fifth, the essentials of an effective budgeting system are as follows:

• There must be top management support.
• There must be a clear-cut organizational structure in the firm.
• The budget system should be planned and integrated into the more comprehensive planning effort.
• Responsibility for the budgeting system must be fixed and understood.
• Budgets should not dominate decisions, that is, they should not replace managerial judgment.
• Accounting jargon should be held to a minimum in budgets and budget reports.
• Care should be taken to assure that the budgeting system does not become too complex, cumbersome, and restrictive.
• Better results will be achieved if budgets have clearly stated standards against which performance is to be measured.
• Proper understanding of the purposes and limitations of budgets must be created throughout the firm.

- The more sporty aspects of budget gamesmanship must be avoided, such as spending surplus the last few days of the budget year simply as a basis for next year's bargaining.
- There must be widespread participation in the development and use of budgets.

Sixth, in working out current intricate interrelationships among costs, price, and production volume, the break-even analysis is simple and can be very effective when properly used.

Seventh, a job-oriented approach to planning, which concentrates on a limited number of objectives where there is a worthwhile payoff, can be a valuable supplement to traditional budget systems, particularly when they become voluminous.

Eighth, management is the dominant key to integrated planning. Management must prevent extrapolations of plans made on the basis of last year's efforts. There must be a careful understanding of the difference between commitments and plans, and actions must result from plans. Finally, and of great significance, top management has a major responsibility in creating an organizational climate that is adaptable to and accepts change.

PART III

Tools for More Rational Planning

12
Rationality in Planning ————

12
Rationality in Planning

INTRODUCTION

The present chapter aims to explore the meaning of rational decision-making in the planning process and to examine some of the major impediments to and aids for making more rational business decisions. This survey will lead into discussion of the realities of the business decision-making process and an analysis of competing theories developed to measure rationality. Since the specialist is being used more and more to help managers in decision-making, and since there are significant problems in the interrelationships between the two, this matter will also be treated at length.

DECISION DEFINED

Like so many other words in the lexicon of planning there are many definitions of the word decision. It is important to define this word, and to classify types of decisions, because methods to make rational decisions vary much depending upon the nature and type of decision to be made.

The word decision is derived from the Latin root *decido*, meaning to cut off (*de*, off; *caedo*, cut). The generic concept of decision, therefore, is settlement, fixed intention, bringing to a conclusive result, judgment, and resolution. A decision is a choice made by a decision-maker about what should or should not be done in a given situation.

Barnard (1954, p. 185) adds another dimension to the concept of decision. He says that acts of individuals may be divided into two parts: those which result from deliberation, calculation, and thought; and those which are unconscious, automatic, and responsive. The first results in decisions, but these decisions also embody subsidiary acts which are the latter.*

* Shackle expresses this thought somewhat differently by stating that decision-making is "the focal creative psychic event where knowledge, thought, feeling and imagination are fused into action." C. F. Carter, Meredith, and Shackle (eds.), 1957, p. 105.

Whenever a decision is made there are present an end to be accomplished and the means to get there. Decision is necessary in choosing both the end to be sought and the means to achieve it. M. H. Jones (1957, p. 5) defines decision largely in these latter terms. He says, "a decision [is] a course of action chosen by the decider as the most effective means at his disposal for achieving the goals or goal he is currently emphasizing—for solving the problem that is bothering him."

Business decisions result from a decision-making process. As Cooper (1961, pp. 43-53) says: "A decision is a point reached in a stream of action." It is a process which is synonymous with the problem-solving steps presented in Chapter 2. Indeed, some writers like Silk (1960a, p. 19) define the decision-making process in these terms. Another definition with this thought is: a decision is a mental event or choice that causes an act or brings about another mental activity which in turn causes an act or another mental event.

SOME MAJOR CHARACTERISTICS OF THE
BUSINESS DECISION PROCESS

In this book all these characteristics of decision and the decision-making process will be in mind. There are also other outstanding characteristics of the decision-making process that should be mentioned because they bear importantly on any concept of rationality of business action. Of most importance are these: decision-making in business is sequential, is exceedingly complex, involves personal values, and is made in an institutional setting.

DECISION-MAKING IS SEQUENTIAL. It is very important to understand that most decisions in business are not isolated events which have no antecedents. Some decisions may appear to be made on the spur of the moment, to be made in one instant of time, to be "snap" decisions. Such appearances may obscure, for the naive, the long chain of previous developments. Only rarely can it be said that important business decision-making is of this sort. A significant business decision is a compilation of many decisions extending over the entire problem-solving spectrum and often over a long period of time. A business decision is made in the course of and grows out of the lengthy, complex, and intricate process of problem discovery, exploration of methods to resolve it, and analysis of means.

As Marion Folsom (1962, p. 4*), for a long time in the top management of the Eastman Kodak Company and one-time Secretary of the Department of Health, Education and Welfare in the Eisenhower Administration, explains, "Decisions generally are the result of a long series of discussions by both line and

* From *Executive Decision-Making* by Marion B. Folsom. Copyright © 1962 by the Trustees of Columbia University. Used by permission of McGraw-Hill Book Company.

staff people after the staff has collected the pertinent material. It is often hard to pinpoint the exact stage at which a decision is reached. More often than not, the decision comes about naturally during discussions, when the consensus seems to be reached among those whose judgment and opinion the executive seeks."

THE DECISION-MAKING PROCESS IS VERY COMPLEX. Many decisions at low levels in the managerial chain may be reasonably uncomplicated, but as decisions are made higher in the administrative hierarchy the complications mount.

The decision-making process, at a minimum, consists of an intricate interrelationship among experts, job responsibility, group deliberation, communication and information systems, questions of administrative feasibility, and codes of morals and ethics. The interrelationships of these elements change as the process flows over time. And always, information is insufficient. Also, the manager who decides frequently finds that equally talented staff and line managers come to opposing points of view.

Seemingly simple decisions may turn out, on analysis, to have wide implications. Chester Barnard (1954, p. 198), a former public utility executive, observed that a decision to move a telephone pole from position A to position B requires 10,000 decisions of many people in many places, and involves successive analyses of environments including social, moral, legal, economic, and physical facts of the environment.*

President Truman used to complain that it was impossible for him to make a simple decision. What he meant was that every decision he made involved an analysis of enormously complex forces, and when the decision was made it generated unbelievably intricate reactions. It took Gross (1953) a full-length book to describe the decisions that led to the passage of the Employment Act of 1946.

THE DECISION-MAKING PROCESS IS FLUID. From company to company and within the same company the decision-making process is always changing. It differs in terms of group size, the way management information systems are set up, the types of decisions which are to be made, the leadership style of managers, and the stage of decision-making.

DECISIONS INVOLVE MANAGEMENT NONQUANTIFIABLE VALUES. In response to a query from the press about how decisions were made in the White House, Press Secretary Moyers replied: "You begin with the general principle that the process of decision-making is inscrutable. No man knows how a decision is ultimately shaped. It's usually impossible even to know at what

* Richard F. Barton defines policy decision with this chain reaction in mind: "A business policy decision is a decision in which the alternative chosen is implemented by becoming a goal in a subsequent decision." (June 1966, p. 120.)

point a decision is made." (*Los Angeles Times,* January 23, 1966, p. 1.)

This insight into Presidential decision-making applies equally to many major business decisions. When asked how decisions were made, Dwight Joyce, President of Glidden, said, "If a vice-president asks me how I was able to choose the right course, I have to say, 'I'm damned if I know.' " John McCaffrey, President of International Harvester, said, "It is like asking a pro baseball player to define the swing that has always come natural to him." (McDonald, 1955, p. 85.)

What Moyers and the business presidents are emphasizing, of course, are the judgmental and the intuitive factors involved in the decision-making process. Whenever decisions can be made automatically, they are not made by managers but by machines, hence all managerial decisions involve judgment. The analysis that is made in preparation for the decision, however, is not at all mysterious. Preceding chapters examined in depth the type of penetrating, scholarly, and voluminous research which is often used as a basis for many managerial decisions. Although most of the process of what should be done to make better decisions is identifiable and clear, that process by means of which a final value judgment of the executive is injected into the process is obscure and inscrutable.

DECISIONS ARE MADE IN AN INSTITUTIONAL SETTING. As demonstrated in previous chapters any company with an organized planning process has an integrated set of institutional arrangements within which decision-making can proceed in an orderly fashion. In this setting there are understood guides for, restraints upon, and stimuli to make decisions. The multiplicity of decisions made in the process are interrelated by a network of aims, decision-making processes, and tests of desirability. To be sure, many decisions in a business may be made outside the organized planning process. But most of the major business decisions are related directly or indirectly to the planning process when that process is well established.

Even though a company does not have an organized planning process, the decision-making, except in the smallest of companies, is made in an institutional setting in which the characteristics of the organization and the people in it bear heavily upon the decision-making process. The way things are done, the way people think, the information systems, and other such elements, influence how decisions are made and carried out. The decision-making that goes on in a company cannot be understood without a comprehension of these environmental forces.

DESCRIPTIVE THEORY OF DECISION-MAKING. In recent years a number of writers have described different parts of a business firm's decision-making process in an effort to develop better theories of decision-making. An ambitious attempt at covering the broad area of setting aims and finding means to reach them is that of Cyert and March (1963). A number of writers are looking at decision-theory models in functional areas. The work of Roberts (1964) is illustrative. In a real sense the present book is a descriptive theory of decision-making in the planning process. But no one has yet developed a descriptive theoretical model for the entire decision-making process in a firm which has been generally accepted.

TYPES OF DECISIONS

There are a number of classifications of business decisions. It is significant to recognize different types of decisions because a method for assuring rationality in one type decision may not be useful in another, or the degree of management understanding of the consequences of one type of action may be much different than for another.

BROAD-COMPREHENSIVE AND TACTICAL-OPERATIONAL DECISIONS. One obvious classification is that which follows the conceptual model of planning presented in Chapter 2. At one end of the model are the broad, fundamental decisions associated with the basic mission of a company and its long-range objectives, policies and strategies. At the other end are the short-range administrative, tactical, and more or less automatic decision-making devices.

ORGANIZATIONAL AND PERSONAL DECISIONS. When an executive acts formally in his role as a company official he makes organizational decisions. Such decisions can be and often are delegated and those at lower echelons then make further decisions based upon them. Personal decisions are those made by an executive acting as an individual member of an organization. These decisions ordinarily cannot be delegated, and if subsequent decisions must be made to implement them the same executive makes those decisions as well. Personal and organizational decisions in practice naturally intertwine; consequently elements of both are found in most decisions (Barnard, 1954, pp. 188-189).

PROGRAMMED AND NONPROGRAMMED DECISIONS. Herbert Simon has developed this useful classification of decisions. In computer language, programmed decisions are those which can be programmed on a computer, and nonprogrammed ones are those which in the present state of the art cannot. Broadly, as Simon describes them, the programmed decisions are repetitive and routine; nonprogrammed decisions are novel and unstructured.

There are different variations of this classification. McFarland (1964, pp. 167-168) speaks of basic and routine types which roughly correspond to Simon's. Another grouping is that of closed and open models for decision-making. These, too, are similar to Simon's programmed and nonprogrammed decisions, respectively.

CERTAINTY AND UNCERTAINTY. For some decisions, for which virtually complete information about inputs and outputs is available, there is very little uncertainty present. The purchase of a short-term government bond belongs in this classification. On the other hand are decisions where probabilities of outcome are not certain but can be stated. These are called decisions under risk. The decision of a roulette player is typical of such a decision. A third type are those where probabilities cannot be stated. These are decisions under uncertainty. The availability of information constitutes the dividing line among these three.

This nomenclature, as that in the preceding subsection, is associated with a new body of knowledge called decision theory. Decision theory is concerned mainly with the mathematical logic of choice under conditions of uncertainty.*

PROBLEM-SOLVING DECISIONS. Anshen (in Bowman and Fillerup, 1963, p. 23) has classified decisions according to the traditional problem-solving and planning steps. They are, first, agenda decisions, or those involved in identifying problems, selecting problems to be examined and assigning priorities among problems. Search decisions are related to the selection of procedures for finding solutions. Also included are decisions concerned with personnel, money, and time to be committed to the search. Allocation decisions are those which commit resources to selected lines of action to solve the problem which initially began the exercise. Implementation decisions are those involved in determining who does what, when, where, and how. Finally, evaluation decisions are those which concern the assessment of performance against predetermined goals and standards. Also included are the development of ideas for modification, innovation, and the generation of new agenda items which inevitably grow out of the evaluation process.

This classification shows that: (1) much creativity and imagination are involved in the decision-making process; (2) decision-making cannot be understood without deep knowledge of the human animal; (3) decision-making covers a multitude of problems having both qualitative and quantitative characteristics; and (4) the process is sequential.†

DEGREE OF CHANGE AND UNDERSTANDING. Chart 12-1 examines decisions in terms of degree of change and understanding of consequences. On the

---

* One group of writers in this field, for example, says: "We shall define decision theory as being primarily concerned with how to assist people (or organizations) in making decisions, and improving the decision process under conditions of uncertainty." Bierman, Jr., Bonini, Fouraker, and Jaedicke, 1965, p. 55.

† See Albert H. Rubenstein, *Organization and Research and Development Decision-making Within the Decentralized Firm*, Evanston, Ill., Northwestern University, 1960 (mimeographed), for a comparable classification developed for and applied to research and development organizations.

Chart 12-1

Classification of Decisions

by Understanding and Change

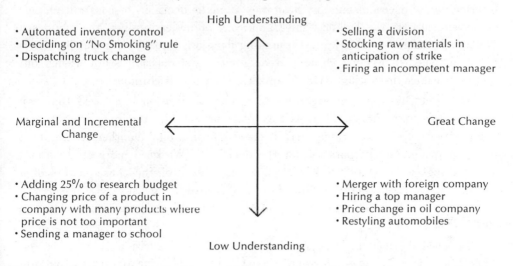

High Understanding

· Automated inventory control
· Deciding on "No Smoking" rule
· Dispatching truck change

· Selling a division
· Stocking raw materials in
  anticipation of strike
· Firing an incompetent manager

Marginal and Incremental
Change

Great Change

· Adding 25% to research budget
· Changing price of a product in
  company with many products where
  price is not too important
· Sending a manager to school

· Merger with foreign company
· Hiring a top manager
· Price change in oil company
· Restyling automobiles

Low Understanding

horizontal spectrum are decisions which range from those causing a marginal or incremental change to those resulting in large and important change. On the vertical spectrum are those ranging from a low understanding of impact to those with a high understanding of consequence.

Programmed decisions tend to be in the left-hand side of the Chart, particularly in the upper left-hand corner. In this area are decisions that primarily relate to the internal allocation of resources. The really fateful decisions frequently lie in the lower-right-hand quartile.

OTHER CLASSIFICATIONS. There are still other groupings which are self-explanatory. Decisions can be classified depending on the organizational level at which they are made, the degree of pressure of time in making them, one-time compared with repetitive decisions, the magnitude of possible results, or satisfactory versus theoretically optimum decisions.

FINALITY OF DECISIONS

When a decision is made it means that a manager is committed to an action. As firms grow larger and decisions become more important a greater degree of permanence tends to involve the commitment made. In other words, a large firm cannot afford the turmoil that would result from constant changes in important decisions.

On the other hand, few decisions can be said to be final. President Truman used to say that he was not fearful of making decisions because they could always be changed.

The indecisive, apprehensive decision-maker can find all sorts of excuses to delay decision or, once a decision is made, to reopen the case. Such an executive is a source of great frustration. In all companies of any size there is an interlocking of decisions and any hesitancy to make decisions or constant change of decision upsets the balance, the framework of understanding, that guides a multiplicity of actions. Hesitancy in making decisions is not wrong, but it creates problems when it becomes chronic. Reopening a past decision is not wrong, but it, too, becomes disrupting to an organization when it is chronic.

Hesitancy to make, or eagerness to reopen, a decision is a game that can be played in many ways. There is the plausible gambit stemming from a new perspective: "Hold everything; here is more information." Another technique is to plead incomplete preparation for the decision: "We need more study about a few things we did not think enough about." Fear of the consequences of a decision may flutter many a faint heart. This executive asks: "Is this *really* what we should do?" There are many other ploys in this delaying game. (Cooper, 1961, p. 47.)

Barnard's (1954, p. 194) standard for making a decision that sticks, is: "The fine art of executive decision consists in not deciding questions that are not now pertinent, in not deciding prematurely, in not making decisions that cannot be made effective, and in not making decisions that others should make."

RATIONAL DECISION-MAKING DEFINED

It was noted above that a decision is concerned with an end to be achieved and the means to do it. A rational business decision is one which effectively and efficiently assures the achievement of aims for which the means are selected. If I am cold and want to get warm it is rational to get close to a fire. If I am in business and want to make a profit it is rational for me to produce goods and try to sell them at a price over cost.

These simple concepts soon get complicated by the fact that rationality in business is a multidimensional concept. What is rational depends upon who is looking. Two oil companies are operating in the Middle East. One pays a generous price for its oil but assumes such a cold and arrogant attitude toward the governments with which it does business that antipathy towards U.S. citizens is high. Another is a sharp bargainer and pays a minimum price but, because the company managers and the foreign government executives communicate well and work together with mutual trust and understanding, there is immense goodwill for everything about the U.S. Which company is acting rationally? At a very different level, management is faced with a decision whether to expense or capitalize a research and development cost. Strong arguments can be developed for each course of action. Which is more rational? (Hawkins, 1963). There is no simple, easy answer to the basic question raised in either case.

Many individuals and groups are interested in every action of a business. Each may have a different objective and, therefore, a different view about what is or is not a rational decision. Merely to list some of the major groups and individuals looking at a business decision is to illustrate the point. They are stockholders, consumers, employees, different government executives and commissions, managers, suppliers, competitors, creditors, professors, and the general citizen.

This suggests, perhaps, that rationality may be defined as the best selection of means to achieve objectives from a system of values acceptable to the evaluator and by which the consequences of the decision can be measured. This means that, if I am a stockholder and have the objective of maximizing rate of return on my investment, I can see and appraise the consequences of decisions with this measure. I may be completely unable to measure the rationality of any one particular decision, but I can determine from and for my scale of values the rationality of the aggregate of decisions over time. But even this turns out to be a very difficult determination because many forces operating on a business may have a great influence on my rate of return. Conceivably, a theoretically irrational decision may turn out to result in a maximization of my rate of return purely as a result of unexpected events. At any rate, in theory at least, each group looking at a business has a system of values and, generally speaking, has measures to determine how well those values are being satisfied by business decisions.

But the question arises: Is a decision "rational" if it turns out to be wrong only because the information available at the time was wrong? If a businessman thinks he should raise a price to preserve his profit position and this action brings down on his company the wrath of the President of the United States, is the decision rational? Or, take the case of a person who bought surplus electronic components from the U.S. government and found he could not dispose of them. Later, however, the government found a need for the components and bought them back at a large loss to itself. Was the original purchase a rational decision?

The only way to extricate oneself from such perplexities is, as Simon (1957, pp. 76-77) suggests, to differentiate among types of rationality. He suggests that a decision is "objectively" rational if it maximizes a given value in a given situation in terms of the discipline used to measure results. A decision is "subjectively" rational if it maximizes attainment relative to the actual knowledge of the subject. It is "consciously" rational to the extent that the process of decision-making is a conscious one. It is "organizationally" rational to the degree a decision is oriented to organizational ends. It is "personally" rational to the extent it achieves an individual's personal goals. These adverbs which describe types of rational action do not exhaust possibilities.

There are yet other ways to look at rationality. Gross (1964, p. 747) suggests three dimensions to determine rationality. First, is the desirability or the extent to which a given action satisfies human interests. Second, is the feasibility or the adaption of means to given ends. Third, is consistency.

THEORIES OF RATIONAL BUSINESS DECISIONS

There have been two main lines of thought about rational decision-making in business which extend back several hundred years. For generations they were reasonably closely related, but in recent years they have splintered into many different approaches to rationality. As a result, there is today no single universally accepted theory of what is a rational business decision.

One old main line of thought was the economist's theory of the firm which, among other things, prescribed, as discussed in detail in Chapter 7, that rational business action was that which served to maximize profits. This was the generally accepted view on the subject up to recent years.

The second main line was that developed by management and organization theorists. This body of thought has always been more diverse and more difficult to classify and characterize than the first.

It is worthwhile to look back over the development of thinking in the second area to help understand better some of the heated current debate about an important element of business theory. This debate is not likely to be settled easily nor soon, and as it continues important choices will be made on the basis of it both in the academic and in the business world.

In tracing this history it should be noted that the development of a theory of management covers a subject considerably broader than rationality of decision-making. It goes without saying that in focusing attention only on rationality full justice cannot be done to the different approaches in the development of a theory of management. But I think the picture will not be too distorted by this focus and will make clear again that the definition of rational business decision depends upon who is looking.

HISTORICAL ANTECEDENTS. From the earliest times of formal organizations and business enterprises there have been theories about wise decisions. (Gross, 1964, pp. 91-234; and Mee, 1963.) Machiavelli's *The Prince* (1950) published in 1532, for instance, is a brilliant discourse on preferred courses of action for leaders. Throughout its history the Christian church has never felt constrained in establishing proper courses of action for businessmen. I am certain that Luca Paciolo (Brown and Johnston, 1963), who so brilliantly described double-entry bookkeeping in 1494, would have said any businessman not using his system was acting irrationally. These few examples merely freshen our memories that history is replete with examples of standards for judging rational business action.

EARLY WRITERS OF MANAGEMENT THEORY. The origins of modern management theory lie in the writings of a few men in the early 19th century. Notable among the early explorers who sought to develop principles of management which would improve business operations and, inferentially, produce more rational decisions, were Babbage and Owen. Babbage (Merrill, 1960, pp. 29-44), a British mathematical scientist, published his book of management principles in 1832. He saw "principles which seemed to pervade many establishments." Owen (1825 in Merrill, 1960, pp. 21-25) pointed out the need for paying attention to human beings at a time when few factory operators had any interest in workers' living conditions, and lays claim to being the father of personnel management and a harbinger of the Mayo experiments. These writings were half a century after Adam Smith's *Wealth of Nations* (1776) and appeared at a time when David Ricardo possessed, and John Stuart Mill was building, an elegant and widely accepted theory of economics. This discipline became one foundation for social and political philosophers who concerned themselves with rational business activity.*

PIONEERS OF CLASSICAL MANAGEMENT THEORY. The founders of the classical school of management wrote at the turn of the century, but their school of thought continues to this day. They took two main approaches to improving efficiency and rationality in decision-making in business. One was the development of principles for more effective management, and the other was the application of scientific methods to improve efficiency. These approaches, of course, are related.

Henri Fayol (1916 translated by Storrs, 1949) stands as the giant in the first approach. He was a successful engineer and manager who felt that management should be taught in the schools and that this could be stimulated by the development of principles, or general guides, to administration. In his most famous work he set forth fourteen basic principles which had general acceptance in schools and in business, and to a large extent, they are still accepted. His principles concerned division of work, authority, discipline, unity of command, unity of direction, subordination of individual interests to the general interest, remuneration, centralization, line of authority, order, equity, stability of tenure of personnel, initiative, and esprit de corps. To Fayol, and those who followed in his footsteps, rational decisions were those made in conformance with his enunciated principles.

A somewhat different approach, but one of major importance, is the work of the great sociologist Max Weber. He sought to develop "ideal" arrangements for all bureaucratic organizations, and listed the characteristics of this ideal in terms of levels of the hierarchical structure and the rules and laws which bound them together. Bureaucratic administration, with its own structure, was to Weber the most rational way to deal with the development of means to achieve

---

* For identification of these early writings associated with the development of management theory, see Mee, 1963, Chapter 1, and Lloyd, 1964.

defined ends for the organization. He called this formal rationality and compared it with substantive rationality, which dealt with the basic need of people in a nation.*

Two contemporary members in good standing of this first approach are Luther Gulick and Lyndall Urwick (1937). Both men built upon the principles laid down by Fayol and stimulated a stream of writers in the same tradition whose works are still important and widely accepted.†

Frederick Taylor is the commanding figure who at the turn of the century stimulated the application of the scientific method to the solution of factory problems. As an engineer who was appointed a gang boss, he became bitterly engaged in a conflict with the workers when he sought to increase output. He decided that the basic cause of the battle was that management did not know what was a proper day's work and, not knowing, tried to increase output by pressure. He, therefore, set about to discover the best ways of performing, and the proper time, for every operation and every component unit of an operation. This meant the best tool, the best use of time, the best machine, and the best flow of work. With meticulous care he devised measures for these elements.‡ To Taylor, rational action was based upon the development of measures of work performance, rules, and mathematical formulations that could be used as standards of performance.

CHALLENGES TO CLASSICAL CONCEPTS OF RATIONALITY. To an ever-widening phalanx of observers and practitioners of business decisions, the older postulates of managerial rationality are being challenged. Some of the challenges have been violent attacks on the classical theorists. Others seek only modifications of the older criteria of rationality. Some only inferentially set up competitive systems of rationality. But, the controversy has been appropriately pictured by my colleague Harold Koontz (1961, pp. 174-188) as "jungle warfare." Students of the subject have not yet settled on a classification system for the different approaches.§ At the risk of further muddying these

* Max Weber was a prolific writer but for his exposition of the "ideal-type" of bureaucracy, see Weber, translated by A. M. Henderson and Parsons, edited by Parsons, 1947.

† For an excellent resume of this classical school, see March and Simon, 1958, Chapter 2.

‡ Among Taylor's major works are "Shop Management," a paper presented to the American Society of Mechanical Engineers in 1903, "Principles of Scientific Management," 1911, and his testimony in Hearings Before Special Committee of the House of Representatives to Investigate the Taylor and Other Systems of Shop Management Under Authority of H. Res. 90, Vol. III, pp. 1377-1508, 1912. These are conveniently found in Taylor, 1947.

§ Efforts to classify approaches to the theory of management can be found in: Koontz, 1961; Suojanen, 1963, pp. 7-17; Filippo, 1968, pp. 91-98; and Gordon, 1963, pp. 290-302.

waters, I shall include the many current approaches to the development of a management theory under four major groupings: the process or operational theorists, the behavioral scientists, quantitative scientists, and miscellaneous observers of business. My purpose is not to try to picture all the current approaches, a subject done well by others. Rather, it is to get the flavor of the approaches.

Process or Operational Theorists

The approach of the process or operational theorists to management theory, says Koontz (1961, p. 175), "perceives management as a process of getting things done through and with people operating in organized groups." It analyzes and explains the process, develops a conceptual structure for it, and builds on this basis a set of principles and guides for management's actions. This school recognizes that firms, especially the larger ones, have multiple objectives and there are multiple interests focused on them. It recognizes that many areas of knowledge are important to and used by managers in the process of devising means to achieve the objectives set for their business. Rationality in this approach would be measured by the extent to which managers established appropriate objectives for their enterprise, developed the means which were most effective and efficient in reaching those goals, and did this with judicial use of available knowledge and wise balancing of various interests focused on the enterprise.

Behavioral Scientists

The behavioral scientists do not so much challenge the idea of principles or guides to rational behavior but rather feel that the classical writers did not consider sufficiently, or misunderstood, the human elements of management. The approaches to this common theme are most diverse and range from the development of useful insights on particular subjects to attempts at the creation of an overall theory to determine rational decision-making.

An early exponent of the individual was Mary Follett (in Metcalf and Urwick, 1942), who contributed a wide variety of fundamental truths and insights concerning people in organizations. She was one of the first to argue that the scientific method could be applied to human relations and that managers too frequently missed the psychological foundations of management.

In a series of empirical studies at the Hawthorne plant of the Western Electric Company near Chicago, stimulated by the urgings of Mary Follett, Mayo (1933 and 1945) and Roethlisberger (1941 and 1954) laid the foundation for a broad search into the human relations phenomenon in business. They found that an individual's sense of participation, a feeling of being a part of a team, is a more powerful motivating force than economic rewards, rest periods, lighting, and comparable material influences.

Another major contributor in this field was Chester Barnard (1954, p. 65.), President of the New Jersey Bell Telephone Company. He viewed the firm as a cooperative system in which individuals worked together to seek the firm's objectives. To him, this system was "a complex of physical, biological, personal, and social components which are in specific systematic relationships by reason of the cooperation of two or more persons for at least one definite end." He did not feel that individual and firm objectives were necessarily identical, but he did see individuals cooperating in a common endeavor. Rational action in a firm to him would be that which assured the communication, coordination, and motivation necessary to weld the organization into a cooperative effort to reach common ends.

To this brief account may be added the discussion of Chapter 7 concerned with behavioral scientists' attitudes towards conflicts between individual and firm objectives. Together with what has been said here, some of the richness of this approach in modifying older concepts of rational business behavior may be appreciated.

Quantitative Scientists

Since World War II there has been a major expansion of work concerned with the application of quantitative analysis to business problems in order to insure more rational decisions. At first this approach was called operations research, but now the more general term is management science. Management science is fundamentally a hybrid science in that it has its origins in many other more basic sciences—mathematics, physics, biology, physiology, engineering, economics, and so on. But it has a central aim and that is to help managers make more rational decisions by applying scientific methods and attitudes and associated techniques, particularly quantitative analysis and mathematical models, to operational problems. The emphasis of management science is to formulate a goal or a problem in quantitative terms, if possible; develop quantitative measures of effectiveness in achieving a solution or reaching a goal; incorporate all pertinent interrelationships in a model, preferably quantified and in a mathematical model; and then test both the model and the solution to find the optimum answer. The more accurately the model duplicates the phenomenon and permits the acquisition of correct quantitative information, the more powerful it is in measuring the output consequences of inputs.

Rationality to management scientists is, in a general way, the rigorous application of the scientific method to problem solving, with heavy emphasis upon mathematics and optimization of output per unit of input. But when one looks at the various types of tools used by management scientists there appear different types of rationality. For instance, industrial dynamicists focus attention on achieving equilibrium in operations as environmental changes take place. In the application of probability theory to decision-making, emphasis is placed on choosing the highest expected values. In many linear programming models the focus is on optimizing profits, or minimizing costs, or both. Chapter 15 will explore this matter more deeply.

Miscellaneous Observers of Business Decisions

We may note, without further discussion, that just about every other major field of knowledge has produced observations relating to rationality of business decisions. In Chapter 7 were noted challenges to the economist's theory of the firm. Fritz Machlup (1967, pp. 3-33) identified ten different concepts advanced by economists and said he probably could find 21 if he tried. Other economists have also identified different approaches to the theory of the firm. (Cyert and March, 1963, pp. 10-13; and McGuire, 1961.) Many writers in other disciplines have sought a theory of the firm and rational managerial action from the point of view of their own expertise. They are too many to mention here but have been summarized by others. (Gross, 1964, Chapter 8.)

CRITERIA FOR RATIONAL BUSINESS DECISIONS. We return to our basic question: What is a rational business decision? The result of the boiling ferment in the development of management theory is that we today have many approaches to rationality and a formidable array of tools for determining it. But there is no universal standard. Each body of doctrine that can be called a discipline views rationality in terms of its own set of values. This does not mean that there is always conflict in these views. Many times the views are different but are complementary in that they look at the same result in a different way. So, there is no recourse but to return once again to the view that what is rational depends upon who is looking.

It is also true, however, that current thinking about the business firm shows clearly there is no universally accepted theory of its operations. This is a major step forward from the time when there was general acceptability of a theory that was more conceptual than operational. It is also true that, as a result of this ferment and interest in management theory in general and the theory of the firm in particular, a very large body of knowledge has been developed and a very large array of methods made available to help the businessman be more rational in terms of the most important values he chooses to use in managing his enterprise.

THE TOOL-KIT OF TECHNIQUES FOR RATIONAL PLANNING DECISIONS

Table 12-1 presents a classification of major methods which can help managers make more rational decisions in the planning process. This is by no means an exhaustive list and there are many variations of many of the methods listed.

Furthermore, the listing is not mutually exclusive. Not only does a semantic problem interfere with a clean-cut classification, but the differences between older and newer methods are not always too clear. For example, simulation as a tool can fit into several of the classifications. Also, the difference between older and newer simulation techniques is a debatable point.

But with all its imperfections Table 12-1 has three virtues. First, it highlights the fact that there is indeed a rich assortment of tools, many of great power, which are available for managers in making decisions more easily and with more assurance that they are more rational. Second, it underscores the fact that the spectrum of useful tools ranges from the old nonquantitative to

Table 12-1 A Classification of Major Tools and Techniques for Rational Decision-Making in Business Planning

I. *NONQUANTITATIVE EMPHASIS*

    A. *Creative mental processes (e.g., creativity, experience, judgment, hunches, intuition, brain storming)*

    B. *Finding the critical factor*
        1. Barnard's principle of the limiting factor
        2. Simple decision chains and tables
        3. Asking the right questions

    C. *Organization per se (e.g., planning organization and budget system)*

    D. *Rules-of-thumb*

    E. *Policies and procedures*

    F. *Simple problem-solving steps*

    G. *General knowledge of the field in which a decision is to be made (e.g., law, economics, physics, etc.)*

II. *GENERAL SYSTEMS METHODS*

    A. *Problem design*

    B. *Nonquantitative simulation model building*
        1. Logical-analytical frameworks
        2. Adaptive search
        3. Work flows

    C. *Accounting systems and models*
        1. Over-all accounting system
        2. Balance sheet and profit and loss statements
        3. Cash-flow analysis
        4. Accounting ratio analysis
        5. Break-even analysis

    D. *Design of information systems*

III. *OLDER QUANTITATIVE METHODS*

    A. *Marginal analysis*

    B. *Return on investment*
        1. Average rate of return
        2. Present value methods

    C. *Quantitative forecasting*
        1. Trend extrapolation
        2. Exponential smoothing
        3. Correlation analysis
        4. Econometric models

IV. *CONVENTIONAL SCHEDULING MODELS*

    A. *GANTT charts*

    B. *Milestone charts*

    C. *Critical path method*

    D. *Line of balance charts*

V. *NEWER MATHEMATICAL TECHNIQUES*

    A. *Probability theory*

    B. *Computer simulation*

    C. *Linear programming*

    D. *Network analysis (Pert/Time and Pert/Cost)*

    E. *Heuristic problem-solving*

    F. *Game theory*

    G. *Cost-benefit analysis*

VI. *COMPLEX METHODS COMBINING MANY TOOLS*

    A. *Systems analysis*

    B. *Social science research*

    C. *Sophisticated corporate planning*

    D. *Program budgeting*

the new highly mathematical. Third, this table will serve as a basis for the discussion of the following three chapters.

PROBLEMS IN MAKING RATIONAL
BUSINESS DECISIONS

Even if there existed universally accepted theories of and techniques for rational business decisions, the actual operating problems of managers would still prove to be major barriers to any continuous achievement of a high degree of rationality. To examine the problems that a businessman has in making rational decisions is certainly not to condone irrational ones. To ignore them, however, is irrational in the development and acceptance of any particular approach to rational decision-making.

CHOOSING THE RIGHT PROBLEM TO SOLVE. The most pertinent question to a businessman is not so much how to do things right but how to find the right things to do. A businessman runs a far greater risk of missing the problem than of missing a reasonable solution. It seems so elementary to underscore the fact that solutions to problems, no matter how elegant, are useless if they solve the wrong problem. But, as Drucker (1954, p. 351) points out, "the most common source of mistakes in management decisions is the emphasis on finding the right answer rather than the right question." A primary job of management is to find the right problem and to define it.

This, however, is not usually an easy thing to do. Very frequently, as Gross (1964, p. 760) points out, to ask the question, "What is the problem?" of members of an organization will, if not summarily brushed aside, lead to acute internal discomfort. The reason is that it usually is a very difficult question to answer. Most organization problems, and all really important ones, turn out to be clusters of many interrelated problems. A firm, for example, may be faced with a decline in sales of its major product. The problem may be due to a competitor's lower price. It may be due to poor advertising policy, an incompetent sales manager, or a poorly designed marketing plan. It might be the result of an incomplete product line and adversely interrelated product demands. The sales manager may see the problem in a different light from the chief engineer, the production manager, or the controller. The real underlying cause(s) of the sales decline may become more difficult to detect and formulate as probing becomes deeper. It may turn out, for example, that the real problem stems from poor communications resulting from inadequate top management direction and coordination. The problem may be due only to a general temporary decline in demand, or it may be a combination of many things.

The story is told of General Verdy du Vernois, who arrived on the battlefield at Nachod and viewed great confusion and despair. He searched his memory for useful doctrines, strategies, and principles which might help to bring order from chaos. Finding nothing, he said, "Let history and principles go to the devil. After all—*de quoi s'agit-il?*" What is the problem? has become a maxim in its own right. (Hansen in Bowman and Fillerup, 1963, p. 134.)

A recognition of the various difficulties in identifying and formulating a problem, and they are formidable, is the first step in rational decision-making. Poor answers to the right problems are far superior to superb answers to the wrong problems. Unfortunately, there are no easy formulas for finding the right problem to solve, particularly when it is sought at the top of the corporate system.

INSUFFICIENT KNOWLEDGE. Businessmen never have as complete information as is required for perfect rationality. Rationality implies complete knowledge about all possible alternatives and complete knowledge about all the possible consequences of each choice. In real life, managers never have more than fragmentary knowledge of all the conditions surrounding their decisions, nor do they have much perception of the consequences of their action as foreseen from their knowledge at the time of decision.

It would be impossible, of course, to get complete information about all the circumstances surrounding a decision, and in practice this is never sought. In practice the volume of information actually gathered for a decision is usually considerably less than is available. One reason is that information is expensive and a manager may feel the advantage of compiling additional information beyond a certain point is not worth the cost. Also, beyond a certain point in data collection, analytical skills become more important and a manager may not have access to such skills or may prefer to use the skills he has available for higher priority purposes. Finally, a manager may accept less information because the picture it provides may, with what he can fill in from his own experience, be enough to choose a reasonably acceptable solution to a problem.

An important function of a manager is to determine when the threshold is reached between insufficient knowledge and enough information to make a decision which he feels is acceptable. But to the extent he does not have complete information a barrier to perfect rationality faces him.

Even though it can be said in truth, as above, that a manager never has full knowledge required for perfect rationality, it is equally true to say that more and more managers today are given more and more data for their decision-making. Indeed, a problem of most managers is to digest the available data and not to be overwhelmed by it. In light of the modern information floods, one is tempted to alter the well-known adage to read: Knowledge is power only if a man knows what facts not to bother with.

With the growing volume of information and techniques to manipulate it, there is a naturally growing tendency to depend more upon solution by formula. It is one thing for a manager to insist upon getting better information and analyzing it rigorously, and quite another to accept quantitative formulations as substitutes for judgment.

NOT ENOUGH TIME TO BE RATIONAL. Eells (1960, p. 146) makes the point that there is never enough time for a manager to be rational. The executive is like a chess player in a 60-second per move game. He must move. Deadlines must be met whether he has or has not what he considers enough information to make a decision.

ENVIRONMENT MAY NOT COOPERATE. Timing of a decision and the forces of environment over which a manager has no control may turn an acceptable solution into a disaster. Many plans have not been successful because of environmental changes. A stock issuance, for example, may be planned while the security market is booming but distributed just as the market declines sharply. It is a moot question as to whether the original decision was rational even though events subsequently proved the results to be disastrous. Whatever the philosopher may say about this issue the fact of hostile environmental forces turning well-laid plans into misfortune must lead only to a conclusion that the net result was much less than rational.

OTHER LIMITATIONS ON RATIONALITY. In an actual operational setting the above factors are by no means the only limitations on a high degree of rationality. There are many, many others which we may pause to mention without elaboration: the force of habit, the need for compromise among different positions, faulty memory, misjudging motives and values of people, poor communications, misappraisal of uncertainties and risks, and the sheer inability of the human mind to handle the available knowledge about facts, values, and human behavior that bear on a decision.

SCIENTISTS, MANAGERS, AND RATIONALITY

In recent years a number of specialists have joined the ranks of business staffs to help managers make more rational decisions. Foremost among them is the management scientist. He has come to management with a set of tools designed to insure rational decision-making, and managers have not always accepted the tools or the scientist as fully as the latter thinks appropriate. There has resulted a conflict of serious proportions between the scientist and the manager which has been the subject of considerable discussion (Churchman and Schainblatt, 1965a, pp. B-69-87; Churchman and Schainblatt, 1965b, pp. B-1-42; Forrester, 1960, pp. 4-5; Good, 1962, pp. 383-393; Hower and Orth, 1963; and Rosenzweig, 1967, pp. 79-86.) This section will explore the dimensions of the problem, the underlying reasons for it, and what might be done about it.

DIMENSIONS OF THE PROBLEM. It must be understood that the modern business of any size uses the services of many experts who, in academic nomenclature, would qualify as scientists. Included, in no order of importance, are economists, lawyers, behavioral scientists, psychiatrists, medical doctors, geologists, physicists, chemists, mathematicians, operating researchers, engineers, and political scientists. In addition, are experts in many fields such as advertising, public relations, union negotiation, planning, organization, real estate, and accounting, many of whom might qualify as scientists, depending upon their background and knowledge.

All these experts at one time or another must come into conflict with general managers if they insist that their expertise be the final arbiter of decision. It is the function of good management to see that the requisite knowledge of the appropriate expert is brought to bear on a problem; it is quite another matter to insist that the expert's judgment be final. Experts are valuable precisely because they have deep and penetrating knowledge of a given discipline. But when problems to be solved break out of the bounds of the routine, the influence of other disciplines of other experts must also be applied. The decision must then be made by a generalist rather than a specialist. If any specialist thinks his solutions are the only "rational" ones, sooner or later conflict with general managers will result.

Two distinguished management scientists, Churchman and Schainblatt (1965b, pp. B-70-71), succinctly describe the issue as follows: "Much of management science has been conducted under the very naive philosophy that a certain kind of reason must prevail, and that once this reason has been made clear, the manager will either accept it or be charged with gross negligence or, still worse, gross stupidity. The counter philosophy consists of asserting that the goals and decisions of managers are so complicated, so elusive, so creative, that they must forever be closed secrets to a mind trained in the objectivity of so-called scientific method."

Differences among specialists and managers will vary a good deal depending upon the persons involved, the companies in which they find themselves, and the problem at hand. Problems between specialists and managers also vary much depending upon the specialty and manager being considered. Lawyers, for example, have gotten along well with management for many years. Economists generally seem to have little trouble with managers. But, as will be noted in Chapter 22, managers are having problems with advanced minds in the physical sciences. It is difficult to generalize, but there are a number of identifiable reasons underlying the schism that exists today between managers and specialists.

SPECIALIST-ERECTED COMMUNICATIONS BARRIERS. Communications barriers raised by the specialist can be a many-headed problem, a few aspects of which follow. First, among some specialists there exists a sort of aloofness from management. One writer, for example, in presenting an article on what a new sophisticated technique could do to help managerial decision-making, concluded in a sort of take-it-or-leave-it attitude that here is the technique and ". . . now it is up to managers to use it."

Second, specialists have on occasion shown an arrogance which inhibits communications not only with managers but with other specialists. One operations research group with which I am familiar was abandoned in large part because the operations researchers appeared to exhibit a sort of intellectual snobbery that considered the man of science superior to the general manager. This attitude was reflected in the management scientist's high intolerance of the fact that his conclusions were not accepted completely. Not only is this view sometimes held with general managers but with scientists in other disciplines who may view and solve problems in different ways.*

Third, is a language barrier. Sometimes by intent but more often because of lack of wisdom, specialists do not communicate except in the esoteric language of their discipline. Today a new language is developed for each new discipline and those not familiar with it have difficulty in mastering it at one exposure.

Fourth, is what Simon (1960, p. 18) has called mathematician's aphasia. He says: "The victim abstracts the original problem until the mathematical intractabilities have been removed (and all semblance to reality lost), solves the new simplified problem, and then pretends that this was the problem he wanted to solve all along. He expects the manager to be so dazzled by the beauty of the mathematical results that he will not remember that his practical operating problem has not been handled." Another writer has spoken of the "acrobatism" of the expert who, in his ardor for the scientific methodology, becomes unrealistic. Both these defects stifle communications with managers. (Stein, 1958, p. 17.)

Finally, there are inherent attitudes of the specialist which, if not recognized and reconsidered in light of managerial attitudes and problems, can lead to a decline in communications. The specialist is often more prone to withholding decision while getting more facts. As noted previously the manager cannot often afford this luxury. The specialist tends to admire the elegant rather than the simple, the intellectually taxing rather than the easy route to solution, the optimum rather than a satisfactory conclusion. By his very expertise he has a trained incapability for considering fully other disciplines in his solution.

MANAGEMENT-CREATED COMMUNICATIONS BARRIERS. Many managers are remiss in creating communications barriers with scientists. Many resist change in the way they do things. When new methods appear which require intensified intellectual effort to understand and employ, their resistance becomes galvanized into blind rejection. They become the victims of innovational sclerosis.

Communication is sometimes effectively stifled when the specialist finds

---

* For a complaint that operations researchers are not taking into consideration behavioral science, see Dutton and Walton, 1964, pp. 207-217.

himself reporting through many organizational tiers. Even though intervening managers may give the research worker full support, the filtering process screens out the researcher-management dialog which often is essential to successful applications. There are many other ways a long organizational filtering process may damage the value of research efforts and thereby erode understanding and acceptance of research results by managers.

Many managers consider their judgment to be superior to any methodology of the scientist. When present this is an attitude that will become apparent sooner or later and will inhibit discussion with scientists just as surely as when the bias operates in reverse.

CHOICE OF PROBLEMS. Some management scientists have naturally tended to direct their efforts to problems that their techniques can readily solve. But these are not always the problems which management, particularly top management, is most interested in solving. It is only when management scientists begin to address themselves to the critical problems which the top manager faces that a basis for recognition and team work exists.

MANAGEMENT PARTICIPATION. In developing solutions to management problems, management scientists have not always sought management participation. Assuming no communications barriers of any significance, line managers can provide guidance to scientists in pointing out and choosing problems, suggesting solutions, and tailoring solutions to assure acceptance of recommendations. A sugar refinery, for example, was interested in different mixtures of raw sugar and asked a management scientist to determine the proper mixes. As he proceeded he was told by managers that mysterious chemical changes took place with certain mixtures and could not be explained. Ignoring these unexplainable conditions he pushed on to a quantitative solution which was never used because it did not solve the problem. A management scientist who does not solicit and succeed in getting the participation of management will fail.

WHAT SHOULD THE RELATIONSHIP BE? Churchman and Schainblatt (1965b) conclude there are four different views about the desired relationship between the scientist and the manager, as follows:

First, is the separate-function concept. This view considers management and the specialist as performing separate functions. "The task of the scientist is to prepare as complete a plan as possible, taking into account as many aspects of the problem as possible, and conforming above all to the standards of scientific research. The completed plan is then presented to the manager, whose responsibility it is to accept or reject what is proposed." (p. B-72.) A far more sophisticated version of this concept is that the scientist should consider operational phases of the design he recommends.

A second concept argues that there should be more understanding by the manager. This is called by Churchman and Schainblatt the communications position. The manager must understand what the scientist is trying to do and why he does what he does. The idea is not that a manager have a "feel" for the work of the scientist but that he in effect become a scientist.

A third position, called the persuaders, says that many OR groups are thoroughly naive in ignoring the issues facing a manager. This concept means that "the problem is not to get the manager to understand the scientist,—since the former is too busy,—but to get the scientist to understand enough about the manager so that he can persuade him to accept the results." (p. B-73.) The principal idea here is for the specialist to "sell" the manager on the validity of his approach and conclusions.

A fourth view is that of mutual understanding. The specialist must understand the politics of decision-making, the intuitive judgment factors involved, and the different approaches of the manager. On the other hand, the manager should understand the creative processes of the specialist. The concept is "something . . . quite complicated and obscure, so complex that we believe extensive research is required to discover its real implications." (p. B-73.)

It is not possible here to examine these views at length. The subtleties of the interrelationship between managers and specialists are many and complex, and this makes generalization dangerous. For instance, under one set of conditions a manager may expect a specialist to reach a conclusion and press for its acceptance. In the development of the conclusion, no relationship with the manager receiving the conclusion is necessary or desired. For most decisions, however, especially the higher up the managerial tier the decision is made, more interrelationships between specialists and managers are desirable.

It does not seem necessary or possible that a manager making a decision has to be an expert in all the specialties which contribute to his decision. It is rather arrogant for one specialist to assert that a manager must be an expert in his specialty. Why his above all the others?

It is always helpful for specialists to know how to "sell" their product to managers. But the more complex is the technique used in coming to a conclusion the more a manager should know about it. A manager should have some understanding of the underlying discipline used in reaching a recommendation. If not, he can only accept a recommendation on faith.

The acceptance of each of these views depends upon many things—the nature of the problem, the needs of the manager, the knowledge of the manager and the trust he has in the specialist, to name a few. For example, Alderson (1965, p. B-6) noted the following managerial motivation matrix:

CHARACTERISTIC	DIRECT NEED	NO DIRECT NEED
Substantive	(1) decision-seeking	(3) service-studies
Negative	(2) conciliating	(4) ritualistic

In area (1) the manager has a problem for which he is in need of expert opinion. He wants a solution, and in getting it he may want to work with the researcher or he may not. In (2) a decision has already been formulated in the mind of the manager and he may want only confirmation. In (3) the manager, for example, seeks expert opinion about possible changes in the environment, or studies of advertising effectiveness. There may be no need for the manager to work closely with the researcher or that he have a penetrating knowledge of the research methodology used for studies of this type. In (4) the manager wants a study so that if top management or a member of the Board of Directors raises a question he can say that "experts examined the problem." There are many other reasons why a manager may want a study from a specialist. This will illustrate, however, the complexity of generalizing about the necessary interrelationship between technical experts and managers.

There is no doubt about the fact that, in general, there are problems between specialists and managers in decision-making. Resolution of the problems would appear to require at least the following.

SOLVE PROBLEMS. Was it Confucius who said, "A management science that does not solve problems for managers is not a management science"? Managers have problems and those who work for and with them should help them solve the problems. Management science must be viewed as a discipline for solving business problems and not as a collection of techniques. The management scientist must not seek a problem to fit his techniques but problems which his techniques can help to solve.

It is important to choose the "right" problem. E. Bright Wilson once said, "Many scientists owe their greatness not to their skill in solving problems but to their wisdom in choosing them." This is good advice for scientists in industry.

Choosing problems to help solve which are of major concern to management inevitably will lead to mathematically messy issues. In his Presidential address before The Institute of Management Sciences, Hertz called upon its members to get interested in such questions. He said: "I suggest that problems to which a management scientist may address himself fall into four categories:

1. Deterministic—where predictable relations exist among the variables at hand.
2. Probabilistic—where the probabilities can be determined.
3. Stable, nondeterministic—where the probabilities can be estimated with some feeling of confidence.
4. Nonstable, nondeterministic—where estimates of the probabilities are subject to varying degrees of uncertainty.

"Some nontrivial problems of management fall into the third class, in which it is possible to manipulate the environment to bring about a reasonably stable system. Most nontrivial management problems fall into category 4, where there are many potential causes of change, some discoverable, but in which the history of the system giving rise to the problem provides little or no basis for forecasting its future state.

"From the point of view expressed in this paper, the only problems worth working on are these latter problems." (Hertz, 1965b, pp. 365-366.)

UNDERSTANDING MANAGERS. The gap between scientists and managers cannot be bridged without considerable understanding by the scientist of the managerial mind and its decision-making world. Hertz has wise words on this point: "The rational mind of the scientist would like to remove all irrationality from this focusing of attention of the manager. The trouble is that in order to do this, we scientists must understand the world of the manager; not a piece of it, but the whole world. If we only understand a piece of the manager's world, we have no justification for asserting that he should pay attention to the piece that we present to him. Thus, in order to recommend important changes to a manager, we must understand the process by which this whole world becomes focused on certain issues and aspects of his environment. Any decision is a snapshot of the universe of the manager. An optimal decision is a snapshot of the rational universe." (1964, p. 364.)

Someone once said that we all want to get the news objectively, impartially, and from our own point of view. This is natural, but at some point in his research the scientist must know when to yield to other disciplines and to the manager who must make the decision. The following cogent lines properly place the roles:

> *"Experts ranked in serried rows*
> *Fill the enormous plaza full.*
> *But only one is there who knows,*
> *And he's the man who fights the bull."*
>
> (attributed to Graves in Smiddy 1964, p. 87)

MANAGEMENT ATTITUDES. It is natural for managers to resist techniques they do not fully understand. On the other hand, successful managers seek and welcome new processes that can lighten their load or help them make better decisions. The manager has a responsibility to break down barriers to communications even though that may necessitate the changing of his attitudes, his ways of working with staff, and his concepts of the organizational role of staff specialists.

The management sciences are not so much a body of techniques as a way of thinking, an attitude. It is an attitude that has faith in the scientific method, that makes a habit of seeking facts and ways to relate facts with each other and the whole of a problem area. Managers cannot understand the practitioners of the newer quantitative decision-making sciences unless they comprehend this view. To communicate with these experts managers must accept comparable attitudes. This does not mean, of course, that the conclusions need necessarily always be accepted. It means that they must be sought, understood, and then blended with other disciplines and their own insights.

Better planning and better decision-making will inevitably result from a proper blending of experts and managers. I do not count myself among those who feel that today's manager is engaged in a holding action until the specialist and the computer take over his job. The manager is and will remain a dominant and unique character in business. I am also convinced that he will become more skilled in his job as a result of new tools for better decision-making, applied through a blend of staff expertise and his own knowledge and experience.

THE MANAGER IS HIS OWN BEST TECHNIQUE. In the final analysis it is the manager, not the expert, who makes the decision. Ralph Lazarus (1963, p. 5), President of Federated Department Stores, Inc., tells the following story which illustrates this point. "Not long ago," he said, "I spent an evening with a veteran magazine editor of national reputation. I asked him this question: 'How can you possibly cram into your head all the things you need to know to judge the hundreds of different stories you publish each year? Politics, atomic energy, sports, medicine, taxes, marriage, foreign relations with Latin America, India, and the Common Market—are you really expert in all these fields?'

"He grinned and said: 'I'm a fraud. I appear to know so much and I really know so little. The complexities of the modern world are totally beyond the grasp of any single man. I don't just judge ideas. I try to fit those ideas into a total picture I have developed of the kind of magazine I want to edit. Most particularly, I judge the people who submit those ideas. Over the years, I've developed an ear that distinguishes the sound of truth from the sound of exaggeration and falsehood. In every issue that I publish I bet my job that my ear has told me right.' "

This editor is doing exactly what every executive must do. Surrounded by experts in finance, law, labor relations, economics, decision theory, politics, and marketing, and with labyrinthian knowledge at their disposal, the manager must depend upon his "ear." This does not mean, of course, solely intuition. It means some conceptual knowledge of the discipline and much knowledge about the personality and competence of the practitioner of the discipline.

An intimate biographer of Winston Churchill said: "He was always deeply interested in techniques of all kinds and listened avidly to experts and professionals, imbibing all they told him with a rare accuracy and grasp. But he never fell a victim to the black magic of specialist infallibility. It was the task of specialists and experts to supply the weights and measures; it was for him to assess them and to reach conclusions." (Carter, 1965, p. 36.)

In sum, the world of the scientist and manager will never be one of complete harmony, but it should be more harmonious than it now is. This can only happen, however, if both strive harder to bridge the gap.

SUMMARY AND CONCLUSIONS

The discussion of this chapter makes it abundantly clear that any determination of what is rational in the decision-making aspect of planning is not easy. Furthermore, there can be no disagreement with Simon (1957b, p. 79) when he says, "It is impossible for the behavior of a single, isolated individual to reach any high degree of rationality."

Nevertheless, the development of knowledge about business decisions leaves no doubt about the fact that a businessman today has at his disposal a formidable array of superior theories and techniques for making more rational decisions. It is true that his problems in being rational are mounting as decision-making becomes more complex. But the result need not be less rationality. What is required is that great care be exercised in choosing the appropriate theories and tools for particular decisions.

Making highly rational decisions in the planning process can result only from a blend of many other highly rational decisions; among them is the determination to develop a completely effective and efficient planning system and all that it implies.

As business problems become more complex, managers find the need to use more specialists who are expert in particular fields of knowledge. Chances are that the more the specialist and the manager work in harmony, or at least understand each other's problems and methods, the higher will be the degree of rationality in decisions.

But in the final analysis, the manager is his own best technique for decision-making. What he considers to be highly rational may be thought irrational by someone else. It all depends upon who is looking.

13
Older Tools
for Making More Rational
Planning Decisions ───────

13
Older Tools
for Making More Rational
Planning Decisions

INTRODUCTION

Business managers have a rich palette of techniques to help them do a better job of planning. The more important ones, particularly from the point of view of top management, were listed in Table 12-1 in the preceding chapter. The present and succeeding two chapters will examine the techniques listed in Table 12-1, except where analysis has previously been given or will be introduced in later chapters.

The point of view taken is that managers do not necessarily need to be experts in using all the techniques available and important to them in planning. But they do need a working concept of each major technique—its nature, how and where it can and should be used, and its strengths and weaknesses at the point of use.

It should be recognized, also, that although the present examination of techniques is more extended than one usually finds in books of this kind, the discussion is still highly condensed. After all, there are books devoted to every technique discussed.

Even though the emphasis is on planning it should be recognized that many of the techniques have usage for both planning and control. PERT is a good illustration.

The definition of technique used here is very broad. It is, as expressed in standard dictionaries, a method, tool, or procedure essential to expertness in executing an art or science. In this sense, the skill of a manager is a major technique as explained in the last chapter. So is a communications system. Methods to stimulate ideas, to motivate people, to organize for decision-making, or to formulate suitable policies are techniques. In this light, many techniques available for planning are omitted from the present discussion. This is especially true in functional areas.

SYNECTIC RELEVANCE

Few if any of the techniques discussed here are used as the sole method for making an important decision in planning. Furthermore, as the planning process proceeds, the combination of techniques to push an issue to decision will change. The manager and his staff have a problem in deciding what the combination should be. This is of great importance not only because, in application, different techniques carry varying price tags, but also because the relevance of a technique changes among issues and over time. There is, therefore, a problem of synectic relevance.

Synectics is a neologism of a Greek term meaning the fitting together of different and apparently irrelevant elements. (Gordon, 1961 and Alexander, 1965.) In the context the term is used here it refers to the combination of people and different techniques, including quantitative and nonquantitative, the mathematical, the hunches, the insights, and the guesses, to advance the decision-making process in planning. But, as noted above, it is essential in fitting these pieces together to make sure that only the techniques relevant to the problem and, indeed, only the relevant parts of each applicable technique are used. This technique is synectic relevance.

Unfortunately, it is not possible today to describe much better than has been done here the way in which this technique should be used. In this light it may be premature and inaccurate to speak of a science of business decision-making as some writers have done. "It is unphilosophical," said John Stuart Mill more than a century ago, "to construct a science out of a few of the agencies by which the phenomena are determined, and to leave the rest to the routine of practice or the sagacity of conjecture. We ought either not to pretend to scientific forms or we ought to study all the determining agencies equally, and endeavor, as far as can be done, to include all of them within the pale of the science; else we shall infallibly bestow a disproportionate attention upon those which our theory takes into account, while we misestimate the rest and probably underrate their importance."

CREATIVITY

Among all the elements entering into planning and the making of plans there is not likely to be any argument about the fact that creativity is the most important. Yet, surprisingly enough, very little has been done to examine what this means. Indeed, very few management textbooks even contain the word creativity in the index of subjects discussed, and those that do dispense with the subject in few words. Research on the subject has been growing in recent years but is still at a comparatively low scale of effort.* Creativity, because of its great value in planning, should receive more than passing notice in any discussion of major techniques for better planning.

DEFINITION OF TERMS. Definitions in the literature on creativity reflect the focus of many different points of view. Our point of view, of course, is managerial and, therefore, is concerned with the relationship of creativity to the business of business. One simple definition of creativity from this point of view is "the ability to develop and implement new and better solutions." (Gary A. Steiner, 1966, p. 2.) † This definition includes the ability to go beyond the conventional patterns of thought and mold new and original thoughts into a plan of action. Notice two elements in this definition: the idea, and its implementation. Ideas in themselves are not productively creative in business if not incorporated in a planned course of action. This is to say, creativity, in the sense of getting a new idea, is not enough in modern business. Most businesses have more ideas floating around than they can handle. The road from a valuable idea to final commercialization and profit is long and hazardous, and creativity can and must flourish throughout the entire journey.

In this sense, hunch or intuition are not the same as creativity, although they can stimulate and are often a part of the creative process. A hunch is a strong, intuitive impression that something will or can happen. It is a common sense form of predictability. Intuition is the power of knowing, or the knowledge obtained, without going through a process of formal reasoning or recourse to conscious inference. It is reason in a hurry. It is innate, instinctive knowledge. Highly creative individuals in all fields have been found to be overwhelmingly intuitive. (Rowan, 1962, p. 11.)

Intuition is not quite the same thing as considered judgment or insight. Considered judgment differs from intuitive judgment in that the logic behind the opinion or conclusion is made explicit. An insight is a faculty for seeing into the inner character of a phenomenon, or apprehending the true nature of a thing, or discerning the underlying truth, by a penetrating mental vision, discernment,

---

* For a brief resume of research on creativity, see William E. Scott, pp. 211-219. Another survey and brief bibliography is that of Hinrichs, 1961.

† Another definition close to this, with a bit more elaboration, is that creativity is "the production of an idea, concept, creation or discovery that is new, original, useful or satisfying to its creator or someone else in some period of time." (Gregory, 1967, p. 182: From *The Management of Intelligence: Scientific Problem Solving and Creativity* by Carl E. Gregory; copyright © 1967 by McGraw-Hill Book Company and used by permission.)

or intuitive understanding. All these, of course, are part of the creative process.

Innovation and invention are two other words closely associated with creativity. Indeed, they are words which describe part of the creative process. Invention is usually thought of as conceiving, devising, or originating something. Innovation is considered to be more the process by which an invention or idea is translated into a plan of action. In the words of a government panel on invention and innovation, "invention and innovation encompass the totality of processes by which new ideas are conceived, nurtured, developed and finally introduced into the economy as new products and processes; or into an organization to change its internal and external relationships; or into a society to provide for its social needs and to adapt itself to the world or the world to itself." (Department of Commerce, 1967, p. 2.)

In business, innovation is more often the outgrowth of recognition and adaptation than of a really new invention. Masaru Ibuka, president of Japan's highly successful Sony Corp., takes pride "in finding unnoticed utility value in others' inventions, seasoning them with original ideas of our own and making them into marketable products." (*Newsweek*, 1966.)

"The creative act in innovation," says Corson, "does not so much involve conceiving something that has no counterpart or antecedent but recognizing the possibility that a new process or concept can be applied to a particular situation." (Corson, 1962, p. 68.) Once there is a recognition, the innovative process may involve "selling" the idea within a company and, when that is accomplished, it includes also all the managerial tasks needed to satisfy a market at a profit. This is the essence of entrepreneurship.*

Peter Drucker (1965) emphasizes in his definition of entrepreneurship the finding and utilizing of opportunity. It is opportunity-focused rather than problem-focused. An entrepreneur looks upon change as an opportunity, and the acceptance of "the leadership of change" is the unique task of the entrepreneur. "The entrepreneur," Drucker says, "is the systematic risk-maker and risk-taker. And he discharges this function by looking for and finding opportunity."

Creativity, then, may involve either technical or nontechnical matters. It is more to the latter that the connotations of innovation and entrepreneurship apply. It is quite possible for a company to be highly innovative and not inventive. It may have a strong marketing and engineering department that is able to take inventions made elsewhere, improve upon them, adapt them to a particular market, and by this combination make a profit. Du Pont has achieved high recognition as a company that invents things. Yet one study of new products

---

* This is Joseph A. Schumpeter's concept. For discussion of his views, see Hartmann, pp. 429-451; and P. M. Sweezy, pp. 93-96. It should be pointed out that Schumpeter felt it was the entrepreneur who perceived and exploited new opportunities and that the manager was more concerned with routine administration and the control of others. This distinction is, of course, false, as amply demonstrated in this book.

introduced by that company between 1920 and 1949 showed that two-thirds were based on inventions made elsewhere. (Mueller, 1962.)

IMPORTANCE OF CREATIVITY. Creativity in the sense presented above is the prime requisite for success in business. Gardner (1962, pp. 2-7) says the only way to keep an organization alive is to let creative people bring change. The organization that does everything by rule, that stifles creativity, is inflexible and on the road to oblivion.

We have already discussed the high importance of being creative and imaginative in the planning process. To reiterate, developing strategies for an enterprise is a creative process of the greatest importance to a company. Their implementation provides a framework for creative activity which will produce products and services that have sufficient competitive edges to be profitable. Many firms have found that stimulating the creative instincts of their employees to cut costs, raise quality, and meet schedules, has been highly productive in increasing profits. The innovative and entrepreneurial elements of creativity are the very essence of the vitality of the private enterprise system. The sharpening of intuitive judgment and insights in the men who manage corporations is a powerful companion to this quality. As Oliver Wendell Holmes once said, "A moment's insight is sometimes worth a lifetime of experience." It is difficult to exaggerate the importance of creativity, and all that is implied in the concept, to the competitive excellence of a company and its ability to achieve the role which society sets for it as well as the aims it sets for itself.

THE CREATIVE INDIVIDUAL. At a research seminar held at the University of Chicago, the seminar director, Gary Steiner (1965, pp. 7-9; and 1966, pp. 3-5), found agreement among a number of scholars and top managers about many of the intellectual and personality characteristics of the creative person. They were as follows:*

"Although measures of general intelligence fail to predict creativity, highs† typically outscore lows in tests of the following mental abilities:

"*Conceptual Fluence.* The ability to generate a large number of ideas rapidly: List tools beginning with the letter t; novel uses for a brick; possible consequences of a situation; categories into which the names of a thousand great men can be sorted—to name just a few of the tasks that have actually been used.

---

* Reprinted from *The Creative Organization* by Gary A. Steiner by permission of the University of Chicago Press. Copyright © 1965 by the University of Chicago.

† "Highs" and "lows" refer to high-creative and low-creative persons. These are relative, not absolute, designations, since in most of the samples studied even the "lows" would qualify as highly creative as compared with the population at large.

"*Conceptual Flexibility.* The ability to shift gears, to discard one frame of reference for another; the tendency to change approaches spontaneously.

"*Originality.* The ability and/or tendency to give unusual, atypical (therefore more probably new) answers to questions, responses to situations, interpretations of events.

"*Preference for Complexity.* Highs often exhibit a preference for the complex, and to them intriguing, as against the simple and easily understood.

"Several closely related personality characteristics distinguish highs and lows in a number of studies:

"*Independence of Judgment.* Highs are more apt to stick to their guns when they find themselves in disagreement with others. In a situation where an artificially induced group consensus contradicts the evidence of their own senses, lows more often yield in their expressed judgment. The same is true when the issue at stake is not a factual one, but involves voicing an opinion on an aesthetic, social, or political matter.

"*Deviance.* Highs see themselves as more different from their peers and, in fact, they appear to be more different in any number of significant as well as trivial characteristics. At the extreme, highs sometimes feel lonely and apart, with a sense of mission that isolates them, in their own minds, from average men with average concerns.

"*Attitudes toward Authority.* A related distinction with far-reaching implications for organizations has to do with the way authority is viewed. The difference between highs and lows is a matter of degree, but to make the point we describe the extremes.

"Lows are more apt to view authority as final and absolute; to offer unquestioning obedience, allegiance, or belief (as the case may be), with respect approaching deference; to accept present authority as 'given' and more or less permanent. Highs are more likely to think of authority as conventional or arbitrary, contingent on continued and demonstrable superiority; to accept dependence on authority as a matter of expedience, rather than personal allegiance or moral obligation; to view present authority as temporary.

"Attitudes toward subordinates are related in the appropriate direction: those who pay unquestioned allegiance tend to expect it, and vice versa.

"Similarly, and in general, highs are more apt to separate source from content in their evaluation of communications, to judge and reach conclusions on the basis of the information itself. Lows are more prone to accept or reject, believe or disbelieve messages on the basis of their attitudes toward the sender.

"'*Impulse Acceptance.*' Highs are more willing to entertain and express personal whims and impulses; lows stick closer to 'realistic,' expected behavior. Highs pay more heed to inner voices, while lows suppress them in favor of external demands.

"So, for example, highs may introduce humor into situations where it is not called for and bring a better sense of humor to situations where it is. And, in general, highs exhibit a richer and more diverse 'fantasy life' on any number of clinical tests.

"Does the more creative man have more inner impulses or fewer inhibitions, or both, and to what degree? The answer is unknown, but there is at least one intriguing finding that suggests a strange combination of two normally opposing traits.

"In the genius and near-genius, a widely used personality test shows 'schizoid' tendencies (bizzarre, unusual, unrealistic thoughts and urges), coupled with great 'ego strength' (ability to control, channel, and manipulate reality effectively). This line of inquiry begins to speak the cliché that the dividing line between madman and genius is a fine one. According to this finding, the line is fine, but firm.

"In sum, highly creative people are more likely than others to view authority as conventional rather than absolute; to make fewer black-and-white distinctions; to have a less dogmatic and more relativistic view of life; to show more independence of judgment and less conventionality and conformity, both intellectual and social; to be more willing to entertain, and sometimes express, their own 'irrational' impulses; to place a greater value on humor and in fact to have a better sense of humor; in short, to be somewhat freer and less rigidly—but not less effectively—controlled."

In his research seminar, Steiner found three characteristics of much interest to management that distinguish the creative problem solvers—the highs, as compared with the lows. First, they are more concerned with and responsive to the basic problem to be solved. They are more task-oriented, work harder and longer, and place higher value on "job interest" than on rewards such as salary and status. Second, they view themselves more as members of a profession than of a business firm. They tend more to seek acceptance from the larger professional community and rise within it, to feel freer to move around from company to company, and to be more cosmopolitan in orientation and aspiration. Highs change jobs to pursue their interests and do not change interests to pursue a job. Third, highs spend more time in the initial phases of problem formulation. Lows are more likely to want to "get on with it."

These are tendencies. On the average, the highs exhibit more of these characteristics than do the lows. But, as Steiner points out, "that is far from saying that all highs have more of each than all lows." (1966, p. 6) There are not very good measuring instruments to choose such people. If many of them are to be employed, some testing devices may increase the odds in favor of choosing the more creative person. But if few persons are to be chosen, and it is important that they all be highly creative (managers, as well as staff experts and scientists), it is doubtful that present testing methods will raise the odds above the currently used procedure of personal appraisal and judgment. Odds are probably raised by appraisal by a highly creative person. This is the application of the rule, "It takes one to know one."

THE CREATIVE PROCESS. A number of investigators have attempted to define the steps in the creative process. The results look much like the problem-solving steps set forth in Chapter 2. There are different sequences but generally they suggest the following: preparation; examining the problem, receiving ideas, and gathering data; accumulating hypotheses and alternatives; letting up, inviting illumination while thinking about other things; synthesis, that is, putting the pieces together, formulating the idea or ideas with clarity; and verification, or judging and testing the ideas by experiments, research, and other means.

A more descriptive sequence is that of Rokeach (Chapter 4 in Gary A. Steiner, 1965): "The creative process is that sequence of thinking leading to ideas or products which, sooner or later, will be regarded as novel and worthwhile because (a) it is an activity characterized by the capacity to distinguish, cognitively, information from source and to evaluate them separately on their own merits which, in turn (b) frees the person to be receptive to, acquire, integrate, and transform new beliefs into new belief systems which violate previously held beliefs and belief systems, (c) all such activity being driven and guided from beginning to end by tension states arising from significant questions put to oneself, significance being cognized as that which has implications or consequences for the ideas, products, feelings, and welfare of other human beings."

While these steps are useful they are more conceptual than operational. The creative process is rarely completed on a clearly delineated step-by-step procedure. It is more often characterized by long delays, quiescence, and then large, unpredictable leaps. The extreme example, of course, is the sudden great insight while shaving in the morning. This process is different from that which characterizes most problem-solving steps in modern businesses, such as those presented in Chapter 2, but both processes can and do operate simultaneously.

THE CREATIVE ORGANIZATION. Steiner has directly related the characteristics of creative individuals with those of creative organizations. The result is shown in Table 13-1. This compilation has many weaknesses and limitations, not the least of which is that it is not complete and the implications of each characteristic vary much depending upon many factors. Nevertheless, it is useful in pointing up some broad distinguishing characteristics of what a creative organization may look like.*

* The characteristics of a creative organization shown in Table 13-1 are quite comparable with those selected by Cummings, 1965, p. 226.

WHAT SHOULD MANAGEMENT DO TO INCREASE CREATIVITY?
If creativity is so important, and if it is possible to identify the elements of a creative organization, what should management do about it? As it turns out, this is not an easy question to answer. Part of the reason lies in the fact that a vast amount of research needs to be done about creativity in organizations before answers can be given with conviction. Furthermore, there are different requirements for creativity in organizations, and they involve different approaches and mixes with more conventional organization theory. There are, however, a few major steps, suggested by research and experience, which management should take to enhance creativity:

1. Top management should make sure that creativity exists at its own level. There is no substitute for a day-to-day example. Furthermore, to stimulate creativity in an organization requires the sort of attitude, posture, and decision that can be found only in a creative management.

2. A carefully designed planning program is essential. Such a program provides channels of communications that stimulate the flow of ideas, reduce communications blockages, and organize idea evaluation systems. A planning system can and should force creativity and innovation not only by its ability to sort out the right problem for analysis but by clarifying the points where creativity has the maximum payoff. Management can expect and, in a sense, command creativity and designate where in the planning process it should be directed.

3. Management in many ways can give encouragement to and stimulate creativity. A philosophy that stresses creativity, takes measures to encourage it, and expects it, is likely to get it. But, in return, many things need be done. If creativity has priority, the awards system should be geared to, and commensurate with, that priority. Those whose creativity is prized must not, as a result of their professional competence, be "penalized" by "promotion" into channels of advancement where their special expertise, and perhaps their type of creativity, might be lost. Rather, advancement and status should be provided within the area of creativity. The necessary accouterments of creativity must be provided and accepted, such as libraries, stimulation of outside contacts, proper research assistance, some privacy, a certain amount of freedom, a receptivity to new and seemingly strange ideas, and a certain amount of permissive management. There should be a willingness to organize in a flexible fashion and to make the organization opportunity-oriented. This means, for example, a willingness to abolish needless communications, to eliminate bottlenecks of inaction, or to change personalities to fit better the identification and exploitation of opportunities.

4. Developing methods to recruit creative managers and staff is a priority managerial responsibility.

5. Top management should try to stimulate creativity through experimentation with such devices as the *ad hoc* team to resolve a problem, "brain storming,"

off-site conferences, hiring consultants for temporary idea stimulation, "opportunity meetings," and comparable techniques suitable to the occasion and the company.

    6. Ways must be found to create a climate for the survival of potentially useful ideas. It is a paradox in industry that most companies have a plethora of ideas and yet there is continuous frustration about the fragility of good ideas. This paradox is largely explainable by the fact that, while there are plenty of ideas, the apparatus to get a proper hearing for them does not always exist. In a letter written in 1957 the late John Williams of RAND expressed another associated problem this way: "As a matter of fact, a new idea is an extremely perishable thing. Its author is likely to be, for a term, its sole supporter, after which it may have none. The normal reaction of most of us to a new idea is either to ignore it, or instantly to seek its defects. Since most new ideas are spurious—including those produced by competent researchers working within their professional specialties—any critic can establish a wonderful batting

Table 13-1 Comparison of Creative Individuals and Creative Organizations

THE CREATIVE INDIVIDUAL	THE CREATIVE ORGANIZATION

Conceptual fluency: able to produce a large number of ideas quickly	Has idea men
	Open channels of communication
	Ad hoc devices:
	    Suggestion systems
	    Brainstorming
	    Idea units free of other responsibilities

Originality: generates unusual ideas	Encourages contact with outside sources Heterogeneous personnel policy Includes marginal, unusual types Assigns nonspecialists to problems Allows eccentricity

Separates source from content in evaluating information; motivated by interest in problem; follows wherever it leads	Has an objective, fact-founded approach
	Ideas evaluated on their merits, not status of originator
	Ad hoc approaches:
	    Anonymous communications
	    Blind votes
	Selects and promotes on merit only

Suspends judgment; avoids early commitment; spends more time in analysis and exploration	Lack of financial, material commitment to products, policies Invests in basic research; flexible, long-range planning

average by just rejecting every new idea. While I have no statistics on the subject, it is my impression that successful ideas often have this history: they are advanced at least once unsuccessfully, and they finally bear fruit when the intellectual climate is so favorable that they are advanced anew practically simultaneously by several independent discoverers."

The climate in an organization must be made favorable to giving new ideas a fair and proper hearing without creating the necessity for the originator or its advocate to spend an unconscionable amount of time "selling" it. A certain amount of this is essential, but in some companies one such major effort is about all the energy a man can muster in his lifetime.

Here again, a planning system can be an invaluable instrument in fostering this climate. But much more is involved—organization, information systems, managerial attitudes, and the nature of people. While a climate and organization may be made more favorable to receiving and analyzing ideas, management

Table 13-1 Comparison of Creative Individuals and Creative Organizations (Continued)

THE CREATIVE INDIVIDUAL	THE CREATIVE ORGANIZATION
	Experiments with new ideas, rather than prejudging on "rational" grounds; everything gets a chance
Less authoritarian; relativistic view of life	More decentralized; diversified
	Administrative slack; time and resources to absorb errors
	Tolerates and expects risk-taking
Accepts own impulses; playful, undisciplined exploration	Not run as "tight ship"
	Allows freedom to choose and pursue problems
	Freedom to discuss ideas
Independence of judgment, less conformity. Deviant, sees self as different	Organizationally autonomous
	Original and different objectives; not trying to be another "X"
Rich, "bizarre" fantasy life *and* superior reality orientation; controls	Security of routine *allows* innovation; "philistines" provide stable, secure environment that allows "creators" to roam
	Has separate units or occasions for generating vs. evaluating ideas; separates creative from productive functions

Source: Gary A. Steiner, "The Creative Individual: His Nature and Nurture," *The McKinsey Quarterly,* Vol. II, No. 2 (Winter 1966), p. 8. An earlier version appears in Gary A. Steiner, *The Creative Organization* (Chicago: University of Chicago Press, 1965), pp. 16-18.

can also reduce the infanticide of new ideas by training creative people to "sell" their ideas.

CONFLICT BETWEEN CREATIVITY AND PRODUCTIVITY. The requirements of an organization to maximize creativity will inevitably collide with organizational patterns needed to maximize productivity in current operations in the sense of optimizing output per unit of input. Examination of the characteristics of a creative organization listed in Table 13-1 will reveal many potential points of conflict with the more traditional structure and rewards system of business organizations. For example, the apparent undisciplined disorder, casual inactivity, and individual independence which can foster creativity is very different from the discipline and control associated with the more routine business functioning of a mass production line. For any organization a desirable balance must be struck between the two. Where this balance lies is a matter for top management to decide. It is not a question easily answered, and once answered it continuously arises for answer again and again.

As organizations evolve, a different dilemma is faced, as stated by John Gardner (1962, p. 5) in the following passage: "The new organization is loose in procedure, unclear in organizational lines, variable in policies. It is willing to experiment with a variety of ways to solve its problems. It is flexible and open to the lessons of current experience. It is not bowed by the weight of tradition. As it matures it develops settled policies and habitual modes of solving problems. In doing so it becomes more efficient, but also less flexible, less willing to look freshly at each day's experience. Its increasingly fixed routines and practices are congealed in an elaborate body of written rules. In the final stage of organizational senility there is a rule or precedent for everything."

LIMITATIONS OF CREATIVITY AS A PLANNING TECHNIQUE. A major limitation of creativity stems from its cost. The greater the creativity sought, and the greater the departure from present practice, the greater is the investment likely to be and the less the chance of a payoff. Financing creativity creates a decision problem comparable to but more difficult to solve than for most capital expenditures. One of the important reasons for the difficulty in coming to really convincing conclusions is the fact that too little is known about how creativity is really found at minimum cost, what reduces uncertainty about payoff, and how a creative organization best relates to traditional organizations. The state of knowledge about such issues does not match their importance. It should be added that the importance of creativity in an organization differs among its parts. It certainly has the highest weight at top management levels, particularly in doing strategic planning. Its significance varies among functional groups, depending upon the function and nature of the company. It is, of course, extremely valuable in the research and development areas of an advanced technology-oriented company. It is of high consequence in the marketing areas in a highly market-oriented company. It may be less important in some other functional departments. The problem for top management, of course, is to determine where it is important, and how important it is, and to nurture and interlace it with other parts of an enterprise so that the net effect is to enhance company vitality and profitability.

OTHER TECHNIQUES WITH
NONQUANTITATIVE EMPHASIS

There are a number of techniques for rational decision-making other than creativity which were included in Table 12-1 of Chapter 12. Since they have been discussed elsewhere, or are rather obvious, comments about them will be brief.

FINDING THE CRITICAL FACTOR. Barnard's principle of the limiting factor was treated at length in Chapter 9, and decision chains and tables will be considered in Chapter 15. Several preceding chapters, especially Chapters 9 and 12, discussed the importance of listing critical questions as a technique in planning and decision-making, and in later chapters this technique will be further illustrated.

ORGANIZATION PER SE. If a businessman is asked how he makes decisions he is most likely to begin to describe how his company is organized. This may not be an accurate response to the question, but it does indicate the importance he attaches to organization in making decisions. Throughout this book has been stressed the fact that organization is of major significance in better planning and decision-making, and it will further be emphasized in later chapters.

RULES-OF-THUMB. A rule-of-thumb is a judgment usually based on practical experience rather than on the result of scientific inquiry. But a rule-of-thumb can grow out of rigorous comparisons of data, actions, and ideas. Every manager develops rules-of-thumb to guide his actions, including convictions about personal strategies, policies, or principles. These are valuable labor-saving devices and, if developed with wisdom and insight, may be of fundamental significance in decision-making.

J. Pierpont Morgan's famous rule-of-thumb was, "If you must think about the cost of your yacht, you should not own one." Rules-of-thumb can pertain to any aspect of the operation of a business, from hiring personnel to replacing obsolete plant and equipment. In a later section of this chapter, quantitative rules-of-thumb concerning important financial relationships will be examined and further illustrate this point.

POLICIES AND PROCEDURES. The importance of this approach to improving rational decision was discussed in detail in Chapter 10.

SIMPLE PROBLEM-SOLVING STEPS. In the first part of this chapter, as well as in preceding chapters, particularly Chapter 2, the power of conceptual and operational steps in improving decision-making was noted. This idea will be illustrated again in later chapters.

GENERAL KNOWLEDGE OF THE FIELD. General knowledge of the field in which a decision is to be made is, of course, significant to planning. If the problem under analysis is legal, production, engineering, political, behavioral, what more useful tool does a manager have than either his personal knowledge of the subject or the expertise of specialists?

Experience is an important element in personal knowledge. Over time a great many problems, solutions, and experiences tend to repeat themselves, not often in precise details but in their fundamentals. These past patterns become the templates for solving today's problems. They are ready-made answers to complex questions like, for example, how to react to a request for a price discount by a big customer, how to react to the loss of a major contract, how to stimulate employees to do better planning, or how to generate creativity among key employees. Frequently, when managers make decisions it is said that judgment or intuition has decided. What has actually happened in many cases is that old solutions have been used in a new setting.

But this can also prove to be a poor technique. The battle in the Pentagon between the military specialists and Secretary McNamara over cost-effectiveness analysis centers precisely on this point. The military are using judgments from old experiences to determine what weapons should be developed and with what configurations. Cost-effectiveness, as will be discussed in the next chapter, approaches the problems in a more rigorous and scientific fashion. There are many reasons why experience is not always the best teacher. Problems may appear but not actually be the same. That is, the problem may be the same, but the setting may differ and result in a set of consequences to a decision radically different from what happened in the past. Memory may be faulty: the solution as recollected and applied to today's situation may not be precisely the one used successfully in a similar situation in the past. An individual may really have forgotten how he solved a similar problem in the past but may not realize that fact.

Knowledge also has sometimes been known to become obsolete. The story is told of Charles F. Kettering, who gave a paper before a convention of automotive engineers and described a new lightweight diesel engine with aluminum pistons, an invention which subsequently became strategic in the revolutionary introduction of diesel power to the railroad industry. After the meeting, one of the attending engineers said to Kettering: "You must be joking. In view of the stresses and frictions in your engine the aluminum pistons simply will not work. They are contrary to every engineering principle I know." "How can you be sure?" asked Kettering. A bit surprised but still holding his ground, the engineer said, "Why—because I'm an engineer." "I know that," said Kettering, "but have you ever been a piston in a diesel engine?"

GENERAL SYSTEMS METHODS

This is a loose classification of methods and approaches to business decision-making which would include, among other techniques, the following.

PROBLEM DESIGN. In a sense, some of the previous techniques, as well as many which follow, are approaches to problem design. But it seems useful to single out this method to underscore the utility of taking a little time to design a problem before seeking a solution. It can be a great time-saver for, as noted elsewhere, the most elegant solution is worthless to a businessman if it solves the wrong problem. This method, applied to research and development, will be presented in detail in Chapter 22.

NONQUANTITATIVE SIMULATION AND MODEL BUILDING. Throughout this book there are illustrations of this approach. Chapter 2 contained a number of conceptual and operational models. These were principally logical-analytical frameworks. The adaptive search method discussed in Chapter 9 could be included in this grouping. Simple work flows designed on paper would also qualify. Enough has been said about the importance of this technique, but it might be added here that a first step in using many of the newer mathematical decision tools is the development of a nonquantitative simulation model of the phenomenon being considered. This point will be explained more fully in Chapter 15.

ACCOUNTING SYSTEMS AND MODELS. Accounting is a quantitative language which records a firm's cash receipts and expenditures. It is a sort of financial housekeeping tool. Although most of the data in an accounting system are in financial terms, there are other types of information collected, such as physical units of production, days absent, relationships between costs and production volume, and so on. It is quite apparent that the typical accounting system is not only a treasury of historical information about the operations of an enterprise, but it is by far the best single model that exists to picture the aggregate operations of the firm in a reasonably simple way. As such it is a major management basis for decision-making.

The balance sheet is a basic accounting document expressing simply the financial position of the company at a moment of time. It is a position statement elegantly expressing the classic accounting formula: assets — liabilities = proprietorship. In early accounting history the balance sheet was considered to be the basic document. During the past century, however, the profit and loss statement has come more to occupy that position. In the planning process, many companies prepare rather complete balance sheets and profit and loss statements for each of the planning years. This constitutes, of course, a beautiful simulation (if done accurately) of the operations of the business and the results to stockholder equity. Both these statements are unexcelled models for relating all planning variables to the financial position of a company. The composition of balance sheets and profit and loss statements is well known to readers of this book and needs no further description here.

Source and application of cash. A cash-flow statement identifies and forecasts all important future sources and uses of cash available to the enterprise. It can be elaborate, as when incorporated in the form of a detailed profit and loss statement, or it can be more simple, as shown in Tables 13-2 and 13-3. These, and forms like them,* can be used to forecast cash flows for any period of time desired—daily, weekly, monthly, etc. The cash forecast model shown in Table 13-2 can be used to start the planning process, as a test of desirability of plans being contemplated, and as a measure of the final results expected from planning. The central focus, of course, is on net cash change, but in preparing the form every facet of the business conceivably can be related to each other and all to net cash change.

Table 13-3 shows a revenue-expense forecast, a somewhat different model. This, too, can be used as a beginning point for long-range planning, especially among smaller companies. It also can be used to test feasibility of the planning being considered and clearly is an important model for testing results if a more descriptive profit and loss statement is not made. In this table, the important elements of costs and revenues are identified and forecast. The difference, of course, is profit or loss, which in turn provides a basis for calculating return on investment rates. Revenue-expense forecasts should be prepared for each product, if possible, and for the firm as a whole. Revenue-expense forecasts for products, as well as any project involving cash income and outgo, should be prepared over the major part of the life cycle of the product or project.

An important feature of this model is that when depreciation is added to net profit the result is cash gain from operations. These two tables are not juggling the same figures in a different pattern. The result of Table 13-3, showing cash gain or loss from operations, is only one input in the cash forecast analysis of Table 13-2. Table 13-2 covers more territory and shows total cash flow. So, when

---

* For different formats, see Schabacker, 1960.

simple revenue-expense forecasts are used in planning they should be accompanied by total cash flow analyses.

It is difficult to exaggerate the importance of these two accounting models. Many businesses have gone bankrupt because they did not keep track of their cash flow in the fashion described here.

Accounting ratio analysis

Accounting ratios are important tools of analysis because they summarize briefly the results of detailed computations and express in capsule form the wisdom growing out of past experience and analysis. They are "rules-of-thumb" as well as normative measures drawn from scientific analysis. Our purpose in this

Table 13-2   Forecast of Cash and Needs

ITEM	TIME PERIODS
Cash sources:	
Opening balance	
Revenue from sales	
Depreciation	
Borrowing on facilities	
Borrowing on inventory and receivables	
Total cash sources	
Cash expenditures:	
Direct labor costs	
Materials purchase	
Payments to subcontractors	
New machinery and tools	
Increases in inventory	
Increases in receivables	
Increases in operating cash	
Payments on loans	
Factory burden	
Officers' salaries	
Selling costs	
Taxes:	
Employer's share of Social Security	
Local property	
Income	
Total cash disbursements	
Net cash change	

section is to illustrate, rather than to present a complete array of, important ratios and their use. Weston lists some eighteen financial ratios which he divides into four categories, as follows: liquidity, leverage, activity, and profitability (Weston, 1962, p. 64). A few illustrations from each category will serve our purposes.

Liquidity ratios are designed to measure the ability of a firm to meet its maturing obligations. These ratios characteristically relate cash or near-cash items to obligations or transactions, as for instance current assets to current liabilities. Liquidity, however, is a matter involving the entire operation of an enterprise and to be sure of conclusions it is necessary to examine the entire stream of cash flows, as noted in the preceding section. Nevertheless, a firm will find in liquidity ratios short-cuts to feasibility testing of plans and helpful measures in planning decision-making.

The current ratio is current assets divided by current liabilities. The rule-of-thumb is that the ratio should be at least 2 to 1 and when it is, it shows that claims of short-term creditors are covered by twice as much assets so that in the

Table 13-3   Revenue-Expense Projection

ITEM	TIME PERIODS
Sales revenues:	
Product A	
Product B	
Operating expenses:	
Direct labor	
Overhead	
Materials	
Selling expenses	
Depreciation	
Total	
Nonrecurring expenses	
Total operating expenses	
Interest and loan amortization	
Net profit before taxes	
Taxes	
Net profit after taxes	
Cash gain from operations (net profit after taxes plus depreciation reserve)	

event of liquidation the likelihood the company will meet all its short-term debts is good. The firm is thus considered to be in a state of short-term solvency.

Not all current assets are as liquid as others and to get a more accurate measure of the extent to which a firm can meet its obligations, assuming the worst conditions, cash plus government securities and other cash equivalents are added together and divided by current liabilities. The result is the quick or acid test ratio.* Inventories are eliminated from current assets as well as only the most certain accounts receivable. The rule-of-thumb is that this ratio should be 1 to 1, which is an obvious conclusion.

Leverage ratios measure the contributions made by owners to the financing of an enterprise, as compared with financing provided by others. If shareholders can get others to finance the firm they obviously reduce their risks and get the benefits of ownership with a comparatively smaller investment. Furthermore, and more importantly, if the firm can borrow funds at a lower cost than the net yield of such funds, the total return to the owners from the business is thereby magnified.

One obvious measure of leverage is the debt to equity ratio. Included is all debt: current liabilities, and bonded debt in all forms (mortgages, notes, debentures). Equity is the ownership fund which includes preferred stock, common stock, capital surplus, retained earnings, and all reserves which earmark surplus or retained earnings for a special purpose. Creditors, of course, prefer a sufficient cushion of ownership funds to avoid losses to them in the event of liquidation. The general rule-of-thumb in industrial corporations is that the debt-equity ratio be at least 1 to 1, that is, the owners have as large an investment as the creditors.

Other leverage ratios are long-term debt to net worth, the rule-of-thumb ratio for which is about 65 percent for industrial companies. The preferred level of current liabilities to net worth is 35 percent. For fixed assets to net worth the general rule is that the ratio should be around 65 percent. These are, of course, maximum levels; the numbers should be no higher. These ratio preferences differ for public utilities and industrial companies with rather certain and steady earnings growth.† (Weston, 1954, pp. 124-135.)

Activity ratios measure the effectiveness with which resources at the command of the company have been employed. Dividing sales by inventory, for example, is a commonly used measure. The calculation can be made either on the basis of selling price or cost; but, whichever is used, the same should be applied to both sales and inventory. There is no standard for this ratio. What is normal will depend much upon the industry and the product as well as upon various policies

---

* Weston distinguishes the quick ratio as being current assets less inventories, divided by current assets, and the acid test ratio as defined here. For both he gives the rule-of-thumb of 1 to 1.

† Various publications of the Securities and Exchange Commission, Washington, D.C., contain averages for industries.

of the company, such as customer service. So, managers must determine what is an acceptable ratio on the basis of past experience, what is the norm in the industry, and their plans for the future. Another activity ratio is sales to fixed assets. Weston feels that if this ratio exceeds two times the mean for the industry it is too high and indicates the firm is overtrading on its assets. (Weston, 1962, p. 62.) If the ratio is low it indicates, of course, the firm has an excessive investment in fixed assets relative to sales. A comparable ratio, of course, is sales to total assets.

There are a number of profitability ratios generally used. Gross operating margin is determined by dividing operating profit by sales. Here again, there is no standard norm, and each management must determine what it desires as a standard. Another useful measure is net operating profit to sales: net profit (after taxes) to sales. Return on assets and return on net worth are even more generally used measures of profitability. These were discussed at some length in the preceding part of this chapter.

There are many other accounting ratios that are highly useful in planning and control. Many have industry-wide utility; others are peculiar to the interests and problems of an industry and company. To illustrate, without analysis: direct to indirect labor, sales per employee, capital investment per employee, floor space per employee, cost per pound of output, productivity per manhour, productivity per unit of production, and so on and on.

The simplicity of these measures must not be allowed to detract from their power. They are excellent short-cuts to handling masses of data in planning, decision-making, evaluating results, detecting problems to be solved, and controlling operations. One great danger in their application exists if only one or a few ratios are used as the basis for decision. The planning process is so complex that it is best done when different ratios are combined and corroborate one another.

Break-even Analysis. This tool was discussed fully in Chapter 11.

DESIGN OF INFORMATION SYSTEMS. The communications and information systems in a company are major factors in stimulating rational decision-making in planning. Their description and use will be presented in Chapters 16 and 17.

OLDER QUANTITATIVE METHODS

Table 12-1 of Chapter 12 listed in this classification marginal analysis, return on investment, and quantitative methods of forecasting. The latter were sufficiently discussed in Chapter 8. The first two are very important and merit more than passing examination.

MARGINAL ANALYSIS. A few years ago Continental Air Lines filled only half the seats on its Boeing 707's, a record some 15 percent worse than the national average. It could have reduced its flights 5 percent and raised its average load to the industry average. But to do so would have resulted in reduced profits. Continental had developed an information system that permitted it to determine with precision whether a particular flight would increase profits, irrespective of the load factor. The key, of course, was to keep out-of-pocket costs below revenues. As discussed in Chapter 7, profits will increase when marginal revenues are greater than marginal costs. Continental found, for instance, that on a late night flight from Colorado Springs to Denver and an early morning flight the other way, the use of a Viscount, which carried some cargo but usually had few passengers, was profitable. The reason was that the net cost of these flights was less than the overnight hangar space rental at Colorado Springs and revenues covered all out-of-pocket costs. (*Business Week*, 1963a.)

If profits are a major objective of a business, marginal analysis is an important method to achieve it. Marginal analysis can be used in many different ways in a business planning program. It can be used to price goods and services. It can be used, as in Continental's case, to determine the worthwhileness of an additional flight. It can be used whenever it is possible to calculate the marginal cost of doing something versus the marginal return. If the cost of taking on one additional salesman, for example, can be related to his value to the company, the marginal principle can apply.

Marginal analysis focuses attention on the question: What difference does the next move make? This is a rather different question than: Will I recover average-cost of the next item I sell or the next flight I authorize? By diverting attention from average-costing, marginal analysis draws attention to the difference of incremental or marginal actions to profits. It accentuates the variables in a situation and underplays averages and constants.

Marginal analysis also stimulates flexibility in planning. Management, for example, is not tied to recovering on each unit sold the average costs calculated in past planning, upon which basis prices were determined. Of course, in the long run average costs must be recovered, but in the short run opportunities are lost if this rule is applied blindly.

As discussed in Chapter 7, a major problem in using marginal analysis is the difficulty in the typical business of getting accurate data about the impact of making a decision to produce or not to produce that last unit. An additional difficulty lies in the fact that the typical business accounting system builds up voluminous historical cost relationships that get projected into future operations and tend to become automatic standards for action. Where these problems can be licked, however, marginal analysis is a strong ally for more rational decisions.

This is not to argue that marginal-costing must replace total or average-costing in pricing. Experience has fully demonstrated that in business planning it is very frequently much easier and far more practicable to project future prices on the basis of estimates of total revenues and expected costs. As noted in Chapter 7, rather typically a businessman will calculate his costs, determine the share of the market he will capture, and then set his price to cover cost and make a profit. But even though this then is fixed in a plan, opportunities for additional profit can be exploited in the implementation of the plan if the marginal principle is recognized and applied.

In sum, marginal analysis has widespread applicability in business planning—beyond pricing—and is a powerful technique for optimizing output with a given input. It focuses attention on the right questions to ask and injects flexibility into planning. Its major limitation stems from difficulties in getting information about incremental income and cost, and from an excessive attachment to historical averages.

RETURN ON INVESTMENT (ROI). A virtually universally used technique in business planning is return on investment (ROI), a simple calculation of the relationship between income and investment cost. Important variations of it are return on assets (ROA) and return on equity or net worth (ROE). ROI is a potent tool in determining the rationality of all decisions relating to expenditures. What more important criterion is there in considering an investment in merchandise, a building, a new machine tool, or a creative scientist, than the prospective profit on the investment? At the same time, of course, the return on investment which is actually received is an important measure of the effectiveness of past planning. Because of its simplicity and concentration on profit, ROI has become a well-used measure of managerial performance both for a company as a whole and for the individual organizational parts of it. Its use for this purpose has been increased greatly by current trends of diversification and decentralization of profit responsibility.* ROI is, therefore, a major technique for both planning and control.

The basic concept of return on investment is deceptively simple. Yet, it can be a dangerous technique if not used appropriately and with caution. Furthermore, neither its calculation nor use is as simple as it first appears. In this part of the chapter will be explored some strengths and weaknesses of this technique and the considerations of importance in making the calculation.

The Du Pont Method

One of the attractive characteristics of the ROI concept is the simplicity with which it relates earnings to the manifold operations of the business. Chart 13-1 shows the Du Pont formulation of ROI (Davis, 1950.) The chart focuses

---

* In one study of 197 companies it was found that 99 percent used ROI as a measure of total company performance, and two-thirds used it as the sole measure. See Miller, 1960, p. 73.

Chart 13-1
Return on Investment

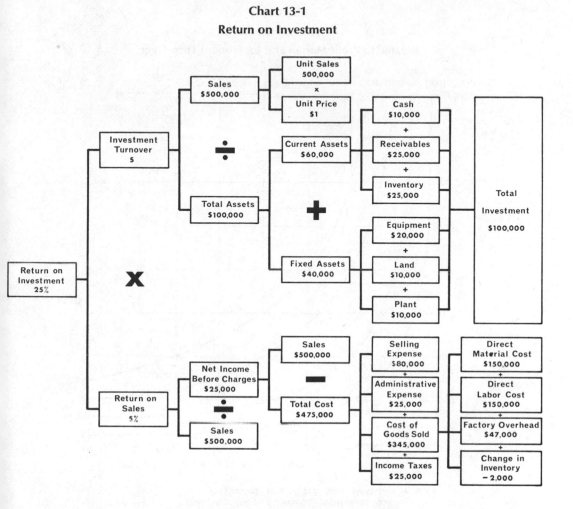

attention on factors that ultimately determine the profitability of a venture, and displays their relationships. (In the Du Pont system the complete breakdown of elements is much finer than shown in the chart.) It is clear from the chart that return on investment is highly dependent upon turnover of capital, or the amount of sales which a given dollar of investment is capable of producing. The chart also shows the significance of cost to earnings.

Given profit margin on sales, and investment turnover, the ROI can be derived. An example is worked out in Chart 13-1. In Chart 13-2 the inter-relationship is further explained. It is clear, for example, that with an investment turnover of 2, and a 15 percent margin on sales, the ROI will be 30 percent.

Importance of Cost of Capital

Simply because one venture may show a return on investment higher than another is no indication that it is necessarily better. Table 13-4 shows two ven-

Chart 13-2

Return on Investment

Related to Profit Margin and Investment Turn-Over

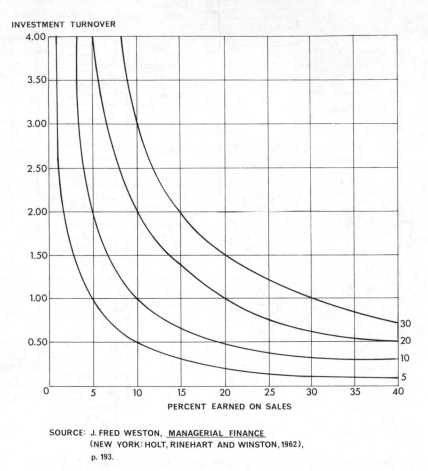

INVESTMENT TURNOVER

PERCENT EARNED ON SALES

SOURCE: J. FRED WESTON, <u>MANAGERIAL FINANCE</u>
(NEW YORK: HOLT, RINEHART AND WINSTON, 1962),
p. 193.

tures, **A** and **B**, and the question is raised as to which is the more successful. Rate of return is one measure and absolute profits is another, and much will depend upon which measure is chosen. Is a high rate of return better than a larger return at a lower rate?

Alfred Sloan (1964, p. 141) in commenting on the importance of ROI in the development of General Motors answered this question in this way: "General Motors' economic objective was to produce not necessarily the highest attainable rate of return on the capital employed, but the highest return consistent with attainable volume in the market. The long-term rate of return was to be the highest expectation consistent with a sound growth of the business, or what we called 'the economic return attainable.'"

Investment A may be less important to operations than investment B; or, investment B may be inconsistent with other purposes of the company; or, different rates of capital may alter the choice of which is more successful. As shown in Table 13-4, if the cost of capital is 17½ percent then only venture A can be called successful. But if it is 12 percent, venture B shows earnings almost twice as high as A's. B seems to be more successful at low rates and A more successful at high rates. There is, therefore, no simple answer to which of several ventures is most successful in terms of the excess of earnings over the cost of employed capital.

Measurement of Income

Because of different accounting conventions and practices it is possible for two individuals to make a different return on investment calculation from the same set of data. To illustrate, a company will undervalue its inventory in a period of rising prices if it uses the last-in, first-out (LIFO) inventory costing method. Just the opposite result will flow from using the first-in, first-out method of inventory costing (FIFO). The latter method will, of course, result in higher reported profits. Items remaining in inventory are the higher priced ones. As a consequence, reported profits will be higher, but amounts in the stated inventory in the balance sheet will be higher. Since replacement of the same physical volume of inventory will require higher costs, it is also said FIFO overstates profits.

Also, the inclusion or exclusion of various costs, aside from inventory, can much influence income calculations. Some costs are capitalized and some are charged off on a current basis. The method of allocating factory overhead, and the han-

Table 13-4   ROI for Two Ventures With Different Costs of Capital

ITEM	Venture A	Venture B
Capital Invested	$2,000	$10,000
Net annual return	400	1,500
Rate of return on capital	20%	15%
Excess of earnings over cost of capital of:		
12%	160	300
14%	120	100
17½%	60	− 200

Source: After David Solomons, *Divisional Performance: Measurement and Control* (New York: Financial Executives Research Foundation, 1965), p. 63.

dling of nonrecurring income can, of course, will affect the income calculation of a division of a company.

Measurement of Investment

There is no general agreement on how total capital employed should be measured. Should fixed assets be priced at book value, original cost, or replacement cost? There are valid arguments for using each of these. Original cost, less depreciation reserves, gives book value and conforms to tax accounting requirements. But this raises problems. Revenues can remain the same but ROI will go up each year. In a period of rising prices this measure will understate the true value of capital. Companies, like Du Pont, that use original cost sometimes have a policy to replace assets on a continuous basis and when the new assets are listed at current cost the average cost of all assets comes closer to replacement cost than to book value. Du Pont reasons that its calculated original cost, in this way, represents top quality plant and equipment and provides the best measure to use in ROI calculations. Public utilities would like to have replacement cost used as a basis for measuring return on investment in rate hearings, particularly in periods of rising prices. Most companies do not use this measure in calculating ROI because of constant changes of the numbers, the fact that they would differ from the accounting data, and because the two measures discussed first are easier to use.

Different methods to calculate ROI. The calculation of ROI varies greatly among companies. The method used should fit the objective of the analysis and, when comparing two proposals or performance, consistency is essential. To illustrate, assume the following proposal to invest in a milling machine. The investment is $1,000,000 and the machine will have a five-year life expectancy. Income from the machine will be $300,000 a year for five years. The total income, therefore, will be $1,500,000. Following are four different methods to calculate ROI. (Pflomm, 1963b.)

Method 1. Annual Return on Investment

$$\frac{\text{Annual Income}}{\text{Original Investment}} \times 100 = \frac{300}{1,000} \times 100 = 30\%$$

Method 2. Annual Return on Average Investment

$$\frac{\text{Annual Income}}{\dfrac{\text{Original Investment}}{2}} \times 100 = \frac{300}{500} \times 100 = 60\%$$

Method 3. Average Return on Average Investment

$$\frac{\text{Total Income-Original Investment}}{\dfrac{\text{Original Investment}}{2}} \times 100 = \frac{500}{\dfrac{1,000}{2} \times 5 \text{ years}} \times 100 = 20\%$$

Method 4. Average Book Return on Investment

$$\frac{\text{Total Income-Original Investment}}{\text{Weighted Average Investment}} =$$

$$\frac{500}{\dfrac{(1,000 + 800 + 600 + 400 + 200)}{5} \times 5 \text{ years}} \times 100 = 16\text{-}2/3\%$$

This by no means exhausts the list of methods to calculate ROI. To illustrate, there are advocates for using the investment base net worth plus intercompany loans, equity plus long-term loans, and total assets less current liabilities. Which will give the best measure? We cannot examine them all and hence will argue the case ROA vs. ROE without specifying precisely how either assets or equity are calculated. First, however, the importance of the time flows of income from an investment must be considered in the ROI calculation.

Importance of Time Discounting

A major fault of all the preceding methods of calculating ROI is that they fail to take account of the time value of net cash flows over the life of the investment. They all yield an average rate of return. In deciding upon future investments it is more important to concentrate on future cash flows and the different values of money in time. A major variation in ROI calculations, therefore, will arise from discounting the flow of income to its present value.

Two basic methods are generally accepted in discounting future anticipated cash flows. The first is the present worth method and the second is the discounted cash flow method. Each has important advantages.

Table 13-5 illustrates the calculation of present worth for investments A and B. The present worth of the future income streams of investment A at 4 percent is $1,287 and of B it is $2,155. Clearly, B is the superior investment in terms of the value of income received over the life of the investment at this discount rate. At 30 percent, however, the two are about equal, and at 40 percent B is clearly the second choice. The reason for this is that investment A returns most of its income in the first two years; the income flow is concentrated in B in the later years. Since money is worth more today than in the future, higher rates of discount will favor A type of investments over the B type. At low rates of discount, the differences will not be as sharp, as shown in the table.

A major question arises in using this method in choosing the rate of discount. The preferred answer is the appropriate cost of capital to a firm. For this reason this method is often called the internal-rate calculation of return on investment. (In Chapter 20 calculation of a firm's cost of capital will be discussed.)

For many investments both the cash inflows and cash outflows vary over time and it is useful to compare them at common points in time from the inception of the project until its completion. The way to do this is to select a rate of return that discounts the cash inflows so that they exactly equal the costs of the project. This is called the discounted cash flow approach. The rate of discount must be found by a trial-and-error process as demonstrated in Table 13-6. Because the discount factor must be found by trial and error, this has been called the external rate of return approach. In this case the discount rate is 22 percent.

Comparison of Methods

Among the ROI calculations discussed here to facilitate choice among investment decisions, the time discount techniques are clearly superior. The present-worth technique has an advantage in that it ranks projects according to the firm's cost of capital. The discounted cash flow approach has merit in discounting of both cash ingo and outgo. Both can be linked with probability estimates of cash flow and thereby provide valuable insights for managers in coming to decisions as will be illustrated in Chapter 20.

Table 13-5 Present Worth Calculation

INVESTMENT = $1,000

Year	A	B
1	500	100
2	400	200
3	300	300
4	200	400
5		500
6		600
7		500

	4%			20%			30%			40%		
Yr.	IF	A	B	IF	A	B	IF	A	B	IF	A	B
1	.96	480	96	.83	415	83	.77	385	77	.71	355	71
2	.92	368	184	.69	276	138	.59	236	118	.51	205	102
3	.89	267	267	.58	174	174	.46	138	138	.36	108	108
4	.86	172	344	.48	96	192	.35	70	140	.26	92	104
5	.82		410	.40		200	.27		135	.19		94
6	.79		474	.33		198	.21		126	.13		78
7	.76		380	.28		140	.16		80	.09		45
Present Worth		1,287	2,155		961	1,125		829	814		1,260	602

Note: Some writers speak of the difference between the cost of the investment and the present worth as present value. In the case of investment A at 4 percent, for example, the present value would be $260. See Weston, *Managerial Finance,* p. 128.

This is not to say that the average-rate-of-return calculation should be discarded as a method to choose among investment opportunities. As a matter of fact most businessmen use it in making some capital budgeting decisions (as will be shown in Chapter 20) over the time discount methods. There are two fundamental reasons for this. First, a large number of investments return cash over a comparatively few years at a rather equal rate. Second, businessmen have a high liquidity preference and tend to choose investments which have a short-term payoff. In these cases the ROI calculations yield much the same results. However, differences between the average-rate-of-return calculation and the discounted cash flow can be very great. Differences between the present values of high near-term costs of investments and far-away income flows can distort the calculation. If costs are spread more evenly over the life of the project, however, comparisons with other measures of return might be closer.

A great advantage of the time discount methods is that they raise important questions for the decision-maker to answer. This, together with an orderly procedure to make decisions, is by and large more important than the differences among the methods for the majority of investments made in business.

In judging managerial performance there are important differences, however, between those return-on-investment calculations which use assets as the investment base and those which use net worth or stockholder equity (the difference between total asets and total liabilities).

It is often observed that ROA is a measure of business performance and ROE is a measure of financial importance. One advantage claimed for ROA is that in a divisionalized company the concern of managers is with the assets employed and not the source of capital. The test of ROA is the ability of managers to use capital profitably from all sources, not just from the stockholders. ROA provides an incentive to increase sales and reduce costs, which may not be the case with concentration on ROE.

On the other hand, concentration on ROA may miss opportunities for profits. For example, as Chamberlain (1962, p. 62) points out, if maximum dollar profit is desired ROE may be the better measure. A lower rate of return on a higher total asset figure might actually produce a better profit showing than a higher rate of return on a lower total asset base.

To illustrate, assume profit of $1,000,000 on sales of $20,000,000 assets of $4,000,000, and a net worth of $2,000,000. ROA and ROE would be calculated as follows (where m=millions):

$$\frac{\$1m}{20m} \times \frac{20m}{4m} \text{ or } 5\% \times 5 = 25\% = ROA$$

$$\frac{\$1m}{20m} \times \frac{20m}{2m} \text{ or } 5\% \times 10 = 50\% = ROE$$

Assume now that profits increase 20 percent to $1,200,000, sales rise to

$40,000,000, and assets double to $8,000,000 as a result of an increase in accounts receivable. The calculations would then be:

$$\frac{\$1.2m}{40m} \times \frac{40m}{8m} \text{ or } 3\% \times 5 = 15\% = \text{ROA}$$

$$\frac{\$1.2m}{40m} \times \frac{40m}{2m} \text{ or } 3\% \times 20 = 60\% = \text{ROE}$$

Thus, an increase in sales and profits on the basis of an ROA calculation would result in a lower evaluation of managerial performance when financing comes from other than equity sources. A strict use of ROA, therefore, can result in lost profit opportunities.

Executives of more than 200 companies were asked what single financial indicator they regarded as most symptomatic of the success of their companies. They replied ROE. (Maurice S. Newman, 1966, p. 18.)

Those who prefer ROE generally consider that it focuses attention on stockholders rather than managers. They insist that, while managers should be measured on their ability to use all sorts of capital in increasing profits, the business operation must begin with equity and a management intent on increasing profits will borrow when such funds earn more than their cost. If profit maximiza-

Table 13-6   The Discounted Cash Flow Analysis

			Rate of Return Analysis		
Year	Expenditures	Cash Advantage	Present Value of $1 at 24%	Present Value of Expenditures	Present Value of Advantage
1962	$ 5,000		.806	$ 4,030	
1963	10,500		.650	6,825	
1964	8,000		.524	4,192	
1965	110,000		.423	46,530	
1966		$ 40,000	.341		$13,640
1967		40,000	.275		11,000
1968		40,000	.222		8,880
1969		55,000	.179		9,845
1970		50,000	.144		7,200
1971		45,000	.116		5,220
1972		15,000	.094		1,410
1973		5,000	.076		380
1974		5,000	.061		305
1975		5,000	.049		245
	$133,500	$300,000		$61,577	$58,125

Table 13-6   The Discounted Cash Flow Analysis (Continued)

			Rate of Return Analysis		
Year	*Expenditures*	*Cash Advantage*	*Present Value of $1 at 22%*	*Present Value of Expenditures*	*Present Value of Advantage*
1962	$ 5,000		.820	$ 4,100	
1963	10,500		.672	7,056	
1964	8,000		.551	4,408	
1965	110,000		.451	49,610	
1966		$ 40,000	.370		$14,800
1967		40,000	.303		12,120
1968		40,000	.249		9,960
1969		55,000	.204		11,220
1970		50,000	.167		8,350
1971		45,000	.137		6,165
1972		15,000	.112		1,680
1973		5,000	.092		460
1974		5,000	.075		375
1975		5,000	.062		310
	$133,500	$300,000		$65,174	$65,440

			Rate of Return Analysis		
Year	*Expenditures*	*Cash Advantage*	*Present Value of $1 at 20%*	*Present Value of Expenditures*	*Present Value of Advantage*
1962	$ 5,000		.833	$ 4,165	
1963	10,500		.694	7,287	
1964	8,000		.579	4,632	
1965	110,000		.482	53,020	
1966		$ 40,000	.402		$16,080
1967		40,000	.335		13,400
1968		40,000	.279		11,160
1969		55,000	.233		12,815
1970		50,000	.194		9,700
1971		45,000	.162		7,290
1972		15,000	.135		2,025
1973		5,000	.112		560
1974		5,000	.093		465
1975		5,000	.078		390
	$133,500	$300,000		$69,104	$73,885

Source: Raymond M. Haas, Richard I. Hartman, John H. James, and Robert R. Milroy, *Long-Range Planning for Small Business,* Bloomington: Bureau of Business Research, Graduate School of Business, Indiana University, 1964, p. 62-63.

tion is the objective, therefore, ROE rather than ROA is the proper measure.

Contract renegotiation between the Department of Defense and military contractors has been based importantly on return on net worth, a practice which has been vigorously resisted by the industry. There are many reasons for the strong feeling against ROE as a measure of performance. It is said, for example, that it favors inefficient contractors. To illustrate, an efficient company selling a product for $1 and making $100,000 on $200,000 of net worth will have a higher rate of return than an inefficient manufacturer selling the product for $1.25 and making $100,000 on a net worth of $500,000. In the first case the ROE is 50 percent and subjects the company to renegotiation of profits. In the second instance the ROE is 20 percent and results in no profit renegotiation. There are many other reasons why defense manufacturers do not like to be measured by ROE criteria, but I mention just this one to show one industry where there is a strong rejection of ROE as a measure of performance. (Weston, 1960.)

Which is the correct measure? The answer, to me, is that neither should be used exclusively as a standard of performance. Each has its advantages but should be used in combination and in light of a larger number of other considerations important in the management of an enterprise. Some of the important reasons for this point of view become clear upon looking at advantages and disadvantages of return-on-investment criteria for planning and performance.

Advantages and Disadvantages of ROI Standards

Some of the more important advantages of the ROI measure is: it focuses attention squarely on the central objective of profits; it is a good measure of the efficiency with which capital is used; it provides a concrete standard against which decisions can be made and performance is measured; it can be established as a goal and provide a broad base for planning; it can be used to control operations; it gets away from a sales growth and sales volume phobia; and it can make clear the responsibility of decentralized managers.

On the other hand the standard is not without shortcomings. It is but one measure in deciding among alternative investments, and to use it exclusively may produce incorrect decisions. Technical progress, morale, stability, and growth, are among factors which may be more governing, on occasion, than ROI *per se*. It gives too much emphasis to capital resources in measuring managerial performance. There are other resources of importance in an enterprise's success. If one division is highly profitable it may have less incentive to do better if other divisions have a lower ROI. Certainly a standard ROI for all operations in a company would be quite inappropriate.

A major shortcoming of ROI as a measure of performance is that it cultivates short-range thinking. This is especially pertinent as division general managers, who are judged principally on ROI, rotate to other jobs after a few years, a tendency which seems to be growing in industry. Today's general division manager may easily develop a better current ROI by a number of decisions, if he has the authority. He can reduce inventory, fail to replace obsolete equipment and machinery, cut down on management training programs, lower advertising expenditures, and chop into his research and development budget. He can exert great pressure on his employees to increase productivity. But all these measures can lead to disaster in the long-run. It can be taken as axiomatic that any divisionalized company that judges its decentralized general managers solely on a current ROI will drive them away from long-range planning and substantially adversely affect long-range profit levels.

Because of these many shortcomings, wise managers in using ROI as a basis for evaluating investment proposals determine a calculation that is best suited to the subject and use that measure consistently. Furthermore, they use it as only one measure in making a choice. Used with caution and used wisely, however, there are few more useful tools for planning and judging results.

CONVENTIONAL SCHEDULING MODELS

Scheduling models facilitate the coordination of activities of an enterprise to achieve optimum utilization of resources in achieving company objectives. These models are useful for a wide range of activities, from a seemingly trivial task of scheduling a plant tour to a very complex job of scheduling activities in a large production program. There is a wide variety of such conventional scheduling models in use, and many variations of them. (Buffa, 1965.) This section will mention only three: simple bar charts, milestone charts, and line-of-balance charts. The Critical Path Method is an older technique which evolved from these; it will be considered in Chapter 14, together with Program Evaluation and Review Technique (PERT). (Holtz, 1966.)

GANTT BAR CHARTS. The Gantt bar charts, or simply bar charts (see Chart 13-3), were developed by Henry L. Gantt in 1917 (1964, pp. 37-38.) The main purpose of bar charts is to describe progress by comparing work done against planned objectives. To plan and control the productive activities of any particular product, several bar charts may be needed to mark the progress of the various components of the given product. Each bar chart may then identify a particular component, which in turn may be subdivided into tasks that go into making the component. These tasks may pertain to activities such as design, drafting, fabrication, testing, and inspection.

Each bar on the bar chart is constructed by plotting the task activity from start to completion date. In essence, the bar chart is a production plan, and management can use it to compare actual progress with plan.

Chart 13-3

Gantt Bar Chart

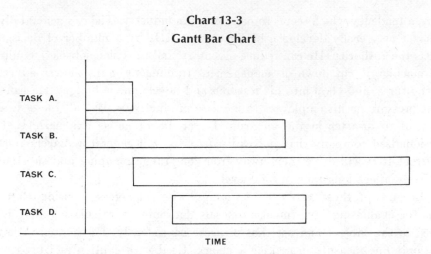

TIME

The Gantt chart method has serious shortcomings for planning and control of complex projects such as those encountered, for example, in large research and development programs. The relationships that exist among activities in a program are not indicated, and they do not provide a framework for resource allocation or costing, both of which are so necessary in planning and control of complex operations. (Miller, 1963, p. 25.)

THE MILESTONE SYSTEM. Under the enormous pressures to catch up in the missiles race following the Korean War the milestone scheduling technique came into widespread use in government agencies supervising prime contractors and, of course, in the plants of the prime contractors. (Wattel, 1964, p. 39.) The milestone system simply lists, as on Chart 13-4, tasks such as design, production, and testing, needed to produce an end item, and identifies milestones important in the program, such as "complete design," or "assembly complete." Milestones are identified in Chart 13-4 by number. The milestone system can be used in almost every type of managerial endeavor that requires planning and control over schedules. It permits a manager to see a complex network of activity flows and those which are most critical in completing the entire task. Being comparable to the Gantt charts, the milestone method is subject to just about the same strengths and weaknesses.

THE CRITICAL PATH METHOD (CPM). CPM is a technique specifically applicable to complex, one-of-a-kind operations. Originally designed to plan and control a construction project by M. R. Walker of E. I. Du Pont de Nemours & Company, Inc., it has expanded rapidly in use and has grown into the more complicated PERT network method. Fundamentally, CPM is developed when the interdependencies of the milestone chart are related and paths in the process of completing a project are identified. CPM, as will be explained in

Chart 13-4

A Milestone Chart

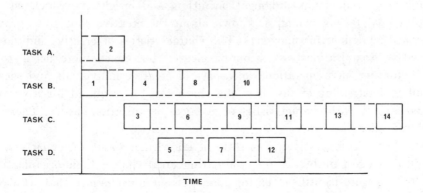

Chapter 15, is a simplified version of PERT. As such, it is better explained later, along with PERT.

THE LINE-OF-BALANCE (LOB) SYSTEM. The above are not the only comparatively simple planning and control methods available in scheduling. Another widely used and much more complicated technique is LOB, developed by George Fouch at the Goodyear Company in 1941 (Robert Miller, 1963, p. 17). It is principally a method for minimizing inventory in production plans with fixed delivery schedules and a repetitive production program not characterized with important uncertainties about deliveries and activities needed to meet deliveries (Holtz, 1966, Section III).

NEWER AND MORE COMPLEX METHODS

The last two classifications of Table 12-1, Chapter 12, concerned the newer mathematical tools and the more complex methods which combine many techniques. These will be discussed in Chapters 14 and 15.

SUMMARY AND CONCLUSIONS

This chapter examined some of the major older tools available to managers to improve their planning. In considering tools useful to planning, whether old or new ones, managers have a difficult problem to determine which should be used at which places in the planning process. This is a problem of synectic relevance, the solution to which is a vital tool in itself.

Among all the older techniques for better planning, creativity of managers and staff stand out by far as being the most important. Creativity in business was defined not alone as the ability to develop a new and original thought, but also the ability to carry an idea through to the point where it is profitably exploited. The differences and complementaries among the words creativity, invention, innovation, entrepreneurship, judgment, intuition, and insight, were defined.

Unfortunately, not enough is known about the creative process to provide unequivocal guidelines for managers. The characteristics of creative individuals and creative organizations are becoming clearer, but much more needs to be known before we have operational measures of creative individuals and reasonably full understanding of just how the characteristics required for a creative organization mix with characteristics of classical organization theory. There are conflicts between the two.

Despite the comparatively low state of knowledge about such matters, top managers have responsibilities for stimulating creativity in their organizations. The following were identified: 1) top management must assure that creativity exists at its own level; 2) a carefully designed planning program is an excellent framework to stimulate creativity; 3) management can and should understand the many ways it can give encouragement to and command creativity; 4) ways must be found to measure and recruit creative managers and staff; 5) top management should try to stimulate creativity through experimentation with different devices; and 6) ways must be found to create a climate for the survival of potentially profitable ideas.

There are, of course, some limitations on the extent to which management should stimulate creativity. It is expensive, and the greater the expected departure from present practice and experience the less is the chance for profitable payoff. Furthermore, the degree and importance of creativity needed will vary among different companies and among the functional organizations in any company. So, top management has a decision to make about where and how much expenditure will be allocated to generate creativity. This dilemma is not unlike most capital expenditure problems but is probably less easily resolved.

Although the analysis was not extensive, the importance of the following methods was emphasized and illustrations were given: nonquantitative simulation and model building, rules-of-thumb, and design of information systems.

Somewhat more attention was paid to marginal analysis as compared with full-cost analysis in decision-making. Marginal analysis is the calculation of the difference between marginal revenue and marginal costs and can be a guide to increase profits when the marginal differences can be calculated.

Return on investment is a major tool used in industry, not only to determine the correctness of proposed decisions but also to measure the performance of managers. The many different methods to calculate ROI were presented and compared. The discussion concluded that different methods of calculating ROI must be fitted to the objective for which they are employed. Whatever method is decided upon should be used consistently in making comparisons. It was concluded, also, that judging managerial performance solely on the basis of short-range ROI calculations might be dangerous and lead to long-range results contrary to the interests of top management.

The high importance of accounting systems as tools for decision-making in the planning process was examined and the conclusion drawn that few models are more illuminating in measuring the impact of operations on profits than accounting models such as balance sheet and profit and loss statements, sources and application of cash statements, and various ratios derived from accounting data.

It would be an egregious blunder for managers or students of management decision-making to ignore, or to underestimate, the commanding significance of these older techniques in better planning, as compared with the newer quantitative inventions. On the other hand, every manager should have a speaking acquaintance with those newer tools which can be singularly helpful to him. These will be considered in the next two chapters.

14
The Systems Approach
to Decision-Making ———————

14

The Systems Approach
to Decision-Making

INTRODUCTION

The new popularity of the systems approach is epitomized in a bill introduced into the U.S. Senate in 1967 by fifteen Senators. This bill (S. 467, 90th Congress, 1st Session) provided for the establishment of a National Commission on Public Management "to study and recommend the manner in which modern systems analysis and management techniques may be utilized to resolve problems relating to unemployment, public welfare, education, and similar national and community problems in the nondefense sector . . ."

In 1965 the U.S. Bureau of the Budget requested all U.S. governmental agency heads to establish an adequate central staff for analysis of many parts of the Planning-Programming-Budgeting System (PPB). The Bureau envisioned "An analytic effort . . . to examine deeply program objectives and criteria of accomplishments." The Bureau went on to say, "Whenever applicable, this effort will utilize systems analysis, operations research and other pertinent techniques."

Within the past half-dozen years the so-called systems approach has become a major instrument in governmental decision-making and is now widely viewed as a unique technique for helping to decide how to resolve many very difficult social problems. Reflecting this development, the systems approach is the subject of renewed attention throughout the business world. I say renewed because this approach has always been used in business but, like long-range planning, there is something different about the approach today as compared with the past.

Despite the rapid growth of the systems approach to resolving governmental, social, and business problems, there is little agreement on precisely what this approach really is. Certainly, there does not exist a ready-made "cook book" to explain how to do it.

In this chapter, the objective is to define the systems approach, and to examine its origins, essential characteristics, importance in managerial decision-making, and its limitations.

WHAT IS THE SYSTEMS APPROACH?

Stafford Beer, an English writer on cybernetics as applied to management, has written (1959, p. 9) that: "Anything that consists of parts connected together will be called a system. For instance, a game of snooker is a system, whereas a single snooker ball is not. A car, a pair of scissors, an economy, a language, an ear, and a quadratic equation: all these things are systems. They can be pointed out as aggregates of bits and pieces; but they begin to be understood only when the connections between the bits and pieces, the dynamic interactions of the whole organism, are made the object of study." The factor of connection, interrelationship, ties together a system. Several pioneer writers on the systems concept emphasize the whole in their definition, e.g.: "A system is an organized or complex whole; an assemblage or combination of things or parts forming a complex or unitary whole." (Richard A. Johnson, Kast, and Rosenzweig, 1963, p. 4.) McGregor (in Bennis and McGregor, 1967, p. 39) links interrelationships with survival in this definition: "A system is an assembly of interdependent parts (subsystems) whose interaction determines its survival."

These definitions make it clear that a system is a very broad concept. It can encompass the universe, a river and its tributary streams, as well as a communications network to complete a decision to purchase an airline ticket.

Now, used very broadly, the systems approach is simple. It is to take account of all the factors or interrelationships relevant to the subject, or system, under study. Put this way, it sounds "commonsensical," trite, and, if taken literally, also completely impossible in practice. It is impossible because in this world everything is connected with everything else and no useful analysis can take into account everything. Very quickly, for a study of any importance, the sheer number of elements which may be considered gets out of hand. Obviously, any practicable systems approach to problem-solving must, therefore, concentrate on a limited number of the most relevant factors.

Before proceeding further with a definition of the systems approach, it is important to note that further specification runs immediately into semantic litter. The following words have been used as being synonymous: the systems approach, systems analysis, systems engineering, systems management, operations research, operation analysis, management science, and cost-effective analysis. There is no point in trying to unscramble definitions for all these terms now. Rather, it is important to distinguish among several major elements of the systems approach, and then to come to grips with this semantic problem in deeper exploration of systems analysis.

Chart 14-1

Conceptual Model of the Systems Approach

to Problem Solving

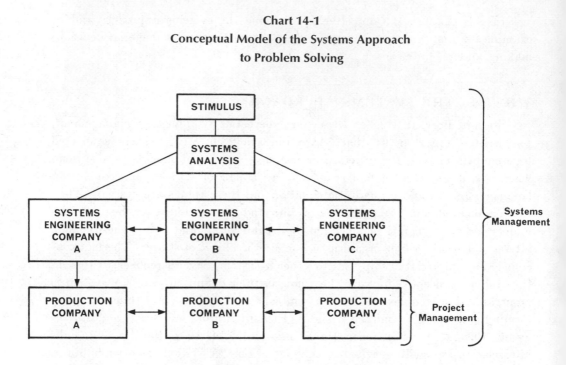

FOUR ROUTES IN THE SYSTEMS APPROACH

The systems approach in decision-making embraces four major elements that are closely interrelated but have distinctive characteristics. Chart 14-1 presents a simple conceptual model that shows these elements and their interrelationship.

It should be realized at the outset that there is no general agreement on definitions of the terms shown in Chart 14-1. Very broadly, systems analysis refers to an orderly analytic study of a system which is designed to help a decision-maker identify a preferred course of action, from among many possible alternatives, to achieve an objective. Thus, weapons systems analysis is a method to identify, say, which of two bomber configurations is the best system in light of defined objectives. A business systems analysis may be the method to determine how selected resources are to be used to maximize profits.

Systems engineering, basically, involves subdividing a broadly defined task into well-defined tasks which can be assigned to people to carry out. The objective of systems engineering is to take a large task, such as the production of the Apollo space craft, and divide it into manageable subtasks which can be assigned to individuals who can do their jobs with minimal concern for or dealings with individuals working on other assignments in the program. The systems engineer has been successful when these individual tasks are completed in conformance with specification, the individual parts of the system fit exactly as required, and the system (the Apollo space craft) fully satisfies all its operational objectives.

Systems management is a term used mostly in the aerospace industry to refer to the whole process of planning, organizing, coordinating, controlling, and directing the combined efforts of a government purchaser (such as the Air Force), private contractors, and any other groups or individuals participating in the completion of a program's objectives. Systems management refers, for example, to the entire program to produce a new airplane, including its development and production, training people to fly it, providing bases from which to fly, and assuring proper maintenance of the equipment over its life. In a broad sense, of course, the chief executive of a company is a manager of a system—his business system—and his work can be called systems management.

Project management shown in Chart 14-1 refers to the administration of a particular part of the whole system. It can be, for example, the management of a team to build a new type valve in a building hardware company, or the management required to build a prototype airplane, or the management of the Apollo space craft which is part of a larger systems management program to land a man on the moon by 1970 and return him safety to earth.

All these terms are used somewhat differently, but I think the above definitions agree generally with practice in those areas where the terms are most frequently used. In later chapters, especially Chapters 18, 19, and 22, project management and systems engineering will be discussed more fully. The remainder of this chapter will be devoted to systems analysis.

THE ESSENCE OF SYSTEMS ANALYSIS

One of the originators and outstanding practitioners of systems analysis defines it as "an approach to complex problems of choice under uncertainty by systematically examining the costs, effectiveness, and risks of the various alternatives." (Quade, 1963, p. v.) It is a technique for grasping a large complex problem by looking at the broad goals to be achieved, alternative methods to achieve them, and then examining the costs and benefits of various approaches to achieve the objectives. In complex problems, such as a systems analysis to choose from among different weapons systems, multiple objectives may exist, and the priority objectives may not at first be clear. System analysis is designed to clarify objectives. It is also a method to discover alternatives and measure their appropriateness in light of all sorts of costs that are relevant to a problem—money, lives, personal satisfactions, machine losses, foregone opportunities for alternative investments, and so on—in light of benefits to be achieved by taking a particular course of action. Benefits may also be of many different varieties—money, lives, time, and so on. In the process of analysis, risks, costs, and objectives are weighed and balanced.

John Rubel called systems analysis "a way of inventing your way to a solution." (Quoted by Terhorst, 1965.) What he means, of course, is that for very complex problems a solution is by no means obvious and systems analysis is a method to help a decision-maker invent a solution. Henry Rowen (1967,

p. 3), President of RAND, had much the same thing in mind in saying: "it is a way of making discoveries. Discoveries not of things, but about objectives or values, or relationships, or facts."

Systems analysis is a systematic way to look at complex problems to assure the achievement of a larger objective more effectively than if its individual parts were examined in isolation. A simple illustration would be the problem of feeding the people of Brazil better diets at a cheaper price by exploiting the great protein resources lying offshore. Systems analysis says that this objective can be accomplished more efficiently and effectively if, instead of directly trying to farm the ocean, all major elements of the system to do this are considered in relation with one another and in respect to the costs and advantages different alternatives embody. This means looking at the need for and types of boats, the methods to fish and farm, offshore and onshore food processing plants, transportation of foodstuffs, and the relationship of this food source to other food supplies in and out of Brazil. The essence of systems analysis, says one wag, is that it has shown that the chicken is the egg's idea of how to get more eggs.

These views suggest, of course, that there is no uniform method for making a systems analysis. Each problem is somewhat unique and each demands that the design of the analysis be carefully prepared for best results. Indeed, says Charles Hitch (1966, p. 54), a distinguished developer of systems analysis in the Pentagon and now President of the University of California, "It is my experience that the hardest problems for the systems analyst are not those of analytic techniques. . . . What distinguishes the useful and productive analyst is his ability to formulate (or design) the problem; to choose appropriate objectives; to define the relevant, important environments or situations in which to test the alternatives; to judge the reliability of his cost and other data, and not least his ingenuity in inventing new systems or alternatives to evaluate."

Systems analysis is still in an embryonic stage, is done differently by different analysts, and varies much depending upon the problem. Although no universal system analysis method exists, there are characteristics which distinguish it from other approaches to complex problem-solving. It is informative to look at some of these for they also help to conceptualize better the meaning of systems analysis. The following discussion of systems analysis will make reference to this activity in decision-making about military and space systems, analysis of huge nondefense problems of major concern to governments, and business problems.

The first characteristic is the blend of many areas of knowledge in the solution of complex problems. Great, ill-structured problems—such as the purchase of nuclear transport ships versus large air transport planes, the best means to achieve urban redevelopment, preferred methods to prevent juvenile delinquency, a decision to acquire a company—require the synthesis of many disciplines if answers are to be useful to decision-makers. Systems analysis permits and encourages the judgment, intuition, and knowledge of experts to be blended in a systematic and efficient manner. Furthermore, systems analysis facilitates the blending of the judgment and intuition of managers with the expertise of specialists. Gene Fisher (1966) has long asserted that the great advantage of systems analysis is that it helps decision-makers to sharpen their judgments. Enthoven (1963) explains these two relationships in the following operational terms: "Systems Analysis can best be described as a continuing dialogue between the policy-maker and the systems analyst, in which the policy-maker (McNamara) asks for alternative solutions to his problems; while the analyst attempts to clarify the conceptual framework in which the decisions must be made, to define alternative possible objectives and criteria, and to explore in as clear terms as possible (and quantitatively), the cost and effectiveness of these courses of action."

A second fundamental characteristic of systems analysis is that it employs and emphasizes the scientific method. Using the term broadly, this means a number of different things.

It means that the method is open, explicit, and results can be verified by other experts. While quantitative data can be mixed with qualitative information, and logic can be blended with empirical evidence, the scientific method requires that the steps in the analysis can be retraced by others. This means that assumptions, data, tests, discussion, evaluations, and so on, can be redone for verification. This does not mean, of course, that the results will be accepted by everyone. For example, to calculate total cost (or total investment) for a new satellite over its lifetime is a difficult and uncertain task. The costs estimated by one person may not be accepted by another, but they can at least be explicitly stated in detail and the methodology of their calculation explained.

It means also that the analysis is systematic and objective. It is systematic in that it follows a prescribed design and is not *ad hoc*. It is objective in that personalities and personal values are submerged to quantitative fact to the extent possible.

It means that each hypothesis is tested and verified by methods appropriate to the hypothesis in question. Some may be tested analytically by rigorous quantitative methods, some only experimentally, some by historical data, and so on.

It means that, to the extent feasible and practicable, information is quantified. When quantified it is more easily manipulated and verified. This is not meant to suggest, of course, that everything can be reduced to numbers. To try to do so in systems analysis would twist some pieces of information and distort results. But the pressure is for quantification rather than vague verbal generalizations. Even where great uncertainties exist efforts are made to quantify. As Enthoven says: "This is not to rule out judgment and insight. Rather, it is to say that judgments and insights need, like everything else, to be expressed with clarity if they are to be useful." (Enthoven, reproduced in Tucker, 1966, p. 141.) *

A third characteristic, which is certainly embraced in the scientific method,

* I have taken the structure for this discussion of the scientific method from this speech.

is the development of a model. The essence of systems analysis is to construct and operate within a "model," or a simplified abstraction of the real situation appropriate to the question. A model provides a structure, hopefully precise, that permits different specialists to communicate, specifies the factual information required and the way it is interrelated, and permits the application of judgment and intuition. This characteristic will be treated at length later.

Fourth, is the evaluation of alternatives by a careful assessment of costs against benefits. So cardinal a feature of systems analysis is cost-benefit analysis that many people mistakenly consider the two to be synonymous. This is not so, for cost-benefit analysis is only one part, albeit an important part, of systems analysis.

Fifth, the time context is the future. Systems analysis does not deal with past problems.

Sixth, the environment of analysis, of course, is surrounded by uncertainties. One characteristic of systems analysis is the attempt to deal explicitly with uncertainty. In weapons systems analysis, Hitch has identified these uncertainties as: uncertainty about planning factors, such as attrition rates, bombing errors, and comparable factors; uncertainty regarding the potential enemy and his reactions; uncertainty about strategic context, such as the period of time covered by an analysis, political constraints, who will be the enemy, and so on; technological uncertainty, such as the existence of or workability of a new technology; and statistical uncertainty, or the type of uncertainty stemming from chance elements in the real world. (Hitch, 1964, pp. 15-16.) He notes that a major attribute of systems analysis is coming to grips with these uncertainties and not brushing them under the rug and ignoring them. They present great imponderables and sometimes simply defy a satisfactory resolution.

There are many ways to resolve the problem, but the point is that in systems analysis all major uncertainties are faced squarely and explicitly.

Seventh, usually the context of systems analysis is very broad and the environmental factors are very complex. Different types of systems analysis will be noted later, but, generally, simple problems where there are single, easily accepted solutions are the exception rather than the rule.

Finally, it may be noted that systems analysis is an art, not a science. Quade's comments on this point in connection with weapons systems analysis are worth repeating. "It is not easy," he says, "to tell someone how to carry out systems analysis. We lack adequate theory to guide us. The attention of the practitioners, when it has turned to methods, has been focused mainly on the development of mathematical techniques. This attention has met with great success. Models have now become easier to manipulate, even with many more variables represented. Computational obstacles cause comparatively little difficulty. It is the philosophical problems, such as occur in providing assurance that the model is meaningful, in devising schemes to compensate for uncertainty, or in choosing appropriate criteria, that are troublesome. This lack of a guiding theory must be expected, for systems analysis is a relatively new discipline." He goes on to say that, because systems analysis is an art and not a science, "we have to do some things that we think are right but that are not verifiable, that we cannot really justify, and that are never checked in the output of the work. Also, we must accept as inputs many relatively intangible factors derived from human judgment, and we must present answers to be used as a basis for other judgments. Whenever possible, this judgment is supplemented by inductive and numerical reasoning, but it is only judgment nevertheless." (Quade, 1966, pp. 6-7.)

In sum, we are dealing with a methodology applied to large complex systems problems, in which specialists combine with decision-makers to blend in a scientific way the best tools available for solving problems that yield to solution in a less satisfactory fashion by any other known method. But each solution is a work of art, not the result of a prescribed methodology or formula that applies to all cases.

TYPES OF SYSTEMS ANALYSIS

It seems useful at this point to illustrate a few types of systems problems in different areas. In the military area, the simplest type problem is one that involves a choice as between two systems within a given category, such as bomber A versus bomber B, or ship A versus ship B, to fulfill a simple mission at least cost. At the other extreme are systems analyses which pit several different types of weapons systems against each other, as, for example, a comparison among bombers, land-based missiles, missile ships, or civil defense programs, to provide the best defense of the continental U.S. at least cost in the 1980's.

In the area of general government, a simple systems analysis might study the question whether the Army Corps of Engineers should spend $10,000,000 on flood control in Missouri versus Colorado. Another illustration is a study of the best method to move traffic in Chicago. At a more difficult level would be a determination of the preferred means of transportation that should be provided and made available for the so-called Northeast Corridor, or the area from Boston to Washington, D.C., in the 1970's. Determining the best allocation of national resources to improve the habitability of U.S. cities would involve a difficult systems analysis.

In the business world, systems analysis runs the gamut from the simple to the complex. A simple systems analysis is illustrated by the problem: What is the proper inventory reorder point in factory X? At a bit more difficult level would be a PERT-type network analysis of work flow (see Chapter 15). At the more complex level is the problem of the International Development Corporation of Litton Industries to use the systems approach in bringing about the development of agriculture, industry, transportation, and recreation in Greece. As noted in Chapter 3, a comprehensive corporate planning program of a company is an important systems analysis for a company.

In sum, the words systems analysis can be used to cover a wide spectrum of analyses. But the concept used here and the power of the methodology is more related to the tough, broad, major, ill-structured type of problem than to the narrow, simple type problem.

TAP ROOTS OF SYSTEMS ANALYSIS

Today's systems analysis finds its tap roots in the development of operations research during World War II, the evolution of the weapons systems contracting concept following World War II, and the synthesis of these with other disciplines at the RAND Corporation in the intervening years to help military decision-makers deal with complex problems. In the meantime, of course, the approach of businessmen to their problems has been a systems approach although the name has only recently been applied to it.

OPERATIONS RESEARCH. What has been called "operations research" (OR) was first systematically employed during World War II by the British and American military services. Although the military services had long used scientists to help solve technical weapons problems, during World War II for the first time groups of scientists were asked to deal with strictly military problems of an operational nature. This was research into operations, hence the name. The types of problems dealt with were as follows: analysis of best patterns to lay underwater mines, the preferred level of depth charges in the North Atlantic, the best altitudes for bombing different targets under different circumstances, and preferred bomb mixes for different bombing missions. When scientists examined such problems they pointed the way to dramatic improvements in efficiency and success. (McCloskey and Trefethen, 1954.)

Following the war there was a constant growth in the applications of operations research methodology to all types of management problems in and out of government. In the military area, the types of problems subjected to operations research analysis broadened to encompass such questions as: What types of weapons systems should be developed in the long-range future? The old label—operations research—still sticks to the analysis of such problems but, as noted above, the preferred words today are systems analysis. In the business and academic worlds the words management science are replacing the words operations research, and both phrases are vaguely blurred with systems analysis, as these words spill over from military usage into the business world.

WEAPONS SYSTEMS CONTRACTING. Beginning about 1953 a new procedure was developed by the Department of Defense for the procurement of weapons. Under the older procedure the military services contracted with individual manufacturers to produce various components of a weapon which were then delivered to a prime contractor who, in turn, completed, assembled, and tested the finished product. Under the new concept the prime contractor was given management, technical, and contractual responsibilities not only over all components of the finished piece of hardware but also for relating the completed weapon with other elements of an entire weapons system, such as bases, training programs, and maintenance over the operational life of the weapon. This was and still is called weapons system contracting.

This new system grew out of problems following World War II as weapons systems became more complex, the demands upon technically qualified people in government simply overwhelmed them, and the necessity for telescoping the time between applied research and production brought new problems. Events such as these gave rise to the new concept of weapons systems which embraced the necessity for a unified approach to managing all major elements incorporated in the actual operation of a weapon. (George A. Steiner, 1961, p. 113.)* The whole program was viewed as a system, a series of integrated parts which fitted into one whole. The fundamental and useful idea was that all parts had to fit together and this could not be done efficiently and effectively if any one were studied in isolation from the others.

WEAPONS SYSTEMS ANALYSIS. Paralleling this development was that of weapons systems analysis (illustrated above) in a number of agencies within and closely associated with the military services. Among the major developers of weapons systems analysis was the RAND Corporation. From the time of its inception following World War II the methods and techniques for analyzing weapons systems have expanded and improved until today the methodology incorporates a wide range of tools, principles, and approaches.

OPERATIONS RESEARCH AND
SYSTEMS ANALYSIS COMPARED

In light of the evolution of narrow operations research methods into broader applications as described above, it is no wonder that the semantics in this field are confusing. Definitions of operations research cover a broad spectrum. At one extreme is the view that operations research is the use of sophisticated mathematical techniques to solve business problems. At the other end are definitions which make operations research synonymous with the scientific method. Examination of the literature in this area will turn up many definitions falling within these two extreme poles.

The melding of operations research into systems analysis raises a question about the distinctions between the two. Quade (1963, p. 2) says there is no clear line of demarcation between the two; the difference is a matter of degree. Kahn and Mann (1956) say systems analysis bears the same relation to operations re-

* For a very detailed analysis see Peck and Scherer, 1962.

search as strategy to tactics. Hitch (1955) says systems analysis and operations research have the same basic elements but that systems analysis is broader and has taken operations research into new dimensions. Enthoven speaks of these words as being synonymous in some of his writings. But in one article he distinguishes between the two in a passage that deserves to be quoted in full.

"It may be helpful to an understanding of the systems analysis approach to have it contrasted with the discipline traditionally known as operations research . . . There are significant differences between the two. Of course, in reality there is a continuum between them, just as there is between physiology and medicine and between physics and engineering. One necessarily must artificially divide a continuous spectrum into discrete segments in order to define the different disciplines. However, I do think it would be useful further to clarify the sense of the systems analysis approach.

"In doing this, I would not want for a moment to suggest that systems analysis is in any sense, intellectually or otherwise, superior to operations research. That would be like suggesting that medicine is superior or inferior to biology. Both have their place. I am reminded of a statement contained in the Carnegie report on excellence to the effect that if a society doesn't respect both its plumbers and its philosophers, neither its pipes nor its theories will hold water.

"Let me contrast operations research and systems analysis in several ways.

"Operations research techniques are applicable to problems such as calculations of optimum inventory levels for spare parts . . ., calculation of the optimum search pattern for . . . forces seeking a submarine in a given area, calculation of the most efficient blend of aviation gasoline, and the like. Systems analysis, on the other hand, is an approach to broader problems such as determining the preferred characteristics for a new attack aircraft, the design of the POLARIS system, a determination of how many POLARIS submarines are required, or the study of the number of antisubmarine ships or the number of attack carriers that should be included in the Navy force structure.

"Generally speaking, operations research accepts specified objectives and given assumptions about the circumstances, the hardware, and the like, and then attempts to compute an optimum solution, usually maximizing or minimizing some objective, given the available resources. Operations research attempts to do an optimization in the small. It may be necessary for the operations researcher first to define the problem, but the operations research techniques themselves are intended for the solution of well-defined problems, that is, problems in which all of the relevant relationships can be specified. Operations research then attempts to select an optimum solution from a predetermined range of alternatives.

"Systems analysis, on the other hand, has a broader orientation. It analyzes alternative objectives and explores their implications. It is focused more on exploring the implications of alternative assumptions than on analyzing in extensive detail the implications of a single set of assumptions. Systems analysis ordinarily is not concerned with computing an optimum solution. If there is optimization involved, it is optimization in the large, rather than in the small. Systems analysis is concerned with avoiding gross error and with giving the decision-maker a menu of choices representing different mixes of effectiveness and cost so that he can make his choice. It is part of systems analysis to question the objectives.

"Systems analysis takes problems that are not defined and attempts to define them. If the problem cannot be well defined, that is specified in all its aspects, systems analysis techniques are still useful in helping the decision-maker by attempting to define those aspects of the problem that can be defined and quantified. Systems analysis emphasizes design of new solutions and widening of the range of alternatives, rather than selecting the best alternative from among a predetermined range. Rather than trying to select a precise maximum or minimum, a motto of the Systems Analysis Office in the Office of the Secretary of Defense is, 'It is better to be roughly right than exactly wrong.'

"The epistemology of operations research is the epistemology of the exact sciences; that is, operations research assumes that the empirical data are accurate, at least accurate enough to make refined and precise calculations worthwhile. On the other hand, the epistemology of systems analysis is the epistemology of the inexact sciences. Statistics may be used although in most major weapon system problems the uncertainties are greater than the statistical variations, so that extensive use of mathematical statistical techniques is not likely to produce useful results. Systems analysis emphasizes techniques for dealing with uncertainty, such as sensitivity tests, the use of ranges, alternative scenarios, and the like.

"Operations research technique emphasizes applied mathematics, such as linear programing, queuing theory, search theory, and inventory theory; that is, a collection of mathematical techniques for maximizing or minimizing something subject to constraints. Also operations research emphasizes the use of computers because its emphasis is largely on efficient and accurate computation of optimum solutions. In effect, operations research is oriented toward problems in which the element of calculation is dominant, and therefore, in which mathematics can be thought of as a substitute for rather than as an aid to judgment.

"Systems analysis, on the other hand, emphasizes basic economic concepts, mostly the simple concepts of marginal product and marginal cost. The systems analysis approach has developed a variety of techniques for analyzing complex problems of decision in such a way as to make calculation the servant of informed judgment. It has, therefore, made use of calculation, but it puts much less emphasis on it than does operations research.

"Who, then, are systems analysts? I am unable to hazard a satisfactory definition of them as a group. There are few courses and no degrees in the subject, and that is doubtless a good thing because it helps to minimize appeals to authority. The main attributes to a good systems analyst, other than those, such as good character and imagination, that are valuable in most professions, are an understanding of scientific method, economic intuition, some facility with mathematics which is the language of science, an appreciation of the limitations as well as the capabilities of his methods. Some very effective systems analysts are officers, some are civilians. No one professional background has proved itself to be best. Representation from a variety of professions and disciplines is clearly beneficial." (Enthoven, 1965, included in Tucker, 1966, pp. 177-180; used by permission of the Naval War College.)

Systems analysis and operations research are both scientific approaches to problem-solving. They blend into one another. But at the extremes, systems analysis is more complex, and less neat and tidy. Although both are highly quantitatively oriented, systems analysis tends to embody a much larger percentage of nonquantitative elements which influence the outcome. Generally, systems analysis is the larger term. Certainly the design of weapons systems of the future, the creation of a new city, or the research-development-production-commercialization process for a major product, are problems for systems analyzing in which operations research may be but a part and not always the most significant or even a significant part.

OPERATIONS RESEARCH AND MANAGEMENT SCIENCE

Over the past half-dozen years operations research has evolved into management science. Management science is a label which also finds definitions by practitioners ranging from the extremes noted above for operations research. I find myself in agreement with Simon (1960, p. 15) when he says, "No meaningful line can be drawn any more to demarcate operations research from scientific management or scientific management from management science." Dantzig, in his Presidential address before The Institute of Management Sciences, said operations research and management science are two names for the same thing—the science of decision and its application. (Dantzig, 1967, p. C-107.)

THE PROCESS OF ANALYSIS

In a very fundamental way the steps in analysis, whether we are speaking of a broad systems analysis or a narrow operations research problem, are quite similar to the basic problem-solving steps presented in Chapter 2. There are some differences, however, which deserve mention.

The process of systems analysis can be diagrammed as shown in Chart 14-2. A problem may be given by a decision-maker to the systems analyst or the systems analyst may be required to formulate the problem. The process of problem formulation includes the detailed description of the task. For instance, if one is to undertake a systems analysis of the transportation problem of a large city the analyst must know what the objectives are. Are they to speed the flow of traffic, reduce the cost of transportation per passenger on public means of carriage, deter-

Chart 14-2

The Process of Systems Analysis

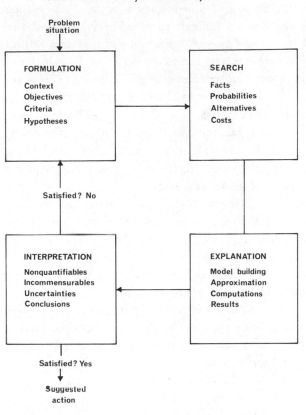

SOURCE: E.S. Quade, "Military Systems Analysis," RM-3452-PR, The RAND
Corporation, Santa Monica, California, January 1963, p. 11.

mine policy of the city with respect to subsidizing public transportation, **or**
determine whether underground highways are feasible and desirable?

Problem formulation also includes the identification of important variables
and a description of the way they interrelate. For example, in the area noted
above, major variables would attach to types of transportation: automobiles, subways, buses, trolley cars, trains, and airplanes. Before proceeding with the study
it is necessary to select criteria for deciding which are preferred alternatives. For
example, if the object is to determine which public means of transportation
should be developed, criteria for choosing among alternatives might be cost in
dollars, cost in passenger comfort, or perhaps cost in terms of air pollution. Correspondingly, benefits must be defined, against which costs can be equated. In
this process, hypotheses may be advanced for testing, such as subways are preferred over buses because they will pollute the air less, or buses may be built
cheaply that will not pollute the air, or double-decking highways is feasible and
costs less than new highways.

The search stage needs little elaboration. Here are sought ideas and evidence to support them, including invention of new alternatives. This is a difficult part of the process because in many instances costs of the elements associated with the systems analysis are difficult to get. For instance, if the problem is one of determining the feasibility and desirability of a system of underground highways in a large city, costs such as the following must be calculated: construction cost per lane-mile in some future time period, right-of-way cost per lane-mile in specified areas in a specified time period, and operating expenses compared with those of traditional highways. In each of these categories are costs that must be identified and calculated. In the last category, for example, are these costs: policing and patrol, night time lighting, debris and wreck removal, pavement and lining repair and maintenance, sign maintenance, emergency call system, traffic control and pacing, and miscellaneous costs.*

Once facts are gathered, it is important to have a method to explain and study them in light of the end objectives of the inquiry. The real world is so complex that some simplifying mechanism is required and a "model" is prepared to do this. This is an idealized version of the real situation but which hopefully contains the relevant forces in the real world that will have the most impact on the final results. The model incorporates major influencing factors, describes how they relate to one another, and how they influence the achievement of the objectives. For example, one type model will list the various cost elements associated with an analysis and relate them to an array of benefits. This model can be both quantitative and qualitative. Usually in a complex systems analysis there is not one but many models. In the development of costs, for example, models may be used to facilitate calculation.

In this part of the process the analyst must come to grips with uncertainties in the future. In a weapons systems analysis they may concern such factors as potential enemy opposition, future attitudes of the Congress, or changes in technology. Comparable uncertainties exist for a business systems analysis. In this part of the study there must be sensitivity analyses, or calculations that show the extent to which results may be importantly altered because of change in one or a few factors. For example, cost-benefit results of a weapons systems analysis may be very sensitive to increasing or decreasing the speed of an airplane. The results of a business analysis may be much influenced by interest rates or actions of a competitor. The results of a demand analysis for a commercial cargo airplane are sensitive to such factors as anticipated competing designs by other manufacturers, cost per ton mile, and cost of manufacture.

The next step is interpretation, or the application of the model's solution in light of real world forces not included in the model. If the results are not good enough, the whole process may be started over again. Or, the answers of the

---

* For a description of a systems analysis concerning underground highways, see George A. Hoffman, *Urban Underground Highways and Parking Facilities*, RM-3680-RC (Santa Monica, California: The RAND Corporation, August 1963).

model, when blended with judgments of the decision-maker, may be sufficient to resolve the problem.

Just as with corporate planning, the whole process is highly iterative, moving through steps in a sequence such as the following: formulating the problem, selecting objectives, designing alternatives, collecting data, building models, weighting cost against effectiveness, testing for sensitivity, questioning assumptions, reexamining objectives, looking at new alternatives, reformulating the problem, selecting different or modified objectives, and so on. (Quade, 1966, p. 10.)

NATURE OF MODELS IN SYSTEMS ANALYSIS

Whenever one approaches a decision-making problem, particularly if it is at all complex, it is easy to see a bewildering mass of forces and relationships which at first appear to be in a state of utter confusion. A primary requirement in systems analysis is to develop some conceptual order for this mass. This is needed to permit the analysis to proceed systematically and with assurance that the major forces and relationships are studied, and that the minor and irrelevant aspects of reality are ignored. A model does this.

Some models are ready-made for particular systems problems, such as an inventory reorder point model. But for most analyses the model must be invented for that study. Model building is an art that requires the analyst to select the right elements to be included and to combine them in a meaningful way. To the extent possible the elements selected for a model and their interrelationships must be made explicit and quantified. As Quade says: "A mark of a good systems analyst (or any wise person communicating with others) is that he states the basis on which he operates. This does not imply necessarily that he makes better assumptions but only that his errors will be more evident." (Quade, 1963, p. 19.)

This is not the only purpose of models. By reflecting known facts and most significant elements in a situation, a model makes it easier to describe and comprehend the facts. Of great importance, too, the model tells the analysts which facts to get and how they relate to one another. The model facilitates the explanation of important relationships. When it is quantified it aids mathematical analysis. It is itself, or serves as a basis for, a theory which explains observed characteristics of a system. The final test of the value of a model is not its complexity, its mathematical elegance, or even its proximity to reality, but whether it can yield predictions with sufficient precision to answer the problems raised.

There is no standard classification of models. They range from objects, through verbal pictures, to precise mathematical formulations. We all use models more than we think. An analogy to explain a point may be considered a model. Thinking and communicating are impossible without the simplifying use of models. A few illustrations of models associated with managerial decision-making may serve to further clarify the idea of models and their use.

Optimizing models contain a measure of the effectiveness of the operations to which they refer. In Chapter 11 a model for break-even analysis, which is an optimizing model, was presented. The return-on-investment model of Chart 13-1 in the preceding chapter is also in this classification. In the next chapter linear programming models will be discussed which also fall in this grouping.

A business organization chart is a schematic model of authority relationships.

For complex systems analysis, detailed diagrams of the flow of analysis are usually prepared and are models. Within each area of analysis there may be not one but several models. For example, a multiple correlation model may be used in forecasting only costs of a system.

Gaming models are frequently used in military systems analysis. They are nonquantitative simulations or scenarios, or war games in which people react to one another and events. A gaming model of this type may not be able to predict what an optimal response should be, but it does make the players aware of uncertainties and complex relationships, and helps in identifying obscure elements for further study.

A description of how a manager should operate while leading a product development team would be a nonquantitative word model. Chart 2-1, Chapter 2, is a nonquantitative model of the process and structure of business planning. Planning on the basis of this complex model will be a systems analysis in which a variety of submodels are present—quantitative, qualitative, physical, and so on.

Balance-sheet and profit-and-loss statements, as noted in the previous chapter, are superb quantitative models of the financial affairs of a business.

Mathematical models are those which contain symbolic language, equations, or quantitative statements of functions. The area of a circle is a mathematical model, viz., $A = \pi r^2$. Following is a more complex model with which systems costs were computed in a missile comparison.*

$$C = C_L m = R C_M N m = C_M (1-R) m,$$

$$N = \frac{aT}{Rrmpk}$$

Where,

R = ground reliability, the fraction of ready missiles which actually fire,

r = air reliability, the fraction of missiles actually fired that do not have to be destroyed,

C_M, C_L = cost coefficients (roughly speaking, the cost per missile fired and the cost of maintaining a missile in a ready state, respectively),

A = a measure of enemy defense strength and of the offense vulnerability,

T = the total number of targets in a target system,

a = The expected number of hits per target needed to give the required confidence that the desired fraction of these targets has been destroyed,

---

* From R. D. Specht, "The Way and How of Model Building," in Quade, *Analysis for Military Decisions*, pp. 66-67.

$m =$ the number of missiles made ready for firing on each salvo,

$k =$ the probability that a delivered warhead will destroy the target. This includes the target characteristics, the weapon yield, and the guidance accuracy (through another model),

$N =$ the number of salvos in the campaign,

$P =$ the probability that a missile survives to the target.

Many other types of models may be important in a systems analysis. Graphic models, pictorial models, presentation models, illustrate the point. The next chapter is full of mathematical models that are useful in business systems analyses.

MODEL BUILDING

How does one approach the problem of developing these models? The answer is, largely, intuitively. Each major systems analysis is a new and unique piece of research. Sometimes past experience is helpful in pointing the way, but if the analysis is to be more than routine it must involve some different characteristics than previously solved problems. The structuring of the models for this part of the analysis is intuitive, meaning thinking which the analyst is unable or unwilling to verbalize. (Morris, 1967b.)

Morris emphasizes the gradual and iterative value in the development of models and sets forth three guides to help the model builder. First, begin simply. Rather than develop at one time a major, complex, and detailed model, the process is more likely to be successful if the model is built gradually. Second, previously developed logical structures can naturally be important foundations upon which to build more elaborate models and should be used in this way. Finally, a process of elaboration or enrichment should involve at least two looping or alteration procedures. One is the practice of working in a sort of tandem with the model itself and the data for the model. Each is tried separately and together in a fashion which avoids one gigantic effort at a grand test of a complex model, a practice not likely to be successful. Another is the continuous interplay, or looping, from assumptions and criteria needed to reach objectives, reworking of the objectives, and development of the appropriate models, to come to acceptable conclusions. (Morris, 1967b.)

A SYSTEMS ANALYSIS OF WATER METERING
IN NEW YORK CITY

An illustration of a broad systems analysis is presented in Table 14-1 to help further clarify the nature of this method.*

---

* This rough outline was prepared by Professor E. H. Blum, now at The RAND Corporation, for use in an informal class exercise he conducted at the Woodrow Wilson School, Princeton University, in 1967.

Table 14-1   General Outline for A Systems Analysis
of Water Metering in New York

POSSIBLE OBJECTIVES

1. *Conserve water—immediate future*

    How: (a) By pointing out probable leaks in mains and other parts of the distribution system.

    (b) By giving detailed information about water usage in industry, offices, and residences.

    (a) In conjunction with leak detection and repair operation.

    (b) Conservation achieved only if information is utilized. May be used:

    (1) To assign charges for water based on actual usage, and so offer economic incentives for decreased usage.

    (2) To point out areas of excessive usage—to permit attack by inspectors (leaks, open hydrants, running faucets, etc.) and/or usage-reduction campaigns (advertising; legal).

    (3) To point out times of high usage—to permit temporary usage-reduction campaigns in periods of unusual consumption.

    (4) To permit monitoring of usage-reduction effectiveness, enforcement of usage-reduction laws.

2. *Conserve water—longer-term*

    How: (a) By (if short-term objectives are met at least in part) reducing the incremental additions to the water supply needed to meet future rising demand (by eliminating or reducing waste in current supply—effectively increasing it—and by reducing the fraction of added supply that will be wasted).

    (b) By giving accurate, detailed data on which to base long-term projections, enabling the city to make more effective use of its sources of additional supply.

    (c) By enabling attention to be focused on chronic over-users of water—leading with time to a reduction of these users' consumption.

    (d) By permitting changes in rate structure appropriate to economic conditions and consumption patterns at future times.

3. *Enhance public cooperation in conservation programs.*

    How: (a) By promoting the idea of "fairness"—charges and penalties based on actual usage, applied to those who deserve them.

    (b) By overcoming feeling of "let my neighbor reduce his use; they'll never know whether I have or not."

Table 14-1 General Outline for A Systems Analysis of Water Metering in New York (Continued)

Some of these objectives may not be practicable or worthwhile. Some may conflict. We will find it hard to refine them or reconcile them, however, without seeing what some of the alternatives, consequences, and costs might be.

UNCERTAINTIES

Major considerations:

1. Current lack of knowledge concerning actual water usage and/or reasonable water usage; i.e., we do not have good information regarding potential savings.
2. Public reaction.
3. Future demand for water.
4. Effect of rate structure on demand.

Minor:

1. Technological developments in sight for metering, reading, data processing.
2. Future redevelopment and construction relative to existing "structure" of industry, offices, and residences.

MAJOR CONSTRAINTS ON ALTERNATIVE PLANS— (SOME QUITE UNCERTAIN)

1. Capital requirements.
2. Operating expenses.
3. Demand for specialized labor: plumbers, electricians, data processing experts.
4. Political environment: probable life of administration; probability of water crisis before system is effective; public reaction to certain "unfair" or "halfway" proposals.
5. Availability of meters desired.

ANALYSIS CYCLE

1. *Design alternative approaches:*

    No meters
    Primary mains only
    Primary and secondary mains

    .

    .

    .

    Every house, office, apartment
    Alternative blocks, with statistical interpolation
        Various levels of detail on metered and less-metered blocks

Table 14-1 General Outline for A Systems Analysis of Water Metering in New York (Continued)

Time-phasing by primary mains, secondary mains, etc.

> by area of city
>
> by area with alternative blocks

Technological alternatives

> Meters
>
> Reading
>
> Data processing

Capital/operating cost trade-off

2. Devise criteria: Measures of effectiveness for principal objectives will have multi-dimensional, possibly conflicting criteria.

3. Quickly work through principal alternatives to assess effectiveness relative to the various criteria. Models at this stage should be simple and aggregative, sufficient to point out major differences between alternative approaches.

   When you have completed this stage, you will have a fair idea of (a) what the various objectives and criteria imply operationally and (b) what sacrifices each of the alternative entails. "Obviously" unsatisfactory objectives and alternatives can be revised or rejected at this point on the basis of the information gained in this first "cut."

4. Revise the list of objectives to include those felt to be most important (including any discovered during the analysis) and exclude those found to be infeasible or unattractive. [But re-question the reasons for rejecting any that initially seemed very attractive.]

5. With this pared-down and revised list of objectives, re-formulate the criteria and measures of effectiveness.

   On the basis of the first analysis, attempt to assign relative measures of importance to the general measures of effectiveness—for example, how will you weigh short-term against long-term, technical efficiency against employment opportunities, etc. These relative measures will clearly be approximate; the importance of this step lies not so much in obtaining useful numbers as in asking important questions and focusing attention on the major issues. You will not be able to combine all the effectiveness measures into a single index that can be maximized or minimized, but you will need some idea of relative importance in order to reduce the number of alternatives you will want to examine closely in the later stages.

6. With the revised criteria, examine the principal alternatives in enough detail to find:

   a. How the most inflexible constraints affect each one.

Table 14-1   General Outline for A Systems Analysis of Water Metering in New York (Continued)

b. Approximately what each will cost:

Capital outlays—timing.

Operating costs—charges with time.

c. Approximately how effective each is according to the various measures of effectiveness; where the major advantages and disadvantages of each lie—with quantitative measures wherever possible.

d. Where there are any potentially catastrophic weak spots in any of the alternatives.

e. How sensitive each is to the important uncertainties.

Models at this stage may need to be fairly detailed and refined, although the careful use of *a fortiori* and dominance arguments (e.g., anything important to us that K-7 meters can do can be done nearly as well by the less complicated K-3, which costs half as much per installed unit) can reduce the calculation considerably. Models should be certain to include what is important for decision-making; even a guess about functional dependence (e.g., statistical uncertainty in the alternate block plan varies roughly in proportion to $1/\sqrt{n}$, where n is the number of metered houses) is better than leaving out an important factor.

Rough models may indicate the areas that require detailed attention and the areas that can be left in rough, aggregative form. They may even suffice to point out significant differences in costs and/or effectiveness that will allow you further to reduce the list of candidate alternatives. The rough models, of course, should take a systems view (e.g., capital cost of *additional* meter = purchase cost (at margin) + administrative cost (purchasing department, etc., at margin) + installation cost + marginal capital costs involved in reading and monitoring system).

7. With these results, re-examine the objectives and criteria to see if modification are needed (e.g., "We expected this plan to look good for the long-term, but the criterion we selected to measure long-term effectiveness did not show the advantages we anticipated."). Check the sensitivity of the results to assumptions (e.g., "We assumed a reduction of 20 gallons per capita per day for the first year, then 10 gpcd for the second year and 2 gpcd for each of the next three years." We don't know this will occur, of course; what happens if the figures turn out to be different?).

Check the key features of the models for their limiting behavior, for their inclusion of important policy variables (e.g., the *net systems* cost to the city of employing 2000 men, currently on welfare rolls, as meter readers).

Table 14-1   General Outline for A Systems Analysis
of Water Metering in New York (Continued)

Check the major differences between alternatives. Is there anything unexpected? Why?

8. Examine the effect on costs and effectiveness results of various crises and extreme contingencies. Do some alternatives have advantages in crisis that do not show up under normal conditions ("insurance")? What does it cost to include this crisis capability in other alternatives that appear better under normal conditions?

9. Examine the results for decision-making implications:

   Costs; effectiveness relative to various criteria

   Trade-offs—strengths, weaknesses

   Combination with other programs.

10. Recommendations? Why?

COST-BENEFIT ANALYSIS*

Very simply, cost-benefit analysis is a technique to measure the costs of an alternative course of action to achieve some objective against the benefits resulting from taking that course. This idea is not new in the business world, where traditionally costs are related to prospective income in deciding a problem. In industry, whenever the costs and prospective income of a proposed undertaking can be measured accurately in dollars, there are many techniques—such as break-even analyses and different return-on-investment calculations—that can be used to relate them in helping managers to choose. But where important factors in a problem cannot be measured in monetary terms, or where such measurement is very difficult and uncertain, or where monetary values are only a part of total values, cost-benefit analysis can be very useful.

Cost-benefit analysis associated with systems analysis has had its greatest development in dealing with military problems. During the past few years, however, as a result of a Presidential directive that all agencies of government adopt the planning-programming-budgeting system (PPB) so successfully developed in the Department of Defense during the administration of Secretary McNamara, this type of analysis has spread rapidly to other government agencies. (Lyndon Johnson, 1965, and Bureau of the Budget, Bulletin No. 66-3.) Recently, the general concept of PPB as used in the federal government has spread to other governmental units and to nonprofit institutions, especially universities.

---

* Cost-benefit analysis is sometimes used synonymously with cost-effectiveness and cost-utility analysis.

Chart 14-3
The Structure of Analysis

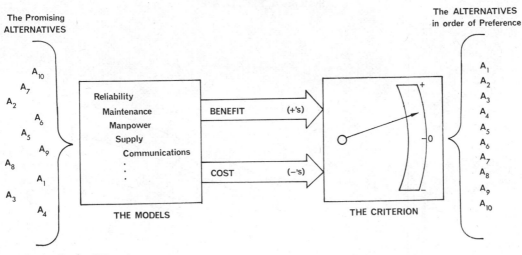

Source: Quade, 1966, p. 9.

It is appropriate to say something here about PPB. Fundamentally, as I pointed out elsewhere (George A. Steiner, 1965, pp. 43-52), PPB is to the federal government what the comprehensive type of planning discussed in this book is to business. In the federal government, as in business, there has always been some long-range planning. But in government today, as in business, the character of that planning has been changed fundamentally during the past few years. The nature of the change has been basically the same in both.

In only a few instances are managers in government able to measure income from an investment and decide whether or not to make the investment on the basis of that standard. The great majority of decisions embody nonmonetary values. Ingenuity is growing in identifying major benefits from proposed activities and quantifying them in such a way that meaningful results are available to decision-makers when these benefits are matched against costs. For broad analyses, as noted previously, calculating reasonably useful costs may be as difficult as determining benefits (Petruschell, 1967). The development of a cost-benefit model for a major systems analysis, therefore, is not cut-and-dried. It is an art and requires invention on the part of the analyst. A major advantage of the method is that it can be tailored to fit a particular problem and is uniquely constructed for that problem. The role of cost-benefit analysis in systems analysis is shown simply in Chart 14-3.

COST-BENEFIT ANALYSIS FOR WEAPONS SYSTEMS. Chart 14-4 shows the costs for five weapons systems as compared with force size. The systems might include ground-based missile systems, long-endurance-aircraft

Chart 14-4

Total System Cost Versus Force Size for Alternative

Systems A, B, C, D, & E

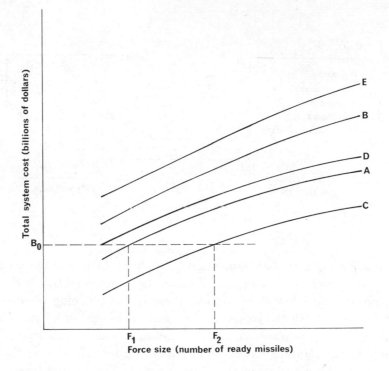

SOURCE : Gene H. Fisher, in David Novick (Ed.), Program Budgeting
(Cambridge, Mass.: Harvard University Press, 1965), p. 113.

systems, missile-launching-aircraft systems, and so on. Force size means number of airplanes or number of missiles in position ready for use. Costs are total, including research and development, costs of the finished product, and all operating costs over the life of the system or for a reasonably long period of time for such systems, e.g., 5 or 7 years.

Chart 14-4 shows that system C is the cheapest and, other things being equal, is preferred. It also shows that if budgets are fixed, a decision-maker can get force F_2, which is twice the size of F_1, for the same amount of money.

Table 14-2 shows quantitative and qualitative information about benefits of importance in evaluating the systems. When used in conjunction with the figures in Chart 14-4, the decision-maker has important information to help him sharpen his intuition. Suppose, for example, that systems A and C are in about the same situation with respect to certain types of variables, such as penetration capability and range, but C is clearly more vulnerable to air attack.

The difference in the systems costs, therefore, is the price paid in system A for getting less vulnerability to air attack. (From G. H. Fisher in Novick, 1965, pp. 112-115.)

COST-BENEFIT ANALYSIS FOR IMPROVED HOUSING. In a study made by Burns (1966) the purpose was to help decision-makers decide about the allocation of resources for improved housing. Table 14-3 shows the type of benefits which the study identified as being important in decision-making and for which, if possible, quantitative monetary values should be found and matched against costs. The major money costs in this case were site acquisition, improvement, structure, and annual operating costs.

Table 14-2   Selected Data Bearing on Utility Considerations for Alternative Systems A, B, C, D and E

DESCRIPTION	ALTERNATIVE SYSTEM				
Quantitative Information	A	B	C	D	E
Effective range (n mi)					
Cruise speed (kn)					
Penetration speed (kn)					
Warhead yield (MT)					
Circular error probability (CEP)					
Single shot kill probability					
Against soft targets					
Against hard targets					
Extended strike option time (days)					
•					
•					
•					
etc.					
Qualitative Information *					
"Show of force" capability					
Multi-directional attack capability					
Ground vulnerability					
In-flight vulnerability					
Controlled response capability					
•					
•					
•					
etc.					

* Some of these items have quantitative aspects to them; but they are very difficult to assess in a study with a short time deadline.

Source: Fisher, in Novick, *Program Budgeting*, p. 114.

COST-BENEFIT ANALYSIS FOR A RESEARCH FACILITY. Any private business that is interested in deciding whether to build a research facility, especially if it does not now own one, can use a cost-benefit analysis as an aid in decision-making. Table 14-4 shows some of the more relevant cost and benefit criteria that bear on such a decision.

IMPORTANCE OF SYSTEMS ANALYSIS
TO BUSINESS

It is appropriate now to highlight a few of the major values of systems analysis to business. (Many of the following values also apply to operations research if it is defined somewhat broadly.)

First, the developments of the past half-dozen years have added immensely to our knowledge about the real nature of systems analysis, its power, and how to go about doing it. It is somewhat like the great value to business in recent clarification of the old nebulous and amorphous concepts of "long-range planning."

Table 14-3   Typology of Benefits from Improved Housing

I. MACRO-ECONOMIC BENEFITS
  A. Increased national or area income
    1. Higher wages and salaries through increased availability for work and higher motivation
    2. Higher product
    3. Higher returns on investment
  B. Reduced public costs
    1. Reduction in hazards such as crime and fire
    2. Reduction in hospital and medical care from injuries and disease

II. MICRO-ECONOMIC BENEFITS
  A. Increased returns on housing investment
    1. Higher rents
    2. Higher interest or other direct returns

III. MICRO- AND MACRO-SOCIAL BENEFITS
  A. Improved family stability
  B. Increased privacy
  C. Improved physical health and nutrition
  D. Improved mental attitude, morale, and aspirations
  E. Greater neighborliness
  F. Better work and study attitude
  G. Higher morals

Source: Burns, 1966, p. 90.

Second, systems analysis reinforces the natural understanding of top managers that they are running a business, a system, which is composed of subsystems within its corporate borders and which interfaces with many systems outside its boundaries. James Culliton (1962) has observed rightly that we are now entering the "age of synthesis." In this age, the predominant approach to decision-making will be through a conceptual scheme that looks at the whole, or the system, and sees all parts operating in a synthesis, as distinct from approaching decision-making from the point of view of individual parts. As business enterprises become more complex the focus of top management attention will logically be on patterns of flow throughout the organization rather than on parts. By looking at a business this way, a top manager is much more likely to avoid or prevent suboptimization of a part at the expense of achieving the desired objectives for the whole. This is hardly a hypothetical danger, for business literature and experience abounds in instances where inventory controls to improve production runs failed to consider needs of customers, or where engineering perfection resulted in a product that was not competitive from a cost point of view.

This view of things will emphasize strategic planning for top management rather than short-range operational planning. It will keep top management atten-

Table 14-4   Cost-Benefit Criteria for a Research Facility

COSTS AND BENEFITS	TYPES OF FACILITY					
Costs	A	B	C	D	E	F
Initial construction costs						
Operating costs:						
salaries						
maintenance						
equipment						
other						
Benefits						
Improving company image						
Improving present products						
Developing new products						
Morale of scientists and engineers						
Relationships with local university						
Stimulating imagination of divisional general managers						
Attracting and holding more competent scientists						
Enhancing company ability to get government contracts						
Improving the manufacturing operation at reduced costs						
Availability of scientists for consulting assignments to divisions of the company						

tion more on the environment and the opportunities that lie ahead than on minor details of today's operations.

Third, the systems approach focuses attention of everyone in the enterprise on the role of the top management as being the head, the director, the leader of a system of which they are a part.

Fourth, the systems approach tells managers that there is a way to deal systematically and scientifically with large, complex, ill-structured problems.

Fifth, the systems approach tells managers that the scientific method complements and does not conflict with his intuition and judgment.

Sixth, the systems approach tells managers that there is a framework within which specialists can work together on major problems, and in conjunction with managers. As with corporate planning, it provides a common understanding, a common approach, and a common language at each interface among specialists. One of the primary advantages to business of early operations research work was that it brought the team approach to management problems. This vital attribute has carried through to modern systems analysis.

Seventh, systems analysis has focused attention on the unique contributions of the scientific method and quantitative analysis in facilitating better choice from among alternatives. Even gross conclusions from quantitative analysis may prove to be better than intuition, although this is certainly not always true. As said before, the scientific method is not necessarily in competition with intuition; rather the two can and should complement one another. But sometimes intuition alone is not reliable. In a room of 25 people, there is a 50-50 chance that two will have the same birthday. Raise the number to 60 and the chance is 99.4%. Would intuition tell one this?

Beyond this, is the importance of the attitude that systems analysis and operations research bring to business. It is not the mathematics, not the quantification, not the body of tools that is of the greatest importance. It is, rather, the attitude that makes these so important. It is the attitude that looks for the scientific method to help managers in their decision-making, that engenders a sort of reverence for facts,* that builds a habit of increasingly looking for hard, accurate facts and ways to relate them to one another and to the whole of a situation.

It cannot rightfully be said that systems analysis and operations research have brought science to management. Charles Babbage two centuries ago began that tradition, and it was accelerated by Frederick Taylor almost a century ago. Many other disciplines today bring "science" to management. But systems analysis and its subset operations research have accentuated, solidified, and organized the movement.

Eighth, and of great significance as Simon (1960, p. 15) has observed, systems analysis (and operations research) has stimulated the interest of scientists,

---

* This is a felicitous phrase of C. C. Herrmann and Magee, 1953, p. 101.

particularly mathematicians and statisticians, in the problems of decision-making of business management. I would add that this wave of interest has also encompassed economists and is now sweeping into the orbit of business affairs sociologists, political scientists, psychologists, and the followers of the new discipline of behavioral science. While some managers may feel uneasy about the ferment that this amalgam of scholarly interest is bringing to the field of management, it cannot, in the end, bring with it anything but advantage to the alert manager.

Finally, all the above explains why a first-rate corporate planning system is such a powerful instrument for business success. It is the systems approach *par excellence*. It provides the framework for the proper participation of various individuals and groups in an enterprise in bringing to bear their particular expertise on the major problems of an enterprise.

SOME PITFALLS AND LIMITATIONS OF SYSTEMS ANALYSIS

The power and value of systems analysis must not blind analysts or managers to the shortcomings of the method. One can think of these shortcomings as falling within two classifications. There are pitfalls, or traps, to ensnare the unwary or naive and cause defective systems analysis. There are also limitations which are inherent in the methodology.

PITFALLS. Ed Quade, a distinguished weapons systems analyst, has given much attention to the pitfalls because he has seen over many years how many exist and how easy it is for an analyst to fall into them. When one looks at the so-called pitfalls out of the context of an actual systems analysis they seem so obvious that one wonders how a reasonably sophisticated analyst can fail to avoid them. But, as Quade so often has said, one has only to examine actual analyses to find how frequently they have resulted in defective conclusions. The following illustrate some of the more frequently mentioned traps.*

First, is the failure to spend enough time deciding what the problem really is and how to go about grappling with it. It is a pitfall, says Quade, to give in to the tendency to "get started" without a lot of thought being given to the problem.

Second, is relying too heavily upon purely quantitative methods and becoming more interested in the model than in the real world. In reading Quade's *Analysis for Military Decisions*, it is easy to see a dominant theme which recurs in the statements of many of the skilled practitioners who contributed to the book. That is, the frequent superiority of rough, common-sense quantitative

* For a thorough analysis, see Quade, 1964, Chapter 16; and 1962; and Kahn and Mann, 1957.

analysis over high-powered optimization techniques. Robert Specht, a long-time observer of systems analysis, has described the markedly changing emphasis in the application of systems analysis to military problems at RAND, as follows:

"Let me put the differences inaccurately but graphically: In our youth we looked more scientific. That is to say, we attached more importance, years ago, to the business of representing that part of the real world with which we were dealing by a single analytical model. With the context chosen, the assumptions determined, the criterion selected, we could turn our attention to the more intriguing questions of how best to apply modern mathematical techniques and high-speed computers to produce a neat solution from which conclusions and recommendations could be drawn.

"There are many problems in the world for which this is a sensible, even a recommended approach. There are problems impossible of solution without the use of the most powerful tools of mathematics and of computers. The optimal distribution of weight and thrust between the several stages of a lunar probe, the determination of its initial trajectory—these are well-defined questions and yield to neat and orderly solution. On the other hand, the stability of the thermonuclear balance or the composition of a strategic deterrent force or the character of the next generation of tactical weapons—these are not questions that may be attacked usefully in this manner, although essential fragments of these problems may be solved analytically. A trivial reason for this is that even modern techniques of analysis are not sufficiently powerful to treat these problems without brutal simplification and idealization. The major reason, however, for the inadequacy of simple optimization procedures is the central role that uncertainty plays in this sinful but fascinating world. No longer are we analyzing a problem with a given and definite context and with specific equipment. We may not have clearly defined objectives. Instead, we must try to design—not analyze—a system that will operate satisfactorily, in some sense, under a variety of contingencies that may arise in a future seen only dimly.

"We have learned that new tools—high-speed computers, war gaming, game theory, linear and dynamic programming, Monte Carlo, and others—often find important application, that they are often powerful aids to intuition and understanding. Nevertheless, we have learned to be more interested in the real world than in the idealized model we prepare for analysis—more interested in the practical problem that demands solution than in the intellectual and mechanical gadgets we use in the solution." (Specht, 1960, pp. 836-838.)

Without elaboration, a few additional pitfalls from Quade's (1964 and 1962) writings are as follows:

"It is clearly a pitfall to expect a man or organization who created a system to discover its faults."

"It is not necessarily true that if enough factual research in a subject area is carried out a valid generalization will somehow automatically emerge."

"There are dangers in oversimplification in the model, although in a general sense it pays to be simple."

"Another dangerous pitfall lies in forcing a complex problem into an analytically tractable framework by emphasizing ease of computation."

"Another pitfall is the effort to set up a complete model which attempts to treat every aspect of a complex problem simultaneously."

"It is a pitfall to put more emphasis on making the 'right' choice between alternatives than on choosing the 'right' objective."

"A very dangerous pitfall is to forget that the question being asked as well as the process being represented determines the model."

"The failure to put sufficient emphasis on the question in the design of the model leads to another pitfall: the belief that there are 'universal' models—one model, say, to handle all questions about a given activity."

"A serious pitfall is to ignore real uncertainty or to try to remove it by assumption."

While the above are directed towards those making systems analyses of military problems, they are completely applicable to systems analyses made for nonmilitary-governmental, or business problems.

INHERENT LIMITATIONS. Considering the top management levels of business firms, there are three fundamental limitations of systems analysis: analysis is necessarily incomplete; measures of effectiveness are inevitably approximate; and ways to predict the future are lacking.

To begin with, systems analysis of major problems at the top of a corporation is complex, and time and money sharply limit the extent of analysis. Costs of getting additional data and pressures of time for decision preclude completely exhaustive analysis. But even if there were no limitations of time and money, systems analysis can never treat all considerations that are relevant in decision-making. In business, for example, a critical issue may be future actions of a competitor. Ways to measure them even approximately rarely exist and must be handled intuitively. But because all such elements cannot be handled, and because a decision-maker's intuition may be different from that of the analyst, the analysis inherently must remain incomplete so far as the decision-maker is concerned.

In both weapons systems analysis and systems analysis in the nondefense area, measures of effectiveness are approximate and sometimes very difficult to invent. Sometimes the highest accomplishment of an analysis is to find a measure that only generally points in the right direction. Deterrence, for example, is something that exists only in the mind of a potential enemy. There are no precise measures of deterrence so only approximations of the impact of a weapons system on deterrence can be measured. In the nondefense field, how does one measure the benefits of an education subsidy for poor students to help pay their way by giving them research grants, as compared with a subsidy for educational buildings? Precise measures are difficult to find in this area. In business, however, much better measures of effectiveness are usually available. They are, of course, profits, return-on-investment, sales growth, and so on. But even here, complete systems analysis often runs into problems in developing measures of effectiveness. Measuring the impact of a program on employee morale, on managerial initiative in becoming more imaginative, or the benefits listed in Table 14-4, are cases in point.

Uncertainties in the future place serious inherent limitations on systems analysis. In weapons systems analysis, for example, there is no satisfactory way to predict a single future for which a "best" system can be designed. It is, therefore, necessary to consider a range of contingencies. For any one future, a preferred course of action may be specified, but there is no way to determine the preferred course of action for the entire range of possibilities. In dealing with business problems there are many ways to treat uncertainties, but in the end for major systems analysis there are also the same sort of fundamental limitations created by uncertainties which plague the decision-maker.

These limitations, of course, are less important to a decision-maker the easier it is to define the problem, the simpler the problem, the more the analysis is concerned with parameters that can be quantified, the narrower the scope of the problem, and the more readily a tested model exists to solve the problem. For example, if an inventory problem is defined as a systems analysis, or a queuing problem as a systems analysis, or the issue of whether or not to replace a milling machine, the limitations described above are of much less importance to management.

SUMMARY AND CONCLUSIONS

The systems approach to rational decision-making is an amorphous phrase that is becoming very popular. This chapter pointed out that there are four major elements of this approach: systems analysis, systems engineering, systems management, and project management. The bulk of the chapter deals with systems analysis.

Systems analysis basically is a methodology that has grown from operations research, weapons systems contracting, and weapons systems analysis. While it has developed principally in governmental decision-making, it has borrowed from and been influential in systems analysis in business. It is a methodology that deals effectively with important, broad, and ill-structured problems. But the words systems analysis also can apply to much narrower problems, such as the development of an automatic inventory reordering system.

Although, fundamentally, systems analysis and operations research are comparable, there are major differences between the two that are pointed out in the chapter.

The chapter also contains the essential procedures to be followed in systems analysis and illustrates the method by describing in some detail the steps to be followed, the nature of models, the nature of cost-benefit analysis, and pitfalls that may trap analysts. Descriptions of systems analysis are given from the military, nondefense governmental, and business worlds.

It was pointed out that the importance of systems analysis to business is derived from these, among other, considerations: it reinforces the natural understanding of the business manager that he is running a business, not subsystems; it focuses attention on the central role of top management in decision-making; it tells managers that the scientific method can be used effectively in dealing with difficult and ill-structured problems; and it has stimulated the interest of scientists in helping managers make decisions easier and better. Limitations of systems analysis to business were also mentioned, such as: for large and important problems, the analysis inherently is incomplete; measures of benefit frequently are only approximate; and uncertainties about the future limit the application of analysis without much judgment.

Systems analysis is an approach to, or way of looking at, complex problems of choice under conditions of future uncertainty. There is no single method universally applicable to do systems analysis. It is not a tool or technique so much as a way of thinking. It is at the present time probably more of an art than a science, in the application of which judgment is of commanding importance. Despite this characteristic, it is a very powerful method of dealing with problems.

15
Newer Quantitative Techniques for Rational Decisions

15
Newer Quantitative Techniques
for Rational Decisions

INTRODUCTION

The phrase "newer mathematical tools" is somewhat of a misnomer because those which are included in this category all have antecedents. But a number of techniques have gained new power in recent years by innovations in their structure and the availability of the computer. There are many newer mathematical methods which have demonstrated their great value to managers. There are also many others that will be used by managers in the future after a period of development. Naturally all cannot be explained in any significant way in a chapter in this book. I have, therefore, selected four major quantitative methods which seem to me to have the most important value to top management in its decision making processes. Indeed, at this writing, there seems to be a ground-swell of usage of these methods in industry, particularly among the larger companies. They are, first, probability techniques, which are concerned with decision-making under conditions of uncertainty. Second, are simulation techniques which are trial-and-error methods to approach reality and to show the results of taking different actions. Third, are programming techniques, which are methods to reach precise quantitative optimizing solutions to extremely complex problems. Finally, are scheduling methods which are valuable in determining allocation of resources in achieving a final objective on schedule. These are not mutually exclusive and sometimes are used in combination. Furthermore, of course, they can be and are used in conjunction with many of the older quantitative and qualitative methods previously discussed.

It is my conviction that managers, particularly top managers, do not need to have a specialist's understanding of the methodology of these tools. But they will find useful a conceptual understanding of them. This conceptual knowledge is important for managers because these tools are so valuable to them. In using them, managers must be in a position to ask staff specialists the "right" questions about their assumptions, methods, and results. Managers should have an understanding about where the tools can be most useful and what their limitations are in different parts of the planning process, for different problems, and in different time phases of planning. Managers should have some knowledge of the methods to be able to adapt the techniques to their own particular problems. Above all, managers must have a conceptual understanding to avoid, on the one hand, being captives of staff specialists or, on the other hand, blindly dismissing the techniques because they refuse to try to understand them. It has been said with some truth that people would rather live with problems they cannot solve than use solutions which they do not understand. Wise managers, however, know that it is not necessary to have an advanced degree in mathematics to understand sufficiently the newer tools to make sure they are used, are used correctly, and with the best results.

There is no doubt that many exaggerated claims are found in the literature concerning the value and use of many of the newer quantitative tools in business decision making. Everyone should recognize that although they are very important when applied to the right problem at the right time they do not make decisions. They serve rather to help managers sharpen their intuition and judgment. As Stockton (1960, p. 112) says, they are not mathematical panaceas that will cure all managerial headaches.

PROBABILITY TECHNIQUES

William Morris has observed that: "It is perhaps not an overstatement to say that no branch of mathematics is more useful in decision making than probability theory, yet none seems more subject to confusion and widespread misconception" (1963, p. 263). The reasons are not hard to find. Probability means different things to different people and there are many different methods to apply probability theory to problems.

As far as business decisions are concerned probability techniques assign values to probabilities of events and actions and permit the selection of preferred courses of action on the basis of the highest projected expected values.* In an important way, probability theory is a method to quantify what is often done by managers in a more "rough-cut" way. But by injecting into management decision-making the rigor of current probability theory it is possible for managers to be more certain about the expected values of actions, to consider far more alternatives, and to find their way through complex alternatives reasonably easily.

It is useful to think of probabilities concerning business decisions in terms of single events or evolving chains of cause and effect. The first would be concerned,

---

* Simply stated, the expected value of an occurrence is the absolute value of such an occurrence times the probability of it actually occurring.

for example, with whether or not a firm is likely to get a specific contract, or whether a union will or will not strike. The second relate to sequential decision making extending into future periods of time. In mind are such decisions as whether or not to produce product A or B, build plant A or not, or penetrate a market or not. These are complex, difficult, and usually fateful decisions about which there is considerable uncertainty at a variety of points in the decision chain. These are the type problems which are in mind in the following illustrations.

THE DECISION TREE. The adaptive search method to developing strategies, presented in Chapter 9, is highly suited to the application of probability theory. The adaptive search tree, it will be remembered, shows possible decisions selected for examination. At selected branches, probabilities may be attached and quantitative outcomes can be measured.

Decision trees have a number of general characteristics which are illustrated in Chart 15-1. In this particular instance the Martin Textile Mill is faced with a 60 percent probability that sales will increase 20 percent next year from today's level of $100,000. There is also a 40 percent chance that sales will drop by 10 percent. If sales increase it will be necessary for the company either to buy new machinery or to pay for overtime work. A combination of the two is possible but is rejected.

The decision tree shows the point of decision, the alternative courses of action, chance events, probabilities, and net cash flow or payoff. In this particular case the cost of new machinery is $50,000 so that at the high level of sales, for example, the net cash flow would be $70,000 ($120,000 sales — $50,000 machinery cost). The cost of overtime is calculated at $10,000 for the higher sales level so the net cash flow would be $110,000 at this level. It is assumed there will be no overtime if sales drop 10 percent. It is clear that given only these facts the company would have a much greater payoff if it used overtime and did not buy the new equipment.

This determination is made by a comparison of the composite payoff, or combined value, of the events and probabilities in each case. This value for the new equipment approach is calculated by multiplying the sales probability .6 by expected sales of $70,000, after deduction for machine cost, which yields $42,000. The same computation at the lower sales level yields $16,000, and a combined total of $58,000. This compares with a total of $102,000 if the company decides to meet higher sales demand with overtime. The net cash flow, after overtime, at the high level is $110,000 and when multiplied by the probability of .6 yields $66,000. The net cash flow at the low level is $90,000 to yield $36,000, and a combined value of $102,000. Paying overtime is clearly the preferred choice.

It should be noted that the combined probabilities emanating from any single chance events adds to 1. This is a fundamental rule in probability theory.

Chart 15-1

A Simple Decision Tree

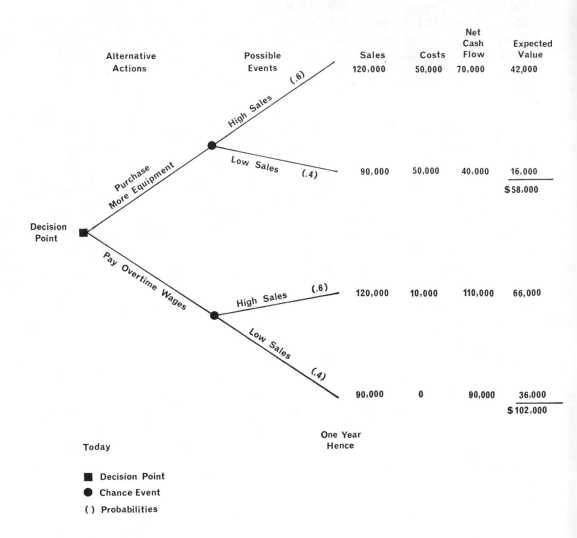

| | | | | Net Cash | Expected |
| | | | | Flow | Value |

The sum of probabilities assigned to any set of mutually exclusive events must add to 1. Furthermore, the weights assigned to any probability are from 0 to 1, 0 meaning no probability whatsoever, and 1 meaning complete chance of occurrence. Thus the probability of any event must be neither less than zero, nor greater than one. The probability of any event is the sum of the probabilities of the basic outcomes constituting that event.

There are, of course, many reasons why the Martin Textile Mill may choose not to hire overtime workers, but buy new machinery despite the fact that the probabilities would be that its net cash flow would be best with overtime. One major consideration of interest in this book is that by extending the branches

Chart 15-2

Decision Tree for The Austin Company

Expansion Program

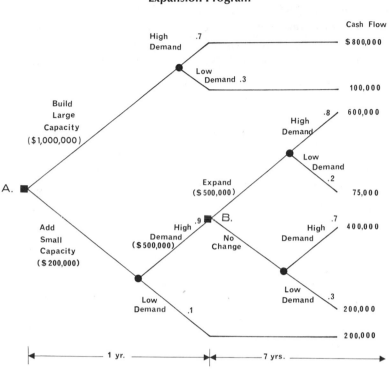

of the tree into future years a very different picture may be presented to management.

When future chance events are considered the decision tree gets complicated rather quickly. Chart 15-2 shows a tree of The Austin Company which is faced with the choice of a large versus a small expansion today, and the possibility that further expansion of the small addition within a year may be appropriate. This is a highly simplified illustration (adapted from Magee 1964b). If the company builds a large addition it estimates the probabilities of a continuing high sales volume and the cash flow of $800,000 per year exclusive of investment costs) will be 70 percent. The probabilities of a low annual net cash flow of $100,000 are 30 percent. For simplicity it is assumed these annual flows will continue throughout the eight-year period. On the other hand, the management estimates that if the addition is small the probability of a one-year high demand of $500,000 is 90 percent and only 10 percent that the low of $200,000 will occur. Following the initial high demand the company estimates that chances will be high for an average annual net cash flow of $600,000 if further expansion is undertaken. If there is no investment the probability of a high net cash flow of $400,000 will be 70 percent, and the probability of a low cash flow of $200,000 will be 30 percent. Should the company expand in a big way now? Or should it undertake a little expansion now and decide later whether or not to add more capacity?

A first step in answering these questions can be taken when a decision tree like that in Chart 15-2 is drawn. This framework is useful in identifying alternative courses of action, chance events, and decision points. When managers calculate probabilities of different events occurring, and have acceptable information about such matters as costs, investment, and income under different alternatives, quantitative analysis of payoffs of different alternatives is then possible.

There are different ways to approach the problem of The Austin Company. One way is to look at decision B and ask whether at that point one year hence an expansion should be made. The simple analysis of comparative expected values is shown in Table 15-1. It is clear that when expected values are calculated and investment costs deducted the expansion is the preferred course of action.

Now, assuming that the correct decision at point B is to expand, what should the original decision be at A? In Table 15-2 the expected value calculations say that the decision at point A should be to make the large expansion, for the expected values are $633,000 higher for this decision.

If the cash flow profiles of different alternatives are rather dissimilar it may be important to calculate discounted expected values. Expected values are discounted in Tables 15-3 and 15-4 and show that the decision at B still should be to expand while the decision at A remains favorable for the large expansion.

SENSITIVITY ANALYSIS. The ability to state a problem with the rigor demonstrated in the decision tree technique opens doors to the handling of one of the prime impediments of quantitative analysis. The normal reaction to the suggestion of trying a new quantitative technique is the one which asserts the inability to quantify some of the data and the inability to estimate closely some of the data. Conceptually, a sensitivity analysis is a determination of how accurately different data must be known in order to be reasonably assured that the problem solution is in fact optimal.

To explain this concept a sensitivity test will be performed on certain of the data used in the preceding decision tree problem. Turning first to Table 15-3 it can be seen that the decision to expand will remain correct for any size investment up to $754,000 (the difference between $2,409,000 and $1,655,000). At this point the discounted expected value of the expansion would equal the discounted expected value of no change. This means that the estimated investment in the expansion would have to be in error by 51 percent before it would result in the decision being incorrect.

To treat another input to the same decision it can be shown that the probabilities assigned to the high and the low demand under the expansion option could decrease from 0.8 to 0.2 respectively to 0.7 and 0.3 before the decision originally reached would be incorrect. If the probabilities assigned to the high and low demand in the no change case were increased from 0.7 and 0.3 respectively to 0.95 and 0.05 then the decision to expand would be reversed.

Table 15-1 Expected Cash Flow at Decision Point B

CHOICE	EVENT	UNDISCOUNTED CASH FLOW	TOTAL CASH FLOW	PROBABILITY	EXPECTED VALUE
Expand	High Demand	$600,000 × 7 yr. = $4,200,000		.8	$3,360,000
	Low Demand	75,000 × 7 yr. = 525,000		.2	115,000
			Total		3,475,000
			Less Investment		500,000
			Net Value		$2,975,000
Do Not Expand	High Demand	$400,000 × 7 yr. = $2,800,000		.7	$1,960,000
	Low Demand	200,000 × 7 yr. = 1,400,000		.3	420,000
			Total		2,380,000
			Less Investment		0
			Net Value		$2,380,000

Table 15-2 Comparison of Decision A for Building Large Plant or Small Addition

CHOICE	EVENT		CASH FLOW	PROBABILITY	EXPECTED VALUES
Large Addition	High Demand	$800,000 × 8 yrs. = $6,400,000		.7	$4,480,000
	Low Demand	100,000 × 8 yrs. = 800,000		.3	240,000
			Total		4,720,000
			Less Investment		1,000,000
			Net Value		$3,720,000
Small Addition	High Demand	1 yr. at $500,000 = $ 500,000			
		Decision B Value = 2,975,000			
		$3,475,000		9	$3,127,000
	Low Demand	$200,000 × 8 yrs. = 1,600,000		.1	160,000
			Total		3,287,000
			Less Investment		200,000
			Net Value		$3,087,000

Table 15-3 Expected Discounted Value of Decision B

PART I

Choice	Event	Cash Flow	Present Value at 10%
Expand	High Demand	$600,000/yr. over 7 yrs.	$2,920,000
	Low Demand	75,000/yr. over 7 yrs.	365,000
No Change	High Demand	400,000/yr. over 7 yrs.	1,947,000
	Low Demand	200,000/yr. over 7 yrs.	973,000

PART II

Choice	Event	Present Value	Probability	Discounted Expected Value
Expand	High Demand	$2,920,000	.8	$2,336,000
	Low Demand	365,000	.2	73,000
		Total		2,409,000
		Less Investment		500,000
		Net Value		$1,909,000
No Change	High Demand	$1,947,000	.7	$1,363,000
	Low Demand	973,000	.3	292,000
		Total		1,655,000
		Less Investment		0
		Net Value		$1,655,000

Table 15-4 Expected Discounted Value of Decision A

CHOICE	EVENT	CASH FLOW	DISCOUNTED VALUE OF YIELD @ 10%	PROB-ABILITY	DISCOUNTED EXPECTED VALUE
Large Plant	High Demand	$ 800,000/yr. over 8 yrs. = $4,268,000		.7	$2,988,000
Large Plant	Low Demand	100,000/yr. over 8 yrs. =	533,000	.3	160,000
		Total			3,148,000
		Less Investment			1,000,000
		Net Value			$2,148,000
Small Plant	High Demand	$ 500,000/yr. over 1 yr. = $ 455,000		.9	$ 409,000
		$1,909,000 (Decision B Value at End of 1 yr.)	1,735,000		1,561,000
Small Plant	Low Demand	200,000/yr. over 8 yrs. =	1,067,000	.1	107,000
		Total			2,077,000
		Less Investment			200,000
		Net Value			$1,877,000

Sensitivity analysis helps managers answer some very important questions. For example, what happens to our calculated demand for electric motors if price is increased 10 percent? In other words, how sensitive is demand to a price change? Or, suppose we cannot reduce the weight of our newly designed airplane. What will the weight over the required specification do to operating costs? Sensitivity analysis shows the implications on final solutions of slight variations of parameters. If an optimum solution is sought, as for example, maximized profit, sensitivity analysis can show for what ranges of changes in values of elements of the analysis the solution is still optimum. Or, it can show the ranges of values which will still yield an acceptable solution to management.

UTILITY PROFILES. It is quite possible that a manager may refuse to accept expected values as a basis for making a particular decision. If, for example, there is a .25 chance that a manager will make $10 million on a contract, a .25 chance that he will lose $10 million, and a 50-50 chance he will make $6 million, the expected value is $3 million ($2.5 + $3.0 — $2.5), as shown below:

EVENT	PROBABILITY	CONSEQUENCE	EXPECTED VALUE
1	.25	+ $10 million	+ $2.5 million
2	.50	+ 6 million	+ 3.0 million
3	.25	— 10 million	— 2.5 million

This manager may observe that he is completely uninterested in any decision which is equally likely to make $10 million or to lose $10 million. This may be his position because to lose $10 million will throw him into bankruptcy. Or, he may be inherently a more conservative person than one willing to accept such risks. The fact of the matter is, of course, that different people have different views about the acceptance of risk. They have different utility profiles.

When faced with a situation such as that presented above the conservative manager will "hedge his bets" in different ways. He may flatly refuse to consider the probabilities stated and express his conservatism in other ways. For example, he may say that he will proceed only if the worst situations he specifies are certain not to occur. In this case, he may say that under no circumstances will he accept a contract which has any risk at all of resulting in negative profit. Or, he will increase those quantitative probabilities associated with undesirable consequences. In this way expected value will decline.

Another approach is to determine a manager's utility or preference curve and apply that to the problem at hand. The results of this approach, of course, may differ sharply from the expected value approach. This simply reflects the fact that a very conservative manager will wish to make choices rather differently from the very optimistic manager and these two will be different from the manager who plays the averages, so-to-speak, or the one that accepts expected value calculations.

Utility curves will naturally differ widely among managers and for each manager in different situations (Swalm, 1966). If, however, a manager's staff can get a reasonably useful preference curve for a given type of decision the manager can be saved the time and frustration of going through each choice at each chance event in a complex decision tree. (For a detailed analysis of this approach see Schlaifer, 1967; Swalm, 1966; and Hammond, 1967).

AN EVALUATION OF THE APPLICABILITY OF PROBABILITY THEORY. The type decision tree and utility analysis presented here has, in my judgment, great potential in improving decision-making at top management levels. Decision tree analysis provides a method for managers to identify fruitful alternative courses of action. It facilitates their placing their subjective values on possible outcomes of decisions. When probability estimates are matched with the object of concern—net cash flow, sales, net asset position, return on investment, present values, etc.—quantitative analysis of expected results can be used as a basis for deciding. When preference curves which register the attitudes of managers towards risk are adapted to the decision tree analysis the results can be brought more closely in line with values of managers. In complex problem-solving under conditions of considerable uncertainty this methodology can be of inestimable value to managerial decision-making.

There are, however, some inherent difficulties with the application of probability theory to business problems of the type which fall within the strategic planning area. In real life situations the decision tree sprouts a large number of alternative branches and very quickly becomes so complex that computers are needed. The number of points at which managerial probability estimates are required quickly tend to become unwieldy.

This condition is further complicated by the fact that there are different degrees of uncertainty which attach to different phenomena. The same distribution is not likely to exist among the chance events in a decision tree concerned with a large problem. The degree of skewness, degree of peakedness, and shape of the curve will vary among chance events to be examined. (Spencer and Siegelman, 1959, p. 14.)

This matter is accentuated because a manager's estimate of the probability distributions will differ depending upon his view of the reliability of estimates of costs, income, and other matters associated with a decision. Estimates of probabilities also may differ depending upon total amounts involved, slopes of curves, and the distance into the future for which estimates are made.

Managers will react differently depending upon the experience they have had with the decision at hand. A top manager of an automobile company will feel much more comfortable dealing with probabilities associated with building a new parts plant than he will in dealing with a potential acquisition in a new field of endeavor to his company.

Furthermore, being human, managers will have different estimates of the probabilities for the same sort of problem from one time to another, and from one problem to another.

For all these reasons, plus others that can easily be conceived, managers up to the present time have had a reluctance to apply explicit probability and preference estimates to particular situations. This is understandable. But in light of the great use of probability theory to managers it is not difficult to predict that they will become less reluctant to use decision tree analysis and apply their probability estimates to chance events. The values to them are too great to be rejected by reluctance to be concrete in their estimates.

APPLICATIONS OF SUBJECTIVE PROBABILITIES. Once managers and their staffs accept the idea of attaching probabilities to alternatives, the range of applications becomes wide. In Chapter 11, for instance, it was noted that managers are now attaching probability estimates to future sales levels which permits an aggregation of all estimates from which alternative future sales curves can be drawn with varied probabilities. If a company is planning to produce a product which will be in competition with that of another company, probabilities can be attached to different sales levels dependent upon variations in the price of the product as compared with the price of a competitor's product. Estimates become more complicated when prices are varied for both products. Later in this chapter will be shown the application of probabilities to a simulation model for capital decisions. Later in this chapter it will be shown how probability estimates may be attached to different discounted cash flows for competing capital investments.

STATISTICAL PROBABILITIES. It should be noted that there is a vast area of probability theory connected with phenomenon for which historical frequency distributions can be used to calculate future probabilities very accurately. For instance, past records make it possible to predict with high precision how many people will die next year per 100,000 of our population, or how many castings out of 10,000 will be faulty, or when a particular type of machine tool is likely to need new drills. This type of calculation has found widespread usage for years in the functional areas of business—inventory control, production control, and quality control—and there are many books which explain it (for instance Buffa, 1961, 1968, and Schlaifer, 1959).

Table 15-5 Johnson Safety Lock Company Actual and Projected Financial Trends ($ In Thousands)

YEAR	SALES	RETURN ON SALES (%)	NET INCOME	EARNINGS PER SHARE*	DIVIDENDS TOTAL†	PER SHARE	STOCK-HOLDER EQUITY	RETURN ON STOCK-HOLDERS EQUITY (%)	ACTUAL HIGH/LOW	STOCK PRICES (DOLLARS) Price Earnings Ratio		
										10	15	20
Actual												
1964	50000	10	5000	5.00	2.5	2.5	25000	20	87/45	50.00	75.00	100.00
1965	55000	12	6600	6.60	3.3	2.3	28300	23.32	100/65	66.00	99.00	120.00
1966	61000	8	4880	4.88	2.44	2.44	30740	15.88	82/70	48.80	73.20	97.60
1967	67000	11	7370	7.37	3.68	3.685	34425	21.41	140/80	73.70	110.55	147.40
1968	74000	10	7400	7.40	3.70	3.70	38125	19.41	150/90	74.00	111.00	148.00
Forecast												
1969	82000	10	8200	8.2	4.10	4.10	42225	19.42		82.00	123.00	164.00
1970	92000	11	10120	10.12	5.06	5.06	47285	21.40		101.20	151.80	202.40
1971	105000	11	11550	11.55	5.77	5.775	53060	21.77		115.50	173.25	231.00
1972	120000	12	14400	14.40	7.20	7.20	60260	23.90		144.00	216.00	288.00
1973	140000	12	16800	16.80	8.40	8.40	68660	24.47		168.00	252.00	336.00
1974	165000	12	19800	19.80	9.90	9.90	78560	25.20		198.00	297.00	396.00
1975	195000	13	25350	25.35	12.67	12.675	91235	27.79		253.50	380.25	507.00
1976	230000	13	29900	29.90	14.95	14.95	106185	28.16		299.00	448.50	598.00
1977	270000	13	35100	35.10	17.55	17.55	123735	28.37		351.00	526.50	702.00
1978	310000	14	43400	43.40	21.70	21.70	145435	29.84		434.00	651.00	868.00
1979	350000	14	49000	49.00	24.50	24.50	169935	28.83		490.00	735.00	980.00

* 1,000,000 shares outstanding

† Dividends are assumed to be 50% of earnings

SIMULATION

Simulation is an exceedingly adaptable and valuable approach to problem solving that is coming into greater use in business planning at all levels—from strategic to short-range operational planning. The scope of simulation is so broad that only the main features can be presented here.

WHAT IS SIMULATION? In a general sense, simulation refers to the representation of reality. In business affairs, simulation means attacking a problem by constructing a model to represent a real business situation and then manipulating the model in such a way as to draw from it conclusions about the real world. Simulation is not so much a technique as an approach to representing the real world in such a fashion that problem-solving is facilitated. In the employment of simulation, however, many different techniques or tools may be employed.

The use of simulation in business is not new. Verbal descriptions, schematic diagrams, or simple tabular representations of reality, for example, have been widely used in the past. A condensed balance sheet and profit and loss statement, for example, as shown in Table 15-5, can be used to simulate reality.

In recent years, however, there have been major improvements in our ability to simulate business situations that make it very new. What is new is the use of mathematical expressions and equations to capture succinctly enormously complex business interrelationships which heretofore could not be easily related, and then to manipulate the model on electronic computers to see in seconds what might happen in reality if the relationships are fixed or are changed in specific ways. Furthermore, with these new tools it is now possible to develop computer programs which can simulate very closely those complex real-world situations which heretofore could not be summarized in a manageable model for problem-solving or easy understanding.

A simulation model is an abstraction of reality but hopefully close enough to the real world to permit useful observations, analysis, or evaluations from it. A road map is an abstraction, or model, of some part of the real world. It omits many real-world details but contains enough information to make it very useful for certain types of problem-solving.

Correspondingly, a model useful in business simulation seeks to eliminate all unnecessary complex detail yet still be sufficiently close to reality to be helpful, when manipulated, in solving some business problem. Because many business planning processes are rather complex, simulation models useful in dealing with them are also complex. In building and using them it often is necessary to apply mathematical symbolic language and equations. But it is very important to note that most of the mathematics used in simulation is not beyond the understanding of most managers.

Although attention in this chapter is focused on newer quantitative techniques, it should be noted that many powerful simulation models, useful at the strategic planning level, can be created very simply and manipulated with ease with or without computers. Table 15-5 presents such a case dealing with important financial matters.

VALUE OF SIMULATION TO MANAGERS. Why are managers interested in simulation? Why do they use models instead of experimenting with the real world? To ask these questions is to reveal rather obvious answers. First, as noted in Chapter 1, the cost of experimentation in the real world is prohibitive compared with simulation on paper or with a computer model. The cost of simulation has been so substantially reduced that even for large systems and large problems it is today a very economical tool. Second, actual changes and interactions in the business world often take much time before their effects are recognized. These long-run implications may be simulated in a matter of minutes with an appropriate model. Third, simulation models help managers to understand better the multitude of interacting variables and interrelationships involved in business systems. Both in the process of creating the model and in using it, the major cause-and-effect relationships of the process simulated are revealed and better understood, the way in which one business system relates to another can be better studied, and the impact of forces from outside on the business system can be seen. With such knowledge, managers can better design new systems, and can make decisions with more understanding of the need for them and their consequences when implemented.

Simulation models have been applied to a wide variety of activities in business, such as: top-management financial allocations in light of probable risk; capital budgeting to maximize return on investment; planning and control of complete refinery operations; railroad car scheduling; inventory decision-making; improving bank lending by simulating customer results from loans; relating production, inventory, and distribution of a finished product; tanker scheduling; personnel planning; steelworks melting operations; equipment redesigning; and designing a bus terminal (Rowe, 1965; Malcolm, 1959).

The range of potential activities that can profitably employ simulation is, of course, very broad. Simulation can be used to predict future possible behavior, to understand the effects of changes in a system, to compare systems, to examine the relationships which exist in a system, or to investigate facts about a system. Simulations can be made to examine conflicts in company goals, help allocate resources, schedule complex activities, study probabilities of expected events, analyze data, train managers, and provide virtually automatic decision-making. Most simulation models, however, are used for three purposes: to investigate the characteristics of some system, such as an inventory or finance system; to make comparisons between different systems, as, for example, relating production, inventory, and distribution; or to study the effects of change within a particular system, such as allocating financial resources in different ways.

Most simulation models to date have been developed for functional area operational problems. But in the past few years simulation has found more and more use in strategic planning and has, therefore, become of direct importance to top management. This is a development which undoubtedly will continue to expand. Indeed, I completely agree with John Dearden (1966, p. 235) when he says that of all the newer mathematical approaches to problem-solving, simulation probably has much greater potential for helping top management than any of the others. Most of the others have greater use to operational management.

Furthermore, simulation is an approach which needs the participation of management at the level where it is to be used. Technicians building and programming a simulation model may not have a feel for the critical interrelationships needed in it, or the way in which parts of it should fit together, or the way in which its manipulation will produce most useful results for management. The judgment of managers may prove to be of decisive importance in the creation of an appropriate model and its acceptable use. Also, if management is to use the simulation model for serious decision-making, or for background understanding, it must know the assumptions entering into the construction of the model.

LIMITATIONS OF SIMULATION. In considering the values of simulation to managers the limitations of the approach should not be overlooked. Perhaps the major problem, especially with respect to a complex matter, is that of inventing the model, developing a computer program for it, and using it properly. Solving the computer programming problem has proven to be a major stumbling block in many simulation applications. This problem has been mitigated, however, by the development of simulation languages such as Simscript (Markowitz, Hausner, and Karr, 1963), DYNAMO (Forrester, 1961), and the General Purpose Simulator (Gordon, 1962).

Another problem grows out of the availability of data and its applicability to real-world situations. Simply because a relationship has been observed between two phenomena—sales and production, for instance—does not mean the relationship can be expected to continue or be the same from one product to another. The probable relationship may be over a wide range of possibilities and, if reality is to be simulated, it is important to consider the probability that it will be at one point as compared with another. This problem has been partly corrected with the development of new techniques for data analysis and evaluation, an important one of which is Monte Carlo sampling, which will be discussed later. These techniques permit a model to be manipulated with a minimum of data and a maximization of the value of the data manipulated.

There are other limitations of and pitfalls to simulation. Some limitations discussed in the preceding chapters of systems analysis apply, of course, to simulation because simulation is an important approach to systems analysis. (Parenthetically, simulation is not synonymous with systems analysis. Systems analysis is the broader term. One of a number of approaches to systems analysis is simula-

Chart 15-3—Simulation of a Strike on Enemy Base in an Air Superiority Campaign

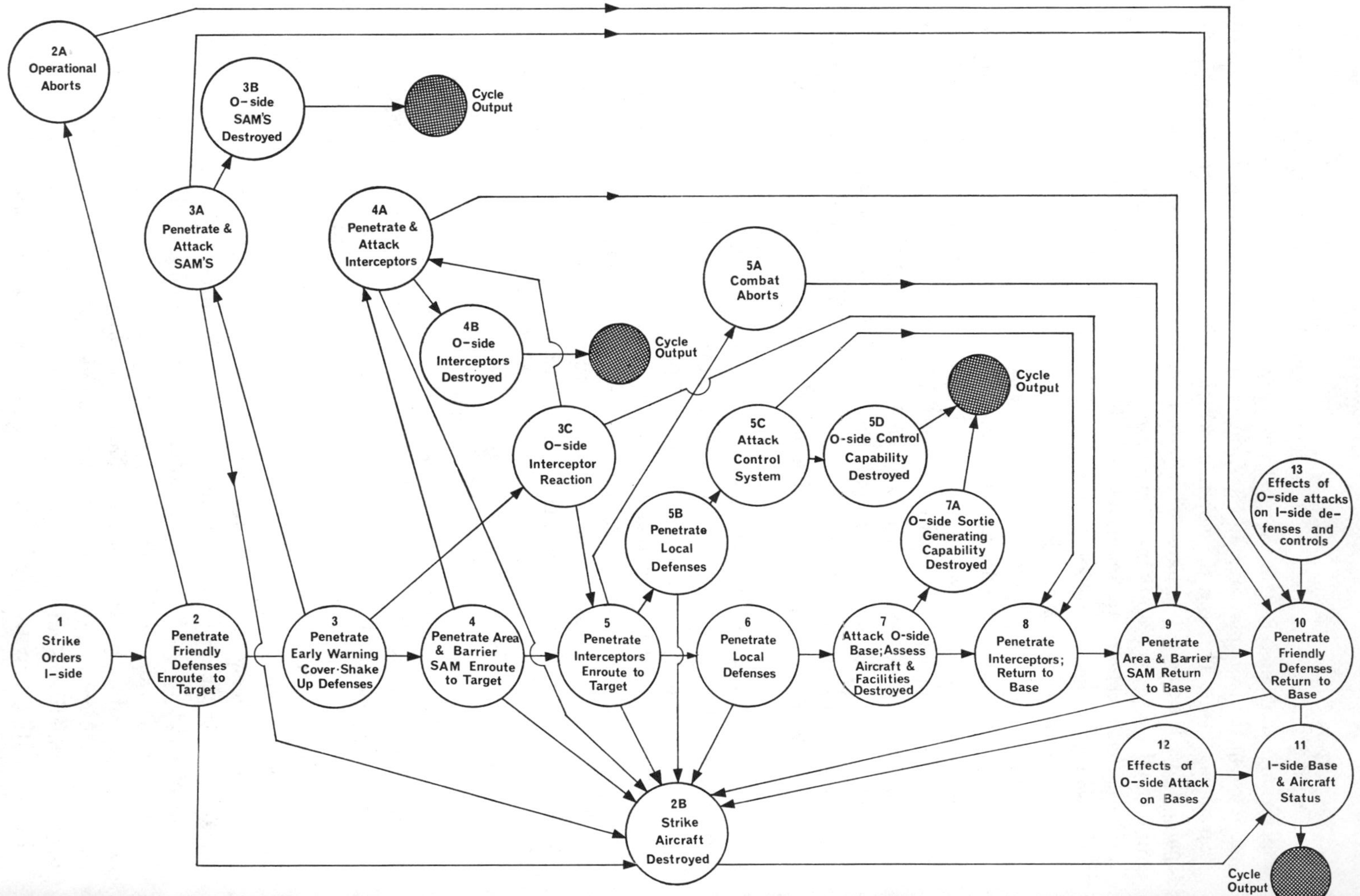

1 Strike Orders I-side

2 Penetrate Friendly Defenses Enroute to Target

2A Operational Aborts

2B Strike Aircraft Destroyed

3 Penetrate Early Warning Cover-Shake Up Defenses

3A Penetrate & Attack SAM'S

3B O-side SAM'S Destroyed

4 Penetrate Area & Barrier SAM Enroute to Target

4A Penetrate & Attack Interceptors

4B O-side Interceptors Destroyed

3C O-side Interceptor Reaction

Cycle Output

5 Penetrate Interceptors Enroute to Target

5A Combat Aborts

5B Penetrate Local Defenses

5C Attack Control System

5D O-side Control Capability Destroyed

Cycle Output

6 Penetrate Local Defenses

7 Attack O-side Base; Assess Aircraft & Facilities Destroyed

7A O-side Sortie Generating Capability Destroyed

8 Penetrate Interceptors; Return to Base

9 Penetrate Area & Barrier SAM Return to Base

10 Penetrate Friendly Defenses Return to Base

11 I-side Base & Aircraft Status

12 Effects of O-side Attack on Bases

13 Effects of O-side attacks on I-side defenses and controls

Cycle Output

SOURCE: G. and S. C. Hayes, Air Superiority Map Exercise Logic and Task Breakdown (Unpublished Document) (Santa

tion.) Other limitations will be noted later in the chapter in connection with specific types of simulation.

ILLUSTRATIVE SIMULATION MODELS. In preceding chapters a number of simulation models were mentioned, such as methods for sales forecasting discussed in Chapter 8, break-even analysis described in Chapter 11, and traditional scheduling shown in Chapter 13. At this point, therefore, it may be sufficient to discuss one simple and highly useful hand simulation and several more complex computer-based simulation models.

A Simple Financial Model. Table 15-5 shows a very simple simulation model of selected financial parameters of a company which can be tied into a company's planning process very easily and hand-manipulated. This model shows how projected sales will reflect in stockholders' return on equity and stock prices, given certain assumptions specified in the model. A top manager may find it very useful to change possible future sales estimates, and return on sales, to see the impact on dividends, return on stockholder equity, and the price of the company's stock on the market. Such a simple model as this can be the basis of significant policy decisions. This model could, of course, be programmed for computers and additional variables added, but it can be manipulated by hand.

A Weapons System Model. In the more complex models are combined many more interrelationships and the probabilities of outcomes are included. The techniques and fundamentals of today's more complex business simulation models were probably first developed by the RAND Corporation in connection with its early military systems analysis (Wohlstetter, Hoffman, Lutz, and Rowen, 1954). Chart 15-3 shows one of the simpler complex types of analysis which is concerned with studying air superiority campaigns. In general, the model simulates the steps (one may say milestones) followed by a friendly aircraft strike (I-side "initiating" in Chart 15-3) in attacking an enemy base (O-side "opposing" in Chart 15-3). It is clear that the model simulates eleven sequential routines from the receipt of strike orders (1) through aircraft status at a friendly base (11). There are additional sub-routines in the simulation. For example, part of the strike force may be assigned the task of "surface-to-air-missile-busting," shown in step 3A. Similarily, another fraction of the strike aircraft may purposefully seek and engage enemy interceptors in "dog-fights" as in step 4A.

Chart 15-3 represents one trial, or one computer-run, in the jargon of "computerese." As the simulation is conducted probabilistically—that is, in terms of probability distributions of the friendly and the enemy orders of battle, for example, as well as in terms of the probability of a given friendly aircraft achieving a particular milestone—a large number of computer runs (or cycles in Chart 15-3) must be made. The runs yield a distribution of results that can be reduced to parameters of a probability distribution. The military planner is then able to say that given such and such a strike, with such and such a flight profile, and some

Chart 15-4

Probability Distribution for Share of Market

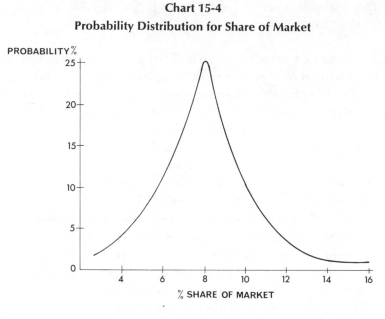

information on the enemy posture and order of battle, the losses incurred by his strike force in attacking an enemy base would on the average be so many aircraft. Furthermore, he can say that if the strike was made repeatedly, under exactly the same conditions, he would lose no more than x and no less than y aircraft in, say, 95 percent of the strikes.

Risk-Analysis Simulation. David Hertz (1968 and 1964) has rightfully pointed out that investment decisions based upon one-point estimates, such as used in conventional measurements like payback period, average annual rate of return, or discounted cash flow rate of return, are highly deficient in that they do not properly deal with uncertainty and risk. Many businessmen know this and try to overcome the deficiency by supplementing their "best guesses" with estimates of "optimistic," "pessimistic," and "probable" for major variables. This is helpful but not good enough, says Hertz. What is much better, he says, is to simulate possible investment outcomes to get a range of probabilities concerning payoff. This is what he calls a "risk-analysis simulation" which yields a "risk-based profile."

Table 15-6 outlines the major steps employed in simulating the possible outcomes of a given investment and in determining a "risk profile," or a probability distribution for future revenues from a given investment. In this case assume the problem is whether to make an investment in a new plant to produce a new product. The simulation deals with one set of investment criteria and, as shown in Table 15-6, starts with a probability distribution for each of a number of major variables. For each, a beta distribution is drawn, as illustrated in the Chart 15-4.

The remaining steps given in Table 15-6 are then followed and a risk profile shown in Chart 15-5 is concluded. Chart 15-5 shows, for example, that the contemplated investment has a 78 percent chance of making more than a 0 percent return on investment and a 22 percent chance of loss. It has a 5 percent chance of making from a 30 to 40 percent return.

Table 15-6   Steps in Risk-Analysis Simulation

1. Construct uncertainty profiles for each important input factor, such as:
     market size
     share of market
     price
     marketing cost
     selling cost
     fixed manufacturing cost
     variable manufacturing cost
     investment

   (This means a distribution of the probability that specific values of each factor will be reached, as shown in Chart 15-4.)
2. The computer simulates an actual situation by selecting one value from each of the above profiles, according to the chances that the values will occur. The selection process is just like spinning a "wheel of chance."
3. The computer then combines the values selected and determines a return on investment for this particular situation.
4. The computer repeats this process of selection and makes an ROI calculation several thousand times.
5. The computer then lists the results and specifies the number of times the ROI falls in a given range, as follows:

ROI RANGES AS %	PERCENTAGE OF SITUATIONS = PROBABILITY OF OCCURRENCE	CUMULATIVE PROBABILITY
30-40	5	5
20-30	19	24
10-20	33	57
0-10	21	78
−10-0	14	92
−30- −10	8	100

6. The cumulative probabilities can then be used to draw a risk profile, as shown in Chart 15-5.

Source: Adapted from David B. Hertz, "Investment Policies That Pay Off," *Harvard Business Review*, Vol. 46, January-February 1968, p. 99.

Chart 15-5

Simulated Risk Profile

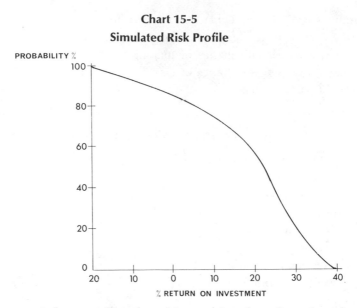

If management does not like the odds or risks of profit or loss, it can alter uncertainty profiles by simulated actions. For example, in the case at hand, a new profile can perhaps be developed by changes in product mix to be produced in the plant, changes in plant design, changes in marketing strategy, or changes in price. The simulation model can then be rerun to see the effect of these changes. Managers can examine risks of different investment policies before operational decisions are made.

Industrial Dynamics. A simulation model encompassing a large, but not the entire, part of a company has been developed by Jay Forrester (1961 and 1964; see also Roberts, 1963). Industrial dynamics is both a concept and a simulation model. In the words of its inventor (Forrester, 1964, p. 7): "Industrial dynamics is a study of the feedback characteristics of industrial activity to show how organizational structure, amplification, and time delays influence the success of the enterprise. It treats the interactions between the flows of money, orders, materials, personnel, and capital equipment, all interconnected by an information network."

Industrial dynamics focuses on the information system in a business because it looks at management as a process of converting information into decisions and action. Information systems have properties that may lead to undesired results. For example, delays and/or amplification may upset a system's equilibrium. If there is a sudden 10 percent increase in sales by retailers, the transmission of this information back through distributors, warehouses, and into the enterprise itself, may result in overreaction and a 40 percent increase in demand at the production level. This sort of amplification can be influenced by information lags, and random fluctuations in behavior of customers, retailers, and wholesalers.

Forrester views an enterprise as a closed loop information feedback system.

Chart 15-6
Operations with Poor Planning and Control

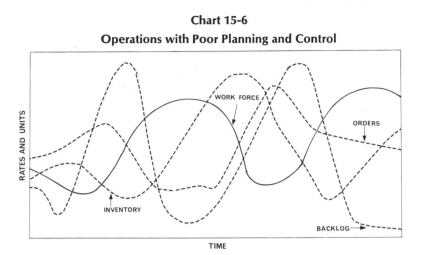

He feels it is possible to improve the stability of the system's behavior by appropriate changes in it. Although a company has no control over its economic environment, it can adjust the design of its system to enable it to react to the given
input in a more efficient manner. What is required, of course, is that sales information at the retail level should be smoothed to eliminate any possibility of excessive impact on the production line, inventories should respond properly to order
rates, order backlogs should not be allowed to drift beyond established ranges,
working capital financing should be kept within proper relationships to production and sales, and the work force should be related to the desired level of production. This does not imply that a firm has total control over its operations
regardless of the input to the system in the form of orders, population growth,
and so on. It does mean that the firm can be designed to respond more quickly
and efficiently to the given input, whatever it is.

Forrester's model, then, examines the firm as an electrical circuit, and determines the informational structure of the firm, the factors that contribute to delays, the length of the delays at each step in the structure, and the policies and
forecasts that contribute to amplification. It determines the successive relationships of these factors and formulates mathematical equations to describe them.
Because the number of equations is great, it was necessary to find some means
to convert the collection of equations to a computer operating program. The
DYNAMO compiler language was developed to accommodate the computer to
this model.

With the model, managers who might have experienced the situation depicted
in Chart 15-6 are able to have a much smoother operation, illustrated in Chart
15-7. These are very simplistic drawings of rather complex comparable charts
derived from the industrial dynamics computer runs. With the model it is possible, of course, to determine policies which enable the improvement of the relationship among the variables and to plan and control accordingly.

Chart 15-7

Operations with the Industrial Dynamics Model

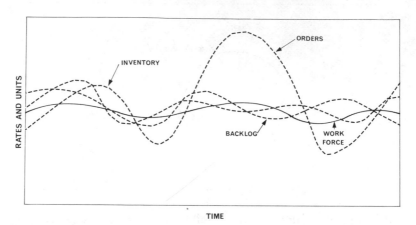

This model, one of the first to encompass a very large part of a business enterprise and interrelate major forces operating in it, brings to management the possibility of getting information of great value in achieving a desired interrelationship among internal activities as dynamic changes from its environment hit on the business. It also provides an excellent laboratory for experimenting and predicting what may happen in a business under specified circumstances.

As with any other managerial tool there are limitations to its use in operations decision-making. First of all, it is complex. Better forecasting of incoming orders, more efficient order handling, better warehouse distribution, enlightened management of information systems, and better internal control of operations, may provide a better basis for management's planning for and controlling of the interrelationships among major segments of the business in a much simpler fashion. Second, the old problem of suboptimization once again appears. Industrial dynamics does not cover all of an enterprise and may, therefore, result in suboptimization at the expense of over-all optimization. Third, there are variables important to the model which are difficult to quantify, such as market strategy, employee or executive motivation, union regulations and activities, and customer service requirements. Fourth, for even a moderate-sized business the number of variables which must be examined becomes so large as to become hard to manage in a model that seeks to come reasonably close to simulating reality. Most of these limitations point to a general question of the extent to which simulation of really large systems can yield sufficient representation to be reliable guides for analysis, planning, and decision-making (Ansoff, 1968). In partial answer to this question the industrial dynamics approach has been used with some success in business operations (Carlson, 1964).

Other Comprehensive Business Simulation Models. There are other large simulation models for business that should be mentioned although space limitations prevent a description of them (Bonini, 1962; Sprowls and Asimow, 1962; and Kagdis, 1962). Another company simulation is that of McMillan and Gonzalez (1965, Chapter 13). A different type of company-wide simulation is the linear programming model which Standard Oil of New Jersey uses in integrating planning and control activities (Rapoport and Drews, 1962). This by no means exhausts the list of possible inclusions, and it is safe to predict that the list will grow.

MONTE CARLO. Monte Carlo is a simulation technique which is of great value in approximating reality. It can easily be adapted to almost any situation so long as alternatives can be quantified. Before a model can be "Monte Carlo-ed," the functional relationships of the real system must be placed in the model. Monte Carlo then produces a quantitative solution by the use of probabilities and random number tables. It is a method widely employed in all types of computer simulation, as noted in the air superiority campaign and the Hertz models described above. Following is one simple illustration of this method (Quade, 1964, pp. 242-243).

Consider a simplified servicing process where items (such as automobiles) arrive randomly at a servicing facility (such as a gas station). The items are handled in series; that is, one at a time. The items arrive in the following manner: 40 percent of the intervals between arrivals are ten minutes long and 60 percent are twenty minutes long. Now suppose that servicing is also random, with ten minutes required to service 80 percent of the items and thirty minutes required to handle the other 20 percent.

From the information given above, it follows that:

Mean arrival interval per item $= 0.4 \times 10 + 0.6 \times 20 = 16$ minutes

Mean servicing time per item $= 0.8 \times 10 + 0.2 \times 30 = 14$ minutes

Mean facility idle time $=$ 2 minutes

The question posed: How long does an item wait on the average? Or, what is the mean waiting time per item?

The above questions may be answered by using a simulation in which a sequence of random numbers represents both the intervals between arrivals and the servicing times. The interval between arrivals is determined by the selection of a random digit: 0, 1, 2, 3, 4, 5, 6, 7, 8, or 9. If the random digit selected is a 0, 1, 2, or 3, the item is assigned an arrival interval of ten minutes. If it is a 4, 5, 6, 7, 8, or 9, the item is assigned an arrival interval of twenty minutes.

The service time associated with the item that comes after an arrival interval has elapsed is specified in a similar manner by selecting a second random digit. If this random digit is a 0, 1, 2, 3, 4, 5, 6, or 7, the item is assigned a servicing time of ten minutes. If the random digit is an 8 or 9, the item is assigned a servicing time of thirty minutes.

The problem is solved in Table 15-7. It is assumed that first arrival takes place at time zero, as shown in Column 4. The digits drawn at random are shown in Columns 2 and 6. These random digits allow the simulation of arrival and servicing times, respectively.

Table 15-7 shows that for the ten samples listed there is a total of 60 minutes waiting time or an average of six minutes per item. This example leaves unanswered many questions such as the number of samples needed to give a good estimate of waiting time. Nevertheless, it does highlight the main features of the Monte Carlo Method as it is used in operations research.

Monte Carlo methods in business problem-solving have found increased use as problems get too complicated for classical analytic and quantitative methods. By simulating the random nature of certain business processes, it can treat problems that are almost impossible to deal with otherwise. Furthermore, the sample size used in Monte Carlo (ten, for example in the problem of Table 15-7) can be increased at little or no cost by use of a computer.

Monte Carlo simulation is less abstract and more flexible than other models of simulation for the following reasons: (1) there is no need in Monte Carlo simulation to specify what is being optimized; (2) it is not necessary to sacrifice complexity or detail to make the solution easy, as the computer can handle

Table 15-7   A Servicing Problem Using Monte Carlo

1	2	3	4	5	6	7	8	9	10
								Number of	Number of
						Minutes			
	First	Arrival	Time	Time	Second	Required	Time	Minutes	Minutes
Item	Random	Interval,	of	Service	Random	to	Service	Item	Facility
Number	Digit	Minutes	Arrival	Starts	Digit	Service	Ends	Waits	Is Idle
1	—	—	0	0	2	10	10	0	0
2	1	10	10	10	8	30	40	0	0
3	9	20	30	40	6	10	50	10	0
4	8	20	50	50	7	10	60	0	0
5	8	20	70	70	9	30	100	0	10
6	2	10	80	100	4	10	110	20	0
7	0	10	90	110	1	10	120	20	0
8	7	20	110	120	3	10	130	10	0
9	4	20	130	130	4	10	140	0	0
10	9	20	150	150	9	30	180	0	10

Note: Column 8 = Column 5 + Column 7
Column 9 = Column 5 — Column 4
Column 10 = Column 5 — Value in preceding row in Column 8

Source: E. S. Quade, ed., *Military Systems Analysis* (Santa Monica, California: The RAND Corporation, R-387-PR, November 1964), p. 243.

complex systems; and (3) the computer simulation program can include provisions for time leads and lags (Burroughs Corporation, 1967, p. 21).

CONCLUDING COMMENT. There is no question about the fact that the computer-based simulation approach to managerial problems is an extremely fruitful one which has virtually unlimited promise for the future. Of major interest to top management is the increasing extent to which it is being used at the strategic planning level. Fortunately, it is an approach which is easy to understand and use by top managers. Simulating a real-life business situation approximates it but also has in it much more, as expressed in an 8th century Chinese poem:

> *I would not paint a face, a rock, nor brooks, nor trees*
> *Mere semblances of things, but something more than these.*
> *That art is best which to the soul's range gives no bound,*
> *Something besides the form, something beyond the sound.*

LINEAR PROGRAMMING

Linear programming is one of the really new quantitative tools that has found increasingly important uses in business. Fundamentally it is a methodology which helps a manager to determine an optimum plan from various alternative courses of action.

The use of linear models to deal with economic problems is not new (Simonnard, 1966, p. IX). But the use of linear programming to solve business problems is new. In 1947 George Dantzig developed the general technique for solving linear programming problems that became known as the "simplex method" (Dantzig, 1949). Although this development laid a basis for the use of linear programming in business, it was the digital computer which made the method of really great practical use to businessmen.

In this section it is impossible to explain in any detail the way problems are solved by linear programming. The reason is that except for the simplest problems the calculations become unmanageable. What I will do, therefore, is to present a few types of problems which linear programming has actually solved in practice and follow this with an elementary description of how a very simple allocation problem can be formulated and solved with this tool. The section then will be closed with a brief analysis of the strengths and limitations of linear programming for management decision making.

SOME LINEAR PROGRAMMING PROGRAMS. The following are problems which managers of different businesses face which can be and have been solved with linear programming methods.

Chart 15-8

A Transportation Problem

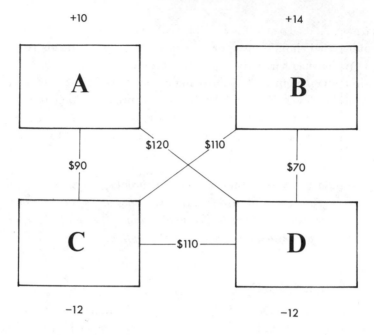

A producer of washing machines makes two models, a deluxe machine and a stripped down version designed to sell in volume at low cost. With limited capacity but a demand for both well above expectations the question arises as to the proper mix for production which will maximize profits. This is a very simple case, which will be solved later, but one which many large and small businesses face.

A railroad must move a number of freight cars about and wishes to do it at the lowest possible cost. A simple problem is illustrated in Chart 15-8. It assumes that 10 freight cars are in location A and 14 are in location B. The problem is to satisfy the demands for 12 in C and 12 in D in such a way that the total cost is the lowest possible or, conversely, the profit will be greatest. In this case it is obvious that the least cost will be achieved when all 10 cars from A go to C, 12 cars go from B to D, and 2 move from B to C. If, however, there were three origins, ten destinations, and 100 cars to distribute, the total number of feasible solutions would be in the millions. This is a type of problem encountered by large multiplant producers in shipping from many production plants and many warehouses. Linear programming can solve such problems quickly with the computer.

An oil company is faced with the problem of determining that blend of gasoline in a particular refinery which will provide a suitable output of required types at the greatest total profit for the plant over a specific period of time.

A large mining company has a problem of determining an optimal twenty-five year production plan which must take into consideration demand, uncertainties about technology, uncertainties about geological conditions, and all other important factors having a bearing upon the problem (Albach, 1967).

A steel mill wants to determine over a long period of time how to use its blast furnaces in order to answer such problems as these: get the least-cost raw material blends, maintain the optimal raw material inventory levels, assure the lowest-cost maintenance program, and schedule specified output to achieve the greatest profit (Fabian, 1967).

The Standard Oil Company of New Jersey is faced with a long-range planning problem in designing its tankers, in terms of size, speed, costs, etc.; determining the number of ships to be purchased; deciding the capacity, cost, production mix, and location of all facilities required at each port; and calculating the required investment and cash flows which will yield the desired profit (Rapoport and Drews, 1962; and Leete, 1967).

The general types of problems to which linear programming is usefully applied are called allocation problems. These are the decisions about what scarce resources should be used in what quantity to reach a desired objective. In business, the resources to be allocated are principally men, equipment, and money. The output, of course, is products and services. Linear programming is a method which can explain how the resource inputs can be used to maximize specified outputs.

The range of applications in business goes far beyond the cases illustrated above and includes such diverse problems as allocating electric supply, assigning parts to be manufactured on existing equipment, allocating salesmen, and even the allocation of resources of banks to loans (Jallow, 1966).

SOLVING THE LINEAR PROGRAMMING PROBLEM. The methodology of linear programming can be roughly divided into four different categories, namely, the graphical, the simplex, the transportation, and special methods. Only the graphical will be presented here. This is the simplest method and can be done by hand. This method becomes cumbersome and unwieldy as problems get more complex. A more efficient and powerful means to identify optimal solutions for more complex problems is the simplex method. While comparable to the simpler method, it reaches solutions by solving sets of simultaneous linear equations. While the simplex method can be used to solve any linear programming problem, there are certain types of problems for which special procedures have been developed to simplify the solution. The transportation method of linear programming is one to deal with the types of problems identified in the second case noted above. Beyond this, of course, are complications, such as in the open-pit mining case and the case of the oil companies, which require special techniques to come to grips with the special problems involved. The methodology in the latter cases tends to get rather complex. Aside from the books referenced in this chapter there are a number of others with both simple and more complex expositions of all linear programming methods (Ferguson and Sargent, 1958; Thompson, 1967; and Vajda, 1958).

FORMULATING A LINEAR PROGRAMMING PROBLEM. A simple approach to formulating a linear programming problem may be illustrated by examining a hypothetical product mix case (after George B. Dantzig, 1963). Assume a furniture company manufactures one model each of five different items. For convenience these may be labeled as item 1, item 2, item 3, item 4, and item 5.

The company can sell all furniture produced. Its profit (revenue less labor costs) per item is as follows:

Item	1	2	3	4	5
Profit	$5	$15	$20	$10	$12

If items 1, 2, 3, 4, and 5 are denoted by x_1, x_2, x_3, x_4, and x_5, respectively, total profit would then be

$$P = 5x_1 + 15x_2 + 20x_3 + 10x_4 + 12x_5 \tag{1}$$

Equation (1) is called the objective function because it represents the goal of the firm. It is seen that the objective function is a linear combination of the un-known quantities of each product, or simply the x_i $(i = 1, 2, \ldots 5)$. The x_i are called decision variables. The goal is to find values for the decision variables such that the objective function as described in equation (1) is maximized.

If the firm had no capacity limitations, the objective function could be maximized by producing an infinite amount of each item. This is absurd, of course, as the firm has a limited capacity; that is, there is a ceiling on the maximum amount of each item produced. This ceiling is called a constraint or a side condition. For the furniture firm, the constraints that determine plant capacity must then be defined. This requires an examination of the manufacturing process.

In the manufacturing process the parts are constructed in the Carpentry Shop. They are next sent to the Finishing Shop for varnishing and polishing, and then are routed to the Assembly Shop. The number of man-hours by items required in each shop is as follows:

ITEMS

Shop	1	2	3	4	5
Carpentry	3	10	20	5	4
Finishing	2	30	40	2	3
Assembly	1/2	3	5	1	2

Plant layout and available equipment limit the amount of labor used within each shop. As a result, the Carpentry Shop can absorb no more than 10,000 man hours for the coming year. Similarly, the labor ceiling for Finishing and Assembly are 6,000 and 1,000 man-hours, respectively.

These constraints may be stated algebraically by the system of linear equalities described in (2). (The symbol "$\leqslant$" denotes less than or equal to; the symbol "$\geqslant$" stands for greater than or equal to.)

$$3x_1 + 10x_2 + 20x_3 + 5x_4 + 4x_5 \leqslant 10,000$$

$$2x_1 + 30x_2 + 40x_3 + 2x_4 + 3x_5 \leqslant 6,000 \qquad (2)$$

$$0.5x_1 + 3x_2 + 5x_3 + x_4 + 2x_5 \leqslant 1,000$$

The furniture company cannot produce a negative number of desks or tables. Therefore:

$$x_i \geqslant 0 \qquad \text{for } i = 1, 2, \ldots, 5. \qquad (3)$$

This formula (3) states that the quantity of each item produced must either be zero or a positive number. This restriction is known as the *non-negativity* condition.

The linear programming problem has now been formulated. The problem is to determine the quantities $x_1, \ldots, x_5$ that would maximize the objective function (1) subject to the side conditions stipulated in (2 and the non-negativity condition in (3).

Based on the above example, generalizations about the structure of linear programming problems may be made. The structure of linear programming problems consists of an objective function, constraints, and non-negativity conditions. The objective function deals explicitly with the goals to be attained: profit maximization or cost minimization. It may be written as

$$P = c_1 x_1 + c_2 x_2 + \ldots \ldots + c_n x_n \qquad (4)$$

where the x_i are the unknowns and the c_i are known $(i = 1, 2, \ldots, n)$.

The constraints may be written as

$$a_{11} x_1 + a_{12} x_2 + \ldots + a_{1n} x_n \leqslant b_1$$

$$a_{21} x_1 + a_{22} x_2 + \ldots + a_{2n} x_n \leqslant b_2$$

$$\vdots \qquad \vdots \qquad \qquad \vdots \qquad \qquad (5)$$

$$a_{m1} x_1 + a_{m2} x_2 + \ldots + a_{mn} x_n \leqslant b_m$$

The non-negativity conditions state that

$$x_i \geqslant 0 \qquad (i = 1, 2, \ldots, n) \qquad (6)$$

The purpose of the linear programming problem is to maximize the objective function (4) subject to the constraints (5) and the non-negativity conditions (6). All of the c_i, a_{ij}, and b_i are assumed to be known. The values of the x_i (the decision variables) that minimize or maximize the objective function are to be determined.

A MAXIMIZATION PROBLEM. To illustrate the basic concepts in the solution of linear programming problems, an example with two decision variables will be used. First, because the example is two dimensional, a graphical solution will be found. Second, the graphical solution will be used to describe the simplex technique.

Practical problems in business and industry where linear programming is applicable typically contain a large number of decision variables which are best solved by the computer. Computer programs that produce quick and economical solutions to complex linear programming problems are readily available.

As an illustration of a problem with two decision variables, consider a firm that produces two models of washing machines (adapted from Theil, Boot, and Kloek, 1962, pp. 4-10). Model A has luxury features and sells for $300; model B, on the other hand, is a stripped-down standard version which sells for $200.

After deducting expenses, the firm finds that its profit margins for the two models are $50 and $30, respectively. The firm cannot produce the more profitable model exclusively, because of plant layout and capacity limitations. The problem is to determine the product mix that maximizes profit, under present circumstances.

If the firm annually makes x_1 units of model A and x_2 units of model B, its total profit would be

$$P = \$50 \, x_1 + \$30 \, x_2 \qquad (7)$$

Equation (7) is the objective function the firm wishes to maximize.

The two models are manufactured in two separate shops, A and B. Shop A produces model A, and Shop B model B. The annual capacity of Shop A is 1,500 units, that for Shop B is 2,000 units. These side conditions may be then written in the form of the inequalities:

$$x_1 \leqslant 1,500$$
$$x_2 \leqslant 2,000 \qquad (8)$$

The firm cannot produce to plant capacity because of an expected shortage in labor supply. The expected labor supply is estimated to be 2,500 man-days. Further, it requires $1\frac{1}{4}$ man-days to manufacture model A and 1 man-day to manufacture model B. Thus, the firm faces the additional side condition:

$$1.25 \, x_1 + x_2 \leqslant 2,500 \qquad (9)$$

Inequality (9) prevents the firm from producing up to the full capacity of

Chart 15-9

Rectangle OABC Fulfills Two Constraints

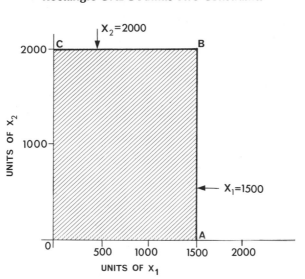

its two shops. Producing to full capacity would require $1{,}500 \times 1.25 + 2{,}000 \times 1.0 = 3{,}875$ man-days, which are not expected to be available for the planning period in question.

GRAPHICAL SOLUTION. The product mix problem described above may be restated as follows:

$$\text{Maximize } 50\, x_1 + 30\, x_2$$

Subject to

$$x_1 \leqslant 1{,}500$$

$$x_2 \leqslant 2{,}000 \qquad\qquad (10)$$

$$1.25\, x_1 + x_2 \leqslant 2{,}500$$

and

$$x_i \geqslant 0 \qquad (i = 1, 2)$$

We know that x_1 and x_2 cannot exceed 1,500 and 2,000 units, respectively. These restrictions can be represented by plotting a vertical line ($x_1 = 1{,}500$) and a horizontal line ($x_2 = 2{,}000$) as shown in Chart 15-9. We label these two lines as AB and BC, respectively. The shaded rectangle $OABC$ conforms to these two restrictions.

In Chart 15-9, the shaded rectangle $OABC$ meets three conditions:

1. Every point in the rectangle is positive, as required by the non-negativity conditions.

Chart 15-10

Triangle OEF Represents 1.25 x$_1$ + x$_2$ ≤ 2,500

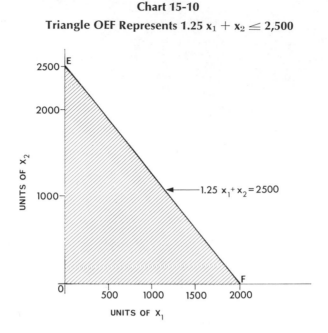

2. Every point in the rectangle fulfills the requirement that any quantity of x_1 produced be less than 1,500 units.

3. Every point in the rectangle fulfills the requirement that any quantity of x_2 produced be less than 2,000 units.

There is, however, another condition that must be met. It deals with the scarcity of labor denoted by the inequality.

$$1.25 \, x_1 + x_2 \leqslant 2{,}500 \tag{11}$$

Inequality (11) can be represented by a right-angle triangle (Chart 15-10) whose legs are the ordinate and the abscissa, and whose hypotenuse is the line

$$1.25 \, x_1 + x_2 = 2{,}500 \tag{12}$$

It is easy enough to plot this line. We need only to find two combinations of x_1 and x_2 that satisfy it. So, when $x_1 = 0$, $x_2 = 2{,}500$; similarly, when $x_2 = 0$, $x_1 = 2{,}000$; and we have the points E (0, 2500) and F (2000, 0) that determine line (12).

Every point in the triangle OEF (Chart 15-10) satisfies the inequality (11) and the non-negativity condition (9). The solution to the problem must then lie in the triangle OEF of Chart 15-10, and also in the rectangle $OCBA$ of Chart 15-9. Combining these polygons, we obtain Chart 15-11.

The pentagon $OCGHA$ in Chart 15-11 satisfies all the stipulated conditions. Any point inside the pentagon conforms to the plant capacity and labor restrictions. The pentagon $OCGHA$ is, therefore, called the feasible region.

Chart 15-11

The Pentagon OCGHA Is the Feasible Region

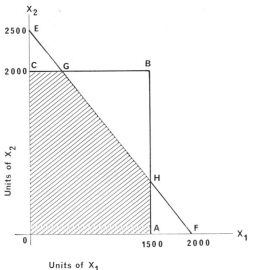

Units of X_1

A solution is now close at hand. We must choose a point in the feasible region that would maximize profit as defined by the objective function (7).

Trial and error will show that the solution must be as far as possible from the origin (Point O) and still remain within the pentagon $OCGHA$. For example, consider Chart 15-12, which reproduces the feasible region. The origin (O) is within the feasible region; but a solution at the origin yields a profit of zero dollars, because at that point $x_1 = 0$ and $x_2 = 0$.

Now, move away from the origin. At point P, $x_1 = x_2 = 600$; and the profit is $50 (600) + $30 (600) = $48,000. Move further from the origin to point Q. At Q, $x_1 = 1,000$ and $x_2 = 800$; and the profit is $50 (1,000) + $30 (800) = $74,000. At point R, $x_1 = 1,200$ $x_2 = 1,000$; and the profit is $50 (1,200) + $30 (1,000) = $90,000. We cannot proceed to point S, as that point is outside the feasible region.

Obviously, the solution must lie on the boundary $CGHA$. There would then be an infinite number of solutions. However, the profit from any combination produced is dependent on the profit margins for products x_1 and x_2. The profit relationship for x_1 and x_2 is expressed by the objective function

$$P = 50\ x_1 + 30\ x_2 \tag{13}$$

Equation (13) may be written in terms of x_2 as

$$x_2 = P - \frac{5}{3}\ x_1 \tag{14}$$

Thus, the objective function may be represented by a straight line, with an

Chart 15-12

Evaluation of Alternative Solutions

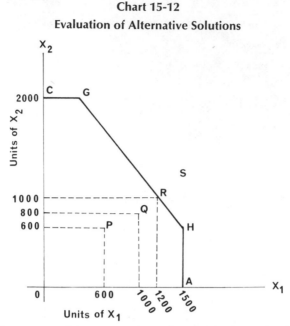

intercept P (unknown at this moment) and a slope of —5/3. A family of such lines (TT_1, UU_1, VV_1, XX_1, YY_1, and ZZ_1) is shown in Chart 15-13, which also includes the feasible region.

It has already been shown that the solution must

1. Lie on the boundary $CGHA$.
2. Be as far away from point O as possible.
3. Conform to the relationship expressed by the objective function.

The solution must then lie on any of the profit lines (TT_1, UU_1, VV_1, XX_1, YY_1) which is as far away from the origin as possible and still contain a point on the boundary $CGHA$. The solution is, therefore, at point H where

$$x_1 = 1,500$$

$$x_2 = \ \ \ 625$$

The maximum profit is then:

$$\$50 \ (1,500) \ + \ \$30 \ (625) \ = \ \$93,750$$

SOME LIMITATIONS OF LINEAR PROGRAMMING. A major limitation of this method is that it treats all relationships as linear. This means, of course, that if the cost of moving a ton of freight one mile is 10 cents, the cost to move it 100 miles will be considered to be $10, and so on. In most economic problems this is not true, for the most relevant relationships are not linear. But, as noted in Chapter 11, for many problems the range of relevance can be considered in linear terms. Also, for some problems dynamic programming may be

Chart 15-13
Family of Profit Lines

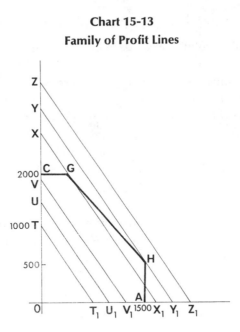

used, which is a method to adapt linear programming to nonlinear relationships.

Second, only those problems are amenable to solution with linear programming which have a number of characteristics, such as: a definite quantitative goal exists, such as most profit, lowest cost, etc.; resources to be allocated have an upper limit, such as capacity of a plant; resource alternatives can be compared; there is a common unit of measure; and the volume of alternatives can be managed.

Third, a large number of management problems have so many variables that the problem grows quickly into a size that linear programming cannot handle. In this event, simplification becomes essential. The issue then becomes one of whether the simplification goes so far as to destroy the usefulness of the conclusions.

Finally, linear programming is expensive. This is not a disadvantage, of course, when cost is less than benefit, but it is a restraining factor in the use of the tool.

BENEFITS OF LINEAR PROGRAMMING. There are many obvious advantages of this method. First, it can resolve some very complex problems which are not amenable to solution in more traditional or intuitive ways.

Second, it can be set up to provide a quick and inexpensive answer to many problems with which a decision-maker is faced and for which he needs a prompt answer. In mind, for example, would be an assessment of the profit implications of taking a few more orders, or the profit implications of deploying a fleet of trucks, or the profit implications of building a new factory.

PROBLEM EVALUATION AND REVIEW TECHNIQUE (PERT)

PERT is partially evolutionary—drawing from Gantt charting, line of balance, and milestone reporting systems—and partially a new creation. The concept of task interrelationships and their graphic representation is old, as noted in Chapter 13. The time and cost concepts, the critical path, and the computerized reporting system used in the technique, are new. The merger of the old and the new in PERT has been called a breakthrough in the art and science of management.

PERT is a powerful tool, when used properly, to facilitate the planning and control of complex programs involving considerable uncertainty. With it, managers can quickly identify schedule problems and allocate resources to overcome them. By cutting across organizational lines of a business it permits an examination of the entire system of activities encompassed in a company's programs. Because of its enormous power PERT was made mandatory in 1964 on larger Department of Defense and NASA contracts. It also has found wide usage in non-defense industry, a development which has been accompanied by PERT programs of most computer equipment manufacturers.

ORIGIN OF PERT. PERT was developed in 1958 by a special study group composed of C. E. Clark, D. G. Malcolm and J. Roseboom of Booz • Allen and Hamilton; R. Young and E. Lenna of Lockheed's Missile Systems Division; and W. Fazar of the Navy's Special Projects Office (SP). It was developed for the Polaris submarine weapon system because, in the words of W. Fazar (1962, pp. 3-4):

"By fall of 1957, it was clear that the various management tools, adopted, adapted or developed for Polaris and which had gained national plaudits for SP, did not provide certain information essential for effective program evaluation and decision making. Not one of these tools, nor all in combination, furnished the following kinds of vital information:

1. Appraisal of the validity of existing plans and schedules for meeting program objectives.
2. Measurement of progress achieved against program objectives.
3. Measurement of the outlook for meeting program objectives."

It was felt by those managing complex projects that the existing state of the art, reflected by bar charts and milestone reports, when applied to complex research and development projects, did not ferret out impending trouble spots quickly and were not adequate for control (Wattel, 1964, p. 42). The study team formed by the SP improved upon the existing technology, particularly the Critical Path Method used for project planning at DuPont, and added statistical considerations to allow for uncertainty. The result was PERT. While the government has always been concerned with predicting program outcomes in terms of

Chart 15-14

PERT Network

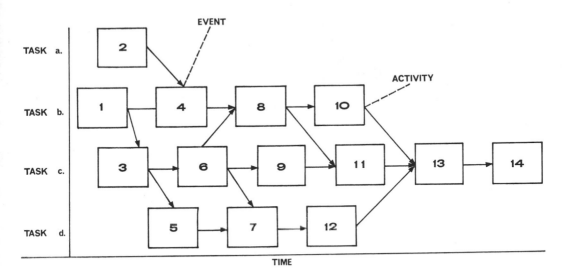

time, cost, and technical performance, the PERT used in 1958 was clearly concerned with time. This aspect of PERT generally became known as PERT/Time.

PERT/TIME. PERT/Time is a method of planning and control distinguished by four characteristics: the PERT network, time estimates, determination of slack and the critical path, and taking corrective managerial action, if necessary. The PERT network shows the sequential steps required to arrive at a predetermined objective. The network defines: (a) events, (b) activities, and (c) constraints.

An event is some specific milestone in a program. An activity is the effort required to arrive at that milestone. A constraint indicates the relationship of an event to a succeeding activity wherein an activity may not start until the event preceding it has occurred. Chart 15-14 is a PERT network of the events shown in the milestone Chart 4, Chapter 13. Just as the milestone chart is a refinement of the Gantt chart, the PERT networks of Charts 15-14 and 15-16 are modifications of the milestone chart.

PERT/Time estimates are based on: (a) planned resources, such as manpower or material, and (b) resource application rates, such as a forty-hour week. Generally, either one or three time estimates are required for each activity of a network such as the one shown in Chart 15-16. When only one time estimate is used, the technique may be called the Critical Path Method (CPM). The Critical Path Method is used in most deterministic projects, such as those of construction, where activity times are usually estimated with great accuracy. The need for more than one time estimate does not exist in those cases.

Chart 15-15

An Example of the Beta Distribution

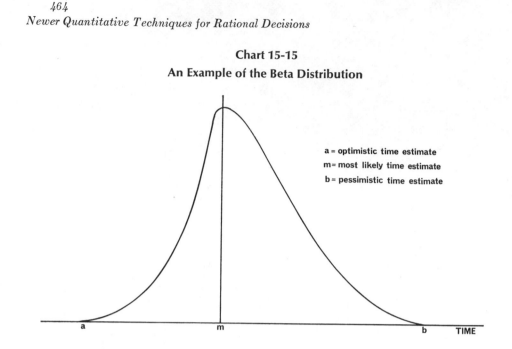

a = optimistic time estimate
m = most likely time estimate
b = pessimistic time estimate

In less certain cases it is recommended that three estimates, rather than one, be made for the time required to complete each activity. The three are: (*a*) the optimistic time, (*b*) the pessimistic time, and (*m*) the most likely time. There are several advantages to having these estimates. First, estimators may make more valid estimates if they can express the extent of their uncertainty. Second, if a single estimate is made it is likely to be the mode, but in estimating activity time the mean is a more representative estimate than the mode.

In more complex programs the uncertainty usually involved makes one time estimate suspect. PERT/Time solves the problem by assuming that the probable duration of an activity is beta-distributed. The beta distribution has the desirable properties of being contained entirely inside a finite interval (*a-b*) where *a* is the most optimistic time estimate and *b* is the most pessimist. The distribution is symmetric or skewed depending on the location of the mode, *m*, the most likely time estimate, relative to *a* and *b*. Chart 15-15 gives an example of one shape of the beta distribution.

The use of the beta distribution serves three purposes. The first is that an "expected elapsed time" (t_e) for an activity can be determined from the three time estimates: *a*, *b*, and *m*. Second, probabilities of completing an activity may be computed from the three time estimates. Thus, in programs with high uncertainty, managers may be able to speak of meeting schedules in terms of probability statements. Third, the use of the beta distribution provides a statistical foundation for the PERT network. The beta distribution is, of course, dependent on subjective time estimates of people.

To make statistical inferences about the timing of future events it is necessary to typify the intervals between adjacent events in terms of their expected values and variances. The expected value is a statistical term that corresponds to the mean. Variance (the square of the standard deviation) relates to the uncertainty associated with the process. If the variance of an activity is large, there is great uncertainty connected with the activity, and vice versa. Two simple equations will produce the estimate of mean and variance for ranges of distribution encountered.

The expected elapsed time, or the mean of the distribution is given by

$$t_e \frac{a + 4m + b}{6}$$

If $a = 5$ months, $m = 7$ months, and $b = 15$ months, the elapsed time, or mean will be 8 months. The mode is, of course, 7 months. The midpoint of the range (or midrange) is $(15 + 5) \div 2 = 10$ months. Note that the mean lies one-third the distance from the mode to the midpoint of the range.

The standard deviation, which is the basis of probability statements, is given by

$$\sigma = \frac{b - a}{6}$$

In the above time estimates, the standard deviation would be 1.67 months, a fairly large deviation (relative to a mean of 8 months) indicating considerable uncertainty.

When expected elapsed times (t_e's) are calculated for each activity they are summed throughout all the network paths to determine the total expected elapsed time for every path of the network. All parallel paths are assumed to be traveled simultaneously but the completion date of the program PERT'ed is dependent on the path which takes the longest time. This path has the highest total elapsed time and is called "the critical path." On Chart 15-16 the critical path is indicated by the heavy arrows.

The total elapsed time of the critical path determines the expected date (T_E) for the completion of the program. Similarly, the expected date of arriving at any event in the network is calculated by summing the elapsed times for each path leading to that event and choosing the highest sum. This is because no event can occur until all activities leading into it have been completed. In Chart 15-16 the expected elapsed times for the initial activities emerging out of Starting Event, for example, are twenty-three, six, and ten.

Once the expected elapsed times (or expected times) for all the activities are calculated, it becomes possible to determine the critical path. There are eleven paths from Starting Event to Production Contract Awarded in Chart 15-16. The critical path is the sum of the expected elapsed times of the series ten, forty-two, ten, five, thirteen, five, and eight. This adds to ninety-three, which is the longest path. The expected date (T_E) for the last event called Production Contract Awarded is then ninety-three.

The expected date (T_E) of any event in the network is calculated in the

Chart 15-16

PERT Network Showing Calculated Times and the Critical Path

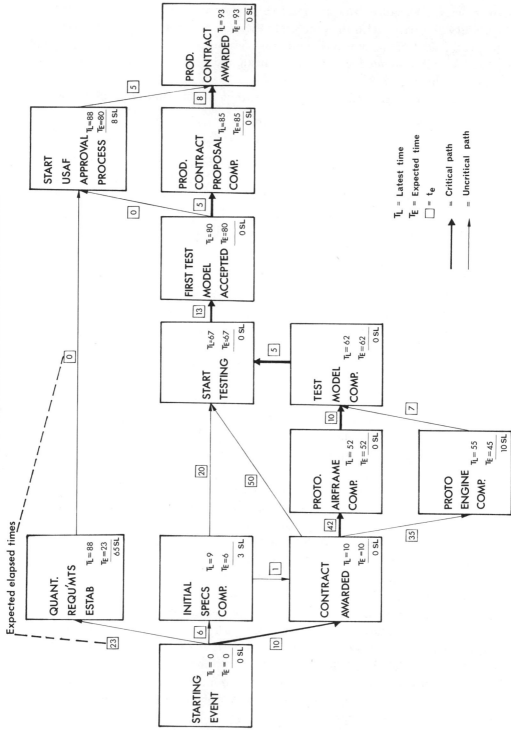

SOURCE: Air Force Systems Command, PERT – Time System Description Manual

same way. For example, there are five paths leading to the event Start Testing. These paths take 26, 31, 60, 57, and 57 units of time. The expected date (T_E) for Start Testing is, therefore, 67.

The latest date on which an event can occur without delaying the completion of the program is called the "latest allowable date" (T_L). In Chart 15-16, the latest allowable date for the end event of the program is assumed, either through design or coincidence, to be ninety-three. The slack, which is the difference between the latest allowable date (T_L) and the expected date (T_E) for the end event, is therefore zero for the example. Zero slack for a program is desirable, though by no means achievable at all times, and the conclusion should not be drawn from Chart 15-16 that expected program completion dates always equal program latest allowable dates.

The latest allowable date for any event in the network is calculated by working back from the end event along the longest path to that event. For example, there are two paths that go back from the end event to the event called First Test Model Accepted. The elapsed times of these two paths are five and thirteen. Therefore, the latest allowable date for the event First Test Model Accepted is ninety-three minus thirteen, or eighty. The slack for this event is also zero.

Slack, the difference between the latest allowable date and the expected date, is an index of the efficiency of a program. Positive slack is "time to spare." For example, the event called Quantity Requirements Established, of the network in Chart 15-16, has a positive slack, or "time to spare" of sixty-five. Events lying on uncritical paths have higher slacks than those lying on the critical path. The critical path is often, therefore, defined as the path with minimum slack. In planning a project, slack times can provide resources for tight schedules. If slack time is excessive, however, the entire network should be reviewed.

The importance of the network concepts described above may be expressed succinctly: if the latest allowable date (T_L) for any event occurs before the expected completion date (T_E) for that event, the manager has cause for concern because the program is falling behind schedule. He then may shift resources to correct the problem or take other appropriate corrective actions.

PERT/cost. PERT/Cost is an extension of PERT/Time, wherein a cost dimension is added. PERT/Cost is distinguished by seven features (USAF, 1963b, pp. 1.3-1.5):

1. A work breakdown structure,
2. Work packages,
3. Networks,
4. Time/Cost interrelationships,
5. Periodic updating of the networks and of the estimates,
6. Program evaluation, and
7. Taking corrective managerial action, if necessary.

Chart 15-17

Planned versus Actual Costs

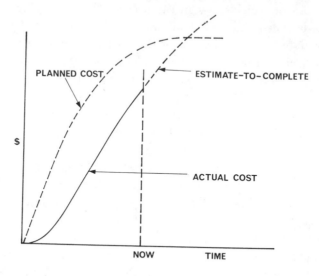

In PERT/Cost overall costs are broken down into successively smaller pieces of hardware, services, equipment, or facilities, until manageable units for planning and control are derived. These units are called work packages (e.g., wing or fuselage). Cost accounting numbers are assigned to the elements of the work packages and these accounting numbers serve to summarize costs of packages at all levels within the work breakdown structure.

Networks that interrelate activities and events for work packages are constructed as in PERT/Time. Either the program schedule, or the cost of the entire program may determine the amount of the physical resources assigned to a particular work package. The critical factor here is how any particular work package fits in the entire program. There is a trade-off between cost and time; generally, however, the schedule considerations of the entire program dictate the cost of an individual work package.

Once the time constraints for a work package are defined, the corresponding resources in terms of manpower, equipment, etc., are calculated. The latter in turn determine the time estimates of the network describing the work package. Time and cost estimates of the work package are then calculated, and each work package is assigned a budget on the basis of these estimates. Thus, a comparison of actual and budgeted amounts for the work accomplished can later be made at the work package level. By the same token, the summarization (or summation) of work package costs (or budgets) throughout the work breakdown structure determines the estimated cost (or budget) of the program within the time constraints used.

Periodically, an estimate-to-complete is made for each work package in progress. The sum of costs already incurred plus the estimate-to-complete determines the estimate at completion for the work package. A comparison may then be made between planned versus actual (including estimate-to-complete) costs, as shown in Chart 15-17 (U.S. Department of Defense and National Aeronautics and Space Administration, 1962).

The networks and the cost estimates are revised periodically to conform to actual and to planned changes in a program. From them, summary reports showing a breakdown of planned versus actual costs are constructed and help a manager to see where corrective action is necessary and possible. Furthermore, a manager is able to forecast future bottlenecks because the time networks can predict schedule slippages, and displays such as Chart 15-17 can predict cost overruns. The manager now has the tools to plan and control simultaneously the time and cost dimensions of his project.

THE USES OF THE PERT TECHNIQUE. In 1966 Jack Hayya identified almost 50 PERT-like techniques in use. Today there are probably 100 or more, and some of these techniques treat a wider range of management problems than PERT. For example, the Trade-off Evaluation System (TOES) developed by the Avco Corporation is a network model which integrates an analysis of the technical performance of a project with PERT/Cost (Diederich, 1962, p. 2). At the other extreme are simple network systems to introduce a product to a new market.

One major strength of PERT is its adaptability to many different management needs. It is not at all necessary that PERT be used completely in the text-book exposition of the method given above. It can be made quite simple and often used without computers. The management planning and control concepts upon which it rests are important and valuable in different situations.

PERT was introduced to help manage the Polaris Program, but it has found wide usage outside the aerospace industry (DeCoster, 1966). Climax Molybdenum Company, a division of American Metal Climax, Inc., reportedly schedules its around-the-clock mining operations with a PERT technique. In a more dramatic operation, a hospital has planned open heart surgery with the CPM technique. It is used widely in construction programs and has been exported to foreign countries (*Business Week,* 1962). It has been employed to program a Broadway play and was widely used by concessionaires for the New York World's Fair.

STRENGTHS AND WEAKNESSES. A system which has been made mandatory in larger military and NASA projects must have great managerial advantages. The major ones seem to be as follows:

First, it forces careful planning of the projects to which it is applied. In complex projects it is impossible to see how events and activities can be planned without fitting the pieces together in a network. Pioneer users of the PERT approach said that 80 percent of its management value was achieved in the initial planning of a project (Booz • Allen and Hamilton, Inc., 1962, p. 9). When PERT is used it assures that planning is done in an enterprise. PERT also forces the development of concrete and specific plans. Also, of course, it provides a solid basis for evaluating the results of plans.

Second, PERT permits simulation and, therefore, experimentation. In more complex and uncertain programs PERT can, when automated, permit managers to determine very quickly and with considerable precision the estimated time and cost implications of taking alternative courses of action. For a complex program such as Lockheed's giant cargo airplane the C-5A, for example, the human mind would be completely incapable of encompassing the many details required for planning. (I have seen computer print-outs of only parts of this program which spanned at least 100 feet!) With the successive summations permitted by the computer, managers are able to look at the entire program and determine appropriate changes in sequencing of events and resources devoted to them.

Third, PERT forces participation in the planning process and pushes it down the managerial line. Operating people make time estimates and in effect help to set objectives and goals in the plan.

Fourth, it permits effective control. Most progress reporting techniques provide management with historic information. PERT, on the other hand, lays a base for anticipatory management action against trouble spots by looking ahead at potential problems. Being forewarned, managers can take action to shift resources or undertake other measures to assure the necessary degree of control. By appropriate summation of data, PERT can provide different levels of management the needed information for each to exercise the proper control. PERT provides a much improved information system for managerial control. Furthermore, it permits concentration of action on the most critical problems because it identifies these problems, current as well as future.

PERT, however, is not without its limitations, especially if used in its classic form. First, in complex systems it can be rather expensive. More computations are required than in any comparable system and the costs can be prohibitive in small contracts. Hayya (1966) found that the Department of Defense was correct in not requiring PERT on contracts under $25,000,000 for this reason. Of course, costs can be reduced if only single time estimates are used.

Second, effectiveness of the method is reduced if estimates are inaccurate. If estimates are too poor, the results can be very serious. This problem may be intensified because there is no way to verify the network estimates. This means, of course, that this system like others is subject to human error. The better the estimates, the more valuable is the method to management.

Third, the aerospace industry has found problems in using PERT/Cost when the packages cut across organizational lines and do not agree with the functional lines on which basic accounting records are kept. While this was an important problem initially it has now been rather well corrected.

USING THE PERT APPROACH. PERT is a technique that cannot be used when the timing of events cannot be predicted, as in the case of basic research. It is usually not used when there exists a sequence of recurring events which are highly predictable, such as in a production line. Because of its comparatively high cost it generally is not used by small companies for small projects, at least in its textbook exposition. PERT is certainly not an "open sesame" to the solution of all management scheduling problems. It is a part of an integrated system of planning and control. Generally, it should not be superimposed on existing systems but should be introduced as an integral part of the company's system which may be modified in part to accommodate the PERT approach. When reasonably good single estimates of time can be made there is no need to have three estimates. When the number of events is less than 100, and single time estimates are used, the processing of information probably can be done by hand. Very important in the effective use of PERT, of course, is the human judgment that is involved in making estimates and allocating resources. Its use must depend upon the ability to make these judgments reasonably accurately.

In sum, PERT is an exceedingly adaptive and powerful managerial tool. When used in specific problems to which it is suited, it can strengthen managerial planning and control decisions over a wide spectrum of problems concerned with scheduling activities to achieve a specified optimum of time, cost, or both.

SUMMARY AND GUIDELINES

In this chapter the major newer quantitative techniques of special interest to top management have been discussed in some detail. They are probability theory, simulation, linear programming, and PERT.

It was concluded that these are very powerful tools of great value to those managers who know how to take advantage of them. Managers do not need to have a detailed expert knowledge of all these methods, but they do need an understanding of how the tools can be used and when and under what circumstances they are most appropriate or of comparatively little aid. Each technique has particular strengths in given situations and each is subject to weaknesses. These were discussed for each method and need not be repeated here. When a manager has a conceptual understanding of these methods he is in position to use his staff expertise more effectively and will know how to apply the methods to his own personality, values, and problems.

16
Management Information Systems

16

Management Information Systems

INTRODUCTION

Information systems are so obviously important in the management of a business that it seems unnecessary to dwell on the matter. But their great significance must be underscored. Without adequate and appropriate communications systems a business simply cannot operate. This applies to small as well as to large enterprises. Information flows are as important to the life and health of businesses as the flow of blood is to the life and health of an individual.

Communication within a business firm has two fundamental purposes. The first is to furnish the information necessary to make decisions to achieve the firm's network of aims. The second is to influence attitudes of people in such a way as to motivate them to direct their activities and interests in reasonable harmony with the firm's network of aims. The first is concerned more with knowledge, and the second deals more with motivation, but the two obviously are closely interrelated. While the attention of this and the next chapter is focused on the former, the latter should not be forgotten.

It is convenient and useful to divide the subject matter of management information systems into two parts. The first, included in this chapter, is concerned with the nature and needs of managers for information. The chapter examines the reasons for deficiencies in information systems and requirements for improving them. The second part, considered in the next chapter, is the present and potential role of computers in improving managerial information systems. A summary of these two chapters and a set of guidelines for developing business information systems will be presented at the end of Chapter 17.

CRITICAL TERMINOLOGY

The semantics associated with information systems is as muddy as any area in business planning. For this reason it is important to devote a little attention to some definitions of major importance in this area.

COMMUNICATIONS. The first rather all-embracing term needing clarification is communication. Communication is derived from the Latin *communis,* meaning common. "When we communicate," says Wilbur Schramm (1954, p. 3.), a long-time student of communications, "we are trying to establish a 'commonness' with someone. That is, we are trying to share information, an idea, or an attitude . . . The essence of communication is getting the receiver and the sender 'tuned' together for a particular message."

Communications is thus the process of conveying meaning from one person to another. It includes any means by which one mind affects another. This can be done by words, symbols, or a multiplicity of human actions—a gesture, a raised eyebrow, a smile, or other such actions.

A broader definition of communication is as follows: "In its broadest sense the term 'communication' refers to the whole process of man's life in relation to the group. It covers a vast and varied field of human action. All the basic social institutions—numbers, language, music, graphic art, science, religion, government—have the function of creating a community of thought, feeling, or action among people. The word 'communication' is therefore merely one way of designating the subject matter of education. Language, however, is the chief means of communication."*

Another definition, close to mine, is that of Keith Davis (1957, p. 228.), who says, "Communication in human relations is simply defined as the process of passing information and understanding from one person to another." A more technical definition is: "Communication is . . . a process for conducting the attention of another person for the purpose of replicating memories." (Cartier and Harwood, 1953, p. 74.)

These definitions stress three important aspects of communications. First, is transmission of ideas; second, is some vehicle for transmission; and third, is a receiver who understands what the sender has in mind. While understanding is a relative matter it is of major importance. A business seeks to achieve objectives, and people in the business are responsible for reaching them. Understanding of objectives and human actions to reach them is quite important. Other things being equal, the greater the understanding the more likely objectives will be achieved efficiently and effectively. I would agree with Scott's definition of communication as follows: "Administrative communication is a process which involves the transmission and accurate replication of ideas for the purpose of eliciting actions which will accomplish company goals effectively. Since administrative communication largely concerns people, the necessity for a high degree of understanding is implicit in the phrase 'accurate replication of ideas.' " (Scott, 1962, p. 173.)

* Reproduced from USAF Extension Course 3A, *Military Management,* Volume 1, "Communications Techniques," through the courtesy of the Extension Course Institute, Air University, Maxwell AFB, Alabama.

If these definitions are accepted, the study of communications covers a very broad area. Communications theory, at least so far as management is concerned, deals with communications in organizations that are managed. It embraces elements of many disciplines, to name a few: administration, behavioral science, mathematics, language, semantics, psychology, political science, and sociology. It has only been in the last handful of years that students of organizations have begun to work diligently on a theory of communications applicable to business.

INFORMATION. Information is a major part of that which is communicated. It is knowledge communicated or knowledge obtained by study and investigation. Information theory, therefore, would be concerned with the acquisition and transmission of knowledge.

These simple definitions are not generally accepted by some students of the subject. A prime characteristic of the above definitions is that the word information conveys the idea of meaning. Some definitions, however, have nothing to do with meaning but refer to information as ". . . a quantitative measure of the amount of order (or disorder) in a system." (Scott, 1967, p. 175.) * Others define information theory in quantitative terms.† Information theory is identified by others as being associated with such diverse disciplines as: ". . . thermodynamics, statistical mechanics, photography, language, models, gambling, cryptology, pattern recognition, and computer technology." (Johnson, Kast, and Rosenzweig, 1963, p. 76. These authors, however, share the broad view I have presented.)

INFORMATION CLASSIFICATION. John Dearden (1966, pp. 115-117.) has classified information that is found and used in a business into five dichotomy groups, all of which are required in planning.

Action vs. Nonaction Information. Action information, as the word implies, requires the recipient to do something when information is received. When an order is received from a customer, for example, specific action follows. Sometimes action may be delayed, as when a bill payable in 30 days is received. Nonaction information may be of several types; one type informs a manager that action has taken place, another may eventually become part of an action report, and another is that which comes from periodicals and books.

Recurring vs. Nonrecurring Information. Recurring information is that which

* Further, states Scott: "Information theory tells how much one needs to know in order to proceed from a state of uncertainty to a state of certainty about the organization of a system." (p. 175). This view is one probably first propounded by two pioneers of information theory, Shannon and Weaver (1949). They say: "The concept of information applies not to the individual messages (as the concept of meaning would), but rather to the situation as a whole . . ."

† See for example, Shull, Jr., 1958, p. 254, who says, ". . . the major characteristics and forces in communication are subject to quantification. A common term applied to this approach is *information theory*."

is generated at regular intervals. Included are a large number of reports in a business covering production, employment, financial conditions, and so on. Nonrecurring information is typified by special one-of-a-kind studies to aid a management decision, such as an analysis of firms which may be acquired.

Documentary vs. Nondocumentary Information. Documentary information is that which is preserved in some written form—punch cards, magnetic tapes, accounting reports. Nondocumentary information is transmitted orally or is received by an individual's observations.

Internal vs. External Information. The distinction here is obvious.

Historical Information vs. Future Projection. The distinction here also is obvious.

Classification, also, could be structured along functional planning informational requirements, such as information needed to plan for and control production, marketing, finance, research and development, employment, and so on.

BUSINESS INFORMATION SYSTEMS. A system, in the sense in which the word is used here, refers to a network of component parts developed to perform an activity according to plan or procedure. The activity here, of course, is flow of information. The system may be composed of procedures, equipment, information, methods to compile and evaluate information, as well as the people who operate and use the information.

It is obvious that each manager is the vortex of different informational systems from which he receives and to which he contributes. Information theory as applied to a business in its broadest terms embraces the study of all these systems. Or, it can pertain to but one element of the overall system, such as mathematical applications to control production, or analysis of the grapevine.

Most information systems embrace elements of many different disciplines and techniques. For example, a production control information system might include elements of disciplines such as linguistics, accounting, mathematics, and management. It might include a variety of transfer and processing methods, such as pattern recognition, computer programming, and command and control complexes. It might also involve both hardware and software, such as computer display equipment, control centers, graphic display equipment, closed circuit television, and general purpose computers.

INFORMATION TECHNOLOGY. Information technology is a word that some writers use to include the application of computers to informational processing.* Some writers refer to information technology as synonymous with the

* See Donald G. Malcolm, and Alan J. Rowe, *Management Control Systems*, New York, John Wiley & Sons, Inc., 1960, who observe: "Many writers have described the era of 'information technology' our society is now entering as one wherein the capability to formulate decision criteria precisely and to process information electronically will create markedly new patterns in management." (p. 187).

technical developments of information systems, such as computers, sensors, display equipment, radar, satellites, and so on. On the other hand, other writers have defined information technology much more broadly to include not only computer applications to management problems but new mathematical techniques as well. (Shultz and Whisler, 1960, p. 3.)

Business information technology, to me, embraces the methods to acquire, use, and disseminate knowledge required to operate a business effectively. This means hardware, software, techniques, plus principles governing their use. The principal difference between information technology and an information system is that the latter term includes people and their activities.

SEMANTIC CONFUSION. This somewhat detailed examination of nomenclature in the area of information theory is presented not with a view to resolving semantic conflicts, but rather to illustrate the confusion of terms which actually exists. It will be a long time before this thicket is torn down and replaced with a clear lexicon. For this reason students of information systems for business must be aware of the precise meaning of writers and practitioners in this field. What seems to make sense may, on further probing, be complete nonsense. And, what at first appears to be nonsense may, with clearer definitions, prove to be significant.

NATURE AND CAUSES OF INFORMATION SYSTEM DEFICIENCIES

In light of the essentiality of information systems to management one would expect to find superior systems in most businesses. This does not, however, square with the facts. In most companies the information systems are defective and are not considered by managements to be good enough. The reasons for this paradox are complex and deserve more than passing attention.

While much has been written recently about improving business information systems there has been little penetrating analysis of what defects exist in present systems and what has caused them. Defects are many and result from a multiplicity of forces. The following are found in most information systems and, because of their significance, cause important deficiencies in systems where they are present.

First, is a lag between organizational changes and information systems to support them. The typical information system in the typical company is designed to meet a set of needs, by specific managers, in a specific setting. As needs, managers, and circumstances change so should information systems. In one company with which I am familiar a serious financial problem forced the president of the company to require each morning a report of the previous day's operations. The report was very detailed and broke down costs to one-tenth of a cent for some items. Once the financial crisis had passed the reports still were made and it was some time before they were stopped.

It is a strange fact of organizational life that rarely does one find a change in informational systems correlated well with changes in organizational responsibilities and needs of managers. One reason may be that it is not easy to change information systems. Another is that managements have only recently become aware of important deficiencies in information systems. Whatever the underlying cause, the result is a much slower rate of change in information systems than in the user needs of the systems. The result is a sort of information lag.

Second, information systems are not usually coordinated with management needs on a company-wide basis. Information systems in most companies have, like Topsy, "just growed." The resulting systems show defects like the following.

The systems are fundamentally accounting systems. Accurate and appropriate reporting of accounting information is of the highest order of importance to a company. Accurate accounting reports are necessary to satisfy various legal obligations of a company, and are most useful in planning for and contracting the basic material operations of a company. This system is a major tool of management, but too many managements have thought of the basic informational needs to run their business only in accounting terms.

This is natural, for accounting information systems provide basic data on profit and loss, inventories, pay rates, production schedules, shipments, and other such activities, all highly important in managing a business. The very significance of accounting reports, however, is responsible for two glaring deficiencies in most business informational systems. One is the obfuscation of the meaning of accounting numbers by technical jargon. To the executive not trained in accounting, the nomenclature of accounting terms and methodology in many reporting systems is a major barrier to understanding. The trouble is that to satisfy a firm's legal responsibilities, accountants must be very careful and very technical. The result is, however, that the technical aspects of accounting have unnecessarily crept into reporting systems for internal managerial planning and control.

Another problem is that accounting systems do not provide major blocks of information needed by management. Accounting information deals with past and current activities inside a business. This information is usually in financial terms. But managers need a good bit of information that is not expressed in dollar terms, such as: share-of-the-market, customer complaints, absenteeism, parts turnover, product defects, and employee complaints. These should be systematically collected and included in management information systems. Furthermore, a steady and disciplined flow of information about what is going on outside the enterprise and what is likely to take place in the distant future is indispensable to the survival of a business. Information systems that have sprung from accounting roots without growing healthy branches to reach for this sort of information are inadequate. Empirical observation leads me to the conclusion that most companies do not have a suitable balance among these informational needs.

Arjay Miller (1958, p. 33), Vice-Chairman of the Board of the Ford Motor Company, has said: "We make very little use of the conventional financial statements, the balance sheet and the operating statement, in reporting to top management. These reports serve a useful purpose in summarizing the Company's current financial position, but they fail to answer the basic questions, 'Why are we where we are?' or 'Where are we headed?'"

Third, today's informational systems in many companies have not kept pace with new technological developments. Great strides have been made in recent years in computer technology and many companies have not profited from them. Some companies have tried to apply the new methods and have not been too pleased with the results. The reason for the most part, however, is misapplication of the technology or management's misunderstanding the critical role it must play in introducing it (Thurston 1959; Dale 1964; McKinsey & Co. 1962 and 1963).

Finally, the problem of building and changing informational systems is enormous and is a root cause of many defects in the systems. The marginal cost of making one or a few changes in information systems is usually well beyond the advantages desired. As a result, the accumulation of debris in the system proceeds until finally it becomes so patently defective that action is taken. Some years ago, for example, John McLean (1957, pp. 95-104.) when a consultant to the Continental Oil Company discovered that some 32 executives of that company received monthly operating reports having 12,000 separate figures. They simply could not digest this mountain of data and the system impeded rather than stimulated and guided action.

When top management decides its information systems need change, action follows. But generally this is a sporadic and not a systematic effort simply because of the difficulty and high costs of making changes.

INFORMATION SYSTEMS ARE FOR MANAGERS

The cornerstone requirement for excellent information systems is understanding of each manager's needs for knowledge. Information is management information only to the extent a manager needs and wants it. Information is useful to a manager only in terms of his scale of values, his accumulated knowledge, his personal responsibility, and the uses he has for it. This seems simple enough on the surface. But developing a manager's needs for information and devising a system to satisfy them is very difficult.

FUNDAMENTAL NEEDS FOR INFORMATION. Before examining problems in understanding management's needs for and production of information, it may be useful to set forth briefly some of the major categories of requirements. Why does an executive need information? He needs information, of course, to manage, to carry out his major functions of planning, organizing, directing, staffing, and controlling. But he faces specific problems in each area. More pointedly he wants information to help accomplish such diverse tasks as the following:

To set objectives for the company.

To formulate major strategies and policies to meet specific objectives.

To report to stockholders the results of operations of the business.

To pay taxes in conformance with law.

To inform the public of selected policies of his company.

To keep abreast of current operations of his business.

To inform employees of various matters.

To prepare long-range plans.

To be warned of major troubles that are ahead.

To see new opportunities that are ahead.

To allocate capital resources.

To exercise the necessary control over day-to-day operations.

To determine product price.

To permit management by exception.

To make decisions about specific matters as they arise.

To provide bases for giving pre-action approval.

To build proper background for outside contacts, such as with legislators, competitors, communities, and governments.

To aid his coaching and educating subordinates.

This list is by no means exhaustive but does illustrate the many varieties of reasons a manager wants information to flow to him or to have a system by means of which information he wishes to impart is transmitted in an appropriate and effective fashion. These type needs vary enormously depending upon many factors, such as the following.

SIZE AND COMPLEXITY OF THE FIRM. In very small companies with less than 50 or 100 people, informational systems are rather simple and center for the most part on the chief executive. He is in daily touch with his employees, gets around to the work areas frequently, and has first-hand and intimate knowledge of the internal operational aspects of his business. Without the means to build formal methods to collect and disseminate information about his environment he gradually develops informal systems to meet his needs.

As the size of companies grow, the need for more formal information systems also mounts. The larger the company the more complex becomes almost every aspect of operations and the more critical is the proper flow of information both with respect to internal and external affairs.

DECISION AREAS. In every business there are areas which are more important than others. These may be termed key decision areas. A parts supplier to the automobile industry must be very careful of his per unit costs. An aerospace company building a manned orbiting vehicle must give extraordinary attention to quality. An architectural and engineering company must be particularly careful about bids on contracts. When developing information systems every company must concentrate on the vital areas responsible for its success or failure.

While the key decision areas in an industry tend to remain the same, they may not have the same priority over time as different problems affect the company. Control of costs is an essential for survival in the automobile industry. Arjay Miller has noted changes in the priorities of cost controls at the Ford Motor Company. Following World War II administrative costs were more a function of recruiting management than acumen in holding down overhead. Manufacturing costs at the time were out-of-line competitively. As manufacturing costs were brought under control, top management's major problem was one of controlling costs designed into a product by stylists and engineers. Once this was brought under better control, attention was focused on an effective purchased material program based on indices of controllable and noncontrollable changes in material prices. Priorities on programs to control other costs were then established and a comprehensive integrated cost-control program was developed. (Miller, 1958, p. 31.)

Identifying the strategic decision areas is only part of the task. There remains the problem of determining what information is needed by different levels of management.

MANAGEMENT LEVELS. Managers at various levels not only need different types of information but need the same information in different forms. Enough has been said about the fact that the president of a company, for example, needs a vastly different mix of information than a manager close to day-to-day supervision of a functional area. Also, top managers want their information in a form different than lower-level managers. A foreman will want on a daily basis specific costs, for example, of men, materials, and machinery under his control. His plant manager may want this information on a weekly basis summarized into department, product, and total plant cost summaries. Top management of the company may wish only monthly reviews of these costs arrayed in higher aggregations. The Board of Directors may wish only annual reports in the form of a balance sheet and profit and loss statement.

ORGANIZATION STRUCTURE AND AUTHORITY. The organizational structure of a company and lines of authority and responsibility must be understood before informational needs of managers at different levels can be established. A highly centralized organization such as an oil company has much different informational flows than a highly decentralized multiproduct company. Degrees of authority will have an important bearing on informational needs. Clearly, also, a chief executive who wants to make all the decisions must have more and different information than one who does not, given the same organizational and economic characteristics.

For a manager to know what his information needs are he must understand clearly his authority and responsibility, his relationships with other managers in other areas, and how he wishes to delegate authority. One major problem in many companies in defining managerial information needs rests in the fact that organizational lines of authority are unclear. In such a situation a manager is hard-pressed to define his needs for information.

MANAGERIAL STYLE. Managers vary a great deal in the way they want to manage. This was partly noted above in commenting upon the relationship between delegation of authority and informational needs. There are other aspects to the matter. Some managers like to get mountains of data, others try to get as little as possible. Some managers like to read reports, others prefer to hear information orally. Some managers like to deal with subordinates on a face to face basis, others deal principally through reports. Some managers deal only with certain problems of their choosing, others let themselves be the victims of expediency. A manager with a technical background may wish his reports to concentrate on technical information. A manager with an accounting background may emphasize accounting reports. Any effort to construct or reform informational systems in a company is doomed to failure if it does not rest on a deep appreciation of these different styles of management, and a thorough knowledge of how the managers affected by the system feel about such matters.

MANAGEMENT'S PERCEIVED NEED FOR KNOWLEDGE. What a manager perceives to be his need for information may differ from what an objective observer may think he needs to perform his job successfully. If a company, for example, runs afoul of the antitrust laws a legal counsel in Washington, D.C., may see a very different need for information than the president of the company involved. The president may be frightened and place a crushing burden on his staff for information. Or, he may be ignorant of what he must know and get too little information.

Another aspect of this condition is what might be called "the data gap." Every manager accumulates his own knowledge about his business which he applies to his problems. His informational systems bring additional knowledge. Unfortunately, there are informational voids between these patterns of knowledge and what is needed with a particular problem. Furthermore, these voids widen and narrow among problems and over time. Understanding the dimensions of these gaps is a prerequisite to the development of information systems.

A major problem is to determine to what extent these gaps should be filled by formal informational systems or by staff work. It is an important duty of staff to detect and rectify such gaps in a manager's storehouse of knowledge. This is not easy to do, and often it accounts for staff innundation of managers with irrelevant information in the hope the gap can be filled. This task is not made easier when managers do not know the dimension of their knowledge deficiency, or are reluctant to display their factual ignorance to subordinates. (Dwyer, 1962, p. 17.)

A MANAGER'S LEVEL OF KNOWLEDGE REQUIREMENTS. David Ewing has cogently pointed out that a manager of a business needs several levels of knowledge. By level he means differences in texture, structure, use, and origin. He observes three levels which, while different at the extremes, merge into each other and intermingle.

The first level is that of methods and techniques. A lawyer uses his knowledge of the law, court procedure, and methods to serve a client. An engineer uses his understanding of methods to build a bridge. Similarly, an administrator uses knowledge about how to solve problems. In mind is knowledge about how to schedule production, lay out a plant, acquire another firm, or install a comprehensive planning system in his company.

The second level is knowledge about reality, about environment. This knowledge concerns such things as the profitability of his company, whether the government is going to take an action which will influence the company, and what sales are likely to be in the future.

The third level has to do with what managers want to happen, conditions they wish, and goals they seek. This level of knowledge is deeply involved in the realm of values. It includes understanding of motivations of people, imaginative insights about individuals and organizations, value systems, and ideas. This type knowledge comes from long experience but also is developed as a manager grows intellectually and as he becomes more aware of his role in administering a business. The level of knowledge in mind here does not deal so much with facts, as do the other two, but is heavily weighted with ideas and intangible bits of knowledge.

Informational flows to satisfy these three levels will be different. So will the capability of individual managers in handling information at these levels. (Ewing, 1964, pp. 127-139.)

MANAGEMENT'S PERCEIVED NEED TO DISSEMINATE KNOWLEDGE. Managers have widely differing views on their obligations to disseminate information—to outside groups and to employees. Views about such matters will vary much from one company to another and among managers within any company. A manager who wishes to keep his employees well-informed about company policy and activities may set up formal informational systems to do this. Many larger companies have public relations staffs to manage dissemination of information to the general public.

MANAGEMENT'S KNOWLEDGE OF INFORMATION TECHNOL-
OGY. What information a manager says he wants will often depend also upon
what he thinks he can get. A manager may wish to have immediate detailed
information about prospective markets for a new exotic product but, knowing he
cannot get it, he will not ask for it. Or, if he does ask for information, his request
will be tempered with an understanding that he wants only "rough estimates." A
manager who understands the capabilities of new computer equipment may ask
for a system which will permit him to have immediate graphic displays of various
forces at play in his business. Or, he may ask for a computerized model of his
business to permit him to make estimates of probable future changes to see the
impact on the financial picture of his company. Naturally, cost relative to need
is an important element in his request.

TIME. The timing of information naturally is important in the development of an information system. Some information is needed daily, some weekly,
some at greater time spans, and some only sporadically. For some classes of information the time span will be dictated by imposed need, such as annual financial
data. For other data, the time requirement will vary with a manager's interests
and line of business.

CONCLUSION. Ralph Cordiner (1965, p. 102*), when Chairman of the
Board of General Electric, commented on the difficulties of developing information systems as follows: "It is an immense problem to organize and communicate
the information required to operate a large, decentralized organization . . . This
deep communication problem is not solved by providing more volume of data for
all concerned, by faster accumulation and transmittal of conventional data, by
wider distribution of previously existing data, or by holding more conferences.
Indeed, the belief that such measures will meet the . . . (management information)
challenge is probably one of the great fallacies in business and managerial thinking. What is required, instead, is a far more penetrating and orderly study of the
business in its entirety to discover what specific information is needed at each
particular position in view of the decisions to be made there."

In light of what was said above a manager may not be joking when he says
he does not know what information he needs. Even when he considers the
matter very carefully he may not come to a conclusive answer. If he does, the
answer may be different in the near future.

The ultimate goal of information systems is to assure that all managers at
all levels are suitably informed, and within appropriate cost, on all developments
which affect them. To do this it is perfectly obvious from the above discussion
that different information systems are required. Any assertions that a single

* From *New Frontiers for Professional Managers* by Ralph J. Cordiner. Copyright ©
1956 by the Trustees of Columbia University. Used by permission of McGraw-Hill Book
Company.

information system can fulfill the informational needs of a business manager are complete nonsense. It should also be clear that the informational systems cannot be moved from one firm to another without important modification. Management needs, style, setting, authority, problems, and other characteristics differ and affect information systems.

While these considerations make the development of information systems a difficult task, it is manageable. The remainder of this chapter is devoted to an explanation of why.

MAJOR INFORMATION SYSTEMS

Information systems may be classified into major and minor systems. Following are the major systems:

ACCOUNTING. The accounting informational system is necessary to develop the vital statistics of a business. It is the first system a business sets up and is the central trunk of any future system of informational flows. The accounting informational system, of course, is composed of many subsystems. Data are needed to comply with governmental regulations, to provide periodic financial reports to stockholders, and to furnish managers at all levels the basic financial facts of the enterprise. The accounting system may provide information on many specific factors such as: profits, standard costs, overhead costs, direct costs, cash flows, break-even analysis, and so on.

PERSONNEL. Most companies maintain much information dealing with employees. Included would be such facts as number of employees, wages paid, loss in production hours, overtime, and measures of labor efficiency (the accounting system in some companies may include this system).

MATERIAL FLOWS. Included in this informational system would be facts about the physical flow of goods through a company, including incoming raw materials, facilities, production, shipments, inventories, and comparable matters.

PERIODIC PLANNING INFORMATION. If a company has a comprehensive planning system it will, of course, need a special type of information on a cyclical basis. This has been discussed before and needs no further elaboration here. In the absence of such a system, a firm may have an annual budgeting program which will provide information combining that in the previous two systems plus goals for the future. This, too, was discussed fully in earlier chapters.

SPECIAL REPORTS. Larger companies require special reports dealing with matters of current or future interest. In mind here are the type reports a long-range planning department will prepare for top managment on future environmental changes; acquisition possibilities; or special internal problems such as changing facility replacement policy. While this system is by no means as formalized as the above systems it is important and must be included here. It also overlaps with the periodic planning cycle and its informational flows.

THE GRAPEVINE. There may be objection to including this informal communications system in this classification of major systems, but it exists in every enterprise, is an important source of information, and is useful in disseminating information. By any standard it is a major information system.

SCANNING. Scanning involves simply an exposure to and perception of information. (Aguilar, 1967, p. 18.) The activity can involve getting information by rigorous methods, such as collecting data about new markets, by statistical sampling, to unstructured conversations with friends. Every manager uses scanning to cover a wide range of his informational needs.

Chart 16-1 shows one model of informational flow in a scanning process to get knowledge for making strategic decisions. The company is in the chemical industry (Aguilar, 1967, p. 170).

MINOR INFORMATION SYSTEMS

Designating the minor information systems is partly a matter of preference, and partly a function of the industry.* Each of the above systems can be divided into subsystems. The following minor systems can be a part of the above major systems.

COMPETITIVE INFORMATION. Too few companies maintain any systematic informational flows about competitors, but all should. Whether formalized or not, most all companies are concerned about information on what competitors are doing and are likely to do. Retail stores often have scouts to survey pricing of competitors. Automobile companies very carefully try to calculate the styling and pricing of competitors' products.

RESEARCH AND DEVELOPMENT. These systems may vary much from one company to another. Included may be network systems, research project selection data, and technical data. For a company that is highly technically-oriented, like an aerospace company, the research and development information system should be a major and not a minor system. Project managers in the aerospace industry have well organized and comprehensive systems of informational flows to and from government monitors of their work. Product managers in com-

---

* John Dearden classifies as major systems those pertaining to financial, personnel, and logistics information. His minor systems are illustrated by marketing information, research and development, strategic planning, and executive observation. (1965, pp. 73-85).

Chart 16-1

The Relative Amount of Strategic Information Obtained
by Gemca's Top Management from Different Sources*

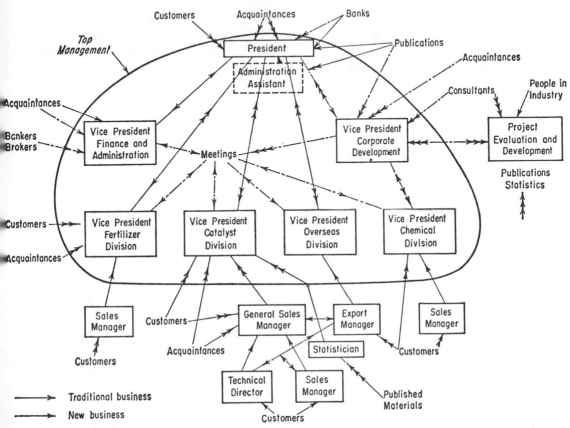

* The relative importance of the flow of strategic information is roughly indicated by the number of the arrowheads: the more numerous the arrowheads, the more important the source of information.

mercial enterprises have very different informational systems to facilitate their work.

SALES FORECASTING. When the time comes for the annual sales forecast to help fix next year's budgets, many companies as noted previously follow a detailed procedure to develop this information.

SPECIAL SYSTEMS. To meet special problems, or to keep abreast of unusual events, temporary systems of information flows may be set up. During World War II and the Korean War, for example, all metal-using companies had to maintain special reporting and control systems concerning their uses of so-called "controlled materials." An aerospace company president set up a special reporting system on details of operations when a major project fell behind schedule and showed a substantial overrun. During a merger a company president will create a special information system.

OTHER INFORMATION SYSTEMS. To conclude this discussion it may be noted that this listing does not exhaust sub- or minor systems. Also, in any company the subsystems vary from time to time and will differ from those of other companies. They, together with the major systems, will vary much in their interrelationships.

It should not be inferred, of course, that all these are well-tailored, consistent, unified, and complete systems, for none of them are. There is, however, a hard-core of consistency and coordination in these systems.

DIFFERENCES AMONG INFORMATION SYSTEMS

The enthusiast who wants to integrate completely management information into one comprehensive system will ignore differences among these systems at his peril. If the basic conceptual model of a comprehensive planning system presented in Chapter 2 is considered, it is perfectly obvious that the different systems discussed above have differing applicabilities. For example, the accounting, material flow, and personnel systems may have very little value, as compared with scanning, in changing the basic purposes of an enterprise. They will have more applicability in strategic planning but not nearly as much there as in the preparation of one-year budgets, or in the day-to-day management of the company. The importance of the major systems and their subsystems also will vary much from one company to another, and within the same firm. For example, a critical path information system may be of prime importance to the president of an architectural and engineering firm during an early construction program. Such a system is of first importance to a project manager who is laying out his engineering development program. The president of his company, however, may have no interest whatever in the results but may want to know what the total cost of the project is likely to be to get an operational prototype.

The applicability of different systems to planning as compared with control will vary much. Daniel (1961, p. 114) has distinguished information system characteristics for these two functions, as follows: *

Planning information:
  • transcends organizational lines
  • shows trends; covers long time periods
  • nonfinancial data important
  • lacks minute details

* Daniel's definition of planning in this article is more akin to our concept of strategic planning and his concept of control, presumably, is more of the day-to-day variety.

- future-oriented

Control information:
- follows organizational lines
- covers short time periods
- nonfinancial data importance
- very detailed
- past-oriented

Systems vary enormously in the extent to which they may profit by computerization. Some companies, for example, find a computerized PERT program to be indispensable. Most companies find computers of major advantage in setting up their accounting, personnel, and logistics systems. One obviously cannot computerize the grapevine, but computers may be helpful in scanning by compiling information.

REDESIGNING THE INFORMATION SYSTEMS

There are three ways to tackle the task of redesigning information systems. The first is the spasm approach. This is a "quickie" examination of current systems, undertaken to spot obvious duplications or to add new sources and flows of information. These undertakings usually are fruitful but do not go far enough and are made too infrequently. A second approach is to mount a thorough-going study of information needs and the systems to meet them. The third is to charge a person or a staff with responsibility to review continuously the major information systems and to keep them up-to-date. The latter two methods are obviously the preferred ones.

The first step in a systematic review of information systems is to select a project leader to head a small task force to do the work. Frequently, when this method is used, the controller is made group leader. This is natural because he is custodian of so much of the information concerning the company's operations. It is important, however, to choose a controller for this post only when he is broad-gauged enough in his thinking to understand thoroughly the needs of managers for both financial and nonfinancial types of information. The required capability on the part of the controller must go well beyond a mere recognition of these needs. It must extend to his capacity and willingness to conceive and design a system to develop the detailed types of information needed by managers at all levels and among different functions. A controller whose experience is wholly financial, and who insists that all reports be balanced to the last penny, is too narrow for this task. There are also others, of course, who can head such a team—a special assistant to a top manager, someone from the long-range planning department, or an outside consultant. The team should include a person well versed in new and evolving information technology.

The next step is for the team to examine the informational requirements of managers, taking into consideration all the factors that influence management needs for information noted previously in this chapter.

The next step is to design the systems to fulfill these needs, a step which must be taken with the full participation of managers. One of the difficulties in recent years in the development of integrated data processing systems has been that computer experts have devised the systems without much conversation with managers. McKinsey and Company several years ago surveyed computer applications of 27 large companies and concluded that: ". . . computer-systems success is more heavily dependent on executive leadership than on any other factor. No company achieved above-average results without the active participation of top management. And where corporate management in effect abdicated its responsibilities, the results were seldom outstanding." (McKinsey and Company, 1963, p. 13.) Technicians, no matter how skilled, cannot alone make decisions about what information managers need.*

Once the systems are developed they should be reviewed and approved by management. For some systems of major significance a hand simulation might be useful to determine feasibility and practicality of results. In 1942 when the Controlled Materials Plan was developed by the War Production Board to allocate scarce metals to American industry, the preliminary reporting requirements were hand simulated. It was found that to run the system on the basis of the original plans would result in a train of freight cars loaded with report forms reaching Washington, D.C., each month. The system was then changed from a monthly to a quarterly reporting cycle and the number of metal shapes and forms on the reports was reduced drastically.

A third method to control information systems is to assign a person or group to study them continuously. In a number of larger companies information systems departments have been established. These departments for the most part, however, have been more responsible for managing computers than for designing overall systems.

---

* This point is made forcefully in Thurston 1962, pp. 135-139.

17
Computers and Management Information Systems

17
Computers and Management
Information Systems

INTRODUCTION

In the last chapter the nature and characteristics of business information systems was discussed. While the fundamental conclusions reached in that chapter will be applicable for a long time to come, the precise way they will be reflected in future informational systems will be much different than in the past. The principal reason for this is growing computer technology.

This chapter summarizes those evolving trends of computer technology which will have the most important impact on business information systems, hypothesizes about the impact of these trends on business information systems, discusses the ways in which business information systems are likely to change, and, finally, presents the more important guidelines for the development of business information systems.

GROWTH OF COMPUTERS IN BUSINESS
INFORMATION SYSTEMS

The modern computer traces its roots back more than 250 years to Pascal, Leibnitz, and Babbage. It was not until 1951, however, that the first business data were fed into a computer,* and it was not until 1954 that a corporation installed a large computer unit. From then on, however, the growth of computer usage has been nothing short of explosive. This growth has paced a remarkable change in business information technology which is destined to continue.

Computer usage has grown rapidly in business information systems because

* For an excellent history of calculating and data processing machines see Robert H. Gregory and Richard L. Van Horn, *Automatic Data Processing Systems*, San Francisco, Wadsworth Publishing Company, 1960, pp. 624-631.

of its unexcelled power. It is well known that computers are unsurpassed in meeting certain types of business informational requirements, such as:

- Large amounts of information need to be stored, added, or processed.
- A large number of interacting variables must be related or analyzed before a problem can be solved.
- Repetitive activities exist the decisions for which can be made more or less automatically by a computer model.
- Accuracy is important or useful.
- Cost per unit of data output should be low.

Over the past ten to twelve years the capability of computers to meet these needs has galloped ahead spectacularly.* These informational processing requirements vary among the information systems discussed previously. In some, such as the accounting and personnel information systems, computers have found major employment. Insurance companies, for example, with their massive record-keeping requirements were among the first to see the great advantages of computers for their data systems. Practically all larger companies have put personnel information on computers. Computers are used very widely in planning for and controlling incoming materials, the production line, inventories, and shipments of finished goods. Computers are finding increasing use in annual planning programs, ranging from the tabulations of budgets to the aggregations of data over the full range of long-term plans. Special reports, of course, take advantage of computers' power. Many of the quantitative techniques discussed in previous chapters are "computerized" to strengthen reports, such as linear programming, econometric models, and decision trees. Among the major information systems only the grapevine is not particularly amenable to computer usage. Scanning is a growing user of computers because of its needs for storing masses of data from which information can be retrieved quickly and analyzed.

The widespread use of computers in business operations is summarized in Table 17-1 which shows the results of a survey of computer usage among 261 companies. It is clear that three-fourths of the firms reviewed use information from computers to measure performance against standards, make decisions, evaluate progress, and forecast. This study asked respondents to specify the type of information which computers provided in different areas. A higher percentage of responding firms use computers to provide information about sales and customers than for any other purpose. The next highest area of response relates to finance; the next to goods produced; and the lowest to manpower.

Manufacturers of nondurable goods are more advanced in the use of computers than are those producing durable goods, or services. (Higginson, 1965, p. 55.)

---

* For excellent resumes of past accomplishments see Nisenoff, 1966, pp. 1820-1835; and Opler, 1966, pp. 1757-1763.

The above survey is impressive in terms of the across-the-board volume of computer applications. Unfortunately, no broad sampling exists of computer usage in terms of sophistication of problem solving. The first important applications of computers were designed to handle routine transactions, mostly of accounting work. The next era of applications dealt with somewhat more difficult problems: inventory control, production scheduling, cash control, finished production distribution. At about the same time, however, some productive facilities, e.g., refineries, were completely automated. A little later some companies, e.g., airlines, developed large integrated information systems.* Empirical observation supports the view that most computer applications today are in the first and second groupings, but the spread of new uses for harder problems is indeed rapid.

COMPUTER-BASED MANAGEMENT IS INEVITABLE

This statement can mean several things, but to me it means that managers in the future, at all levels, will rely importantly on computers in their decision-making. It means, further, that the elements of the information system of the business will be automated. An information system is composed of five basic components, as shown in Chart 17-1. In a manual system, human beings perform

Table 17-1 Use of Computers in Planning, Controlling, and Administering

PURPOSE	NO. OF COMPANIES
Planning:	
Evaluating progress	231
Forecasting	220
Setting objectives	186
Allocating resources	157
Seeking new products, companies, markets	135
Controlling:	
Measuring performance	236
Setting standards	179
Administering:	
Decision-making	227
Communicating	146
Coordinating	142
Delegating	72

Source: M. Valliant Higginson, *Managing with EDP, A Look at the State of the Art* (New York: American Management Association, 1965), p. 53.

* For illustrations see Shultz and Whisler, 1960; Higginson, 1965; Gentle, Jr., 1960; and Gallagher, 1961.

Chart 17-1
Basic Components of an Information System

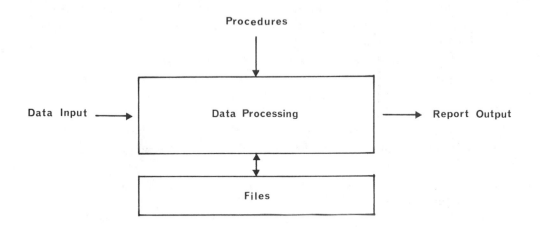

Procedures

Data Input → Data Processing → Report Output

Files

the five basic functions. In a computer-based system these functions are performed by equipment. On the input side, source data collection devices or optical character recognition equipment is used. The process of computing, of course, is done by high-speed computers with included procedures in stored programs. Files embrace any one of many storage media: high-speed core memory, magnetic tapes, discs, drums, or photographic retrieval devices. The outputs also may be of different sorts: high-speed printer, punched cards, remote typewriter, or remote display consoles. (Rowe, 1967.) Implicit in this system are remote inquiry consoles that can be used to interrogate files and manipulate data.

To say that future management will be computer-based does not mean there will be complete reliance on the computer, or that one massive integrated information system will be found in the typical company. It does mean that computers will become increasingly important to and a dominant tool at all levels of management. This view is justified by anticipated evolving technological trends, discussed in the next section, and their clear implications for management information systems.

MAJOR EVOLVING COMPUTER
TECHNICAL TRENDS

Rapid technological developments, in both computer software and hardware, make somewhat hazardous any predictions of future computer systems and their implications for business informational systems. (Software refers to procedures and routines associated with computers. Included would be program directions, compilers, library retrieval routines, documents, and manuals needed for the operation of the machines. Hardware refers to the physical equipment which makes up a computer system; such as mechanical, magnetic, electrical, and optical equipment. Cabinets, display panels, keyboards, etc., are hardware.) Nevertheless, current and near-term future computer technology advances are reasonably clear and their implications for business information systems can be projected with some accuracy.

First, past and current trends will continue for increasing computer speed, raising storage capacity, reducing storage space, and lowering cost per unit stored. The dimensions of these trends during the past ten to fifteen years have been most impressive. With the three generations of computers produced during this time period, storage costs in dollars per million additions have dropped from $10 to 1¢; and computing speed has jumped from 500,000 additions per second to one billion per second.

The development of large-scale integrated circuits, which can contain thousands of active electronic elements on a single small silicon chip, will assure the continuation of trends such as these. By 1975 central computer processing speeds may be increased by a factor of 200, central computer processing units reduced in size by a factor of 1,000, costs cut by a factor of 500, and total U.S. computing power raised by a factor of 1,000. (Boehm, 1967.) Large-scale random access memories will have capacities up to 100 billion bits. Optical character readers will be available with a capability of handling from 500 to 1,000 characters per second and with a cost of up to ten times less than key punching.

The precise accuracy of such forecasts is not so important here as the certainty of the direction. These trends will permit the development of giant data banks where retrieval is fast and inexpensive. The implications for business data systems, as will be discussed in a moment, are enormous.

Second, computer time-sharing will grow rapidly. Time-sharing makes it possible today for many separate customers, using their own desk-top keyboards or Teletype machines, to put data in a central computer and to get back answers over a telephone line. Not only does this development permit an important reduction in the cost of computers to each user but makes it possible to gain immediate access to data base stores not otherwise available. As the number of customers that tie into such a system increases the cost per customer naturally will drop to a fraction of what a computer would cost.

Time sharing is in practice today and will grow rapidly in the future. G. J. Feeney has set the stage in these words: ". . . in terms of technology that exists right now, if 200 individuals get together—or are brought together by an entrepreneur—they can have desk-side access to a system that will look to each of them like a 16K—50—100 micro second processor with a million-character supporting file system, a comprehensive compiler, enough software to get into and out of the system and maintain program and data files with relative ease, and a teletype keyboard and printer with paper tape attachment as the input-output device, all for about $10 per hour. While no existing system quite comes up to these performance *and* cost specifications it is safe to say that such systems will be fairly common next year and will be very widely available the year after. And we can anticipate that they will provide increasing performance scope and decreasing unit cost as time passes." (Feeney, 1967, p. C-114.)

Third, is simplification of man's ability to "speak" to the computer. In recent years there has been a move toward the standardization of languages to program computers. Today, three languages are widely used—Algol, Fortran, and Cobol. There are, of course, a great many special languages, such as those needed for telecommunications, graphics, simulation, or language translation.

Another important direction is toward implicit or descriptive language. In the above languages, the operator writes actions to be done in the performance sequence required. In an implicit language, the writer describes the initial status, and the desired final status, of his computation and a processor called a compiler then develops a program to meet the requirement. They are programs that translate instructions of one language (other than machine language) into an acceptable program for a computer. Furthermore, compilers are now available to permit the easy application of a language developed for one machine to be used on another. (Opler, 1966, p. 1761.) For example, a program developed for the IBM 7094 can be run on the IBM 360 with the use of an off-the-shelf compiler.

The language with which a businessman can communicate with a computer is getting simpler and simpler. For example, the RAND Corporation has had in operation since January 1964 its JOSS (Jonniac Open-Shop System) in which ten remote typewriter consoles are served concurrently by time sharing in one central computer. With but one easy-to-learn typewritten page of instructions (Table 17-2) this system permits a user, working with a standard key typewriter, to converse with the computer in a fashion illustrated in Table 17-3.*

Experiments are now being made to permit speaking in the English language directly to the computer. This is proving to be a tough problem to solve, but it may be developed in the not too distant future. (Grosch, 1967, pp. 42-47.)

Fourth, very rapid strides will be made in computer graphics. This is a new and exciting technology made operational only since 1963.† Computer graphics refers to the concept of man's communication with computers by means of graphical symbols, such as lines, curves, dots, and so on. The equipment to communicate with the computer is a cathode ray tube, a light pen or voltage pencil, and a function keyboard. The graphic input is made by a light pen or

* For a description of this and comparable systems see Chasen and Seitz, 1967, pp. 48-55. Also Shaw 1965, p. 3149.

† The first significant presentation was by I. E. Sutherland when he described his "Sketchpad" work at Lincoln Laboratories in 1963. The Lockheed-George Company began to develop its Man-Computer Graphics System in 1964, and other operational systems began from that time. (Chasen and Seitz, 1967, p. 51.)

Table 17-2   JOSS One-Page Summary

DIRECT or INDIRECT

Set x = a.

Do step 1.1.
Do step 1.1 for x = a, b, c(d)e.
Do part 1.
Do part 1 for x = a(b)c(d)e, f, g.

Type a, b, c, ——.
Type a, b in form 2.
Type "ABCDE."
Type step 1.1.
Type part 1.
Type form 2.
Type all steps.
Type all parts.
Type all forms.
Type all values.
Type all.
Type size.
Type time.
Type users.

Delete x, y.
Delete all values.

Line.

Page.

INDIRECT (only):

1.1 To step 3.1.
1.1 To part 3.

1.1 Done.

1.1 Stop.

1.1 Demand x.

DIRECT (only):

Cancel.

Delete step 1.1.
Delete part 1.
Delete form 2.
Delete all steps.
Delete all parts.
Delete all forms.
Delete all.

Go.

Form 2:
dist. = ... accel. = ——.——

  x = a.

RELATIONS:

   $= \neq \leqslant \geqslant < >$

OPERATIONS:

   $+ - \cdot / * () [] ||$

CONDITIONS:

   if $a < b < c$ and $d = e$ or $f \neq g$

FUNCTIONS:

sqrt (a)	square root
log (a)	(natural logarithm)
exp (a)	
sin (a)	
cos (a)	
arg (a, b)	(argument of point [a, b])
ip (a)	(integer part)
fp (a)	(fraction part)
dp (a)	(digit part)
xp (a)	(exponent part)
sgn (a)	(sign)
max (a, b)	
min (a, b, c)	

PUNCTUATION and SPECIAL CHARACTERS:

   , ; : ' " —— # $?
   ——.—— indicates a field for a number in a form.
   . . . . indicates scientific notation in a form.
   # is the strike-out symbol.
   $ carries the value of the current line number
   * at the beginning or end kills an instruction line.
   Brackets may be used above in place of parentheses.
   Indexed letters (e.g. v[a], w[b]) may be used above in place of x, y.
   Arbitrary expressions (e.g. $3 \cdot [\sin(2 \cdot p + 3) - q] + r$) may be used above in place of a, b,
     c, ...

voltage pencil on the cathode ray tube face and the results appear on the scope face. For example, an operator may draw a line on the scope and by the use of the function keyboard direct the computer to straighten the line. Or, a sketch of an automobile design may be drawn and the computer directed by the keyboard to turn the design around and display the car at different angles. In developing design, a single cog of a wheel may be drawn by pen on the scope and the machine asked to draw all the other cogs on the wheel, which it can do. A designer can, with this system, interact with the computer and conduct an immediate and continuous "dialogue."

Computer graphics have been used up to the present time only by very large companies in engineering design work. The technology has shown remarkable value in this work. The Lockheed-George Company estimates, for example, that it has reduced part programming time on the order of 6 to 1. (Siders, 1966, p. 22.) Automobile design time has been reduced by a comparable factor. (Siders, 1966, p. 126.)

Table 17-3   A Simple JOSS Conversation

A simple JOSS conversation. User inputs are in light type. JOSS responses are in boldface. Lines beginning or ending with an asterisk are considered commentary only.

Type time.
   time: 10:13
Type 3.1416 + 2.7183.
3.1416 + 2.7183 =   5.8599
Type 3.1416 + e.
e = ???
Set e = 2.7183.
Type 3.1416 + e.
       3.1416 + e =   5.8599
qwertyuiop
Eh?
*Solving a transcendental equation.
   Kepler's equation:
*$M = E - e \sin E$.
*Find E, given $M = 1.210$, $e = 0.260$.
1.1 Set $M = e - e \cdot \sin(E)$.
1.2 Type*
1.2 Type E,M in form 1.
Set e = 0.260.
Do part 1.
Error at step 1.1: E = ???
Set E = 1.
Do part 1.

**Error at step 1.2: I can't find the required
   form.**
Form 1:
   $E = \text{—•——}$ $M = \text{—•——}$
Do part 1.
   E = 1.000   M = .781
Do part 1 for E = 1.1 (.1) 1.5.
   E = 1.100   M = .868
   E = 1.200   M = .958
   E = 1.300   M = 1.049
   E = 1.400   M = 1.144
   E = 1.500   M = 1.241
*By inspection, I can see the **answer is
   about E = 1.47.**
Do part 1 for E = 1.468 (.001) **1.472.**
   E = 1.468   M = 1.209
   E = 1.469   M = 1.210
   E = 1.470   M = 1.211
   E = 1.471   M = 1.212
   E = 1.472   M = 1.213
*The solution, to three decimal places:
   E = 1.469.
Type time.
   time: 10:19
Type users.
   users: 15
*There are now 14 other people
   simultaneously using
*JOSS.

At the present time graphic representations are two dimensional, but there are expectations that they will be three dimensional in the future. It is also expected that in the future computers will be programmed through pen writing on the scope face. (pp. 149-150.)

There are many problems along the way before computer graphics will be widely used. At the present time the system is extremely expensive and faces major problems in developing software programs, but these problems will be overcome and computer graphics will spread beyond engineering use to meet informational needs of management.

FUTURE BUSINESS INFORMATION SYSTEMS TRENDS

The above trends in computer technology will have an important influence on business information systems. Since the implications of computers for management decision-making were discussed in previous chapters, the interest here is principally upon the impact of computers upon information systems *per se* as compared with their use in making decisions. But the two are so related that the latter cannot be completely ignored here. The following trends are in no particular order of importance.

First, managers will have access to information in large data banks. It is altogether likely that data banks of certain types will be geographically distributed throughout the country and linked together. These decentralized centers will probably be linked to data banks in Washington, D.C.

The future of the computer utility lies ahead. In 1965 the first computer utility, Keydata Corp., began operations in Cambridge, Mass. This particular company only operates a time-sharing computer. Companies like this will in the future, however, store data of all types for business usage and make it available to customers for a fee.

With this sort of system the market research director of a company in Los Angeles may by a console in his office request information from a computer utility in Los Angeles about consumer disposable income in the southwestern part of the U.S. He may also request national historical information on consumer disposable income which the Los Angeles utility will get directly from a data bank in Washington, D.C. It is conceivable that data banks will exist for different types of specialized information, such as literature in different fields (e.g. finance, accounting, marketing), legal cases, medical knowledge, and scientific and engineering technical data. These banks of information may be tied to computer utilities and they, in turn, to individual company systems.

Second, individual company information systems may be enriched by information developed by others and placed on magnetic tapes for a management's use. For example, those in the drug or chemical industry can now buy on magnetic tape the UNITERM index of drug and chemical patents. Tapes are also available with information on the direction of drug research and competition. The F. W. Dodge Division of McGraw-Hill supplies a computerized tabulation of data on the construction industry. The volume of this type data will grow. (Rowe, 1966.)

Third, real-time informational systems will expand in usage. There is some disagreement about what a real-time information system is, but a majority of interested students of the subject would probably agree with the following. "A real-time system is one where: (a) information is stored on random access equipment; (b) the information is updated frequently enough to be considered correct at all times; and (c) the information can be retrieved as quickly as needed." (Dearden, 1966, p. 275.) Some experts would insist, however, that real-time means instant availability of information as activity takes place. Donald Malcolm defines the term as follows: "The meaning of the word 'real-time' lies in the fact that information is used as it develops and that elements in the system are controlled by the processed information immediately, not after the fact or by making periodic forecasts of the expected future state of the system." (Malcolm, Rowe, and McConnell 1960, p. 208.) A familiar application is the American Airlines Sabre System. From hundreds of locations it is possible to ask the computer if space is available for many days in advance on well over a thousand flight legs. If space is available, the computer will temporarily allocate the space until the customer decides whether he wants it. When he decides, the push of a button reserves the space for him. If space wanted is not available, alternatives are flashed back. But the system provides real-time information going far beyond passenger reservations. A central computer maintains detailed information on flights, crews, competition, and many other elements important in running the airline. The computer will answer virtually instantaneously not only information on reservations, but flight status, costs, revenues, crew scheduling, and so on.

Enthusiasts predict that more and more of a firm's information system will be real-time and forecast the day when a chief executive will run his business surrounded by computer consoles feeding him real-time data. There are several reservations which one should consider in such projection. (Dearden, 1966b, pp. 123-132.) A very large amount of information needed to operate a business cannot be produced by a real-time computer system, and real-time information systems are also expensive.

If advocates for a firm-wide real-time system, however, lower their anticipations it is easy to see increasing applications at all levels of management. Top managers in the largest companies cannot and will not operate their enterprises with real-time systems. One of the most cherished requirements for these men is time to think, time to digest and evaluate information. The last thing they want or need is a continuous battering of petty and detailed real-time information overwhelming them. On the other hand, as will be discussed shortly, it can be anticipated that top executives will become more intimately associated with computers on a man-to-machine basis. Part of this experience may be associated with real-time informational flows.

At lower managerial levels the spread of real-time information systems will be much greater. This is particularly true with managers who are responsible for such functions as production, or shipping products. An increasing number of companies are currently installing real-time systems to manage such activities as these.

Fourth, new man-machine communications systems will help managers to get information quickly and to manipulate the data for better decision-making. More and more managers will have their own connection to a central computer. This will permit them to get information as quickly as they need it. As noted above, a linkage between his company's computer and that of a central data bank will give a manager quick access to very large volumes of information.

If programs are developed which simulate his business, or permit him to play with models on the basis of inputs he decides upon, he can sit at his desk and manipulate data to help in his decision-making. With computer graphics the inputs and outputs of such models may be displayed on a cathode ray screen. Computer graphics will also permit engineers to work directly at a computer with marketing, production, and financial personnel in the development of new products.

Newer languages will make it easy for managers to communicate with computers. No matter how easy it is to communicate they will want to do so by voice, and if their demand is insistent enough that, too, will someday be possible.

Fifth, cost reductions in storing and retrieving data, growth of storage capacity, and inter-machine communications, will permit top managers to bring together in an integrated fashion far more information about their business than is now feasible. It will be possible to get quickly information about activities in all the far-flung divisions of a company, and it will be possible to relate scattered pieces of information. Computers will permit, if not force, a systems orientation in management. The systems approach, as described in Chapter 14, recognizes that a business in its entirety is a system, but that within the larger system there are many subsystems. Computers will permit managers easily to look at parts of the system and to relate the parts to the whole. For a very large company this capability does not exist without computers.

Sixth, time sharing will make it possible for even small companies to have access to computers. Since they will not have to bear the cost of original equipment, but only a rental cost shared by others, the net cost to them will be a fraction of what it otherwise would be.

Seventh, as discussed in previous chapters, computers will make it much easier for managers to take advantage of new powerful mathematical tools, such as PERT, linear and dynamic programming, probability theory, and simulation.

Of course, the use of these techniques is not dependent upon computers, but for complex problems computers are frequently the only practicable way to a solution.

Eighth, automated planning, control, and decision-making of entire plants will continue to expand. Today, there are many plants that are operated by computers. (*Business Week*, 1960.) To operate a plant with computers, of course, will necessitate a much different informational system for managers than before.

Information systems in the functional areas will become more computerized. In the production area, for example, real-time planning and control systems will expand. In numerically controlled production systems computers will take a part drawing, prepare a machine tool tape for it, and run the machine tool to produce it.*

Finally, as a result of new developments business information systems will be more versatile, be more flexible, be more accurate, have a quicker response time, and be easier to manipulate and change. The variety of new techniques will open up many new ways to receive, send, and manipulate information. Technology will permit managers to change the information system easily, and access to wider ranges of information will make the systems more powerful.

Mike Kami (1958, p. 77.), some time ago, correctly understood the application lag between *technical* capability and actual use. He said: ". . . While technological progress itself can be revolutionary . . . , *methodological* progress is by its very nature evolutionary. We cannot expect to achieve the rosy picture of the integrated data processing applications, the 'fast time' business simulation, 'optimum' production scheduling and automatic 'decision-making' functions by an explosive and revolutionary breakthrough. It is going to take a long, evolutionary process, involving hard and persistent work on the part of all of us, before we shall be able to use computers for all the tasks they are technically capable of performing."

DATA MANAGEMENT

These developments have given rise to a "total information systems" concept and the creation of staff positions in companies to take advantage of the new technology. "Total systems," "management information systems," and "integrated information systems," are often used synonymously in the literature. What is in mind is ". . . a network of related subsystems developed according to an integrated scheme for performing the activities of a business. It is a means of uniting men, materials and machines to accomplish the objectives of the business. It specifies the content and format, the preparation and integration of information for all functions within a business that will best satisfy the planning, organizing,

* For a thorough description of this method see Chingari, 1967.

directing and controlling needs of the various levels of management." (Sklar in Radamaker, 1963, pp. 21-4.) This really is more of a philosophy than an operational concept, although there are those who take the idea literally to mean one single integrated system serving all needs. Comments will be made about this view later in the chapter.

This philosophy, however, is important because it looks at a business as an integrated system which encompasses all departments and subsystems of the business. Information systems should reflect this fact and interrelate all parts of the system. This is different from a concept which sees independent information systems satisfying individual departments and managers, with only a loose, if any, over-all integration.

To take fuller advantage of computers in providing better integrated informational systems some companies have created top-level staff positions, such as vice president of data management or information technology. The functions of these executives vary a great deal—some are managers of a more or less clerical electronic data processing operation while others are involved in developing computer-based information systems to serve a large part of the informational needs of a company.

In the approach to the integrated information system it is necessary for at least three groups to collaborate, namely, information systems specialists, management scientists, and managers. (Ackoff, 1967, p. B-156.) In any important alteration of a business's information system there also probably should be present staff specialists of different types (e.g., accounting, planning, market research) in the areas involved.

The approach to more integrated information systems will fail unless all these groups participate and seek a realistic understanding of how decisions are made in a company, the different types of decisions that are made, the informational requirements to make the decisions, and the preferred means to get the required information to the right managers. (Elwell, 1967, pp. 40-59, and Ackoff, 1967.)

Big problems lie in designing software. A major job is that of designing the data structure to be sure the needed information is available, obsolete information can easily be erased from the system, and appropriate information is selected to provide a proper response to an acceptable question. To achieve this will also be expensive.

In the preceding chapter much was said about the types of managerial information needs, but at this point it is worthwhile to comment on information versus facts. Most managers have an over abundance of irrelevant information. Their big problem is to get necessary relevant information.

It is relatively easy to collect statistics but quite another thing to develop only that information which is useful for a manager, at a particular time, and to help him solve his problem of the moment. No system can fulfill this idea completely, but too many systems provide more data than illumination. Richard Neuschel has commented wisely on this point, as follows: "There is no question but that electronic equipment (and, indeed, punched-card equipment) can produce more information faster than can be generated by any other means. But, because this is true, one wonders whether our ability to generate information has not far outstripped our ability to assimilate it and use it intelligently in the running of the business. In any event, all levels of management face the persistent danger of becoming so fascinated by the lure of office automation that they lose sight of a far greater need to sharpen their skills in determining *what information is of real worth*. This need is born of the fact that most managements are already flooded with too much information—a good part of which is of the wrong kind . . . The real need in applying high-speed computers to the management of large-scale enterprises is not so much that of using such machines to manipulate existing knowledge as it is one of identifying much more clearly . . . the factors that affect business health and in what specific ways and . . . to what degree each of these factors exerts its influence in any given situation." (Neuschel, 1960, pp. 206-208.*)

THE NEAR-FUTURE BUSINESS
INFORMATION SYSTEM

While changes in information systems will generally be made at an evolutionary pace, there will be growing differences as time goes on. Chart 17-2 shows a type of informational system which seems likely to be widespread in the 1970-1980 time range. In this time period, there will still exist for the average company not one but many information systems. Most of the important ones, however, will be connected to the same data base. Since this data base will be connected with others the scope of available information will be enormous. By means of this connection a manager also, for example, will be able to "talk" through the computer with his banker and his subcontractors.

The manager will have available in his office the means for instantaneous communication with computers, both through print outs and through graphic display. Since the use of these instruments is his choice to make he can use real-time information as he wishes. Many managers may have their own small desk computers.

The average manager, however, will still have a variety of other elements in his information system, as depicted in the chart. Friends, acquaintances, fellow managers, the printed word, and other information systems will be important to him.

* From *Management by System*, 2nd ed., by Richard F. Neuschel. Copyright © 1960 by McGraw-Hill Book Company, Inc., and used by permission.

Chart 17-2

"Typical" Business Information Systems of the Future

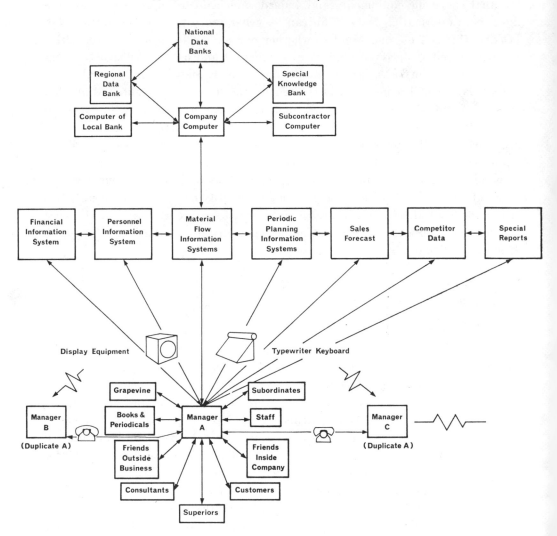

IMPACT OF COMPUTERS ON CENTRALIZATION

The changes which computers have brought about and will continue to make in management information systems have given rise in recent years to a spirited debate about the extent to which management decision-making will be centralized. On the one side are those who assert that the organization chart of a typical company in the future will look like a football balanced on a bell—middle management will be eliminated. On the other hand are those who say no such thing will happen. On the contrary, it is asserted, the use of computers is sure to expand the job content of middle managers; they not only will fail to disappear but will be much more useful managers. The principal arguments of this debate, and the results of research into the issues, deserve comment here.

THE CASE FOR ELIMINATING MIDDLE MANAGEMENT.* Some scholars feel that the following trends are sure to take place. There will be an upward shift of the boundary between planning and performance and, as a result, a large part of a firm's planning responsibilities will be removed from middle managers. The assumption is that most of the decision-making of middle managers can be programmed. That is, the decisions are routine, repetitive, and predictable relations exist among variables, and consequently inputs to a decision can be quantified to achieve a specified quantitative output. In such a case, a program can be prepared for computers which will automatically perform the necessary calculations and prescribe the optimum course of action. This argument assumes that a large part of middle management's work is devoted to such programmable problems as determining optimum inventory levels, filling customers' orders, matching raw material flows with production lines, scheduling shipments of finished goods, and comparable repetitive and routine type decisions. Such tasks a machine can do better than the middle manager.

It is recognized that there are unprogrammed, nonrepetitive, and ill-structured type problems facing middle managers. Product styling, pricing, and dealing with customer complaints are among them. It is assumed decisions about such matters will be distributed between top and lower management levels.

A natural concomitant, it is said, will be a recentralization of industrial organization. Top managers will assume more responsibilities to plan, innovate, and create. This will result in reversal of a decentralization trend of the post World War II era.

Accompanying this trend will be the growth in number and influence of central analytical expert staffs, such as management science groups. The assumption, of course, is that because of capability of making more centralized decisions top managements will in fact do so and, in order to help in this process, expert staff groups will be created in more and more companies.

THE CASE FOR RETENTION OF MIDDLE MANAGEMENT.† Opposition to the above case rests on several grounds. First, the death knell of middle management, it is said by this group, is based upon an assumption that more of the middle manager's task is concerned with routine matters than is really the case. There is no question about the fact that where a middle manager's only, or virtually total, task is to make routine decisions, the computer probably would

* See, for example, Leavitt and Whisler, 1958, pp. 41-48; Shultz and Whisler, 1960; Simon in Anshen and Bach, ed., 1960; and Simon, 1960.

† See, for example, Anshen, Chapter 2 in Bowman and Fillerup, 1963; Burlingame, 1961, pp. 121-126; Jacoby, 1962, pp. 31-43; Koontz, 1959, pp. 78-84; and Gallagher and Axsmith, in McKinsey and Co., 1961.

replace him. But the average middle manager makes many nonprogrammed, one-of-a-kind, novel, and complex decisions. Strides have been made in solving some of these problems with computers, but so far there is a capability of using computers for only a minor part of the volume of such decisions made by middle managers. Progress in this area will continue, but the pace in resolving them not only is likely to be slower than enthusiasts anticipate but also likely not to match the increase in volume of nonroutine business problems.

Second, and of major importance, is the fact that the case for the demise of the middle manager rests on a rather significant misunderstanding of his task. Even though automation will bring an important transfer of decision-making responsibility from managers to machines, the net impact will be to widen the middle manager's job. There will be an important change in his job content, in the nature of the tasks he undertakes.

This group claims that computers will reduce the number of routine tasks now performed by middle managers and leave them more time to do creative, imaginative work. Just as with top management, the development of new analytical tools will help middle managers sharpen their intuition and judgment. Furthermore, they will be freed to devote more attention to tasks which they previously had to slight, such as longer-range planning; dealings with employees, customers, labor unions, and people in the communities where they work; improving relations with central headquarters officers; and educating themselves to be better managers. Freed of routine tasks, the middle manager will be able to spend more time working with human problems in his organization so as to motivate, lead, and teach those associated with him. As a matter of fact, rather than leave the middle manager a useless appendage, the computer may make one of its most valuable contributions in freeing him to broaden his job and become more valuable to his enterprise.

Third, the case for decentralization is probably more persuasive than that for centralization, say the opponents of the middle-management-disappearance thesis. Businessmen are faced with growingly complex enterprises where ill-structured problems are increasing more rapidly than technical methods to deal with them. The pressure to stimulate people, improve their creativity, and ignite their imagination, is destined to increase, not alone to solve better the problems of the enterprise but to meet the growing expectations of people in becoming a more important part of their company. Decentralization is more likely to meet this need than centralization. Here again, computers will aid all levels of management in getting better facts and in shifting burdensome calculations to machines, and in so doing will permit them to make greater contributions to themselves and to their firms.

WHAT HAS HAPPENED? Studies which have been made of the impact of computers on middle management help to evaluate these opposed points of view. Shaul interviewed 53 middle managers and 14 top managers in eight companies, all of which had several years' operating experience with electronic data processing equipment. His findings rejected the thesis that middle managers will disappear or become engaged solely in routine matters. His findings fully support the view that the role of the middle manager will expand. Of the managers he interviewed 60 percent said they now work longer on planning activities than before and they have much more time for considering new opportunities. The middle managers he interviewed felt that with computers their decisions were better than before. They were unanimous in concluding that their status had not been lowered. In fact, they said the middle manager's status had been raised. His job was now more complex, he had a greatly increased volume of information to analyze problems in depth, he was using more experience and judgment, and computers added to his activities or replaced some with more responsibility. (Shaul, 1964a and 1964b.)

Schwitter (1965, p. 236.) studied the impact of computers on middle management among 47 firms. He concluded that in only two of the companies was there a change in content of top management jobs, and the changes were only in the jobs of the controller and vice president in charge of purchasing. Middle management jobs showed slightly more increases than decreases in job content. Lower management jobs showed a definite decrease in job content. These jobs were those of supervisors of stores, payrolls, time-keeping, standards, and machine accounting where computers actually took over their routine tasks. He concluded that his findings ". . . do not support the conclusion that middle management jobs would become 'more specialized and highly programmed.' " His conclusions, he say, ". . . support . . . (those) who predict that middle management jobs of the future would require more initiative, vision and knowledge."

In 1962 the Westinghouse Electric Company installed a Tele-Computer Center. (Gaddis, 1967, pp. 5-18.) The computer is linked to the largest Westinghouse plants and processes about 90 percent of all its industrial orders, sending shipping instructions in three seconds to the warehouse nearest the customer. It updates inventory records on a real-time basis, permits real-time cash accounting in some 230 banks in which the company has accounts, and handles the bulk of the company's accounting records. This system resulted in the disappearance of large clerical groups, and overall, computers shrank the number of managers at middle levels. Those who remained, however, found their job content expanded. Divisional accounting managers, for example, now function as financial planners. Computers cut down the manual calculation of engineers and permitted them to concentrate more on design. (*Business Week*, 1966b.)

THE OUTLOOK. Specialists have a way of looking at management solely in terms of their expertise, and computer specialists are no exception. While their views of the impact of computers on organization may be exaggerated, there is truth in their expectations. On the other hand, this element of truth conflicts with other forces operating in business which serve to counteract any forecast of the end of middle management.

A more realistic appraisal of the future impact of computers on organization would seem to be as follows:

First, for those firms committed to and operating best through centralization, such as oil and insurance companies, information technology advances and new decision-making tools will tend to reinforce and speed up the trend.

Second, automated factories will continue to expand in numbers, as will computerized production lines.

Third, the trend to decentralize management will be accentuated as companies continue their heterogeneous product lines and find necessity for increasing rather than decreasing delegation of authority. Among such companies the mix of decision-making as between headquarters and divisions will change. A closer meeting of minds about company aims will provide a clearer environmental set of rules within which decentralized managers can "have their head." Better informational communications between headquarters and divisions will permit quicker and more accurate surveillance of performance.

Finally, while there will be elimination of middle managers who have only routine tasks, the opportunity will be present and accepted for expanding middle management job content. The net result is more likely to be an increase in middle managers in numbers and, more importantly, an enhancement of middle management's contribution to company aims.

FAR-DISTANT TECHNICAL TRENDS

What new developments will occur in automation following 1980 is a matter of fascinating speculation. There can be no doubt, however, that there will be great new developments which will importantly affect business organization and information systems. Some of the possibilities anticipated by a group of experts at the RAND Corporation in a rough order of their approximate appearance after 1980 are: automatic language translator with correct grammar; widespread use of automatic decision-making at the management level for industrial and national planning; automated interpretation of medical symptoms; widespread use of robot services for refuse collection, as household slaves, as sewer inspectors, and so on; widespread use of computers in tax collection, with access to all business records—automatic single tax deductions; availability of a machine which comprehends standard IQ tests and scores above 150 (where comprehend is to be interpreted behavioristically as the ability to respond to questions printed in English and possibly accompanied by diagrams); evolution of a universal language from automated communication; and man-machine symbiosis, enabling man to extend his intelligence by direct electro-mechanical interaction between his brain and a computing machine. (T. J. Gordon and Helmer, 1964, fig. 8.1.)

MANAGERS, MANAGEMENT, AND DECISION-MAKING

The developments observed in this chapter should leave no doubt about the importance of computer technology to managers. There will, however, be no diminution of the responsibilities of managers for managing. Theirs will not be a world of automatic decision-making by computer-based information systems, nor will it be a world in which large blocks of managers will be replaced by computers. What will happen, of course, is that managers will have better, quicker, and more information acquired at low costs to help them in their decision-making.

One important event that will take place will be a change in influence of computers on decision-making. Today the computer has widespread impact on decision-making in a number of functional areas, especially production. As time goes by, the influence will rise up the managerial hierarchy. Today the computer really has had little impact on top-level managerial decision-making. (Brady, 1967, p. 7.) In the 1970's, however, there seems little doubt that computers will have great influence in top management decision-making. Beyond the 1970's the impact will be even deeper. (Ozbekan, 1967; Myers, 1967; and Greenberger, 1962.)

SUMMARY AND CONCLUDING GUIDELINES FOR DEVELOPING INFORMATION SYSTEMS

The last chapter pointed out that the flow of information in a business is of major importance to a manager's making rational decisions. Despite its significance, however, most companies find a number of important deficiencies in their information systems. These were noted. Examined in the chapter also were the different type needs by managers for information, and the fact that there is not one but a number of information systems which must exist in a business to satisfy properly these needs.

The most outstanding catalyst of business information systems today and into the future is the computer. In the present chapter, therefore, evolving computer technology trends were examined and it was shown how they will bring about important changes in business information systems. The possibilities for and values of looking toward more computer-based integrated business information systems were examined, and a conceptual model of a "typical" business information system in the 1970-1980 period was advanced. Some problems in the development of more integrated information systems were also discussed.

Throughout both chapters a number of guides were advanced for designing business information systems which may now be brought together. The use of the word system in the following set of guides does not refer to one set of procedures for collecting and disseminating information. Rather what is in mind is that many informational systems exist in a company but that there should be an integration among them. One may, therefore, speak of an integrated system which would include subsystems with common data bases and coordinating links. But, as noted in the preceding chapter, I prefer to think of major and minor systems which would be reasonably interrelated. I reject the view that there can or should be a single all-encompassing system that provides all the informational needs of all managers.

First, the system should provide to each executive information needed for: identifying and choosing among alternative courses of action, planning the end results for which he is responsible and the specific actions to achieve these end results, measuring his own and his subordinates' performance, and taking corrective action. First and foremost, information systems are designed to help managers to manage. This means aiding them in their decision-making principally with respect to planning and control, and providing information required by government regulations.

Second, the system must concentrate on developing information rather than facts. It should provide the relevant and omit the irrelevant data.

Third, the system must conform to and reflect the company's organizational structure and delegations of authority so that controllable elements of performance of each organizational unit may be measured accurately in terms of contribution to company-wide goals. This means, of course, that information about one organizational unit, especially when used to plan and control, will contain data only connected with that unit. Performance reports of unit A which includes cost elements of unit B will not truly reflect results of operations of either unit.

Fourth, the system should be integrated, so that information available at all levels of management and for subsystems tie together into a consistent body of data and in such fashion that reports become more condensed the higher the level of management. This simply reflects a correlation of value of data with detail. Lower-level managers generally need more detail than upper-level managers. The flows of data should reflect the fact, too, that information needs at lower levels of management are generally for much shorter time periods than for higher levels. Different types of information, therefore, have different values as among the levels.

Fifth, the system must recognize that information needed for planning is often different from that needed for control, although the two must be developed in recognition of each other.

Sixth, data developed by the system must be timely; cover past, present, and future anticipations, where appropriate; and be complete. Completeness here refers to coverage of critical nonfinancial as well as financial factors, and long-term as well as short-term information.

Seventh, the system should be reasonably integrated in the sense that to the fullest extent possible common data should be used, relevant parts of different individual informational systems should be related and be comparable. But flexibility should be assured by providing for new informational systems within the overall structure to deal with new sources of information and new problems.

Eighth, it must be recognized that for most of the information systems used by a manager, particularly higher-level managers, human communications is indispensable to understanding. Very frequently, data are not meaningful to an executive unless it is explained. Sometimes information supplied by subordinates is unintentionally, or willfully, misleading. (See on this point, R. N. McMurry, 1965.) Often, decisions are made at the time information is received, and participation in the decision may be necessary by those who will carry it out.

Ninth, the system should emphasize and amply cover, to the extent possible, information about those operational elements of a business, and environmental forces, which will be most responsible for the success or failure of an enterprise.

Tenth, in the development of information systems the technical interests of staff experts must be submerged to the interests of managers, but the two must cooperate in developing systems. Staffs must avoid rushing into informational systems design without management participation and approval. Managers must not abdicate their responsibility to staff in this work.

Eleventh, efforts should be made to assure to the extent possible that information collections and flows fit the management styles of managers. This is not always easy because management styles may differ. But to the extent that workable balances can be arranged this guideline will have been followed.

Twelfth, specific printed reports in the system should adhere to guides such as the following:

   a. cover the most significant elements in light of end results desired.
   b. facilitate measurement of performance by drawing the correct comparisons.
   c. include only essential facts so that the reader can learn without being confused.
   d. be easy to understand and read.
   e. be distributed only to those needing them.
   f. be issued as promptly as possible on fixed schedules.
   g. be prepared economically.
   h. cover the proper periods of time for the subject.
   i. use the best techniques known and acceptable to management in the presentation format.

Thirteenth, computers must be used appropriately in the system. It must not be inferred that because computers are widely used in a company that it has an effective informational system, nor conversely, that because it has not widely used computers its information system is poor. Computers are extremely important in information systems but not the whole story. They may be widely used, for example, in controlling payrolls and production but the company may still have a very poor overall information system.

Fourteenth, the greater the knowledge of managers of the capabilities of computers the more computer systems can offer. The more management knows about computer systems the more willingly it will use and accept advanced computer techniques, and the more acceptable will be computer automated decision-making.

Fifteenth, management should be willing to experiment with new computer and information technology. Changes are coming swiftly. Any new important change in information systems is likely to go through a period when "bugs" will have to be eliminated. Managers should also be interested in and should press their staffs for help in understanding and using new methods.

Finally, the system should be placed under continuous review for improvement, but should not be altered repeatedly in minor details.

PART IV

Planning in Selected Major Functional Areas

18
Marketing Planning ───────────

18
Marketing Planning

INTRODUCTION

Planning in the marketing area is the keystone in the arch of comprehensive planning in most companies, and corporate success generally is synonymous with marketing success. It is fitting, therefore, that Part IV of this book on functional planning begin with marketing planning.

As will be explained shortly, marketing planning covers a far wider spectrum of activities than can be encompassed in this chapter. Many things have already been said in previous chapters about and applicable to marketing planning. Also, Chapter 19 on product planning, and Chapter 22 on research and development planning, also fall within the perimeters of marketing planning. In this light, this chapter will seek to set a framework for organizing thinking about marketing planning in general, and will examine in detail a few selected elements of the subject. Emphasis will be laid on the meaning of marketing planning, alternative marketing organizations, how marketing plans are developed, the functions of marketing managers, and selected problems in determining the "marketing mix."

Parenthetically, I want to mention here that the treatment of the subject matter is not uniform in the chapters in this part of the book. The intent in this part of the book is not to develop a comprehensive treatment of planning in each area. Nor is the intent to develop a conceptual sequential description and analysis of the planning process or its structure. Much of this was done previously. Rather, the objective is to build on the materials in the preceding parts of the book in such a way as to present major considerations in the development of plans in each area that are of prime concern to top management and essential in better planning in each area. Emphasis is placed on basic guidelines and methods important in doing this planning.

WHAT IS MARKETING?

Marketing planning, of course, is concerned with marketing. This is not too helpful because there are no generally accepted definitions of marketing. A few definitions are as follows: "Marketing is the performance of business activities

that direct the flow of goods and services from producer to consumer or use."
(Alexander, 1960, p. 15.) "The activities and organizations, other than the
original production of materials and their manufacture, by which all these things
(e.g., products consumed at breakfast), are assembled simultaneously for consumption are known collectively as marketing." (Vaile, Grether, and Cox, 1952,
p. 3.) "Marketing is the performance of business activities that direct the flow of
goods and services from producer to consumer or user in order to satisfy customers and accomplish the firm's objectives." (McCarthy, 1964, p. 16.) One
excellent textbook on marketing avoids a definition and observes: "The authors
believe that formal definition of so amorphous a field is in a sense too limiting
and far less useful for students than the establishment of a genuine feel for the
breadth and animation of the areas covered . . ." (Matthews, Buzzell, Levitt and
Frank, 1964, p. 14*). This is a view with which I find myself most sympathetic.
But I think what authors of the above definitions are reaching for can be said
in a slightly different way and capture the essence of the marketing function. A
fundamental distinction between marketing and other functions in a firm is that
marketing focuses upon exchange between the firm and its customers. It can be
seen "as those activities necessary and incidental to bringing about exchange
relationships." (Holloway and Hancock, 1968, p. 4.)

The late Wroe Alderson (1957, especially Chapter VII) looked at marketing
in this light. He considered exchange as an act which improves the assortments
held by two parties to an exchange. The assortments, to him, are the heterogeneous collections of products and services designed to serve the needs of some
behavioral system. In marketing terms, exchange takes place in order to increase
the utility of assortments of both parties in the transaction. In a barter economy,
a mutually beneficial exchange of assortments takes place, say, when one group
with excess wheat exchanges it for wool produced by another group. In a money
exchange, the mutual enhancement of improving assortments is partially hidden
but nonetheless is there. It is the essence of the marketing function, says Alderson,
to make such exchanges of assortments as mutually beneficial as possible. Indeed,
he says, "marketing is . . . the source of all ultimate value in use." (p. 198.) The
fundamental objective is to match the needs of the individual with a suitable
product, and this the marketing function does.

A great deal of the operation of a business is, therefore, subsumed under
marketing. Marketing looks at the assortments held by individuals in particular
settings and seeks to make various resources available to the firm to meet these
needs to the value of both parties.

Another way to say the same thing is as follows. Marketing deals with two
flows of action and utilities. First is that which creates form utility by the

process of production and then creates both a place and time utility through distribution. A second stream of action is a counterflow of cash and orders from consumers. Marketing matches these two flows in such a way as to maximize customer satisfaction and enterprise profits. This means that all activities of a company in matching needs and resources, and in sorting resources to meet needs, are marketing activities.

IMPORTANCE OF MARKETING

Put in this way, there can be no doubt about the importance of the marketing activity in a company. There are, however, a few other things that should be said about it.

Marketing becomes increasingly significant in a society as a separation occurs between the point of consumer need or demand and the source of supply to meet it. Marketing reconciles the discrepancies between the needs of buyers and the supply available to them. In a simple economy these discrepancies are few because needs are modest and the means available to meet them are virtually homogeneous, that is, there is no or little product differentiation. The vast separation of consumption from supply, and the intermediate machinery needed to reconcile these discrepancies, brings about a basic heterogeneity of both products and wants. This complicates the marketing process but at the same time makes it a source of increasing value in society.

The complexities of moving from a simple to an advanced society have given rise to the egocentric point of view of businesses. A producer of steel, or rubber, or computers, for example, faces extraordinary problems in the fundamental task of producing his products. Preoccupation with this difficult job tends to lead him away from considerations of changing market needs, away from the marketing point of view expressed above.

Some writers have said that this is all wrong, that the only sensible point of view is to discover needs of customers and then back up from that point of view to determine the needed supplies. Although this is a useful concept it is not practical in many cases, such as in those where a firm's investment is very heavy in particular material resources, and skills, and manufacturing techniques. In such cases, for example, selling and advertising can perform a useful function by bringing customers to recognize values in improving their assortments which may be ignored or misunderstood.

The importance of the marketing function lies in its value in matching needs with resources. From a social point of view its value rests in doing this in such a fashion as to maximize consumer utility, while at the same time using resources in such a way as to achieve the greatest social benefit. From a company point of view, the importance of the marketing function lies in balancing needs with resource possibilities in such a fashion as to meet profit and other objectives.

It is worth noting here that the importance of marketing is also reflected in the fact that around 50 percent of the consumer's dollar is absorbed in marketing costs. (Stewart and Dewhurst, 1939.) About half the nation's workers are engaged in this activity.

THE MARKETING CONCEPT

Adam Smith, as noted previously, built a theory of economics which placed the consumer at the very center of the production and distribution process. To him, business revolved about the consumer, not the other way around. This view today is embraced in the so-called "market concept." But between Adam Smith and today's concepts there have been many changes. Indeed, some writers describe the more recent changes as bringing about a "marketing revolution." The evolution of production and marketing in the Pillsbury Company illustrates the major changes which have taken place. (Keith, 1960, pp. 35-38.) The company was formed in 1869 and from its inception to the 1930's it was production oriented. The idea for the formation of the company came from the availability of wheat and water power, not from the availability and proximity of market areas or consumer demands for less expensive flour products. The concern of the company was with production, not with marketing. The philosophy of the company during this period might have been stated as: "We are professional flour millers. Blessed with a supply of the finest North American wheat, plenty of water power, and excellent milling machinery, we produce flour of the highest quality. Our basic function is to mill high-quality flour, and of course (and almost incidentally) we must hire salesmen to sell it, just as we hire accountants to keep our books."

This was an era, especially up to 1920, of mass distribution. Immediate demand for goods of many industries was running behind ability to produce and a major problem, therefore, was the development of better ways to get goods to consumers.

Pillsbury moved into a second stage in the 1930's which was sales oriented. In this era, generally, the productive processes were capable of turning out a high volume of goods and there was a tendency for goods to accumulate at factories and in warehouses without aggressive selling. In this era, an awareness of the importance of selling emerged and along with it the dominance of aggressive sales managers who sought to stimulate consumer's desires.

Pillsbury, like other companies, became more conscious of and considered their consumers, desires, wants and prejudices as being very important in business success. The company recognized the importance of distributors and set up a commercial research department to get facts about the market. Pillsbury's thinking in this era might have been summed up as: "We are a flour-milling company, manufacturing a number of products for the consumer market. We must have a first-rate sales organization which can dispose of all the products we can make at favorable prices. We must back up this sales force with consumer advertising and market intelligence. We want our salesmen and our dealers to have all the tools they need for moving the output of our plants to the consumer."

The decade of the 1960's began the marketing era. In this period a number of factors made it quite clear that more system was needed. Pillsbury, like many other companies, was in a position to produce literally hundreds of new and different products and it needed a system to screen and evaluate products which should be manufactured, an organization to operate the system, and to maximize sales of products selected for production. The criteria for product selection fundamentally were "those of the consumer herself." The company's purpose was no longer to mill flour, or to manufacture a wide variety of products, but to satisfy the needs and desires, both actual and potential, of our customers." The philosophy in this period could have been stated as: "We make and sell products for consumers."

This turn in basic philosophy was marked by institutional changes. The small advertising department was transformed into a marketing department. The brand-manager was created and given total accountability for results. He directed the marketing of his products as if he were the owner of the business. Production did his bidding and finance kept his accounts.

This change of attitude, this point of view, is called the market concept. It is a posture that is now being assumed in many companies.

Today, Pillsbury is moving into a fourth era—that of the marketing company. In this era, marketing will assume an even more dominant position than today. A marketing company in the future will be one which will not consider itself to be engaged in producing and marketing, but rather it will accept the idea that its reason for being will lie in its merchandising and marketing activities. Marketing will guide and control the entire operation, and manufacturing will be a service activity to supply the goods demanded by consumers as conceived by marketing managers and staff. (Bell, 1966, p. 8.) * Marketing will be the king pin in matching consumer needs with company resources in Alderson's concept.

This means, of course, that marketing will become more important in comprehensive corporate planning, and top management will become more deeply involved with it. Indeed, the marketing revolution has paralleled the revolution in corporate planning, and for somewhat the same reasons. The decisive factor in successful marketing planning may be excellence in overall corporate planning.

The new concepts in marketing are important philosophies to guide opera-

* Bell has a slightly different set of dates for the marketing revolution. To him, the mass distribution stage was between 1900 and 1920; the aggressive selling stage existed in the 1920's and 1930's; the marketing concept stage emerged in the 1940's; and in some companies today the marketing company stage presages the wave of the future. (See pp. 6-8.)

tions. They do not exalt marketing but rather underscore its importance in business success. The new view makes clear the idea, as Alderson and Green nicely put it, that: "There is no pay-off for the scientist in his laboratory, for the production manager in the most modern plant, or for the wizard of finance except as the company's products find acceptance in the market."*

With this background, a formal definition of marketing which fits the approach of this book may be given. It is: "Marketing is the management task of strategically planning, directing, and controlling the application of enterprise effort to profit-making programs which will provide customer satisfactions—a task which involves the integration of all business activities (including manufacturing, finance, and sales) into a unified system of action." (Bell, 1966, p. 22.) While this definition is given with approval it must be reiterated that marketing, like comprehensive planning itself, has many facets, not the least of which is philosophical, and to try to capture the whole with a formal definition is to obscure its broad scope and real essence.

IS YOUR COMPANY MARKET ORIENTED?

Accepting the importance of the customer as the major basis for company activities in the marketing and related fields of activities implies the acceptance of many other operating rules of conduct. For instance, the Vice President— Marketing of American Radiator & Standard Sanitary Corporation says that a marketing oriented company will respond affirmatively to questions such as the following (Buell, 1965, pp. 11-12):

" • Does your chief marketing executive participate in company decision-making, particularly those decisions involving major capital commitments?

• Do plant expansion plans result from marketing forecasts or are they initiated by the production department?

• Do plant and equipment expansion plans assume that today's product lines will be manufactured throughout the payout period?

• Do the marketing manager and his staff spend as much time planning to meet future market conditions as they do on management of current operations?

• Are new-product ideas checked out by marketing before investments are made in technical research and engineering?

• Are research and engineering departments provided with new and revised product specifications based on customer research?

• Do these specifications include elimination of maintenance or provide for easy maintenance and repair for the customer or serviceman?

* Reprinted with permission from Alderson and Green, *Planning and Problem Solving in Marketing* (Homewood, Ill.: Richard D. Irwin, Inc., 1964), p. 5.

- Is your ratio of marketing research people to technical research or engineering development personnel in proper balance?

- Is your customer service department provided with accurate facts on deliveries? Does it have the authority to get action for the customer when needed?

- Does your marketing organization devote time to studying environmental change so as to anticipate new customer needs and wants?

- How long has it been since your channels of distribution have been studied to see whether there is a more efficient way to reach and serve your customers?

- Are your advertising messages based on factual studies of customers' buying motives?"

This list of questions could easily be expanded, but it makes the point. How many companies will find when they approach these questions with an open mind that (a) they still are trying to sell to customers what they want to sell rather than finding out what customers want and satisfying those needs; or, (b) instead of harmonious relationships among functional groups servicing marketing, as well as within the marketing area itself, there is internecine warfare?

CORPORATE AND MARKETING PLANNING

The theme of this book is that the best framework for the best marketing planning is the over-all corporate planning system. The fundamental economic and noneconomic purposes of a business, which are explicitly stated or implicitly assumed as the starting point of a corporate planning program, provide basic guides to the entire marketing planning effort. The determination of specific lines of business to be pursued by a company has an obvious direction power over marketing planning. In a fashion examined at length in previous chapters, marketing planning is both guided by and has an influence on the development of long-range objectives, policies, and strategies which are developed in the strategic planning process. At this level, marketing is one of a number of subsystems in the total corporate system, and interrelated with finance, facilities, management, employees, and other functional elements making up a company. Similarly, marketing must be interrelated with other functions in the development of medium-range programs and short-range plans.

This is another way of saying that successful marketing begins at the top of the company. Only top management has the entire perspective of the relationship of the company to its environment, and of the major balances which must be maintained within the company, to guide the marketing planning. Only top management in the over-all planning process can make sure marketing objectives relate properly to relevant corporate objectives, and that strategies are developed for them in conformance with these company objectives. Within these guides, of course, tactical marketing planning can better be devised at the proper lower levels of management.

Two prominent marketing management consultants have concluded that top managers of successful market-oriented businesses manage this way. These managers are well-informed about the consumers served by their companies and about the strategies their companies and their competitors are following to strengthen their position with customers and to improve their shares of the market. These managers spend much time on formulating fundamental objectives and policies, rather than on reviewing day-to-day program details. (Pearson and Wilson, 1967, p. 2.)

MARKETING PLANNING STEPS. As amply demonstrated in previous chapters there is no universal way to make a comprehensive corporate plan, nor is the process simple in actual practice. It was also pointed out, however, that conceptually the process is comparatively simple. These observations also apply to marketing planning.

Conceptually, marketing planning consists of two fundamental steps. First, is the selection of particular markets, that is, customers in particular settings to whom the company wishes to appeal. Second, is the development of the marketing mix, or the selection and combination of marketing components that the company wishes to use in meeting the identified market needs.

Identification of markets turns out usually to be a difficult task because for all products they are multiple. A market grid for electric fans, for example, may identify markets such as the following: homes, retail stores of different types, hospitals, restaurants, schools, business offices, automobiles, airplanes, trains, ships, and various military markets. Each of these may be classified into geographic regions, such as East, West, North, South, European, and South American.

The problem of marketing planning is to determine in which of the markets the company will try to conduct an exchange, in Alderson's words, which is profitable to both customers and the company. This identification is initially in terms of location but must eventually be determined in terms of size.

The next step, as noted above, or really one which is iterated with the above, is that of selecting the marketing mix. McCarthy has reduced the mix variables to four in his conceptual model, namely, product, place, promotion, and price. (1964, p. 36.) Under product are such activities as adding, dropping, or modifying product lines; branding, packaging, standardizing, and grading. The need, of course, is to develop the proper product for the identified market. Place refers to getting the right product to the right market at the right time. This principally concerns choosing channels of distribution. Promotion is concerned with the way the firm communicates with customers about products and channels of distri-

Table 18-1 Comparison of Marketing Planning Steps

A	B	C
Define the Planning Task		
The Preplan Audit	Analyze Marketing Situation	Develop Necessary Information
Forecasting: Demand and Competition		Examine Problems
	Assessing the Opportunity	Assess opportunities
	Identification of Marketing Targets	Determine objectives
Generation of Strategies	Determining Scale of Effort	Develop strategies and policies
	Consideration of Alternative Approaches	
	Developing the Marketing Mix	
The Preliminary Program	Completing the Marketing Plan	Plan the plan
Clarification of Objectives		Plan the controls
Determining Sequence of Activities		Plan the implementation
Providing for Coordination of Activities		
Testing by Simulation and other Methods		
Administrative Detailing of Program		
Consideration of Org. Changes		
Acceptance of Plan	Final Approval of the Plan	Contingency plans and budgets
Installation of Plan		
Review of Planning Procedure		

Source: A is from Wroe Alderson and Paul E. Green, Planning and Problem Solving in Marketing (Homewood, Ill.: Richard D. Irwin, Inc., 1964), pp. 633-636; B is from Martin L. Bell, Marketing Concepts and Strategy (New York: Houghton Mifflin Co., 1966), pp. 374-381; and C is from John M. Brion, Corporate Marketing Planning (New York: John Wiley & Sons, Inc., 1967), pp. 37-38.

bution. Under this heading, of course, are advertising, sales promotion, development of salesmen, and personal selling. The price problem is to set the correct price for the product. This decision will rest on many factors such as cost, competition, volume, and the company's product mix in a given market. It will also be influenced by markups, discounts, volume buying practices, and other terms of sale.

All the above four P's are conceptually of equal importance, and all are considered more or less simultaneously in marketing planning. But, as McCarthy notes, some sequence must be followed in planning and a logical one is to move in the order in which the P's are discussed above. He says (p. 40), there is some logic in this sequence in that the first step is the identification of the product which can best meet a market demand. The next step is to get it there. The next step is to promote it to let customers know it is available and designed for them. Finally, it must be priced so they will buy it in sufficient volume. In practice, however, these are intermixed as the decision-making process in planning proceeds.

Table 18-1 compares marketing planning steps advanced by three authors. The above two steps—identification of markets and determining mix—can be seen in each of these sequences of steps. But each sequence in Table 18-1 gets closer to steps actually taken in practice. Chart 18-1 adds a time dimension to the set of actual operational steps of one company in its development of a marketing plan.

COMPLEXITIES OF MARKETING PLANNING. Within each of the P's is a long list of possible variables which the planning manager must take into consideration in any planning situation. The sheer number of factors which must be considered quickly becomes astronomical. If there are, for example, under consideration 10 products having 10 variables, the number of variables to be considered is 10^{10}. Consider the marketing planning problem of the American Can Company with over 2,000 different products!

To the variables included in the P's must be added environmental considerations. Important in marketing planning would be the forces in the firm's external environment. The internal environment of the firm aside from the P's, constitutes another set of variables. In mind, for example, are the resources available to the firm, the value systems of managers, and corporate-wide objectives.

To go one step further, Alderson and Green note that "There is no phase of human culture which cannot enter into a marketing problem and perhaps turn out to be the crucial factor in its solution."[*] This opens up a wide range of variables, a concept which Chart 18-2 tries to capture.

---

[*] Reprinted with permission from Alderson and Green, *Planning and Problem Solving in Marketing* (Homewood, Ill.: Richard D. Irwin, Inc., 1964), p. 51.

Chart 18-1

Schedule of Annual Marketing Planning Steps

	MONTH AND WEEK																			
	July				August				September				October				November			
	1	2	3	4	1	2	3	4	1	2	3	4	1	2	3	4	1	2	3	4
Marketing Manager gives top management necessary market information																				
Top management, with the help of the marketing manager determines company sales and profit goals and major strategies																				
Product managers establish preliminary plans within these guidelines, including sales programs, costs, profits, etc.																				
Marketing manager reviews and approves these preliminary plans																				
Product managers review these plans with Field Sales Managers to determine feasibility																				
Product Managers prepared written summaries of agreed-upon plans																				
Marketing manager reviews product plans and submits them to top management for approval																				
Field Sales Managers assign district sales objectives																				
District Managers work with salesmen to agree upon sales objectives and plans																				
Field Sales Managers aggregate agreed upon sales objectives and plans																				
Product Managers prepare financial summaries of final working plans																				
Controller prepares company operating budget																				
Top management reviews and approves final plans																				

Chart 18-2

Areas of Knowledge Applied to Marketing Planning

Another fact of life is that the nature of marketing problems varies a great deal from one company to another and within the same company. For instance, GW Electronics is a small newly formed company in Los Angeles which markets only AM-FM radios imported from Japan. These radios can be plugged into an automobile tape recording system in the same way as a tape recording. How different are the marketing problems of this firm from those of General Motors. Or, consider the difference between marketing planning in the McDonnell-Douglas Company between a follow-on program for the Manned Orbital Laboratory as compared with that relating to the new DC-10.

Another problem is that of establishing long-range marketing objectives and relating them to other company objectives. To do this necessitates answering some very important questions about markets, company desires, and trade offs with other company activities.

As viewed here, marketing must be considered as a behavioral system rather than a mechanistic system with fixed input-output matrices. Marketing involves motivating buyers all along the line from the ultimate consumer back to the raw material buyer and seller. This is a very complex process in which human motivations and behavior are of dominant consideration. It is this complexity that is partly responsible for the difficulties in and costs of marketing. This very complexity also provides great opportunity for marketing planners to make more and better use of new methods of analysis in the quantitative as well as the behavioral science areas.

Other problem areas in marketing planning would include organization, the

---

Table 18-2   Table of Contents of a Marketing Plan

INFORMATION BASE AND BUSINESS ANALYSIS

A. General background economic indicators for past five years and future 10 years, such as GNP and its components, especially disposable consumer income; population growth; and commodity price trends

B. Data and analysis of past (5 years), present, and projected (10 years), as appropriate for:
1. Total markets for each product
2. Characteristics of markets of interest to company
3. Sales potential and expected volume for each product and share of each market
4. Current posture for each product, including major strengths and weaknesses relating to product acceptance, distribution channels, promotion, and pricing.

C. Data and analysis of competition, including for past and present such matters as:
1. Share of market
2. Product acceptance
3. Future potential product, price, promotion, and channel distribution changes
4. Strengths and weaknesses of competitor marketing

D. Analysis of future changes in strategic factors for marketing success for each product and each market

E. Analysis of problems and opportunities in integration of the company's functions in supporting marketing

---

development of proper information systems, relating short and long-range planning, and applying properly available analytical tools.

A MARKETING PLAN TABLE OF CONTENTS. Marketing plans differ among companies but should contain certain characteristics and meet certain requirements. Some of the requirements of a good marketing plan may be stated as follows (adapted from Bell, 1966). Parts or all of the plan must be kept confidential. The plan must be properly welded into the total planning effort of the company, and be appropriate to what the firm wants to do, the risks it can take, what is necessary from marketing to achieve all firm objectives. The plan must be feasible, that is, it is capable of being achieved. The plan must be comprehensive and complete and not leave for a later date the development of im-

---

Table 18-2   Table of Contents of a Marketing Plan (Continued)

F. Conclusions pinpointing changes in the firm's environment, as well as those within the company, which constitutes new and important opportunities or important problems.

MARKETING OBJECTIVES AND GOALS (LONG AND SHORT RUN)

A. Objectives and goals concerned with volume, profit, share of the market.

B. Objectives and goals concerning main elements of marketing, such as product, promotion, channels, and pricing.

MARKETING STRATEGIES (LONG AND SHORT RUN)

A. Product development

B. Distribution techniques

C. Pricing

D. Promotion

E. Profitability

F. Share of the market

TEN-YEAR PLANS

(In this section are detailed plans for five years and a targeted general statement for the 10th year.)

A. Product development   B. Etc., as above

ONE-YEAR DETAILED PLANS

(Included here are the specific action steps necessary to accomplish marketing objectives, such as promotion, display, support of other departments, etc.)

FINANCIAL SUMMARY

A. Analysis of income, cost, and profit results (10 years).

portant parts. The plan must be flexible to meet changing circumstances. It should include a schedule, a sequence of events to be followed. It should include a short-term budget to guide current efforts. The plan should provide for, or rest upon, the precise methods for carrying it out. It should be based upon a system for periodic review. It also, of course, should be written.

The marketing plan should, of course, follow the framework of the conceptual model presented in Chapter 2, and incorporate in it the major variables discussed above in this chapter. Each over-all marketing plan, and detailed current marketing plans, have different emphases. Table 18-2 shows a general outline for a rather complete marketing plan.

Upon the basis of this broad discussion of marketing, planning attention may now turn to selected subjects which have great importance to the marketing manager and to the student of marketing planning.

THE MARKETING MANAGER

Having discussed the function of marketing, it is now desirable to look at the many tasks of a marketing manager. As a company embraces the marketing concept and pushes towards becoming a marketing company, the functioning of the marketing manager changes and his activities expand in number and scope. In a study of 52 divisionalized companies it was found that at the corporate level 40 have a rather broad view of the marketing function. Generally, the person in charge of this activity in these companies is a vice president, usually has the word marketing in his title, and reports to the president. (Stieglitz and Janger, 1965, p. 80.)

There is, of course, no standard list of functions of marketing managers, but tabulation of functions of many marketing managers would undoubtedly show the following activities to be included in the job responsibility of more than one:

market research	industry and customer relations
new product development	customer service
product pricing	sales organization
branding	distribution channels
personal selling	physical distribution
advertising	marketing field organization
promotion	marketing law
display	general marketing administration

Seldom, if ever, will one find all these activities performed by one marketing manager. These activities also may overlap, depending upon definitions, and they may be further subdivided.

The marketing concept is, of course, a systems concept. All the above activities, for example, may be considered subsystems to the larger marketing system of a company. (Adler, 1967b, pp. 105-118.)

The responsibility of the marketing manager may vary with respect to each of these activities. For example, he may be responsible for making recommendations to the president concerning policy in each of the areas. He may be responsible for management of activities in some of the areas, such as management of salesmen. He may be responsible for coordinating actions among different functional groups, such as in new product development.

The mix of these activities and responsibilities will, of course, vary much from case to case. In small firms the marketing manager is obliged to perform just about all these functions, with whatever help he can pick up from others. In a larger company, however, there must be substantial delegation of authority and complex interrelationships with other functional and operating groups.

ALTERNATIVE MARKETING ORGANIZATIONS

Planning the marketing organization is a major responsibility of top management. This necessitates decisions about such matters as which functions a marketing manager will perform, how authority is distributed among managers in the marketing organization, and what are the authority relationships among functional and operating managers.

There are three fundamental ways of organizing marketing activities, viz., by function, by product, and by market. Chart 18-3 illustrates the functional approach, which simply means organizing the work to be done around marketing functions and under a marketing manager. As growth takes place and products increase in numbers, conflicts may arise among the functional areas which can be resolved by organizing around products, as shown in Chart 18-4. In this type of organization, very characteristic of the packaged goods industry, product managers have authority over functional areas contributing to their job. Product managers in this type of organization have varying degrees of functional authority, ranging from very little to much, over employees in other functional areas contributing to their work. If particular markets become important, or the number of products marketed nationally increases, the marketing task may be organized better around markets, as shown in Chart 18-5. Tire and chemical companies, among others, have used this type of organization to assure better coordination of effort at local levels.

The varieties of organization developed from these three basic types is limited only by human ingenuity. To illustrate a few, organization may emphasize a type customer, several product managers may be set up within a division and each be given direct responsibility over all functional personnel, organizations may emphasize manufacturing process or technology employed, or they may be

Chart 18-3
Functional Arrangement of Authority in a Marketing Organization

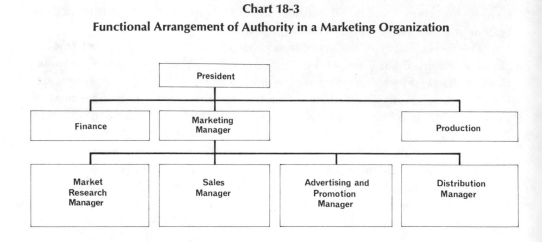

Chart 18-4
Marketing Organization with Product Managers

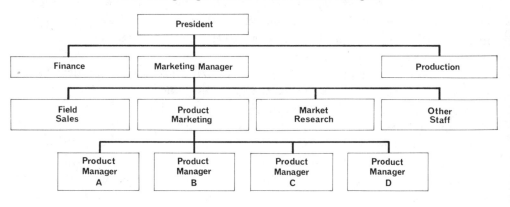

Chart 18-5
A Marketing Organization with Geographic Decentralization of Authority

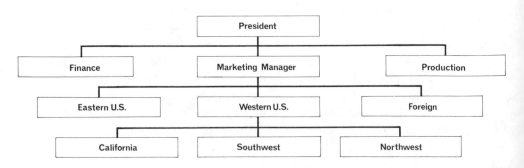

divided according to defense or nondefense markets, or they may emphasize raw materials. (Evans, 1964, p. 15.)

When organizations move away from the classical functional set up several inherent problems appear. Responsibility is more difficult to define and is shared by specialists and market product managers. Because of this the problems in developing coordinated strategies and plans increase. For reasons such as these Pearson and Wilson (1967) point out that companies should stick with functional organization as long as possible and that functional organizations have success-fully been used by large complex companies with a line of similar products, one dominant product line, and several large product lines.

Many executives have found, much to their embarrassment, that changing the marketing organization from a functional to a product type, has not brought beneficial results, and that the same type organization which succeeds in one company does not always fare well in another. This suggests there probably are underlying actions that are required to be sure the more complex organizational arrangements actually work well. Pearson and Wilson (1967) have identified five.

First, the limits of the product manager's role and responsibility for the management of a product must clearly be set forth. A product manager who is given full responsibility for a product and then is denied authority over adver-tising, promotion, or product development, is clearly heading for trouble.

Second, there should be developed a strategy and process review to guide and measure performance of a product manager's operations. There should be an over-all strategy for the company which is stated in as clear and concrete terms as possible. Without this strategy, product managers may have great diffi-culty getting plans approved. But with this, and an orderly process for reviewing and approving his subplans, there is a firm basis for measuring a product man-ager's performance. This sort of thing, as said so frequently before, is nicely accomplished in a comprehensive formal planning program.

Third, when a product manager must use a functional staff, the possibility for conflicts between him and the function staff should be considered in apprais-ing his performance.

Fourth, a process should be created which will force to the top management levels all important conflicts of interest between product management and func-tional line management. Obviously, if conflicts are submerged and allowed to fester, the chances for damage increase.

Fifth, establish a system for measuring the results of a product manager's performance which is consistent with his responsibilities. A fundamental measure of performance should be profits, but many problems arise in trying to measure performance on this basis. (Some were mentioned in Chapter 13 in the discussion of ROI.) A system should be established which can register for each product manager the normal cost of elements under his control and standard cost of all elements not under his control. With this information it would be possible to hold a product manager accountable for profitability and to watch any trade-off of long-term profits for short-term gains.

THE ROLE OF MARKET RESEARCH IN MARKETING PLANNING

What was said above makes abundantly clear the importance to marketing planning of market studies. Further comment on this matter by way of elaboration and illustration is in order here.

For many years whatever the H. J. Heinz Co. made had to bear the Heinz keystone label. But since 1964 this company has aggressively sought private-label business in soups and baby foods. (*Business Week,* 1967d.) A few years ago, Univis, a producer of optical lenses, discovered some cracks in its distribution system and covered them by creating two completely new and separate specialist sales forces to complement the sales force selling to distributors. (*Dun's Review and Modern Industry,* April 1965, pp. 83-84.) The circulation of *The Observer* had fallen from 250,000 in early 1962 to 136,000 in mid-1963. Following a series of changes the circulation of this paper hit over 400,000 in two years. All these developments resulted from thorough market research.

Marketing research has many purposes. Sometimes it is to provide information for decision-making, sometimes data are collected only for background knowledge, sometimes a study is made to help determine what questions should be asked for further study, sometimes studies are made to test theories held by managers and scholars about the marketing process, and sometimes market research may help a company to prove a theory that gives it a competitive advantage. The field of marketing, and its theory, is still being developed and as a result much market research in business is concerned with testing and developing theories about various parts of the process. There is just about no aspect of marketing which does not deserve research, and in the research it is possible to use many disciplines and areas of knowledge, as illustrated in Chart 18-2. Of highest importance to most companies, however, is research in four areas: sales potential, competition, general environmental trends, and special studies. The following comments are designed only to illustrate the scope and direction of such studies, and their important uses, rather than to describe how they may be conducted.

THE MARKETING AUDIT. Some writers in the marketing field draw a line of demarcation between the marketing audit and marketing research, but I shall consider the audit as a type of marketing research. The marketing audit generally is considered to be an over-all comprehensive survey of the marketing system, practices, policies, philosophy, organization, and management of a company. It is concerned with the fundamental conceptual and operational basis of a firm's marketing activities. Covered are every aspect of the marketing function—products, sales, promotion, distribution, channels, pricing, and so on. The audit looks at past history, current interrelationships among actions and objectives, and the implications of current activities for future developments. This type of information, of course, will reveal possible ways to improve policies, objectives, and strategies. For instance, in one firm that made such a survey it was found that the price of one product gradually was reduced over time until costs became higher than the price. Just the reverse was found in another product of the same company. An audit may show a decline in productivity per salesman, or that important policies are not being followed, or that a company needs to retrain marketing managers, or that the entire distribution system needs revision.

SALES POTENTIAL. In seeking to determine sales potential a market researcher wants an answer to two fundamental questions: what is the market over a given period of time, and what is the character of that market? These two questions, when answered, are basic to decision-making about new as well as old products. Quite obviously, a company is not likely to introduce a new product on the market, or continue an old one, if there is no market. Furthermore, study of the market and its character may pinpoint a new opportunity which was not clear before, or identify a previously unseen threat.

Some of the questions which must be answered in determining *what* the market is over a period of time, or at one point in time, for a particular product, are:

Who are the customers?
How much will they buy?
Where will they buy?
At what price will they buy what volume?
What is the major competition likely to be?
What are the probabilities of different levels of sales potential?

To determine the *character* of the market other questions must be answered, such as:

What are the characteristics of customers? What are the major segments of the market? These questions involve analysis which looks for such distinctions as the following: age distribution, income distribution, rural versus urban, foreign versus domestic, government versus non-government, and so on.
Who are the major customers?
Is sales growth based on fad, or strong long-term trends?
What does the customer desire in terms of satisfactions?

Why does the customer purchase one product rather than another?
(Price? Quality? Service? Advertising? Selling?)
What are the customers' main methods and patterns of buying?
What changes are likely in customer buying habits?
What is the elasticity of demand?
What are the preferred channels to customers in terms of their interests?
Are they the least cost channels?

This list can easily be expanded but I think the nature of the required research is indicated by them. Getting acceptable answers to questions such as these is difficult, especially for new products. For example, electronic companies have spent years and much money in trying to get better figures on potential sales of military electronics and they are today unhappy with their ability to forecast the market more accurately. However, when questions such as the above can be answered, even reasonably accurately, a strong base for marketing planning is laid.

COMPETITION. Market research may be pursued in this area as a part of the above types of study, or as a separate problem. To note a few of the major questions which should be answered is to illustrate the significance of this research. (See also Table 8-1, Chapter 8.)

Who are our major competitors?
What is the share of the market of major competitors?
What are the major strengths and weaknesses of our competitors in each important marketing area?
How active are our competitors likely to be in introducing new products, cutting prices, changing distribution methods and channels, in promotion, and so on?
What specific important actions from our point of view are competitors likely to take in these areas?
What marketing plans must be made in our company to offset competitive threats?

GENERAL ENVIRONMENTAL TRENDS. Here, the research should cover important environmental factors that will have an influence on marketing planning. To illustrate: changing consumption patterns, buyer attitudes, price changes for raw materials and finished products, style trends, government regulations, community acceptance of different communications media, changing consumer buying habits, and so on. The importance of studies such as these were discussed at length in Chapter 8.

SPECIAL STUDIES. Market research also would include, of course, such special studies as warehouse location, plant location, store location, measurement of sales performance, and the characteristics of specific retail trading areas, to name a few.

WHO CONDUCTS MARKET RESEARCH? The primary responsibility for market research, of course, is in the marketing area. But, as noted in Chapter 8, the analysis of marketing phenemenon which is important in business decision-making is often made in other areas of the company independent of, as well as in conjunction with, marketing. Engineering, for instance, may be mostly responsible for examining future technical capabilities of competitors. Accounting may participate with marketing in making pricing studies. And, research and development may work with salesmen in designing a new product to meet identified consumer demands. Studies about whether a company should make or buy a component are also a significant type of market research for many companies.

To a growing number of companies the possible scope of market research is becoming so large and important that major problems arise about the depth of research to be done by the staff of the company, and whether and what kind of research shall be purchased. In conjunction with the first point, of course, are major decisions about the special competence that a company will want to have in its own staff.

A MATRIX OF MARKETING OBJECTIVES

Marketing objectives generally grow out of market research. For instance, a forecast of the sales potential for a product may dictate the sales objective. If the company has 25 percent of the market for a product today and can see no way to increase that share, nor any threat to that level, the sales objective is determined by the market forecast. Market research can also identify market segments, distribution channels, or brand preferences which also may serve as a basis for formulating new objectives. American Motors identified a segment of the automobile market which it exploited profitably with its first compact Rambler. It has had problems, however, in protecting its position from encroachment by the major automobile manufacturers.

Marketing objectives also, of course, are derivative from higher over-all company objectives. For instance, the following sequence can easily be conceived for sales objectives:

Over-all Company Objectives:
—Increase sales volume by 10 percent each year over the next five years.
—Increase profits 12 percent each year over the next five years.

Marketing Vice President Objectives
Preliminary sales, profit, and share objectives for all product groups are as follows:

Product Group	SALES VOLUME Year 1 2 3 4 5	PROFITS Year 1 2 3 4 5	MARKET SHARE Year 1 2 3 4 5
A			
B			
C			
D			
E			
F			

Corporate Sales Manager

District sales and profit objectives for each product group, in terms of volume in each district, and for each market segment, for each of the next five years, are as follows—

District Sales Managers

Sales and profit volume for each product group, for each market segment, and for each salesman, for the next five years, are as follows—

Salesmen

Sales and profit volume for each major account, and other customers, for each product group, for the next five years, are as follows—

A comparable hierarchy of objectives should exist for other marketing elements, such as cost reduction, advertising and promotion, distribution, and so on. These objectives also should relate horizontally at each major level of management.

MARKETING STRATEGIES

Each of the elements of marketing planning, and the entire market plan, is founded upon one or more central ideas or strategies to achieve predetermined objectives. All that was said in Chapter 9 about strategies applies to marketing strategies. That chapter, among other things, identified a number of significant approaches to the development of strategies which certainly apply to marketing. But there are aspects of strategy which apply somewhat uniquely to marketing which deserve additional comment.

SOME ILLUSTRATIONS OF MARKETING STRATEGY. Money companies seek a continuously high sales volume, with commensurate profits, for specific products. To do this requires that a company achieve a maximum differential in competitive strength in a market segment.* The Mallory Battery Company, a major division of P. R. Mallory and Company, Inc., successfully did this when it decided that the best way to take advantage of its technology was to get its batteries into consumer devices as original equipment. It designed its batteries, in light of this strategy, for Instamatic camera flash, Accutron watches, Zenith hearing aids, and tape recorders. It then pushed sales in retail stores throughout the world as replacement batteries for the original equipment. At the same time the company licensed production of two important batteries on which it held patents—mercury and manganese-alkaline—to several of its competitors because of their marketing ability in getting into "the nooks and crannies of retailing." (*Business Week*, 1967a.)

In Chapter 9 it was noted that one approach to the development of a strategy was finding a niche in a market. The Volkswagen found a niche in the American automobile market which it was able to perserve and, indeed, strengthen. It had two important advantages in the American market. First, American manufacturers could not dislodge the Volkswagen niche with modifications of American automobiles. Second, American manufacturers could not bring their economies of scale to the disadvantage of Volkswagen. The Polaroid Land Camera found a competitive niche (in taking pictures and printing them simultaneously) which it has been able to maintain for a long period of time.

The strategy chosen should be coordinated with other strategies of a company and seek optimization of the whole rather than the parts. It will be recalled that Winchester chose new marketing channels while trying to maintain its past distribution system. This failed because strategies conflicted. The idea here is to avoid optimization of sub-systems which prevent optimization of the entire business. To be avoided, of course, is a pricing strategy which keeps an obsolete product moving at the expense of total business profits.

In every major area of marketing there is a variety of strategies from which to choose. To show how complex a matter it is to choose strategies, it is interesting to examine the principal factors in Table 18-3, which 146 companies said were taken into consideration in pricing new products, and then imagine the number of separate strategies that might be associated with each one. Comparable possibilities exist for the other three P's of McCarthy.

STRATEGIES SHOULD BE SPECIFIC. A company could establish a strategy in these terms: "In order to increase the share of the market for product Y, additional funds will be devoted to product design and advertising." The objective, as well as the way resources are to be deployed, is too vague. It would be much more helpful to marketing planning if the statement could be made more concrete, such as: "The decline in market share of product Y will be halted and

---

* I am indebted to Charles W. Faris (1967), for this and the following principle, which he called "conditions to be met."

reversed by (a) complementing it with a jumbo-sized package, (b) increasing advertising in high-brand development areas, (c) increasing promotion spending in weaker share areas, and (d) redesigning packaging for greater sales appeal." The objective is established, although it could be more specific if actual share-of-market numbers were used. Strategy is much more clear.

STRATEGIES FOR CONTROLLING PRODUCT LIFE CYCLES. Every product goes through a life cycle like that shown in Chart 18-6. The product life cycle is based on the observable fact that the sales volume of a typical product follows an s-shaped curve such as that shown in Chart 18-6. During its introduction on the market a product usually passes through a low-volume production phase. Then it enters a period of rapid growth to reach a sales peak at maturity, and then sales gradually decline. Notice that the profit curve shows a declining rate of growth and absolute decline before corresponding sales. Of course, each product has its own particular profile but the average one follows the curve illustrated. In every case the end is the same—obsolescence and disappearance. Before this happens a product may go through a series of new life cycles.

Table 18-3   Principal Factors in Pricing New Products

PROFIT AND COST CONSIDERATIONS
Profit (general)
   Return on investment (or sales)
   Cost plus profit
Volume-cost-price relationships
Costs (general)
   Production costs
   Development costs
   Selling or promotional costs
Financial risk

COMPETITIVE CONSIDERATIONS
Competition (general)
Price of competitive products
Price of substitute products
Degree or type of competition
Anticipated reaction of competitors

PRODUCT CHARACTERISTICS
Value to customers (general)
   Economic justification to customers
   Product utility
Product uniqueness (general)

Quality
Service
Patent control
Importance to product line
Product's expected proprietary strength
Product life

MARKET OR SALES EXPECTATIONS
Market size or potential
Estimated sales volume for company's new
   product
Share-of-market goal or potential

OTHER FACTORS
Anticipated reaction of prospective
   customers
Maximum price obtainable
Stability of industry price structure
Consistency with product-line price structure
Psychological pricing factors
Unused production capacity
For sale in domestic or foreign market
Corporate-image implications

Source: National Industrial Conference Board, *Appraising the Market for New Industrial Products,* Studies in Business Policy, No. 123 (New York: NICB, 1967), p. 74.

Chart 18-6

The Basic Life Cycle of New Products

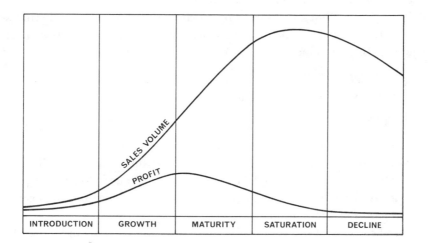

| INTRODUCTION | GROWTH | MATURITY | SATURATION | DECLINE |

This phenomenon creates two fundamental opportunities for imaginative strategy. First, is to reshape and control the life cycle of each product. Second, is to develop a mix among individual product life cycles which will best achieve company objectives. (Clifford, 1965, pp. 48-60; Cox, 1967, pp. 375-388.)

Special strategies are needed at each stage of a product's life cycle and in the different marketing areas. For example, in the introduction stage the product is competing with old goods and, as a result, advertising may be directed mostly at informing the public about the uses and advantages of the product. When Corfam first came on the market its advertising was directed in this way. When the product approaches maturity there will be competition with sellers of the same type of product, sellers of other products, and threats from new products. Here, advertising may seek to induce consumers to ask for the product by its brand name.

Marketing mix will also vary among the different life cycle stages. For example, in the maturity stage brand advertising may be mixed with cost reduction to make the product more competitive, repackaging to give it a new competitive status, new channels of distribution to open up new markets, and other advertising which points out to consumers possible new uses for the product. Jell-O and General Foods have successfully created a new life cycle for many of their products through a mix such as this.

In the stage of saturation, the product is competing with new products, it is becoming obsolete, consumers may be getting "tired" of it, or it has lost its identity as a result of the expansion of private brands of distributors. These conditions suggest a much different mix of marketing strategies than noted above.

In order to retain old customers, service may be expanded, advertising may be directed more toward brand names, redesign of the product may be needed to breathe new life into it, or it may be abandoned.

In sum, there are many approaches to the development of marketing strategies and many possible strategies which will pay off. It is the art of marketing management to determine which are the "right" strategies.

NEWER QUANTITATIVE TECHNIQUES IN MARKETING PLANNING

Marketing decisions have long been dominated by intuition based upon experience—and this will continue. This is not because there is apathy to using new decision-making methods but rather to the enormous intrinsic complexity of marketing problems which defy quantification so characteristic, for example, of most production planning problems.

Nevertheless, all the quantitative methods discussed in previous chapters are now finding more applications in the marketing area. Elementary textbooks in the marketing field are becoming more quantitatively oriented.* There are also a number of books concerned solely with quantitative methods in marketing. (Frank, Kuehn, and Massy, 1962; Ferber, Blankertz, and Hollander, Jr., 1964; Weinberg in Alderson and Shapiro, 1963; and Frank and Green, 1966.) The professional journals, and the more popular magazines for managers, are also printing more quantitatively-oriented marketing articles. (Kotler, 1965b; and *Business Week*, 1965b.)

In addition to all the methods presented in previous chapters, there are others which are of particular significance to marketing which can only be mentioned here. Sampling theory, tests of consumer intentions, and special tools for determining location of retail stores, are obviously important in marketing planning, and illustrate the point.

Of all the newer developments in marketing planning none compares with the importance of computers. Computers permit marketing managers to do things today that were impossible before computers. In addition to their uses in applying new tools to aid decision-making, consider this illustration of its use at J. C. Penney. At J. C. Penney, as in some other large merchandisers, the small punched tickets, removed from merchandise sold at all stores during the day, are sent to New York City or Los Angeles. These little tickets are coded to show many facts and, when fed into the computer, can match a store's planned stock against actual stock; if there is a deficiency, the computer can order an appropriate amount of new stock. As discussed previously, computers also permit the application to marketing problems of such powerful tools as linear programming

---

* See especially Alderson and Green, 1964; and Charvat and Whitman, 1967.

(to improve physical distribution, for example), and simulation (to determine market mixes, consumer preferences, sales forecasts, potential competitive behavior, and pricing, for example).

THE POLITICAL AND LEGAL AND SOCIAL AND CULTURAL ENVIRONMENTS

At the beginning of this chapter it was pointed out that marketing plans must be made in recognition of various environmental forces, some of which a firm may influence and some of which it cannot alter, at least in the short run. Of great importance to marketing are the political and legal and the cultural and social environments. It is not always understood that planning in marketing can be a complete waste of time if it is contrary to forces in these environments.

POLITICAL AND LEGAL ENVIRONMENT. In the U.S., as in most countries of the world, there exists a pattern of relationships between the business community and government. Business influences government, and government, of course, directly affects business. A classic example of misunderstood relationships between the two led, in 1962, to withdrawal of a price increase by the steel companies after the strongly expressed displeasure of President Kennedy. Any marketing plan for a foreign country which does not consider political conditions in that country may be disastrous. For example, a plan to market a product in a particular country may be blocked by a sudden protectionist wall built as a result of internal political considerations.

Laws which affect marketing are massive, very complex, and often reflect contradictions in social attitudes. Aside from many inconsistencies among the laws are uncertainties about how they will be applied. For these reasons an understanding of the complex body of laws bearing particularly on marketing and the way they are likely to be enforced, is highly important in determining the feasibility of a marketing plan.

The antitrust laws of the federal government are the foundation for laws having an important influence on marketing. The first major piece of legislation in this area was the Sherman Antitrust Act (1890) which clearly specified (Section 1) that "Every contract, combination in the form of trust or otherwise, or conspiracy, in restraint of trade or commerce . . . is illegal." This law was passed upon the insistence of producers who were being victimized by monopolistic distributors, and by small competitors who were being driven out of business by gigantic trusts. This law still stands as a rampart against monopolistic practices. It has, however, been amended in many important ways, and associated statutes have been passed in many areas, so that today the laws regulating business practices are very complex. This complexity should be illustrated here.

In 1911, for example, the Supreme Court said there were both reasonable and unreasonable restraints of trade: the former do not violate the law, while the latter do.* This was the so-called "rule of reason," and the Congress responded approvingly by passing the Federal Trade Commission Act (1914), establishing the Federal Trade Commission, to administer this interpretation. The Act gave the FTC substantive regulatory powers the most prominent of which were over (Section 5) ". . . unfair methods of competition in commerce, and *unfair or deceptive acts or practices in commerce* . . ."† The FTC was given authority to issue cease and desist orders against actions which the law said were illegal.

In the same year the Clayton Antitrust Act was passed "to supplement existing laws against unlawful restraints and monopolies." Probably the most significant part (Section 7) stipulated that no corporation engaged in interstate commerce could acquire the stock of another corporation also engaged in interstate commerce when the effect was "to substantially lessen competition" between the two. (The Celler-Kefauver Amendment of 1950, known as the Anti-Merger Act, prohibited the acquisition of assets as well as stocks when the effect was to reduce competition.) But the Clayton Act also specifically prohibited tying agreements which substantially lessened competition or attempted to create a monopoly in any line of commerce. It prohibited interlocking directorates which limited competition in violation of the antitrust laws, and it also dealt with price discrimination.

During the depression of the 1930's small grocers felt they were unjustly threatened by the competition of chain stores and were instrumental in the passage of the Robinson-Patman Act (1936). Section 2 of the Clayton Act was designed to prevent temporary local price-cutting by a firm with large resources from eliminating a competitor who was not strong enough to withstand a price war even though he might be just as efficient. The Robinson-Patman Act strengthened this provision by stating that price discrimination was unlawful where the effect might be "to injure, destroy, or prevent competition with any person who either grants or knowingly receives the benefit of such discrimination, or with customers of either of them." This law was anti-chain store and was directed more to the survival of small competitors than to maintenance of competition in general. Nevertheless, this Act has resulted in a complex mass of administrative interpretation and court action concerning what is and what is not permissible price differentials.

Among other pieces of legislation with which certain marketing managers should be familiar are the following. The Lanham Trademark Act (1946) which is concerned with trademarks. A number of laws concern products, such as the Wool Products Labeling Act (1939), the Fur Products Labeling Act (1951), the Textile Fiber Products Identification Act (1958), and the Federal Hazardous

* *United States v. Standard Oil Co. of New Jersey,* 221 U.S. 1 (1911).

† The italicized parts were added by the Wheeler-Lea Act of 1938 which also gave the FTC more power to enforce its orders.

Substances Labeling Act (1960). In the foods area, laws such as the following have special impact on certain types of producers: the Federal Food, Drug and Cosmetic Act (1938), and the Federal Aviation Act (1958) which concerns, among other things, certification of airplanes. To federal regulations must be added state and local laws and ordnances concerning advertising, distribution and selling methods, trade agreements, and pricing.

Resale price maintenance, for example, is a special aspect of laws concerning pricing. Known as "fair trade" acts, resale price maintenance laws permit a manufacturer or distributor of products bearing a trade-mark, brand, or name of the producer, to fix by contract the minimum or actual wholesale and retail price of such products as they move to the consumer. Most states now have laws which permit some form of retail price maintenance. These laws were approved by the Congress in the Miller-Tydings Act (1937) which amended the Sherman Act to exempt resale price agreements in interstate commerce when commodities move into states where resale price maintenance contracts are legal. This Act also stipulated that such laws shall not be considered as unfair competition under Section 5 of the Federal Trade Commission Act. Resale price maintenance is a subject of considerable controversy but it is legal.

This brief survey is given only to underscore the fact that legislation exists which is important in making marketing plans. There are many valuable textbooks on marketing law such as Howard (1964); Simon (1956); and Grether (1966). A few illustrations of its impact on marketing objectives and strategy may further illuminate this consideration. Before doing so, however, a word should be said about social attitudes.

SOCIAL AND CULTURAL ENVIRONMENT. The marketing plan must be made in awareness of attitudes of people and other cultural forces in the community. The public generally, and important segments of it particularly, have views about the various aspects of marketing which a marketing manager ignores at his peril. Advertising, for example, which violates a deep feeling, custom, or taste of a people may doom a product to failure. In Germany, for instance, the young, vivacious, attractive blonde model that is used to advertise automobiles in the United States does a better job if she is not too young, not too gay, not too frivolous. (*Wall Street Journal*, April 27, 1965, p. 1.)

Differences in habits, values, and ways of doing things naturally have a bearing upon marketing success. Colgate-Palmolive has found, for instance, that it must vary its soap formulas from country to country in Western Europe. Italians, for example, like heavily scented soap while the Swedes do not. General Mills introduced Betty Crocker cake mixes into Great Britain in 1960 and withdrew them three years later because the British people found them too sweet. Nationalism in foreign countries leads companies like Singer, Woolworth, National Cash Register, and Heinz, to maintain a low corporate silhouette and a high product image. In the United States just the reverse is sometimes the preferred strategy.

Intellectual leaders and other opinion makers are concerned with business practices and their views may either restrain or advance certain marketing practices. Some prominent writers, for example, have violently attacked marketing persuasion as the source of distortion of social values, production and consumption priorities, and social resource allocations. In some current literature the consumer is pictured as a bedeviled focus of business pressures to buy what he does not want, may not need, and cannot afford. (Galbraith, 1966, especially Chapter XVIII; Packard, 1957; and Packard, 1960.) There is no question about the fact that advertising may lead a consumer to buy what he does not want or need. But Galbraith, for instance, would divert persuasion through taxation from the promotion of luxuries to the advancement of better education, more housing, cleaner air, purer water, and improved recreation parks. These views have not gone unchallenged (Sandage, 1961, pp. 71-80, Alderson, 1957, Chapter IX, and Grether, 1968, pp. 9-13) but they are accepted by many influential thinkers. Whether valid or not, the point is that they are most relevant to long-range marketing planning. Executives must be aware of moral as well as legal restraints that are placed upon them by society as a whole and by influential groups in it.

LEGAL IMPACTS ON MARKET STRATEGY. Some of the laws pertaining to marketing practices are clear and unequivocal. But there is a vast gray area where legality depends upon many circumstances such as the size of the company whose practices are being judged, the share of the market of the product concerned, and the jurists or governmental administrators who are interpreting the law. The following observations are designed to illustrate this.

A company that acquires too large a market may find itself in trouble with the antitrust laws.* This problem is complicated by the fact that the Supreme Court will not permit itself to be pinned down as to what constitutes an illegal share of the market. Furthermore, there usually are problems in defining what is the market to be measured.

Since the "model" statute drawn up by Printer's Ink in 1911 concerning false and deceptive advertising, the mounting legislation on this subject indicates a declining tolerance by society of advertising which is deceptive and which takes

---

* What is too much is not clear, but in *United States v. Aluminum Co. of America,* 322 U. S. 716 (1945), the Supreme Court held that 90 percent of an industry was in itself objectionable. On the other hand, in *United States v. Columbia Steel Co.,* 334 U. S. 495 (1948), 51 percent of the market was not considered objectionable. In *Brown Shoe Company v. United States,* 370 U. S. 1 294 (1962), however, the Court ruled that a merger of the Brown Shoe Company and the G. R. Kinney chain of retail stores violated the antitrust laws since the combined shares of the merged companies exceeded 5 percent of the total market for children's and women's shoes in the areas served.

advantage of consumers' ignorance or gullibility. The FTC has issued cease and desist orders against a long list of unfair advertising practices. Not only is false advertising contrary to law, but excessive amounts of advertising also is unfair competition.*

Price fixing is a thorny area in which several very large companies recently ran afoul of the law and temporarily importantly damaged their images. Pricing decisions that are made in cooperation with other sellers are illegal *per se*, with the one exception of resale price maintenance as noted above. On the other hand, pricing which is reached independently by a company, and which does not discriminate against competing producers or result in a restraint of trade, is legal. But in between are many circumstances where only intimate knowledge of the law will permit a judgment as to what is legal or illegal.

SUMMARY AND CONCLUDING GUIDELINES
FOR MARKETING PLANNING

This chapter examined at some length the meaning of marketing, the way in which marketing has grown in importance in most companies, tests of marketing orientation, the nature and characteristics of marketing planning, marketing organization, and special topics of importance in marketing planning. The latter included the nature and role of market research; the matrix of marketing objectives; marketing strategies; the use of newer quantitative techniques in marketing planning; and the relevance of political, legal, social, and cultural environmental factors on marketing planning.

Some of the more important conclusions and guidelines for marketing planning are as follows:

1. There is no generally accepted definition of marketing. The one most favored in this chapter is that marketing deals with the goods and service exchange between consumers and the firm in such a way as to improve the assortment to the mutual benefit of each.

2. Today's advanced marketing company has gone through four stages in marketing development during the past hundred years, and in each the marketing function has been elevated in importance. Also, in each stage the consumer has assumed a more central position in marketing planning.

3. Marketing is becoming more important as society becomes more complex. This is illustrated by the fact that today about 50 percent of the consumer's dollar is for marketing costs.

4. The chief executive is the principal marketing officer. His participation in marketing planning is important in its success and marketing planning is important in the success of his company.

* *American Tobacco Co. v. U. S.*, 328 U. S. 781, 797 (1946).

5. The responsibilities of marketing managers vary with each company and industry, but they are expanding rather than contracting.

6. There is no single best marketing organization. Acceptable alternative arrangements are variations of three basic patterns of marketing organization— by function, product, and region.

7. Product organizational arrangements generate conflicts of authority not found in functional arrangements. There are, however, practices that can be followed to reduce these frictions to tolerable proportions.

8. A formal corporate planning program is the best framework within which marketing planning problems can be resolved.

9. There are identifiable steps in marketing planning which, when followed, will improve the marketing planning process. The operational steps, however, are tailored to each company's situation.

10. The identification of markets, and analysis of the characteristics of markets, are products of market research and fundamental in finding marketing opportunities and threats and in formulating marketing objectives and strategies.

11. A hierarchy of objectives and goals exists in better marketing planning to relate marketing aims to company objectives, to tie objectives and goals in each major marketing function to higher objectives, and to relate at each level of management the aims of each marketing function. The degree of interrelatedness will vary, of course, but marketing planning should develop and proceed upon the basis of such a network.

12. Once objectives and strategies are formulated, the next problem in marketing planning is to develop the marketing mix, or the combination of all the many marketing elements needed to achieve objectives. The bewildering variety of these elements may be classified in one of the following four categories: product, place, promotion, and price. The marketing mix is unique to each plan.

13. While intuition and experience are still and will continue to be major determinants of decision in marketing planning, newer quantitative methods are being used more and more to help managers.

14. The political, legal, and social, and cultural environments are so important to marketing planning that marketing managers should be knowledgeable about aspects of these fields, which touch upon their current and potential interests.

19
Product Planning ⸻

19
Product Planning

INTRODUCTION

In the preceding chapter it was pointed out that the success of a company depends upon how well it mixes the four P's of marketing elements: product, place, promotion, and price. This chapter deals with the first of these because of its huge significance to a business firm. While all elements of a marketing mix are important in the final outcome of a new product development, the action usually begins with and is focused on product.

The subject of product planning is much larger than can be confined in the few pages of this chapter, so attention will be focused on selected issues. They are the nature and importance of products and product planning, the nature of preferred organizational arrangements for new product development, the process of selecting and screening ideas, and product elimination. The reader will remember that aspects of product planning were treated in previous chapters, and he may take note that the subject will be touched upon in later chapters.

NATURE AND IMPORTANCE OF PRODUCT
AND PRODUCT PLANNING

WHAT IS A PRODUCT?   At the outset it is useful to define what is meant by a product. It can, of course, be described as a physical thing or commodity. But, in line with the discussion of the preceding chapter, it can and should be described in much broader terms. Consumers do not buy products because of their physical appearance, chemical content, or construction. They buy products for the satisfaction, use, utility, and profit which they expect to get from the product.

This concept of product as a bundle of satisfactions or benefits has importance in considering product planning. It says that a product is not only the physical thing but all the elements associated with it that are designed to enhance consumer satisfactions. Included, of course, are appearance or packaging, price, service, location, and other marketing elements. Product planning, therefore, embraces not only the technical development of a product but the relationship of all marketing elements to enhancing its satisfaction and benefit to consumers.

PRODUCT FAILURE CHANCES. Every manager should have a firm understanding of the sobering statistics of product failure. (George A. Steiner, 1966b, pp. 52-62, *passim*.) While no reliable data are available the rules of thumb for all industry are probably well within the following ranges.

The chances that a new idea will result in a commercial success are at least less than one in 100. In some industries, for certain types of products, the odds against development of an idea are greater. The Pharmaceutical Manufacturers' Association, for instance, reports that the odds are more than 6,000 to one that a newly discovered drug will never reach the market. In 1962, 168,000 substances were tested in pharmaceutical laboratories, of which only twenty-eight became marketable drugs (Chas. Pfizer and Co., Inc., 1968, p. 10). J. H. Whitney and Company says that out of 2,100 new product propositions, only seventeen were considered to have merit; out of these only two were conspicuously successful, five were moderately successful, six were borderline, three were still too young to appraise, and one was a distinct failure even though its production was recommended. (Arnoff in Ewing, 1964a, p. 318.) Another observer has reported that out of 540 new ideas for chemical products proposed for further analysis, 98 were regarded as pertinent, 8 were approved for development, and 1 went to market. (Ralph Jones, 1958.)

For ideas that actually are introduced into a company's planning program and are sufficiently attractive to warrant at least a preliminary technical-business review, the chances of commercial success are one in forty, as shown in Chart 19-1. (Booz • Allen and Hamilton, 1960). For products that have been market-tested and then distributed nationally to consumers, the success ratio (in the sense of profitable production and sale) is one in five.

The world will not always beat a path to the door of the man who makes a better mousetrap. A few years ago, Chester M. Woolworth, President of the Animal Trap Company of America, of Lititz, Pa., decided that he would produce a better trap than the conventional five-cent (now higher-priced) mousetrap. He was sorry he did. He built a new trap that worked like a charm—it was highly efficient, rather good-looking, and relatively cheap at twelve cents. This product was developed upon the basis of careful research into the habits of the pests, was skillfully designed and tested in the laboratory, and then was market tested. Everything pointed to a product success and the trap was distributed nationally. Troubles quickly appeared, however, and losses forced the company to withdraw the product from the market.

Chart 19-1

Decay Curve of New Product Ideas

By Stage of Evolution

(80 Companies)

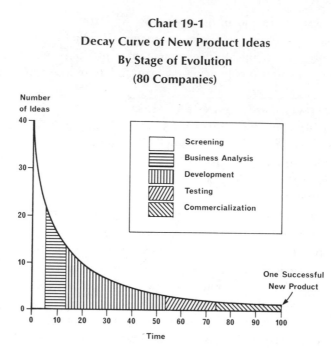

Source: This extract is reprinted with the permission of Booz • Allen & Hamilton, International Management Consultants.

What happened? The marketing and psychology tests proved inadequate. Post mortem research uncovered the fact that, typically, the husband buys the traps and the wife disposes of the mouse by tossing it and the trap into the trash. This new trap, although clearly superior to the old, obsolete product, looked too expensive to cast aside, so she was left to consider the mouse and the trap until her husband returned from work in the evening. Furthermore, once he disposed of the mouse, the trap had to be cleaned and stored. This she did not like. (Woolworth, 1962, pp. 26-27; Matthews, Jr., Buzzell, Levitt, and Frank, 1964, pp. 3-6.)

Some years ago the Pioneer Tool & Die Co., of Akron, Ohio, built a baitless, odorless, automatic trap that catches mice by the dozens. This device, about the size of an attache case, lures curious rodents, one at a time, through a hole and trap door and along a corridor that eventually leads to their deaths. The company built 5,600 of these traps and lost $63,000 when only 400 were sold at $29.95 each. The company finally scrapped 5,000 traps and at this writing is still trying to sell 200 at $15 each. Mr. Zinkann, the president of the company, says, "Our big mistake was that nobody ever found out whether anyone wanted to buy a mousetrap as elaborate as ours for the original high retail price." (*Wall Street Journal,* March 6, 1967, p. 1.)

High mortality of new products is found in both large and small companies, in those that are sophisticated and in those that are naive, and in the profitable

Chart 19-2

Industrial Goods Manufacturers' Dependence on

New Products

(173 Reporting Companies)

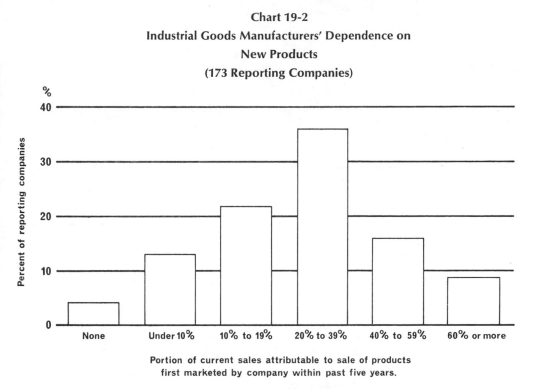

Portion of current sales attributable to sale of products
first marketed by company within past five years.

Source: Roger M. Pegram and Earl L. Bailey,"The New-products Race," in The Marketing Executive Looks Ahead,
1967 National Industrial Conference Board, Inc., p. 39.

as well as the impoverished. For most companies there is an obvious requirement
for better new product planning.

NEW PRODUCTS AND FUTURE SALES. The future sales importance
of new products to the average business firm is framed in Charts 19-2 and 19-3.
In both the industrial and consumers' goods industries, most companies report
that from 20 to 39 percent of current sales are for products first marketed by the
company within the preceding five years.

THE PRODUCT LIFE CYCLE, COSTS, PROFITS, AND TIME. In the
preceding chapter the typical life cycle of products was discussed, and portrayed
in Chart 18-6, and some of the implications of the cycle for product planning
were examined. Several additional characteristics of today's typical life cycles
create difficult problems in product planning and are examined here.

One, which has been mentioned previously, is the shortening of time between
the introduction of a product and the peak of its sales volume. To illustrate, the
Gillette Razor Company dominated the razor blade market for decades with its

Chart 19-3

Consumer Goods Manufacturers' Dependence on

New Products

(50 Reporting Companies)

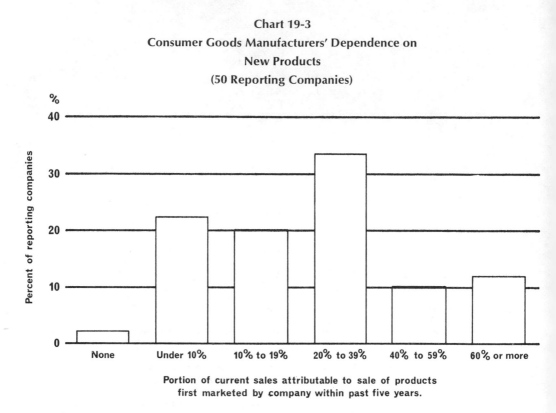

Portion of current sales attributable to sale of products
first marketed by company within past five years.

Source: Pegram and Bailey, "The New-products Race," p. 38.

Blue Blades. About 1960 Super Blue Blades were introduced with a prospect, based upon past experience, of decades of growth and profitability ahead. Within three years, however, the stainless steel razor was introduced and the Super Blue Blade was obsolete.

An important characteristic of the product life cycle, irrespective of its length, is the degree of correlation of the sales and profit volume. As shown on Chart 19-4, the two curves are rather different. During the product's introduction, the heavy marketing costs needed to launch it, the high costs of development allocated to each unit, and the low volume result in low unit profit. As growth occurs the profit volume increases rapidly. During the late growth and maturity stages, however, competition cuts into profit margins and eventually total profits begin to decline, but before sales volume drops.

For many products there is a growing inverse relationship between cost of development and product life. This is illustrated in Chart 19-5 for the transportation industry.

This phenomenon is most important when related to the slope of the profit curve noted above. Management is typically faced with the necessity for recouping heavier product development costs in a shorter period of time during which

Chart 19-4
Product Cash Flow

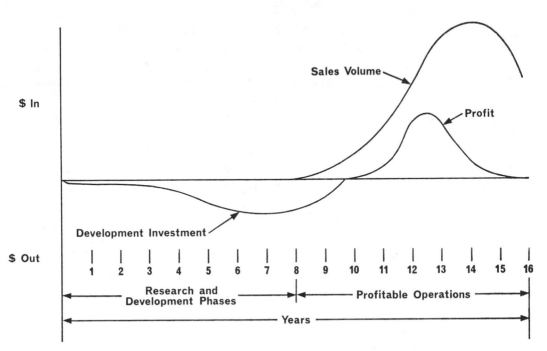

Chart 19-5
Relationship Between Product Development
Cost and Product Life

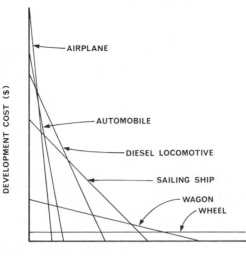

profits are made on the product. This problem becomes even more difficult as the development costs rise and pay-out period recedes into the future, as in the case for a highly technical product, such as color television or an airplane.

There is an important dilemma facing management in considering this cost-profit-time problem. Catching competitors by surprise is an old strategy to increased profits. On the other hand and up to a point, other things being equal, the longer the development and the greater the testing the less uncertainty about marketability. The more developing and testing of products, however, the greater is the initial investment. So major questions of timing arise: When to stop developing? When to stop testing? When to introduce the product? In today's business world, because of the communications network, it is very difficult to surprise a competitor. But a management that rushes to market without adequate testing may wind up far worse than if it delays and gives competition a chance to catch up. Last year, for example, a giant food company developed a fruit-filled toast waffle. It was tested carefully at a cost of about $500 thousand, and everyone thought it would be a great success. So did a major competitor who was watching the proceedings and went into production with a duplicate product. Without market testing the product was launched nationally, beat the first competitor by six months, and now enjoys a lead over the originator. (Weingarten, 1967, p. 45.)

WHY NEW PRODUCTS FAIL. There are several different ways to look at the question of why new products fail. Of major importance is the attitude of managers. If top management does not recognize the importance of new products to the prosperity and survival of the total business, and does not make unmistakably clear that it expects results in this area, the new products program may fail. Problems will arise also if top management does not recognize that there is an evolutionary process in the development of new products which is controllable by management. The basic truth, in my opinion, is that new products fail principally because of a management failure.

This is borne out by various surveys that have been made on this subject. One recent study by the National Industrial Conference Board listed the following major reasons for new product failure: (Cochran and Thompson, 1964, p. 11.)
  • Inadequate market analysis
  • Product defects
  • Higher costs than anticipated
  • Poor timing
  • Competition
  • Insufficient marketing effort
  • Inadequate sales force
  • Weakness in distribution

More than 50 percent of the 87 company respondents in this survey mentioned the first three factors. About one-third said the first item was the most important reason for the disappointing showing of new products, 25 percent mentioned the second as a primary cause, and 15 percent noted the third as the most important reason for failure.

There are, of course, many different aspects of each of these. For example, inadequate market analysis may mean there was insufficient knowledge of markets or misjudgment of markets. This could result from inaccurate forecasts of the market, incorrect estimates of the share of the market which the firm would enjoy, erroneous estimates of probable competition, acceptance of inadequate market tests, or adverse environmental forces over which the firm had no control. A major economic decline might be in this category.

This survey did not deal with organization; but if it had it might well have concluded, as did an earlier survey, that most problems of new product development were organizational in nature. A survey of hundreds of companies showed that 84 percent of them said their most significant problems were in the area of organization. Half the problems mentioned by all companies fell in this area. (Booz • Allen, and Hamilton, 1960.) Asked specifically where there were opportunities for improvement in organization the respondents mentioned these in order of importance: organization structure, definition of responsibilities, top management, systems and procedures, communications, working relationships, reporting relationships, and size of organization. Other organizational problems include executives who cannot agree on what new products are needed, idea men whose brain child is too often unjustifiedly squashed, products with sales engineered out of them, and sales department rejection of new products.

Returning to the comment made at the beginning of this discussion about management's responsibility in product success or failure, it is clear that all the reasons discovered in these surveys for failure cannot be dumped at the door of management. It can be said, however, that management has the responsibility for preventing these shortcomings from hampering successful product development, and when the shortcomings appear management has been less effective than it should have been.

WHY OLD PRODUCTS LAST. There are exceptions to the general rule that product life cycles are shrinking. For many products life is robust and appears to be unlimited. In the 1840's William and Andrew Smith peddled their "cough candy" to stagecoach riders, and today, Smith Brothers' cough drops are sold widely. Many other products enjoy a seemingly unending life, such as Hershey's milk chocolate, Life Savers, Diamond matches, Prince Albert tobacco, and Coca Cola. The following are some of the major reasons for such longevity (Adams, 1965, pp. 47 ff.) :

• Fulfillment of a basic, elementary need or desire, more real than created. The product is still being used for its original purpose, whether it is to taste better, heal faster, or clean more thoroughly.

• Graphic trademark. The product has an easily recognized and memorable trademark which identifies it in the customer's mind. Last year Listerine changed the packaging of its long-lived mouthwash to dress it up and give it more appeal. Sales promptly dropped and did not rise again until the old easily identified yellow paper packaging was restored.

• Reliability. Little change over time has been made in the product, name. or trademark. This in itself has served to symbolize uniformity and quality.

• Word-of-mouth advertising. Information has passed from one generation to another so that the product in effect becomes a household word. The product takes on a generic meaning, such as Kleenex.

• Door-to-door selling has maintained sales of many old products.

• Multiple outlets and mass distribution of mass consumption items is an important factor in successful longevity.

• Low price. Most long-term best sellers are priced in cents, not dollars, and are directed toward the stable consumption, repeat market. Furthermore, mark-ups have not kept pace with rising prices. The change has been in reduced size, such as in the old 5-cent candy bars.

• Less-than-successful imitation. Attempts to imitate for various reasons have failed.

• Profitability. The products continue not because of their name but because they have earning power.

While most companies are looking for such low-risk and high payoff products, the majority of products on the market are not in this category. Even when many of these factors are present, changes in competition, consumer tastes, or other vagaries of competitive life bring about decline.

VARIETIES OF NEW PRODUCTS. There are a number of different types of new products each of which has its own set of problems and all differ from others. The major varieties are: (Fulmer, 1966, p. 17.)

• New model. This is a new product which is an improvement over, packaging change in, or incorporates some other modification of, an existing product. It usually is designed to be sold to the same customers for the same uses as the current product. An automobile, a cake mix, or a detergent, are illustrations.

• A new product in a familiar market. In this case, the product is new to a company but the market in which it is sold is one the company knows because it is the same as that for present products. For example, a company may be making and selling herbicides to control broad-leaf weeds. Now, it decides to sell a new product which is a herbicide to control narrow-leaf or grass-like weeds.

• A product not new to the market it serves but new to a company. Transistor-grade silicon was a new product for Monsanto Chemical, for example, but it was being produced at the time by other competitors and sold in markets served by Monsanto.

• A totally new product introduced into a totally new market. An example is **Du Pont's Corfam** to replace shoe leather.

Problems associated with the success of products in each of these categories will naturally differ, and the differences will be accentuated by other dimensions, among which the following are important: risks of capital loss, capital investment required relative to a firm's equity, importance of the product to future sales and profits, nature of major customers (i.e., masses of consumers versus a single customer), size of company, organizational arrangements for product development, and experience of the company in product development of the type undertaken.

A new model development generally is considered to be a low-risk undertaking, especially if it is developed from an established product, in a complete product line, and the change is clearly indicated as being needed and accepted by customers. On the other hand, when Lockheed modified its famous F-104C fighter airplane to an all-weather bomber-intercepter for production in western European companies, risks associated with the resulting F-104G were substantial. Risk will increase in direct relation to the degree a new product departs from the engineering, manufacturing, and distributing experience of a company. Risks are very high for a company that wants to market a new product and does not have the distribution structure or know-how, or is developing a product requiring new advanced engineering skills which it does not have, or decides to produce abroad a product it has never manufactured and sold at home.

It can be accepted as a sort of iron law of product development that the more a product differs from those a company now makes and knows thoroughly, the greater are the odds that it will not contribute a dollar of profit. A company must be very sure of the probabilities of success before deviating from this lesson of experience.

KEYS TO IMPROVED NEW PRODUCT DEVELOPMENT

In light of the above-described significance of new products to a company, and the high risks usually associated with their development, it becomes of the greatest importance to management to find those touchstones which are most likely to assure the success of a new product. A few of the outstanding keys to success are set forth in this section, and several of them will be described in more detail in the remainder of the chapter.

The fundamental key to new product success is the existence of creative and imaginative ideas coupled with the ability to develop them. This is the key to a drawer full of keys and is found only when many elements are present in a firm's planning system.

A second outstanding key to new product success is an effective comprehensive corporate planning program. The methodical stimulation and development of new product ideas fostered in such a system is a major necessary ingredient to product success. Table 19-1 shows how the major steps in product development relate in a very broad way to principal structural elements of comprehensive planning. These steps will be discussed in detail later in the chapter.

Organization for new product planning is of major importance to new product success for it facilitates creativity and the more efficient use of all resources needed for success. From the first development and evaluation of an idea through its phase-out after successful commercial exploitation, different combinations of expertise in a company must be coordinated. For example, there usually are involved specialists from sales, research, production, and finance. Each of these look at problems from a different orientation; sales and promotion personnel are market-oriented and highly concerned about salability of product; research personnel are more technically oriented and more interested in scientific feasibility and value of product. Production specialists center their attention on physical plant and machinery, and the way products are constructed, so as to optimize the use of this productive capability; and finance experts are concerned essentially with the financial results of a new venture, particularly in terms of cash flow and final return on investment. The greater the expertise of these representatives, the more diverse are their views likely to be about a product. Yet, successful new product development requires a blending of their talents to get the proper mix of McCarthy's four P's. The proper organizational arrangement within which they do this is a major method to resolve this problem.

A critical reason for many product failures is the inadequate technical-economic analysis of new product proposals. A minimum requirement for success, therefore, is an appropriately competent appraisal of the business potential and financial results of a given technical configuration. Here again, organization and procedures will help solve this problem, but managerial attention to the problem, plus staff expertise, plus appropriate research techniques, are additional requirements.

Table 19-1   Relating Over-All Planning Sequence and New Product Development Steps

NEW PRODUCT SEQUENCE \ OVER-ALL PLANNING	STRATEGIC PLANNING	MEDIUM-RANGE PROGRAMMING	SHORT-RANGE PLANNING
EXPLORATION	X	X	•
SCREENING	X	X	X
BUSINESS ANALYSIS	X	X	X
DEVELOPMENT		X	X
TESTING		•	X
COMMERCIALIZATION			X

X High overlap
• Less overlap

Of course, the fundamental principles and guidelines to planning which have been discussed in preceding chapters are applicable and essential in product success.

Further elaboration of procedural steps, organizational arrangements, and feasibility testing and analysis follow. While we are obliged here to describe steps in detail it must be emphasized that too many procedures can be specified which may stifle the creativity needed in product development. A major problem of management is to assure an acceptable balance between method and flexibility.

ILLUSTRATIVE PROCEDURAL STEPS

Table 19-1 presents the broad categories of steps which are taken in any new product development. Both in theory and practice the details in each category are many and complex, as illustrated in Table 19-2 and Chart 19-6. Although the steps in these tables and chart are somewhat self-explanatory, a little elaboration is in order.

The exploration stage involves the process of identifying areas of interest, generating ideas for exploration, and collecting suggestions. The over-all company planning process should be a main source of broad guidance to the new product search. Customers, competition, consumers, and technical developments will be fruitful sources of ideas. As discussed in Chapter 22, research and development laboratories are becoming ever-more important as sources of new ideas even among industries that consider themselves as having little technical orientation.

The next stage is a provisional screening of the new ideas to determine whether further and more expensive evaluation is justified. Product ideas at this stage are screened quickly and with a minimum of resource expenditure.

If the product passes through this first large sieve, a more rigorous business analysis should follow. In this step a team may be created to study markets, costs, product characteristics, and other factors to determine whether the product will be as profitable as required and whether it will meet other requirements determined by the company. In this process the technical feasibility and specifications of the product may be determined. If the product passes muster, this step may conclude with a detailed plan for future product development.

The development phase takes the product through to the prototype. As this stage proceeds, the product is continuously subject to further business analysis and technical design developments until a prototype which can be tested is made available.

A useful step then is to test the product in a limited market area to see whether it should be launched nationally. While market testing proceeds, laboratory tests can continue, further business analysis will proceed, cost structures will be refined, and final decisions on design, production, marketing, and financing will be made.

Table 19-2 Points for Improvement in a Program of New Product Evolution

The following list of points, made without comment, has helped increase success in many companies seeking to analyze, change and improve their new product programs.

EXPLORATION

1. *Determine the product fields of primary interest to the company.*
   Analyze major company problems.
   Evaluate the company's principal resources.
   Identify external growth opportunities ready for exploitation—expanding markets, technological breakthroughs or rising profit margins.

2. *Establish a program for planned idea generation.*
   Identify idea-generating groups.
   Give them a clear concept of the company's interest fields.
   Expose creative personnel to idea-generating facts.
   Conduct exploratory technical research.
   Utilize team approach.
   Minimize distractions from current problems.

3. *Collect ideas through an organized network.*
   Designate an idea collection point.
   Establish comprehensive idea-collection procedures.
   Cover selected outside sources of ideas.
   Solicit ideas actively and directly.
   Consider each idea first on a "can-do" basis.
   Treat the idea man with care.

SCREENING

1. *Expand each idea into a full product concept.*
   Translate the idea into business terms.
   Identify the key business implications of the product concept and its development.
   Prepare a written proposal of the product idea.

2. *Collect facts and opinions, which are quickly available, bearing on the product idea as a business proposition.*
   Select evaluation techniques to fit the specific idea.
   Identify the best sources of facts and qualified opinions.
   Use quick and inexpensive fact-gathering methods.
   Apply strictly the principle of "diminishing returns" to fact-gathering.

Table 19-2   Points for Improvement in a Program of New Product Evolution (Continued)

3. Appraise each idea for its potential values to the company.

Estimate the magnitude of the profit opportunity.

Assess the investment, time and risk requirements.

Check the idea against other selection criteria.

Provide for subsequent review of ideas discarded or shelved.

BUSINESS ANALYSIS

1. Appoint persons responsible for further study of each idea.

Select a small product team, representing major departments that would be affected by the product.

Tailor team size and composition to the nature of the product.

Select team members on the basis of their self-interest.

2. Determine the desirable market features for the product and its feasibility.

Determine characteristics of the market and its trends.

Appraise both competitors and their products—existing and potential.

Conduct experimental market and technical research, within budget limits established for preliminary investigation.

Identify "Appeal" characteristics that would differentiate and sell the product.

Establish feasibility of developing and manufacturing a product with these features.

3. Develop specifications and establish a definite program for the product.

Evaluate various business alternatives to determine desired product specifications.

Establish a timetable and estimate expenditures to evolve this product through succeeding stages.

Reduce the proposed idea to a specific business proposition in terms of time, costs, manpower, profits and benefits.

Get top management approval or revision of the product idea in terms of its specifications and program before authorizing the development stage.

DEVELOPMENT

1. Establish development projects for each product.

Explode the product proposal into as many projects as are required for administrative control.

Schedule these projects within the approved budget and timetable for the product.

Maintain the product team for company-wide coordination.

Pin-point responsibility of all team members and identify them in all reports and records.

Establish yardsticks for measuring performance and progress.

Table 19-2   Points for Improvement in a Program of New Product Evolution (Continued)

2. *Build product to designated or revised specifications.*

Exhaust available information.

Maintain security against outside information "leaks."

Continue market studies as a basis for enhancing product salability.

Hold to agreed specifications or make formal revisions by repeating the specification stage.

Keep top management informed; report promptly anticipated changes in objectives, schedule or budget.

3. *Complete laboratory evaluation and release for testing.*

Complete laboratory tests adequate to determine basic performance against specifications.

Provide checks and balances through organization and procedure to assure objectivity of product appraisal.

Apply commercial rather than scientific standards to determine product "release" point.

Prepare management report summarizing product description and characteristics; report project completion.

TESTING

1. *Plan commercial experiments necessary to test and verify earlier judgments of the product.*

Expand product team, if required.

Outline the nature and scope of commercialization phase.

Identify the major factors that must prove out to support successful commercialization.

Establish the standards by which product performance and market acceptance will be judged.

Plan test methods, responsibility, schedule and cost.

Construct a testing program and recommend it to top management for approval.

2. *Conduct in-use, production and market testing.*

Continue laboratory testing.

Design and test production facilities.

Submit products to customer use for "abuse" testing.

Conduct test marketing programs in line with plans for commercialization.

Survey company, trade and user reactions to the product and its commercialization program.

Table 19-2   Points for Improvement in a Program of New Product Evolution (Continued)

3. Make final product decision; freeze design.

Interpret test findings objectively; drop or modify products which fail tests.

Incorporate test findings in product design and commercialization plans.

Detail the program for full-scale production and sales with a schedule, budgets and manpower.

Recommend the product and its commercialization program, with full supporting data, to top management for final product decision.

COMMERCIALIZATION

1. Complete final plans for production and marketing.

Establish patterns for over-all direction and coordination of the product.

Expand product team to encompass all departments involved.

Designate individuals responsible for each part of the commercialization program.

Assure that these individuals work out all program details to fit coordinated plan.

2. Initiate coordinated production and selling programs.

Brief all participating personnel.

Maintain established program sequence and schedule.

Provide feed-back mechanisms for program corrections.

3. Check results. Make necessary improvements in product, manufacturing or sales.

Make design changes promptly to correct "bugs."

Work continuously for cost reduction and quality control.

Shape the product and its program to meet competitive reaction and changing internal pressures.

Maintain necessary team members until the product is a "going" commercial success, absorbed by established organization.

The management concepts outlined here "take some doing" to bring actual improvement in new product results. The vital "how to" factors are not easily generalized. The specifics of a program for one company, even if well understood, tend to be useless and often dangerous in another company.

Source: This extract is reprinted with the permission of Booz • Allen & Hamilton, International Management Consultants.

Chart 19-6
Work Flow in Market Development at Kaiser Aluminum & Chemical Corporation

DEVELOPMENT STEPS	Primarily the Responsibility of				
	Over-all Aluminum Division Mgmt.	Profit Center Operating Division	Product Development	Market Research	Other Aluminum Divisions and Corporate Staff Functions
1. Initiate new product ideas.	x	x	x	x	x[1]
2. Screen new product ideas.		x	x		
3. Approve orders; approve for predevelopment evaluation.	x	x			
4. Examine market and economic feasibility.		x	x	x	
5. Examine technical feasibility.		x	x		x[2]
6. Request project approval.			x		
7. Approve.	x	x			
8. Set timetable and budget.			x		
9. Detailed study of the market.				x	
10. Design and engineering.			x		
11. Request approval for prototype or limited manufacture.			x		
12. Approve limited manufacture and marketing.		x			
13. Obtain product for test.			x		
14. Prepare test marketing program.		x	x	x	
15. Supervise test marketing.		x		x	
16. Evaluate test marketing results.		x		x	
17. Obtain and evaluate manufacturing cost data from test.			x		
18. Prepare detailed plan for marketing and manufacture.		x	x		x[3]
19. Prepare and submit request for capital funds.		x			
20. Approve capital fund request.	x				
21. Supervise facility construction and start-up.		x	x		x[4]
22. Assume marketing and manufacturing responsibility.		x			

[1] Various
[2] Research
[3] Central Engineering, Real Estate, Legal, Controller
[4] Central Engineering

Source: Letter from Company to Author

The next step, then, is commercialization, which means actual production and coordination of other functional areas to make the new venture a success in the market.

The actual sequence of steps in an operating setting will, of course, vary, but the basic set of steps must be followed—none can be eliminated or circumvented and each must be given its deserved emphasis. Many products have failed, for example, because 99 percent of the investment has been in product technical development and 1 percent in market analysis. Chart 19-6 shows the work flow in product development for the Kaiser Aluminum & Chemical Corporation. The basic steps specified in Tables 19-1 and 19-2 are covered, but the sequence and the details differ. This chart is worth study also because it shows the decision-making points, and the interrelationship of responsibility among line and staff, as the process proceeds. All companies set up procedures which fit their particular needs at the moment. So, as with over-all corporate planning, although the conceptual model has universal applicability the precise way it is used will vary among companies and products.

In the case of Kaiser Aluminum & Chemical Corp., there are five principal operating divisions (Aluminum, Chemicals, Refractories, Nickel, and Real Estate), each of which operates autonomously and is self-sufficient as far as special skills in the areas of development, research, engineering, and marketing are concerned. Chart 19-6 refers to the Aluminum Division, but other divisions operate in a comparable way. There are five subdivisions in the Aluminum Division, as follows: Electrical Products, Mill Products, Fabricated Products, International, and Metals.

Although an effort is made to separate new product development from day-to-day activities, the two are inextricably interwoven. The sequence is as shown in Chart 19-6 but is less formal than it appears in the chart.

All new ideas are given a preliminary screening for their technical, marketing, and economic feasibility. This is done either by the operating division ultimately responsible for manufacture and sale of the product, or by the Aluminum Division staff Product Development group. The Aluminum Division has staff groups performing services for the five subdivisions noted above; the two of most importance in this discussion are Product Development, which is basically technically-oriented, and Marketing Research.

Preliminary screening is done by Market Research and, if favorable, the Product Development department prepares a development program including prototype production, testing marketing, and a complete development budget. Beyond this, the work flow and procedural steps are much the same as shown in Chart 19-6. So, as with over-all corporate planning, although the conceptual model has universal applicability the precise way it is used will vary much among companies and products.

ORGANIZATIONAL ARRANGEMENTS

There are two opposite types of organization for new product development. One exists in a functionally organized company where all new product planning is done centrally. The other exists in a multidivisional company where all new product planning is done in product divisions. Possibilities and practices within this spectrum are many, but there are about seven basic patterns, as shown in Chart 19-7 (adapted from Fulmer, 1966).

BASIC PATTERNS. These arrangements permit different emphasis, such as involvement of top management, involvement of staff experts, high creativity, action orientation, functional orientation, decision-making authority, and type products for development. For instance, Chart A permits lodging full responsibility for development in one person, whereas the arrangements of Charts F and G provide for committee coordinated decisions. Chart C permits orientation to one major function. In this instance it is research and development, but it could be marketing or engineering. In the detergent business product management is highly market-oriented, but in the aerospace industry it is more technically-oriented. A number of the patterns obviously permit, and may force, top management involvement. Chart E shows a new product department, as compared with the integrated approach of Charts D, F and G. But the arrangement in Chart E could also be integrated, depending upon how the department acts with respect to other functions.

Four main approaches shown in Chart 19-7 which deserve more attention here are new product committees, product managers, new product departments, and project teams.

NEW PRODUCT COMMITTEES. An AMA study of 140 companies showed that product planning is assigned to a committee in 58 percent of the cases as compared with the assignment in 42 percent of the cases to an individual. Among the large companies, 73 percent said they used the committee approach, whereas in small companies, as might be expected, the distribution was rather evenly divided. This study also showed that in 1963 the committee approach was new to 50 percent of the companies during the preceding two years. (Tietjen, 1963.)

The committee device is used by companies in a number of different ways. Frequently, the president's staff committee may serve as a sounding board for new product ideas and developments. Some companies, the Ford Motor Company for instance, maintain new product committees at both the corporate and divisional levels. In many companies *ad hoc* or temporary committees are formed to deal with particular phases of the product development, such as preliminary design, a problem with respect to a particular technical feature, market analysis,

Chart 19-7
Organizational Patterns for New Product Development

A. A Product Manager

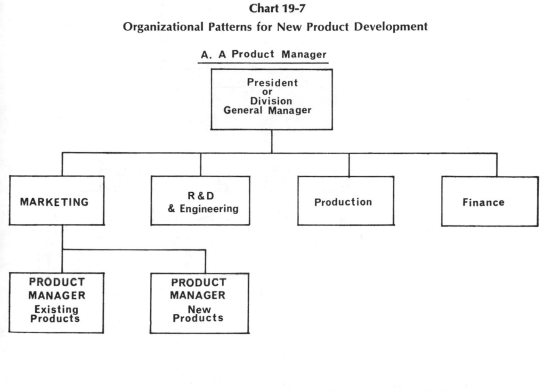

B. A New Product Department Under Marketing Staff

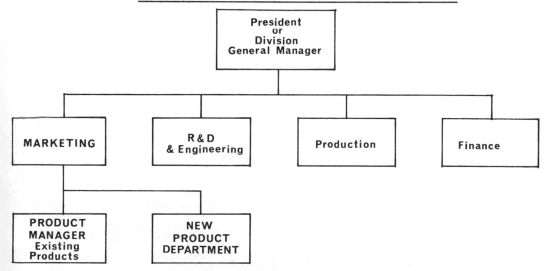

Source: Robert M. Fulmer, ed., Organization for New-Products Development, Experiences in Marketing Management, No. 11 (New York: National Industrial Conference Board, Inc., 1966), pp. 28-32.

Chart 19-7
Organizational Patterns for New Product Development (Continued)

C. A New-Product Department under R&D

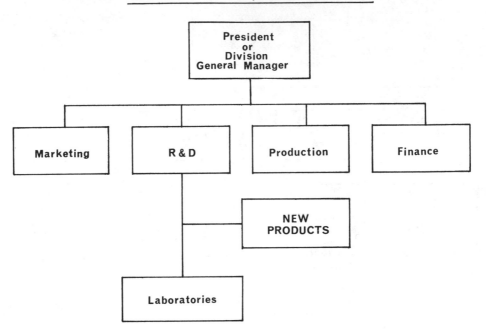

D. A New-Product Department

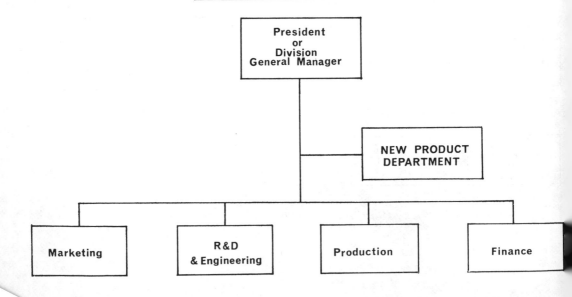

Chart 19-7
Organizational Patterns for New Product Development (Continued)

E. Separate Department

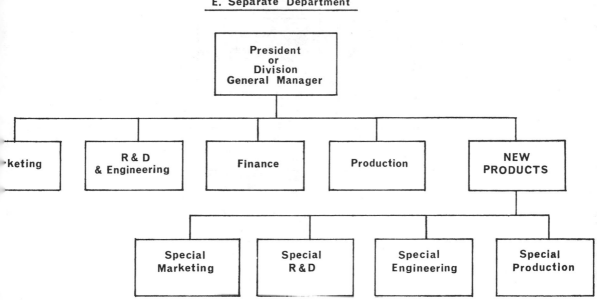

F. New Product Committee

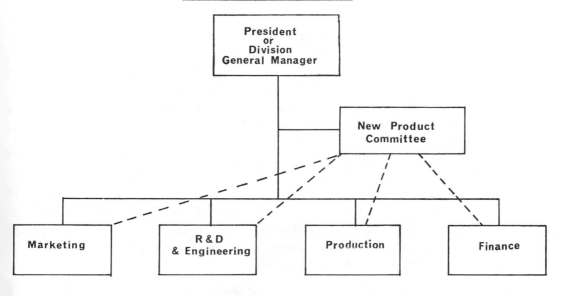

Chart 19-7

Organizational Patterns for New Product Development (Continued)

G.   Task Force Teams

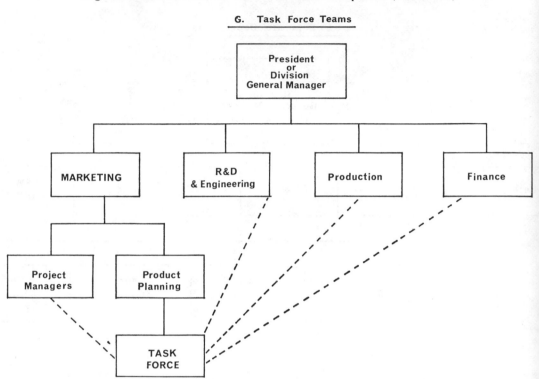

or distribution. A variety of permanent committees are used by some companies to deal with the whole or parts of the development cycle.

A major function of committees is to coordinate various functions. Lorsch found that a system of permanent cross-functional coordinating committees provided a setting which enhanced product innovation.* With proper selection of people, proper use of the committee method, and proper relationships between the committee and other authority centers in a company, committees can be effective coordinating and communicating centers.

The Plumbing and Heating Division of American-Standard, for example, has a product development committee reporting directly to the president. The committee is composed of representatives from sales, manufacturing, research, and purchasing, and oversees the product development process. Once this committee approves a proposal for further development, a project team is appointed to produce a preliminary design specification. The product development committee reviews this, together with data concerning the expected profitability of the product, and if the green light is on, the product is released to manufacturing for production. (Lear in Newgarden, 1958b.)

* See Lorsch, 1965, and a summarized version of this study by Lorsch and Lawrence, 1965.

PRODUCT MANAGERS. Product managers are growing in numbers and importance in American business, and their functions and practices are so varied, however, that no single definition will be suitable to describe the way they operate. Throughout the arrangements shown in Chart 19-7 there may be differing degrees of authority granted to marketing and project managers, and they may be given responsibility for different subject matter.

At the most authoritative position is a project manager, who acts as an entrepreneur or head of a business. In some companies the president is, indeed, the chief product manager. In the case where a company gives a manager full funding, full authority, and all needed people reporting directly to him, he is a business entrepreneur. At the other extreme is the product manager who is given responsibility over a product but has no functional authority over personnel in other departments who must help him in discharging his duties. This has obvious problems associated with it. In between is a "matrix-type" organization, illustrated in Chapter 22, where a project manager may get help from other departments but have some functional authority over the personnel used on his projects. This, too, has problems, some of which were mentioned in Chapter 18 and will be discussed more fully in Chapter 22.

In the fuller authority type of product management, the range of responsibilities will run from the development of basic strategy recommendations through the management of the life cycle or cycles for the product. In the consumer goods industries, for instance, product managers are more concerned with market analysis, sales promotion, and advertising. In the industrial products field, however, the attention is more on technical design and special consumer requirements, and less on sales promotion. In the aerospace industry, for example, project management is largely technically-oriented, and in the perfume field it is almost wholly sales-oriented. In most instances today, products are sold as brands and the manager is spoken of as a brand manager (Fulmer, 1965; Sanford and Bailey, 1965). They are usually given full authority over functions needed in their managing the life cycle of the brand under their control. If they only have authority for initiating action in one area—marketing for instance—and then must negotiate with others to get the task done, they do not have the decision-making capability of managers and perhaps should be called something other than managers. Fulmer (1965, p. 72) suggests product specialists.

A major advantage of a product manager with full authority is, of course, that one central focus exists for relating all functions concerned with the product. Centralizing authority also generally is accompanied by enthusiasm, which is important, and more efficient direction of efforts. There are, however, problems with this method. Too much power in the hands of a project manager can create antipathies elsewhere in an organization. If a project manager, on the other hand, shares his authority this also is an obvious source of difficulty.

A survey of 189 product managers among 27 companies showed the following wide range of duties and responsibilities, in descending order of importance:

pricing
new products
product improvement
sales forecasting
define advertising and literature needs
initiate market analysis and/or
   marketing research
service policies/methods

product elimination
direct sales force toward
   target accounts
develop one-year marketing plans
distribution policies and methods
department budgets
profits
field testing

Others included application engineering, development of five-year marketing plan, return on investment, and manufacturing budget. (Fendrich, 1966, p. 7.) A comparable survey, were it made, of project managers in advanced technological industries would show much the reverse emphasis, e.g., great stress on research and engineering development and very little on marketing.

NEW PRODUCT DEPARTMENTS. Some companies have created a new product development department at the divisional level. Others, like the National Biscuit Company, have created one at the corporate level. Prior to 1959, all new product and new-variety activities at Nabisco were centered in the production department. With an ever-increasing need for new products, a necessity for tightening relations between production and marketing, and in recognition of the priority of longer-range planning for new product development, the company created a separate department to oversee new product development.

Directors in the department are responsible, respectively, for marketing studies, product-concept generation programs, product development, marketing research, and marketing. The department's responsibilities range from concept generation, through the test market and final evaluation of a product's performance, and on to the recommendation to the president concerning the operating department to which the product should be assigned for national distribution. In this department is assembled a group that can look at the company as a whole, tap its best resources, and avoid duplication of effort. (Fulmer, 1966, pp. 56-61.)

Here again, the exact duties of such departments vary a great deal among companies. In some instances they are self-contained units such as the Advanced Project Department of "Kelly" Johnson at the Lockheed Aircraft Corporation. More frequently, they embody many but not all functions necessary to product development, such as that at Nabisco.

PROJECT TEAMS. A project team is a form of working committee that is created to carry out a particular assignment associated with a product development. Such a team may be formed for the entire process, which is unusual, or for particular stages in product development, which is more usual. It may report to a committee, a product manager, or a department head. Once a product is launched the group may be disbanded, which is usual, or it may be given an operating responsibility to manufacture and sell the product, which is not usual.

At American Standard's Plumbing and Heating Division, for example, once a preliminary favorable review of a new product is accepted, a project team goes to work. It is composed of a representative from the research department, who is chairman, and a representative from both sales and manufacturing. Its responsibility is to discuss and evaluate design, costs, etc., and produce a preliminary specification. If the design is approved it is then picked up in the operating departments. At Johnson's Wax, sponsor groups are formed to formulate proposals and guide the development of products, but once a product is ready for exploitation a product committee is formed, the nucleus of which is the sponsor group, to take the product through full-scale commercialization.

ORGANIZATIONAL LESSONS FROM EXPERIENCE. While product development organizations among companies are often very difficult, there are some outstanding lessons of experience which are helpful in guiding the creation of these organizations. Ten major ones are as follows.

First, things happen faster and generally with more likelihood of success if there is an advocate of a proposal who either is responsible for its success or participates importantly in its development. If this person is the originator of the proposal, so much the better.

Second, success requires the coordination of different functions throughout a product's development and life. A function of product committees is to bring together these interests, particularly sales, research, finance, and manufacturing.

Third, committees should be given a staff, not a line function. If committees are asked to produce some product or result, the chairman should be made responsible, not the committee.

Fourth, responsibility for each major phrase of product development should be pinpointed in some individual.

Fifth, a written plan for the development of a product should be prepared.

Sixth, all procedures in each phase should be spelled out in some detail and checklists of things to be done and questions answered should be available, but care should be taken to avoid either the preparation of too much instruction or the blind insistence that it all be followed to the letter.

Seventh, flexibility in product development should be stimulated and encouraged. All products are not the same, and each must be handled in just a little different manner.

Eighth, information and reporting systems are important in controlling the process. Different managers and staff become involved in different phases of the process, yet there is need for a continuous and related series of decisions. Suitable reporting relationships among those involved must be organized and followed so that information not only is available at the right time and place for decision-making but is useful in controlling the development of a product. At the completion of different phases, especially market testing, early commercialization, and the end of a product life cycle, case histories of lessons of experience and evaluation should be assembled.

Ninth, it has been found in some organizations where project managers use personnel in functional areas, who are under the control of functional officers, that productivity increases despite the violation of older unity of command principles. This is a matter which will be discussed at length in Chapter 22.

Finally, proposed products should be actively pursued and not allowed to lie dormant. A system which gets cluttered with inactive committees, inconclusive studies, and ideas held in limbo, will choke on its own uncertainties.

To these, of course, should be added the many guidelines for effective organization which may be found in management textbooks.

DEVELOPING PRODUCT IDEAS
AND STRATEGIES

In previous chapters, especially Chapter 9, approaches to and illustrations of the development of product strategies were presented. While an intensive treatment of this subject is not, therefore, necessary here, a few additional comments and illustrations may be useful.

Developing a product strategy can begin at a number of different points. Some of the major starting points for most companies, divided into external and internal stimuli, are as follows: Externally, customer needs may exist but are not being met completely satisfactorily by existing products. There is a need, for example, for subsonic vertical take-off and landing transports which is not now being met and some company eventually will step in to meet this need. Many companies develop a product and create a demand for it, such as a new soap, perfume, or dog food. Companies may also anticipate a future demand which must be met and get prepared to meet it.

Internal stimuli may flow from examination of a company's strengths and weaknesses. For example, a firm may find there is excess capacity in one of its plants. Another product to fill this capacity may be priced competitively because it does not have to bear the entire burden of facility and machinery investment. A firm may have a complete product line except for one price range or one type product. To fill this niche may provide an advantage much greater than if the product stood alone. Plants, or raw material resources, may be strategically located in areas that permit the firm to exploit a particular market. A company may have a valuable patent, specialized research talents, unique managerial skills, or excess cash that open the door to profitable development.

In the actual process of product planning the flows of ideas can be in orderly textbook model progression, from missions to broad product areas, to specific products. Or, as is much more typical, ideas spring from many different sources and are fitted into or bring about a change in over-all strategic plans.

As noted in Table 19-2, a prime step in idea exploration is the determination of the company's fields of interest. It is just as easy to stimulate ideas within a defined objective, product and market area, or technology, as to leave the field of inquiry completely open-ended. Indeed, it is more likely that better ideas will be stimulated with higher potential pay-off with some over-all company areas in view than if none are identified and expressed. The more specific can be the fields of interest expressed for the company, the more direction will be provided to those working on new ideas.

Another important management responsibility, as noted in Table 19-2, is to develop a system for stimulating new product ideas. The comprehensive planning program is a prime step forward in doing this, but many other courses of action can be taken, such as identifying and stimulating idea-generating groups. Some years ago, for example, Thiokol Chemical Co. decided to stimulate its employees to develop new products by creating seven five-man research teams. These teams were manned by volunteers and they worked after regular hours and on weekends without extra pay. They were dubbed the "seven hills of wisdom," and were strongly motivated because they knew if they developed a good idea that resulted in a profitable product their careers with the company would be enhanced. Furthermore, if they were successful they might become the project managers for the new product. The results were excellent.

Management must understand the fragility of a new good idea and study the best methods within the company for giving birth to new ideas. This is a very difficult task and must not be underestimated, for the more radical the idea the more resistance is likely to be generated against it.

One study of 71 major companies showed the source of new product ideas to be as follows: marketing, 32.4 percent; research and development, 26.5 percent; top management, 13.1 percent; customers, 10.6 percent; new products department, 6.7 percent; manufacturing, 3.7 percent; and all others, 7.0 percent (Randle, 1960, p. 13).

Of course, the more interesting question is the origin of ideas within these different areas. Although this sort of question has not been the subject of much research, it is beginning to attract scholars. (Rubenstein, in Dean, 1963.)

Most top managers with whom I have talked say they have far more ideas than they can possibly exploit. Indeed, many assert the mere volume of ideas creates a problem for them. While this may be so, every management should encourage the development of new product ideas and maintain an orderly system for the purpose. While the formal planning program may provide a framework for advancing new ideas, it would seem effective for management to set up an idea collection point which circumvents the chain of command. As noted above, surprising resistance can be developed to combat a new idea, and the channels of transmission to points where ideas can be considered reasonably objectively must not be clogged.

SCREENING AND SELECTING IDEAS

It is perfectly obvious from the failure rates of new products that improvement can be made in the screening processes of most companies. Although, as noted in Chapters 6 and 7, business motivations are more complex than profit maximization and new products may be added to a firm's line for other purposes, such as to increase volume, maintain employment, improve market share, or fill

Chart 19-8
The New Product Screening Process

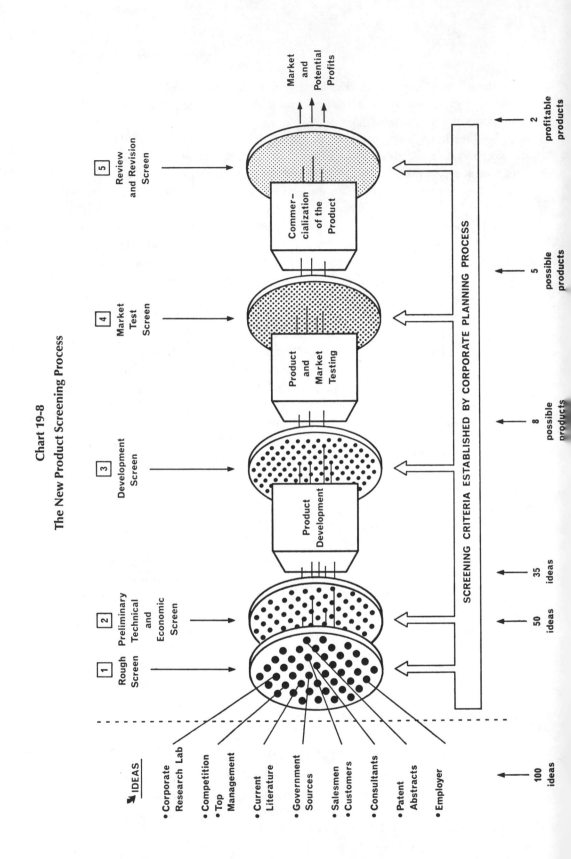

a product line, in most companies the critical issue at each stage of a new product development is prospective profitability in a narrow cash sense, such as return on investment.

Prospective profitability rests on a number of factors including: (1) the nature and extent of the competitive advantage of the product, (2) the slice of the market it captures, and (3) the margin of price over cost. While these factors can never be calculated with complete certainty, continued analysis of the elements making up each of these factors can yield progressively more accurate results as a product moves to and into commercialization. No company with any imaginative flow of ideas, however, can afford to put each one through the type of analysis that yields high accuracy. The costs would be excessive. As a result, each idea should be put through a screening process, pictured in Chart 19-8, where the holes in the screen become progressively smaller and smaller as the analysis becomes more and more rigorous.

All methods listed in Table 19-2 have some applicability in this screening process. Some have pertinence at one point in the process and not at others; some are applicable throughout the process, and some are not; and the value of the tool will vary depending upon the product under consideration. Space does not permit here an examination of each tool for its applicability to the product screening process. It is useful, however, to examine a few outstanding techniques which are used as an idea moves from the left to the right in Chart 19-8. What is said here does not replace the suggestions of Table 19-1, but complements them.

SIMPLE INITIAL SCREENING. A very simple approach to an initial screening which I call the "chicken scratch method" is shown in Chart 19-9. This method asks a few simple standard questions, the answers to which can be quick reactions. The idea here is to rate the product for each factor to reveal a profile. If a product has a profile which is more prominent to the left of the dotted line it becomes a candidate for further review. If more line is to the right, the project is rejected for the time being. While simple, this is a powerful and very economical method.

It is possible, of course, to build upon such simple sets of questions as shown in Chart 19-9. Given a satisfactory answer to a quick preliminary screening, the next step may be to examine more carefully some of the factors to be considered and their values. For instance, more care may be taken to define just what is very good, good, average, and so on.*

WEIGHTING. The next step, in more rigorous analysis, of course, would be to put weights on some of the questions asked, because some of them are much more important to a company than others. Here, as with the preceding technique, the issue is to determine the general "fit" of the new idea. The assumption is that

---

* For an excellent list of factors and subfactors for new product screening, together with qualitative descriptions of values, see O'Meara, Jr., 1961, pp. 84-85.

Chart 19-9

Illustrative Preliminary Screening Profile for a New Product Year

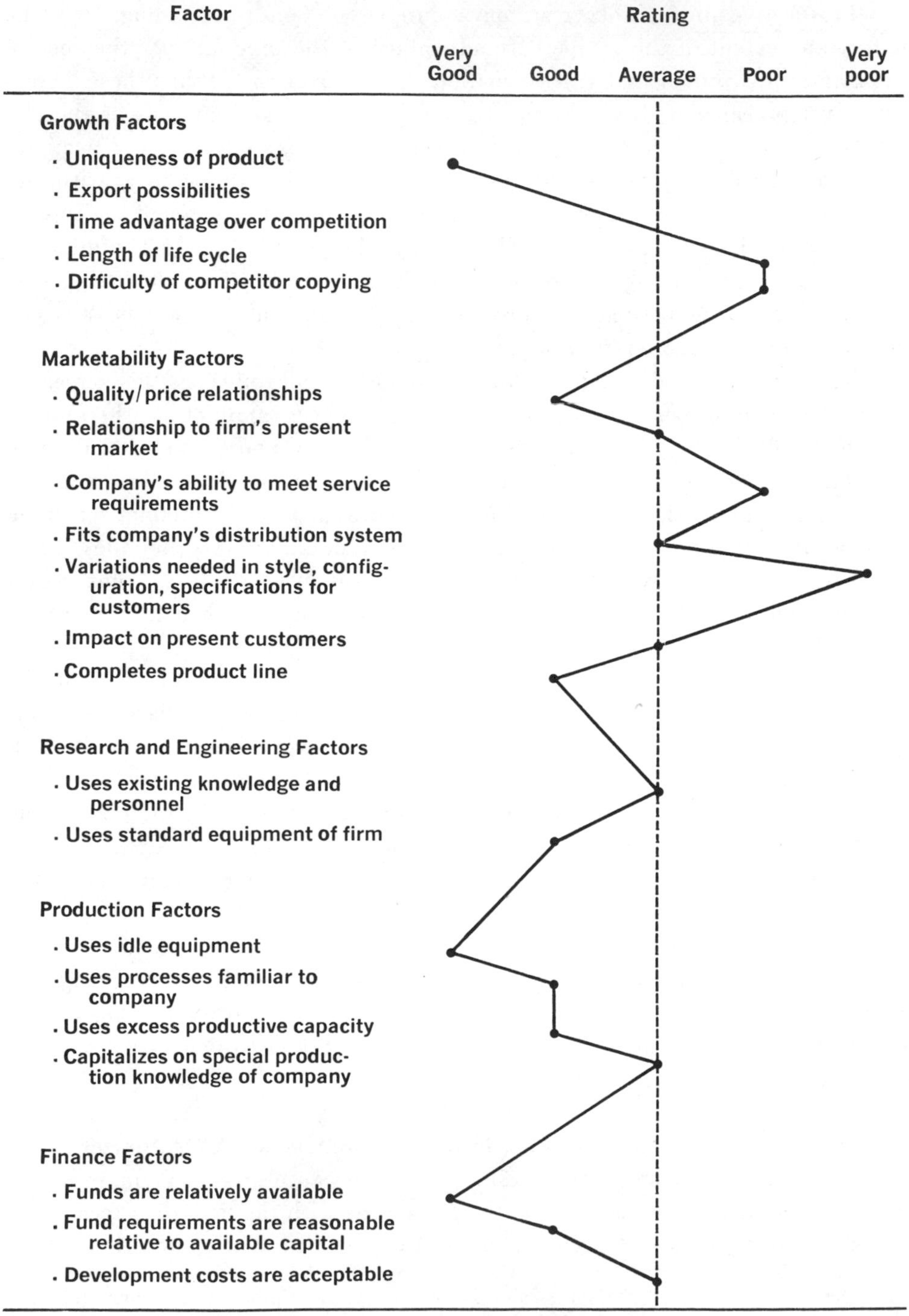

Factor	Very Good	Good	Average	Poor	Very poor
Growth Factors					
. Uniqueness of product	•				
. Export possibilities					
. Time advantage over competition					
. Length of life cycle				•	
. Difficulty of competitor copying				•	
Marketability Factors					
. Quality/price relationships		•			
. Relationship to firm's present market				•	
. Company's ability to meet service requirements				•	
. Fits company's distribution system			•		
. Variations needed in style, configuration, specifications for customers					•
. Impact on present customers			•		
. Completes product line		•			
Research and Engineering Factors					
. Uses existing knowledge and personnel			•		
. Uses standard equipment of firm		•			
Production Factors					
. Uses idle equipment	•				
. Uses processes familiar to company		•			
. Uses excess productive capacity		•			
. Capitalizes on special production knowledge of company			•		
Finance Factors					
. Funds are relatively available	•				
. Fund requirements are reasonable relative to available capital		•			
. Development costs are acceptable			•		

a poor "fit" will be most unlikely to contribute to the profits of the company and, therefore, deserves no further attention.

Assigning weights to particular factors can be rather simple or elaborate. Table 19-3 shows a simple evaluation matrix, the explanation of which is rather obvious.

The addition of probability estimates is shown in Table 19-4. (Suggested by O'Meara, 1961, p. 86.) In this table, weights are given for each item of marketability and each scale (very good, average, poor). The evaluator then assigns a probability to each of these. In the illustration, he obviously felt that the probability of a very good quality/price relationship was just a little less than average. (Each individual probability estimate is made on the basis of 1 being perfect.) He then multiplies his probability estimate by the value assigned to each item. The value attached to "very good," for instance, is 10 and since the probability is .4 the total expected value is 4.0. When the evaluations are completed, the expected values are added and multiplied by the subfactor weight in column (B) to get the subfactor evaluation in column (G).

The analysis can be carried one step further. Going back to Chart 19-9, weights can be given to the major characteristics specified: growth, marketability research and engineering, production, and finance. These weights can be multiplied by the total factor values made by analysis such as in Table 19-4 and a final single index number derived for a product.

Table 19-3   Evaluation of Product Fit

(A) Factors	(B) Weight	(C) Product Compatibility Values											(D) B x C
		0	.1	.2	.3	.4	.5	.6	.7	.8	.9	1.0	
Marketability	.20				x								.080
Growth	.10					x							.050
Research and Engineering	.5								x				.040
Finance	.40						x						.240
Production	.25				x								.100
TOTAL													.710

Rating Scale: .7 - .8 = good
     0 - .3 = poor   .9 - 1.0 = excellent
     .4 - .6 = fair   Minimum acceptance value = .70

Note: Suggestion for this table is from Barry M. Richman, "A Rating Scale for Product Innovation," *Business Horizons,* Vol. 5, No. 2 (Summer 1962), p. 43.

Table 19-4 Evaluation Sheet for Marketability*

(A) Subfactor	(B) Subfactor weight	(C) Very Good (10) EP	EV	(D) Average (6) EP	EV	(E) Poor (2) EP	EV	F Total EV	(G) Subfactor Evaluation (Col B x Col F)
Quality/Price Relationship	3.0	.4	4.0	.5	3.0	.1	.2	7.2	21.6
Relationship to firm's present market	2.0	.5	5.0	.4	2.4	.2	.4	7.8	15.6
Company's ability to meet service requirements	1.0	.6	6.0	.8	4.8	.0	.0	10.8	10.8
Fits company distribution system	1.0	.2	2.0	.8	4.8	.0	.0	6.8	6.8
Variations in style, etc.	1.0	.4	4.0	.8	4.8	.0	.0	8.8	8.8
Impact on present customers	1.0	.8	8.0	.4	2.4	.1	.2	10.6	10.6
Completes product line	1.0	.2	2.0	.5	3.0	.4	.8	5.8	5.8
TOTALS	10.0								80.0

Note: EP = expected probability, and EV = expected value.
Source: Suggested by John T. O'Meara, Jr., "Selecting Profitable Products," Harvard Business Review, Vol. 39, January-February 1961, p. 86.

A variation of weighting is to make an evaluation on the basis of a simple formula. There are a number of different ones, among which is the following (Miller, 1957, p. 31):

$$\frac{\begin{array}{c}\text{Chances of} \\ \text{Technical} \\ \text{Success}\end{array} \times \begin{array}{c}\text{Chances of} \\ \text{Commercial} \\ \text{Success}\end{array} \times \begin{array}{c}\text{Annual} \\ \text{Volume}\end{array} \times (\text{Price-Cost}) \times \text{Life}}{\text{Total Cost}} = \frac{\text{Project}}{\text{Number}}$$

This formula, of course, is nothing more than expected total net profit compared with total cost. Its virtue lies in the fact that it points out important elements necessary for success. There have been many modifications of this simple formula, some of which are rather complex. Jantsch (1967, pp. 191-200) describes most of them.

PROFIT MEASURES. The measure of profits soon becomes significant in screening, and the question arises as to what concept of profits should be used. The basic choice lies between some concept of incremental profits and net profits over full-cost. Incremental profits refers to the net addition to a firm's profits which the new product makes. In this case, new products are credited with the entire increase in profits and may show better profitability because they benefit from previous investments not charged to them as costs. Net profits on the other hand mean that each product bears its full burden of fixed overhead costs. As a result, cost burdens of existing products are correspondingly lightened.

There are occasions for the use of each of these measures, or a combination of each. In order to get a foothold in a new market a firm may use incremental profit. When the life cycle of a product is very short, as, for example, a short-term licensing program, a subcontract to fill a capacity gap, or a special product to meet a customer's need, incremental profit may be used. Generally speaking, however, most product analyses proceed on the basis of calculating full-cost (including the product's share of overhead) against long-term income.

There are different ways to relate these two money streams, the most usual of which is to calculate return on investment. But as noted in Chapter 13, there are a number of ways to calculate ROI. Whatever method is used by a company it should be consistent when product possibilities are compared.

One other point deserves mention in connection with profits. The level of acceptance must be related to a number of factors, such as the long-range profit objectives of the company, what other products are returning, and the best alternative uses of the monetary and non-monetary investment to be made. For example, a product may have a very high ROI but the profit volume may be so small relative to other products in the company that it is not worthwhile to apply existing managerial talents to its development.

MORE RIGOROUS ANALYSIS. As the screening process continues there should be ever-more rigorous analysis of three major factors: market, development costs, and technical feasibility where that is appropriate. At each step in the process of deciding to put a product into production the market appraisal looms ever-more important. Clearly there should be at an early stage a reasonable estimate of total sales which may be anticipated. This reflects, as noted in Chapters 8 and 18, such considerations as total industry sales and the share expected to be captured by this product, what competitors are likely to do; and the impact of evolving general economic changes, price competition, distribution channels, advertising. The more fateful the decision to go ahead, the more rigorous should be this analysis.

Matched against this are the anticipated costs of product development broken down at least by engineering development, market testing, business research, required facility and other costs to move into production, and costs of production.

Closely associated with both the market and costs (for more and more products) are the technical aspects of the product. A decision, for example, to produce a new commercial transport airplane is deeply influenced by technical considerations which also affect market and cost.

When these factors have been studied and estimates made, it is possible to develop cash flows showing income and outgo over a long period of time. This is an aspect of financial planning which was treated in Chapter 13. When products are important to a company it is usual to develop complete estimates of their cash inflows and outflows throughout their life cycles. Such a calculation ought to be made for most products, if for no other reason than to see what the simple rate of return on investment is likely to be. For products which necessitate major capital investments the analysis should be much more penetrating. It should at the very least include cash flow statements, probably worked out on a present value flow basis; over-all company balance sheet and profit and loss statements with the product in and with it omitted; detailed estimates of costs by time period; and a technical plan prepared in considerable detail. If the product, for example, is an automobile, engineering should be complete enough to show detailed configuration and specification.

As the screening process goes on there are, of course, market tests which may be made for a product. These tests open up a whole new range of tools for analysis including sampling theory, consumer motivation testing, and consumer attitude tests. What is an appropriate array of tests will vary among products.

The point is ultimately reached where for major product decisions the intensity of analysis and the rigor applied to it is very great. Thus, for a comparatively simple decision such as Revlon's Futurama lipstick the core analysis is housed in a three-inch thick onionskin typewritten volume! For a product like the Apollo space vehicle, the SST, or the Edsel, the volume of analysis reproduced on paper is literally weighted in the tons! The more important are the decisions to be made, the more every relevant decision tool known to man is employed.

ADVANCED ANALYTICAL METHODS. In product screening, industry is gradually beginning to employ some of the more advanced methods which were described in preceding parts of this book, particularly in Chapter 8 and Part III. There are two broad applications: one is the use of specific tools for an analysis, and the other is the use of models to interrelate various important elements entering into a new product decision. A few illustrations follow.

Already noted are ways that probabilities may be attached to different estimates of anticipated sales, costs, and profits. (Additional examples will be found in Chapter 20.) From such estimates it is possible, of course, to find ranges of probabilities of loss and profit with respect to individual products. If very many estimates of probabilities are made, the computations quickly become manageable only by computers. Decision trees with probabilities, as discussed in Chapter 15, are being used more frequently. The critical path method, and in some cases the textbook version of PERT, may be useful in plotting the many moves necessary to bring an idea to the market. (Busenbury, 1967.)

New methods are being developed to interrelate the many factors that must be assessed in product development. One mathematical model takes subfactors like those presented in Chart 19-9, makes probability distributions for each of the evaluations of very good, good, etc.; and, when placed on the computer, the model can provide detailed probability distributions of expected values. With this method, managers may try different probabilities and see immediately the results of their assumptions. (Freimer and Simon, 1967.)

Simulation models are becoming more popular. "Sprinter"* is a simulation model, for example, that interrelates such elements important in a decision to go ahead with a product as demand, cost, profit, competition, price, advertising, distribution channels, and other products of a firm (Urban, 1967). Responses from customers under various circumstances can be simulated throughout the life cycle of the product. The end sought in the model is the calculation of the maximum expected value of the total discounted differential profit for a product. This is the difference between total profit of the firm with the product, and total profit without the product. The differential profit is compared with the investment needed to achieve it, and a decision can then be made depending upon the return promised. This model can examine uncertainties surrounding the project, help to determine whether further input data would be worth the cost, and develop probabilities of profits at different levels.

* "Sprinter" is derived from Specification of Profits with Interaction under Trial and Error Response.

PRODUCT ELIMINATION

One final aspect of product planning to be discussed is product elimination, which usually, but not always, is the result of unsatisfactory profit or sales behavior. Product elimination can be forced, for example, by antitrust action as when Rockwell Manufacturing in 1967 eliminated its executive airplane in order to meet the requirements of the Department of Justice for merging with North American Aviation.

When a product's sales and profits are unsatisfactory there are a number of choices open to a company. It can, for example, improve its efficiency of production and distribution, reduce cost, cut price, and make the product more attractive to customers. Or the product itself may be improved by better packaging or redesign. Sometimes better servicing of the product to customers may change its profit outlook. If these avenues do not produce desired results the product may be produced but sold to others in bulk for them to market. In some instances the firm may find it profitable to get someone else to produce the product at a lower cost. If these choices fail to produce desired results the logical next step is to stop making and selling the product.

When considering abandonment, the question of profit standard to be applied naturally arises. One method is to calculate, if possible, sales attributed to the product, costs incurred in making it, and the resulting profit. This net profit may then be related to the investment devoted to the product to get a return on investment, and if the product does not return what is considered desirable for the company it becomes a candidate for disposal.

A second approach is to calculate the cash revenues lost by discontinuing the product and the cash expenses that would be thereby avoided. The difference can then be related to an investment base which is the net disposal value of the investment upon abandonment. This base is the receipt of sale of plant and equipment and the reduction in inventories, receivables, cash, and current payables that can be achieved. When this value is found, rate of return can be approached in two ways. It can be determined by dividing indicated net cash earnings lost by the recoverable investment. Or, it can be determined by projecting the stream of earnings into the future and finding a discounted cash flow rate of return.

These two methods should lead to about the same conclusion unless the pattern of cash flows is highly unusual. The simple rate of return calculation is probably somewhat easier to make because it can be derived from existing accounting data, but the cash flow technique is more sensitive to the timing of the income-outgo cash stream. Ease of calculation is a relative term, for in both cases, severe problems are usually involved in getting reasonably accurate data. In the first approach, problems in accurately calculating the impact of deleting a product from the whole of a firm's operations are formidable. The total loss of revenue, for example, may for a number of reasons be greater or less than the sales of the product in question. There is also the problem of disentangling costs of the product when it is produced with investments common to a number of products. Estimates needed to make the cash flow analysis also encounter many obvious problems.*

With product line detractors, as with new products, the depth of analysis depends much upon the importance to the company of the product surveyed.

CONCLUDING GUIDES FOR IMPROVED PRODUCT DEVELOPMENT

This chapter was concerned with an over-view of the importance of new products to the prosperity of a company and the risks entailed in developing them. The main focus of attention was on organization to develop new product, the development of new product ideas, and methods to screen and select from among them. The more outstanding conclusions about and guidelines for product planning are as follows.

1. It should be quite clear from the discussion in this chapter that new product development is of prime concern to top management. What attention top management gives it will vary, of course, from case to case. If the product is one which may risk the entire equity of a company the chief executive is likely to, and should, get deeply involved in the process of selection and development. If the product is one among hundreds, the concern of the chief executive may be limited to overseeing the broad planning program and assuring that a suitable mechanism exists in his company for ordering the product decision-making process in an effective and efficient manner.

2. A prime guide to better product planning is a firm recognition of the critical role products play in the success of a company and the high risks that are typically entailed in their successful development. Among other things, such an understanding will provide insight into the great financial savings that, in the typical firm, will follow from improvement in the product planning process.

3. The best product development exists where over-all comprehensive company planning is matured and operates effectively and efficiently. In such a case, over-all company strategic plans provide clear guidance to product development, and details are hammered out in the programming process.

4. The keys to successful product planning rest in the degree of creativity which exists in stimulating new imaginative ideas, and in the suitability of the organization to develop and examine the ideas. There is no substitute for bright new ideas that give a company a competitive edge. Unfortunately, there are no sure-fire methods to make these ideas available in a company, but there are many things that can and should be done to achieve the potential.

5. A number of different organizational methods are being used successfully

---

* For an analysis of these problems see Shillinglaw, 1957.

today. Top management's responsibility is to assure a proper blending of the different organizational devices for product development. In addition, and of high importance, is the need to select competent product managers.

6. In the product development process there is a continuous intermeshing of planning and control as the activity moves from the idea incubation stage to full successful commercialization. Carefully drafted procedures must be prepared for each phase of this development to make sure that bright ideas are not scotched and that appropriate resources, and no more, are matched with risk, uncertainty, and magnitude of investment. Specific steps in the process must be identified and procedures formulated. Guidelines for and principles important in taking each step must also be specified. This means many things, such as, cost-value analysis should be made at appropriate spots in the product development cycle on the basis of written procedures and principles suitable to their application. It means, too, that the feasibility analysis must be appropriate to the subject. Using an elephant gun to hunt a flea is as unrewarding as hunting elephants with fly-swatters.

7. There are new advanced methods for improving decision-making in the product development area, behavioral as well as mathematical, that top management should press both line and staff to examine and use when appropriate. In the behavioral area the developments of most relevance are in group decision-making, and hence organizational. In the quantitative area the new methods are found principally in the screening and selection process.

8. Product managers should be required to produce written plans. This forces a product manager to think things through, provides a base for top management to evaluate what is going on, and creates a framework within which coordination of relevant functional activities can be more readily assured.

9. When a company needs a number of product managers, or has product teams, and especially when work gets done in a matrix organization, conflicts of authority are inevitable. An understanding top management can do much to assure that these abrasions do not create serious injury to products, people, and the organization.

10. Two major profit measures in comparing products are incremental and net. Each has value under different circumstances.

11. Product elimination is a problem which often needs to be faced. There are two profit measures which may be used in this analysis. One is to calculate sales attributed to the product, cost incurred in making it, and the resulting profit. The other is to calculate cash revenues lost by discontinuing the product and the cash expenses saved. Both are difficult calculations to make.

20
Financial Planning ──────────

20
Financial Planning

INTRODUCTION

Financial planning cannot be considered a function separate and distinct from other types of planning if comprehensive corporate planning is to be a meaningful concept. But throughout the planning process there are financial aspects of planning that deserve special treatment. It is the purpose of this chapter to bring together a number of these aspects which were treated in previous chapters, and to add to them considerations not examined previously. Special attention is paid to capital expenditure planning and control. Other subjects treated in less detail are the planning responsibilities of finance executives, the maintenance of liquidity, cost reduction programs, financial simulation models, and financial functional plans.

DUTIES OF FINANCIAL OFFICERS

The finance function is performed principally by various financial officers of a company, who are generally considered to be the vice-president of finance, the controller, the treasurer, or combinations of the three. In a functional sense, chief executives and long-range planners also have duties in the finance function.

Responsibilities of officers who are involved in the finance function vary much depending upon the firm. But generally, the treasurer is largely responsible for obtaining capital from external sources and for managing the cash, valuables, and property of the business. The controller is responsible for assuring the financial health of the enterprise through his accounting and auditing systems. He, for example, sees that funds are used honestly, efficiently, and in conformance with policy. The vice-president of finance, if one exists, is usually a manager who makes financial policy and is the channel for the various financial activities of the company from top management to managers handling the different financial functions.* From what has been said before, the roles of chief executives and long-range planners in this area are clear.

Table 20-1 lists the principal functions of different finance officers as performed in 165 companies. It is quite apparent that the duties of these managers are broad and of the greatest significance to the success of a company.

Table 20-1 Functions Allocated to Treasurers, Controllers, and Others in the Finance Area

FUNCTION	TREASURER Per Cent	CON- TROLLER Per Cent	TREASURER AND CON- TROLLER EQUALLY Per Cent	OTHER RESPONSES Per Cent	NO ANSWER Per Cent
Accounting, corporate, general, cost	4	90	2	4	—
Annual reports, preparation of	28	41	2	26	2
Auditing, internal	11	78	1	7	3
Banking relations	79	4	4	12	—
Budgeting	17	57	7	14	5
Capital expenditures	32	21	2	41	5
Cash management	74	15	1	9	—
Credits and collections	64	20	1	15	—
Customer claims and claims against customers	44	22	1	30	3
Dividends, disbursement of	66	14	1	15	4
Economics and statistics	23	39	4	25	10
Financial statements, preparation of	8	84	4	4	—
Insurance	54	19	4	22	—
Inventories (turnover, maximum and minimum)	12	44	5	37	3
Legal (supervision of legal staff)	24	3	—	57	16
Office services (centralized)	12	52	2	26	9
Payroll (confidential), preparation of	42	46	—	12	1
Payroll (general), preparation of	14	67	1	18	1
Real estate, buying, selling, and leasing of	33	4	1	55	8
Records, custody, retention and destruction of	13	64	3	19	1
Systems and procedures	7	77	3	10	3
Taxes	28	50	6	14	2

Source: Edward T. Curtis, *Company Organization of the Finance Function,* AMA Research Study 55 (New York: American Management Association, Inc., 1962), p. 18. Responses are expressed as a percentage of total, and the table is based only on companies which have both a treasurer and a controller. Because of rounding, some percentages do not add to 100.

* For an elaboration of the functions of these officers, together with other combinations of names, see Curtis, 1962, pp. 11-15; and Plummer and Moller, 1962.

As has been well demonstrated in previous chapters, a comprehensive corporate plan blends all major elements in an enterprise, only one of which is financial. Financial officers contribute to corporate planning in different ways in different companies; but in the aggregate, and at a minimum, they must meet the following requirements for the effective discharge of their responsibilities in planning and its implementation. These are not necessarily in order of importance.

First, there must be a system for and a translation of plans into financial terms. This means, for example, the development of balance sheets, profit and loss statements, and other accounting forms which show the quantification of plans in monetary units.

Second, the financial executive participates, often with others, in making forecasts to be used in planning, such as of sales, costs, and income.

Third, the financial executive is a part of the planning team which evaluates alternative courses of action and the final plan. In this role he must establish and maintain financial standards for choosing from among alternative courses of action and for testing the feasibility of plans in financial terms, e.g., standards for making capital expenditures, judging performance, or making philanthropic gifts. In this role he must assure that plans are rigorously analyzed and evaluated in terms of these standards.

Fourth, the financial executive must make certain that the company is and will continue to be financially liquid. He must make sure, for example, that plans and operations produce proper relationships between working capital and current liabilities, between long-term debt and income to pay principal and interest, and between dividend payments and retained earnings.

Fifth, the financial executive determines the feasibility of financing requirements as between internal and external sources.

Sixth, maintenance of the dominance of the profit objective is a major financial requirement for all planning. Financial executives are not necessarily the custodian of this central motivating force but do have a special responsibility, along with the chief executives, to keep it in the forefront of planning.

Seventh, the financial executive must exert continuous pressure for cost reduction and methods to achieve it.

Eighth, the financial executive must maintain a suitable system for translating plans into current actions, such as short-range budgets.

Ninth, the financial executive must assure proper coordination of various financial aspects of corporate plans.

Tenth, the financial executive participates with others in developing financial objectives, policies, strategies, and tactics for financial objectives such as dividend policy, credit and collection policy, borrowing policy, and profit objectives.

Eleventh, the financial executive is responsible for maintaining major parts of the control system which permits top management to assure that operations are taking place in conformance with plans.

Each of these requirements includes a long list of subactivities, far too many to discuss in this chapter. A critically significant part of business planning not discussed before concerns capital budgeting, a subject which now will be discussed at length.

CAPITAL EXPENDITURE PLANNING
AND CONTROL PROCEDURES

SIGNIFICANCE OF CAPITAL EXPENDITURES. There are three ways to go broke running a business. One is to spend too much, another is to spend too little, and the third is to invest in the wrong thing.

Unwise investments, while they may not bring bankruptcy, can cripple a company by increasing operating expenses, by absorbing an excessive amount of company funds, and by reducing profits. On the other hand, failure to invest may reduce quality of product, increase costs, or cause a company to fall behind its competition. Not only is capital expenditure policy of major importance to a company but it is of great significance to an industry as well as to the national economy. Excessive capacity in an industry, for example, can result in cut-throat competition which may not only create unnecessary problems in the industry but also have national repercussions. Either excessive or too little capital investment on the part of industry generally has major impact on general economic conditions.

BASIC REQUIREMENTS FOR MANAGEMENT OF CAPITAL EXPENDITURES. In light of the significance of capital expenditures it is not at all surprising that larger companies have prescribed procedures for planning and controlling them. (One study of 424 companies showed that 93 percent had capital expenditure budgets (Sord and Welsch, 1958, p. 91).) Another study showed that 75 out of 100 companies had capital budgets (Pflomm, 1963b, p. 6). There are two basic requirements for the effective management of capital expenditures. The first is an administrative program to provide management with timely and comprehensive information on investment opportunities, together with a mechanism for making wise decisions. The second is a set of reliable techniques which management may use for assessing the merits of individual investment proposals and for ranking them in some order of priority.

Management's responsibility, therefore, covers the development of an administrative procedure over the flow of capital decision-making as well as the techniques for helping management to make the decisions. This means, of course, a comprehensive planning system as well as special procedures for and methods of decision-making set up for capital allocations.

NATURE OF CAPITAL EXPENDITURES. Capital expenditures can be classified and defined in different ways. A capital expenditure in the economic sense is one which is expected to produce benefits over a period of time, usually longer than one year. In typical accounting practice there are expenditures which may be capitalized as compared with those that are "expensed," although the distinction is not universally held among accountants. By capitalizing expenditures, an accountant will charge their cost to a later period of time as the activity to which they are associated produces income to which costs can be charged. Expenditures for physical plant and equipment clearly fall within this category. Expenditures for such items as advertising, basic research, or training costs, are frequently "expensed" or fully charged off as current operating costs. Some capital expenditures can produce identifiable future income, but benefits from some types of expenditures may not produce clearly identifiable cash income. In the latter category are investments for training a manager by sending him to school, building an employee recreation hall, or building a new laboratory for a research scientist.

Obviously, the problems in making decisions for these classes will not be the same. For this reason, most companies classify capital expenditures. Westing-

Table 20-2 Facility Project Classification of Westinghouse

TYPE	DEFINITION
Major Projects:	Any project for any purpose in which the final cost to the Company is $1,000,000 or more.
All Other:	
Class 1 Expansion Projects	Projects primarily intended to provide greater output or to manufacture new products.
Class 2 Product Improvement Projects	Projects primarily in support of product redesign or broadening of line primarily for purpose of improved saleability.
Class 3 Cost Reduction Projects	Projects primarily intended to reduce costs or expenses by improvement of facilities to achieve reduction in labor, materials or expense.
Class 4 Necessity Projects	Projects essential to operations not lending to classification in one of the three above classes.
Class 5 Government-Owned Facilities	Expenditures for facilities directly reimbursable and with title vested in Government.

Source: Planning and Control of Facilities' Expenditures (Pittsburgh, Pa.: Westinghouse, 1964), p. 2.

Chart 20-1

Conceptual Model of Capital Expenditure
Planning and Control

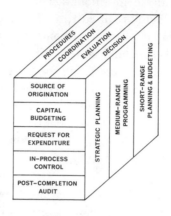

house, for example, uses the classification shown in Table 20-2. Another classification is as follows: *

1. Cost Reduction Program
2. Expansion for Increased Production
3. New Models or Products
4. Quality Improvement
5. Sales and Distribution
6. Replacement of Existing Facilities
7. Research and Development (Product Engineering)
8. Administration

Some classifications rest on income-producing versus non-income producing investments. Some are based on size of capital expenditures. Some are divided according to whether they maintain operations or are for growth. Some classifications combine several of these groupings. Westinghouse, for example, classifies proposals by size in addition to the groupings of Table 20-2.

CONCEPTUAL MODEL OF CAPITAL EXPENDITURE PLANNING AND CONTROL. Chart 20-1 sets forth a conceptual model which explains simply the main elements of a capital expenditure planning and control structure and process.† The process cannot be explained without considering at least three dimensions. The model reflects the fact that the process of developing and evaluating capital expenditure proposals is deeply intermingled with the entire planning process. The whole planning process provides a basic setting for the

---

* For others, see *The Capital Expenditure Control Program*, Accounting Practice Report No. 7, *N.A.A. Bulletin*, March 1959, pp. 8-9.

† In developing this model I benefited from the model prepared by Usry, 1960, pp. 23-25.

development and evaluation of capital expenditure proposals. There is also in many companies a specific step-by-step procedure followed in advancing, evaluating, and following-up capital expenditure decisions. Although most of these concern short-range planning they reflect longer-range planning. Finally, the whole process at different stages in planning is guided by procedures, coordination, evaluation, and decision, as shown in the model. As Usury notes, these latter are activities that permeate the entire process as compared with the preceding ones, which are sequential implementing activities. (p. 25.) Before examining these sequential steps and permeating activities in more detail it may be useful to present a typical plan for programming and approving facilities expenditures, as illustrated by Westinghouse's system.

In the fall of each year, each division prepares a proposed *Facilities Program*, projecting facilities expenditures for three years and specifying in detail projects to be initiated during the next calendar year. Projects are classified as "major" (over $1,000,000), and "all others," and are combined in the *Annual Budgeted Facilities Program*. These are forwarded to the Group Vice Presidents for review and submittal to the Capital Expenditures Committee. The consolidated requirements of all divisions are balanced by the Capital Expenditures Committee with the corporate funds available for facilities expenditures, and the *Facilities Programs* are adjusted, if necessary, to bring the total within available funds. Recommendations of the Capital Expenditures Committee are submitted to the President, who, in turn, submits them, after review and approval, to the Board of Directors for acceptance. Following Board acceptance the divisions may initiate *Appropriation Requests*, which, when approved, permit authorized expenditures. The final step is a post-audit of results. (Westinghouse, 1964, p. 1.)

SOURCES OF ORIGINATION. The planning process is, of course, a major stimulant to new capital expenditure suggestions. As objectives are hammered out and strategies devised to achieve them, proposals for capital expenditures obviously will be generated. As the planning proceeds, there should be arrangements made to encourage new ideas at all levels in a company. Although most companies have far more proposals than funds to support them, it is important to stimulate new ideas continuously, with the hope that some may eventually be funded and make profits that otherwise might have been lost.

Specific stimuli to capital-investment opportunities are many. Studying future markets and profit opportunities for the company is a fertile field. Stimulating creative thinking at all levels of an organization is bound to produce new ideas for capital expenditures. An audit of the economic effectiveness of existing facilities should turn up good ideas. A comparison of the firm's present and prospective physical plant with those of competitors may suggest new programs. Examination of educational needs for managers and skilled technicians may turn up good ideas. Creating an organized research organization will be stimulating. Cost-effective analysis of computer installations may support the need for the purchase of such equipment. All these sources, and many more, exist in an effective comprehensive planning program, and if the program does not stimulate more ideas than the company can profitably use there is something wrong with the planning system.

CAPITAL BUDGETING. A capital budget is a basic management tool in developing, evaluating, and controlling capital expenditures. It is in its approved form an array of expenditures to be made for selected classes of projects in future periods of time. Table 20-3 shows a summary of a facilities program and a forecast of expenditures. Capital budget requests usually include information for classes of projects. The time period varies but extends generally from one to three years. These short-range budgets, of course, are operational tools of management, reflecting decisions actually made. (Many companies prepare longer-range capital budgets covering the full length of the planning period, often five and frequently ten years. But these are not budgets in the sense the term is used here. Rather they are estimates of future capital expenditures needed to implement proposed plans.) The capital budget requests are accompanied, generally, with back-up details about why the expenditures are required and what their profit implications are calculated to be. This is expressed, for example, in terms of return on investment, cost-reduction savings, or profit potential.

There are many advantages to having capital expenditure budgets. Management is in a much better position to determine the extent to which proposed facility expenditures are programmed properly with longer-range plans, required plant capacity, cost and profit objectives, available funds, available manpower, and general economic conditions. There is considerable advantage to management in evaluating programs side by side, which can be done when capital budgets are prepared. Since cash requirements for capital expenditures are large in most companies, relative to other outlays, it is important to know what they are likely to be in order to permit better management of total cash flow.

Among companies not using capital budgets, the following are reasons given: informal controls are adequate, capital budgets lead to extravagance, capital budgets are unrealistic, and capital budgets reduce flexibility (Pflomm, 1963b, p. 7).

REQUEST FOR EXPENDITURE. Generally, top management approval of the capital budget expresses agreement with the proposed plan for capital expenditures, but this is not the same as an actual authorization of the expenditure. Authority to commit and spend funds generally follows some sort of request-for-expenditure procedure. In some firms full authority is granted at the time annual budgets are prepared. In these instances the volume of detail associated with the decision is considerably greater than among firms where a further authorization is required. In such cases, the capital budget that is approved by top management is much less detailed than the back-up material required on requests for actual expenditure. In the latter cases, information such as the following may be required: detailed economic justification, engineering justification, costs, and schedules of expenditure.

In most firms, the authority of managers to make capital expenditures is held at surprisingly low levels. It is not at all unusual, for example, to find that a plant manager of a large company may commit funds only up to around $1,000, or a vice president up to $2,500, or a president up to $15,000 to $20,000. In order to shove more authority down into divisional levels, the Gulf Oil Corporation in 1966 permitted managers in the field to make expenditures up to $500,000 without approval from the company's headquarters in Pittsburgh. Before, the ceiling was $25,000. Although such broad authority is now rare, the trend is toward raising the authority levels.

IN-PROCESS CONTROL. The authorization to proceed with a project is an authorization to proceed at a specific cost, time schedule, and specification. In order to assure that action follows this approval, there is need for some control. The type of controls employed are most frequently periodic status reports covering accounting cost controls and engineering and architectural controls for physical plant.

POST-COMPLETION AUDIT. Most companies make some type of post-completion audit. There are three major purposes of the post-completion audit. First, management's attention is directed towards unsuccessful projects or those that do not meet their previous expectations. Decisions can be made about what to do and lessons may be learned about avoiding performance failures in the future. Second, the integrity of future capital expenditure proposals is preserved. Competition for funds, or incompetently prepared justifications, may result in exaggerated claims that are not detected in the screening process. Post audits serve notice on everyone that a day of reckoning may reveal past misjudgments. Third, examination of results of past actions should provide a basis for improving the future capital expenditure planning and control process.

Most companies select the type of projects to be audited, such as large items with major significance to the company. Some select projects for audit on the basis of dollar amount involved, such as $10,000 and above. The thoroughness of the audit varies among companies with some making a cursory survey and others requiring a very detailed report. (Pflomm, 1963b, Chapter 6; and Istvan, 1961, Chapter 5.)

For the most part the post-completion audits are made by the staff of one of the finance executives, often in the accounting group. Other personnel, however, may be involved, such as the chief engineer, a plant manager, or persons responsible for the project.

Table 20-3   Facilities Investment Plan Summary

WESTINGHOUSE FORM 29066 G
(DOLLARS IN THOUSANDS)

FACILITIES INVESTMENT PLAN SUMMARY

FORM 4

MAJOR PROJECTS OR ACQUISITIONS				APPROP. EXPENDITURES		TIMING OF APPROR. EXPENDITURES			
PROJECT TITLE	PROJECT INITIATION DATE	RETURN ON INVESTMENT %	TOTAL INVESTMENT $	EXPENSE	TOTAL	19	19	19	AFTER 19
1									
2									
3									
4									
5	TOTAL - Major Projects								

ANNUAL BUDGETED FACILITIES PROGRAMS

	1st YEAR PROGRAM	BY CAPITAL & APPROPRIATION EXPENSE - COST RANGE			APPROPRIATION REQUEST		19 EXPENDITURES	
		UNDER $50,000	$50,000 TO $99,999	$100,000 & OVER	EXPENSE	TOTAL	EXPENSE	TOTAL
6	VOLUME IMPROVEMENT (Class 1)							
7	PRODUCT IMPROVEMENT (Class 2)							
8	COST IMPROVEMENT (Class 3)							
9	REPLACEMENT & OTHER (Class 4)							
10	TOTAL - 1st Year Program							
11	FORECASTED 2nd YEAR ANNUAL BUDGETED FACILITIES PROGRAM							
12	FORECASTED 3rd YEAR ANNUAL BUDGETED FACILITIES PROGRAM							
13	TOTAL - ALL COMPANY FINANCED PROJECTS - NEXT 3 YEARS (5+ 10+ 11+ 12)							
	PRIOR YEARS PROGRAM	Major Projects						
14	REMAINING EXPENDITURES AFTER DECEMBER 31 THIS YEAR	All Others						
15	ON ALL COMPANY FINANCED PROGRAMS REMAINING OPEN							
16	AFTER DECEMBER 31.	Total Open						
17	TOTAL - ALL COMPANY FINANCED PROJECTS (13 + 16)							
18	NEXT YEAR'S LEASE COSTS		DIVISION			FOR YEAR		
19	TOTAL OUTSTANDING LEASE COMMITMENTS					19		
20	NEXT YEAR'S DEPRECIATION		SIGNED - DIVISION MANAGER			DATE		
21	NEXT YEAR'S RETIREMENTS							
22	NEXT YEAR'S GOVERNMENT FINANCED PROJECTS							

Source: Westinghouse Electric Corporation, 1968 Planning Procedures, Pittsburgh, Pa., June 30, 1967.

All of the above steps take place more or less sequentially in the different planning stages, with variations appropriate to the planning stage and the type expenditure under consideration. As noted above, there are activities in capital expenditure planning and control that are not sequential, but cut across the sequential steps and permeate the whole process. These now deserve brief comment.

PROCEDURES. Many companies have specified procedures for capital expenditure planning and control, particularly with respect to the short-term capital budget and actions taken on the basis of it. Although this procedure fits into comprehensive planning programs when they exist, it is also separated, in part, from them.

A new development in planning activity is the growth of capital appropriations committees. In a recent study of 87 companies, the NICB found 23 had capital appropriations committees, 15 placed responsibility for passing on capital expenditures in other committees (e.g., finance committee, budget committee, or executive committee of the board of directors), and the remainder did not use any form of financial committee for controlling capital expenditures. (Pflomm, 1963a, Chapter 3.)

Practices among the committees vary much. Generally, many of the following functions are performed: review procedures for capital expenditure planning and control, encourage managers to make more realistic proposals, set up more uniform evaluation procedures, review the proposals of capital expenditures, control the expenditure of capital funds, monitor the progress of projects, and review post-completion audits.

Committee membership usually includes at least one member of top management, and financial executives are well represented. Many also include managers from sales, manufacturing, engineering, and research.

COORDINATION. Long-term capital expenditure programs theoretically, of course, should be carefully related to the objectives a company seeks and should reflect an efficient deployment of resources. This might be considered a vertical coordination, as compared with a horizontal coordination which reflects a proper interrelationship among all capital expenditure programs in all functional areas. Actually, of course, such precision is neither possible nor desirable. But it is a coordination which capital expenditure programs should approach in a manner fitting to each company's situation. This may be considered substantive coordination, as distinguished from procedural coordination which lays out the administrative methods to accomplish it.

EVALUATION AND DECISION. Evaluation and decision are two other aspects of capital expenditure planning and control which permeate the process.

Throughout there is continuous evaluation and decision-making. The tools of analysis will differ at stages in the process, as will the nature of the decision. As with the product selection process, the initial screening may involve rather simple evaluation techniques and result in only rough screening decisions. As the final decision for a fateful investment approaches, the evaluation becomes more sophisticated and the decision-making much more serious. Although capital investment decisions are based upon many considerations, there are important financial techniques which managers have at their disposal.

TECHNIQUES FOR FINANCIAL EVALUATION OF CAPITAL EXPENDITURES

The most important techniques are: the payback period, the simple rate of return, the time-adjusted rate of return, the MAPI special formula for equipment, and risk analysis. Several of these techniques were discussed in Chapter 13 but will be re-examined here in connection with capital expenditures.

PAYBACK, OR PAYOUT, METHOD. This method simply measures how long it will be before income from an investment (before depreciation but after taxes) will equal cost. If a screw machine costs $15,000 and returns $5,000 each year (before depreciation and after taxes) the payback period is three years. The shorter the payback period, the more favorably a project is regarded.

This is a rather widely used technique. Terborgh has reported that 60 percent of firms surveyed used this method. Among firms using this criterion, 28 percent adopted the three-year payback period and 34 percent used a five-year payback (Terborgh, 1958). Istvan (1961, p. 91) found that of 48 companies he investigated 34 used this method.

A major shortcoming of this measure is that it does not consider total project profitability. In the following case, for example, project A would be preferred on a typical payback criterion even though project B would yield greater profits over the life of the project.

Project	Cost	Annual Return	Annual Payback Period	Annual Life
A	$12,000	$4,000	3	3
B	$12,000	$3,000	4	6

Why is it that this method is used with such an obvious shortcoming? Several answers are as follows. First, this method has a built-in conservatism. It emphasizes liquidity, but does this sometimes at the expense of profitability. It also recognizes increasing uncertainties as time goes by. It is true that the longer the future, the greater the uncertainty. The solution, however, is not to use an arbitrary cut-off but rather to recognize uncertainties, to make judgments about the degrees of uncertainty, and to decide on that basis. Second, a company may be hard-pressed for cash in the next few years, and the payback method is used as an evaluation criterion not because it is the best but because there is no better solution.

RETURN ON INVESTMENT. Return on investment derives the percentage yield of anticipated income to the investment outlay. As noted in Chapter 13, there are different ways to make this calculation. Many companies that use the method ask penetrating details about the calculation, as shown in Table 20-4. Istvan reported that 32 of the 48 companies he surveyed used a return-on-investment criterion for facility decisions, and that in 24 of the 32 companies it was the primary measure. (p. 85.)

This technique has obvious advantages over the payback formulation inasmuch as it does take account of income over the entire life of a project. Nevertheless, it also embodies a major weakness (like the payback method) because it fails to consider the time value of money. The timing of income flows is obviously of great importance to a company, especially for a large investment. This is a consideration explicitly examined in present worth methods for measuring investment worthiness.

TIME-ADJUSTED RATES OF RETURN. Two basic methods to take into consideration the value of income flows over time in relation to cost are the discounted cash flow and the present worth techniques, demonstrated in Chapter 13. Each of these techniques has its strengths and weaknesses. Those who prefer the present worth technique point to the fact that the discounted cash flow concept is difficult to get managers to understand, the method of computation is tedious, it can mislead if there are losses as well as earnings in a project's life, and it assumes that earnings received during an investment's life are reinvested at the same rate of return yielded by the project being measured. (Pflomm, 1963b, p. 44.)

The present worth method has an advantage over the discounted cash flow technique because it alone reflects changes in the firm's cost of capital. It also, however, assumes the reinvestment rate and the discounting rate to be equal, an assumption usually contrary to practice.

Despite theoretical differences, the two techniques yield about the same results. Lorie and Savage (1955) conclude that for the great majority of investments made by businesses the two methods will rank the proposals just about the same.

Despite the obvious advantages in using the time-adjusted methods to help choose among investments, why are they not more generally found in use? As

Table 20-4 Strategic Projects Return on Investment Worksheet
Discounted Cash Flow

DOLLARS IN THOUSANDS

DIVISION	PROJECT NO.	DATE
PRODUCT LINE	PROJECT PURPOSE	
PROJECT DESCRIPTION		

INVESTMENT

	AMOUNT
1. FACILITIES EXPENDITURES - CAPITAL	
2. FACILITIES EXPENDITURES - EXPENSE	
3. FACILITIES EXPENDITURES - TOTAL	
4. OTHER STRATEGIC EXPENSE	
5. NET WORKING CAPITAL INVESTMENT	
6. LESS - SALVAGE VALUE OF PRESENT EQUIPMENT	
7. LESS - **STRATEGIC EXPENSE TAX EFFECT**	
8. **TOTAL PROJECT EXPENDITURES** (SUM OF LINES 3, 4 AND 5 MINUS LINES 6 AND 7)	

OPERATING RESULTS (AVERAGE ANNUAL SALES, COSTS AND INCOME)

9. SALES BILLED AFFECTED BY PROJECT	
10. APPLICABLE DIRECT PRODUCT COSTS	
11. INCREMENTAL COMMITTED AND MANAGED COSTS (EXCLUDING DEPRECIATION)	
12. INCREMENTAL IBT ON SALES BILLED AFFECTED (LINE 9 MINUS SUM OF LINES 10 AND 11)	
13. NET COST IMPROVEMENT ON BASE VOLUME	
14. DEPRECIATION (LINE 1 ÷ YEARS OF DEPRECIATION LIFE)	
15. INCREMENTAL IBT ON PROJECT (SUM OF LINES 12 AND 13 MINUS LINE 14)	
16. FEDERAL INCOME TAXES (48% OF LINE 15)	
17. **INVESTMENT CREDIT**	
18. **INCOME AFTER TAXES**	
19. **AVERAGE ANNUAL CASH FLOW (LINE 18 PLUS LINE 14)**	

20. PAYOUT PERIOD (LINE 8 ÷ LINE 19)	
21. YEARS OF ECONOMIC LIFE	
22. DISCOUNTED CASH FLOW RATE OF RETURN ON INVESTMENT	%

SUPPLEMENTAL DATA

	1ST YEAR	2ND YEAR	3RD YEAR
A. TIMING OF TOTAL PROJECT EXPENDITURES (LINE 8)			
B. IMPACT ON PERSONNEL		PRIOR TO	PROPOSED
HOURLY PRODUCTIVE			
HOURLY EXPENSE			
SALARY			

	YES	NO	COMPLETE	TO BE COMPLETED BY
C. PERSONNEL PLANNING REQUIRED				

Source: Westinghouse Electric Corporation, *1968 Planning Procedures,* Pittsburgh, Pa., June 30, 1967.

noted previously, one reason is high liquidity preference. With a high liquidity preference, the simple payback or return-on-investment calculations will yield more acceptable results to a manager, with easier calculations. Furthermore, a number of firms feel that the more complicated techniques increase costs without a corresponding increase in profits. In those instances, for example, where a firm has an extensive interrelationship among capital facilities, and where joint costs and joint revenues are many and important, the complications of the sophisticated techniques are great. (Istvan, 1961, p. 101.) Also, the fact should not be overlooked that many managers feel there is higher payoff to them in concentrating their time on getting better investment proposals, searching for better information about cost and benefit, and administering the capital investment program, than in refining the computations. This attitude probably is more prevalent among small than larger enterprises. After intensive investigations of smaller enterprises, Solomon thinks this view is justified, for he concluded that "small businessmen should not worry greatly about their failure to use refined analyses but should be more concerned with discovering new opportunities and collecting better information. The real need in small business investments is for greater imagination and creativity." (Solomon, 1963, p. 125.) * There undoubtedly is much truth in this conclusion. But for both small and large businesses the great importance of the more sophisticated techniques is that they tell managers what very important questions should be asked about investments whether they do or do not actually make the detailed calculations.

THE MAPI FORMULA. An important exception to this evaluation is the use of the formula developed by George Terborgh of the Machinery and Allied Products Institute for management use in considering replacement of machinery. His method has been called an adjusted after-tax rate of return. The MAPI formula seeks to calculate what will be a next-year's rate of return from an investment in new equipment if action is taken now rather than waiting one more year. The calculation is shown in Table 20-5. Fundamentally, the next-year's rate of return from the MAPI calculation is a discounted cash flow rate of return. Whereas the formulation of the discounted cash flow rate of return must be tailor-made for each case (as shown in Chapter 13), MAPI's is a "cookbook" formulation that all managers can easily use when considering machine replacement. Here again, even if a manager does not choose to use the prescribed path to make the calculation, he can find in it the right questions to be asked about the investment.

RISK ANALYSIS. A major weakness of all the preceding techniques for evaluating the desirability of an investment is that they do not take into consideration probabilities concerning important aspects of the decision. The discounted cash flow return on investment, for example, may show that investment

* See also Haynes and Solomon, Jr., 1962, pp. 39-46.

Table 20-5   MAPI Return-on-Investment Calculation

MAPI OPERATING FORM
(Averaging Shortcut)

PROJECT   Roundness Measuring Instrument

ALTERNATIVE   Continuing as is

COMPARISON PERIOD	(YEARS)	(P)	1
ASSUMED OPERATING RATE OF PROJECT	(HOURS PER YEAR)		230

I. OPERATING ADVANTAGE

(NEXT-YEAR FOR A 1-YEAR COMPARISON PERIOD,* ANNUAL AVERAGES FOR LONGER PERIODS)

A. EFFECT OF PROJECT ON REVENUE

		Increase	Decrease	
1	FROM CHANGE IN QUALITY OF PRODUCTS	$ 3,500	$	1
2	FROM CHANGE IN VOLUME OF OUTPUT	1,500		2
3	TOTAL	$ 5,000 X	$ Y	3

B. EFFECT ON OPERATING COSTS

4	DIRECT LABOR	$ 410	$	4
5	INDIRECT LABOR			5
6	FRINGE BENEFITS	100		6
7	MAINTENANCE		6,400	7
8	TOOLING			8
9	MATERIALS AND SUPPLIES	50		9
10	INSPECTION			10
11	ASSEMBLY			11
12	SCRAP AND REWORK		700	12
13	DOWN TIME			13
14	POWER	5		14
15	FLOOR SPACE	85		15
16	PROPERTY TAXES AND INSURANCE	30		16
17	SUBCONTRACTING			17
18	INVENTORY			18
19	SAFETY			19
20	FLEXIBILITY			20
21	OTHER			21
22	TOTAL	$ 680 Y	$ 7,100 X	22

C. COMBINED EFFECT

23	NET INCREASE IN REVENUE (3X — 3Y)	$ 5,000	23
24	NET DECREASE IN OPERATING COSTS (22X — 22Y)	$ 6,420	24
25	ANNUAL OPERATING ADVANTAGE (23 + 24)	$11,420	25

* Next year means the first year of project operation. For projects with a significant break-in period, use performance after break-in.

Table 20-5   MAPI Return-on-Investment Calculation (Continued)

II. INVESTMENT AND RETURN
A. INITIAL INVESTMENT

26	INSTALLED COST OF PROJECT	$29,800		
	MINUS INITIAL TAX BENEFIT OF	$ 2,085	(Net Cost)	$27,715	26
27	INVESTMENT IN ALTERNATIVE			
	CAPITAL ADDITIONS MINUS INITIAL TAX BENEFIT	$		
	PLUS: DISPOSAL VALUE OF ASSETS RETIRED			
	BY PROJECT*	$	$	27
28	*INITIAL NET INVESTMENT* (26 — 27)		$27,715	28

B. TERMINAL INVESTMENT

29 RETENTION VALUE OF PROJECT AT END OF COMPARISON PERIOD

(ESTIMATE FOR ASSETS, IF ANY, THAT CANNOT BE DEPRECIATED OR EXPENSED.
FOR OTHERS, ESTIMATE OR USE MAPI CHARTS.)

Item or Group	Installed Cost, Minus Initial Tax Benefit (Net Cost)	Service Life (Years)	Disposal Value, End of Life (Percent of Net Cost)	MAPI Chart Number	Chart Percentage	Retention Value $\left(\dfrac{A \times E}{100} \right)$
	A	B	C	D	E	F
Roundness Measuring Instrument, Etc.	$27,715	15	10	1A	90.8	$25,165

	ESTIMATED FROM CHARTS	(TOTAL OF COL. F)	$25,165		
	PLUS: OTHERWISE ESTIMATED		$	$25,165	29
30	DISPOSAL VALUE OF ALTERNATIVE AT END OF PERIOD*			$	30
31	*TERMINAL NET INVESTMENT* (29 — 30)			$25,165	31

C. RETURN

32	AVERAGE NET CAPITAL CONSUMPTION $\left(\dfrac{28 - 31}{P} \right)$	$ 2,550	32
33	AVERAGE NET INVESTMENT $\left(\dfrac{28 + 31}{2} \right)$	$26,440	33
34	*BEFORE-TAX RETURN* $\left(\dfrac{25 - 32}{33} \times 100 \right)$	% 33.5	34
35	INCREASE IN DEPRECIATION AND INTEREST DEDUCTIONS	$ 3,650	35
36	TAXABLE OPERATING ADVANTAGE (25 — 35)	$ 7,770	36
37	INCREASE IN INCOME TAX (36 × TAX RATE)	$ 3,885	37
38	AFTER-TAX OPERATING ADVANTAGE (25 — 37)	$ 7,535	38
39	AVAILABLE FOR RETURN IN INVESTMENT (38 — 32)	$ 4,985	39
40	*AFTER-TAX RETURN* $\left(\dfrac{39}{33} \times 100 \right)$	% 18.9	40

* After terminal tax adjustments.

Note: The number found in 29 (E) is derived by locating service life (B) and disposal value (C) on MAPI Chart I-A. MAPI has different charts which must be consulted. With these charts the value for column (F) is easily derived.

Source: George Terborgh, *Business Investment Management, A MAPI Study and Manual* (Washington, D.C.: Machinery and Allied Products Institute and Council for Technological Advancement, 1967), pp. 205-206.

A will yield 30 percent and investment B, 20 percent. Other things being equal, it is clear that investment A is preferred. But other things may not be equal. A determination of probabilities may show (see Chart 20-2) that there is better than a 1 in 10 chance that A may lose money and that it has only a 4 in 10 chance of returning 30 percent. On the other hand, investment B has no chance of losing money and has an 8 in 10 chance of making 20 percent. It may be, of course, that a company will choose A because it is willing to take the risk. On the other hand, if it cannot afford to lose money it will choose B.

Managers always consider risks of loss and compare them with probabilities for profits. Until recently, however, the estimates and calculations have been made mentally by the managers as the decision-making process evolved. But now, with risk analysis and the speed of the computer, managers may put explicit probabilities on important elements associated with capital investments to get graphic pictures of probabilities concerning expected values of investments.

As noted in Chapter 15, in any investment of magnitude many factors will have an important bearing on the ultimate payoff. Among them are market size, selling price, market growth rate, share of market, and operating costs. Risk analysis begins with the selection of these factors. Then managers and staff experts prepare probability distributions for each of these elements. Once these are prepared, probability points are chosen at random from among the distributions and computers calculate a rate of return for each combination. The process is repeated many times until a probability distribution of the rate of return for the investment is developed (Hertz, 1964). The steps to be followed, and the results achieved, are shown in Table 6 of Chapter 15.

Chapter 15 discussed the problem of management's placing probabilities, in explicit quantitative terms, on variations expected for different factors of a decision. This will not be repeated here but should be recalled as part of this discussion.

MAJOR CONSIDERATIONS IN CAPITAL EXPENDITURE DECISION-MAKING

Capital expenditure evaluations and decisions are among the most complex and difficult with which top management must be concerned, and there is no easy way to make these decisions. The above techniques are very valuable in capital allocation decisions but they are not the whole story by any means. In this section, therefore, attention is focused on a number of aspects of this decision-making process that have an important bearing on an understanding and appreciation of the process.

CONSISTENCY WITH PLANS. The probability that a given investment will produce the profits or other results predicted depends in part on how it fits into a company's long-term development plan. A new plant may promise a high yield, but if the development of managers to run it and the acquisition of engineers to use it do not coincide with its completion, the expected profits may not appear. A number of projects may promise high yield when viewed individually, but when all are undertaken simultaneously the total expected profit may not appear for any number of reasons. A company may calculate that a given investment will not yield an acceptable return on any economic criterion but may be considered desirable in light of other considerations, such as improvement of company image, or because of the assumption of community responsibilities. Regulatory commissions may require a company to make investments for specific purposes, such as smog control devices for automobiles or safety devices on airplanes. Recent regulations and legislation with respect to both these activities will necessitate the expenditure of millions of dollars by the companies involved. In this light, it is quite apparent that few important capital investments, if any, can be made automatically by the application of one criterion. Capital investment is a singularly important activity that demands for its success the deepest attention of top management aided by the best staff brains available in the company. It is an exceedingly complex problem that must be considered in light of both long- and short-range plans in all important areas of a company. In this connection, too, there should be recalled the difficulties standing in the way of a manager in being rational that were presented in Chapter 12.

EVALUATION TECHNIQUES VARY WITH INVESTMENT. The financial techniques discussed above are of greatest use in those instances where costs and income from investments can be measured with some reasonable degree of accuracy. Such projection is impossible and often irrelevant for many investments, such as the following: improving the physical surroundings of a plant as a matter of community pride or to add to the satisfactions of employees, research on a particular "blue sky" idea, building a new restaurant for employees because the old one is obsolete, or continuing to operate a marginal plant in an economically distressed community. Hunches, intuition, value systems of managers, and politics are basic determinants of such investments. Cost-benefit analyses might be useful for such investment decisions.

There are also other types of investment that are not readily amenable to financial-type evaluations. Such are those which are indispensable to operations, like the replacement of a burned-out motor which runs the machine tools of a plant.

Joel Dean (1966), in a prize-winning article, says that advertising should be considered a capital investment and that the discounted cash flow analysis is a suitable yardstick for decision-making. Gary MacDougal (1967), in another prize-winning article, says that companies should consider dividend boosts as possible investments because, judiciously given, they can raise the price of the

Chart 20-2

Risk Analysis for Return on Investments A and B

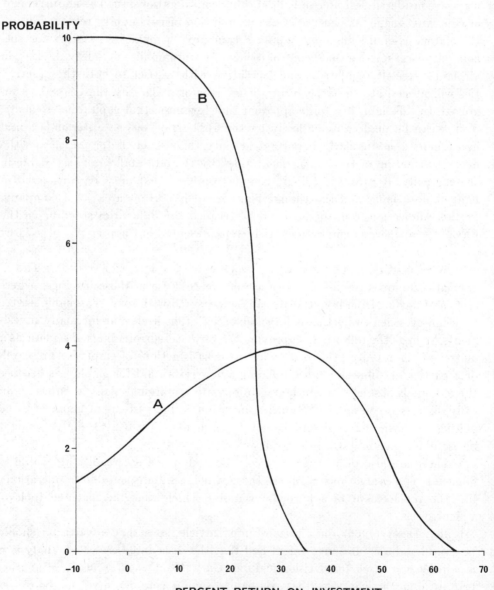

PROBABILITY

PERCENT RETURN ON INVESTMENT

company's stock and thereby reduce the number of shares to be used in acquisitions. Here, too, a financial yardstick can be applied in decision.

Financial analysis is applicable for the majority of investments. With it, managers can rank investments and use the resulting evaluations as a first and major step in decision-making. This does not mean that the results of financial evaluations will always govern the decision.

PROJECT RANKING AND CRITERIA. Whatever financial system of evaluation is used, management must make a choice of criteria to be used to determine the desirable investments. It may decide to use the current average company return on investment, the return on investment of competing companies, the average return on investment of the industry, a predetermined return on investment for each division or plant, a rate of return for specific project classes, the cost of capital of the firm, or the cost of borrowing.

Companies that classify capital expenditure proposals usually have different criteria for different classes. For example, a company may decide that all expansion and cost-reduction projects must return 30 percent or more on investment to be eligible for approval. Of course, the method to calculate return on investment is also specified.

Many companies rank their investment proposals in terms of return on investment, and use urgency rankings (e.g. A, indispensable; B, high; C, average; D, low). In this way the total volume of required financing can be arrayed by yield and urgency and matched against available funds. If funds available in the firm are insufficient to satisfy all legitimate needs, the company then must decide whether to go outside the company for additional financing.

COST OF CAPITAL. The cost of a firm's capital is simply the cost of the capital employed by a firm. By comparing the company's cost of capital with the prospective profits of new investments, the gain to present stockholders to be derived from seeking outside funds can be measured. Theoretically, there is no point in using outside funds unless there is a gain to the stockholders. Although the concept of cost of a firm's capital is simple enough, there is much controversy about how to make the calculation. Following is a simple calculation:

CAPITAL	CAPITAL STRUCTURE	COST RATES	COST OF CAPITAL
Bonds	5%	5	.25%
Preferred Stock	10%	6	.60%
Common Equity	85%	10	8.50%
TOTAL	100%		9.35%

In this case, of course, the cost of capital is 9.35 percent. In making this calculation, average rates may be used if funding costs have varied from time to time.

There is not agreement on the method of calculation, however. For example, some authorities use the dividend-yield basis for calculating cost of common stock and others use the price-earnings ratio. In industries with stable dividends the dividend yield might be suitable. But where dividends fluctuate greatly the price-earnings ratio may be better. There are problems in using the price-earnings ratio, however, especially since the ratio will fluctuate over time. Furthermore, what to do with glamor stocks is a question. If the price-earnings ratio is 1/10, a 10 percent cost of capital is indicated. But if the ratio is 1/50, the cost of capital at 2 percent is hardly useful as a criterion for investment. If this were used as a cut-off criterion, it would not be long before the company would have to go to the market for funds and the price earnings ratio would hardly hold up. Other issues are whether to use past, current, or anticipated rates; how to cost retained earnings; and handling of underwriter fees, taxes, and other costs. (Weston, 1962, Chapter 11.)

CALCULATING COST AND INCOME.   In theory, a firm should make capital investments where the difference between capital costs and income will add to company profits. This assumes a number of things, such as: the company has access to capital markets and can in fact use the new investments profitably. This latter raises a point of major importance, namely, the accuracy of cost and income calculations. Investment costs are not generally harder to calculate than income, although maintenance costs, ultimate salvage values, and costs of a complex highly technical product, may be difficult to calculate with much certainty. The greater problem usually is that of figuring income with reasonable accuracy, especially if the investment lasts over more than a few years. The greater the possible error in measuring income, and the more strategic the investment decision, the more intuition and hunch will challenge quantitative calculations. Probability estimates will help more than averages but neither, in such a case, can be relied upon.

FINANCIAL POLICY.   A firm may find that it has investment opportunities, for which the indicated return is above its cost of capital, that cannot be financed from funds in the business. The question of outside financing then arises. This immediately raises basic questions of financial policy. Should a firm go deep into debt to finance growth? Some companies have a policy that growth will be financed only from internal funding sources. Should a company pass up a dividend to finance new investment opportunities? This, of course, raises a whole battery of new problems. There is no need to describe other implications on financial policy in financing new investment proposals. The point is that when the question arises it is not answerable by a calculated yield, for before a decision can be made many policy issues will be raised for answer.

THE MANAGEMENT OF FUNDS

The management of company funds includes a number of areas, such as assurance of the liquidity of the company both in the short- and long-run, the determination of what sources of funds to use or tap in both the short- and long-run, and the internal flow and control of funds in current operations. Each of these, of course, includes many sub-areas.

In Chapter 13 two financial statements were presented: a revenue-expense forecast and a forecast of the source and use of funds. These two statements, together with pro forma balance sheet and profit and loss statements, are derived from the planning process and are models for deciding what to do about the management of company funds.

THE SHORT-TERM CASH CYCLE AND LIQUIDITY. Many small businessmen, and some large ones too, have been very surprised at how they got into serious financial difficulties while rapidly expanding sales. The problem centers in the way working capital is managed, as illustrated in the following transactions.

In Balance Sheet I, in Table 20-6 (adapted from Weston, 1962, pp. 263-265), the firm is in a liquid position, but making nothing. An order for metal castings is received and work begins. Balance Sheet II shows that the purchase of materials and payment of workers is financed by a reduction of cash and an increase in current liabilities. The working capital of the firm (current assets — current liabilities) is unchanged in Balance Sheet II compared with Balance Sheet I. But the current ratio (current assets divided by current liabilities), which should be at least 2 to 1, has deteriorated to 1.67. Furthermore, the debt-equity ratio has jumped to 56 percent. The financial position of the firm is weakening.

In Balance Sheet III it is shown that to process the castings the firm has had to draw down cash and borrow from the banks. The current ratio has dropped to 1.46, the acid test ratio (cash divided by current liabilities) has declined to 1.15, and the debt-equity ratio has risen to 81 percent.

In Balance Sheet IV finished castings have been shipped and accounts receivable recorded for the price. Note that in order to pay wages and accounts payable, and to retain a minimum cash balance, the firm has had to borrow an additional $45,000 from the banks. The retained earnings represent the mark-up from the value of finished goods in inventory to accounts receivable. While the financial ratios have improved in Balance Sheet IV, the total debt is large and the cash position with relationship to current liabilities is much too low.

At this point the firm may get into a tough financial problem, or improve its position, depending upon many circumstances. If those holding accounts finance their commitment promptly, the firm will be in a sound position as shown in Balance Sheet V. But if there are delays which are compounded by requirements for financing new orders, or if there is any major problem, such as defective castings, the firm may get into serious financial difficulties. Many small firms crash on these rocks. But large firms sometimes get into comparable difficulties. One of the great ironies of this age, for example, was the extraordinary success of the Douglas Aircraft Company in selling its great line of commercial transports, and in providing the highest quality of technically advanced equipment to the Department of Defense and NASA, and still running into this type problem. The problems, of course, were far more complicated than in the simple illustration shown here, but the end result was grave enough to bring about the

Table 20-6 Comparative Balance Sheets

BALANCE SHEET I

Assets		Liabilities	
Currents Assets			
Cash	$30,000	Capital Stock	$80,000
Fixed Assets			
Plant & Equipment	50,000		
		Total Liabilities and Net	
Total Assets	$80,000	Worth	$80,000

BALANCE SHEET II

Assets			Liabilities	
Current Assets			Acc't Payable	$30,000
Cash	$15,000		Accrued Wages Payable..	15,000
Inventories:			Total	$ 45,000
Work-in process:				
Materials	30,000			
Labor	30,000			
Total		$ 75,000	Capital Stock	80,000
Fixed Assets				
Plant & Equipment	50,000			
Total Assets		$125,000	Total Liabilities and Net Worth ..	$125,000

BALANCE SHEET III

Assets			Liabilities	
Current Assets			Acc't Payable	$30,000
Cash	$ 5,000		Notes Payable	20,000
Inventory:			Accrued Wages Payable..	15,000
Fin. Goods	90,000			
Total		$ 95,000	Total	$ 65,000
Fixed Assets			Capital Stock	80,000
Plant & Equipment	50,000			
Total Assets		$145,000	Total Liabilities and Net Worth ..	$145,000

merger in 1967 of Douglas with McDonnell to form the McDonnell-Douglas Company.

LONGER-RANGE LIQUIDITY MANAGEMENT. Financial management concerning liquidity must, of course, look beyond current operations. When the longer-range is considered, major policy questions arise with respect to dividend policies versus retained earnings; the structure of debt relative to cash flow; and the nature of the securities, if any, to be used in financing. Some companies as a matter of policy have a fixed annual dividend (e.g., American Telephone and Telegraph for years had a $9 annual dividend rate); others pay no cash dividend but periodically issue stock dividends (e.g., many fast-growth companies do this); and others split net profits about fifty-fifty between stockholders and the internal needs of the business. Obviously, many factors influence dividend policy: net profits, anticipated future demands for cash, needs to repay debt, legal requirements of state of incorporation, access to capital markets, current and prospective rates of interest if borrowings are needed, and many others.

There obviously can be no fixed rule to prescribe how financial management will answer questions in dealing with matters such as these. But over a long period of time business financial experience in different industries and with particular types of companies has evolved a body of principle, strategy, and practice,

Table 20-6   Comparative Balance Sheets (Continued)

BALANCE SHEET IV

Assets		Liabilities	
Current Assets		Notes Payable $65,000	
Cash .... $ 5,000			
Acc't Rec. 140,000		Total Current Liabilities	$ 65,000
Total	$145,000	Capital Stock 80,000	
		Retained Earnings 50,000	
Fixed Assets			
Plant & Equipment	50,000	Total Net Worth	130,000
Total Assets	$195,000	Total Liabilities and Net Worth ...	$195,000

BALANCE SHEET V

Assets		Liabilities	
Current Assets		Capital .... $ 80,000	
Cash .... $ 80,000		Earned Surplus 50,000	
Fixed Assets			
Plant & Equipment ...	50,000	Total Liabilities and Net	
Total Assets	$130,000	Worth	$130,000

which provides guidance. Space does not permit any resume of this body of knowledge here, but it is generally available in the business literature on the subject. (Weston, 1962.)

COMPUTER SIMULATION IN FINANCIAL PLANNING

The problem of financial management today is not so much one of developing a theory for operations, for the present-day theory is well advanced, as it is to use available tools and to develop new ones to assure a quicker and more informed response to possible alternative courses of action in the extraordinary maze of possible actions in financial management. This book describes many tools which financial managers have today to do this. At this point, however, I want to draw attention to the growing use of computer simulations for financial management.

Computer simulations, as shown in Chapter 15, can be at any level of detail and cover any desired scope of the financial planning process. At one level of abstraction, for example, is a computer simulation which permits management to ask the question "What would happen if . . . ?" and to get a prompt response. If, for example, financial management says that it is the basic objective of the enterprise to maximize stockholder equity (using that word in the lay sense), there are many possible financial interrelationships which, if optimized, will do that. For example, dividends should be retained in the business if the company can earn more through reinvestment in the business than can the average stockholder. A company should increase its outside borrowings so long as earnings on these investments will yield more than the company's cost of capital and so long, of course, as other considerations indicate the desirability of such borrowing. A constraint on this sort of activity, however, will be the maintenance of a proper debt-equity ratio, which, in turn, is a matter of managerial policy influenced by many other considerations. But many of these considerations can be programmed on a computer. A simulation model can relate these, and many other determinants, to increasing stockholder equity.

When this is done, management may ask such questions as the following and experiment with the results in the development of financial planning: If we retain all earnings over the next five years and apply them to growth by these kinds of investment . . . , what will be the return on equity over this period of time? Can we increase the rate of return on equity by paying out half our earnings in dividends and borrowing the remainder needed for internal investment by the issuance of bonds? What happens to return on equity if we finance prospective growth through stock? If we invest in this volume over the years, increase sales in this way, hold costs to this level, and borrow in these specific ways and in these amounts at these rates of interest, what will be the cash flow and what will be the resultant impact on stockholder equity?

These interrelationships, of course, are merely illustrative of a vastly larger number in the real world. But the point is that simulation models can handle a large number of these variables in this type problem and permit management to simulate the financial future as a better basis for decision-making.

Chart 20-3 shows a simulation model which can be used to answer a number of questions such as these. This model will quickly get very complex when decision rules and probability distributions are added. But, as illustrated in Chapter 15 (Table 15-5), simple hand simulation models can also be valuable in helping managers to answer such questions as the above. This is an appropriate place to note that linear programming models have been developed for banks' financial management, although they are not yet being used (Jallow, 1966).

COST-REDUCTION PROGRAMS

All well-managed companies strive to improve their profit position by making sure that costs of operation are held at the lowest possible levels consistent with other objectives of the company. One way to do this is to see that cost-reduction programs are systematically analyzed in the long-range planning process and put into effect in current operations. Although this is a type activity that involves all managers throughout a company it rests heavily on financial planning and control.

The financial executive finds his activities important in cost-reduction programs in many ways. He is, for example, the custodian of much past historical information about standards for costing. He is deeply involved in the development of current budgets which set the standards for cost control. He is often responsible for the information system that reports progress of the programs to management. Finally, his internal auditing group not only is a source of intelligence for additional cost reduction but also evaluates practice with respect to current programs.

Crash cost-reduction programs may work temporarily, but in the end they are likely to do more harm than good. The far better technique surely is to approach cost reduction as a long-range continuing program to be managed in light of all other operational requirements of a company. One NICB study canvassed over 200 companies and concluded that two-thirds of them accepted this philosophy and put it into practice (Walsh, Jr., 1964).

Executives of the companies participating in this study agreed that the active leadership of top management was indispensable to the success of any cost-reduction program. Some of the executives felt that the coordinator of the program should be a production executive because of his understanding in an area where major cost reduction emphasis should be placed. Others felt that the financial executive could be an effective coordinator because of his control of budgeting and reporting. Others, however, felt the financial executive should be only a scorekeeper, not the manager or coordinator of the program.

Traditionally, internal auditing has been adopted to review a firm's opera-

Chart 20-3

Flow Chart of a Simplified Financial Planning Model (Simulation)

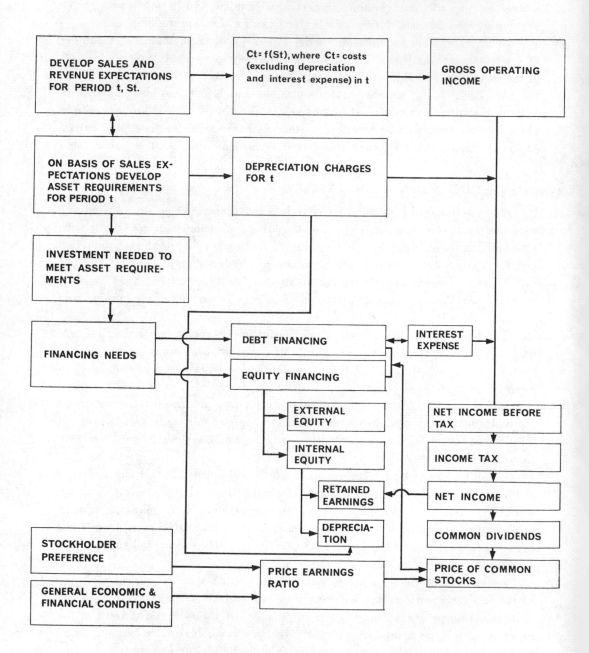

tions by its own independent appraisal department placed in the finance organization. Generally, the job has involved verification of accounts. In recent years, however, there has been an important shift in the work of internal auditors from conventional audits to more managerial-type activities. For example, they may determine the adequacy of the system for internal control, investigate compliance with company policies and procedures, appraise personnel performance, and assist in profit improvement and cost-reduction activities. (Jerome, 1961, Chapter II; and Walsh, 1963.) Managers have found that the special training of internal auditors has given them insight into operational areas where savings can be effected, and if they are asked to make management-type audits as well as financial audits they can be much more productive.

FUNCTIONAL PLANNING

Each of the financial officers of a firm also must plan for activities in his own functional area. Table 20-1 suggests areas for which functional plans should be made. As noted in a previous chapter, it is not always necessary that these functional plans mesh nicely with the over-all company plans, although there certainly should be some interrelationship. For example, if the controller is planning to change his accounting system over the next two or three years, he may not be obliged to relate these changes to production, or sales, or research. But he should, of course, relate the plans to profit objectives if the changes will influence the way profits are to be reported.

If electronic data processing plans are the responsibility of a financial manager, and they usually are, there may be need to relate them carefully to other types of plans. This equipment is a major expense and may have a bearing on the financial position of the firm. Furthermore, there may be shifts of existing personnel brought about by the introduction of this equipment and the need for new skills and talents in the firm.

Plans in the financial functional area are both quantitative and qualitative. For example, the treasurer may set his plan to develop closer relationships with the financial community since his company will be obliged to go outside for additional funds. This would be a qualitative plan and may have many detailed subplans. Plans to add to the staff to make evaluations of new candidates for acquisitions can be quantitative and qualitative.

FINANCIAL COMMITTEES

A growing number of companies in recent years have established committees to aid in their financial management, an expansion that has taken place for many of the same reasons that comprehensive corporate planning has grown. There are six types of committees that may be found in all types and sizes of companies: the finance committee, capital appropriations committee, budget committee, pension or retirement committee, salary committee, and general accounting committee. Committee membership is made up of top management.

These committees have brought special skills and experience to bear on financial problems; provided a forum for representation of major interests; permitted better coordination in planning, evaluation, and control; helped to bring about impartial decisions which have avoided favoritism; and given executives who are responsible for decision-making the advice and counsel of diverse views. On the other hand, they have fallen into some of the common pitfalls in the use of committees. These are inability to reach decisions, tendency to compromise, tendency to accept a least controversial decision, acceptance by the committee of decisions which should be made by an individual, domination of the committee by a powerful individual, unpreparedness for the meetings, and wasting time of members.

A strong chairman can correct many of these problems. Proper membership on the committee also is important for successful use of this system. The purpose and authority of the committees ought to be carefully defined, membership should be small rather than large, meetings should be regular rather than *ad hoc*, staff work should be done effectively for the committee, and the committee should not be asked to make decisions that should be made by individuals.

A survey of almost 200 companies (Pflomm, 1963a, pp. 8-9) showed that the following were the reported duties of three major committees of particular interest in this chapter. The finance committee deals with: "accounting policy and procedures, appointment of depositories, appointment of public accountants, capital budgets and expenditures, contracts, contributions, corporate taxes, depreciation policy, dividend policy, equity financing, expansion programs, forecasts and future planning, information for financial analysts, investment portfolios, long-term borrowing, mergers and acquisitions, operating budgets, price changes, salaries, short-term borrowing, and subscriptions and memberships."

Capital appropriations committees are used to: "encourage local managements to make more realistic proposals, effect uniform evaluation of capital projects, avoid overlapping of projects, select projects that best meet the company's needs, control the expenditure of funds, and monitor the progress of capital projects." (Pflomm, 1963a, p. 21.)

Budget committees review, recommend, or approve short-term budgets and are sometimes responsible for review of actual operations as compared with budgeted targets. Some of them have even broader responsibilities, which include: "forecasting, profit planning, establishing operating costs, counseling operating department heads, recommending budgetary procedures, approving expenditures not provided for in budget, and passing on capital budgets and authorizing the expenditure of funds." (Pflomm, 1963a, p. 33.)

SUMMARY AND CONCLUDING GUIDELINES

Among the aspects of financial functional planning discussed in this chapter, most emphasis was placed on capital expenditure decisions and the techniques used in making them. Emphasis was also laid on administrative and organizational procedures important in capital budgeting. Although discussed, less emphasis was placed on financial management of all company funds, cost-reduction, and finance committees.

Some of the more significant conclusions reached in the chapter are:

First, the duties of financial officers are very broad and show no uniform profile in industry.

Second, there are, however, a number of major responsibilities of financial officers which are assumed by most financial officers, such as translating plans into financial terms, helping to make financial forecasts for planning, establishing financial standards for evaluating financial results of plans, helping to evaluate plans, and others noted in the chapter and in the following.

Third, there are two basic requirements for an effective capital expenditure program. The first is an administrative program to guide the process; the second is a set of reliable techniques for decision-making.

Fourth, many companies have a formal set of procedures for making capital allocation decisions. Most companies divided capital expenditures into different categories of need and urgency, and most have capital budgets.

Fifth, the major financial measures used in deciding capital allocations are the payback period, return on investment, time-adjusted rates of return, the MAPI formula, and risk analysis which includes the use of probability theory in simulation models. Each has special advantages and disadvantages.

Sixth, while financial measures are of great importance in capital allocations they may not always be applicable nor, when applicable, decisive. Evaluating techniques and their importance vary with the type of investment being considered.

Seventh, the principle is clear that investments should be made when potential yield is greater than the cost of a firm's capital. This simple rule, however, is difficult to follow because of calculation problems, and is not always governing.

Eighth, a major responsibility of financial executives is to assure the liquidity of a company in the short- and long-run. The many pitfalls which must be overcome before liquidity can be assured were discussed in the chapter.

Ninth, computer simulation is a new powerful instrument to help managers answer quickly many difficult and puzzling questions about the future financial policy and practice of their companies.

Tenth, more companies are establishing finance committees to help in financial decision-making.

21
Diversification Planning ──────

21

Diversification Planning

INTRODUCTION

Diversify or die, and diversify by plan, are two managerial imperatives.* In the long run, a business firm must diversify or die. Cope's law of the survival of the unspecialized asserts that: ". . . the animals which survive are those close to the main lines of evolutionary development representing major animal improvisations. These animals enjoy the benefits of all the large-scale inventions of their evolutionary ancestors but do not make the dangerous specializations—expensive but relatively less useful—that land their less canny relatives at the end of the evolutionary limb." (LaBarre, 1954, p. 27.)

H. W. Smith, in *Kamongo,* adds to this concept in these words: "It is so common to find excessive specialization just preceding the extermination of a race that ones comes to associate them together, and to accept the one as a sign of senescence presaging the other. The highly specialized animal is reaching the end of its blind alley." (H. W. Smith, 1962, p. 85.)

The course of evolution is strewn with beasts that concentrated too much on one characteristic. The tusks, the horns, the teeth, the jaws, the size of many animals became specialized to exploit a given environment. Specialization resulted in their undoing, for when the environment changed they could not adjust.

So it is with business enterprises. Enterprises must specialize to exploit a given environment. But all environments change, and they must, therefore, diversify to permit adaptation to new environments. If they do not diversify they will become extinct. Hence, the injunction: diversify or die.

Chance has and will continue to play an important role in successful diversification. In the long run, however, the "luckiest" will be those whose diversification is rooted in thoughtful and soundly conceived planning. This is not news to most managers, but precisely what to do about it is not always clear. The litera-

* In this chapter I have borrowed from my article, 1964, pp. 11-18, without specifying where direct quotes have been used.

Chart 21-1
Expansion vs. Diversification

Products \ Markets	Present	New
Present		///Diversification///
New	///Diversification///	///Diversification///

ture purporting to tell a manager what to do is rather voluminous, but the pieces are scattered and not always consistent. Nevertheless, there is a growing body of knowledge and experience from which are discernible a number of major guides for better planning of diversification. This chapter seeks to identify those outstanding policies, strategies, and actions which have brought successful diversification.

MEANING OF DIVERSIFICATION BY ACQUISITION AND MERGER

Diversification means entry into new product lines, processes, services, or markets. Does this mean a firm is diversified when it makes submarines and ocean-going liners? Is it diversified when it has a chain of restaurants and motels? A beginning can be made at identifying diversified firms by using the broad U.S. business groupings in the *Standard Industrial Classification Manual*. (Bureau of the Budget, 1957.) All business and services are classified in the SIC into 89 major groups (called 2-digit categories). At a minimum, diversification may be said to exist when a company does business in two or more of these broad categories. But they are, perhaps, too broad. For instance, the category "electrical machinery, equipment, and supplies" includes such diverse products as highpower transformers, household stoves, refrigerators for homes, telephones, spark plugs, and x-ray equipment. A better classification to determine degree of diversification probably is the next level of classification. For transportation equipment, for instance, the next level of classification includes these groups: motor vehicles and motor vehicle equipment; aircraft and parts; ship and boat building and repairing; railroad equipment; motorcycles, bicycles, and parts; and miscellaneous transportation equipment.

More generally, diversification may be defined as producing a new product or service, or entering new markets, which involves importantly different skills, processes, and knowledge from those associated with present products, services, or markets. The simple diagram in Chart 21-1 illustrates the spectrum.

Diversification defined in this way can proceed upon the basis of research on and development and production of new products within a company, or mergers and acquisitions.* The first, of course, is designed to produce internal growth and the second is called external growth. Chapter 19 dealt with new product developments, a subject which will also be treated in Chapter 22.

HISTORICAL DIVERSIFICATION PATTERNS

To provide a little perspective for this chapter some reference should be made to diversification movements of the past. Diversified firms have existed as long as enterprise has been organized. The House of Fugger, for example, was probably one of the most famous business establishments of the sixteenth century. This organization engaged in banking; owned thousands of cloth-making looms; conducted an extensive trade in spices throughout Europe; and owned copper mines in Hungary, silver mines in the Tyrol, and mercury mines in Spain. While international finance was its main interest, considerable differences existed in types of financial activity. Not only did the House finance trade but it served as banker to the rulers of Europe, including the Popes. Diversification for this enterprise paid off. Jacob Fugger (1449-1525), founder of the house, noted that his profits were a steady 54 per cent over the last sixteen years of his life. (Mueller, 1963, pp. 187-188.)

In a time leap, note the great trading joint-stock companies (such as the East India Company) of the 17th century—the forerunners of our modern corporate form of organization. They also combined under one management an amazing variety of activities, ranging from colonization to trade (Davis, 1897, 1961).

The values of diversified enterprise were recognized in early America when in 1791 the legislature of New Jersey passed an act incorporating "the Society for Establishing Useful Manufactures." This company, one of the most pretentious of our pioneer industrial corporations, was promoted and aided by Alexander Hamilton while he was Secretary of the Treasury, and was designed to be highly diversified. Even though it was not a successful manufacturing concern, it was not dissolved until 1945 (Davis, 1917).

Recent American history has recorded three bursts of diversification activity, which have been reflected in merger waves, and which are generally remembered and need only a casual reference here. The first occurred during the latter part of the last century, from about 1898 to 1903, when vertical combinations (which joined the manufacturing processes from raw materials to finished product) and horizontal mergers (which embraced competitors in the same product lines) were designed to secure domination in particular fields. An impressive upsurge of mergers of formerly competing companies in these few years was a direct outgrowth of a previous long period of intensive, often destructive, and certainly

* In this book acquisitions and mergers for convenience will be considered as being synonymous. For a glossary of terms concerned with combinations of two companies, see Mund, 1955, pp. 135-136.

bitter competition. Most major lines of business were represented in the merger movement.

The next thrust of activity took place in the period from 1918 to 1929. This movement was characterized by the growth of large holding companies, considerable product differentiation of a primary line (such as various makes of automobiles in one company), and combinations to exploit the expanding American and world markets.*

The third movement began after World War II and is still continuing exuberantly. This period has been characterized by annual rates of product additions substantially above previous levels. (Gort, 1962, p. 28.) Diversification through merger and acquisition has dominated the wave. While I have seen no studies which measure the growth of new products through internal business methods, I would guess that diversification through this route as compared with past periods has also been impressive. Recent acquisition activity has emphasized less the vertical and horizontal integration, and more the concentric and conglomerate integration, two terms which will be discussed later in the chapter. Ralph Nelson studied the 100 largest contemporary companies in the U.S. and concluded that 63 percent of them had at least one important merger in their history without which they would not be in the present-day "elite one hundred" list. (Nelson, 1959.)

While diversification is as old as business history, the phenomenon has assumed striking dimensions in recent years and, unless impeded by applications of the antitrust laws, is likely to continue at a rapid pace. The possibility of legal barriers is noted because of a new drift in Supreme Court decisions which, if continued, may slow down the acquisition process. (Markham, 1963; and Stanford Research Institute, 1963.)

MAJOR REASONS FOR DIVERSIFICATION

A business, being a dynamic organization run by individuals with diverse and multiple motivations, finds many reasons for diversification. While most of what is said in this section is applicable to internal diversification, and diversification through penetration of old products in new markets, the focus is on acquisitions and mergers. There are many very important things an acquisition can do for a company which explain its popularity, as follows:

GROWTH. Charles Thornton, Chairman of the Board of Litton Industries, one of the most spectacular growth companies in recent years through acquisi-

---

* For a brief resume of merger movements in the U.S., see J. Fred Weston, *The Role of Mergers in the Growth of Large Firms* (Berkeley, Calif.: University of California Press, 1961); and Dudley F. Pegrum, *The Regulation of Industry* (Homewood, Ill.: Richard D. Irwin, Inc., 1949).

tions, said: "We grow not just to stay in business but to have a virile, stimulating atmosphere. The strength of the U.S. is in an industrial base that is ever-growing. Growth is associated with progress, the means to accomplish more things. Profit is only one of the motives. A stronger motive is a deep, pioneering spirit."* By all odds, growth is the most outstanding reason for diversification through mergers.

If a firm has an objective in the future to reach a specified level of sales, and there appear to be no prospects that this objective can be reached by internal product developments or the penetration of new markets, there is only one alternative and that is acquisition. The pressures for growth as an objective reside in the continuous expansion of the U.S. industrial base, as Charles Thornton noted above. Any company in an industry that is growing must expand at least at the average for the industry or open itself to problems attached to retrogression. Norton Simon, Chairman of the Finance Committee of Hunt Foods, another fast-growing enterprise, says that companies "will make all sorts of excuses and pretenses why 'it makes sense' for a certain merger. But the pure fact is that as companies see limitations or slower growth in their own field, they will move into another."†

Aside from these considerations, the growth objective is felt by many executives to be accompanied with other benefits. It is deep in American management thought that growth is stimulating *per se*, that it represents a fulfillment of the entrepreneurial drives of businessmen. It is considered to be stimulating because it favors the creative and imaginative in searching for and exploiting new opportunities.

There are some, but not many, companies that wish to be big for bigness' sake. There are many managers who wish to expand because of the economic power attached to size. These are not as popular views in business or in society as the above, and are not as motivating as some of the other benefits of growth given above, but they exist as driving forces.

AVOID DEPENDENCE ON ONE PRODUCT LINE. If a company feels that it cannot achieve its objectives by sticking to its traditional line of business, it may offset this uncertainty by acquisition. W. R. Grace, an old shipping company, decided its traditional business was not good enough and today is an important producer of chemicals, operates an airline, is engaged in outdoor advertising, makes paper, and produces oil.‡ After about 75 years of great success with one product, the Coca-Cola Co. decided a few years ago to diversify into new

---

* Reprinted from the September 30, 1967, issue of *Business Week* by special permission. Copyrighted © 1967 by McGraw-Hill, Inc.

† Reprinted from the March 12, 1966, issue of *Business Week* by special permission. Copyrighted © 1966 by McGraw-Hill, Inc.

‡ For a brief resume of this history, see "The Changing Face of W. R. Grace," *Dun's Review*, July 1967, pp. 22 ff.

types of soft drinks, blends of citrus juices, coffee, and tea. (*Business Week*, 1963b.) The rapid increase in product obsolescence discussed in previous chapters is a root stimulus for diversification to avoid disaster if the sole source of income loses consumer favor.

STABILITY. Like growth, although not as much a fetish, American businessmen are strongly motivated to seek continuous sales and profit growth with a minimum of fluctuations about the trend line. Instability can result from many events. Cyclical, seasonal, and secular shifts in demand are important causes, but changes in models, in the life cycles of different products of the line, the impact of variations of raw material prices on finished goods prices and demand, or delays in getting component parts, can bring instability.

Most managers are not satisfied with fluctuations in sales and seek to do something about them. One reason for this interest is to maintain reasonably stable levels of employment for employees because that builds loyalty, and because it fits into an ever-growing desire of American managers to make their companies "good places to work." Obviously, stabilizing income and profits is of advantage to stockholders, and it also avoids pressures on managers in periods of income dips. The fact is clear that there are many unpleasant consequences of income instability and it is better to avoid it if possible. Textron is a company that has a policy of acquiring companies which do not have cycles of activity that run concurrently so as, of course, to foster stable growth.

FURNISH NEEDED TECHNICAL KNOW-HOW. This is a motivation of growing significance which has many aspects. A company may wish to get into a new line of business, for example, for which it does not have the technical know-how, and does so by acquisition. Or, a company may wish to add to its present technical know-how by acquisition, such as the purchase of Stavid Engineering by the Lockheed Aircraft Corporation to acquire a particular electronic capability.

REDUCE COSTS BY USING COMPANY DISTRIBUTION SYSTEMS. It is quite possible, of course, for a company with an effective distribution system to reduce cost per unit distributed by adding new lines. A number of the food distributors have sought this objective in recent years. Campbell Soup, for example, added Pepperidge Farm products to its system for this reason. Boise Cascade, a fast-growing conglomerate, has expanded from lumber and building materials into paper, packaging, prefabricated houses, and residential developments, a main purpose of which has been to develop and use marketing capability in related fields.

BREAKING INTO INTERNATIONAL MARKETS. U.S. expansion abroad raises problems not found when tried at home, and many businessmen have found the most expedient method to make foreign entry is to acquire an interest in or merge with a foreign-based firm. General Electric's acquisition of Machines Bull in France is an illustration of this company's efforts to break into the computer market in Europe. Campbell Soup has acquired a biscuit maker in Belgium, Heinz has acquired food processors in Holland, and BeechNut has acquired Tetley Tea in England. A number of large European companies have reversed this process in the U.S.

ACQUISITION OF TAX WRITE-OFFS. Many acquisitions have been made simply because the acquirer wants the benefit of the operating tax loss carry-forward of the acquired. When Textron acquired American Woolen and Robbins Mills, this apparently was in mind and did reduce substantially the company's effective federal income tax.

SOLVE COMPETITIVE PROBLEMS. Competitive threats create the occasion for business marriages. If you make shortening and find that ready-made mixes are cutting into your market, you do as Procter & Gamble did and acquire Duncan-Hines and make cake mixes yourself.

OTHER REASONS FOR ACQUISITIONS. This by no means exhausts the list of reasons for acquisitions. A few others may be given without illustration or comment, as follows: to use surplus cash, to offset unfavorable geographic locations, to utilize waste or by-products, to use basic raw materials, to use excess productive capacity, to capitalize on distinctive knowledge, to capitalize on a company's basic research, to limit competition, to control patents, to complete a product line with a sufficient spread of models and prices, to take advantage of tax laws, to acquire new and needed management, and to increase borrowing capacity. A different type of motivation was behind the 1967 merger of the huge North American Aviation Company and Rockwell-Standard. It was the idea of stimulating technology transfer from one company to another, in this case the exploitation of the technical research of the giant aerospace company by a non-defense consumer-oriented company.

WHY DIVERSIFY RATHER THAN BUILD FROM WITHIN?

Many of the above objectives can be met by internally-managed diversification. There are a number of compelling reasons, however, why many companies wish to meet their objectives by acquisition or a combination of external and internal growth, rather than relying on internal diversification.

Acquisition saves a company time. It takes time to develop a research organization, particularly in an advanced technology industry; and it takes time to build a new productive facility and operate it. Where time is important, companies can save themselves years by acquiring these resources in another company.

One element of business risk may be eliminated. If a company is not familiar with the management or substance of a new research effort, a new engineering problem, or a new productive operation, there may be less risk in finding these activities in a suitable state of performance in another company and acquiring it.

The cost may actually be less to a company by acquiring another rather than duplicating its capabilities by building from within. Following World War II, for instance, many companies found they could gain productive facilities through acquisition much more cheaply than through their own construction programs. This also was obviously much faster and permitted companies to take advantage of a great surge in consumer demands. Sometimes, too, it is possible for a company to find another whose book value is below replacement costs.

Sometimes it is possible for a company to finance an acquisition more easily than to finance internal expansion. This can happen, for example, when a large flotation of securities by a company at a particular time might not be well received. In such a case, the company might acquire another company by an exchange of stock and require no public acceptance of securities.

This does not exhaust the reasons why a company may wish to acquire another rather than build from within, or to solve other problems through internal means, but it does specify the more important ones.

WHY DO COMPANIES WISH TO BE ACQUIRED?

It takes two to make a marriage and, while some are "shot gun," most weddings in the industrial world as in the social world are arranged with mutual advantages in mind. We have discussed the many reasons why one company may wish to acquire another. Now, how about the motives of the acquired?

Two types of sellers should be distinguished. First are owner-investors, such as banks, financial holding companies, pension funds, and other financial investors in businesses, including stockholders. The second class are owner-managers who, while having financial interests in a company, actually manage the companies. The motivations of the two for merging are very different. In the first case, the investors usually wish to sell because they prefer cash. The motivations of the second group are much more complex.

There can be distinguished both business and personal reasons for wishing to be bought. One ever-present reason lies in the problems of the federal estate tax, which ranges up to 77 percent and must be paid in cash. Furthermore, it is not easy to predict what evaluation will be placed on a business for estate tax purposes. If an owner of a closely held company has built up his estate through the growth of his own company, if most of his assets are stock in the company, and if cash is not available except through sale of the stock to satisfy the estate tax, it is obvious that the family will have to sell stock to outside interests. Not only may they lose control but they may be forced to sell at a time when the price will be much below real value. Aging owners of closely held corporations who want to avoid these problems on their deaths put their businesses up for acquisition. These owners can "go public," of course, but this raises other problems. Frequently, the best solution is to arrange a merger.*

A company may find that it has a narrow product line which is being threatened. Its resources may be insufficient to correct this problem, and the best solution may lie in being acquired by a company with resources to meet the need. A company may get into financial difficulties, as did the Douglas Aircraft Company in 1967, and merge with another one having the financial resources to provide the needed assistance. There are a number of inventors who develop their own companies and wish to sell out so that they may use the resources to exploit another of their inventions, or retire. Dissension among partners, or owner-managers of a company, may become serious enough to motivate them to seek a purchaser.

ACQUISITION INDIGESTION

The statistics on successes and failures of business acquisitions are not much more reliable than those presented about new product developments in Chapter 18. But the broad dimensions are reasonably clear and show a substantial volume of failures.

One consultant in this field concluded that "as you examine the records . . . you come to the conclusion that no more than half of the mergers turned out to be really worth while." (Roehl, 1962.) He cites the results of a survey of a management consulting firm which showed that among companies making one or two acquisitions the results were good in 27 percent of the cases, doubtful in 50 percent, and in 23 percent the acquired companies were sold or liquidated. One encouraging fact, however, is that by the time the companies had gained experience in making five or ten acquisitions the results were much better, for in this case 62 percent of the acquisitions were rated good.

The National Bureau of Economic Research made an extensive study of diversification from 1929 to 1954 and came to the melancholy conclusion that there appears to be only a mild positive correlation between diversification and company growth during that period of time. (Gort, 1962, p. 15.) (One may ask, of course: What would have happened to the companies studied if they had not diversified? One may also ask: What might have happened had these companies planned better?) Furthermore, the correlation between profit rates and diversifi-

* For further discussion see Drayton, Jr., Emerson, and Griswold, 1963.

cation was not at all clear. (pp. 65-78.) For the companies examined, the influence of diversification on profits was not in itself enough to overcome other causes of variation in rates of profit return. Diversification was not the key to prosperity for the average company. (One may ask, however: What would the profit return have been for these companies had they not diversified?)

A *Fortune* survey of the acquisition activities of manufacturing companies among the 500 largest in the U.S. concluded: "It is hard to quantify the case, but one hypothesis suggested . . . is that the most successful of the conglomerates are relatively new companies that become conglomerates at some early stage in their development—rather than older companies that began diversifying heavily in response to problems and anxieties about the original corporate operations." (O'Hanlon, 1967, p. 177.)

The roll call of companies that have gotten indigestion from acquisitions includes highly successful enterprises. To illustrate, among companies with multimillion dollar acquisitions that have not yet paid out are General Electric's acquisition of Machines Bull (Wierzynski, 1967, pp. 92 ff.) and the Ford Motor Company's acquisition of Philco. (Siekman, 1966, pp. 116 ff.)

On the other hand, acquisition has been the major source of growth and earnings for many companies. Table 21-1 shows a selected number of so-called conglomerate companies among the largest 500 in the U.S. which have grown rapidly through the acquisition route.

Table 21-1 Average Annual Growth in Earnings Per Share of Selected Large Companies Which Have Grown Through Acquisitions

COMPANY	AVERAGE ANNUAL GROWTH IN EARNINGS PER SHARE	
	1961-66	*1956-66*
Avco	13.67	—
Borg-Warner	14.28	2.28
Eagle-Picher	21.98	1.79
Eltra	21.99	19.44
Food Machinery Corp.	20.34	13.37
Fairchild Camera	15.47	24.54
Grace, W. R.	18.30	7.32
Gulf & Western	26.79	—
International Telephone & Telegraph	71.89	7.55
Litton Industries	35.09	36.53
Minnesota Mining & Mfg.	12.15	12.90
Textron	27.93	16.15

Source: O'Hanlon, "The Odd News About Conglomerates," *Fortune,* June 1967, p. 177.

PLANNING STEPS AND PRINCIPLES

There are two different approaches to diversification, namely, the *ad hoc* and the planned. There also may be a third, a blend of the two. There have been successful diversification moves by managers who, on the spur of the moment and without plan, decided to acquire another company. A less spontaneous, but not well-planned, approach frequently occurs when a company by plan acquires another and then finds itself with an asset it does not particularly want or know how to handle. Such was the case of the Norge refrigerator produced by Borg-Warner. Borg-Warner was organized in 1928 as a federation of automobile parts makers who felt that by pooling their assets they could bargain better with the larger automobile manufacturers. Norge Corporation was acquired only for its transmission manufacturing subsidiary, the Detroit Gear & Machine Co. During the great economic depression of the 1930's, however, Borg-Warner decided it should move into the household appliance field by using the Norge refrigerator as a base. By 1937 it had so advanced this diversification that this line of business accounted for 35 percent of total company sales.

There can be little question about the fact that the planned acquisition program is more likely to be the more successful. Very well, what is sound planning for a particular company or problem? There is no single approach to diversification that can guarantee success; there does not exist any one series of steps and procedures which a company can adopt to solve its diversification planning problems. Every company differs from every other and diversification problems of a particular company may differ over time.

There do exist, however, fundamental procedural steps and principles which, when understood and wisely adapted and applied to particular situations, can assure successful diversification. These fundamentals appear behind all successful diversification planning. Detailed surface differences among diversification programs should not blind one to the importance of these underlying steps and principles.

A number of suitable how-to-do-it diversification planning steps exist in the literature.* They naturally vary depending upon the company and writer. A brief series of steps is shown in Table 21-2.

* From among many publications setting forth procedures for both in-house new-product development and acquisition including merger, the following are cited: Theodore A. Andersen, H. Igor Ansoff, Frank Norton, and J. Fred Weston, "Planning for Diversification Through Merger," *California Management Review,* Summer 1959; Thomas L. Berg and Abe Schuchman, ed., *Product Stategy and Management* (New York: Holt, Rinehart and Winston, Inc., 1963). This is a book of readings many of which deal with procedures. Also note Sidney Cottle, "Four Steps to Diversification Planning," *Business Quarterly,* Summer 1963; Myles L. Mace and George G. Montgomery, Jr., *Management Problems of Corporate Acquisitions* (Boston, Mass.: Division of Research, Graduate School of Business Administration, Harvard University, 1962); and J. F. Weston, "Planning for Corporate Merger," *California Management Review,* Spring 1963.

In a planned acquisition program the sequence of steps is more or less governed by a natural life cycle of the acquisition. Through the stages of this life cycle there are a number of lessons learned from experience which can help to produce more successful acquisition programs. The remainder of this chapter is devoted to these steps and lessons of experience.

ROLE OF CORPORATE PLANNING. Effective comprehensive corporate planning is indispensable to top-quality diversification planning. This, together

---

Table 21-2   One List of Diversification Steps

1. Establish comprehensive and integrated over-all corporate objectives, goals, strategies, and policies.
2. Develop specific objectives, goals, and policies for new-product internal growth or diversification by acquisition and merger.
3. Develop and explore new ideas for (a) new products and their internal development or (b) acquisition or mergers, or (c) both.
4. Screen new ideas through appropriate criteria to sort out those deserving further analysis and development.
5. Gather facts and analyze them to determine the economic and technical feasibility of further development or acquisition proposals.

The above sequence of steps is suitable both to internal product development and acquisition. Beyond this point, requirements are sufficiently different to justify a separate sequence for each type of diversification.

INTERNAL PRODUCT DEVELOPMENT:

6. Complete research and development.
7. Test the prototype for production and sale.
8. Produce and sell.
9. Control to insure that actions take place in conformance with plans and to achieve basic objectives and goals.

ACQUISITION AND MERGER:

6. Discuss with prospective marriage partner the proposed acquisition or merger and explore problems and opportunities.
7. Negotiate the terms of acquisition or merger.
8. Integrate the two companies to the extent desirable.
9. Periodically review the results to determine whether actions are in conformance with plans.

Source: George A. Steiner, "Why and How to Diversify," *California Management Review*, Vol. VI, No. 4 (Summer 1964), p. 17.

with actual experience in acquisitions, is a fundamental principle for successful acquisitions. Litton is a classic illustration of successful diversification through thorough planning. One of the participants in Litton's growth has written:

". . . Charles B. Thornton, Roy L. Ash, and H. W. Jameson, studied the total electronics industry and decided upon a program to establish leadership in several parts of that industry. This plan was to be accomplished through acquisitions as well as through internal research and development. The major initial areas selected were electronic tubes, military equipment and systems, communications, business machines, and certain components. There was nothing fortuitous about Litton's growth; the acquisitions and internal growth were planned in detail. Each year the top executives review the five-year plan, extend it where appropriate, and embark on a continuous effort to create a large, profitable, and successful company." (Mace and Montgomery, 1962, pp. 62-63.)

In the planning process a number of activities take place which give the diversification program direction. While these have been elaborated at length elsewhere they have not been discussed with reference to diversification as such and should, therefore, be illustrated from the point of view of this activity.

It is difficult to see how a diversification program can be successful without a clear definition of objectives. It is highly probable that the acquisition of another company without a clear purpose in mind will result in failure, or, putting the matter another way, developing clear objectives will force a number of activities which should greatly enhance chances of success. Acquisitions are means to ends and in making them it obviously is important to know what the ends are.

In determining objectives, and in devising means to achieve them, the strengths and weaknesses of the diversifying company must be honestly and penetratingly set forth. There is no substitute for a company identifying its own particular capabilities and limitations. These, in conjunction with objectives, provide invaluable clues to the most appropriate diversification moves. A company with a weak research department may see clearly its need to acquire a company with a strong technological team. A company that knows it has a poor distribution capability may more easily see the need for merging with one having a strong marketing arm than if it does not recognize the magnitude of its weakness.

The evaluation should cover thoroughly the traditional elements of a company, such as marketing programs, technical talent, managerial capabilities, financial strength, and so on. It should also probe deeply into unique strengths and weaknesses. These may suggest opportunities which would otherwise be undiscovered. Some skills to look for in such a penetrating probe are capability in dealing with strong and militant unions, in living with unstable prices, in exploiting new product ideas, in sensitivity to consumer needs, and in exploiting new distribution techniques. (Conrad, 1963.)

Broad strategic approaches may be of four types: vertical, horizontal, concentric, and conglomerate. Vertical mergers are those in the same product line (or line of business) and involve integration from basic raw materials to the ultimate sale to consumers. A steel ingot producer acquiring an iron ore mine as well as a steel fabricating company would be engaging in vertical merger. Ford's acquisition of Electric Autolite Co. in 1961 to break into the auto replacement-part business is in this category.

Vertical integration, of course, has many advantages. It may benefit from specialization and the continuous control over the flow of materials. In this way, sales and profits may be improved through reduced costs, and may be more stable. But there are also dangers. Diseconomies of scale of parts of the integration may adversely affect profits, and a company may find itself in competition at too many points in the flow of materials. Vertical integration may also encourage federal antitrust action.

Horizontal mergers are those which join producers of similar products at the same stage of manufacture and distribution. A chemical company acquiring other chemical companies, or an electronic company acquiring other electronic companies, is involved in horizontal integration through merger. BVD Co., Inc., an old and well-known underwear maker, decided around 1962 to acquire companies horizontally. It has acquired a long list of companies making apparel such as neckwear (Beau Brummel Ties, Inc.), knitwear (Mullins Textile Mills, Inc.), lingerie and sleepwear (Flexees International, Inc.), men's clothing (Timely Clothes, Inc.), and knitwear (Wonderknit Corp.). It also has begun to acquire distributors, moving in a vertical direction.

Acquisition of a company producing the same or very closely related products also, of course, permits specialization with consequent efficiencies. Such a merger may help a company to produce at closer to capacity, thereby improving profitability. If an acquisition is too close to the product line of the acquiring company, however, it may be guilty of reducing competition by acquiring competitors and run afoul of the antitrust laws.

Concentric mergers are those in which the merged parties have a common thread of interest. This common thread may be in product areas, as when a shortening manufacturer acquires a cake mix producer; it can be in the manufacture of comparable products, which is close to horizontal merger; or it can be in terms of a common marketing arrangement as has been the case with mergers in the food industry. It may result from technical complementarity as when Litton Industries acquired Monroe to provide cross-fertilization between its computer scientists and office machinery know-how to make and market a desk computer. "Automatic" Sprinkler Corp., a fast-growing company, seeks to find a company to acquire which can become the nucleus of acquisitions having a common interest. Ducommun Metals has diversified into products using the same marketing channels.

Conglomerate mergers bring unrelated product lines of business into a company. The growth of Ling-Temco-Vought, for example, has been principally in unrelated lines of business. As a matter of fact, James Ling, the driving force behind this company, has a conscious strategy to move into new fields of business, rather than to take over companies in the same line of business, in order to avoid court action under the antitrust laws. Textron is another fast-growing conglomerate with the same strategy.

Acquisitions in recent years have been dominated by the concentric and conglomerate types largely, I suspect, to avoid possible antitrust action. The full extent of this movement is not easy to picture. *Fortune* examined the largest 500 companies in the U.S. and came to a conclusion which was surprising: that conglomerates are still the exception rather than the rule among this group. It measured lines of business in these companies in each of 78 major categories in the *Standard Industrial Classification Manual* and found that 102 of the 500 are still operating in a single category. (O'Hanlon, 1967, pp. 175-177.) This does not tell the whole story, however, because, as noted above, these 2-digit groupings are broad and companies may be considerably diversified in the sense of producing very different products within a broad 2-digit classification. Examination of these companies on the basis of more refined product codes would show considerably more diversification among the "top 500."

This is partly borne out by another study of 22 companies having 181 mergers during the period 1960 to 1965. This study concluded that a little less than half the mergers were of the conglomerate type. Concentric mergers were about 27 percent of the total (14 percent technical and 13 percent marketing), horizontal acquisitions constituted 25 percent, and 5 percent were vertical integrations (Kitching, 1967, p. 86).

Thorough planning and imaginative management are required to select those acquisition strategies fitting each company. It is this fact, rather than the specific strategies, that I wish to emphasize here. A company should, however, have a comprehensive and unified diversification strategy; strategies should be developed for approaching prospective sellers, for completing the transaction, for assuring proper relationships between two merged managements, and for assuring that diversification produces the desired results.

SCREENING CRITERIA. Once the basic objectives and strategies have been established it is important to develop more detailed screening criteria. These may be considered tactics, but actually they represent a combination of strategy and tactics. The basic purpose of this further elaboration obviously is to provide a better basis for searching for and evaluating prospective acquisitions. Screening criteria not only save much time but also should make more certain that objectives are met.

The Borden Company's basic objective in its acquisition drive, in the words of Chairman of the Board Francis Elliott, is "not only to strengthen our organization immediately but, more importantly, to broaden the foundation on which we can build for the future." Some of the screening requirements are as follows: The company must be well-established in its own business, be able to upgrade Borden earnings, and be guided by astute, experienced management. It must also have growth potential through expansion by adding new products or by a deeper penetration of markets—a tactic described by Elliott in one of his favorite phrases as "geographic roll-out." (Levy, 1967, p. 81.)

The Maytag Co. says any diversification it attempts must meet two basic criteria, namely, the acquisition must make use of Maytag's skills in machining and metal working, and it must not upset the company's vertical integration. Also, the financial condition of the company to be acquired must be acceptable and, importantly, the management of the acquired company must want to stick with Maytag. (*Business Week*, 1965a.)

Screening criteria vary, of course, among companies. Generally, however, it would seem important that the following categories (not in any particular order of importance) be considered in developing the standards against which new ventures must be judged. Where appropriate, standards should take into account past trends and, more importantly, future prospects.

Size of company. There are obvious reasons for placing limitations on the size of companies to be acquired. This standard can be expressed in terms of sales, net profits, assets, and/or investment required to acquire.

Market share. A minimum market share today and for some future point of time may be stipulated.

Growth potential. Similar to, but not the same as, the above is growth potential of the company, which may be expressed in financial terms such as sales, profits, and assets; in capabilities for becoming a nucleus for other acquisitions; or as a source of new technical capabilities. Stability of growth may be important to a company, and used as a criterion.

Type of business. While broad objectives and strategies may lay down guidance as to the types of business which interest a company, more details may be set forth in the screening criteria. It is one thing, for example, to be in the automotive manufacturing business as a supplier of a quality low-cost component for which a firm has weak competitors, and quite a different matter to be an assembler of finished automobiles competing with the "big-three."

Profitability. This is an obvious criterion and can be expressed in different ways, such as absolute amounts, per share, return on investment, and annual prospective growth rates.

Use of and additions to company strength. It may be worthwhile to specify the extent to which an acquired firm should take advantage of the acquiring company's strengths, especially if this is an important reason for an acquisition. Also, it is often important to define explicitly just what strengths the new acquisition is to bring to the combined company.

Price and financing. Naturally, the price of a company is important. Some companies insist that no acquisition dilute the equity of the stockholders of the acquiring company. Others may accept a temporary dilution if future prospects are promising. If a company with a low stock price-earnings ratio acquires one with a high stock price-earnings ratio, it is possible to dilute the equity of the stockholders of the acquiring company. This takes place, as shown in Table 21-3, because there may be a greater increase in shares relative to the increase in stockholders' equity of the acquiring company. This is, of course, important but the far greater consideration is the future of the two companies. Dilution of stockholders' equity is one useful item to consider in acquisition but it is not as important as other considerations, and any wise company will accept some temporary dilution, if necessary, to advance its stockholders' interests in the future. But, other things being equal, dilution is not desirable. The much preferable position is just the reverse, as shown in Table 21-4 (page 653).

Methods of financing may be specified in criteria; some companies may want to acquire solely with cash, others entirely through an exchange of stock, and others with different mixes.

Management compatibility. Many acquisition negotiations have failed when

Table 21-3   How an Acquisition Can Dilute Stockholder Equity

ITEM	COMPANY A	COMPANY B
Asset value on books (10 times earnings)	$20,000,000	$20,000,000
Liabilities	14,000,000	14,000,000
Net worth or stockholder equity	6,000,000	6,000,000
Shares outstanding	2,000,000	2,000,000
Earnings per share	1	1
Price-earnings ratio	20	10
Stock price on market	20	10
Stockholder equity per share	$3	$3
Stock exchange when B acquires A 2 for 1		
Share value	$40,000,000	
Number of shares		4,000,000
Combined Company		
Assets		$40,000,000
Liabilities		28,000,000
Net worth or equity		12,000,000
Stock outstanding		6,000,000
Stockholder equity per share		$2

one or the other of the parties to the prospective arrangement has said, "They are not our kind of people." Compatibility can be defined in many ways: as a matter of philosophy, or a way of looking at things generally; a style of management; the blending of skills of managers; scales of value; treatment of employees; personal ambitions; and so on. These are important elements of an acquisition and merit some specification of standards for evaluation.

Other criteria. Other criteria can be considered, to name a few: research and development strength and fit, timing of entry into a new field, timing of acquisition, marketing methods, type of manufacturing process, antitrust considerations, potential for joint product development, joint marketing potential, and location.

Each firm must consider factors such as these and determine for itself which are important in an acquisition. Once done, it also may be desirable to place weights on the more significant factors. (Mace and Montgomery, 1962, pp. 168-174.)

LOCATING COMPANIES TO ACQUIRE. With a carefully developed statement of objectives, strategies, and tactical screening standards as described above, a company is in a strong position to find the "right" company.

Many of the larger companies have a staff group to help top management in acquisition programs. Frequently this staff is in the corporate planning group, as noted in previous chapters, but sometimes it is a separate group. A case can be made for either organizational arrangement, but in most instances it probably would be better to have the corporate planning group deeply involved in diversification acquisitions, at least up to the point of actual integration.

Staff work in the search stage may involve an analysis of industry sales projections to find those with growth potential of interest to a company, and identification of particular concerns which might fit the acquirer's needs. (Andersen, Ansoff, Norton and Weston, 1959.) In many other ways, staff can narrow the focus so that approaches can be made on a "rifle-shot" and not a "buck-shot" basis.

Good staff work builds up an enormous amount of information over time that is indispensable to a company with an active continuous acquisition program. Although expensive, the probable payoff of effective staff work is very high relative to cost.

A source of information about companies to be acquired, which may and should parallel acquisition staff activities, are members of the board of directors. Other important sources are investment bankers, commercial bankers, consultants, and business brokers who concentrate on acquisitions. In dealing through brokers it is very important to be sure to get a reputable one for excessive liabilities can be incurred in dealings with less reputable ones. (Mace and Montgomery, 1962, Chapter V.)

EVALUATING PROSPECTIVE CANDIDATES FOR MERGER. If companies are acquired according to specification, as they would be with the type of screening standards discussed above, it will be possible often to tell at a quick glance whether a company deserves fuller evaluation. For a major acquisition the evaluation should, of course, be thorough and rigorous. Among other things this would include the following:

1. *General History and Background of the Company.* Included here would be a brief history of the development of the company; the identification of and brief biographical statements on the officers; stock ownership distribution; important recent changes in organization, management, products, etc.; reputation in the industry for integrity, quality products, etc.; and similar matters. This background information should, of course, be prepared and evaluated in terms of the interests of the acquiring company.

2. *Financial Evaluation.* Included should be collection and evaluation of balance sheet and profit and loss statements over an appropriate period of time. This evaluation should penetrate deeply into the current financial condition of the company, its liquidity, its financial problems, the extent to which it corresponds to standard financial ratios of the industry and the acquiring company, the extent to which it will strengthen or weaken the financial position of the acquirer, the possible ways to finance acquisition, whether the acquisition will or will not dilute the acquire's stockholders' equity, and the price which seems appropriate to pay for the acquisition.

To make such evaluations the financial data should be reviewed to assure that financial statements are comparable and can be evaluated properly with those of the acquiring company. For example, it will be important to know whether assets are valued at original cost less depreciation, or on some other basis.

Of critical significance, of course, are the financial prospects for the future if the firm is acquired. This is partly a matter that can be evaluated on purely financial grounds; e.g., an elimination of bonded indebtedness may alter importantly financial prospects, or complete overhauling of a cost accounting system may turn loss into profit. It is more fundamentally, however, a result of operations and management, and the financial prospects cannot be forecast without analysis of these elements.

3. *Operations.* Under operations would be included the collection and evaluation of information about products manufactured. Included would be the type of products, volume, costs in relation to sales price, quality, stage in life cycle, and other considerations of importance to the acquiring company. Markets served also must be examined in terms of share held, nature of

consumers, consumer loyalty, geographic distribution, etc. The location of the plants of the company might be included, together with an examination of the productivity of facilities, replacement needs, operating capacity, and actual capacity being used. It may be important to have a complete analysis of research and development capability, capability in managing production lines, and competence in distributing products.

Analysis of future prospective demand for the products usually is important. This should be related to prospective costs of production to determine potential profit. The analysis may include methods by which the acquiring company may increase output per dollar of capital outlay, reduce product cost by engineering improvements, raise quality without raising cost, and in other ways enhance profit prospects. By eliminating some plants, or by expanding capacity of some plants, the profit picture may be much improved. At any rate, the real emphasis must be on the future and not the past.

4. *Management Capabilities.* If the acquiring firm wishes to retain present management in the acquired firm, there ought to be an analysis of the quality of management and its compatibility with management in the acquiring firm. The quality of management is not as easy to evaluate as financial and operating data, but in a real sense the marks given the company on these evaluations are a direct reflection of managerial capability. But other matters must be considered, such as motivations, loyalty, reputation, competence in specific functions, innovative capabilities, and age distribution.

5. *Resume of Fit.* If there is a prescribed set of standards for acquiring firms, the net conclusion should specify the kind of a fit the acquired company has with the screening criteria. Should it be acquired? If so, what is the price that ought to be paid? How should the acquisition be financed? What does the acquiring company have to do to assure that the prospects for the future as projected in the evaluation actually are achieved?

Top management need not necessarily get involved in this evaluation, but there are several considerations concerning top management relations to a staff group making such evaluations which deserve mention. If management has a staff to help search for and evaluate prospective candidates for acquisition, top management should studiously avoid ignoring staff and making an acquisition without staff knowledge. This is especially unfortunate if the move turns out poorly. Also, top management must avoid passing on to staff, and expecting a thorough analysis of, every proposal that comes to management's attention. Staff may be able to dispose of many cases quickly and devote more attention to more promising companies. Finally, top management must demand top-quality staff studies. This means that top management must understand what is involved in a thorough and competent study and expect it from staff. It is not the mass of detail, or the manhours spent, that determines the quality of a study, but the rigor with which it has been analyzed, the extent to which the correct factors have been identified and evaluated, and the intelligence that the results display.

NEGOTIATING THE ACQUISITION. When all the above has been accomplished, the acquiring firm must then determine its strategy for approaching the prospective partner. In setting this strategy the acquiring company should be in a position to answer a number of questions. For example, if the to-be-acquired company is healthy and successful there must be an answer to such questions as: Why should we merge with you? What is our advantage? If we do sell, how will our company fit into yours? What, precisely, will be the relationship of our top management with yours? What are your plans for our managers and employees?

These are natural questions and if the answers to them are not thought through, or are unsatisfactory to the receiver, the acquisition is not likely to take place. If they are answered to the satisfaction of the prospective acquired, the conversation quickly may get into more detailed areas suggested by the interests of the acquired. For instance, if an objective is to distribute the acquired's products through the acquirer's distribution system, the acquired will want to know just how this is to be done and what it will do for and to his organization.

The actual approach can be made in different ways. For example, two presidents may get together, the president of the acquiring company may have with him a friend of the president of the prospective acquisition company, or arrangements can be made through investment bankers.

In whatever approach is used, secrecy should be a guiding consideration. Rumors of impending negotiations bring with them too many problems for both companies. Changes in stock price may jeopardize financing plans, employees of either company may get upset, other firms may become interested in the prospective merger and try to stop it, and so on.

The list of causes for a breakdown of negotiations is long, but probably the one most frequently of highest importance is price and financing. Coming to a conclusion about what is a sound purchase price is difficult and inevitably a matter of controversy between buyer and seller. It will depend not alone on financial considerations but on prospects in an uncertain world and the bargaining power of both sides. A first approach to the question is to ask what is being purchased. What is being purchased, of course, are assets used in a going operation. One measure of the value of the business will be the current market price of all shares outstanding. There are obvious difficulties in accepting completely this answer. Another approach is to capitalize earnings. The future earnings of the company can be projected and capitalized at a rate which presumably a prudent investor would pay. Perhaps a better approach is to examine the business in considerably more detail by evaluating major assets and relating them to major liabilities and earning power. In this way a return on assets or stockholder equity can be calculated and compared with the same ratios in the acquiring company. This, of course, is not an easy task since it involves among other things an evaluation of intangibles, such as going-concern value, the worth of a company's good will, the value of a favorable market position, and an estimate of future earnings.

For a company whose securities are listed on an exchange, the minimum price would be the total market value. For an unlisted closely-held company, of course, this price is not available and makes more difficult the calculation of a minimum acceptable price for the company being acquired.

Beyond all this, many factors will have an influence on price. The price will be different if prospective earnings will be enhanced by the acquirer's action than if the acquired will improve the acquirer's profit position. It may be advantageous from a tax point of view to acquire by an exchange of stock, and this will reflect on the price the buyer is willing to pay. Much will depend, of course, upon how anxious both parties are to merge.*

When the purpose of an acquisition is to get access to talented managers or scientific and technical brains, the traditional methods of financial valuation are not too applicable. Employment contracts, stock options, and pension arrangements must be considered along with financial valuations. These factors also may be reviewed in a straight-forward acquisition, but they become more important in this type of situation.

INTEGRATING THE COMPANIES. Planning for the integration of the companies once the acquisition is agreed to will depend much upon the motive for the acquisition and the plans for its relationship to the acquired. For example, if the acquired company is in effect allowed to be a decentralized, virtually autonomous profit center under its old management, the problems of integration will be considerably less than if the new company is to be completely managed by the acquiring firm. In either event, however, there will be very important "people problems" as well as operational problems.

This is not the place to lay out in any detail guidelines which should govern integration planning and operating. A few points may be made, however, as illustrations. (Linowes, 1964)

First, the acquiring company should have a set of policies governing many matters relating to the relationships of people, such as promotion, filling managerial vacancies, compensation and benefits, and replacement. It is natural for people in merging organizations to be filled with anxiety, and the more quickly

* For an examination of these factors, see Wellington, in Newgarden, 1958a, pp. 65-72.

this anxiety can be dispelled, the more productive and smooth-running will be the merger.

Second, there should be explicitly stated policies about managerial planning and control. As quickly as possible the acquiring company's planning and control system should be installed.

Third, an effort should be made to create good communications between the two companies in order to build up an atmosphere of mutual trust and understanding. There should be a forthright facing of problems and issues. David Kilmer says: ". . . good communications with acquired management must exist at all levels. From the very start, successful acquirers show their concern for clear communications and mutual understanding with the management of the acquired company. They indicate broadly what they plan to do after the acquisition is consummated, show how the meshing will improve the stockholders' return, and make it clear that good producers need not be afraid of losing their jobs. As each move is made, they explain what is behind it and what its impact will be on the new division and its people, quelling unfounded rumors before they develop. They find that drastic decisions are much better received when presented forthrightly." (Kilmer, 1967, p. 6.)

Fourth, if operations and organizations are to be integrated, the sooner the task begins the better. Preplanning should avoid delays and procrastination which can only bring headaches.

Fifth, unprofitable assets should be disposed of as quickly as possible. These should have been discovered before negotiations get under way and probably should have been discussed in negotiations.

Sixth, managers of the acquired company should be architects of change and properly motivated. One study which examined in detail the acquisition successes of 22 companies concluded that the critical element in success was the existence of managers of change. The acquiring company either brought in new managers of change or motivated the old management. (Kitching, 1967.) Obviously to do this successfully requires careful planning of the integration in which management tasks are evaluated, managers to fill them are identified, and the means to motivate managers are determined.

Seventh, when managers in the acquired company fail to measure up to what is expected of them, they should be removed promptly. There are many reasons why a manager who has done well in an independent company may not perform effectively in a merged company; or the evaluation of the acquiring company may not have revealed an important weakness of a key manager. Whatever has happened, however, prompt changes should be made among personnel who are not performing properly.

POSTAUDIT. The final step in merger should be a postaudit of results. This should, of course, be tailored to each situation, but the principle of review is sound since it requires an examination of past mistakes and successes from which future experiences can benefit. A postaudit should provide a sober evaluation of the profitability of the venture. If it turns out that all or part of the venture is a loser, that which is not working out should be sold. It is easy to become wedded to a past decision, and it is human to find it hard to admit error. If a company has a policy to disinvest unprofitable parts of a business, and if it matches that policy with a rigorous postaudit, it will be easier to get rid of failing acquisitions.

MAJOR CONSIDERATIONS IN
SUCCESSFUL ACQUISITIONS

A number of fundamental principles and guidelines have been given above for successful acquisition. In reviewing the literature on this subject written by those who have had extensive and successful experience in making acquisitions, and from my own empirical observation of companies having success in this activity, I have derived six fundamental factors for successful acquisition that stand above all others.

INVOLVEMENT OF THE CHIEF EXECUTIVE. Mace and Montgomery (1962, p. 75.), after having examined the experiences of many companies in acquiring other companies, concluded: "We found that in every company in which there was a successful acquisition program, the chief operating executive was personally involved. There were no exceptions." In the larger companies, staff groups make important contributions to the acquisition program, as explained above, but there is no substitute for the personal involvement of the chief executive.

There are many reasons for this. The president must provide the driving force, the initiative, in acquisition. No acquisition program will move without his consent and interest. Even though his interest is expressed, it is still necessary for him to get involved personally if the program is to succeed. Another reason he should get involved is that acquisition is his job, and if he does not get personally involved he clearly will not be doing his job. (In an autonomous division or subsidiary, the general manager is the focal point.) Also, I have found that company presidents like to talk to other company presidents, not to their junior officers, when serious business is discussed. The acquisition program, therefore, will probably go more smoothly if negotiations are conducted at appropriate stages between the two presidents. Furthermore, the president often must get approval from his board of directors for his acquisition program, which, of course, makes this a matter demanding his personal attention. Finally, the chief executive has experience in the industry, knows people, knows how they think, and has information about candidates for acquisition that staff may not possess. This point is more pertinent for acquisitions of companies in the same or a similar line of business as that of the acquirer. In general, however, the experience of the chief executive gives him an insight, an intuitive feel for important considerations, that is of great value in making successful acquisitions.

The question arises, of course, as to what is the precise role of the chief executive? This is a many-faceted question and, as with planning in general, the answer will vary considerably from one case to another. In a general sort of way, the chief executive should be deeply involved in initiating and stimulating an acquisition program. In the development of objectives and strategies he should be heavily involved. In the stages of searching for and evaluating companies the staff can act without much of his attention. In negotiations with a company to be acquired the chief executive ought to be deeply involved at proper points. Once integration takes place, his involvement becomes the same as for comparable operating segments of the business.

IMPORTANCE OF PLANNING. Companies that have been most successful have learned the value of formalizing their approach to acquisitions and have made full-time staff assignments to do this. The formalization of acquisition procedures encompasses thorough planning throughout the entire process as well as clear and detailed methods for evaluations through the decision-making stages. To paraphrase a current product's slogan, things go better with planning.

IMPORTANCE OF THE EXPERT. Acquiring other companies is a complex activity that brings together the expertise of many disciplines—investment banking, tax analysis, accounting, law, economics, and management, to name a few—details of any one of which may, if ignored, turn success into disaster. A management entering this field for the first time, therefore, should have at its disposal the services of reputable experts on acquisitions.

VALUE OF HIGH STOCK PRICE-EARNINGS RATIOS. Price-earnings ratios are of great significance in the growth of many companies. The reason is that if a company with a high stock price-earnings ratio acquires one with a low price-earnings ratio, and after the merger the price-earnings ratio continues to be high, there is a net gain to stockholders of both companies. This is shown in Table 21-4. In this simplified case it is clear that after the acquisition shown, stockholders of the acquiring Company A have a share of stock worth $26.60, whereas before the stock was worth $20.00. Shareholders of acquired Company B, who gave up a share of stock priced on the market at $10, now find that, although they have only half as many shares as before, the price of each share is $26.60 and the value is equal to $13.30 for each old share. (Smalter and Lancey, 1966.)

AVOIDANCE OF COMPANIES IN DISTRESS. Some companies look for others in distress with the hope of adding something to the combination that will correct a deficiency and revitalize an ailing enterprise. With few exceptions these integrations do not work out much better than the situation of the girl who marries a man to reform him.

THE QUALITY OF MANAGEMENT IS A MAJOR CONSIDERA-TION. While some companies have sought others with weak managers and, by replacing them with strong managers, have made handsome profits, this is not a game with odds in its favor. Generally, rapidly growing companies have not enough top managers to put into failing enterprises.

Litton top management has often been asked about its ability to place managers in its acquisitions; the response has been that Litton is not using its managers but is acquiring other good managers. There is no substitute for good management in the acquired company. This suggests a very important planning policy, namely, once top quality management is acquired, do what is necessary to keep it. Several years ago a large electronics company acquired a smaller company in a slightly different field with a top quality scientist-manager. Because of differences between this manager and the acquiring company—differences which should have been ironed out before the merger—he left. The company has been trying to find a suitable replacement for several years and, in the meantime, is not nearly as successful as it should be.

There is no substitute for competent management in the acquiring company.

Table 21-4 Value of a High Price-Earnings Stock Ratio In an Acquiring Company

ITEM	COMPANY A	COMPANY B
Before merger:		
Net income	$2,000,000	$2,000,000
Shares outstanding	2,000,000	2,000,000
Earnings per share	$1	$1
P/E ratio	20	10
Stock price on market	$20	$10
Market value of company	$40,000,000	$20,000,000
Acquisition		
Exchange of stock	1,000,000	1 A for 2 B
Value	$20,000,000	
After merger:		
Combined income	$4,000,000	
Shares outstanding	3,000,000	
Earnings per share	$1.33	
P/E ratio	20	
Stock price on market	$26.60	
Stock equivalent value		$13.30

If a company's diversification philosophy is to move into related product areas, it is important to have depth of management and understanding of the business so that it can apply imagination to the new additions. If, on the other hand, the philosophy is one of entry into unrelated product lines, the requirement for capable management is still strong.

So important is this principle to Signal Oil & Gas Company that Forrest Shumway, the President, says, "We'll look at anything, so long as it makes money and can take care of its own management." (*Los Angeles Times*, May 14, 1967, p. 1.) A major guideline in International Telephone & Telegraph Corporation's acquisition is, in the words of Harold Geneen, Chairman and President, that the acquired company have a good management, preferably of able young men. (*Wall Street Journal*, October 28, 1965, p. 1.)

SUMMARY AND GUIDELINES FOR DIVERSIFICATION PLANNING

This chapter defined diversification, presented a brief historical review of major diversification movements, discussed at length basic reasons why one firm might want to acquire another and why the second might be willing to be acquired, looked briefly at the record of and reasons for diversification failure, and then discussed at length the principal steps in effective diversification planning and fundamental actions found by experience to be essential in successful corporate weddings.

Some of the more outstanding conclusions about and guidelines for successful diversification are as follows:

1. Diversify or die is a managerial imperative.

2. It is not easy to define diversification, but generally it means producing a new product (or service) or entering new markets which involve importantly different skills, processes, and knowledge from a firm's present products and markets.

3. There have been three major waves of diversification in U.S. industrial history, the third of which is now moving forward with considerable thrust.

4. Among the major reasons why one company wishes to acquire another are: to grow (as measured by sales, profits, employees, or geographic regions), avoid dependence on one product line, get stability in growth, furnish needed technical capability, reduce costs by using the same distribution system, break into international markets, acquire tax write-offs, solve competitive problems, and acquisition is often cheaper and faster than diversifying from within.

5. Companies are willing to merge for many reasons, such as owners may need cash to pay inheritance taxes, may need the cash resources of the acquiring company, or may simply wish to sell and retire.

6. Although the statistics of unsuccessful acquisitions are not reliable, they do indicate that many corporate marriages have gone sour.

7. The most important avenue to successful acquisition is a thoroughly planned program. Acquisition planning involves the following major steps: setting policies and strategies within a comprehensive corporate planning program; developing criteria for screening prospects at the different stages of decision-making, locating companies to be acquired, evaluating candidates, negotiating the acquisition, integrating the companies, and making a postaudit of success and failure.

8. Experience has shown the following to be indispensable to the success of mergers:

a. The chief executive must be personally involved. His needed involvement, however, varies at different stages in the process.

b. The best acquisition programs are planned.

c. Acquisitions involve extremely complex matters, and the company that has little or no experience in the process should use the services of reputable experts.

d. It is most advantageous for a company to have a high price-earnings stock ratio. In such a case stockholders of both companies are promised an increase in stock price.

e. Companies that have looked for and acquired companies in distress have generally not profited.

f. The quality of management found in, or placed in, the acquired company is of paramount importance in the success of the merger. There is no substitute for capable management, and if managers in the acquired company for any reason do not measure up to their responsibilities, replacement should be as quick as possible.

22
Research
and Development
Planning

22
Research
and Development
Planning

INTRODUCTION

Although the bulk of R&D planning in the U.S. is confined to a comparatively few companies, the impact of these companies on the U.S. economy is far beyond their relative numerical count. Furthermore, the inevitable impact of a rapidly dynamic economy is an increase in R&D planning among more companies. A growing number of companies are coming to understand the significance of a comment reportedly made by Charles Kettering that, "By its very nature research is a gamble . . . but the only risk that is greater than doing research is not doing it." This is not quoted to mean that all companies must engage in research and development programs, for this is not true.

The scope of subject matter which may properly be discussed in this area is so wide that only selected issues can be examined in this chapter. Following a discussion of the meaning and spectrum of R&D planning, the role of comprehensive planning in guiding detailed R&D planning will be examined. This will be followed with case illustrations of R&D planning in different types of companies, methods to organize the R&D function, principles governing the total dollar R&D budget, methods to forecast technology, and concluding guidelines for better R&D planning.

THE GROWTH OF RESEARCH AND
DEVELOPMENT EXPENDITURES

Everyone is aware of the recent growth and present high volume of industrial R&D expenditures in the U.S., shown in Chart 22-1. This chart makes clear that the increase in industrial R&D is due to rapid expansion in federally-funded as

Chart 22-1

Trends in Funds for Industrial R&D

Performance by Source, 1953-65

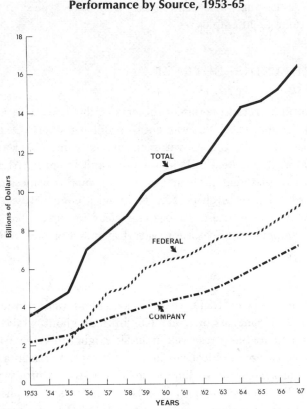

Source: National Science Foundation, "Reviews of Data on Science Resources," NSF 66-33, No. 10, December 1966, U.S. Government Printing Office, Washington, D.C.: p. 1; 1966 (actual) and 1967 (estimate) from a telephone call to the NSF, April 1968.

well as company-funded research. This is, of course, not the total research expenditure in the U.S. In addition in 1968, for example, approximately $6.5 billion was spent on R&D by the federal government itself plus federal support to universities and colleges.

The bulk of R&D funds is spent on aircraft and missiles, electrical equipment and communication, chemicals and allied products, motor vehicles and other transportation equipment, and machinery. Indeed, these five areas account for about 85 percent of all expenditures.

Among these industries, the federal government is a major contributor to aircraft and missiles expenditures. Private industry contributes heavily too, but not as much as the Government, in the electrical equipment and communications industries.

The National Science Foundation (1966, Tables 3, 15) estimates that in 1964 there were 13,400 companies performing research and development, a low number relative to the total number of perhaps 275,000 manufacturing companies in the U.S. Among these companies, 87 percent of the funds were spent by those having more than 5,000 employees, and only 5 percent was spent in those with less than 1,000 employees.

THE NATURE AND SPECTRUM OF R&D PLANNING

The range of managerial planning problems in the R&D area is indeed wide. At one end are monumental governmental problems of R&D planning that would include, for example, U.S. Government plans to match or excel potential technical developments of the USSR in weapons and in space. At the other end of the spectrum are planning problems of a very small businessman who feels the need to improve his research posture to avoid a competitive threat. At the outset, therefore, it is important to become clear on just what we mean by research and development and to appreciate the range of major R&D planning problems.

WHAT IS RESEARCH AND DEVELOPMENT? While there is no consensus on the definitions of R&D, there is a general understanding of major categories. Table 22-1 contains one set of definitions about which there can be some general agreement. Basic research includes original investigations which do not have specific commercial objectives in view. If undertaken in a business firm the scope would not necessarily be limited to the present or prospective interests of the company. The major distinction between basic and applied research is that in the latter are identified possible applications of basic research to meet objectives of a business. Product development is concerned with the technical nonroutine activities associated with translating scientific knowledge into marketable products. At minimum, product development may produce tests of feasibility; at maximum, the production of a prototype. Finally, a product is produced for further research and development or for sale.

A number of modifications of this classification may be found. For instance, some writers divide basic research into pure and fundamental, in which pure is undertaken on the basis solely or principally of the intellectual curiosity of an individual. Fundamental research, on the other hand, is a search for knowledge without reference to specific applications, but that hopefully will result in discovery of benefit to a firm's interests. There still, however, are no specific commercial objectives in mind. Development and production are also divided into a number of stages, as shown in illustrations later in this chapter.

While the R&D process can be considered sequential, from basic through the other stages shown in Table 22-1, it can be iterative like planning, and many of the stages can be performed concurrently. Concurrence will inevitably increase costs but savings in time may be worth it. It goes without saying, of course, that each of the stages shown in Table 22-1 can be, and is in practice, divided into many finer categories. This will be illustrated later in the chapter.

It should be noted that the National Science Foundation excludes from its definition of research and development, "routine product testing, market research, sales promotion, sales service, research in the social sciences or psychology, and other nontechnological activities or technical services." In this book, however, R&D planning in business will include many of these activities since the success of technical research and development is so heavily dependent upon a blending

Table 22-1 Research and Development: Steps, Activities and Promises for the Future

STEP	ACTIVITY	PROMISE
I	Basic Research Experimental Research Basic Development Advanced Research	Understanding of universe and organization of knowledge about it to: a. Permit major changes in ways of looking at phenomena and activities; b. Create new devices and methods for accomplishing objectives; and c. Identify phenomena and activities which permit revolutionary changes in existing products, methods and approaches. Its promise is great but not identified to specific purposes and the possibility of fulfillment is *highly uncertain.*
II	Applied Research Advanced Development Basic Evaluation Basic Testing	Singling out or identifying specific potentials or applications with a view to developing devices or methods for utilizing the new general knowledge obtained in Step I. Application or usefulness is identified but the economy, efficiency and acceptability of the proposals remain uncertain. Promise is for great new things.
III	Product Development Product Testing Product Evaluation Pilot Production	Specific devices or methods appear as likely solutions but must be brought reasonably close to final application to determine effectiveness, economy and acceptability. Do-ability has been established and major advances are promised.
IV	Product Application Application Research Applied Testing Application Evaluation	New uses and applications or modifications of existing uses or applications are sought for existing methods, products or components: may result in substantial benefits to users or producers. Some success is reasonably assured since it is evolutionary rather than revolutionary.

Source: David Novick, "What Do We Mean by Research and Development?" *California Management Review,* Vol. II, No. 3 (Spring, 1960) p. 9.

Table 22-2   Spectrum of Management Problem Areas for R&D Plans

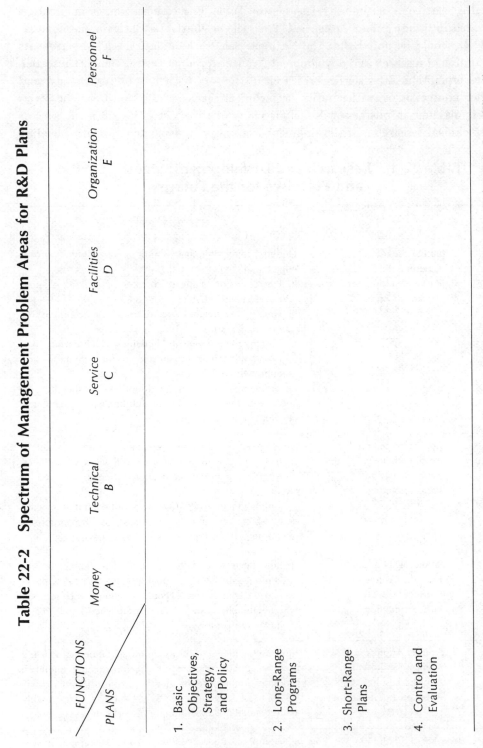

FUNCTIONS / PLANS	Money A	Technical B	Service C	Facilities D	Organization E	Personnel F
1. Basic Objectives, Strategy, and Policy						
2. Long-Range Programs						
3. Short-Range Plans						
4. Control and Evaluation						

Source: Suggested by Robert N. Anthony, *Management Controls in Industrial Research Organizations* (Cambridge, Mass.: Harvard University Press, 1952), p. 11.

of all these activities. Indeed, as noted in Chapters 18 and 19, the success of even a highly technical product may depend far more on research in these latter areas than in the technical areas. And for products with low new technical content the balance is even more heavily weighted to the social science end.

Planning problems and activities will vary much depending upon which of the stages in Table 22-1 and Chart 22-2 are being considered. But there are also other dimensions of the R&D planning problem.

TYPES OF R&D PLANS. Cursory examination of Table 22-1 shows there are different types of R&D plans. Tables 22-2 and 22-3 further elaborate varieties of R&D plans. The range of problems to which R&D planning is addressed is obviously rather wide. For instance, the issues in box 1A may concern whether

Table 22-3   Project Planning Matrix

PLANNING TASKS	TYPES OF PLANS				
	Project Definition	*Project Operating Plan*	*Contingency Plan*	*Project Expansion or Contraction Plan*	*Project Termination Plan*
Organizing Project Team					
Developing Project Design					
Defining Work Tasks					
Scheduling					
Engineering Drawing Procedure					
Budgeting and Cost Control					
Profit Plan					
Quality Control					
Staff Organization					
Subcontracting					
Facilities					
Reporting to Customer					
Internal Informational Reports					
Project Expansion					
Project Completion					

Source: George A. Steiner and William G. Ryan, *Industrial Project Management* (New York: The Macmillan Co., 1968), p. 42.

the company will or will not do any basic research, as compared with applied research, and if so, how much? Here should be established the directions and financial size of the R&D effort. As has been amply demonstrated in previous chapters, approaches to planning in box 1A are radically different from, say, those of 4F which may concern methods to measure individual performance.

Table 22-3 further amplifies the planning spectrum by presenting the problem from the point of view of an individual project manager in a large organization. In mind, for example, is a manager of an R&D project to develop, say, a satellite having specific requirements, who is working in an organization having other project managers. In this context, he operates within basic objectives, strategies, and policies of the company and must plan in the areas shown in Table 22-3.

In looking at the types of possible R&D plans shown in Tables 22-2 and 22-3 it should not be assumed that every R&D project must have complete plans in every one of the areas and that they all must tie together neatly. The problem of management is to determine at which point in this spectrum to devote planning efforts and at what point in time to do it. This art, of course, is another dimension to the problem.

OTHER DIMENSIONS OF R&D PLANNING. Some of the major problem areas which a fuller examination of R&D planning certainly would examine in detail are the following (those marked with an asterisk will be discussed at some length later in the chapter) :

*Problems in managing and planning R&D which is funded by the Federal Government are considerably different from those of a private company doing the same type of research.

*Perhaps of more fundamental concern generally is the distinction between research performed in a highly technologically-oriented company and that of a highly market-oriented company with low technology.

*There is an important difference between the demand-pull and the technology-push approach to R&D. The first approach is illustrated by George Heath, Director of Research for Imperial Chemicals Industries, who asserts that there is little question but that 25 to 30 years ahead technology can do just about anything demanded of it. His problem, therefore, is to determine today what the future demands for technology will be so that he can organize his R&D now to be in a position to meet the needs. On the other hand is the approach of inventing the better mouse trap with the conviction that when invented the demand for it will exist and be expressed in the marketplace.

It is worthwhile to digress a little to note that economists for a long time have assumed that technological innovation was "exogenous," that is, it came to the economy from the outside, or arose from non-economic forces. The idea has long held, also, that when a major invention appeared it gave rise to a new wave of major discoveries and applications. This is a most attractive view since it is perfectly obvious that technological developments have been growing very rapidly and have been reflected in a comparable increase in new commercial applications. The net result of this line of thought, of course, is that as technology develops in the future there will be an exponential growth of innovations as the impact fans out into new inventions and products.

Schmookler found, in a study of important inventions from 1800 to 1957 in agriculture, petroleum refining, papermaking, and railroading, that ". . . in no single instance is a scientific discovery specified as the factor initiating an important invention in any of these four industries. . . . When the inventions themselves are examined in their historical context, in most instances either the inventions contain no identifiable scientific component, or the science they embody is at least twenty years old." (Schmookler, 1966.)

Scientific progress and innovation do not move in tandem. What is the spur to the applications on the market of scientific discovery? Schmookler's answer is very simple. Inventions are mainly "demand-induced" rather than "knowledge-induced"; most inventions are stimulated by a market opportunity, present or potential, which offers a profit.

*Forecasting consumer wants and technology to match them in the future becomes a very important business consideration in R&D planning.

*Organizing the process is an obvious major planning problem for a company doing very much R&D.

*The selection system for projects is rather complex and also of obvious importance.

*Scientists and engineers doing research must blend their talents and interests with others in a company. To do this effectively requires careful planning and competent management.

For companies with large and expanding R&D programs the anticipated shortage of scientists and engineers may be intensified by greater imbalances in demand and supply in certain disciplines. For these companies future plans to avoid problems resulting from recruitment difficulties are important.

A very important subject of planning in companies with large engineering activities is the rapidly growing use of computer graphics in engineering design. This subject was touched upon briefly in Chapter 17.

Among those companies doing business with the government which requires R&D there are significant and growing problems concerned with what the companies consider excessive surveillance, documentation, and conformance to prescribed procedures.

Timing R&D expenditures is obviously important.

An important consideration in R&D planning concerns activities to improve the technology transfer process and to encourage and improve imagination, creativity, and innovation in the R&D process.

THE ROLE OF CORPORATE PLANNING

It is true that the Edisons, Ketterings, and Steinmetzes in this world were very successful without the benefit of a comprehensive corporate plan, and there will be others who will be successful in contributing importantly to their companies who will feel more restrained than benefited by a formal planning program. But for the bulk of R&D plans in most successful companies, a formalized planning program is a prerequisite for success. Why is this process so important to the successful R&D program? The reasons are that top management becomes involved in R&D and makes decisions of the highest importance to it, the process answers questions providing positive guidance to the effort, and a framework is available for coordination of R&D with other activities.

TOP MANAGEMENT'S CONTRIBUTIONS. A study made by McKinsey and Company among firms active in R&D concluded that in successful R&D top management became deeply involved in the research process. Furthermore, the study found that half the good research ideas developed in the chemical, electronic, and drug industries were suggested originally by top management (Hertz, 1965, p. 49). This is a finding just the reverse of what has been generally thought, a thought which, no doubt, has been a basis for much of top management's reluctance to get too involved in R&D planning.

There are many reasons why top management may be effective in guiding R&D. For example, it is freer to think of various alternatives, and its lack of scientific training makes it less likely that technical constraints will inhibit thinking. Also, top managers have intuitive skills, honed by hard experience, which are very important and valuable in guiding R&D efforts.

Precisely how involved top management should be in guiding R&D is a complex subject. In the basic research area, for example, top management of a large company may be involved only in such matters as total dollar allocations and decisions to commercialize when new products seem to be marketable. At the other extreme, if a company decides to expand importantly through in-house R&D efforts, top management should decide the directions.

CORPORATE PLANNING GUIDANCE FOR R&D. R&D planning, in the general case, is tied into over-all comprehensive planning in the same way that all other major functional areas are. This has been amply illustrated in previous chapters but a few more samples associated with R&D may be appropriate.

Fundamental guidance is given to specific R&D projects through the determination of business lines of a company, basic company objectives, major policies, and strategies developed in the planning process. If an oil company determines that it will grow by 10 percent a year largely through the internal development of low-cost and palatable foods from petroleum, it has established a basic set of guidelines for its R&D department. The heart of the R&D project selection process is this sort of guidance. (O'Donnell, 1967, Conclusion.)

Strengths and weaknesses, it will be remembered, are probed in the strategic planning process. Several years ago Gladding McBean looked at its technological posture and decided to stick with highly sophisticated ceramic science rather than dissipate its efforts in other possible areas.

Of special importance to R&D planning are technological forecasts which enable a company to avoid unexpected surprises. With a forecast of potential technological changes which may affect its products, a company is in a position to determine which technological positions it must defend at all costs and, when found, undertake research to secure those positions. Pharmaceutical and electronic companies are constantly engaged in this game. Technological forecasts permit a company to compare its technical capabilities with those of competitors and to determine what must be done to maintain its position. One chemical company has a policy which prescribes that research in all fields in which the company has an interest shall be at such a level that if it is surprised from any source it can regain its competitive position within four years.

The entire planning mechanism provides a suitable setting for coordinating R&D with other functional activities. At the highest levels, R&D objectives and strategies are related to financial capability, facility expansion, market strategies, profit plans, and so on. In the medium-range programming phase of planning, more detailed R&D projects can be more directly related to other functional areas. For instance, if a company thinks it feasible to reduce costs of a product by 10 percent over the next few years, R&D may be assigned specific duties in connection with product redesign. This may entail new facilities for R&D, new personnel or personnel shifts, and close relationships with marketing. Frequently, as noted in Chapters 18 and 19, planning product committees are created to perform this integration.

This coordination clearly is important to be sure, among other things, that scientific and engineering designs are in harmony with market needs, that designs permit the lowest cost compatible with optimum sales appeal, and that research and development costs are in harmony with ultimate anticipated profit. Furthermore, as Donald Pelz (1964) has discovered after intensive survey, the technical man performs better when these types of decision-making influences are involved in his goal setting.

Every company should have a reasonably satisfactory system for answering two basic questions: What technology do we need to meet a competitive threat, to exploit a new market opportunity, or to alter and improve a present product? What technology is available to answer the first question?

These questions can be answered effectively by communication in the planning process. In larger companies a planning staff can link the technical and nontechnical groups in answering the questions. In very large companies a single focal point for technical communications within the company, and between the company and outside sources, may be established to facilitate technology transfer (George A. Steiner, 1966).

Broad guidance from the top down is matched in R&D planning with ideas flowing up from the bottom. Each stream of activity influences the other. A new brilliant discovery in a laboratory can, for example, open up a new product line for a company as when Du Pont's metallurgists accidentally discovered Detaclad, a process for bonding metals such as the present "sandwich coins."

R&D PLANNING PROFILES

The way different industries and companies go about their R&D planning varies much and is illustrated by the following cases.

INNOVATE TO ORDER. A very large number of companies fall into this category, and parts of the R&D planning of even very sophisticated technically advanced companies may be so classified. In this situation, technology is dominated by other considerations and is a comparatively minor problem.

For instance, a company may wish to repackage and produce a product with different ingredients, as, for example, a pharmaceutical manufacturer producing a new vitamin pill. Or, the requirement may be to redesign a product, such as an electric motor, a pump, or a valve. Or, the need may be satisfied by the application of a simple technology, such as the use of aluminum in place of copper in certain automobile parts—a problem faced by automobile manufacturers during the Korean War in order to conserve copper. In adapting existing technologies, the engineers will work closely with others to relate the technology to cost, market need, packaging size, or consumer psychology. A need for technology may be internal, such as a technical change requested in a machine tool to increase productivity or to reduce cost.

The characteristics of innovation to order are: the design requirement is rather well fixed, the technology required is generally known and readily applied to the problem, and the actual application is rigidly supervised to assure meeting the specified requirement. There is little R&D planning as such; rather, the R&D activity is a derivative from other planning.

ADVANCED TECHNOLOGY-DOMINATED R&D PLANNING. At the other extreme are the large aerospace companies who have much different R&D planning characteristics. Here, R&D planning is a major determinant of the success of the company. R&D planning involves identification in the far distant future (5 to 20 years) of important military and space missions, determination of technologies that will be important in their success, and decision to begin currently to achieve the required competence to meet mission requirements. In the process of doing so, the companies must not only transfer vast amounts of technology from outside their company but must literally assume the responsibility for new inventions. A study made by the Department of Defense, for example, showed that among twenty large systems about 35 percent of the major events necessary to the ultimate performance of the system were made after the development contract award date (Sherwin and Isensen, 1966).*

R&D planning is a large effort in both industry and government in the aerospace industry. This is not confined, of course, to identification of future R&D needs. An even larger part of R&D planning concerns the operational planning which follows a contract to proceed. This in turn begins an elaborate series of R&D planning stages resulting eventually in a prototype, production, or both. The whole process is unbelievably complicated, as one might expect in such a gigantic application of resources to achieve new technological developments. Elaborate efforts, therefore, have been made to develop policies, procedures, analytical models, and other guidelines to improve the effort. While there have been important advances made in R&D planning in the aerospace industry there does not exist by any means, either in government or in industry, complete satisfaction with the methodology.

The decisions made by an aerospace company to undertake specific types of research are very important for there is no question about the fact that the bulk of contracts are given to those companies which have the greatest technical strengths and can produce the required product at acceptable costs and on required delivery schedules. The required technical strength cannot be built overnight, nor can even the largest of the aerospace companies be strong in all fields. As a consequence, the R&D decisions made by an aerospace company today will determine the contracts which it will win or lose five or ten years from now.

Chart 22-2 presents my over-all portrayal of the R&D planning problem and structure in the aerospace industry. The government, as shown at left, is continuously making surveys of future needs and future technical developments upon which basis specific requirements are established for equipment. Requests for proposals are then sent to industry and bidding for contracts proceeds.

In the meantime the aerospace companies, as shown in Chart 22-2, are continuously appraising the possible future needs of the government, upon which basis future R&D needs are determined and decisions made about which needs a company wishes to fulfill to be in the best position to win specific types of contracts. (Another dimension not shown on this chart is the application

* An event in this report is defined in two categories: undirected science in which the objective of the work is the advancement of knowledge for its own sake, without regard for application; and applied or directed science, in which a specific application is in view.

Chart 22-2

Planning Research and Development Programs in the Aerospace Industry

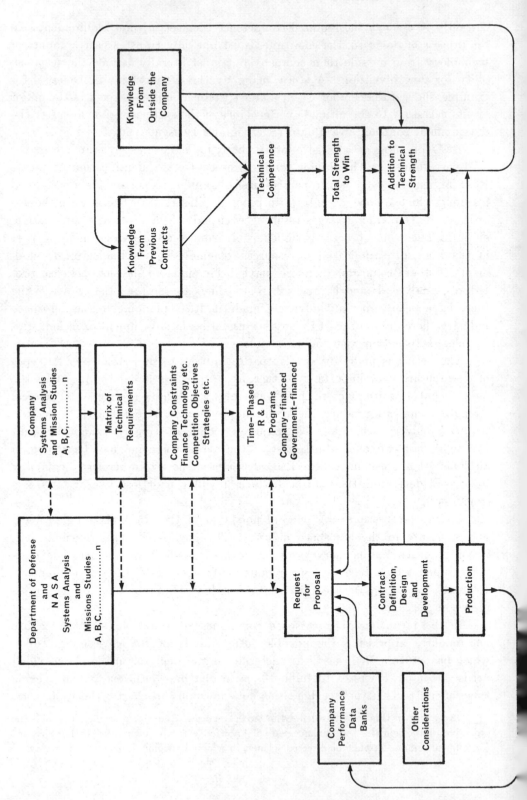

of aerospace technology, growing out of government contracts, to nondefense uses. The most spectacular illustration, of course, is the development of commercial airplanes.)

Throughout this process, as illustrated in Chart 22-2, there is continuous dialogue and informational interchange between the government and the industry. This does not mean, of course, that each tells the other everything about its business and interests, but there is an awareness on the part of each of the major potential developments concerning each.

Of fundamental importance are the mission studies, or systems analyses, made in both the government and industry. What is involved in these studies is a thorough examination of future political, economic, military, and technical events in light of national security and space objectives. Such studies reveal hardware requirements to meet national security and space exploration objectives. These are deep studies that employ elaborate analyses and probe into the future for great distances—some move into the next century*

From their mission studies, aerospace companies develop a matrix of technical needs for new potential products and use this as a basis for their R&D planning. A very simple illustration is shown in Table 22-4.

Details among matrices will, of course, differ, but under each of the major technologies will be identified more specific problem areas, as illustrated under propellants. A tabulation such as this will, of course, relate the needed time-phasing of different technologies where that is appropriate, identify the areas where the company is strong and where it is weak, establish priorities for various technological developments if the mission objective is to be achieved, calculate risks in being able to overcome particular technical problems, examine strengths of competitors, and project timing requirements for technical solutions.

When such an evaluation is made a company is in a position to determine which technical programs it wishes to pursue in order to be in a position to compete effectively for a future potential contract. This decision is based upon the objectives of the company, its present technical capabilities, available funding, and other comparable considerations.

The next step, as shown in Chart 22-2, is to determine specific technical programs, for specific periods of time, and assure their necessary funding. This will, when added to the transfer of technological information from previous contracts and from sources outside the company, result in a technical strength which hopefully will win contracts. This is not the place to examine the bases

---

* For an illustration of the technique, see Harold Linstone, 1967. Another illustration of a slightly different but no more elaborate methodology is Klass, 1964, pp. 56-59; and Klass, 1965, pp. 54-58. This is a system called Pattern, standing for Planning Assistance Through Technical Evaluation of Relevance Numbers, developed by Honeywell. Pattern is reported to have cost $250,000 to set up and may involve between $50,000 and $100,000 a year to update and operate. See Jantsch, 1967, p. 127.

for government's choosing a particular contractor, but technological strength obviously has to be of great importance. Technological strength as reflected in proposals is related to data banks of information in the government concerning past experience with a contractor, other considerations, and a choice made.

If the aerospace contractor has chosen the correct **R&D** path in the future, has performed well on previous contracts, has a good design with acceptable costs and time schedule, the chances of winning a contract are high.

Underlying all **R&D** planning in both the Department of Defense and NASA is the life cycle concept. Simply stated, the cycle is composed of four distinct phases: concept formulation (which may take many years), contract definition (which make take a year or two), acquisition (which may take one to eight years), and operation (which may extend over many years). **R&D** planning in the more technically oriented commercial enterprises can learn much from the

Table 22-4 Technical Requirements for Alternative Missions

	MISSION				
TECHNOLOGY	Mars Flyby	Venus Flyby	Manned Recoverable Reentry Vehicle	Space Station	etc.
Propellants					
1. Rubber-based					
2. Nitrosplastisol					
3. High Energy					
4. Gas Generator					
Conventional Rocket Motors					
Advanced Rocket Engines					
Inertial Guidance					
Aerodynamics					
Biomedicine					
High Temperature Thermodynamics					
Particle Physics					
Solar Physics					
Planetary Defluidization					
Etc.					

military and space experience because the many intricate processes in each stage have been identified and incorporated in the procedural steps that must be followed. (The official regulations concerning the life cycle are conveniently found in Steiner and Ryan, 1968, Appendix A.) There are a number of models of the life cycle process which explain in detail the steps to be followed (Thome and Willard, 1966; Kane, 1967; Kaprielyan, 1966; and *Aviation Week & Space Technology,* 1967).

It is very difficult to generalize about this whole procedure, but the main characteristic of planning in the industry are determined by such considerations as the following:

1. There is an elaborate effort made both by the industry and the government to identify today those evolving technical requirements which will be needed to complete potential missions over a long period of time, up to 20 or more years.

2. The specific design of these future missions is, of course, uncertain, so technology planning cannot be completely coupled to long-range future specific need. Companies, therefore, try to maintain a technical competitive strength in an area, such as tactical missiles, fighter airplanes, or experimental satellites, rather than in specific detailed versions of products in these areas.

3. The government provides a very large part of the R&D funding of the industry and, therefore, has an important voice in R&D programs to be undertaken.

4. In the stage of mission identification and near-term R&D to fulfill long-range future program needs, there is more emphasis upon research than upon development and more freedom is permitted to contractors. As a program approaches the final design stage, and moves into the development of a prototype or the final product, government surveillance and direction become strict.

5. Technical superiority is generally favored over dollar costs of production.

In sum, the aerospace industry is unique not only because of its close relationship with government but also because of the fact that no other industry has as much R&D activity and experience in planning it. For these and other reasons, the R&D planning programs of this industry are of general interest.

TECHNICALLY MOTIVATED INDUSTRIAL COMPANIES. In between these two types are companies in the industrial world who seek to push back the frontiers of technology in their lines of business, who want to expand by internal new product R&D, and who want to employ modern technology wherever it can be done to their advantage. For want of a better name, I call these technically motivated companies, illustrations of which are Du Pont, General Electric, Westinghouse, 3M, Union Carbide, and Celanese.

Generally, there are two broad types of research done both in the divisions and/or central laboratories of such companies. One type will apply presently known technology to meet specific market demands, redesign products, and so on. This is innovation to order. Second, central laboratories will have flexibility in developing new products which hopefully will be added to existing lines of business and marketed profitably. This is technology-push. The patterns of individual companies, however, differ much. We can do no more than illustrate this type company.

One pattern is that of Texas Instruments, Inc. This company has a number of decentralized product divisions which have their own research and development divisions and are virtually autonomous. There is also a Central Research and Engineering group that has both staff responsibilities for coordinating and integrating the total technical effort of the company and also for creating new technology and products in its laboratories (From Teal, 1962).

Plans are submitted twice a year in this company, and the Central Research and Engineering group on these occasions submits to management what it deems to be a compilation of worthwhile projects. To be "worthwhile," a project must have the following characteristics: generate good industrial technology; produce new product ideas or ideas for product improvement; enhance company prestige in the scientific community; challenge, extend, and train technical personnel and project leaders; have a reasonable probability of success; and have the enthusiastic support of a project manager.

The selection is based upon company objectives, the nature of the company's present business, the technical capability of research personnel, areas in which the company may market, and products which the company may develop and manufacture. In considering such factors as these, the company makes a technological forecast to find technical areas of interest for the company and to detect what competitors are doing. Careful review is also made of the programs of the product divisions. All this work results in proposals for initiating new projects, continuation of present projects, and elimination of some existing projects.

Projects are classified into four groups. First, are "major directed projects," or those having a high degree of economic confidence in the sense that the end product is clear and there is assurance that it can be marketed successfully. Second, are "directed projects," which are those that provide specific technology needed in an established product line in one of the divisions and for which economic confidence is high. Third, are "major exploratory projects," where there may be a clear view of potential product but there is a lack of technology in the company to develop it. These projects generally result from long-term exploratory projects from which some reasonable estimate of the probability of developing the needed technology can be derived. Finally, are the "long-term exploratory projects," which have a low level of economic confidence because it is not clear what the specific end product will be. The research here is predominantly basic in nature, and there is a great deal of freedom given to scientists. The scope of the work is generally restricted only to the technological areas of present and anticipated major interest to the company. In some cases, the selection of the project is simply that of interest to a scientist of high capability who has interests paralleling those of the company.

The Bell Telephone Laboratories illustrates a little different R&D planning system. Aside from specific service requests, the scientists and engineers have considerable freedom to think and work with the mild yet purposeful objective of advancing the interests of the company. A classic illustration extends back to 1910 when some of the more farsighted engineers began to think about the future and, looking at the projected curves of telephone growth, decided that unless self-dialing telephones were developed the company within a generation could not hire enough operators for the system. Looking at population data, they concluded that if every eligible girl of the right age and education were hired by AT&T, there would not be enough. The result was technical planning to resolve this problem (Hunt, 1954).

In some companies, the director of research is given considerable leeway in devising his research program. This is especially the case when his responsibility is to engage in basic research to develop new technology for new products. The Central Research Department of Du Pont has a budget which is divided 50-50 for explorations into (a) entirely new fields not connected with present company manufacturing interests, and (b) sponsored research by individual departments of the company bridging the gap between new discoveries in the pioneering effort and the development of new processes of interest to the departments. For example, the Central Research Department discovered a broad class of linear condensation polymers having a crystaline structure. When it was discovered that these could be spun into fibers, the Textile Fibers Department supported research in the Central Research Department and initiated further work in its own laboratories. A polyamide called nylon 66 was the first one selected for commercialization. The Plastics Department initiated production of nylon bristles and also undertook research for manufacturing nylon intermediates from petroleum or coal. Other departments of the company also found new products in the basic discovery (Salzberg, 1963, p. 79).

In companies such as these, the interplay between marketing and R&D is virtually continuous. Marketing is immediately determining in the division laboratories, while in the central laboratories it becomes gradually more important as a new invention comes closer to commercialization. Chart 22-3 shows this interrelationship in a schematic way and also shows other steps in the R&D process which are of interest in light of what was said previously. In this case, research began with the thought that a market would exist for a product having the properties of Kapton.* But it was some time before market research began to play an important role.

---

* Kapton polymide is a new ultra-high temperature film, used for electrical insulation, printed circuits, capacitors, fire protective clothing, magnetic and pressure sensitive tapes, hose and tubing, and other specialized comparable applications.

Chart 22-3
Stages in the Development of
Du Pont's "Kapton" Polyimide Film

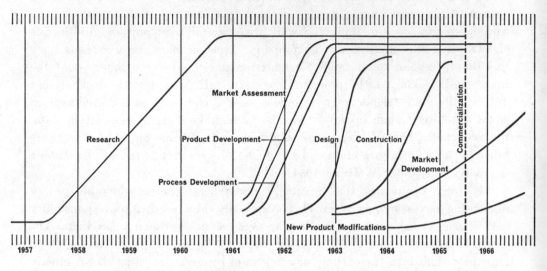

Source: "The D of Research and Development" *This is Dupont 30* (Wilmington, Delaware: E. I. Du Pont de Nemours & Company, 1966), pp. 14-15. Courtesy E. I. du Pont de Nemours & Company (Inc.).

COMPETITIVE R&D TEAMS. A few companies have created two competitive teams to develop a product. For example, General Electric's Flight Propulsion Division deliberately supports two teams to develop the same jet engines, on the grounds that the final product will thereby be better. The Mustang of the Ford Motor Company is the product of no fewer than seven rival design teams (Mapes, 1966, p. 1). William McLean of the U. S. Naval Ordnance Training Station at China Lake has gone one step further. He set up one fully funded team to build an all glass bathysphere. At the same time he named a small creative team whose goal was to beat the first group, but with 10 percent of the first team's budget!

This competitive approach, of course, is designed to prevent one group of scientists from concentrating on limited alternatives and to prevent the inclination of one group to become excessively enamored with one set of alternatives. Rivalry also stimulates endeavor in the groups. On the other hand, there are critics of this approach who think it leads to wasteful duplication and internal battles that may leave scars which take a long time to heal. This approach may be effective in the more creative areas of R&D, but because of dangers and costs it probably will not expand rapidly.

CRITERIA FOR PROJECT SELECTION. A word should be added here on criteria for project selection. In addition to what has been said above about criteria for project selection, there should be noted as applicable to certain types of projects many of the techniques discussed in previous chapters, such as cost-utility analysis, return on investment, check-off lists, risk analysis, and so on. An excellent analysis of 30 different methods to select R&D programs is contained in Cetron, Martino, and Roepcke (1967).

Albert Rubenstein made a survey of 37 laboratories in 29 companies to find out what criteria (indicators, measures, variables) they used to judge the progress and/or results of R&D work. His conclusions are of interest here and are given in Table 22-5.

PURCHASING R&D. A company, of course, need not have its own R&D establishment nor completely depend upon it when it supports one. A small company may not have the resources to support an R&D staff. Sometimes a company may have technical limitations which it can fill more readily and with less cost by purchasing R&D. For these and other reasons, companies use the services of universities, nonprofit research institutes, profit-making research organizations, trade association laboratories, the federal government, and any other sources that may be available. Purchasing R&D is by no means confined to very small enterprises for large companies also engage in this practice.

ORGANIZATION OF R&D

Until very recently whatever research was conducted in the typical corporation took place with an air of improvisation and experimentation as a sideline to the production process. More and more companies today, however, are creating research (used in a broad sense) organizations with the directors reporting to the chief executives. Among divisionalized companies, R&D has taken its place alongside other functional officers such as finance, law, personnel, manufacturing, corporate planning, and marketing.

THE RESEARCH AND DEVELOPMENT DIRECTOR. The functions of this individual will depend upon his role in the corporation, the size of the company, and so on. However, general R&D functions to be discharged include the following:

1. See that the technical R&D activities of the company are conducted in conformance with company objectives, strategies, and policies.
2. See that the corporation places proper emphasis on changing technology of interest to it and integrates it into its operating programs.
3. See that technological developments of interest to the corporation are communicated to those in the corporation who are most concerned.
4. See that technological developments within the corporation are communicated properly to others in the corporation who are most interested.

Table 22-5 Criteria Used to Judge Progress and/or Results of R&D in 37 Laboratories*

	*Number of Companies**
1. Related to effect on sales volume or revenue: Increased business; increased output without increasing investment; share of the market; percent of products from research; consumer acceptance; effect of new products on old product sales; new customers.	19
2. Related to effect on savings in materials, labor, or other costs: Royalty payments saved; use of by-products, wastes, idle facilities or personnel, or less profitably employed facilities; reduction of product line; closer control of manufacturing quality; better process yields; etc.	17
3. Related to effect on profits: Profit on research vs. nonresearch products; profit and loss analysis for whole R&D effort; payoff time on projects; percent return on investment.	13
4. Related to time and cost of the technical solution: Frequent re-estimates of time and cost; progress on project or program phases; actual vs. budgeted expenses; actual vs. scheduled progress; proportion of budget spent vs. progress.	28
5. Related to customer satisfaction: Number and nature of complaints; broadening of product line.	10
6. Related to information output: Number of valuable ideas; percent of ideas from inside laboratory; learning about new processes and materials; sources of new ideas; training individuals; development of specifications; evaluation of information output to application groups; information developed for sales; repeat requests for work.	17
7. Related to success of technical solution: Number of problems successfully handled; number of patents— written up, applied for, granted; number and nature of project failures.	16

* Indicates use by a company in at least one of its laboratories.

Source: Albert H. Rubenstein, "Setting Criteria for R&D," *Harvard Business Review*, Vol. 35, No. 1 (January-February 1957), p. 97.

5. Give competent and imaginative advice and counsel on technical matters to top management, including the board of directors, and all operating divisions.

6. See that technology within the corporation is blended properly in the planning and operation program, with other relevant activities.

7. See that technological knowledge is available and used properly in the corporation to create new and improved products, to minimize costs of production, to provide standards for quality production, to provide technical standards for purchase of materials and equipment, and to provide technical assistance to manufacturing.

8. Maintain required technical liaison with and surveillance of customers and competitors.

9. Work with other managers in formulating the company's R&D programs in the applied and development research fields.

10. Recommend research programs to the chief executive.

11. Recommend, develop, and administer company strategies, policies, and procedures concerning the technical R&D program.

12. Make recommendations concerning, and administer a program for, improving the productivity of R&D personnel through the imaginative use of aids to relieve them from tedious and unnecessary work.

13. Assure that the most competent research talents are made available to, and kept in, the corporation.

14. Administer the R&D organization within the corporation.

The director of research in the modern corporation has a responsible job to perform. His importance rises the more the corporation concerns itself with basic and fundamental research which, while having some of the flavor of research unfettered from commercial interests, is conducted with an eye to the future interests of the company. In such a case the imagination, leadership, intuition, and intellect of the project director is the basic means to allocate resources and to stimulate fruitful research.

The R&D director is also responsible for assuring a proper balance between a required control and freedom of inquiry. The closer a project is to basic research, the less will be administrative control and the more freedom of exploration. In examining the activities of sixteen project managers in the aerospace industry who produced technically superior projects at minimum time and cost to prototype, William Ryan and I found that in the design phase these men all administered their programs with great looseness (Steiner and Ryan, 1968). As the projects moved toward the prototype stage and into production, however, these project managers insisted on much tighter control. The freedom of scientists and engineers, therefore, was correspondingly reduced. Through the process from basic research to production, the successful project manager maintained a proper balance between the two, a posture that required great skill.

Chart 22-4

Corporate Unit Does All Research

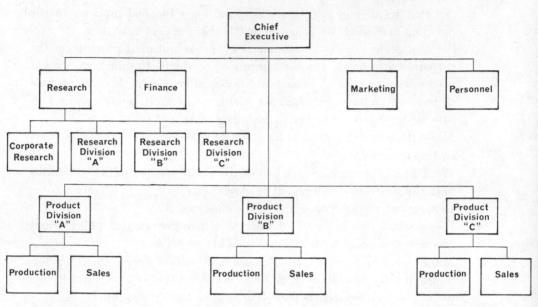

Source: From *Top Management Organization in Divisionalized Companies* (New York: National Industrial Conference Board, 1965).

ALTERNATIVE ORGANIZATIONS. Among the more general organizational arrangements are those shown in Charts 22-4 through 22-6. (Stieglitz and Janger, 1965, pp. 74, 75, and 77.) In Chart 22-4 all the work is done in a central research organization. When the volume of research done is small and the primary emphasis is on the development of products for internal diversification, this may be a suitable arrangement. In a large divisionalized company, however, there may be problems generated between the divisions and the central research unit about allocation of resources. To forestall them, and to give the divisions more control over their destiny, the model in Chart 22-5 may be used. In this arrangement a split is made between corporate central laboratory research and division research. In this case, the central laboratory research may be more basic research, research covering several divisions, or specific research paid for by the divisions. Division work may be more directly related to short- and long-range divisional profits. There are many companies, however, who place all R&D in the divisions and do not support a central research organization. In Chart 22-6 no research is conducted at corporate headquarters, but a functional office exists there; also, a division is created to do nothing but R&D work comparable to that done by the central laboratories in Chart 22-4, and the divisions then perform research and development associated with their own programs and future progress.

Project managers are more and more being given responsibility for specific research and development projects which have a specific terminal date and which

Chart 22-5

Divisions Do Own Research

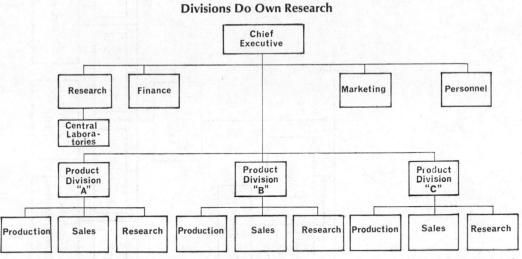

Source: From *Top Management Organization in Divisionalized Companies* (New York: National Industrial Conference Board, 1965).

Chart 22-6

Corporate Unit Does No Research

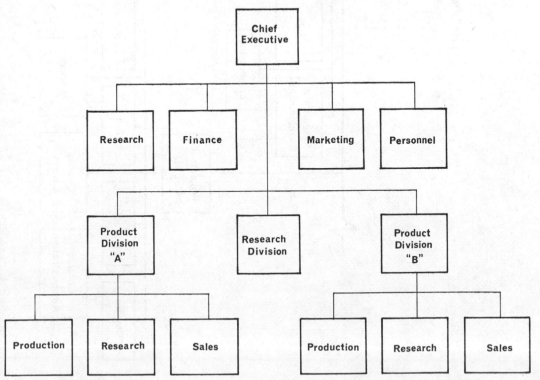

Source: From *Top Management Organization in Divisionalized Companies* (New York: National Industrial Conference Board, 1965).

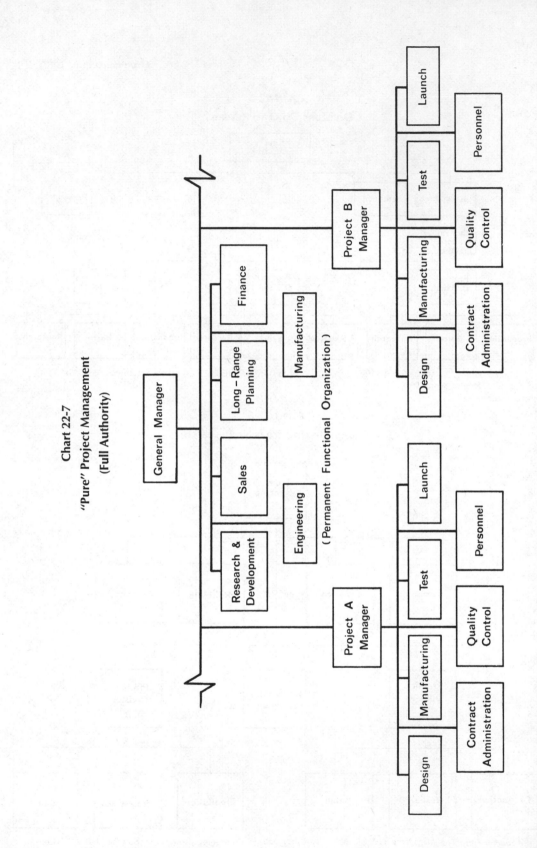

Chart 22-7
"Pure" Project Management
(Full Authority)

involve important risks and higher-than-average technical uncertainties. Three fundamental types of organization are used in technically oriented companies, as shown in Charts 22-7, 22-8, and 22-9. In the "pure" form, as shown in Chart 22-7, the project manager may have virtually full authority within his company to complete his assignment with resources placed at his disposal. Chart 22-8 shows a "matrix" form of organization, where the authority of the project manager is splintered and shared with functional managers. Here, the project manager may have under his immediate direction a small staff who are temporarily assigned to him, but most of the work is done through personnel in functional areas. Functional managers retain direct line authority over these personnel. The project manager determines the "what" and "when" of the project's activities, and the functional manager assigns the necessary support from his area. The third type of organization shown in Chart 22-9 portrays a situation where the project manager has no authority over work being done in the functional areas. He is more of a monitor, or an expediter, than a true manager, integrator, or coordinator, as in the first two arrangements.

HOW MUCH SHOULD THE R&D BUDGET BE?

There is no ready answer to this question. Common practice, however, has revealed a number of standards for answering it, such as the following:

- Establish the total R&D budget at some percentage of sales.
- Try to match what competitors are doing.
- Find the industry average and stick to that.
- Take a past historical average for the company and increase it by an amount equal to the internal rate of growth that is set as a company objective. If, for example, the company decides to grow at 8 percent per year through internal product developments, then increase the budget for research and development by 8 percent each year.
- "Cost" out R&D needed to meet specific product objectives and add a percentage for independent research to be determined by those doing it.
- Give the R&D staff what is requested if the amount is reasonable in light of the firm's financial ability.
- Develop in the planning process a balance among R&D and all other activities.

Any automatic method for determining the total R&D budget is incorrect and, if used, indicates that a company is not thinking through its real needs. Certainly, finding out what competitors are doing and then matching the amount is not to be considered an effective approach. Asking the research people what they want also is not a sound approach unless the amount is related to company objectives and strategies by the research staff in developing their aggregate needs.

Chart 22-8
"Matrix" Project Management
(Shared Authority)

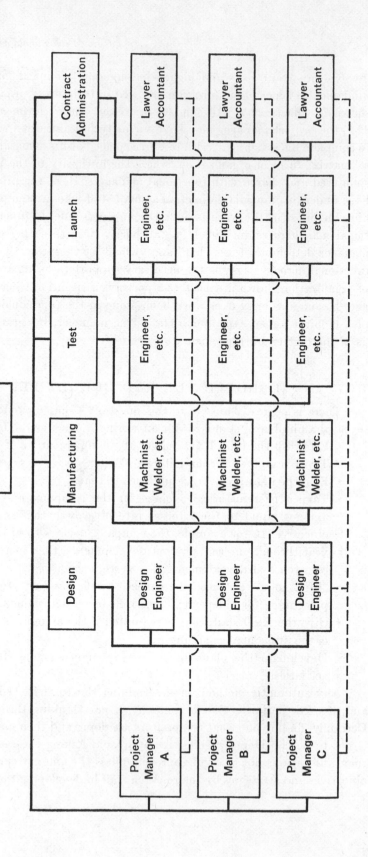

Chart 22-9
"Influence" Project Management
(Monitoring Authority)

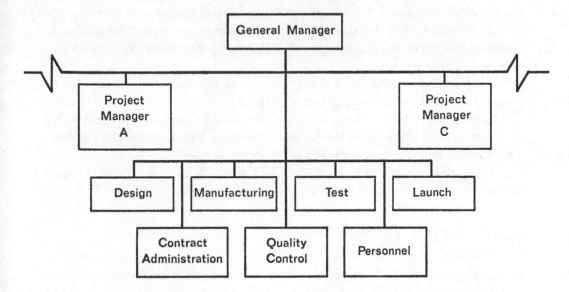

If this is done, management can review the totals on the basis of proper stand-ards. An assumption that future sales results will be proportionate to research expenditures has been proven wrong. Following a detailed survey of the major inventions made by E. I. Du Pont de Nemours & Company from 1920 to 1950, Willard Mueller (1962) concluded, among other things, that the Company's success in making important product and process improvements did not increase proportionately to its increasing research and development budget. Furthermore, as is well known, large sales volume has often grown from products the research costs of which were minor, and vice versa. Varian Associates of California, for example, reportedly invented the klystron tube on a budget of $100.

Certainly, if research costs can be related to potential payoff this is a solid basis for determining a large part of the budget. This method cannot be used, however, to determine how much of the budget should be for basic research which may ultimately improve the image of the company, or how much to satisfy the independent intellectual interests of scientists in the laboratories.

There are considerations which can govern the size of the R&D budget, as follows:

What is needed to achieve the long-range objectives of the company? If a company has a long-range planning program, it will know what it wants to achieve and can, therefore, begin to cost out the research and development ex-penditures needed to meet objectives.

There is an "ideal" level of research and development which may be calculated and, if so, will have a bearing on the totals. If the totals are higher than in the first cut above, then the company objectives may be raised, and vice versa.

Is the company in a position to finance the levels of research projected in the above? If a company is in temporary financial troubles it may have to reduce its "ideal" budget. But this should be done only after much care. The usual proclivity of businesses to cut research and development first when there is a downturn is probably not wise.

R&D budgets should be reasonably stable to maintain momentum and to keep the required complement of technical talent.

Some amount for basic research may be added to support the interests of the scientists and engineers in the company's research and development program. This amount today is very low for industry in the aggregate.

Table 22-6 shows one type of R&D budget which can be helpful in determining amounts for specific purposes and for all together.

FORECASTING TECHNOLOGY

For many reasons noted previously, technology forecasting is important in the development of R&D planning, especially among the more technically-oriented companies. While it is not new, it has emerged in recent years as a serious art and more companies are becoming concerned with it.

Table 22-6   Budget Classifications of Research and Development by Product and Purpose

TYPE OF RESEARCH	NEW PRODUCT RESEARCH	NEW PROCESS RESEARCH	PRODUCT IMPROVEMENT RESEARCH	TOTAL RESEARCH BY	TOTALS
	Product A B C	Product A B C	Product A B C	Product A B C	
Basic					
Applied					
Product Development					
Product Application					
Total for Product					
Grand Total					

Source: Adapted from James Brian Quinn, "Budgeting for Research," in Carl Heyel, ed., *Handbook of Industrial Research Management,* New York, Reinhold Publishing Corp., 1960, p. 284.

WHAT IS TECHNOLOGY? Technology basically is a very broad term including the entire notion of technique and knowledge not only in the physical sciences but in such fields as medicine, behavioral science, and also business maagement. In the present context, technology refers to scientific and technical information which is involved in the development of new inventions, new designs of present products and services, and new products and services. In mind are new products such as computers, the supersonic transport, Corfam, or automation of machine tools.

Information is the essential ingredient of technology, and it is the principal output of science and technology. This information may exist in the minds of scientists and engineers, in technical books and periodicals, computer memories, and other depositories. It is known as knowledge, understanding, skill, technical data, and know-how.

In this light, says Hartman, "Technological forecasting is the process of estimating, as a function of time in the future, the amount of technical information that will exist in a well-defined field of technological activity." (Steiner and Cannon, 1966, p. 244.) From a little different point of view, technological forecasting involves the probabilistic assessment of the future patterns of transfer of technical information. This would also include, of course, an appraisal of the availability of certain types of information. (Bright, 1967.) Another pragmatic definition of technological forecasting is as follows: "The description or prediction of a foreseeable invention, specific scientific refinement, or likely scientific discovery that promises to serve some useful function." (Prehoda, 1966, p. 12.)

The area of activity with which this chapter is concerned was described in Table 22-1. But this is not the whole of the spectrum of levels of technology transfer. (Jantsch, 1967, pp. 24-25.)

LEVELS OF CAUSALITY. The feasibility of technological forecasting varies depending upon levels of future causality and the precision which is sought. I have classified levels of causality for present purposes as follows: (1) breakthrough, (2) demand-induced technical advance, and (3) economic and social consequences.*

By breakthroughs are meant new, comparatively unexpected, technical advances. In mind are such modern inventions and discoveries as the telephone, the radio tube, penicillin, the transistor, and the laser. All these new inventions were built on some old technical information but the appearance of the new product was unpredictable, at least with any precision.

The second category is of much more immediate interest to individual firms. Here one finds technical developments which are supplied to meet a demand.

---

* For a different classification, see S. Colum Gilfillan, "The Prediction of Technical Change," conveniently located in Bright, 1964, pp. 747ff; see also Jantsch, 1967.

There are many old ideas and technology which have lain dormant for years but which tomorrow will result in important new products. They will develop when a commercial receptivity exists for them.

Historically, it is easy to demonstrate an impressive time lag between invention and profitable commercialization. Gilfillan, for example, examined 19 inventions introduced in the quarter-century before 1913 and concluded there was a time interval of 176 years between the first thought about the technology and the first working machine or patent; another 24 years to the first practical use; 14 more years to commercial success; and another 12 years to important use. (Gilfillan in Bright, 1964, p. 740; and Gilfillan, 1935, p. 96.) The idea of the computer, for example, was conceived and a working model was made by Charles Babbage almost 150 years ago. The typewriter was around for many years before successfully produced and sold for a profit.

There are many reasons for this lag. To illustrate—lack of precision parts (the computer), lack of exploitable commercial demand (airplanes), too high cost (home video tapes), or lack of receptivity (birth controls).

The third category of economic and social consequence of new technology is important to businesses because of the direct impact on an enterprise as well as longer-range potential indirect implications. In mind here, of course, is the meaning of a new technology to the products of a firm. The diesel locomotive, for example, was destined to affect the lives of the old steam locomotive manufacturers in a fashion they completely underestimated. Also, new technology changes environment which in turn affects a company. While the automobile at the time it was introduced did not directly affect most businesses, its indirect impact has been felt by every business.

METHODS OF FORECASTING TECHNOLOGY. Even though technology forecasting is in its infancy, there are many methods which have been developed to do it.* Among them, it seems to me that five categories are most important for business usage. They are optimism, trend extrapolation, correlation, simulation, and informed judgment. Of course, as with sales forecasts, a methodology which uses many approaches may also be considered a distinct method. Each of these has been the basis of past successful predictions but the experience has varied much from time to time, technology to technology, and the degree of precision of the forecast.

Optimism refers to the idea of the wish being father to the thought that a particular event will happen. Mere optimism is not wholly without merit, for two reasons. Whatever an "imagineer" may dream about—a color television set, a wrist television receiver and transmitter, an electrically controlled automobile, or the end of smog—is probably or can be desired by millions of others. A re-

* For a penetrating analysis of elements of some 100 techniques, see Jantsch, 1966, especially pp. 119-121. For further descriptions of methods, see Cetron, 1967. See also Lenz, Jr., 1962; and Sweezy, in Lesser, Jr., 1966.

ceptive market, therefore, exists which stimulates invention. It may also serve to counteract pessimism of those who think the event cannot be made to occur.

Extrapolation is a better method for predicting technology. This is a technique, as with sales forecasts, which extends past trends into the future. When past regularities and patterns have been rather persistent, this method can be used with some confidence. But the past data and that projected must be significant, accurate, and generally available. For example, if one plots on a chart data over a long time period about such matters as aircraft speed, engine thrust, lumens per watt, or engineering yield strength of materials, fairly accurate forecasts of developments may be made for reasonable distances into the future. In some areas of technology this method has produced very acceptable results. (Isenson, Chapter 16, in Steiner and Cannon, 1966; for a mathematical method to extrapolate technology trends, see Floyd, 1967.)

Other technology forecasts can be made with better assurance of success when correlation methods are applied. When a controlling factor can be found, prediction may be rather easy when the current situation of that factor is found. For example, it is not difficult to predict future speeds of commercial transports when speeds of today's military aircraft are known. The invention of the first steam engine pointed clearly to the development of the steamship and the steam locomotive. Increasing strength of materials will determine the future height of buildings and maximum bridge span. In order for this method to be useful there must be at least one significant function which now exists or can be predicted with reasonable certainty.

An extension of this technique is that of simulation. This method makes forecasts on the basis of present or discernible future events in subordinate functions of the principal technology the subject of the forecast. For example, the use of credit cards to buy merchandise and have the cost debited to the purchaser's bank account at the moment of purchase is easy to predict. Credit cards are now in widespread use, and the use is growing. The day of time-sharing computers is here and the technique will expand. A number of other technologies needed for the success of this system are either here or readily perceived in the near future. Thus, it is comparatively easy to apply these developments in future situations and simulate their uses.

A final technique is that of informed judgment. There are, of course, many variations which are possible in using this very general method. One is the very interesting Delphi Technique. Rather than taking one man's opinion, or using open discussion to reach a consensus, the Delphi method seeks a series of agreements upon the basis of new information inputs. This technique, in the words of its inventors, "eliminates committee activity altogether, thus . . . reducing the influence of certain psychological factors, such as specious persuasion, the unwillingness to abandon publicly expressed opinions, and the bandwagon effect of majority opinion. This technique replaces direct debate by a carefully designed program of sequential individual interrogations (best conducted by questionnaires) interspersed with information and opinion feedback derived by computed consensus from the earlier parts of the program. Some of the questions directed to the respondents may, for instance, inquire into the 'reasons' for previously expressed opinions, and a collection of such reasons may then be presented to each respondent in the group, together with an invitation to reconsider and possibly revise his earlier estimates. Both the inquiry into the reasons and subsequent feedback of the reasons adduced by others may serve to stimulate the experts into taking into due account considerations they might through inadvertence have neglected, and to give due weight to factors they were inclined to dismiss as unimportant on first thought." (Helmer and Rescher, 1959, p. 47; and Dalkey and Helmer, 1963). An informative and useful application of this technique in forecasting a wide range of new developments into the 21st century was made by Gordon and Helmer (1964). The Thompson Ramo Wooldridge Company is now using a variation of this method (called Probe) to project new technical developments in areas of interest to the Company in the next twenty years.

APPLICABILITY OF FORECASTING METHODS. These methods have different degrees of applicability, depending upon the level of causality considered and the degree of specificity sought. In Table 2-7 the methods are rated as to value of results for three dimensions. The evaluations obviously are judgmental and degrees of utility will vary for technology details within each of the levels of causality.

The value of the different techniques depends much upon whether the strengths of the technique can be applied. For example, if a critical lead technology now exists, a correlation technique can be accurate. Generally, however, over a wide range of technological developments informed judgment (Delphi) probably over-all is the best technique. Of course, none of the techniques ought to exclude some variation of informed judgment and intuition.

REQUIREMENTS FOR A "GOOD" TECHNOLOGICAL FORECAST. In a basic sense, those criteria for a useful technological forecast are much like those of a standard sales forecast. But there are enough differences to warrant their identification here. One writer designates them as follows:

"a. The forecast must cover all significant fields of technology affecting the future of the organization using it.

b. The forecast is specifically directed toward the technical problems confronting the organization using it.

c. The projections and interpretation are free from bias introduced through justifications of previous decisions, defense of current activities, or blindness to alternative technical possibilities.

d. The projections are expressed in quantitative terms using a figure of merit, time scale, and if possible, the level of confidence of the estimate.

e. The forecast is terminologically valid to the professional and gives clear implications in the language of the operational executive.

f. The forecast is constantly under review and revision to reflect changing technology and the improvement of forecasting technique.

g. The language of the forecast is common with that of technical and operational plans.

h. The projections and interpretation reflect the technovative organization's considered professional judgment.

i. The forecast covers a time period sufficiently long to include normal lead time for exploitation of changes in technical capability, permit adequate response time for the organization, and permit sufficient reexamination to build confidence to a level for decisions with minimum achievable uncertainty.

j. The forecast is considered to be and is used as a crucial, separate part of the organization's planning process.

k. The forecast is confidentially prepared and protected in order that the organization may evaluate all information from whatever source with ruthless objectivity, and can communicate it unambiguously throughout the organization" (Sweezy, 1966, p. 28).

Table 22-7   Rating of Technological Forecasting Methods

Purpose and Method	Break Through	Demand Pull	Economic and Social Consequences
Rough Estimate of Happenings			
optimism	P	P	P
extrapolation	P	G	P
correlation	P	G	G
simulation	P	G	G
informed judgment (Delphi)	F	G	G
Time and capability specification			
optimism	P	P	P
correlation	P	G	G
extrapolation	P	P	P
simulation	P	G	G
informed judgment (Delphi)	F	G	G

RESULTS: G—Good   F—Fair   P—Poor

SUMMARY AND CONCLUSIONS

This chapter included data about the phenomenal growth of R&D in the U.S. and its concentration in different industries. The nature and spectrum of R&D was described to explain why there cannot be one but must be different approaches to R&D planning. The relationship of a comprehensive corporate planning program to R&D planning was discussed, and different R&D planning profiles among companies and industries were presented. Basic organizational patterns for R&D were presented, the question of how much the R&D budget should be was considered, and the nature and methods of forecasting technology were examined.

Among the more important conclusions and guidelines for improving R&D management planning are the following:

First, R&D is a many-faceted phrase and the problems of planning for it vary depending upon which aspect of the subject is treated.

Second, advancing technology makes it imperative that every business become more concerned about planning an R&D program at a higher level than it did in the past. This does not mean, of course, that every business must allocate dollars to R&D, but it means that all should at least be aware of it more than in the past.

Third, the best basis for R&D planning is in an over-all comprehensive planning framework. The fundamental rules governing the best use of this system also apply to R&D planning.

Fourth, the best R&D program starts with a clear statement of company objectives, strategies, and policies. These provide an effective guideline for all R&D planning with the possible exception of a very small amount of basic research, although even in this case the objectives and interests of the company may be used as guidelines.

Fifth, top management involvement in choosing R&D programs is important whether or not it considers itself technically qualified.

Sixth, best results follow in development when there is a proper blend of activity among R&D, engineering, marketing, and finance personnel. This is not only possible but it is a responsibility of management to see it takes place.

Seventh, R&D planning must be flexible to deal with the different phases of the program. A scientist in doing basic research may be guided by few if any plans, but as R&D moves closer to development and production, planning specifications and targets must be finer and adhered to more rigorously.

Eighth, there is no single best method for evaluating R&D projects, nor is there a single best organizational arrangement for the activity.

Ninth, there is no single answer to how much a company should allocate to R&D, although there are a number of considerations which can help a top management decide what the totals should be.

Tenth, technological forecasting is feasible within limits and there are many different methods available for companies that need to make such forecasts.

23
Planning
in Other Functional
Areas

23
Planning
in Other Functional
Areas

INTRODUCTION

Planning problems, practices, and principles in the five major functional areas were discussed in the previous chapters. Depending upon the company and its needs, long-range plans may be required in a number of other functional areas. The purpose of the present chapter is to identify these other areas and to make a few comments about the topics of planning which they may address.

The skimpy treatment given these areas in this chapter (except for planning in the international area, which is more detailed than the others) is clearly no measure of importance. Rather, it is recognition of the fact that this book cannot contain all that is pertinent to corporate planning. Furthermore, once the subject matter of planning in an area is identified, the general way to proceed in planning in it has been amply described in previous chapters.

INTERNATIONAL PLANNING

With the help of the Institut Européen d'Administration des Affaires, I conducted, in the fall of 1965, a five-day conference at the Palais de Fontainebleau, France, which dealt with multinational corporate planning. From the deliberations of this conference, at which were present corporate planners and officers of the largest multinational corporations of the world, it was concluded that the fundamental principles, practices, processes, and structures discussed in this book apply equally to a company's national and international planning. However, the conclusion was also reached that very important dissimilarities exist between the two. (Steiner and Cannon, 1966.) A few of the primary areas of difference are noted in the following discussion.

THE INTERNATIONAL COMPANY. A major determinant of the nature and scope of international planning will be, of course, the degree of commitment and point of view of management about worldwide opportunities. A company that is toe-deep in international markets with a few exports of domestically-produced products adds a minor dimension to its domestic activities, including planning. But when a company has vast investments around the world and engages in global thinking about their disposition, the nature and scope of its planning is very different. Such companies think in terms of worldwide alternatives open to them. This means, for example, that decisions about the investment of company funds, deployment of key personnel, location of production facilities, marketing strategies, and organization will be determined or importantly influenced by the comparative worldwide competitive advantages to the company.

One important change resulting from this type of thinking is that company headquarters should be organized "so that the entire upper-management echelon will (a) be exposed to and become skilled in international management problems, and (b) retain in its hands full responsibility for strategic planning and decision making, regardless of national or other geographic boundaries." (Clee and Di-Scipio, 1959.) *

THE FEDERATIVE PRINCIPLE. A secret of successful management of international companies lies in the simple principle: centralize responsibility for strategic planning and decentralize responsibility for local planning and operations. Successful overseas operations are most usually those which are oriented to local conditions; the unsuccessful ones are those which seek to run foreign operations from the U.S. As one executive commented, "You can't run a day-to-day business with a 13,000-mile umbilicus." (Pierotti, 1967, p. 57.) This is not to say, of course, that American managerial methods and techniques are not transferable to foreign lands. They are. But it does mean there must be important modifications to fit local conditions. A variety of dissimilarities with domestic planning stems from this necessity.

Large successful multinational companies have adopted the federative principle in their planning. The great Philips Company of the Netherlands, for example, has been very successful thanks in part to the adoption of this principle. In practice the principle has three aspects: (1) considerably autonomous national

---

* For the same view see also John J. Beauvois, "Internationalism: A New Concept for U.S. Business," *California Management Review*, Vol. 2, No. 2 (Winter 1960), pp. 28-37; and John Fayerweather, "LRP For International Operations," *California Management Review*, Vol. 3, No. 1 (Fall 1960), pp. 23-35.

organizations bound into the "World Federation of Philips Organizations," (2) product divisions at company headquarters in Eindhoven which determine broad lines of worldwide policy for product families, and (3) a Board of Management which issues general lines of policy and strategy that serve as flexible guides to both national organizations and to product divisions. (Steiner and Cannon, 1966, p. 101.) National plans are reviewed at central headquarters for their relationship to established policies and other national plans, and then are approved for operations. National organizations have heavy planning responsibilities. It is their job, for example, to develop the entire marketing operation over the full breadth of the company's product range under their management. This style is also typical of many American companies with far-flung and important international operations, such as H. J. Heinz, Union Carbide, Celanese, and Singer, to name but a few.

There are many illustrations of the need for adaptation to local conditions. Sears Roebuck and Co., for example, encountered great difficulties in Spain when it tried to merchandise under its own brand names, because this practice ran counter to the fierce pride Spanish producers take in their own names. In Great Britain, the Betty Crocker brand was introduced in 1959, heavily promoted, and withdrawn in 1963 because it did not fit the buying habits of the British housewife. (Sommers and Kernan, 1967, and Yoshino, 1967.) Heinz pickles made in England satisfy British tastes but are considerably different from the U.S. product, and the same thing is true with other products such as soups. The fact of the matter is, of course, that in different countries there are great variations in all sorts of environmental conditions that have an important bearing upon business success. Attitudes of people, moral values, social conditions, the legal system, politics, education, traditions, and so on, in one way or another may make or break a product or service.*

Philips feels that the federative system offers great advantages over the centralized system in these important ways:
"1. Autonomy stimulates creative thinking.
2. Company activities in a given country are completely integrated into the economy of that country.
3. The company can draw fully on international diversity of talent.
4. Action can be taken quickly and can be adapted to local needs.
5. The disadvantages of central bureaucracy are avoided." (Steiner and Cannon, 1966, p. 102.)

MODE OF ENTRY. Problems differ depending upon the method chosen to get into a foreign market. The usual first contact of a company with a foreign market is through the export of its product. The next logical step is to license a

---

* For a systematic analysis of these factors see Farmer and Richman, 1966.

foreign producer. Local manufacturing then may follow, and later this plant may become a manufacturing site for export to other countries.

A company must make choices about the strategy of its capital investment. At one extreme is licensing a foreign producer without making an investment in his operations; at the other extreme is financing a wholly-owned subsidiary or division. In between are other possibilities such as acquiring an equity position in a foreign company, entering into a joint venture arrangement, or operating on a service or management contract. All these methods have their own particular advantages and disadvantages which planning must consider.

THE DATA BASE. Effective planning, as noted in previous chapters, demands thorough knowledge of markets, technology, social patterns, and many other environmental forces. In the U.S. vast amounts of data exist from which these analyses can be made and on the basis of which risks and uncertainties can be better balanced. The availability of the same type of data is rarely, if ever, found in comparable measure in foreign countries.

NATIONAL AND COMPANY PLANS. In a growing number of countries of the world there are comprehensive long-range plans which govern not only the activities of the government but in one way or another relate to planning done by business within the countries. In some countries, business planning must relate closely to government plans to be eligible for investments, credits, and other needs. An American company in India recently planned for the introduction of an American-produced product but failed to note that the long-range plan of India prohibited the importation of this product because the plan said it had to be made in India.

NATIONAL INTERESTS AND COMPANY INTERESTS. A major planning problem may arise as a result of conflicts between national interests and interests of an international company. A company may wish to attract skilled workers in a country to produce successfully a product planned for the country. In order to attract the workers the company may be willing to offer pay somewhat higher than local standards. To do so, however, may upset wage patterns in the country and create difficult social and economic problems for the country.

Some countries maintain strict laws concerning what may be imported and what must be produced within a country. These laws may run counter to the best allocation of company resources. Monetary regulations of countries also sometimes conflict with local regulations. U.S. antitrust regulations that apply to American companies operating abroad may make it difficult for an American company when it is faced with monopoly power permitted by a foreign country.

While there are many areas of conflict, there are also areas of common purpose. An American company serving its own economic purposes in an underdeveloped country may also raise the entire standard of living of that country. (Lilienthal, 1960.) I stated elsewhere that multinational corporations, "In their search for markets, reduced production costs, competent management, and other opportunities for profit, . . . are capable of spreading the great productive benefits of the more technically advanced businesses of the world much more widely. They can, therefore, raise the worldwide level of economic well-being importantly." (Steiner and Cannon, 1966, p. 4.)

FINANCIAL PLANNING. Recent publicized problems of the U.S. with its balance of payments deficit have brought home the complicated financial problems which affect international business operations. Controls over direct foreign investments by American companies, regulations associated with income of foreign activities, curbs on overseas lending, complications arising from devaluation of foreign currencies, and exchange regulations of foreign countries, create problems and opportunities which generally do not affect planning of activities in the U.S.

OTHER PLANNING PROBLEM AREAS. Other problems that differ much from domestic planning issues include managerial training for overseas assignment; choosing and training local managers; integrating accounting systems; determining the degrees and methods of transferring U.S. know-how, both managerial and technical; and establishing the degrees and areas of local managerial authority. Each of these, as with the issues discussed above, can be subdivided into many different problems for the planner.

CONCLUSION. This is a brief sketch of the great complications in international planning and the areas of important dissimilarity with corporate planning of purely national companies. Although these are very important it still is correct to say that the fundamental principles, practices, and methods of corporate planning presented in this book are as applicable to international as to domestic planning.

MANUFACTURING PLANNING

This is such an important subject that it would be easy to justify a chapter devoted exclusively to it. I have not done so, however, simply because it would duplicate much that has been said previously. In previous chapters there are many references to the interrelationships among major functional areas of which manufacturing is one. Furthermore, any extensive penetration of manufacturing planning quickly gets deeply involved in minute planning details that are not of as much interest to top managements in most companies as broader objectives, policies, and strategies which give guidance to detailed manufacturing planning. So, at this point it seems enough to describe the scope and subject matter of manufacturing planning.

The manufacturing executive should have three major responsibilities in the long-range planning process, as follows: (1) to appraise his present position and state trends within his industry with respect to subjects which are his responsibility; (2) to work with other functional managers, especially marketing, finance, and research and development, on the feasibility of plans as seen from the manufacturing manager's point of view; and (3) to prepare a detailed plan for all his major activities, in as much detail as required and with as close interrelationships with other company activities as needed, to make sure the objectives, policies, and strategies of the top management are met. (Payne, 1963, pp. 177-178.)

In no particular order of importance, the following could be included among the major areas of concern to a manufacturing manager:

Tooling and other production equipment
Plant facilities and plant location
Personnel
Production planning and control
Maintenance
Health and safety of employees
Manufacturing research and development engineering
Industrial waste control
Manufacturing organization

Other items that might be mentioned, such as cost control and quality control, are subsumed under several of the above categories.

A major area of activity not dealt with previously concerns production planning and control. It may be useful, therefore, to mention a number of possible elements which are incorporated in planning in this area, as follows:

Planning and control systems for production, fabrication, subassembly, assembly, final assembly, functional test, and checkout
Scheduling of material, parts, and components purchases
Subcontracting relationships and schedules
Quality control
Cost control
Inventory planning and control
Conversion to automatic numerical controls
Interrelating production planning and control with other functions of manufacturing and other company activities

In each of these areas, of course, many subdivisions are obvious.

Most of these subjects are important elements of the comprehensive plan in its major parts—strategic, medium-range programming, and short-range. Details about planning in this area beyond what has been said previously are beyond the scope of this book.

STAFF DEPARTMENT PLANS

All companies of any size have staff services, and in larger companies these are organized into staff departments or divisions. In large divisionalized companies, staff groups and/or departments exist at both headquarters and in the divisions. "Staff" refers to a group which is not charged with the responsibility for the primary activities of a business. The accounting personnel, for example, are engaged in service activities and are staff to line groups which turn out the primary products or services of a company. Such staff groups, or general office functional executives, advise and assist the president and other line managers with respect to their functional areas. These groups frequently have "functional" authority over other groups. By functional authority is meant power which a staff manager has over process, practices, policies, and other matters in departments other than his own. This functional authority, of course, is limited to the area of responsibility of the functional manager, but it also often applies throughout a company, at headquarters as well as among divisions. Thus, the chief accounting officer of a company will have functional authority over accounting matters throughout the corporation. This authority can be exercised by line or service departments, depending upon the responsibilities they possess. A customer service department, for example, may be given functional authority among different divisions in matters pertaining to specific types of customer services.

Functional executives are responsible in their areas for developing policies, recommending policies to the president, providing guidance to other departments, assuring proper coordination with other company activities, and reviewing company actions in or affecting their functional areas. There are many variations in the degree of authority of these groups, both with respect to activity and type of company.

All groups having staff and/or functional authority should have long-range plans that fit into the over-all comprehensive plans of a company. The degree of fit, in many cases, need not be tight, and each area should work out the relationship on the basis of experience. For instance, most of the contents of a legal plan need not be intimately integrated with other plans. But if a company is anticipating difficult problems ahead which will have a bearing on many activities of the firm, there should be some association of these legal threats with planned activities in other areas. On the other hand, employee recruitment and retirement plans should be more closely related to production plans.

Plans in staff and functional areas should be developed on the basis of some acceptable table of contents and cover the major programs in the area. One com-

pany requests its functional areas to develop long-range plans on the basis of
the following outline:
- Briefly describe the activities covered in the function.
- Specify the objectives sought for the function and major activities.
- Assess current posture by making an analysis for the function and activity
  of strengths and weaknesses to achieve objectives, and in relation to the
  posture of competitors.
- Describe special functional opportunities, problems, and threats.
- Set forth the strategy to achieve objectives, to exploit opportunities, to
  solve problems, and to avoid threats.
- Lay out the programs or tactical activities required to carry out strategies.

There seems little need to examine in depth the many possible functional
staff plans. So, this chapter will conclude with selected comments about the nature
of the activities in major functional staff areas which might, depending upon company interests and problems, be the subject of long-range plans.

PERSONNEL FUNCTIONAL PLANNING.   The personnel function's
elevation to a high position at the corporate level is of relatively recent origin.
Historically, the personnel department developed as a record-keeping department
which maintained data on workers, such as date hired, jobs held in the company,
wages paid, and so on. In the 1920's, businesses assumed a growing number of
services for employees to offset, in a more or less paternalistic fashion, the growing strength of trade unions, and also in response to union demands. During the
1930's, the work of personnel departments expanded to include negotiation with
trade unions and direct dealing with employees in working out problems between
them and the company. While this change was the result of rising union strength,
there was also behind it a growing awareness of the importance of human relations. Following World War II, and continuing up to the present time, personnel
departments have expanded their responsibilities in response to a number of other
important trends.

There is today among more and more companies a recognition of the great
importance of people to a business. There is a recognition, for example, that the
greatest competitive advantage of a company in the long run is the competence
of its people. At the same time there is a growing demand by people in organizations for greater satisfaction from their work experience. This is especially true of
managerial and skilled technical personnel. For these and many more reasons,
personnel departments are assuming more and more functions.

Among the major functions which may be found in the personnel (or industrial, or employee, relations) department of a large company are:

Recruitment and placement
Communications, including company newspaper

Wage and salary administration

Employee benefit programs, including insurance, pensions, and savings and
credit plans

Training services and management development

Labor relations and union negotiations

Special services, including:

Medical

Safety and fire protection

Recreation, restaurant, etc.

Counseling

Conceivably, long-range plans may be desirable in all these areas. To illustrate, plans concerning management might include:

Schedule of needs for managers at all levels. This would be derivative from
plans of the company for production, research, etc., and from estimates of
retirements, promotions, and resignations from the company.

Inventory of skills, potential, and job competence of present executives.

Strategies and programs to fill the gaps, e.g.:

Training of managers through rotation, schools of the companies and universities, broadening assignments, understudy programs, etc.

Financial support to managers to improve their education.

Recruitment from outside through acquisition and direct hiring.

A number of large companies have well-developed long-range management
plans. The Personnel Planning Division of the Royal Dutch Petroleum Company,
and Shell Transport and Trading Company, Ltd., for example, is concerned with
long-range plans for some 9,000 middle and upper managers. It makes detailed
plans concerning jobs, and candidates to fill them, for time periods up to 15 years.
For instance, its estimates of need are made 15 years ahead because it feels that
is the average time required to develop a promising recruit into a manager. Individual career plans are made for seven-year periods, and some other types of plans
for lesser spans.

A Los Angeles bank has developed a network program for selecting and
determining the appropriate training for personnel to fill needed jobs in the
future. This program identifies potential jobs to be filled, the responsibilities to
be assumed, and the training and job sequences in the bank which would best
qualify a manager for the posts. The program then searches present personnel
files which are on computer memories, identifies a number of potential candidates, and lays out the job path which each should follow to fill the new posts to
be vacant some years hence. This program, of course, is not automatic because
naturally it permits managers to choose candidates to be trained for new jobs and
also, naturally, depends on the acquiescence of the manager to be trained.

The objectives, strategy, and detailed plans for technical personnel, and for
hourly employees, would differ from those for general managers. For example, a

problem in highly technically-oriented companies is to forecast the precise types of new technologies which will be important to the company and, upon that basis, lay plans both for getting this expertise and determining implications for new products and services. Also, to illustrate further, the kinds of training, upgrading, and personal improvement programs undertaken for hourly employees would be somewhat different than for scientists, engineers, and general managers.

MANUFACTURING STAFF PLANNING. There are many companies, and the number is growing, that have established manufacturing staffs at central headquarters. These units do not manufacture anything but, rather, see that various production-oriented services are performed, and bring to the company-wide manufacturing process knowledge, especially in planning and control, that will improve the company's actual manufacturing programs. Following are some of the functions performed by vice presidents of manufacturing:

Lay out policies and procedures for the corporate-wide development of manufacturing plans in conjunction with the corporate planning department.

Establish objectives, policies, and strategies for a wide variety of activities, such as material purchases, inventories, manufacturing facilities, and the production process.

Stimulate the development among the divisions of newer techniques to improve the production process, such as the use of automatic numerical controls.

Develop standards for measuring performance in major manufacturing elements, such as use of facility capacity, quality control, cost control, tool replacement, and maintenance.

Advise the divisions on manufacturing and engineering matters, including new methods of planning and control.

Evaluate the performance of manufacturing employees.

Serve as the company's principal manufacturing representative in industry, community, and governmental activities.

Provide technical advice to divisions.

Stimulate and coordinate technology transfer among the divisions and between the company and outside sources.

Improve the manufacturing information systems.

Review, evaluate, and aggregate the company's facility requirements and make recommendations for approval to top management.

Review and evaluate all manufacturing plans and make recommendations to top management concerning their implementation.

Develop policies for the company's air and water pollution abatement program.

Again, this list is not exhaustive but it does, I think, illustrate the type of activity of manufacturing staff groups.

Top management, especially in the larger companies, wants to plan and control production on a broad aggregate basis. The combined activities of a comprehensive corporate planning program, together with the use of expertise such as that found in manufacturing staff, is very helpful in doing this. New techniques are also being developed to facilitate top management's dealing with production on an aggregative basis which eliminates details of individual products and facilities (Buffa, 1967).

All these subjects, of course, can be the subject of plans, long and short. Precisely what should be done is determined by the circumstances existing in each company at a particular point in time. Details must be omitted here, for the purpose of this section is to suggest and not to define.

ORGANIZATION PLANNING. The objective of organizational planning should be, of course, to determine the types of organization for a company that will be best to permit it to achieve its objectives efficiently and effectively. This is an important objective to be met because ill-conceived or unplanned organizational structures can play havoc with people and efficient operations. It is not sensible to prepare an organization for a business and assume that, although unchanged, it will serve well over a period of time. A business is a dynamic living thing and changes taking place within it necessitate reorganization. Furthermore, new developments are constantly appearing in organizational arrangements that an alert top management recognizes and uses.

There are several dimensions to organization planning. One is the relationship between plans in functional areas and organization. Another is planning to implement organizational change.

In the first area the problems and issues may be illustrated in the following way. If the plans of a major division materialize, should the new business developments be split off and a new division formed? If so, when should this be done? Where should it be located? Who should manage it? Or, conversely, as new products are developed in different divisions, and new acquisitions are made, should there be any transfers of products among divisions or consolidations of divisions? If a company is centralized, should it be decentralized? If a company is divisionalized, what should the relationships be between headquarters and the divisions? If a company wishes to move into foreign operations, what should the form of organization be in foreign operations? As foreign operations increase in volume, should there be any organizational changes at the home office, such as elevating the head of a foreign division to a vice presidency and giving him functional authority in all divisions having exports?

Once decisions are made about organization structures, careful planning is required to introduce changes. Two students of organization have pointed out: "The best designed plan cannot make its own way. Approval at the top does not insure its successful penetration throughout the organization. Whether the detailed changes are eventually introduced depends on the skill and drive with which the implementation of the plan is carried out. Implementation is the pay-off in every program of change. Astute diagnosis, imaginative planning, skillful presentation are desirable—in fact, necessary—if the plan is to succeed. But they are not sufficient. Crucially important are the actions that top management takes to alter and adjust their own attitudes and practices, and to help others to adjust theirs, so as to buttress and support the multiple changes engendered by the plan." (Ginzberg and Reilley, 1967, pp. vii-viii.) A poorly timed plan for an organizational change, for instance, can create chaos in its execution. Any important organizational change will have an impact on people and their psychological reactions must be considered carefully.

There are also many other elements which are important in effecting organizational change in an optimum manner. This is not the place to consider them, but it should be noted here that organizational planning is related to structure and institutional order as well as to the manner in which change is brought about.

PUBLIC RELATIONS PLANNING. A growing number of companies are creating public relations staffs. In some companies these are subordinated to the marketing or personnel manager, but in more companies these staffs are not adjuncts to other functions. They are separate groups with corporate-wide responsibilities. The functions of public relations staffs vary, of course, but the definition of their functions which is contained in Webster's *New Collegiate Dictionary* is acceptable. It is: "The activities of an industry, union, corporation, profession, government, or other organization in building and maintaining sound and productive relations with special publics such as customers, employees, or stockholders, and with the public at large, so as to adapt itself to its environment and interpret itself to society."

A public relations officer has three important connections with comprehensive corporate planning. First, he should bring to the process an understanding of the public's needs, desires, interests, opinions, etc., about important actions contemplated by his company. Second, he should participate in the decision-making process, so far as his expertise and judgment make appropriate, so that he can properly interpret past, current, and proposed actions of the company. Finally, he should have his own plans for his own activities.

As noted in previous chapters, the larger a company becomes, the more "publics" have an interest in it. One major reason, of course, is that its power has a deeper potential impact on more people. It becomes most important, therefore, for it to understand potential impacts of its actions on those who have an interest in it so that it can conduct its actions accordingly. Richard Eells points out that there are two main purposes of public relations. First is to relate the corporation to its social environment, both by assuring that messages from a company's publics are heard and proper responses are developed. Second is to assure that the company's underlying objectives are formulated into realistic public relations terms and that they contribute to the development of a desired image. (Eells,

1959.) To do this, of course, public relations can be no mere appendage to some other function in a company. It must be a major function.

Public relations departments in large companies have a wide scope of functions, including the following, most of which deserve to be the subject of long-range planning:

Conduct research on and report public reactions and attitudes to and about the company.

Prepare public speeches, articles, and statements for company executives and determine programs of such activities and documents to best enhance company objectives.

Manage consumer, dealer, and company publications.

Develop policies, strategies, and plans for communications with all the company's publics.

Arrange company shows, exhibitions, and moving pictures for educational and publicity purposes.

Develop policies, strategies, and plans to assure proper relationships with government, community, and civic organizations, and represent the company in dealings with these institutions where appropriate.

Develop research programs as a basis for advising company officials about proper positions on legislation and public affairs issues affecting the interests of the company.

Advise, assist, and concur in the selection of managers having posts with important public associations.

Exercise functional authority over public relations activities throughout all departments of the company.

Advise top management concerning, and administer, the philanthropic programs of the company.

It seems obvious that some of the above functions can have a profound impact on company activities, good and bad, depending upon how they are performed, for public relations activities can indirectly influence customers, legislators, employees, and investors. The development of one type of public image can serve to lift a company's price/earnings ratio, a great asset if the company is acquisition-minded. The public relations department that prevents a chief executive from saying the wrong thing at the wrong time and successfully gets him to say the right thing at the right time can be worth much. Proper public relations planning will help a company to achieve its tangible aims and may be one of the strongest methods to help it achieve its intangible aims.

ACCOUNTING FUNCTIONAL PLANS. A good bit has been said in previous chapters about plans for, or involving, accounting. But these were directly related to the development of comprehensive company plans. Depending upon circumstances, a company may wish to develop functional accounting plans which may or may not directly relate to the comprehensive planning process. For instance, the accounting staff may lay plans for the introduction of computers in its accounting system. This may not be of concern at all to the general corporate planning process except possibly for its impact on finance. But it will have deep impact on the accounting system—people, organization, information flows, and practices. The chief accountants and finance officers of insurance companies, for instance, have gone through this planning exercise and can attest to its importance.

Accounting staffs are responsible for an important branch of the total information system of a company and may want to lay plans for improving the system and making it of more use to management in its decision-making. For instance, the staff may lay plans for developing accounting simulation models to help management.

Because of the great changes taking place in business accounting, a company may want to make plans for retraining its accountants and take advantage of new knowledge in this field.

Other topics of accounting functional plans may be accounting organization, functional authority in the accounting organization, new policies concerning such matters as costing capital expenditures, accounting policies to be followed in dealing with changes in foreign currency restrictions and devaluations, or consolidating accounting practices in acquired companies. Here, as elsewhere, a requirement for a long-range functional plan may stimulate the formulation of new imaginative programs.

CORPORATE STAFF PLANNER PLANS. A corporate planning staff in a large company ought also to be obliged to prepare a functional long-range plan for the company's comprehensive planning activities. This probably will not be an elaborate plan but might well include subjects such as the following:

Introduction of computers in the planning process.

Introduction of new decision-making techniques to improve planning and plans.

Changes in the planning procedure and organization as planning evolves and the company grows.

Matching the demand for and supply of particular specialties in the planning process.

As amply demonstrated in this book, the corporate planning process is dynamic and a company that wishes to get the greatest payoff from it must be alert to new developments within the company which will change the system as well as new knowledge that will make the system of greater use to managers. Watching these trends and assuring that the company benefits from them is a job for the corporate planning staff.

PURCHASING AND TRAFFIC FUNCTIONAL PLANNING. Purchasing may be under the headquarters' manufacturing staff unit, and traffic may be placed with marketing, but in some companies staff functional responsibilities in these areas are lodged in a separate central corporate officer. Companies where these functions exist as separate units on the corporate staff have several common characteristics. For example the products of the company come from one common element, such as crude oil. Frequently they are vertically integrated, and their divisions are both customers of and suppliers to other divisions.

The less homogeneous a company's production operations, the more a purchasing unit's activities are associated with the actual management of production. But even among companies with highly decentralized product divisions there may be some central purchasing. Purchasing units may also be involved in company-wide purchasing planning, analysis of purchasing activities, scheduling of purchases, compliance with government regulations concerning purchasing, and dealings with suppliers. If a purchasing unit is set up, it may also have some of the other functions noted above under manufacturing.

A traffic unit is concerned with incoming and outgoing shipments. Here again, this function may be performed in individual product divisions, but in some companies separate staff units exist at headquarters and have a variety of functions, including the following:

Negotiate with common carriers about rates, schedules, and freight classifications.

Represent the company before public utility commissions and regulatory agencies.

Prepare policies and procedures for moving materials into and out of the company.

Administer claims against shippers and from customers.

Assure adequate facilities to meet incoming and outgoing material and product flow schedules. (Stieglitz and Janger, 1965, pp. 95-100.)

OTHER FUNCTIONAL PLANS. There are other functional activities for which functional plans may be developed which may be noted with little elaboration. For instance, many companies have legal staffs who may find challenging the development of a plan for their area. The requirement for a functional plan may perhaps be of importance for a company's treasurer who has responsibilities, among others, for managing a company's stock certificates and other corporate documents. If he happens to be responsible for stockholder relations, with or in place of a public relations officer, plans may be needed in light of future important programmed events affecting their interests. A chief scientist of a company, or a vice-president of engineering, may not only evaluate scientific and engineering plans of the entire company but may also himself be asked to plan ahead for this corporate function.

SUMMARY AND CONCLUSIONS

This chapter discussed the nature and scope of planning and plans among a number of functional areas not previously treated. Where a company has an important international program it will obviously be a focal point for planning. It was pointed out in this chapter that while the basic fundamental principles and practices of planning discussed in this book apply equally to national and international business planning, there are many important dissimilarities in the substance and practice of planning in these two areas. Manufacturing planning was discussed, but not in as great detail as international planning, largely because many major aspects of it were treated in previous chapters. The rest of the chapter concerned planning and plans among separate staff units often found in the headquarters of companies and having company-wide functional authority. Illustrations of the subject matter of plans in the following staff units or departments were presented: personnel, organization, public relations, accounting, planning staff, and purchasing and traffic.

It was concluded that the precise type of planning in these units varied much among companies. It was also concluded that the interrelationship between planning in any area and the comprehensive planning activity varied much depending upon experience, managerial attitudes, and demonstrable value.

PART V

Concluding Observations

24
Concluding Observations: The Current State of the Art and the Future of Comprehensive Corporate Planning

24
Concluding Observations:
The Current State of the Art
and the Future of
Comprehensive
Corporate Planning

INTRODUCTION

Rather than try to pull together the major threads of thought in this book into a summary and conclusions section, this last chapter instead will focus on the questions of where we are now with respect to understanding comprehensive corporate planning, and where we are heading.

THE CURRENT STATE OF THE ART OF
CORPORATE PLANNING

An assessment of the state of the art of corporate planning means an inquiry into the status of the theory. At the outset, and before I lose the business practitioner, I want to emphasize that when speaking of a theory of planning the most practicable and powerful ideas for business practice are in mind. Frequently, when businessmen speak of theory they mean what is irrelevant to them, or what is so theoretical as to be valueless to them in practice. Actually, a better theory of planning has immense value to the man who is planning. One of the characteristics I have found in most managers is their willingness to use better knowledge when it can be of help to them. This means understanding and appreciation of theory. There is no more practical thing than a good theory.

THE NATURE OF A THEORY OF PLANNING. Once again a semantic problem arises, for there is no generally accepted definition of a theory. A theory can cover a wide variety of things. For instance, in the words of the dictionary it can be contemplation, or speculation; hypotheses; a general or abstract body of facts and principles, such as the theory of medicine; more or less plausible or scientifically acceptable general principles offered to explain phenomena, for example, the theory of demand and supply, or the theory of organizational behavior; or a body of theorems, principles, and laws, presenting a rounded systematic view of a subject, such as the theory of foreign exchange or the theory of relativity.

When the words "theory of planning" are used here, what is in mind is an accumulation of truths, principles, and laws, that comprehensively, reasonably clearly and accurately relate phenomena within the area of planning. Included are the general conceptual models used in planning, identification of major interrelationships among phenomena, classification of knowledge, the tools of the trade, and, perhaps, the relationship of knowledge to need.

This is an aggregate body of theory that has a number of characteristics. First, it should have a set of principles and laws with broad applicability. Second, these should have predictive value. Third, the detailed theories should be tested and found to be valid. Fourth, the theory must explain and describe the phenomenon of planning in total and in its parts. Fifth, it must be useful in actual practice. Sixth, the theory must organize effectively and classify properly the relevant knowledge and experience. Finally, it should give direction to research and teaching of the subject.

Before assessing the state of corporate planning theory today, some comments are needed about the nature of parts of the theory, particularly hypotheses, principles, and laws. Here again, the expressions are ambiguous. Generally, an hypothesis is an untested proposition. Frequently used synonymously with an hypothesis are theory, principle, generalization, and laws. When used in this way they are propositions that have been tested by the finding that they permit predictions to be made within reasonable degrees of accuracy. The only true test of the validity of an hypothesis, a principle, or a law, is to compare predictions with experience. Therefore, to ask the question: do we have a theory of planning, is to ask: do we have propositions that enable us to make predictions? (Weston, 1955.) From a pragmatic point of view, when inquiry is made into the state of theory of planning today, the issue is really whether there exists a body of guidance which helps a businessman improve his planning, and helps a student of business to understand better what is and what should be going on in this area.

There is another matter of importance, however, that concerns the precision of the predictions that can be made. Obviously, the greater the accuracy of predictions, and the fewer the exceptions, the more powerful is the theory. Furthermore, the more simply the theory can be stated, the wider its applicability; and the greater its predictability qualities, the more powerful it is. (Friedman, 1953.)

Theories are built by observation and contemplation of what is important. Carl Alsberg's wise comment comes to mind, namely, "If, in the social sciences and especially economics, more attention were devoted to the recording of what seem important facts and to the analysis of their significance, I am confident we should not need to worry about theory." (In Davis, 1948, pp. 139-140.) What he means, of course, is that theory that is valuable will follow from careful observation and analysis. Former Dean Donham of the Harvard School of Business elaborates on this point in the lead article of the first volume of the *Harvard Business Review*, as follows:

"The task of developing business theory scientifically is first, the recording of facts; second, the arrangement of these facts into series and relationships; third, the development of generalizations which can be safely made only upon the basis of such recorded facts. Except in so far as this method is applied consciously on a large scale, the generalizations of business will be largely hypotheses more or less fantastic in their nature, and the executive must often gamble with his most important problems." (Donham, 1922, p. 10.)

Before an assessment of planning theory, I want to comment on the meaning of the word principle. In this book this word has been generally avoided in preference to guidelines, actions required, or lessons of experience. This was done only because there is a widespread misconception of the meaning of the word principle as used in the social sciences in general and in management in particular. A principle is widely considered to be something of an immutable law that always works and has no exceptions. It is the incontrovertible law of the physical scientist that is so often in mind.

What should be pointed out is that there is a range of immutability in conceiving of a principle, both in the physical and in the social sciences. Furthermore, for many reasons, laws and principles can be accepted in the social sciences as being powerful even though there are exceptions. Considerable ambiguity is and must be tolerated in the social sciences.

These points deserve illustration. At one extreme, a principle can assert an invariable relationship among phenomena, amounting to a law, such as excessive inventory will reduce profits in the long run, or large organizations cannot function efficiently without specialization of labor. At the other extreme, a principle may be considered an hypothesis which has been partly tested in practice and has exceptions, such as the wider in scope a plan is, the more participation there should be in its preparation to assure acceptance and implementation. In between, are other propositions that have been tested in varying degrees and have different predictive certainties.

In the social sciences exceptions can be found in principles or laws and they still may be accepted as having useful predictive value. Helmer and Rescher point out (1958, p. 12): "In order for a law in the inexact sciences to be valid, it is only necessary that, if an apparent exception should occur, an adequate explanation be forthcoming, an explanation demonstrating the exceptional characteristics of the case in hand by establishing the violation of an appropriate (if hitherto unformulated) condition of the law's applicability."

This is a looseness which makes the rigorous-minded uncomfortable. But it is a looseness which is not due to slipshod workmanship or misunderstanding of the facts. Rather, it is a reflection of the inherent complexities in the social sciences. I think the words of Alfred Marshall (1890), the great neoclassical economist, deserve to be recalled to support further this very important point. He said:

"The laws of economics are to be compared with the laws of the tides, rather than with the simple and exact law of gravitation. For the actions of men are so various and uncertain, that the best statement of tendencies, which we can make in a science of human conduct, must needs be inexact and faulty. This might be urged as a reason against making any statements at all on the subject; but that would be almost to abandon life. Life is human conduct, and the thoughts and emotions that grow up around it. By the fundamental impulses of our nature we all—high and low, learned and unlearned—are in our several degrees constantly striving to understand the courses of human action, and to shape them for our purposes, whether selfish or unselfish, whether noble or ignoble. And since we *must* form to ourselves some notions of the tendencies of human action, our choice is between forming those notions carelessly and forming them carefully. The harder the task, the greater the need for steady patient inquiry; for turning to account the experience, that has been reaped by the more advanced physical sciences; and for framing as best we can well thought-out estimates, or provisional laws, of the tendencies of human action."

This does not mean, of course, that efforts in business planning or in economics should not be made to find those laws and principles that can be rigorously stated and never be subject to exception. But, because of the nature of business planning, it would be hopeless to try to erect a structure as complete, esthetically and logically structured, and as simple, as the exact theory of the physical sciences.

AN ASSESSMENT OF THE STATE OF THE ART OF PLANNING. "It is scarcely too much to say," says Talcott Parsons, "that the most important single index of the state of maturity of a science is the state of its systematic theory." (Parsons, 1954, p. 212.) As noted above, important components of a theory are the conceptual schemes to tie together the main parts of the discipline, logical interrelationships among parts, classification of the tools, and the number and power of principles and laws. Where does the theory of comprehensive corporate planning stand in these areas?

As noted in this book there are emerging basic conceptual models of corporate planning and its parts which have been tested in practice and found applicable and valuable. The main broad conceptual framework, I think, does exist, but it needs to be more generally understood and refined.

The integration of elements of planning and their classification into a logical order has progressed remarkably rapidly in the past decade. As given in this book they do provide a good description of how corporate planning is and should be done. Many hypotheses concerning interrelationships have been tested. The classification framework does provide a place to hang old and new facts related to the system. In some parts of the theory the description of the interdependent parts has advanced rapidly in recent years and is today excellent—for instance, in business policies, or controlling the life cycle in an advanced technologically oriented product development. In other areas, classification is acceptable but interrelationships are still inadequately identified, as, for instance, in relating R&D to long-range objectives. In some cases both classification and interrelationships are not well perfected, as, for instance, the social responsibilities of business.

Rapid progress has been made in the development of principles and "laws" to guide both practice and to further research. The going has been rough, however, because every organization is unique. Each has its own customs, mores, ways of doing things, and value systems. Yet, underneath, it is becoming clearer that there are fundamental planning generalizations, or principles, which apply to all organizations.

There have been a number of these principles discovered about the planning process which this book has sought to identify and describe. But there are also two facts which are clear. Those that have been discovered are only a small part of the total body of theory which is needed. And, those which have been discovered need to be more rigorously defined and narrowed so as to be more prescriptive. For example, it is clear and can be taken as a "law" that without top management support of corporate planning the corporate planning process will fail. This is a most important guide to action and is a principle with predictable value. But what is needed beyond this is a series of guidelines which will prescribe in much more detail precisely what support means and what will be the consequences of its absence (Dale, 1959).

In many areas of planning there do exist principles and practices which, together, constitute the basis upon which fast strides should be made in the future in building a stronger theory and better practice. Great advances, for instance, have been made in the theory of quantitative methods in business planning. The theory of forecasting is growing stronger. In these and other disciplines associated with planning, research has identified many new guides to practice, but much testing is needed before they can be considered operational. (Haire, 1964.)

There are undoubtedly practices today which are successful but which will disappear in the future. Some of the cherished guidelines in present-day theory will certainly be discarded; some will rise to higher levels of value. In presenting the many lessons of experience, and the tested principles in this book, space simply has not permitted full discussion of all qualifications associated with their application. The danger is that they be taken as scientific laws when they are really only provisional guides to actions and should be used only under certain specified circumstances. This sort of qualification does not mean they are unimportant. They may still contain significant information, ideas, and guidance when all their limitations are recognized. The theory of planning today, however, has not sufficiently sorted out all these considerations.

Turning now to the tools available for business planning it can be concluded that their number and power have increased impressively. Many old tools still have high significance, such as the accounting system, and newer tools, such as the mathematical, have radically eased many formerly perplexing managerial decision problems and made their solutions much more accurate. The planning process is much more scientific in a quantitative sense. But important strides still can and should be made in forging new tools and applying more fully those that now exist.

How about the state of the theory in light of the need? Assessment is difficult here because in some areas theory and technique are probably equal to need, as for instance in inventory replenishment. But at the strategic planning levels both the theory and methodology reveal gaping holes.

In light of the unevenness of the development of planning theory an over-all assessment is difficult. On net balance, however, it seems to me that great strides have been made in the past decade, today's status is contributing importantly to operations, and the total theory and methods are approaching but have not yet reached maturity. Some of the shortcomings to be overcome and gaps to be filled will support this evaluation.

CHALLENGES AHEAD FOR MANAGERS, PLANNERS, AND STUDENTS OF PLANNING

A few competent observers have concluded that U.S. industry is not doing as good a planning job as it knows how to do. Indeed, Marvin Bower (1966, p. 1*) says, ". . . in most companies planning is still underdeveloped as a managing process . . . better planning is still one of the new frontiers of better managing."

There is a double challenge here for managers. First, is to avoid major pitfalls by accepting the guidance of today's knowledge. Second, is to master present and

---

* From *The Will to Manage* by Marvin Bower. Copyright © 1966 by Marvin Bower. Used by permission of McGraw-Hill Book Company.

evolving planning theory so as to be better prepared to meet the rapid changes of business life which lies ahead.

PITFALLS TO BE AVOIDED. Following are 21 pitfalls that stand out as the more important ones into which some managers have fallen. There are more, but my purpose here is to highlight a few of the major shortcomings of comprehensive corporate planning that my observations, and those of many others, have found in practice. Some of them could be included in several of the following groupings. Since many of them have been the subject of detailed analysis in previous chapters, additional comments will not be made about all of them. For several, however, a few additional remarks are fitting.

A. Pitfalls in Getting Started:
1. Top management's assumption that it can delegate the planning function to a planner.
2. Rejecting planning because there has been success without it.
3. Assuming that the present body of knowledge about planning is insufficient to guide fruitful comprehensive planning.
4. Assuming that a company cannot develop effective long-range planning in a way appropriate to its resources and needs. This implies that a company cannot gradually begin long-range planning and get better and better at doing more and more complex planning—all within its capabilities.

B. Pitfalls Related to a Misunderstanding of The Nature of Planning:
5. Forgetting that planning is as much a political as a rational process.
6. Ignoring the fact that planning is and should be a learning process.
7. Assuming that planning is easy. It is hard work but should not be dreary. Hard work itself is not dreary, but superficial work is always boring.
8. Assuming that corporate comprehensive planning is something separate from the entire management process.
9. Assuming that effective total planning can be done piecemeal or that integration of major parts is unnecessary.

C. Pitfalls in Doing Planning:
10. Extrapolating rather than thinking through future alternatives and making choices. In mind here, of course, is the practice of taking last year's plans and adding one more year to them by extrapolating trends rather than rethinking the future in light of current and prospective future changes.
11. Developing such a reverence for numbers that irreverence for intuition and value judgments predominate the thinking going into planning.
12. Seeking precision of numbers throughout the planning horizon. This

is a failure to see that precise numbers become less and less meaningful the longer the planning horizon. The farther out in time is the horizon, the less is the need for and possibility of accuracy. As time is extended, numbers shade into trends and ranges.

13. Assuming that older methods to choose from among alternatives should be discarded in favor of newer techniques. The pitfall here, of course, is failing to keep in mind that some older techniques for quality planning are quite valuable.

14. Doing long-range planning periodically and forgetting it in between cycles.

15. Developing a rigid structure and process for planning that rules out flexibility, looseness, and simplicity. By the nature of the exposition of this book, it has been necessary to speak in terms of high integration of the different elements of planning and to emphasize the complex nature of the process. Also, however, the periodic admonition was made that planning should be kept as simple as possible. Furthermore, the methodology for doing it should be as flexible and loose as possible to stimulate innovation, creativity, and vitality. It is a major pitfall to allow the planning machinery to eliminate or erode these qualities of the process. It is a pitfall to try to plan everything, and all major elements of a plan cannot be neatly compartmentalized and meshed into all other parts throughout the planning horizon.

16. Assuming that equal weight should be given to all elements of planning. This is associated with point 15 above and has two parts which need comment. In pursuing planning, the consideration which is given to various multiple objectives should be on some priority scale. Profit clearly, for example, is the dominant objective. Furthermore, each company needs to determine which part of the planning process is of most importance to it and concentrate on that.

D. Pitfalls in Using Plans:

17. Assuming that plans once made are in the nature of blueprints and should be followed rigorously. A thread running through this book is the significance to management of flexibility, adaptability, and agility in meeting new conditions. It is a major pitfall to lose this quality in the implementation of plans.

18. Approaching the planning task, and using the results, on the assumption that it is possible to eliminate uncertainty in the future. This may be an elaboration of the above pitfall, but it is so important as to be worth an additional comment. It is not possible to be certain about the future and certainty should not be sought by pretending to have found it.

19. Assuming that planning must meet a single test of rationality. This

is a pitfall, of course, because what is rational to one mind may be irrational to another.

20. Assuming that planning is an interesting and useful exercise but that resulting plans should not be taken seriously.

21. Assuming that, because plans must result in current decisions, it is the short-run that counts and planning efforts as well as evaluations of results should concentrate on the short-run.

THE CHALLENGE TO KEEP ABREAST OF GROWING PLANNING KNOWLEDGE. Another important thread running through this book is reference to the rapid current changes taking place both in the internal affairs and the external environment of businesses. The pace of these changes is likely to accelerate in the future and presents a challenge to managers and planners to keep pace with new knowledge about planning in order to meet confidently new planning complexities. More top managers than middle and lower-level managers seem to understand this. One study asked 705 top managers what their educational needs were in terms of "should have," "could use," and "don't really need." The results were that 50 percent felt they "should have" more knowledge in long-range planning and forecasting for corporate growth, and in over-all strategy and goals. (Dubin, Alderman, and Marlow, 1967.) There were only two subjects which got a higher percentage response, and only two others received a 50 percent response. Middle managers did not mark long-range planning in their "should have" category although it is entirely possible they included it in a "management development" classification which 66 percent rated highest.

CHALLENGES TO STUDENTS OF PLANNING. In this section will be illustrated the rich opportunities for significant research in corporate planning. Although answers will not be found in the near future for all the proposals that follow, it can be taken as a certainty that the frontiers will be pushed back and new research of significance to business will be completed. The suggested areas and topics of research were prepared by looking back over this book and choosing a few of the major gaps in planning knowledge which were discussed. I also profited from Drucker (1958) and Ansoff and Brandenburg (1967).

A. *Fundamental Nature of Planning.*

1. Research on the fundamental nature of planning concerns the basic concept, purpose, and nature of comprehensive corporate planning. Perhaps one of the most needed and most difficult tasks is to devise a theory of the firm that will modify or replace the economist's profit maximizing principle to provide a better and more realistic standard of rationality in decision-making.

2. Probing into this question may be fruitful: What is the proper planning

process for different sized firms, for different type operations, and for various conditions?

3. An urgent problem is that of devising a legal system which will prevent and resolve serious conflicts between multinational corporate interests and the interests of nations, particularly the developing countries, in which they have an interest. This is, of course, a problem broader than that of planning, but it also has a direct impact on the nature and practice of business planning.

4. The over-all conceptual model of corporate planning needs to be refined to fit different types of situations in different companies. The interrelationships among the major parts of the model need better clarification, especially to reflect different situations. Better models of parts of the planning process need to be forged, as, for example, in developing the proper marketing mix.

5. Perhaps research may help to get planning out of its present semantic jungle, although I am not at all sure research is the road to doing this.

6. As government and business planning come closer together there will be significant need for better understanding about how they relate one with another. Especially important will be the development of a theory about how they can be coordinated to achieve social objectives better and at the same time preserve the fundamental characteristics of today's business enterprise and political system.

B. The Behavior of People.

7. One of the phenomena of recent times is the growing awareness of the importance of people in enterprises. The attitudes, activities, and interrelationships of people in organizations will become more important in the future. Although there is much research activity among behavioral scientists, there still are vast plains of unanswered questions in the area of planning. For instance, what are the appropriate degrees of participation by people in the planning process? What better guides can be prepared to determine the needed degree of correlation between company objectives and those of individuals? What are the best methods to stimulate creativity in planning which are appropriate to different companies, different levels of employees, and different conditions? Are there better ways to improve organizational acceptance of important changes resulting from plans? What methods may managers employ to ensure that planning is vigorously rather than perfunctorily pursued? What are the impacts and implications of styles of management on people that improve or impede effective planning?

8. What is the proper role of the chief executive in the planning process in different type organizations, and under different circumstances, with respect to different managers and staff?

9. Different managers have different capabilities and reservations about applying probabilities to events. What are the main inhibitions of managers in

applying probabilities? Can techniques and programs be devised to make it easier for them to apply probabilities?

C. The Process and Its Results.

This is a large catch-all category which concerns the way plans are actually prepared and how results are achieved and measured. A large part of, but by no means all, the research suggested here falls within the management science area in which newer quantitative tools and the computer will play a significant role. The behavioral scientist, as well as the researcher in other disciplines, however, will also have important work to do. There is hardly an end to exciting research topics in this category.

10. Overall is the need to develop criteria for the applicability of different conceptual and quantitative ideas and techniques to different phases of the planning process and to different circumstances. In this general area is the problem of developing a cost-benefit analysis for the entire planning process to help managers know when they have achieved the proper balance between the two parts of this equation.

11. Another important area for research is the large question of developing better methods to handle uncertainty.

12. At the objectives level the following come to mind: What methods may be devised to assure a clear concept of, a proper mix among, and measures of performance relating to, a network of aims? What principles and practices can be devised to relate better the network of aims without excessive entanglement in detail? What measures can be devised to help managers of different sized companies, and in different industries, to determine what their social responsibilities are and the degree to which they should be pursued?

13. The strategic planning area is one which scholars have neglected for too long. Vital issues suggest themselves here, such as: What better methods can be devised to help managers determine the best strategies? More work on simulation models at this level may well be the best approach to this question. More research into the strategic factors responsible for business success might also be helpful. What are the best methods to relate strategies to objectives? How can strategies of central headquarters be better related to tactics in divisions? Does style of management have any relationship to types of strategies? How do personal and company strategies relate in top managers? Does experience tell anything about the best strategies to use in prescribed situations?

14. Although there has been important improvement in forecasting techniques, much remains to be done. In industries with long lead-time technical products, this question still has not been answered satisfactorily: How can future market needs be best translated into specific current research and development programs so that the payoff in terms of sales in the future is maximized?

15. The area of resource programming opens up new challenges for the introduction of quantitative and computer techniques. For example, there is the need for simple and powerful simulation models to help managers make easier and better decisions about choice among alternatives in marketing mix, in relating physical and financial activities, and in tying capital expenditures to production needs. An important unanswered question today is: What technique can be devised to tell a manager what he should allocate to research and development?

16. Not very acceptable rules are available to tell managers what elements of planning should be tightly related, what should be loosely related, and the precision of data which needs to be applied in planning over the time spectrum.

17. The entire area of organization, including authority relationships and information systems, has in it challenging opportunities for research. For example, what is the best over-all organizational structure for comprehensive corporate planning among different sized companies and industries? What is the relationship between organizational arrangements and the improvement in or impedance to planning? This opens up a range of topics, such as: What authority relationships in different organizational patterns will provide the most efficient planning? When and under what circumstances should a company divide its headquarters' planning staff into strategic planning and operational planning? At what point should marketing organizations change from a functional to a product structure?

18. Information systems and communications provide fertile areas of exploration. As new information techniques are developed and incorporated in data systems, major questions arise about the best structure and flow of information for planning. Also, many old questions about improving communications among people in organizations still remain.

In looking at this list of challenges, it is obvious that scholars from a great many disciplines, as well as planners and managers in business, can make a contribution to the development of better planning theory. Also, all major types of research are required, that is, basic, applied, empirical, inductive, and deductive.

FUTURE EVOLVING TRENDS IN COMPREHENSIVE CORPORATE PLANNING

The future characteristics of comprehensive corporate planning will be considerably different from those of today if present trends persist. Some of today's characteristics, however, will still be important. A few suggestions of the profiles of the future—perhaps the next 15 years—may be ventured as follows:

First, more companies will undertake formal comprehensive corporate planning, and the number of corporate staffs created to help management do the planning job will expand.

Second, there will be an increase in planning activity relative to total corporate activity in terms of the number of people and the time devoted to the task.

Third, there will be an expansion of the functions of planning staffs so that their responsibility will include strategic planning; review or development of short-range operational plans, depending upon organizational structure; organizing for top management the growing flood of information submitted and required for decision-making; and some measure of control over the implementation of plans. This latter is a drift that is fraught with dangers. The future will see a much closer working relationship between these staffs and top managements, with the result that the corporate planning process will be even more significant to business operations than it is today.

Fourth, there will be changes in the degree of integration of plans. In the very large corporations, the tendency will grow to avoid over-all integration of corporate plans of all divisions and functions. At headquarters there will be developed strategic plans which will not be completely integrated. Individual division and subsidiary plans will be integrated with company strategic plans, but except for a few elements the detailed plans of the divisions will not be coordinated into one total company plan. Naturally, such elements as sales goals, anticipated profits, and capital expenditures will be aggregated. But details will not be aggregated for all divisions. To do so would be too complex. Sufficient coordination will come through reviews of division plans by top management, corporate planners, and functional officers at headquarters. In the medium-large and smaller companies there will be more coordination, e.g., strategic planning will be more closely related to programming, and programming more coordinated among divisions and for major elements of plans. There will be much closer relationships between strategic planning and research and development in most companies. More functional areas will be tied into the whole process in all companies.

Fifth, the competence of the planning process will be much enhanced by such characteristics as: more careful examination of environmental forces; wider range and better examination of alternatives; deeper exploration into more distant time horizons; much greater use of new powerful tools, and a better blend of the old methods with the new and of the newer quantitative techniques with nonquantitative values.

To illustrate, in the strategic planning area, there will be superior theories to test rationality of plans; there will be better techniques to assure needed creativity, to blend quantitative facts with qualitative considerations, to probe more surely for the critical limiting factor in choosing courses of action; and there will be better procedures to guide the effort while at the same time permitting a maximum of creativity and flexibility.

There will be a great expansion in the use of computers and newer quantitative techniques in the process, especially in operational planning. Computers will be used importantly in the strategic planning area to develop alternatives and to weight them, one against another. This will free management and staff to explore further than today ranges of nonquantitative elements bearing upon decision-making. Harold Smiddy thinks that during the next fifty years advances in management's understanding of values will equal the advances in the past fifty years in management's understanding of the particular kinds of knowledge and skills most appropriate in achieving professional and profitable managerial results (Smiddy, 1964, p. 89).

In operational planning there will be an important growth of computers to total activity. The translation of strategic plans into medium- and short-range detailed plans will be largely programmed on computers. I have in mind not only the feasibility testing of various alternative choices, but tying together into a programmed network the many intricate procedural flow patterns of product development from research through engineering testing to production, tying this process into marketing and sales, and relating income to product development plans. Human value judgments, intuition, and innovation will be as important if not more important than today, but most of the basic work will be done by computers.

With all these helpful developments there will not be available in the near future a "cookbook" on corporate planning that will lay out nicely and precisely exactly what should be done in each situation. Along with the growth of knowledge and techniques will be expansion of complexities in planning. Managers will still be their own best technique for planning. This will place on them an even heavier burden than today in keeping abreast of knowledge so that they can depend upon themselves for many answers that arise in planning.

Sixth, there will be more decision-making in the planning process by groups, and more specialists will be involved. For instance, information experts and psychologists may be added to specialists now generally involved in the process.

Seventh, in the planning process there will be growing recognition of the importance of intangible assets as compared with tangible assets. In mind are management capabilities, creativity of people, technological capability, and the entrepreneurial spirit among managers. This latter force is one which, according to my bright clear vision, will receive more attention from top management in the future.

Eighth, new words and phrases are likely to be developed for the planning process because of nomenclature problems and the shortcomings of present definitions in conveying meaning clearly and exerting the proper motivation of people.

Ninth, there will be a much closer relationship between business and government planning in the U.S. Throughout the world the trend toward closer government-business planning is clear and strong. It is particularly evident among the industrial nations of Western Europe (Verdoorn and Massé, in Steiner and

Cannon, 1966). It is a well-known trend among the underdeveloped nations of the world (Waterston, 1965). Among the communist nations, business has been controlled by the central government, but in recent years in the Soviet Union business planning has been more decentralized. (Richman, 1967, pp. 3-16.)

Closer relationships between government and business planning in the U.S. will result from reasons such as the following. The mere fact that comprehensive long-range planning is growing rapidly in both government and business will mean that business will more and more reflect government plans. It is becoming clear that many of the great social problems which exist in the U.S. cannot be solved without the combined efforts of federal, state and local governments, and business. This will also bring the two together in their planning.

Except for those instances in which government and industry cooperate in a team effort to solve a problem such as coordinating efforts to rebuild a city, or organizing the economy in a major war, the characteristics of the U.S. government-industry relationship will be much the same as today. That is, government will lay forward plans, such as setting national goals, working out long-range plans for individual agencies, and expressing the national views of the society most people seem to want, and industry voluntarily will react to these plans. The plans and visions will be premises in business planning. There will be no organized effort to get business and government together, as for instance in France (Schollhammer, 1967), to develop a national plan for the U.S.

This seems to be a reasonable view for the next fifteen or so years. Thirty and more years from now the scenario may be very different, for all sorts of incredible events may serve to change society, the business institution, attitudes, and techniques (Kahn and Wiener, 1967).

THE SOCIAL SIGNIFICANCE OF BETTER CORPORATE PLANNING

From what has been said in this book, one of the great advantages of corporate planning derives from its help to managers in utilizing much better the resources at their disposal. Planning facilitates not only the better interrelationship between a company and its external environment but also is a process for assuring more efficient internal resource processing. In this light, planning helps business to fulfill its basic social responsibility of using its resources more efficiently to satisfy society's wants.

The view has been expressed that planning does indeed help businesses to use their resources more efficiently, but they use this power in their own rather than in the interests of consumers. This is the view, in oversimplified words, that whereas in the past the producer worked to satisfy consumer wants he now controls consumer wants. In the past, says J. K. Galbraith (1967), there was "... a unidirectional flow of instructions from consumer to market to producer ..." which can be called "the Accepted Sequence." (p. 211.) Today there is "The

Revised Sequence," he says, in which "the producing firm reaches forward to control its markets and on beyond to manage behavior and shape the social attitudes of those, ostensibly, that it serves." (p. 212.)

If this is true, then planning helps management to perform a social disservice. But it is not true. The older system was not quite so unidirectional as generally supposed, and it is a fact that today producers do influence consumers, but business planning has not replaced the market mechanism. This book is filled with illustrations attesting to this fact. The much better description of what really happens in the great bulk of corporate planning is found in the marketing concept described in Chapter 18 and other accounts scattered throughout this book.

Advertising is frequently singled out as a whipping boy to show how industry controls the consumer. Of course advertising is persuasive or there would be none. But I think the quality of advertising often is confused with its real power over consumers. I am reminded of a little poem (Economos, 1968, p. 28.) that says:

> *"The quality of commercials is not restrained;*
> *It droppeth as the general brain unleavened*
> *Sinks infinitely lower."*

In some instances advertising does in fact, and regrettably, induce consumers to buy what they do not want and perhaps should not have for their own advantage. But this power is probably relatively small to the basic interests of consumers as they see them.

A service is always performed when abuses of power are identified for correction. To point out examples of abuses to consumers does not, however, make the case that business controls consumers. Consumer wants are still decisive in most business activity. If this were not so, the statistics of product failure would not be so shocking.

A case can always be made that industrial output mix really is not what it should be to meet the needs of society. It may be that industrial output ought to be less concentrated on new gadgets that have low utility value and a short life, and more concentrated on providing goods and services to help the underprivileged at home and abroad. But these are personal judgments. To the extent that society can and does reveal a consensus about wants, the industrial system and government are reasonably effective in reacting accordingly.

Indeed, as noted in this book, a major problem which corporate planning tackles is that of trying to identify society's needs in the future. Once these are identified, the resources at the disposal of a company can then be directed to meeting them. Through the long-range planning of government, society is getting better at identifying its future wants. But there are still vast areas which today are unidentified. Thousands of business firms, independently of government and one another, are trying to foresee these wants in their planning programs. When they are wrong in their forecasts, there is an automatic correction in the market place, and when they are right they profit. This feedback mechanism, as imperfect as it is today in parts, still seems to be producing a better and better utilization of resources in conformance with individual and social utility scales.

Furthermore, a case can be made that corporate planning serves to sharpen competition with an inevitable beneficial social result. As companies become more able to assess properly their environment, including what their competitors are likely to do, the result will be keener competition. For instance, technological forecasting of larger companies which includes activities of competitors, has brought forth, and will do so more frequently in the future, the same new products in many companies. For example, a number of companies produced at about the same time artificial leather, color television sets, ready-cooked baking mixes, jumbo-jet airplanes, and computers. If only one company had patent control of such products, there obviously would be a less competitive situation than what actually developed in each case and a consequent diminution in social benefit.

Closer relationships between government and business planning can have enormous social advantage. The U.S. today is facing unprecedented social problems, such as air pollution, water pollution, training unskilled and unemployed workers, congested transportation, and the need for new cities. The unique capabilities of three resources must be applied to these problems for solution: the money that is at the disposal of the federal government; the intimate knowledge of local political, social, and economic conditions which must be understood before solutions are possible; and the managerial and technical talents of industry. There is likely to be no or inadequate solution to many great social problems of today if each of these three agencies acts alone. Solution can only come from their cooperation. This is recognized and, as a consequence, it is inevitable that government and industry work together with present institutional arrangements and that new ones be invented. In either event there will be a meshing of government-industry long-range planning.

If this cooperation takes place in this fashion and if, as a result, these social problems become reduced in magnitude and gradually solved, the social advantage cannot be calculated. No less than the preservation of our political-social-economic system is at stake.

I do not mean to say that corporate planning will solve these problems, nor that they will be solved easily. What is in mind is that better long-range planning in both government and business can be a key technique to solving these problems, provided other enabling actions take place in the political area.

A projection of closer relationships between government and industry planning in the U.S. does not herald a planned economy. This is not the place to argue this case but, in keeping with the broad brush strokes of this chapter, a few points are permissible. Government controls associated with its planning have been of two basic types—indirect and direct. Generally speaking, direct controls have expanded in use and restrictiveness in periods of national crises, such as wars, and declined in use and loosened following the end of the emergencies. The prevailing attitude in the U.S. is to exercise government controls wherever possible through indirect rather than direct means. The result is a broadly prescriptive framework within which individuals can be freed to pursue their own self-interests. A classic illustration, of course, is the use of monetary policy to stimulate economic activity in a slump or to restrain excessive consumer and business spending which might be inflationary in a boom. No pejorative conclusion should attach to growing governmental planning as such. There is a case that can readily be made that, by virtue of planning and the use of indirect rather than direct controls, the free market mechanism may be preserved rather than replaced and the totality of freedoms of the people can be expanded rather than reduced (Finer, 1945; and Clark, 1948).

There are yet other social benefits of better corporate long-range planning. For instance, there was noted in Chapter 23 the potential of the multinational corporation in improving life in the underdeveloped countries of the world. This is one of a number of expectations of corporations which surely will be more and more felt in corporate planning. Throughout this book, and especially in Chapter 7, the growing recognition of social responsibilities in larger companies was discussed.

In sum, better government planning, better business planning, and closer relationships between the two, can be powerful forces for important social benefits. There are dangers in these trends, but they ought to be held in check without too much difficulty. As a result, it is not too much to say that better corporate planning is one important influence in helping this society preserve the best features of the private enterprise system. Comprehensive corporate planning (in industry and government) may turn out to be one of the great social inventions of the twentieth century.

SUMMARY

In a sweeping sort of way this chapter has tried to portray the knowledge which has been accumulated about comprehensive corporation planning relative to the needs of the times. Major pitfalls which exist in current practices were identified and future trends in planning were projected. Finally, a few comments were made about the social significance of corporate planning done in a business and as related to government planning. A few of the major conclusions are as follows:

First, although knowledge about corporate planning has been accumulating rapidly, the body of theory which captures it is far from perfect. There are gaping holes which must be filled. But, on the other hand, the body of theory contains powerful ideas and tools.

Second, in discussing the state of the theory of planning it was pointed out that many highly useful principles and guidelines to action, based both upon empirical observations and deductive reasoning, are available for managers to use. The principles, however, are considerably looser than those in the physical sciences.

Third, important challenges for the future exist for managers in overcoming many pitfalls found in current business practice.

Fourth, great challenges exist for scholarly research in improving the theory and practice of planning.

Fifth, important changes will take place in future corporate planning, such as: more companies will have formal long-range planning; planning will increase relative to total activity in the typical firm; there will be rapid expansion in the use of computers in planning; quantitative techniques will grow in use and planning will become more of a science, but intuition will still be important and planning still will also be an art; there will be more group participation in planning; and government and business planning will be more interrelated.

Sixth, corporate planning will take on increasing social significance for a number of reasons. It will facilitate society's ability to "invent" the futures it wishes; in cooperation with governments it will help solve major socio-economic problems; it will increase rather than reduce competition; it will help business to utilize resources more efficiently in meeting the wishes of consumers; and it can raise productivity in underdeveloped nations. There are dangers ahead in the use of corporate planning capability, and in its joining government planning, but these are not likely to get out of bounds.

THE SPIRIT OF PLANNING

The insightful Spanish Jesuit Baltasar Gracian three and one-half centuries ago captured the spirit of modern planning in words which fittingly set the tone of this book (as translated by Lockley, 1967, p. 45):

"Think in anticipation, today for tomorrow, and indeed, for many days. The greatest providence is to have forethought for what comes. What is provided for does not happen by chance, nor is the man who is prepared ever beset by emergencies. One must not, therefore, postpone consideration till the need arises. Consideration should go beforehand. You can, after careful reflection, act to prevent the most calamitous events. The pillow is a silent Sibyl, for to sleep over questions before they reach a climax is far better than lying awake over them afterward. Some act and think later—and they think more of excuses than consequences. Others think neither before nor after. The whole of life should be spent thinking about how to find the right course of action to follow. Thought and forethought give counsel both on living and on achieving success."

References

ACKOFF, RUSSELL L., "Management Misinformation System," *Management Science*, Vol. 14, December 1967.

ADAMS, VELMA A., "Why the Old Products Last," *Dun's Review & Modern Industry*, April 1965.

ADLER, LEE, ed., *Plotting Marketing Strategy* (New York: Interpublic Press and Simon and Schuster, Inc., 1967a).

————, "Systems Approach to Marketing," *Harvard Business Review*, Vol. 45, May-June 1967b, pp. 105-118.

AGUILAR, FRANCIS JOSEPH, *Scanning the Business Environment*, Studies of the Modern Corporation, Graduate School of Business, Columbia University (New York: The Macmillan Co.; London: Collier-Macmillan Ltd., 1967).

ALBACH, HORST, "Long Range Planning in Open-Pit Mining," *Management Science*, Vol. 13, June 1967, pp. B-549-568.

ALBROOK, ROBERT C., "Participative Management: Time for a Second Look," *Fortune*, Vol. LXXV, May 1967.

ALCHIAN, ARMEN A., "Uncertainty, Evolution, and Economic Theory," *Journal of Political Economy*, Vol. 58, June 1950, pp. 211-221.

ALDERSON, WROE, "Commentary," *Management Science*, Vol. 12, October 1965.

————, *Marketing Behavior and Executive Action* (Homewood, Illinois: Richard D. Irwin, Inc. 1957).

————, and PAUL E. GREEN, *Planning and Problem Solving in Marketing* (Homewood, Illinois: Richard D. Irwin, Inc., 1964).

————, and STANLEY J. SHAPIRO, *Marketing and the Computer* (Englewood Cliffs, N.J.: Prentice-Hall, Inc., 1963).

ALEXANDER, R. S., *Marketing Definitions: A Glossary of Marketing Terms* (Chicago: American Marketing Association, 1960).

ALEXANDER, TOM, "Synectics: Inventing by the Madness Method," *Fortune*, Vol. 71, August 1965.

ALFRED, A. M., *Discounted Cash Flow and Corporate Planning*, Woolwich Economic Papers, No. 3 (London: Woolwich Polytechnic, 1964).

ALLEN, J. KNIGHT, "The Rising Acceptance of Corporate Strategy," *Stanford Research Institute Journal*, Feature Issue I, 1965.

ALMON, CLOPPER, JR., *The American Economy in 1975* (New York: Harper and Row, 1967).

AMERICAN ASSEMBLY, *The Report of the President's Commission on National Goals* (New York: Columbia University, The American Assembly, 1961).

AMERICAN MANAGEMENT ASSOCIATION, *Achieving Full Value From R&D Dollars* (New York: American Management Association, Inc., 1963a).

————, *Company Organization for Economic Forecasting*, Research Report No. 28 (New York: American Management Association, Inc., 1957).

————, *Control through Information*, Management Bulletin 24 (New York: American Management Association, Inc., 1963b).

————, *Computer-Based Management for Information and Control*, Management Bulletin 30 (New York: American Management Association, Inc., 1963c).

————, *Marketing Harnesses the Computer,* Management Bulletin 92 (New York: American Management Association, Inc., 1967).

————, *Data Processing Today: A Progress Report,* Report No. 46 (New York: American Management Association, Inc., 1960).

————, *Sales Forecasting, Uses, Techniques, and Trends,* Special Report No. 16 (New York: American Management Association, Inc., 1956).

American Tobacco Co. v. United States, 1946.

AMES, CHARLES B., "Keys to Better Product Planning," *Business Horizons,* Vol. 9, Summer 1966, pp. 49-58.

AMMER, DEAN S., *Manufacturing Management and Control* (New York: Appleton-Century-Crofts, 1968a).

————, *Materials Management,* rev. ed. (Homewood, Illinois: Richard D. Irwin, Inc., 1968b).

————, *Materials Management* (Homewood, Illinois: Richard D. Irwin, Inc., 1962).

AMSTUTZ, ARNOLD E., *Computer Simulation of Competitive Market Response* (Cambridge, Massachusetts: The M.I.T. Press, 1967).

ANDERSEN, THEODORE A., "Coordinating Strategic and Operational Planning," *Business Horizons,* Vol. 8, Summer 1965, pp. 49-72.

————, H. IGOR ANSOFF, FRANK NORTON and J. FRED WESTON, "Planning for Diversification Through Merger," *California Management Review,* Vol. 1, Summer 1959, pp. 24-36.

ANSHEN, MELVIN, "Organization Structure and the New Decision-Making Technology," in Donald M. Bowman and Francis M. Fillerup, *Management: Organization and Planning* (New York: McGraw-Hill Book Co., Inc., 1963), Chap. 2.

————, "Price Tags for Business Policies," *Harvard Business Review,* Vol. 38, January-February 1960, pp. 71-78.

————, and G. L. BACH, *Management and Corporation 1985* (New York: McGraw-Hill Book Co., Inc., 1960).

ANSOFF, H. IGOR, *Corporate Strategy* (New York: McGraw-Hill Book Co., Inc., 1965a).

————, "The Firm of the Future," *Harvard Business Review,* Vol. 43, September-October 1965b.

————, and RICHARD C. BRANDENBURG, "A Program of Research in Business Planning," *Management Science,* Vol. 13, February 1967, pp. B-219-239.

————, and DENNIS P. SLEVIN, "An Appreciation of *Industrial* Dynamics," *Management Science,* Vol. 14, March 1968, pp. 383-397.

————, and JOHN M. STEWART, "Strategies for a Technology-Based Business," *Harvard Business Review,* Vol. 45, November-December 1967, pp. 71-83.

ANTHONY, ROBERT N., "Framework for Analysis in Management Planning," *Management Services,* March-April 1964, pp. 18-24.

————, *Management Controls in Industrial Research Organizations* (Boston: Graduate School of Business, Harvard University, 1952).

————, *Planning and Control Systems: A Framework for Analysis* (Boston: Harvard University Press, 1965).

————, "The Trouble with Profit Maximization," *Harvard Business Review,* Vol. 38, November-December 1960, pp. 126-134.

APPLEBAUM, WILLIAM, and RAY A. GOLDBERG, *Brand Strategy in United States Food Marketing* (Boston: Division of Research, Graduate School of Business Administration, Harvard University, 1967).

ARCHER, STEPHEN H., "The Structure of Management Decision Theory," *Journal of the Academy of Management,* Vol. 7, December 1964, pp. 269-287.

ARGYRIS, CHRIS, "Human Problems with Budgets," *Harvard Business Review*, Vol. 31, January-February 1958.

———, "The Individual and Organization: Some Problems of Mutual Adjustment," *Administrative Science Quarterly*, Vol. 2, June 1957a.

———, *Personality and Organization* (New York: Harper and Brothers, 1957b).

ARNOFF, E. LEONARD, "Operations Research and Long-Range Company Planning," in David W. Ewing, ed., *Long-Range Planning for Management* (New York: Harper and Row, 1964).

Aviation-Week and Space Technology, "System Life Cycle," Vol. 87, Mid-December 1967.

AVOTS, IVARS, "The Management Side of PERT," *California Management Review*, Vol. 4, Winter 1962, pp. 16-27.

BABBAGE, CHARLES, *On the Economy of Machinery and Manufactures* (Philadelphia: Carey & Lea, 1832).

BARNARD, CHESTER I., *The Functions of the Executive* (Cambridge, Massachusetts: Harvard University Press, 1954).

———, *Organization and Management* (Cambridge, Massachusetts: Harvard University Press, 1948).

BARNETT, C. C., JR., and Associates, *The Future of the Company Utility* (New York: American Management Association, Inc., 1967).

BARNHILL, J. ALLISON, "Marketing and Cultural Anthropology: A Conceptual Relationship," *University of Washington Business Review*, Vol. 27, Autumn 1967, pp. 73-84.

BARTON, RICHARD F., "Reality and Business Decisions," *Journal of the Academy of Management*, Vol. 9, June 1966, pp. 117-122.

BASSIE, V. LEWIS, *Economic Forecasting* (New York: McGraw-Hill Book Co., 1958).

BATES, KENNETH O., "Establishing and Achieving Corporate Goals," American Management Association (mimeographed and undated).

BAUMGARTNER, JOHN STANLEY, *Project Management* (Homewood, Illinois: Richard D. Irwin, Inc., 1963).

BAUMHART, RAYMOND C., "How Ethical are Businessmen?" *Harvard Business Review*, Vol. 39, July-August 1961.

BAVELAS, ALEX, "Some Problems of Organizational Change," *Journal of Social Issues*, Vol. 4, No. 3, Summer 1948, pp. 48-52.

BEAUVOIS, JOHN J., "Internationalism: A New Concept for U. S. Business," *California Management Review*, Vol. 2, Winter 1960, pp. 28-37.

BEER, STAFFORD, *Cybernetics and Management* (New York: John Wiley and Sons, Inc., 1959).

BEISE, S. C., "Planning for Industrial Growth: An Executive View," in remarks before Milan Conference on Planning for Industrial Growth sponsored by the Stanford Research Institute, Milan, Italy, 1963.

BELL, MARTIN L., *Marketing, Concepts and Strategy* (New York: Houghton Mifflin Company, 1966).

BENNIS, WARREN G., *Changing Organizations* (New York: McGraw-Hill Book Co., Inc. 1966).

———, and CAROLINE McGREGOR, eds., *The Professional Manager* (New York: McGraw-Hill Book Co., 1967).

BERG, NORMAN, "Strategic Planning in Conglomerate Companies," *Harvard Business Review*, Vol. 43, May-June 1965, pp. 79-92.

BERG, THOMAS L., and ABE SHUCHMAN, eds., *Product Strategy and Management* (New York: Holt, Rinehart and Winston, Inc., 1963).

BERLE, A. A., JR., "Corporate Powers as Powers in Trust," *Harvard Law Review*, 44: 1049, 1931.

———, *Power Without Property* (New York: Harcourt, Brace and Company, 1959).

———, *The 20th Century Capitalist Revolution* (New York: Harcourt, Brace & World, 1954).

———, and GARDINER C. MEANS, *The Modern Corporation and Private Property* (New York: The Macmillan Company, 1933).

BESSE, RALPH M., "Company Planning Must Be Planned," *Dun's Review and Modern Industry*, Vol. 69, April 1957, pp. 46-48 and pp. 62-69.

BIERMAN, HAROLD, JR., *Managerial Accounting, An Introduction* (New York: The Macmillan Company, 1963).

———, CHARLES P. BONINI, LAWRENCE E. FOURAKER, and ROBERT K. JAEDICKE, *Quantitative Analysis for Business Decisions* (Homewood, Ill.: Richard D. Irwin, Inc., 1965).

———, and SEYMOUR SMIDT, *The Capital Budgeting Decision* (New York: The Macmillan Company, 1960).

BLACK, GUY, "Systems Analysis in Government Operations, *Management Science*, Vol. 14, October 1967, pp. B-41-58.

BLOOD, JEROME W., *The Management of Scientific Talent* (New York: American Management Association, Inc., 1963).

BLOUGH, RAY, *International Business: Environment and Adaptation* (New York: McGraw-Hill Book Co., Inc., 1966).

BLUM, E. H., Subpanel Chairman, *Subpanel on Transportation System Requirements, Commerce Technical Advisory Board, Panel on Electrically Powered Vehicles, Third Draft Report*, Santa Monica, The RAND Corporation, multilithed, September 29, 1967.

BOCK, BETTY, *Mergers and Markets: A Guide to Economic Analysis of Case Law*, 3rd ed., Studies in Business Economics, No. 85 (New York: National Industrial Conference Board, 1964).

BOEHM, BARRY W., "Keeping the Upper Hand in the Man-Computer Partnership," *Astronautics and Aeronautics* (Santa Monica, California: The RAND Corporation, April 1967).

BONINI, CHARLES P., "Simulation of Information and Decision Systems in the Firm" (Graduate School of Business, Stanford University, Stanford, California, May 1962).

BOOZ • ALLEN & HAMILTON, *The Management Implications of PERT* (New York: Booz, Allen & Hamilton, Inc., 1962).

———, *Management of New Products* (New York: Booz, Allen & Hamilton, 1960).

BOULDING, KENNETH E., "The Ethics of Rational Decision," *Management Science*, Vol. 12, No. 6, February 1966, pp. 6-19.

———, *The Image* (Ann Arbor, Michigan: Ann Arbor Paperbacks, 1956).

BOWEN, HOWARD, *Social Responsibilities of the Businessman* (New York: Harper & Row, 1953).

BOWER, MARVIN, *The Will to Manage* (New York: McGraw-Hill Book Co., Inc., 1966).

BOWMAN, DONALD M., and FRANCIS M. FILLERUP, *Management: Organization and Planning* (New York: McGraw-Hill Book Company, Inc., 1963).

BRADY, RODNEY H., "Computers in Top-Level Decision-Making," *Harvard Business Review*, Vol. 45, July-August 1967, pp. 67-76.

BRANCH, MELVILLE C., *The Corporate Planning Process* (New York: American Management Association, Inc., 1962).

———, "The Corporate Planning Process, Plans, Decision, Implementation," *Operations Research*, Vol. 6, July-August 1958, pp. 539-552.

———, "A Missing Link in Planning," *California Management Review*, Vol. 6, Fall 1963, pp. 75-80.

———, *Planning: Aspects and Applications* (New York: John Wiley & Sons, Inc., 1966).

———, "A View of Corporate Planning Today," *California Management Review*, Vol. 7, Winter 1964.

BRANNEN, T. R., and F. X. HODGSON, *Overseas Management* (New York: McGraw-Hill Book Co., Inc., 1965).

BRATT, ELMER C., *Business Forecasting* (New York: McGraw-Hill Book Company, 1958).

BREECH, ERNEST R., "Planning the Basic Strategy of a Large Business," in Edward C. Bursk and Dan H. Fenn, Jr., eds., *Planning the Future Strategy of Your Business* (New York: McGraw-Hill Book Co., Inc., 1956).

BRIGHT, JAMES R., *Research Development and Technological Innovation* (Homewood, Illinois:: Richard D. Irwin, Inc., 1964).

———, "Technology Forecasting for Industry," Program for the First Annual Technology and Management Conference, Lake Placid Club, May 22-25, 1967.

BRION, JOHN M., *Corporate Marketing Planning* (New York: John Wiley & Sons, Inc., 1967).

BROOKS, JOHN, *The Fate of the Edsel and Other Business Adventures* (New York: Harper and Row, Publishers, 1959).

BROWN, GENE, and KENNETH S. JOHNSTON, *Paciolo on Accounting* (New York: McGraw-Hill Book Company, Inc., 1963).

BROWN, JAMES K., STUART C. DOBSON and G. CLARK THOMPSON, "Company Growth: Mostly Planned, But Sometimes Painful," *The Conference Board Record*, Vol. III, October 1966, pp. 7-15.

———, SAUL S. SANDS and G. CLARK THOMPSON, "The Status of Long-Range Planning," *The Conference Board Record*, September 1966.

BUELL, VICTOR P., "The Major Challenge to Marketing Management," *Emerging Trends in Marketing, Marketing Management* (New York: National Industrial Conference Board, 1965), pp. 11-12.

BUFFA, ELWOOD S., "Aggregate Planning for Production," *Business Horizons*, Vol. 10, Fall 1967, pp. 87-97.

———, *Models for Production and Operations Management* (New York: John Wiley & Sons, Inc., 1963).

———, *Modern Production Management* (New York: John Wiley & Sons, Inc., 1965).

———, *Production-Inventory Systems: Planning and Control* (Homewood, Illinois: Richard D. Irwin, Inc., 1968).

BURGESS, WILLIAM H., "'Calculable Growth' Means Corporate Vitality," *Management Review*, Vol. 54, September 1965, pp. 4-10.

BURLINGAME, J. F., "Information Technology and Decentralization," *Harvard Business Review*, Vol. 39, November-December 1961, pp. 121-126.

BURNS, LELAND S., "Cost-Benefit Analysis of Improved Housing: A Case Study," *Cost-Benefit Analysis of Social Projects* (Geneva, Switzerland: United Nations Research Institute for Social Development and Office of Social Affairs, 1966), pp. 88-111.

BURNS, TOM, and G. M. STALKER, *The Management of Innovation* (Chicago: Quadrangle Books, 1961).

Burroughs Corporation, *Simulation* (Detroit, Michigan: Burroughs Corporation, 1967).

BURSK, EDWARD C., and DAN H. FENN, JR., eds., *Planning the Future Strategy of Your Business* (New York: McGraw-Hill Book Co., Inc., 1956).

BURTON, PAUL, *Corporate Public Relations* (New York: Reinhold Publishing Corp., 1966).

BUSENBURY, WARREN, "CPM for New Product Introduction," *Harvard Business Review*, Vol. 45, July-August 1967, pp. 124-139.

Business Week, "Computers Start to Run the Plants," November 5, 1960.

————, "Shortcut for Project Planning," July 7, 1962.

————, "Airlines Take the Marginal Route," April 20, 1963a.

————, "Coke Tries New Ways to Refresh," August 24, 1963b.

————, "Maytag Hangs Its Wash on a Hometown Line," April 10, 1965a.

————, "Computers Begin to Solve the Marketing Puzzle," April 17, 1965b.

————, "Where Pennsalt Got Its New Pep," June 19, 1965c.

————, "Why Companies Seek Greener Fields," March 12, 1966a.

————, "How Computers Liven a Management's Ways," June 25, 1966b.

————, "Why the Ink Is Black at Harris-Intertype," December 31, 1966c.

————, "Where Tiny Cells Power Big Sales," January 14, 1967a.

————, "Turning Deaf Ear to Rich Suitors," January 14, 1967b.

————, "Corporations: Where the Game Is Growth," September 30, 1967c.

————, "H. J. Heinz Pours It on In Products and Profits," November 11, 1967d.

BUTLER, WILLIAM F., and ROBERT A. KAVESH, *How Business Economists Forecast* (Englewood Cliffs, N. J.: Prentice-Hall, Inc., 1966).

BYLEVELD, HERBERT, "Donations Practices of Canadian Companies, 1965," *The Conference Board Record*, Vol. IV, February 1967, pp. 21-26.

CAMPBELL, ROBERT MOORE, *A Methodological Study of the Utilization of Experts in Business Forecasting* (Los Angeles: Graduate School of Business Administration, UCLA, 1966) (unpublished doctoral dissertation).

CANNON, J. THOMAS, *Business Strategy and Policy* (New York: Harcourt Brace & World, Inc., 1968).

CARLSON, BRUCE, "Industrial Dynamics," *Management Systems*, Vol. 1, May-June 1964, pp. 32-39.

CARLSON, JOHN A., "Forecasting Errors and Business Cycles," *American Economic Review*, Vol. LVII, June 1967, pp. 462-481.

CARTER, C. F., G. P. MEREDITH and G. L. S. SHACKLE, eds., *Uncertainty and Business Decisions: A Symposium* (Liverpool: Liverpool University Press, 1957).

CARTER, MARTIN B., WALTER WEINTRAUB and CHARLES A. RAY, eds., *Management Challenge and Response* (New York: Holt, Rinehart and Winston, Inc., 1965).

CARTER, VIOLET BONHAM, *Winston Churchill: An Intimate Portrait* (New York: Harcourt, Brace and World, Inc., 1965).

CARTIER, F. A., and K. A. HARWOOD, "On Definition of Communication," *The Journal of Communication*, November 1953.

Celanese World, Special Issue: Planning at Celanese, Vol. 8, January 1966.

CETRON, MARVIN J., "A Survey of Technological Forecasting—Concepts, Comparisons and Experiences," paper presented at the First Annual Technology and Management Conference, the Lake Placid Club, May 22-25, 1967.

————, JOSEPH MARTINO, and LEWIS ROEPCKE, "The Selection of R&D Program Content —Survey of Quantitative Methods," *IEEE Transactions on Engineering Management*, Vol. EM-14, March 1967, pp. 4-13.

CHAMBERLAIN, NEIL W., *Enterprise and Environment* (New York: McGraw-Hill Book Co., Inc., 1968).

——, *The Firm: Micro-Economic Planning and Action* (New York: McGraw-Hill Book Company, Inc., 1962).

——, *Private and Public Planning* (New York: McGraw-Hill Book Co., Inc., 1965).

CHANDLER, A. D., JR., *Strategy and Structure: Chapters in the History of the Industrial Enterprise* (Cambridge: The M.I.T. Press, 1962).

CHARVAT, FRANK J., and W. TATE WHITMAN, *Marketing Management—A Quantitative Approach* (New York: D. C. Heath and Company, 1967).

CHASEN, S. H., and ROBERT N. SEITZ, "On-Line Systems and Man-Computer Graphics," *Astronautics & Aeronautics*, Vol. 5, April 1967, pp. 48-55.

CHINGARI, GASTONE, *Digital Simulation of Numerically Controlled Production Systems*, NASA Research Paper No. 14, NASA Research Project (Los Angeles: Graduate School of Business Administration, UCLA, mimeographed, 1967).

CHURCHMAN, C. W., and A. H. SCHAINBLATT, "Commentary on the Researcher and the Manager," *Management Science*, Vol. 12, October 1965a, pp. B-1-42.

——, and ——, "The Research and the Manager: A Dialectic of Implementation," *Management Science*, Vol. 11, February 1965b, pp. B-69-87.

CLARE, ARTHUR C., *Profiles of the Future* (New York: Harper & Row, 1962).

CLARK, JOHN M., *Alternative to Serfdom* (New York: Alfred A. Knopf, 1948).

——, *Competition as a Dynamic Process* (Washington, D.C.: The Brookings Institution, 1961).

CLARK, JOHN W., *Religion and the Moral Standards of American Businessmen* (Chicago: South Western Publishing Co., 1966).

CLEE, GILBERT H., and ALFRED DI SCIPIO, "Creating a World Enterprise," *Harvard Business Review*, Vol. 37, November-December 1959, pp. 77-89.

CLEVELAND, HARLAN, "Crisis Diplomacy," *Foreign Affairs*, Vol. 41, July 1963, pp. 638-649.

CLIFFORD, DONALD K., JR., "Managing the Product Life Cycle," *The McKinsey Quarterly*, Vol. I, Spring 1965, pp. 48-60.

COCHRAN, BETTY, and G. CLARK THOMPSON, "Why New Products Fail," *The Conference Board Record*, Vol. I, October 1964, pp. 11-18.

COLBERT, BERTRAM A., "Pathway to Profit: The Management Information System," *Management Services*, Vol. 4, September-October 1967, pp. 15-24.

COLE, ARTHUR H., *Business Enterprise in Its Social Setting* (Cambridge, Massachusetts: Harvard University Press, 1959).

COLLINS, ORVIS F., DAVID G. MOORE and DARAB B. UNWALLA, *The Enterprising Man* (East Lansing, Michigan: Graduate School of Business Administration, Michigan State University, 1964).

COLM, GERHARD, and PETER WAGNER, *Federal Budget Projections* (Washington, D. C.: Brookings Institution, 1966).

CONRAD, GORDON R., "Unexplored Assets for Diversification," *Harvard Business Review*, September-October 1963.

CONTROLLERSHIP FOUNDATION, "Planning, Managing and Measuring the Business: A Case Study of Management Planning and Control at General Electric Company," Series II, Business Planning and Control, Report No. 3 (New York: Controllership Foundation, Inc., 1955).

COOPER, JOSEPH D., "Making Decisions—and Making Them Stick," *Management Review*, August 1961, pp. 43-53.

CORDINER, RALPH J., "Managerial Strategy for International Business," Speech before

World Trade Dinner, National Foreign Trade Council Convention, Waldorf-Astoria, New York, November 1960.

———, *New Frontiers for Professional Managers* (New York: McGraw-Hill Book Co., Inc., 1956).

COREY, E. RAYMOND, "The Strategy of Market Introduction for Industrial Products," in David W. Ewing, ed., *Long Range Planning for Management*, rev. ed. (New York: Harper and Row, 1964), Chapter 38.

CORSON, JOHN J., "Innovation Challenges Conformity," *Harvard Business Review*, Vol. 40, May-June 1962, pp. 67-74.

COTTLE, SIDNEY, "Four Steps to Diversification Planning," *Business Quarterly*, Summer 1963.

COX, WILLIAM E., JR., "Product Life Cycles as Marketing Models," *The Journal of Business*, Vol. 40, October 1967, pp. 375-388.

CROSS, HERSHNER, DONALD I. LOWRY, A. R. ZIPF, GEORGE KOZMETSKY and ROBERT ANTHONY, *Computers and Management* (Boston: Graduate School of Business Administration, Harvard University, 1967).

CULLITON, JAMES W., "Age of Synthesis," *Harvard Business Review*, Vol. 40, September-October 1962.

CUMMINGS, LARRY, "Organizational Climates for Creativity," *Journal of the Academy of Management*, Vol. 8, September 1965, pp. 220-227.

CURTIS, EDWARD T., *Company Organization of the Finance Function* (New York: American Management Association, Inc., 1962).

CYERT, RICHARD M., and WILLIAM DILL, "The Future of Business Education," *The Journal of Business*, Vol. XXXVII, July 1964, pp. 226-228.

———, ———, and J. G. MARCH, "The Role of Expectations in Business Decision-Making," *Administrative Science Quarterly*, Vol. 3, December 1958, pp. 307-340.

———, and JAMES G. MARCH, *A Behavioral Theory of the Firm* (New York: Prentice-Hall, 1963).

DALE, ERNEST, *Decision-Making Process in the Commercial Use of High-Speed Computers* (Ithaca, N. Y.: Graduate School of Business and Public Administration, Cornell University, 1964).

———, *Management Theory and Practice* (New York: McGraw-Hill Book Co., Inc., 1965).

———, "The Social and Moral Responsibilities of the Executive in the Large Corporation," *American Economic Review*, Vol. LI, May 1961.

———, "Some Foundations of Organization Theory," *California Management Review*, Vol. II, Fall 1959, pp. 71-84.

———, and LYNDALL F. URWICK, *Staff in Organization* (New York: McGraw-Hill Book Co., 1960).

DALKEY, N., and O. HELMER, "An Experimental Application of the Delphi Method to the Use of Experts," *Management Science*, Vol. 9, 1963.

DANIEL, D. RONALD, "Management Information Crisis," *Harvard Business Review*, Vol. 39, September-October, 1961.

———, "Team at the Top," *The McKinsey Quarterly*, Vol. 1, Spring 1965, pp. 19-20.

DANTZIG, GEORGE B., *Linear Programming and Extensions* (Princeton, N.J.: Princeton University Press, 1962).

———, "Management Science in the World of Today and Tomorrow," *Management Science*, Vol. 13, February 1967.

——, "Programming of Interdependent Activities; II Mathematical Model," *Econometrica*, Vol. 17, July-October, 1949, pp. 200-211.

DARLING, CHARLES M., III, and THOMAS J. DIVINEY, "Business in Public Affairs Today," *The Conference Board Record*, May 1966, pp. 8-15.

DAVIS, J. S., Ed., *Carl Alsberg, Scientist at Large* (Stanford: Stanford University Press, 1948).

DAVIS, JOHN P., *Corporations, A Study of the Origin and Development of Great Business Combinations and of Their Relation to the Authority of the State* (New York: Capricorn Books, 1961); previously published in 1897.

DAVIS, JOSEPH STANCLIFFE, *Essays in the Earlier History of American Corporations*, Vol. I (Cambridge, Mass.: Harvard University Press, 1917).

DAVIS, KEITH, *Human Relations in Business* (New York: McGraw-Hill Book Company, Inc., 1957).

DAVIS, RALPH C., *The Fundamentals of Top Management* (New York: Harper and Brothers Publishers, 1951).

DAVIS, T. C., *How the Du Pont Organization Appraises Its Performance*, Financial Management Series No. 94 (New York: American Management Association, Inc., 1950).

DEAN, BURTON V., ed., *Operations Research in Research and Development* (New York: John Wiley & Sons, 1963).

DEAN, JOEL, *Capital Budgeting* (New York: Columbia University Press, 1951).

——, "Does Advertising Belong in the Capital Budget?" *Journal of Marketing*, Vol. 30, 1966, pp. 15-21.

——, "How to Find the Moment When Modernizing Pays Best," *Business Week*, September 27, 1958.

——, *Methods and Potentialities of Break-Even Analysis* (London: Sweet and Maxwell, Ltd., 1952).

——, and W. SMITH, "On The Economic Advantages of the Growth of Firms," *Economie Appliquée*, July-September 1965.

DEARDEN, JOHN, *Computers in Business Management* (Homewood, Illinois: Dow Jones-Irwin, Inc., 1966a).

——, "How to Organize Information Systems," *Harvard Business Review*, Vol. 43, March-April 1965, pp. 73-85.

——, "Limits on Decentralized Profit Responsibility," *Harvard Business Review*, Vol. 40, July-August 1962a, pp. 81-89.

——, "Mirage of Profit Decentralization," *Harvard Business Review*, Vol. 40, November-December 1962b, pp. 140-154.

——, "Myth of Real-Time Management Information Systems," *Harvard Business Review*, Vol. 44, May-June 1966b, pp. 123-132.

DeCOSTER, DON T., "Time Networking in Retrospect," *Business Review*, Vol. XXVII, October 1966, pp. 44-54.

DE JOUVENEL, BERTRAND, *The Art of Conjecture* (New York: Basic Books, Inc., 1967).

DIEBOLD, JOHN, "What's Ahead in Information Technology," *Harvard Business Review*, Vol. 43, September-October 1965, pp. 76-82, 123-132.

DIEDERICH, F. W., *Trade-Off Evaluation System* (TOES) (Wilmington, Mass.: Avco-Research and Advanced Development Division, Engineering Management Report No. 3, May 19, 1962).

DILL, W. R., D. P. GAUER and W. L. WEBER, "Models and Modeling for Manpower Planning," *Management Science*, Vol. 13, December 1966, pp. B-142-167.

Dodd, E. Merrick, "For Whom are Corporate Managers Trustees?" *Harvard Law Review*, Vol. 45, 1932, pp. 1145-1163.

Donham, Wallace B., "Essential Groundwork for a Broad Executive Theory," *Harvard Business Review*, Vol. 1, October 1922.

Drayton, Clarence I., Jr., Craig Emerson and John D. Griswold, *Mergers and Acquisitions: Planning and Action* (New York: Financial Executives Research Foundation, 1963).

Drucker, Peter F., "Big Business and the National Purpose," *Harvard Business Review*, Vol. 40, March-April 1962.

———, "Business Objectives and Survival Needs: Notes on a Discipline of Business Enterprise," *The Journal of Business*, Vol. XXXI, April 1958.

———, "Entrepreneurship in the Business Enterprise," Commercial Letter, Canadian Imperial Bank of Commerce (Toronto), March 1965.

———, "Long-Range Planning," *Management Science*, Vol. 5, April 1959a, pp. 238-239.

———, *Managing for Results* (New York: Harper & Row, 1964).

———, "Potentials of Management Science," *Harvard Business Review*, Vol. 37, January-February 1959b.

———, *The Practice of Management* (New York: Harper & Row, Publishers, 1954).

Dubin, Robert, *Human Relations in Administration*, 2nd Edition (Englewood Cliffs, N. J.: Prentice-Hall, Inc., 1961).

Dubin, Samuel S., Everett Alderman and H. Leroy Marlow, *Managerial and Supervisory Educational Needs of Business and Industry in Pennsylvania* (University Park: The Pennsylvania State University, 1967).

Dun's Review & Modern Industry, "The Changing Face of W. R. Grace," Vol. 90, July 1967.

———, "Sales $ Marketing," April 1965, pp. 83-84.

Du Pont Company, *This Is Dupont 30*, "The D of Research and Development" (Wilmington, Delaware: E. I. Du Pont de Nemours & Company, 1966).

———, *Executive Committee Control Charts* (Wilmington, Delaware: E. I. Du Pont de Nemours & Company, 1959).

Dutton, J. M. and R. E. Walton, "Operational Research and the Behavioral Sciences," *Operational Research Quarterly*, Vol. 15, 1964, pp. 207-217.

Dwyer, Edmund D., "Observations on Information Systems," *Advances in EDP and Information Systems*, Report #62 (New York: American Management Association, Inc., 1962).

Economos, Judith, *UCLA Alumni Magazine*, Vol. 42, Spring 1968.

Eells, Richard, *Corporation Giving in a Free Society* (New York: Harper & Row, 1966).

———, "The Corporate Image in Public Relations," *California Management Review*, Vol. 1, Summer 1959, pp. 15-23.

———, *The Government of Corporations* (New York: The Free Press of Glencoe, 1962).

———, *The Meaning of Modern Business* (New York: Columbia University Press, 1960).

Eisner, Robert, *Determinants of Capital Expenditures*, Studies in Business Expectations and Planning No. 2 (Urbana: Bureau of Economic and Business Research, University of Illinois Press, 1956).

Elwell, Harry H., "Data Information Management System," *Management Services*, Vol. 9, November-December 1967, pp. 40-59.

Emerson, Harrington, *The Twelve Principles of Efficiency* (New York: The Engineering Magazine Company, 1912).

ENGLAND, GEORGE W., "Organizational Goals and Expected Behavior of American Managers," *Journal of the Academy of Management,* Vol. 10, June 1967a, pp. 107-118.

————, "Personal Value Systems of American Managers," *Journal of the Academy of Management,* Vol. 10, March 1967b, pp. 53-68.

ENTHOVEN, ALAIN C., "Systems Analysis and the Navy," originally published in *Naval Review 1965* and included in Samuel A. Tucker, ed., *A Modern Design for Defense Decision; A McNamara-Hitch-Enthoven Anthology* (Washington, D.C.: Industrial College of Armed Forces, 1966).

————, "The Whizziest Kid," *Time Magazine,* June 28, 1963.

ERIS, RENE L., and BRUCE N. BAKER, *An Introduction to PERT-CPM* (Homewood, Illinois: Richard D. Irwin, Inc., 1964).

EVANS, GORDON H., *The Product Manager's Job,* Research Study 69 (New York: American Management Association, Inc., 1964).

EVANS, MARSHALL K., "Profit Planning," *Harvard Business Review,* Vol. 37, July-August 1959, pp. 45-54.

————, and LOU R. HAGUE, "Master Plan for Information Systems," *Harvard Business Review,* Vol. 40, January-February 1962, pp. 92-104.

EWING, DAVID W., "Corporate Planning At a Crossroads," *Harvard Business Review,* Vol. 45, July-August 1967.

————, ed., *Long-Range Planning for Management* (New York: Harper and Row, 1964a).

————, *The Managerial Mind* (New York: The Free Press of Glencoe, 1964b).

FABIAN, TIBOR, "Blast Furnace Burdening and Production Planning—A Linear Programming Example," *Management Science,* Vol. 14, October 1967, pp. B-1-27.

FARIS, CHARLES W., "The Relationship Between Corporate Strategy and Market Segment Research," Boston Marketing Series, The Boston Marketing Group, 1967.

FARMER, RICHARD N., and BARRY M. RICHMAN, *International Business: An Operational Theory* (Homewood, Illinois: Richard D. Irwin, Inc., 1966).

FAULHABER, THOMAS A., *Manufacturing: Strategy for Growth and Change* (New York: Holt, Rinehart, and Winston, 1962).

FAYERWEATHER, JOHN, *Facts and Fallacies of International Business* (New York: Holt, Rinehart, and Winston, 1962).

————, "LRP for International Operations," *California Management Review,* Vol. 3, Fall 1960a, pp. 23-35.

————, *Management of International Operations* (New York: McGraw-Hill Book Co., Inc., 1960b).

FAYOL, HENRI, *General and Industrial Management* (1916), translated by Constance Storrs (London: Sir Isaac Pitman and Sons, Ltd., 1949).

FAZAR, WILLARD, "The Origin of PERT," *The Controller,* December 1962.

FEENEY, G. J., "Time Sharing, Management, and Management Science," *Management Science,* Vol. 13, February 1967.

FENDRICH, C. WELLES, JR., "The Industrial Product Management System," Management Bulletin 80 (New York: American Management Association, Inc., 1966).

FERBER, ROBERT C., D. F. BLANKERTZ, and S. HOLLANDER, JR., *Marketing Research* (New York: The Ronald Press Co., 1964).

————, and GEORGE FISK, "The Role of the Subconscious in Executive Decision-Making," *Management Science,* Vol. 13, April 1967.

FERGUSON, R. D., and L. F. SARGENT, *Linear Programming* (New York: McGraw-Hill Book Co., Inc., 1958).

FETTER, R. B., and C. DALLECK, *Decision Models for Inventory Management* (Homewood, Illinois: Richard D. Irwin, Inc., 1961).

FILIPPO, EDWIN B., "Integrative Schemes in Management Theory," *Journal of the Academy of Management*, Vol. 11, March 1968, pp. 91-98.

FINER, HERMAN, *Road to Reaction* (Chicago: Encounter Paperback, 1963).

FISHER, GENE H., "The Analytical Bases of Systems Analysis," The RAND Corporation, Santa Monica, California, May 1966, mimeographed.

———, "Illustrative Example of Cost-Utility Considerations in a Military Context," in David Novick, ed., *Program Budgeting* (Cambridge, Mass.: Harvard University Press, 1965).

FLOYD, A. L., "Trend Forecasting, A Methodology for Figures of Merit," A Talk Prepared for the Industrial Management Center, Lake Placid, New York, May 1967; Burbank, Lockheed Aircraft Corporation, mimeographed.

FOLSOM, MARION B., *Executive Decision-Making* (New York: McGraw-Hill Book Co., Inc., 1962).

Forbes Magazine, "Who Says the Edsel was a Flop?" Vol. 100, August 15, 1967, pp. 32-35.

FORD, H. P., "Long Range Management Planning," *Long Range Planning in British Industry* (Bradford, England: The Management Centre, University of Bradford, 1967, mimeographed.).

FORD, HENRY, II, "What America Expects of Industry," speech delivered at the Annual Meeting of the Michigan State Chamber of Commerce, Detroit, Michigan, October, 1962.

FORRESTER, JAY W., "The Changing Face of Industry—The Role of Industrial Dynamics," Graduate School of Business Administration, University of Southern California, February 1964.

———, "The Impact of Feedback Control Concepts on the Management Sciences," Foundation for Instrumentation Education and Research (The FIER Distinguished Lecture 1960).

———, *Industrial Dynamics* (Cambridge: Massachusetts Institute of Technology Press, 1961).

Fortune, "Cunard Bets on a Pair of Queens," Vol. 75, January 1967, pp. 57-58, 62.

———, "Have Corporations a Higher Duty Than Profits?" Vol. 62, August 1960, pp. 108-109 and 146-153.

FOURRE, JAMES P., *Understanding Linear Programming*, Management Bulletin 94 (New York: American Management Association, Inc., 1967).

FOWLER, HENRY H., "National Interests and Multinational Business," in George A. Steiner and Warren M. Cannon, eds., *Multinational Corporate Planning* (New York: Crowell-Collier and Macmillan, 1966), Chapter 8.

FRANK, RONALD E., and PAUL E. GREEN, *Marketing Management Analysis* (Englewood Cliffs, N. J.: Prentice-Hall, Inc., 1966).

———, ALFRED A. KUEHN, and WILLIAM F. MASSEY, *Quantitative Techniques in Marketing Analysis* (Homewood, Ill.: Richard D. Irwin, Inc., 1962).

FREEDGOOD, SEYMOUR, "What Happened at Burlington When the King Dropped Dead," *Fortune*, Vol. 69, June 1964.

FREIMER, MARSHALL, and LEONARD S. SIMON, "The Evaluation of Potential New Product Alternatives," *Management Science*, Vol. 13, February 1967, pp. B-279-292.

FRIEDLAND, SEYMOUR, "How to Evaluate Investment Proposals," *California Management Review*, Vol II, No. 2, Winter 1960, pp. 47-56.

FRIEDMAN, MILTON, *Capitalism and Freedom* (Chicago, Ill.: University of Chicago Press, 1962).

———, "The Methodology of Positive Economics," *Essays in Positive Economics* (Chicago: University of Chicago Press, 1953).

FRIEDMANN, JOHN, "A Conceptual Model for the Analysis of Planning Behavior," *Administrative Science Quarterly*, Vol. 12, September 1967, pp. 225-252.

FULMER, ROBERT M., ed., *Organization for New-Product Development* (New York: National Industrial Conference Board, Inc., 1966).

———, "Product Management: Panacea or Pandora's Box," *California Management Review*, Vol. 7, Summer 1965, pp. 63-74.

FURST, SIDNEY, and MILTON SHERMAN, *Business Decisions* (New York: Random House, 1964).

GABOR, DENNIS, *Inventing the Future* (New York: Alfred A. Knopf, 1964).

GADDIS, PAUL O., "The Computer and the Management of Corporate Resources," *Industrial Management Review*, Fall 1967, pp. 5-18.

———, *Corporate Accountability* (New York: Harper and Row, 1964).

GALBRAITH, JOHN K., *The New Industrial State* (Boston: Houghton Mifflin Company, 1967).

GALLAGHER, JAMES D., *Management Information Systems and the Computer* (New York: American Management Association, Inc., 1961).

———, and DOUGLAS J. AXSMITH, "Data Processing in Transition," in *EDP The First Ten Years* (New York: McKinsey & Co., Inc., 1962).

GARDNER, FRED V., *Profit Management and Control* (New York: McGraw-Hill Book Co., Inc., 1955).

GARDNER, JOHN W., "You Can Tell a Creative Company by the People It Keeps," *Think*, Vol. 28, November-December 1962, pp. 2-7.

GARRETT, LEONARD S., and MILTON SILVER, *Production Management Analysis* (New York: Harcourt, Brace & World, Inc., 1966).

GELLERMAN, SAUL W., "The Company Personality," *The Management Review*, Vol. 48, Part 1, 1959.

GENERAL ELECTRIC COMPANY, *General Electric's Organization*, Book Two, *Professional Management in General Electric* (New York: General Electric Company, 1953-55).

GENTLE, EDGAR C., JR., *Data Communications in Business* (New York: American Telephone and Telegraph Company, 1965).

GILFILLAN, S. COLUM, "The Prediction of Technical Change," in James R. Bright, *Research Development and Technological Innovation* (Homewood, Ill.: Richard D. Irwin, Inc., 1964).

———, *The Sociology of Inventions* (Chicago, Illinois: Follett Publishing Co., 1935).

GILMORE, FRANK, and R. G. BRANDENBERG, "Anatomy of Corporate Planning," *Harvard Business Review*, Vol. 40, November-December 1962, pp. 61-69.

GINZBERG, ELI, DALE L. HIESTAND and BEATRICE G. REUBENS, *The Pluralistic Economy* (New York: McGraw-Hill Book Co., Inc., 1965).

———, and EWING W. REILLEY, *Effecting Change in Large Organizations* (New York: Columbia University Press, 1957).

GOETZ, BILLY E., *Management Planning and Control* (New York: McGraw-Hill Book Co., Inc., 1949).

———, *Quantitative Methods: A Survey and Guide for Managers* (New York: McGraw-Hill Book Co., Inc., 1965).

GOLDE, ROGER A., "Practical Planning For Small Business," *Harvard Business Review,* September-October 1964.

GOLDFARB, NATHAN, and WILLIAM K. KAISER, eds., *Gantt Charts and Statistical Quality Control* (Hempstead, N. Y.: Hofstra University, 1964).

GOOD, I. J., "How Rational Should a Manager Be?", *Management Science,* Vol. 88, July 1962, pp. 383-393.

GORDON, G., "A General Purpose Systems Simulator," *IBM Systems Journal,* Vol. I, September 1962.

GORDON, PAUL J., "Transcend the Current Debate on Administrative Theory," *Journal of the Academy of Management,* Vol. 6, December 1963, pp. 290-302.

GORDON, R. A., *Business Leadership in the Large Corporation* (Washington, D.C.: The Brookings Institution, 1945).

GORDON, T. J., and OLAF HELMER, *Report on a Long-Range Forecasting Study,* P-2982 (Santa Monica, Calif.: The RAND Corporation, September 1964, multilithed).

GORDON, WILLIAM J. J., *Synectics, The Development of Creative Capacity* (New York: Harper & Row, 1961).

GORT, MICHAEL, *Diversification and Integration in American Industry,* a study by the National Bureau of Economic Research (Princeton, New Jersey: Princeton University Press, 1962).

GRACIAN Y MORALES, BALTASAR JERÓNIMO, *The Science of Success and the Art of Prudence,* translated by Lawrence C. Lockley (Santa Clara, Calif.: University of Santa Clara Press, 1967).

GRANT, E. L., and W. G. IRESON, *Principles of Engineering Economy* (New York: The Ronald Press Company, 1960).

GREEN, PAUL E., "Bayesian Statistics and Product Decisions," *Business Horizons,* Vol. 5, Fall 1962, pp. 101-109.

GREEN, TIMOTHY, "Cunard Fights For Survival," *Fortune,* Vol. 75, January 1967, pp. 57-62.

GREENBERGER, MARTIN, ed., *Computers and the World of the Future* (Cambridge: The M.I.T. Press, 1962a).

———, ed., *Management and the Computer of the Future* (Cambridge: The M.I.T. Press, 1962b).

GREENE, TERRELL E., and J. C. HAYYA, *Air Superiority Map Exercise Logic and Task Breakdown* (Unpublished Document) (Santa Monica, Calif.: The RAND Corporation, April 23, 1964).

GREGORY, CARL E., *The Management of Intelligence: Scientific Problem Solving and Creativity* (New York: McGraw-Hill Book Co., Inc., 1967).

GREGORY, ROBERT H., and RICHARD L. VAN HORN, *Automatic Data Processing Systems* (San Francisco: Wadsworth Publishing Company, 1960).

GRETHER, E. T., "Galbraith Versus the Market: A Review Article," *Journal of Marketing,* Vol. 32, January 1968, pp. 9-13.

———, *Marketing and Public Policy* (Englewood Cliffs, New Jersey: Prentice-Hall, Inc., 1966).

GROSCH, H. R. J., "The Computer Downstairs," *Astronautics & Aeronautics,* April 1967, pp. 42-47.

GROSS, BERTRAM M., *The Legislative Struggle* (New York: McGraw-Hill Book Company, Inc., 1953).

———, *The Managing of Organizations* (New York: The Free Press of Glencoe, 1964).

GROSS, DONALD, and JACK L. RAY, "A General Purpose Forecast Simulator," *Management Science,* Vol. 11, April 1965.

GROSSMAN, ADRIAN J., "Inner-Directedness in Planning," *Management Technology,* Vol. 4, December 1964, pp. 92-114.

GULICK, LUTHER, *Administrative Reflections from World War II* (University, Alabama: University of Alabama Press, 1948).

————, and L. URWICK, eds., *Papers on the Science of Administration* (New York: Institute of Public Administration, 1937).

GUNN, WILLIAM A., "Airline System Simulation," *Operations Research,* Vol. 12, March-April 1964, pp. 206-229.

————, and LEE R. HOWARD, "Management Aspects of Airline System Simulation" (Burbank, California: Lockheed-California Company, 1966).

GUTH, WILLIAM D., and RENATO TAGIURI, "Personal Values and Corporate Strategies," *Harvard Business Review,* Vol. 43, September-October, 1965, pp. 123-124.

GUTMAN, PETER M., "Strategies for Growth," *California Management Review,* Vol. 6, Summer 1964.

HAAS, RAYMOND M., RICHARD I. HARTMAN, JOHN H. JAMES and ROBERT R. MILROY, *Long-Range Planning for Small Business* (Bloomington: Bureau of Business Research, Graduate School of Business, Indiana University, 1964).

HAEFFELE, JOHN W., *Creativity and Innovation* (New York: Reinhold Publishing Corp.; London: Chapman & Hall, Ltd., 1962).

HAIRE, MASON, "The Social Sciences and Management Practice," *California Management Review,* Vol. VI, Summer 1964, pp. 3-10.

————, EDWIN E. GHISELLI and LYMAN W. PORTER, *Managerial Thinking* (New York: John Wiley and Sons, Inc., 1966).

HAMILTON, EDITH, *The Greek Way* (New York: *Time Incorporated,* 1963).

HAMMERSLEY, J. M., and D. C. HANDSCOMB, *Monte Carlo Methods* (New York: John Wiley & Sons, Inc., 1964).

HAMMOND, JOHN S., III, "Better Decisions With Preference Theory," *Harvard Business Review,* Vol. 45, November-December, 1967, pp. 123-141.

HANNOCH, JULIUS, and IRWIN GOLDMAN, "Corporate Planning at Merck," in George A. Steiner and Warren M. Cannon, eds., *Multinational Corporate Planning* (New York: Crowell-Collier and Macmillan, 1966).

HANSEN, HARRY L., "Planning Product Strategy," in Donald M. Bowman and Francis M. Fillerup, *Management: Organization and Planning* (McGraw-Hill Book Co., Inc., 1963).

HARBISON, FREDERICK, and CHARLES A. MYERS, *Management in the Industrial World* (New York: McGraw-Hill Book Co., Inc., 1959).

HART, ALBERT G., *Anticipations, Uncertainty, and Dynamic Planning* (New York: Augustus M. Kelley, Inc., 1951).

HARTMAN, LAWTON M., "The Prospect of Forecasting Technology," in George A. Steiner and Warren M. Cannon, eds., *Multinational Corporate Planning* (New York: Crowell-Collier and Macmillan, 1966).

HARTMANN, HEINZ, "Managers and Entrepreneurs: A Useful Distinction?" *Administrative Science Quarterly,* Vol. 3, March 1959, pp. 429-451.

HAWKINS, DAVID F., "The Case of the Dubious Deferral," *Harvard Business Review,* Vol. 41, No. 3, May-June 1963, pp. 162-188.

HAYEK, FRIEDRICH A., *The Road to Serfdom* (Chicago: University of Chicago Press, 1944).

HAYNES, W. WARREN, and MARTIN B. SOLOMON, JR., "A Misplaced Emphasis in Capital Budgeting," *Economics and Business,* Vol. 2, February 1962, pp. 36-46.

HAYYA, JACK C., *A Study of the Appropriate Use of PERT in Procurement Contracts,* unpublished doctoral dissertation, Graduate School of Business Administration, UCLA, 1966.

HEIN, PIET, "The Road to Wisdom," *Life,* October 14, 1966.

HELMER, OLAF, *Social Technology* (New York-London: Basic Books, 1966).

————, and NICHOLAS RESCHER, "On the Epistemology of the Inexact Sciences," P-1513, Santa Monica, The RAND Corporation, 1958, and in *Management Science,* Vol. 5, 1959.

HEMPEL, EDWARD H., *Top Management Planning* (New York: Harper & Row Publishing Co., 1945).

HENDERSON, A., and R. SCHLAIFER, "Mathematical Programming," *Harvard Business Review,* Vol. 32, May-June 1954, pp. 73-100.

HENDERSON, BRUCE D., "Preventing Strategy Obsolescence," (Boston, Mass.: Boston Consulting Group, Inc., undated printed matter).

————, "Strategy Planning," *Business Horizons,* Vol. 7, Winter 1964.

HENRY, HAROLD WILKINSON, *Long-Range Planning in Industrial Corporations: An Analysis of Formalized Practices* (Ann Arbor: The University of Michigan, doctoral dissertation, 1965).

HERRMANN, C. C., and J. F. MAGEE, " 'Operations Research' for Management," *Harvard Business Review,* Vol. 31, July-August 1953.

HERTZ, DAVID B., "Investment Policies That Pay Off," *Harvard Business Review,* Vol. 46, January-February 1968.

————, "The Management of Innovation," *Management Review,* April 1965a.

————, "Mobilizing Management Science Resources," *Management Science,* Vol. 11, January 1965b, pp. 361-368.

————, "Risk Analysis in Capital Investment," *Harvard Business Review,* Vol. 42, January-February 1964.

HETRICK, JAMES C., "Mathematical Models in Capital Budgeting," *Harvard Business Review,* Vol. 39, January-February 1961, pp. 49-64.

HEYEL, CARL, ed., *Handbook of Industrial Research Management* (New York: Reinhold Publishing Corp., 1960).

HIGGINSON, M. VALLIANT, *Managing with EDP, A Look at the State of the Art,* AMA Research Study 71 (New York: American Management Association, Inc., 1965).

————, *Management Policies, I* and *II,* AMA Research Studies 76 and 78, respectively (New York: American Management Association, Inc., 1966).

HINRICHS, JOHN R., *Creativity in Industrial Scientific Research,* Bulletin No. 12 (New York: American Management Association, Inc., 1961).

HITCH, CHARLES J., "Analysis for Air Force Decisions," in E. S. Quade, ed., *Analysis for Military Decisions,* R-387-PR (Santa Monica, Calif.: The RAND Corporation, 1964), Chapter 2.

————, "An Appreciation of Systems Analysis," P-699 (Santa Monica, California: The RAND Corporation, August 18, 1955).

————, *Decision-Making for Defense* (Berkeley and Los Angeles: University of California Press, 1966).

————, "The New Approach to Management in the U.S. Defense Department," *Management Science,* Vol. 9, October 1962, pp. 1-8.

————, and ROLAND N. McKEAN, *The Economics of Defense in the Nuclear Age* (Cambridge: Harvard University Press, 1960).

————, and ————, "What Can Managerial Economics Contribute to Economic Theory?" *American Economic Review*, Vol. LI, May 1961, pp. 147-159.

HITCHCOCK, F. L., "Distribution of a Product From Several Sources to Numerous Localities," *Journal of Mathematical Physics*, Vol. 20, 1941, pp. 224-230.

HOFFMAN, GEORGE A., *Urban Underground Highways and Parking Facilities*, RM-3680-RC (Santa Monica, California: The RAND Corporation, August 1963).

HOLLOWAY, ROBERT J., and ROBERT S. HANCOCK, *Marketing in a Changing Environment* (New York: John Wiley & Sons, Inc., 1968).

HOLMES, PARKER M., RALPH E. BROWNLEE and ROBERT BARTELS, *Readings in Marketing* (Columbus, Ohio: Charles E. Merrill Books, Inc., 1963).

HOLTZ, J. N., *An Analysis of Major Scheduling Techniques in the Defense Systems Environment*, RM-4697-PR (Santa Monica: The RAND Corporation, October 1966).

HOOPES, ROY, *The Steel Crisis* (New York: The John Day Company, Inc., 1963).

HOOPES, TOWNSEND, "The Corporate Planner (New Edition)," *Business Horizons*, Vol. 5, No. 4, Winter 1962, pp. 59-68.

HOWARD, M. C., *Legal Aspects of Marketing* (New York: McGraw-Hill Book Co., Inc., 1964).

HOWELL, JAMES E., and DAVIEL TEICHROEW, *Mathematical Analysis for Business Decisions* (Homewood, Illinois: Richard D. Irwin, Inc., 1963).

HOWER, RALPH M., and CHARLES D. ORTH, III, *Managers and Scientists* (Boston: Graduate School of Business, Harvard University, 1963).

HUGHES, CHARLES L., *Goal Setting: Key to Individual and Organizational Effectiveness* (New York: American Management Association, Inc., 1965).

HUNT, MORTON M., "Bell Labs' 230 Long-Range Planners," *Fortune*, Vol. 49, May 1954, pp. 120-123 and pp. 129-136.

ISAACS, ASHER, and REUBEN E. SLESINGER, *Business, Government and Public Policy* (New York: D. Van Nostrand Company, Inc., 1964).

ISENSON, RAYMOND S., "Technological Forecasting: A Planning Tool," in George A. Steiner and Warren M. Cannon, eds., *Multinational Corporate Planning* (New York: Crowell-Collier and Macmillan, 1966).

ISTVAN, DONALD F., *Capital-Expenditure Decisions*, Indiana Business Report No. 33 (Bloomington, Ind.: Bureau of Business Research, Graduate School of Business, Indiana University, 1961).

JACKSON, HENRY M., "To Forge a Strategy for Survival," *Public Administration Review*, Vol. XIX, Summer 1959.

JACKSON, THOMAS W., and JACK M. SPURLOCK, *Research and Development Management* (Homewood, Illinois: Dow Jones-Irwin, Inc., 1966).

JACOBY, NEIL H., "Impacts of Scientific Change Upon Business Management," *California Management Review*, Vol. 4, Summer 1962, pp. 31-43.

JALLOW, RAY, *The Development and the Contribution of an Asset Management Methodology to the Long-Range Planning Function in the Banking Industry*, a doctoral dissertation, Graduate School of Business Administration, UCLA, 1966.

JAMISON, CHARLES L., *Business Policy* (Englewood Cliffs, N.J.: Prentice-Hall, Inc., 1953).

JANTSCH, ERICH, *Technological Forecasting in Perspective* (Paris: Organization for Economic Cooperation and Development, 1967).

JAPAN MANAGEMENT ASSOCIATION, *Long-Range Business Planning in Japan* (Tokyo: Japan Management Association, 1966).

JEROME, WILLIAM TRAVERS, III, *Executive Control—The Catalyst* (New York: John Wiley and Sons, Inc., 1961).

JOHNSON, LYNDON B., "The Great Society," Commencement Address, The University of Michigan, May 22, 1964.

———, Memorandum to Heads of Departments and Agencies, dated August 25, 1965.

JOHNSON, ORACE, "Corporate Philanthropy: An Analysis of Corporate Contributions," *The Journal of Business*, Vol. 39, October 1966.

JOHNSON, RICHARD A., FREMONT E. KAST and JAMES E. ROSENZWEIG, *The Theory and Management of Systems* (New York: McGraw-Hill Book Co., Inc., 1963).

JONES, MANLEY HOWE, *Executive Decision-Making* (Homewood, Illinois: Richard D. Irwin, Inc., 1957).

JONES, RALPH, "Management of New Products," *Journal of Industrial Engineering*, September-October 1958, pp. 429-435.

KAGDIS, JOHN, "The Mark I Business Simulation Model," TM-708/200/00, (Santa Monica, California: System Development Corporation, December 1, 1962).

———, and MICHAEL R. LACKNER, "A Management Control Systems Simulation Model," *Management Technology*, Vol. 3, December 1962, pp. 145-166.

KAHN, HERMAN, and IRWIN MANN, "Techniques of Systems Analysis," RM-1829-I (Santa Monica, California: The RAND Corporation, 1956).

———, and ———, "Ten Common Pitfalls," RM-1937 (Santa Monica, California: The RAND Corporation, July 1957).

———, and ANTHONY J. WIENER, *The Year 2000: A Framework for Speculation on the Next Thirty-Three Years* (New York: The Macmillan Co., 1967).

KAIDEN, MARTIN R., *Planning for Tomorrow: How Large Industrial Companies Plan for the Future*, master's dissertation, mimeographed (New York: New York University, 1967).

KAISER ALUMINUM & CHEMICAL CORPORATION, *Planning Guide*, February 1964.

KAMI, MICHAEL J., "Electronic Data Processing: Promise and Problems," *California Management Review*, Vol. 1, Fall 1958.

KANE, FRANCIS X., "Plans for Future Satellites Must Consider User Equipment," *Aerospace Management*, Vol. 2, Fall-Winter 1967, pp. 55-60.

KAPPEL, FREDERICK R., "The Information Revolution: Every Manager's In It," *Columbia Journal of World Business*, Vol. 1, Winter 1966.

KAPRIELYAN, S. PETER, "NASA Management at the Crossroads," *Aerospace Management*, Vol. 1, Summer 1966, pp. 3-11.

KAST, FREMONT E., "Motivating the Organization Man," *Business Horizons*, Vol. 4, Spring 1961.

———, and JAMES E. ROSENZWEIG, *Management in the Space Age* (New York: Exposition Press, 1962).

———, and ———, eds., *Science, Technology, and Management* (New York: McGraw-Hill Book Co., Inc., 1963).

KEITH, ROBERT J., "The Marketing Revolution," *Journal of Marketing*, Vol. 24, January 1960, pp. 35-38.

KELLEY, EUGENE J., and WILLIAM LAZER, *Managerial Marketing: Perspectives and Viewpoints* (Homewood, Illinois: Richard D. Irwin, Inc., 1962).

KERR, CLARK, JOHN T. DUNLO, FREDERICK H. BARBISON and CHARLES A. MYERS, *Industrialism and Industrial Man* (Cambridge, Mass.: Harvard University Press, 1960).

KILMER, DAVID C., "Growth by Acquisition: Some Guidelines for Success," *The McKinsey Quarterly*, Vol. III, Spring 1967.

KITCHING, JOHN, "Why Do Mergers Miscarry"? Vol. 45, November-December 1967, *Harvard Business Review*, pp. 84-101.

KLASS, PHILIP J., "New Approach Pinpoints Vital R&D Needs," *Aviation Week & Space Technology*, December 28, 1964, pp. 56-59.

———, "Rating System Gives Planning Priorities," *Aviation Week & Space Technology*, January 4, 1965, pp. 54-58.

KLEIN, HARRY T., "The Way Ahead," Address at Texaco Old-Timers' Dinner, New York, April 7, 1952.

KLINE, CHARLES H., "The Strategy of Product Policy," *Harvard Business Review*, Vol. 33, July-August 1955, pp. 91-100.

KNIGHT, W. D., and E. H. WEINWURM, *Managerial Budgeting* (New York: The Macmillan Company, 1964).

KOHLER, E. L., *A Dictionary for Accountants* (Englewood Cliffs, N. J.: Prentice-Hall, Inc., 1956).

KOONTZ, HAROLD, "The Management Theory Jungle," *Journal of the Academy of Management*, Vol. 4, December 1961, pp. 174-188.

———, "Top Management Takes a Second Look at Electronic Data Processing," *Business Horizons*, Vol. 2, Spring 1959, pp. 78-84.

———, ed., *Toward a Unified Theory of Management* (New York: McGraw-Hill Book Co., Inc., 1964).

———, and CYRIL O'DONNELL, *Management: A Book of Readings* (New York: McGraw-Hill Book Co., Inc., 1964a).

———, and ———, *Principles of Management*, 3rd edition (New York: McGraw-Hill Book Co., Inc., 1964b).

KOTLER, PHILIP, "The Competitive Marketing Simulator—A New Management Tool," *California Management Review*, Vol. 7, Spring 1965a, pp. 49-60.

———, "Competitive Strategies for New Product Marketing Over the Life Cycle," *Management Science*, Vol. 12, December 1965b, pp. B-104-119.

———, "The Use of Mathematical Models in Marketing," *Journal of Marketing*, Vol. 27, October 1963, pp. 31-41.

KRUPP, SHERMAN R., "Theoretical Explanation and the Nature of the Firm," *The Western Economic Journal*, Vol. 1, Summer 1963.

LA BARRE, WESTON, *The Human Animal* (Chicago, Illinois: University of Chicago Press, 1954).

LAPORTE, LOWELL, *Investor Relations* (New York: National Industrial Conference Board, 1967).

LARSON, R. L., "How to Define Administrative Problems," *Harvard Business Review*, Vol. 40, January-February 1962, pp. 68-80.

LAZARUS, RALPH, "The Case of the Oriental Rug," *Michigan Business Review*, Vol. XV, November 1963.

LAZER, WILLIAM, "Perspectives of Sales Forecasting," *Business Topics*, Vol. VII, Winter 1959.

LEAR, ROBERT W., "The Product Planning Committee: Its Opportunities and Responsibilities," in Albert Newgarden, ed., *Establishing a New Product Program*, Management Report 8 (New York: American Management Association, Inc., 1958).

LEARNED, EDMUND P., C. ROLAND CHRISTENSEN, KENNETH R. ANDREWS and WILLIAM D. GUTH, *Business Policy* (Homewood, Illinois: Richard D. Irwin, Inc., 1965).

———, and AUDREY T. SPROAT, *Organization Theory and Policy, Notes For Analysis* (Homewood, Illinois: Richard D. Irwin, Inc., 1966).

———, DAVID N. ULRICH and DONALD R. BOOZ, *Executive Action* (Boston: Harvard University Press, 1951).

LEAVITT, HAROLD J., *Managerial Psychology* (Chicago: The University of Chicago Press, 1958).

———, *The Social Science of Organizations* (Englewood Cliffs, New Jersey: Prentice-Hall, Inc., 1963).

———, and THOMAS L. WHISLER, "Management in the 1980's," *Harvard Business Review*, Vol. 36, 1958, pp. 41-48.

LE BRETON, PRESTON P., *General Administration: Planning and Implementation* (New York: Holt, Rinehart and Winston, 1965).

———, and DALE A. HENNING, *Planning Theory* (Englewood Cliffs, New Jersey: Prentice-Hall, Inc., 1961).

LECHT, LEONARD A., *Goals, Priorities, and Dollars, The Next Decade* (New York: The Free Press, 1966).

LEETE, GURDON W., "The EMSI Story," *The Lamp*, Vol. 49, Winter 1967 (Standard Oil Company of New Jersey publication) pp. 6-9.

LEMKE, B. C., and JAMES DON EDWARDS, eds., *Administrative Control and Executive Action* (Columbus, Ohio: Charles E. Merrill Books, Inc., 1961).

LENZ, R. C., JR., *Technological Forecasting*, Aeronautical Systems Division (Wright-Patterson Air Force Base: Defense Documentation Center Cat. No. AD-408085, June 1962).

LESHER, RICHARD L., and GEORGE J. HOWICK, *Background, Guidelines and Recommendations for Use in Assessing Effective Means of Channeling New Technologies in Promising Directions* (Washington: National Commission on Technology, Automation, and Economic Progress, November 1965).

LESSER, ARTHUR, JR., ed., *Decision-Making Criteria for Capital Expenditures*, Papers of the 4th Summer Symposium (Hoboken, New Jersey: *The Engineering Economist*, Stevens Institute of Technology, 1966).

LEVIN, RICHARD I., and C. A. KIRKPATRICK, *Quantitative Approaches to Management* (New York: McGraw-Hill Book Co., Inc., 1965).

LEVITT, THEODORE, "The Dangers of Social Responsibility," *Harvard Business Review*, Vol. 36, September-October 1958.

LEVY, ROBERT, "Borden's Land of Milk and Honey," *Dun's Review & Modern Industry*, May 1967.

LEWIN, KURT, *Field Theory in Social Science* (New York: Harper Torchbooks, Harper & Row, 1951).

LEWIS, JOHN P., *Business Conditions Analysis* (New York: McGraw-Hill Book Co., Inc., 1959).

LIKERT, RENSIS, *New Patterns of Management* (New York: McGraw-Hill Book Co., Inc., 1961).

LILIENTHAL, DAVID, "The Multinational Corporation," in Melvin Anshen and G. L. Bach, *Management and Corporation 1985* (New York: McGraw-Hill Book Co., Inc., 1960), pp. 119-158.

LINOWES, DAVID F., "Neglected Areas in Acquisition Evaluations," *Management Services*, Vol. 1, November-December 1964, pp. 13-21.

LINSTONE, HAROLD A., "On Mirages," Burbank, California: Lockheed Aircraft Corporation, May 25, 1967 (mimeographed).

LITCHFIELD, E. H., "Notes on a General Theory of Administration," *Administrative Science Quarterly*, Vol. 1, June 1956.

LLOYD, HUMPHREY, *Biography in Management Studies* (London: Hutchinson of London, 1964).

LOCKHEED-CALIFORNIA COMPANY, *Supersonic Transport Impact on the Commercial Airplane Market*, Study Three (Burbank, California: Lockheed Aircraft Corporation, 1966).

LORIE, J. H., and L. J. SAVAGE, "Three Problems in Capital Rationing," *Journal of Business*, Vol. XXVIII, October 1955.

LORIG, ARTHUR W., "Where Do Corporate Responsibilities Really Lie?" *Business Horizons*, Vol. 10, Spring 1967, pp. 51-54.

LORSCH, JAY W., *Product Innovation and Organization* (New York: The Macmillan Company, 1965).

———, and PAUL R. LAWRENCE, "Organizing for Product Innovation," *Harvard Business Review*, Vol. 43, January-February 1965, pp. 109-122.

LUNDBERG, CRAIG C., "Administrative Decisions—A Scheme for Analysis," *Journal of the Academy of Management*, Vol. 5, August 1962, pp. 165-178.

LYON, ROBERT, "Profit Maximization and Motivation," *Economics and Business Bulletin*, Temple University, 1962.

McCARTHY, E. JEROME, *Basic Marketing: A Managerial Approach*, rev. ed. (Homewood, Illinois: Richard D. Irwin, Inc., 1964).

McCLELLAND, DAVID C., *The Achieving Society* (New York: D. Van Nostrand Company, Inc., 1961).

McCLOSKEY, J. F. and F. N. TREFETHEN, *Operations Research for Management*, Vol. I (Baltimore, Md.: John Hopkins University Press, 1954).

McCORMICK, FOWLER, "The Philosophy and Ethics of Management," speech at UCLA, February 25, 1953 (mimeographed).

McDONALD, JOHN, "Georgia-Pacific: It Grows Big on Trees," *Fortune*, Vol. 65, May 1962.

———, "How Businessmen Make Decisions," *Fortune*, Vol. 52, Part 1, August 1955.

———, "The Men Who Made T. I.," *Fortune*, Vol. 64, November 1961.

———, "Sears Makes It Look Easy," *Fortune*, Vol. 69, May 1964.

McDONALD, J. D., *Strategy in Poker, Business and War* (New York: W. W. Norton, 1950).

McDONOUGH, ADRIAN M., *Information Economics and Management Systems* (New York: McGraw-Hill Book Company, Inc., 1963).

McFARLAND, DALTON E., *Management: Principles and Practices*, 2nd ed. (New York: The Macmillan Company, 1964).

McFARLANE, ALEXANDER N., "The Search for Purpose," *The Conference Board Record*, Vol. 11, February 1965.

McGREGOR, DOUGLAS, *The Human Side of Enterprise* (New York: McGraw-Hill Book Co., Inc., 1960).

———, edited by Warren G. Bennis and Caroline McGregor, *The Professional Manager* (New York: McGraw-Hill Book Co., Inc., 1967).

McGUIRE, JOSEPH W., "The Concept of the Firm," *California Management Review*, Vol. III, Summer 1961, pp. 64-88.

———, "The *Finalité* of Business," *California Management Review*, Vol. VIII, Summer 1966, pp. 89-94.

McKEAN, R. N., *Efficiency in Government Through Systems Analysis* (New York: John Wiley and Sons, Inc., 1958).

McKINSEY & COMPANY, INC., *Getting the Most Out of Your Computer* (New York: McKinsey & Company, Inc., 1963).

———, *EDP The First Ten Years* (New York: McKinsey & Company, Inc., 1961).

McKINSEY, JAMES O., "Adjusting Policies to Meet Changing Conditions," General Management Series, No. 116 (New York: American Management Association, Inc., 1932).

———, *Budgetary Control* (New York: The Ronald Press Company, 1923).

McLAUGHLIN, CHARLES C., "The Stanley Steamer: A Study in Unsuccessful Innovation," *Explorations in Entrepreneurial History*, Vol. 7, October 1954, pp. 37-47.

McLEAN, JOHN G., "How to Evaluate New Capital Investments," *Harvard Business Review*, Vol. XXXVI, November-December 1958.

———, "Better Reports for Better Control," *Harvard Business Review*, Vol. 35, May-June 1957, pp. 95-104.

McMILLAN, CLAUDE, and RICHARD F. GONZALEZ, *Systems Analysis: A Computer Approach to Decision Models* (Homewood, Illinois: Richard D. Irwin, Inc., 1965).

McMURRY, ROBERT N., "Clear Communications for Chief Executives," *Harvard Business Review*, March-April 1965, Vol. 43, pp. 131-147.

MacDOUGAL, GARY E., "Investing in a Dividend Boost," Vol. 45, *Harvard Business Review*, July-August 1967, pp. 87-92.

MACE, MYLES L., "The President and Corporate Planning," *Harvard Business Review*, January-February 1965.

———, "The President and International Operations," *Harvard Business Review*, November-December 1966.

———, and GEORGE G. MONTGOMERY, *Management Problems of Corporate Acquisition* (Boston: Division of Research, Graduate School of Business Administration, Harvard University, 1962).

MACHIAVELLI, NICCOLO, *The Prince and the Discourses* (New York: Modern Library, 1950).

MACHLUP, FRITZ, "Theories of the Firm: Marginalist, Behavioral, Managerial," *The American Economic Review*, Vol. LVII, March 1967, pp. 1-33.

MAGEE, JOHN F., "Decision Trees for Decision Making," *Harvard Business Review*, Vol. 42, July-August 1964a, pp. 126-138.

———, "How to Use Decision Trees in Capital Investment," *Harvard Business Review*, Vol. 42, September-October 1964b, pp. 79-96.

MAINER, ROBERT, "The Impact of Strategic Planning on Executive Behavior," Boston, Mass., Boston Safe Deposit and Trust Company, multilithed, 1965.

MALCOLM, D. G., "The Use of Simulation in Management Analysis—A Survey and Bibliography." SP-126, Santa Monica, California, System Development Corporation, November 1959.

———, ALAN J. ROWE, and LORIMER F. McCONNELL, eds., *Management Control Systems* (New York: John Wiley & Sons, Inc., 1960).

MALOTT, JUDITH, *Company Organization for Economic Forecasting*, Research Report No. 28 (New York: American Management Association, Inc., 1957).

Management Methods, "How Management Tackles Advance Planning," Vol. 13, January 1958.

MAPES, GLYNN, " 'In-House' Rivalry," *Wall Street Journal*, September 14, 1966.

MARCH, JAMES G., and HERBERT A. SIMON, *Organizations* (New York: John Wiley & Sons, Inc., 1958).

MARGOLIS, J., "The Analysis of the Firm: Rationalism, Conventionalism, and Behaviorism," *The Journal of Business*, Vol. 31, July 1958.

MARKHAM, JESSE W., "Antitrust Trends and New Constraints," *Harvard Business Review*, May-June 1963.

MARKOWITZ, H., B. HAUSNER, and H. KARR, *Simscript: A Simulation Programming Language* (New York: Prentice-Hall, Inc., 1963).

MARSHALL, ALFRED, *Principles of Economics* (New York: The Macmillan Company, 1890).

MARSHALL, A. W.,"Experimentation by Simulation and Monte Carlo," P-1174 (Santa Monica, Calif.: The RAND Corporation, January 28, 1958).

MARTING, ELIZABETH, ed., *Developing a Product Strategy* (New York: American Management Association, Inc., 1959).

MASLOW, A. H., "A Theory of Human Motivation," *The Psychological Review*, Vol. 50, July 1943, pp. 370-396.

MASON, EDWARD S., "The Apologetics of 'Managerialism,'" *The Journal of Business*, Vol. XXXI, January 1958.

————, ed., *The Corporation in Modern Society* (Cambridge, Mass.: Harvard University Press, 1960).

MASON, R. HAL, "Organizing for Corporate Planning," in *Proceedings of the Long Range Planning Service Client Conference, February 7-9, 1962* (Menlo Park, Calif.: Stanford Research Institute, 1962).

MASSÉ, PIERRE, "National Planning and Business Enterprise in France," in George A. Steiner and Warren M. Cannon, *Multinational Corporate Planning* (New York: Crowell-Collier and Macmillan, 1966).

MASSEY, WILLIAM F. (Compiler), *Planning and Decision-Making in Marketing: A Selected Bibliography* (annotated) (Cambridge: School of Industrial Management, Massachusetts Institute of Technology, 1961).

MATTHEWS, JOHN B., JR., ROBERT D. BUZZELL, THEODORE LEVITT and RONALD E. FRANK, *Marketing: An Introductory Analysis* (New York: McGraw-Hill Book Co., Inc., 1964).

MAURER, HERRYMON, *Great Enterprise* (New York: The Macmillan Company, 1955).

MAYO, ELTON, *The Human Problems of an Industrial Civilization* (New York: Viking Press, 1960).

————, *The Social Problems of an Industrial Civilization* (Boston, Mass.: Harvard University Graduate School of Business Administration, 1945).

MEE, JOHN F., "The Creative Thinking Process," *Indiana Business Review*, Vol. XXXI, February 1956, pp. 3-7.

————, *Management Thought in a Dynamic Economy* (New York: New York University Press, 1963).

MERRILL, HARWOOD F., ed., *Classics in Management* (New York: American Management Association, Inc., 1960).

METCALF, HENRY C., and LYNDALL URWICK, eds., *The Collected Papers of Mary Follett* (New York: Harper and Brothers, Publishers, 1942).

MEYER, HERBERT H., EMANUEL KAY, and JOHN R. P. FRENCH, JR., "Performance Appraisal—A New Approach," *Harvard Business Review*, Vol. 43, January-February, 1965.

MILLER, ARJAY, "New Roles for the Campus and the Corporation," *Michigan Business Review*, November 1966.

————, "Reporting to Top Management at Ford," *California Management Review*, Vol. 1, Fall 1958.

MILLER, DAVID W., and MARTIN K. STARR, *Executive Decisions and Operations Research* (Englewood Cliffs, N.J.: Prentice-Hall, Inc., 1960).

MILLER, ERNEST C., *Objectives and Standards Research Study 74,* (New York: American Management Association, Inc., 1966).

———, *Objectives and Standards of Performance in Marketing Management,* AMA Research Study 85 (New York: American Management Association, Inc., 1967).

MILLER, JAMES H., "A Glimpse at Practice in Calculating and Using Return on Investment," *N.A.A. Bulletin,* June 1960.

MILLER, ROBERT W., *Schedule, Cost and Profit Control With PERT* (New York: McGraw-Hill Book Co., Inc., 1963).

MILLER, STANLEY S., *The Management Problems of Diversification* (New York: John Wiley & Sons, Inc., 1963).

MILLER, THEODORE T., "Projecting the Profitability of New Products," in *The Commercialization of Research Results,* Special Report No. 20 (New York: American Management Association, Inc., 1957).

MITCHELL, W. E., "Cash Forecasting: The Four Methods Compared," *The Controller,* Vol. 28, April 1960.

MONSEN, R. J., B. O. SAXBERG and R. A. SUTERMEISTER, "The Modern Manager, What Makes Him Run?" *Business Horizons,* Vol. 9, Fall 1966.

———, *Modern American Capitalism: Ideologies and Issues* (Boston: Houghton Mifflin Company, 1963).

MONTANA, PATRICK J., *The Marketing Executive of The Future* (New York: American Management Association, Inc., 1967).

MOORE, FRANKLIN G., *Management Organization and Practice* (New York: Harper and Row Publishers, 1964).

MOORE, G. H., ed., *Business Cycle Indicators,* Vols. I, II, National Bureau of Economic Research (Princeton, N.J.: Princeton University Press, 1961).

———, and JULIUS SHISKIN, *Indicators of Business Expansions and Contractions: A Reviewed List* (New York: Columbia University, 1966).

MOORE, WILBERT E., *The Conduct of the Corporation* (New York: Random House, 1962).

MORGENSTERN, OSKAR, *On the Accuracy of Economic Observations* (Princeton, N. J.: Princeton University Press, 1963).

MORRIS, WILLIAM T., "Intuition and Relevance," *Management Science,* Vol. 14, December 1967a, pp. B-157-165.

———, "On the Art of Modeling," *Management Science,* Vol. 13, August 1967b, pp. B-707-717.

———, *Management Science in Action* (Homewood, Illinois: Richard D. Irwin, Inc., 1963).

MUELLER, WILLARD F., "The Origins of the Basic Inventions Underlying DuPont's Major Product and Process Innovations, 1920 to 1959," in National Bureau of Economic Research, *The Rate and Direction of Inventive Activity* (Princeton, N.J.: Princeton University Press, 1962).

MULLER, HERBERT J., *Freedom in the Western World* (New York: Harper & Row, 1963).

MUND, VERNON A., *Government and Business,* 2nd ed. (New York: Harper & Row, 1955).

MURDIC, R. G., "The Long-Range Planning Matrix," *California Management Review,* Vol. 7, Winter 1964, pp. 35-42.

MYERS, CHARLES A., ed., *The Impact of Computers on Management* (Cambridge: The M.I.T. Press, 1967).

MYERS, M. SCOTT, "Conditions for Manager Motivation," *Harvard Business Review,* Vol. 44, January-February, 1967.

NATIONAL ASSOCIATION OF ACCOUNTANTS, *Cash Flow Analysis for Managerial Control*, Research Report No. 38 (New York, 1961).

———, *The Capital Expenditure Control Program*, Accounting Practice Report No. 7, *N.A.A. Bulletin*, March 1959.

NATIONAL AERONAUTICS AND SPACE ADMINISTRATION, *DOD and NASA Guide, PERT Cost*, Office of the Secretary of Defense (Washington, D. C., June 1962).

———, *An Administrative History of NASA, 1958-1963* (Washington, D.C.: National Aeronautics and Space Administration, 1966).

NATIONAL BUREAU OF ECONOMIC RESEARCH, *The Rate and Direction of Inventive Activity* (Princeton, N. J.: Princeton University Press, 1962).

NATIONAL INDUSTRIAL CONFERENCE BOARD, *Appraising the Market for New Industrial Products*, Studies in Business Policy, No. 123 (New York: N.I.C.B., 1967).

———, *Forecasting Sales*, Studies in Business Policy, No. 106 (New York: N.I.C.B., 1963).

———, "Long-Range Planning Pays Off," *Business Record*, October 1956.

———, *Managing Company Cash*, Studies in Business Policy, No. 99 (New York: N.I.C.B., 1961).

NATIONAL PLANNING ASSOCIATION, "*The Use of Economic Projections in Long-Range Business Planning: Results of a Questionnaire Survey*," National/Regional Economic Projections Series, Report No. 66-J-5 (Washington, D.C.: December 1966) (Mimeographed).

NATIONAL SCIENCE FOUNDATION, *Basic Research, Applied Research, and Development in Industry, 1964* (Washington, D.C.: U.S. Government Printing Office, 1966a).

———, "Reviews of Data on Science Resources," N.S.F. 66-33, No. 10, December 1966 (Washington, D.C.: U.S. Government Printing Office, 1966b).

NAYLOR, THOMAS H., JOSEPH L. BALINTFY, DONALD S. BURDICK and KONG CHU, *Computer Simulation Techniques* (New York: John Wiley and Sons, Inc., 1966).

NELSON, RALPH, *Merger Movements in American Industry 1895-1956*, National Bureau of Economic Research, Report #66 (Princeton, N.J.: Princeton University Press, 1959).

NEUSCHEL, RICHARD F., *Management by System* (New York: McGraw-Hill Book Co., Inc., 1960).

———, "Profit Improvement as a Way of Corporate Life," *The McKinsey Quarterly*, Vol. 1, Spring 1965, pp. 38-47.

NEUSCHEL, ROBERT P., "Physical Distribution: Forgotten Profit Frontier," *The McKinsey Quarterly*, Vol. III, Spring 1967, pp. 51-63.

NEWELL, WILLIAM T., JR., *Long-Range Planning, Policies and Practices: Selected Companies Operating in Texas*, Research Monograph No. 25 (Austin, Texas: Bureau of Business Research, The University of Texas, 1963).

NEWGARDEN, ALBERT, ed., *Corporate Mergers and Acquisitions*, Management Report No. 4, (New York: American Management Association, Inc., 1958a.)

———, ed., *Establishing a New Product Program*, Management Report 8, (New York: American Management Association, Inc., 1958b).

NEWMAN, MAURICE S., "Return on Investment: An Analysis of the Concept," *Management Services*, Vol. 3, July-August 1966.

NEWMAN, WILLIAM H., *Administrative Action* (Englewood Cliffs, N. J.: Prentice-Hall, Inc., 1951).

———, "Shaping the Master Strategy of Your Firm," *California Management Review*, Vol. 9, Spring 1967.

———, and JAMES P. LOGAN, *Business Policies and Central Management*, 5th ed. (Chicago, Ill.: South-Western Publishing Company, 1965).

——, and ——, *Management of Expanding Enterprises* (New York: Columbia University, 1955).

——, and CHARLES E. SUMMER, JR., *The Process of Management* (Englewood Cliffs, N. J.: Prentice-Hall, Inc., 1961).

Newsweek, "Sony: How to Grow Big by Thinking Small," Vol. 65, June 13, 1966, pp. 88-90.

NISENOFF, N., "Hardware for Information Processing Systems: Today and in the Future," *Proceedings of the IEEE*, Vol. 54, December 1966, pp. 1820-1835.

NORDQUIST, GERALD L., "The Breakup of the Maximization Principle," *Economics and Business*, Vol. 5, Fall 1965, pp. 33-46.

NOVICK, DAVID, ed., *Program Budgeting* (Cambridge, Mass.: Harvard University Press, 1965).

——, "What Do We Mean by Research and Development?" *California Management Review*, Vol II, Spring 1960.

ODIORNE, GEORGE S., "A Search for Objectives in Business—The Great Image Hunt," *Michigan Business Review*, January 1966.

——, *Management by Objective* (New York: Pitman Publishing Corp., 1965).

O'DONNELL, CYRIL, "Highlights of the Seminar Discussion" in George A. Steiner, ed., *Managerial Long-Range Planning* (New York: McGraw-Hill Book Co., Inc., 1963).

——, "Coordination of the Firm's Plans and the Nation's Economic Objectives," *Economie Appliquée* (Institut de Science Économique Appliquée, Paris), Winter 1965.

——, ed., *The Strategy of Corporate Research* (San Francisco: Chandler Publishing Company, 1967).

O'HANLON, THOMAS, "The Odd News About Conglomerates," *Fortune*, Vol. LXXV, June 1967.

O'MEARA, JOHN T., JR., "Selecting Profitable Products," *Harvard Business Review*, Vol. 39, January-February 1961.

OPINION RESEARCH CORPORATION, *The Conflict Between the Scientific Mind and the Management Mind* (Princeton, New Jersey: Opinion Research Corporation, 1959).

OPLER, ASCHER, "New Directions in Software 1960-1966," *Proceedings of the IEEE*, Vol. 54, December 1966, pp. 1757-1763.

OPTNER, STANFORD L., *Systems Analysis for Business and Industrial Problem Solving* (Englewood Cliffs, New Jersey: Prentice-Hall, Inc., 1965).

OTTEN, P. F. S., In *Proceedings, International Industrial Conference, 1961* (Co-sponsored by the National Industrial Conference Board and Stanford Research Institute.) (Menlo Park: Stanford Research Institute, 1961).

OTTO, D. D., "Principles of Planning as Applied by Philips," in George A. Steiner and Warren M. Cannon, eds., *Multinational Corporate Planning* (New York: Crowell-Collier and Macmillan, 1966).

OWEN, ROBERT, *A New View of Society* (New York: E. Bliss and E. White, 1825); part of this can be found in Harwood F. Merrill, ed., *Classics in Management* (New York: American Management Association, Inc. 1960).

OXENFELDT, ALFRED R., *Developing a Product Strategy* (New York: American Management Association, Inc., 1959).

OZBEKHAN, HASAN, "Automation," *Science Journal*, Vol. 3, October 1967, pp. 67-72.

PACKARD, V., *The Hidden Persuaders* (New York: D. McKay, 1957).

——, *The Waste Makers* (New York: D. McKay, 1960).

PARNES, SIDNEY J., and HAROLD F. HARDING, eds., *Toward a Theory of Creativity* (New York: Charles Scribner's Sons, 1962).

PARSONS, TALCOTT, *Essays in Sociological Theory* (New York: The Free Press of Glencoe, 1954).

PAYNE, BRUCE, *Planning for Company Growth: The Executives Guide to Effective Long-Range Planning* (New York: McGraw-Hill, 1963).

PEARSON, ANDRALL E., and THOMAS W. WILSON, JR., "Making Your Marketing Organization Work" (New York: Association of National Advertisers, Inc., 1967).

PECK, MERTON J., and FREDERICK M. SCHERER, *The Weapons Acquisition Process: An Economic Analysis* (Boston: Graduate School of Business Administration, Harvard University, 1962).

PEGRAM, ROGER M., and EARL L. BAILEY, "The New-Products Race," *The Marketing Executive Looks Ahead* (New York: National Industrial Conference Board, Inc., 1967).

PEGRUM, DUDLEY F., *The Regulation of Industry* (Homewood, Illinois: Richard D. Irwin, Inc., 1949).

PEIRCE, JAMES L., "The Budget Comes of Age," *Harvard Business Review*, Vol. 32, May-June 1954.

PELZ, DONALD C., "Freedom in Research," *International Science and Technology*, February 1964, pp. 54-66.

———, and FRANK M. ANDREWS, *Scientists in Organizations: Productive Climates for Research and Development* (New York: John Wiley & Sons, Inc., 1966).

PENROSE, EDITH TILTON, *The Theory of the Growth of the Firm* (New York: John Wiley & Sons, Inc., 1959).

PESSEMIER, EDGAR A., "Forecasting Brand Performance Through Simulation Experiments," *Journal of Marketing*, Vol. 38, April 1964, pp. 41-46.

———, *New Product Decision: An Analytical Approach* (New York: McGraw-Hill Book Co., Inc., 1966).

PETIT, THOMAS A., "The Doctrine of Socially Responsible Management," *Arizona Review*, Vol. 14, December 1965a.

———, "Making Socially Responsible Decisions," *Journal of the Academy of Management*, Vol. 9, December 1966, pp. 308-317.

———, "The Moral Crisis of Big Business," *Arizona Review*, Vol. 14, November 1965b.

PETRUSCHELL, R. L., "Project Cost Estimating," P-3687 (Santa Monica, Calif.: The RAND Corporation, September 1967).

PFEFFER, IRVING, ed., *The Financing of Small Business: A Current Assessment* (New York: Crowell-Collier, Macmillan, 1967).

PFIZER, CHAS. & CO., INC., *Annual Report, 1963*, New York.

PFLOMM, NORMAN E., *Financial Committees*, Studies in Business Policy, No. 105 (New York: National Industrial Conference Board, Inc., 1963a).

———, *Managing Capital Expenditures*, Business Policy Study No. 107 (New York: National Industrial Conference Board, 1963b).

———, *Managing Company Cash* (New York: National Industrial Conference Board, Inc., 1961).

PHILLIPS, JR., CHARLES F., "What is Wrong With Profit Maximization?" *Business Horizons*, Vol. 6, Winter 1963, pp. 73-80.

PIATIGORSKY, GREGOR, *Cellist* (New York: Doubleday, 1965).

PIEROTTI, ROLAND, Executive Vice President, Bank of America, *Time*, December 29, 1967.

Planning-Programming-Budgeting, Hearings Before the Subcommittee on National Security and International Operations of the Committee on Government Operations, U.S.

Senate, 90th Congress, 1st Session, Washington, D. C., U.S. Government Printing Office, 1967.

PLUMMER, GEORGE F., and GEORGE MOLLER, "The Financial Executive," *The Controller* (New York: Financial Executives Institute, January 1962, pp. 16-18, 22, 34-35).

PORTER, LYMAN W., *Organizational Patterns of Managerial Job Attitudes* (New York: American Foundation for Management Research, 1964).

POSTLEY, JOHN A., *Computers and People* (New York: McGraw-Hill Book Co., Inc., 1960).

PREHODA, ROBERT W., *Designing the Future: The Role of Technological Forecasting* (Philadelphia: Chilton Book Co., 1966).

PRINCE, THOMAS R., *Information Systems for Management Planning and Control* (Homewood, Illinois: Richard D. Irwin, Inc., 1966).

PRYOR, MILLARD H., JR., "International Corporate Planning: How Is It Different?" *Management Technology*, Vol. 4, December 1964, pp. 139-148.

QUADE, E. S., ed., *Analysis for Military Decisions* (Santa Monica, California: The RAND Corporation, 1964).

———, "Military Systems Analysis," RA-3452-PR (Santa Monica, California: The RAND Corporation, 1963).

———, "Pitfalls In Military Systems Analysis" (Santa Monica, California: The RAND Corporation, 1962).

———, "Systems Analysis Techniques for Planning-Programming-Budgeting," P-3322, (Santa Monica, California: The RAND Corporation, March 1966).

———, and W. L. BOUCHER, eds., *Systems Analysis and Policy Planning: Applications in Defense* (New York: American Elsevier Publishing Co., 1968).

QUINN, JAMES BRIAN, "Budgeting for Research," in Carl Heyel, ed., *Handbook of Industrial Research Management* (New York: Reinhold Publishing Corp., 1960).

RADAMAKER, TED, *Business Systems,* Vol. II (Cleveland, Ohio: Systems and Procedures Association, 1963).

RANDALL, CLARENCE B., *The Folklore of Management* (Boston: Little, Brown and Co., 1959).

RANDLE, C. WILSON, "Generating New Product Ideas," *California Management Review*, Vol. 2, Winter 1960.

RAPOPORT, LEO A. and WILLIAM P. DREWS, "Mathematical Approach to Long-Range Planning," *Harvard Business Review*, Vol. 4, May-June 1962, pp. 75-87.

RAUTENSTRAUCH, WALTER, *Economics of Enterprise* (New York: John Wiley and Sons, Inc., 1939).

RAVENCROFT, E. A., "Return on Investment," *Harvard Business Review*, Vol. 38, No. 2, March-April 1960.

REICHARD, ROBERT S., *Practical Techniques of Sales Forecasting* (New York: McGraw-Hill Book Co., Inc., 1966).

REISMAN, DAVID, *The Lonely Crowd* (New Haven, Conn.: Yale University Press, 1950).

REVSON, CHARLES, "The Development of the Futurama Lipstick Case," in Sidney Furst and Milton Sherman, *Business Decisions* (New York: Random House, 1964).

REYNOLDS, WILLIAM H., "The Edsel Ten Years Later," *Business Horizons,* Vol. 10, Fall 1967, pp. 39-46.

RICHMAN, BARRY M., "A Rating Scale for Product Innovation," *Business Horizons,* Vol. 5, Summer 1962.

————, "The Soviet Educational and Research Revolution: Implications for Management Development," *California Management Review*, Vol. IX, Summer 1967, pp. 3-16.

RILEY, JOHN W., JR., and MARGUERITE F. LEVY, eds., *The Corporation and Its Publics: Essays on the Corporate Image* (New York: John Wiley and Sons, Inc., 1963).

RINGBAKK, KJELL-ARNE, *Organized Corporate Planning Systems* (Madison, Wisc.: Graduate School of Business, University of Wisconsin, doctoral dissertation, 1968).

ROBERTS, EDWARD B., "Industrial Dynamics and the Design of Management Control Systems," *Management Technology*, Vol. 3, December 1963, pp. 100-118.

————, *The Dynamics of Research and Development* (New York: Harper & Row, 1964).

ROBINSON, DWIGHT E., "Fashion Theory and Product Design," *Harvard Business Review*, Vol. 36, November-December 1958.

ROBINSON, MARSHALL A., HERBERT C. MORTON, and JAMES D. CALDERWOOD, *An Introduction to Economic Reasoning*, 4th ed. (Washington, D. C.: The Brookings Institution, 1967).

ROBINSON, RICHARD D., *International Business Policy* (New York: Holt, Rinehart, and Winston, 1964).

ROCKEFELLER, DAVID, *Creative Management in Banking* (New York: McGraw-Hill Book Co., Inc., 1964).

ROEHL, ORA C., "The Pitfalls and Potentialities in Acquisitions and Mergers," Speech at Tenth Annual Management Conference, University of Chicago, March 14, 1962 (mimeographed).

ROETHLISBERGER, F. J., *Management and Morals* (Cambridge, Mass.: Harvard University Press, 1941).

————, and W. J. DICKSON, *Management and the Worker* (Cambridge, Mass.: Harvard University Press, 1939).

————, *et al.*, *Training for Human Relations* (Boston: Graduate School of Business Administration, Harvard University, 1954).

ROKEACH, MILTON, "In Pursuit of the Creative Process," in Gary A. Steiner, ed., *The Creative Organization* (Chicago: University of Chicago Press, 1965).

ROMAN, D. D., "The PERT System: An Appraisal of Program Evaluation Review Techniques," *Journal of the Academy of Management*, Vol. 5, April 1962, pp. 57-65.

ROOSEVELT, ELEANOR, *Tomorrow is Now* (New York: Harper & Row, 1963).

ROOT, L. EUGENE, and GEORGE A. STEINER, "The Lockheed Aircraft Corporation Master Plan," in David W. Ewing, *Long Range Planning for Management*, rev. ed. (New York: Harper & Row, 1964).

ROSENZWEIG, JAMES E., "Managers and Management Scientists (Two Cultures)," *Business Horizons*, Vol. 10, Fall 1967, pp. 79-86.

ROSTOW, EUGENE V., "To Whom and For What Ends is Corporate Management Responsible?" Chapter 3 in Edward S. Mason, ed., *The Corporation in Modern Society*, (Cambridge, Mass.: Harvard University Press, 1960).

ROWAN, HELEN, "The Creative People: How to Spot Them," *Think*, Vol. 28, November-December 1962.

ROWE, ALAN J., "Computer Simulation—A Solution Technique for Management Problems," *Proceedings, Fall Joint Computer Conference, 1965*.

————, "Information Technology in the 1970 Era," July 21, 1967 (mimeographed).

ROWE, MALCOLM J., "Assessing Future Opportunities for Growth," National Industrial Conference Board, Inc., Midwest Marketing Conference, May 10-11, 1966 (mimeographed).

ROWEN, HENRY, *Statement Before the Special Subcommittee on Scientific Manpower Utilization of the Senate Committee on Labor and Public Welfare*, January 27, 1967 (mimeographed).

RUBENSTEIN, ALBERT H., "Field Studies of Idea Flow and Project Selection in Industry," in Burton V. Dean, ed., *Operations Research in Research and Development* (New York: John Wiley and Sons, 1963).

———, *Organization and Research and Development Decision-Making Within the Decentralized Firm* (Evanston, Ill.: Northwestern University, 1960, mimeographed).

———, "Setting Criteria for R&D," *Harvard Business Review*, Vol. 35, January-February 1957.

———, MICHAEL RADNOR, NORMAN R. BANKER, DAVID R. HEIMAN and JOHN B. McCOLBY, "Some Organizational Factors Related to the Effectiveness of Management Science Groups in Industry," *Management Science*, Vol. 13, April 1967, pp. B-508-518.

RUSH, HAROLD M. F., *Managing Change* (New York: National Industrial Conference Board, Inc., 1967).

ST. THOMAS, CHARLES E., *Practical Business Planning* (New York: American Management Association, Inc., 1965).

SALES AND MARKETING EXECUTIVES' ASSOCIATION OF LOS ANGELES, *A Study of the Marketing Executives' Role in Long-Range Company Planning*, A Study Conducted by The Sales and Marketing Executives Association of Los Angeles, Research Projects Committee, 1965.

SALZBERG, PAUL L., "Progress Through Coordinated Effort," in Jerome W. Blood, *The Management of Scientific Talent* (New York: American Management Association, Inc., 1963).

SANDAGE, C. H., "Sandage Defines the Role of Advertising," *Advertising Age*, May 15, 1961, pp. 77-80.

SANDS, SAUL S., *Setting Advertising Objectives*, Studies in Business Policy, No. 118 (New York: National Industrial Conference Board, Inc., 1966).

SANFORD, RALPH S., and EARL L. BAILEY, *The Product Manager System*, Experiences in Marketing Management, No. 8 (New York: National Industrial Conference Board, Inc., 1965).

SAYLES, LEONARD R., and GEORGE STRAUSS, *Human Behavior in Organizations* (Englewood Cliffs, N.J.: Prentice-Hall, Inc., 1966).

SAYRE, WALLACE, "The Triumph of Technique Over Purpose," *Public Administration Review*, Spring 1948.

SCHABACKER, JOSEPH C., *Cash Planning in Small Manufacturing Companies*, Small Business Administration (Washington, D.C.: U.S. Government Printing Office, 1960).

SCHAFFIR, WALTER B., "What is Corporate Planning? What Should it Be?" *Chapter Newsletter* (American Marketing Association), Vol. 19, November 1963.

SCHIFF, MICHAEL, and MARTIN MELLMAN, *Financial Management of the Marketing Function* (New York: Financial Executives Research Foundation, Inc., 1962).

SCHLAIFER, ROBERT O., *Introduction to Statistics for Business Decisions* (New York: McGraw-Hill Book Co., Inc., 1961).

———, *Analysis of Decisions Under Uncertainty* (New York: McGraw-Hill Book Co., Inc., 1967).

———, *Probability and Statistics for Business* (New York: McGraw-Hill Book Co., Inc., 1959).

SCHMOOKLER, JACOB, *Invention and Economic Growth* (Cambridge, Mass.: Harvard University Press, 1966).

SCHODERBEK, PETER P., "A Study of the Applications of PERT," *Journal of the Academy of Management*, Vol. 8, September 3, 1954, pp. 199-210.

SCHOLLHAMMER, HANS, *French Economic Planning and Its Impact on Business Decisions* (Bloomington: Graduate School of Business, Indiana University, 1967, doctoral dissertation).

SCHRAMM, WILBUR, *The Process and Effects of Mass Communication* (Urbana, Illinois: University of Illinois Press, 1954).

SCHUMPETER, JOSEPH A., *The Theory of Economic Development*, translated by Redvers Opie, *Harvard Economic Studies*, Vol. XLVI, 1934.

SCHWITTER, JOSEPH P., "Computer Effect upon Managerial Jobs," *Journal of the Academy of Management*, Vol. 8, September 1965.

SCOTT, BRIAN W., *Long-Range Planning in American Industry* (New York: American Management Association, Inc., 1965).

SCOTT, WILLIAM E., "The Creative Individual," *Journal of the Academy of Management*, Vol. 8, September 1965.

SCOTT, WILLIAM G., *Human Relations in Management: A Behavioral Science Approach* (Homewood, Illinois: Richard D. Irwin, Inc., 1962).

————, *Organization Theory* (Homewood, Illinois: Richard D. Irwin, Inc., 1967).

SHANNON, CLAUDE E., and WARREN WEAVER, *The Mathematical Theory of Communication* (Urbana, Illinois: University of Illinois Press, 1949).

SHAUL, DONALD R., *The Effects of EDP on Middle Management* (Graduate School of Business Administration, University of California, Los Angeles, 1964a, doctoral dissertation).

————, "What's Really Ahead For Middle Management?" *Personnel*, November-December 1964b, pp. 8-16.

SHAW, J. C., "JOSS: Experience With An Experimental Computing Service for Users at Remote Typewriter Consoles" (Santa Monica: The RAND Corporation, May 1965).

SHEEHAN, ROBERT, "It's a New Kind of Ford Motor Company," *Fortune*, Vol. 65, February 1962.

SHERWIN, C. W., and R. S. ISENSON, "First Interim Report on Project Hindsight" (Summary), Office of the Director of Defense Research and Engineering, Department of Defense, Washington, D. C., June 30, 1966.

SHILLINGLAW, GORDON, "Profit Analysis for Abandonment Decisions," *The Journal of Business*, Vol. XXX, January 1957, pp. 17-29.

SHONFIELD, ANDREW, *Modern Capitalism: The Changing Balance of Public and Private Power* (London-New York: Oxford University Press, 1965).

SHULL, FREEMONT A., JR., *Selected Readings in Management* (Homewood, Illinois: R. D. Irwin, 1958).

SHULTZ, GEORGE P., and THOMAS L. WHISLER, eds., *Management Organization and the Computer* (Glencoe, Illinois: Free Press, 1960).

SIDERS, R. A., *et al.*, *Computer Graphics* (New York: American Management Association, Inc., 1966).

SIEGEL, IRVING H., "Technological Change and Long Run Forecasting," *Journal of Business*, Vol. XXVI, July 1953.

SIEKMAN, PHILIP, "Henry Ford and His Electronic Can of Worms," Fortune, Vol. LXXIII, February 1966.

SILK, LEONARD, *The Education of the Businessman* (New York: Committee for Economic Development, Supplementary Paper No. 11, 1960a).

————, *The Research Revolution* (New York: McGraw-Hill Book Co., Inc., 1960b).

————, *Forecasting Business Trends* (New York: McGraw-Hill Book Co., Inc., 1963).

SIMON, HERBERT A., *Administrative Behavior* (New York: The Macmillan Company, 1957a).

————, "A Comparison of Organization Theories," *Review of Economic Studies*, Vol. 20, 1952-53; reprinted in Herbert A. Simon, *Models of Man* (New York: John Wiley and Sons, Inc., 1957b).

————, "The Corporation: Will It Be Managed by Machines?" in Melvin Anshen and G. L. Bach, eds., *Management and Corporations 1985* (New York: McGraw-Hill Book Co., Inc., 1960a).

————, *The New Science of Management Decision* (New York: Harper & Row, 1960b).

SIMON, M. J., *The Law for Advertising and Marketing* (New York: W. W. Norton & Co., Inc., 1956).

SIMONNARD, MICHEL, *Linear Programming* (Englewood Cliffs, N.J.: Prentice-Hall, Inc., 1966).

SKLAR, NORMAN E., "Integrated Information Systems," in Ted Radamaker, ed., *Business Systems*, Vol. II (Cleveland, Ohio: Systems & Procedures Association, 1963).

SLOAN, ALFRED, JR., *My Years With General Motors* (Garden City, N.Y.: Doubleday and Company, Inc., 1964).

SMALTER, DONALD J., "The Influence of D-O-D Practices on Corporate Planning," *Management Technology*, Vol. 4, December 1964.

————, and RODERIC C. LANCEY, "P/E Analysis in Acquisition Strategy," *Harvard Business Review*, Vol. 44, November-December 1966, pp. 85-95.

SMIDDY, HAROLD F., "Planning, Anticipating and Managing," *Management Technology*, Vol. 4, December 1964, pp. 83-91.

A. P. Smith Manufacturing Company vs. Barlow et al., 26 N.J. Super. 106, 1953.

SMITH, ADAM, *An Inquiry into the Nature and Causes of the Wealth of Nations*, edited by Edwin Cannan (New York: The Modern Library, 1937).

SMITH, H. W., *Kamongo* (New York: The Viking Press, 1962).

SMITH, RICHARD AUSTIN, "How A Great Corporation Got Out of Control," Parts I and II, *Fortune*, January 1962 and February 1962.

SOLOMON, MARTIN B., JR., *Investment Decisions in Small Business* (Lexington: University of Kentucky Press, 1963).

SOLOMONS, DAVID, *Divisional Performance: Measurement and Control* (New York: Financial Executives Research Foundation, Inc., 1965).

SOMMERS, MONTROSE, and JEROME KERNAN, "Why Products Flourish Here, Fizzle There," *Columbia Journal of World Business*, Vol. II, March-April 1967, pp. 89-97.

SORD, BURNARD H., and GLENN A. WELSCH, *Business Budgeting, A Survey of Management Planning and Control Practices* (New York: Controllership Foundation, Inc., 1958).

————, and ————, *Managerial Planning and Control* (Austin, Tex.: University of Texas Printing Division, 1964).

SORENSEN, CHARLES E. (with SAMUEL T. WILLIAMSON), *My Forty Years With Ford* (New York: W. W. Norton, 1956).

SPECHT, R. D., "RAND—A Personal View of Its History," *Operations Research*, Vol. 8, November-December 1960, pp. 836-838.

SPENCER, MILTON H., and LOUIS SIEGELMAN, *Managerial Economics* (Homewood, Illinois: Richard D. Irwin, Inc., 1959).

SPRINGER, CLIFFORD H., ROBERT E. HERLIHY and ROBERT I. BEGGS, *Advanced Methods and Models* (Homewood, Illinois: Richard D. Irwin, Inc., 1965).

SPROWLS, R. CLAY, and MORRIS ASIMOW, "A Model of Customer Behavior for the Task Manufacturing Corporation," *Management Science*, Vol. 8, April 1962, pp. 311-324.

STANFORD RESEARCH INSTITUTE, *Corporate Development Through Diversification, Proceedings of the Client Conference, Long-Range Planning Service*, September 25-27, 1963a, mimeographed (Menlo Park, California: Stanford Research Institute).

———, *Planning Research Highlights* (Menlo Park, California: Stanford Research Institute, 1963b).

STARR, MARTIN K., "Planning Models," *Management Science,* Vol. 13, December 1966, pp. B-115-142.

STEIN, KARL H., "Resistance to Super-Scientific Management," *Economics and Business Bulletin,* Vol. 11, September 1958.

STEINER, GARY A., "The Creative Individual: His Nature and Nurture," *The McKinsey Quarterly,* Vol. 2, Winter 1966.

———, ed., *The Creative Organization* (Chicago: University of Chicago Press, 1965).

STEINER, GEORGE A., "Approaches to Long-Range Planning for Small Businesses," *California Management Review,* Vol. X, Fall 1967, pp. 3-16.

———, "Approaches to Long-Range Planning For Small Business," in Irving Pfeffer, ed., *The Financing of Small Business: A Current Assessment* (New York: Columbia University Press, 1967).

———, "Basic Approaches to Long-Range Planning," *Proceedings of the 1962 Annual Meeting of the Academy of Management* (New York: AMA, 1963a).

———, "The Critical Role of Top Management in Long-Range Planning," *Arizona Review,* April 1966; also in *Financial Executive,* July 1966a.

———, *Government's Role in Economic Life* (New York: McGraw-Hill Book Co. Inc., 1953).

———, "Improving the Transfer of Government-Sponsored Technology," *Business Horizons,* Vol. 9, Fall 1966b.

———, "Making Long-Range Company Planning Pay Off," *California Management Review,* Vol. IV, Winter 1962.

———, ed., *Managerial Long-Range Planning* (New York: McGraw-Hill Book Co., Inc., 1963b).

———, *National Defense and Southern California, 1961-1970* (Los Angeles: Southern California CED Associates, 1961).

———, "Program Budgeting, Business Contribution to Government Management," *Business Horizons,* Vol. 8, Spring 1965, pp. 43-52.

———, *Strategic Factors in Business Success* (New York: Financial Executives Research Foundation, 1968).

———, "Why and How to Diversify," *California Management Review,* Vol. VI, Summer 1964.

———, and WARREN M. CANNON, eds., *Multinational Corporate Planning* (New York: Crowell-Collier and Macmillan Company, 1966).

———, and WILLIAM G. RYAN, *Industrial Project Management* (New York: Crowell-Collier and Macmillan, 1968).

STEWART, PAUL W., and J. FREDERIC DEWHURST, *Does Distribution Cost Too Much?* (New York: The 20th Century Fund, 1939).

STEWART, ROBERT F., "A Framework for Business Planning," Report No. 162, Long Range Planning Service (Menlo Park, California: Stanford Research Institute, February 1963).

———, "Summary Tabulation of Responses, 1966 Survey of Business Planning," (Menlo Park, California: Stanford Research Institute, March 1967, mimeographed).

———, and MARION O. DOSCHER, "The Corporate Development Plan," Report No. 183

(Menlo Park, California: Industrial Economics Division, Stanford Research Institute, September 1963).

————, J. KNIGHT ALLEN and J. MORSE CAVENDER, "The Strategic Plan," Report No. 168, Long Range Planning Service (Menlo Park, California: Stanford Research Institute, April 1963).

STIEGLITZ, HAROLD, and ALLEN JANGER, *Top Management Organization in Divisionalized Companies*, Studies in Personnel Policy No. 195 (New York: National Industrial Conference Board, Inc., 1965).

————, and ————, "When the Chairman is Chief Executive," *Business Management Record*, August 1963, pp. 7-11.

STIGLER, GEORGE J., "The Cost of Subsistence," *Journal of Farm Economics*, Vol. 27, 1945, pp. 303-314.

STOCKTON, R. STANSBURY, *Introduction to Linear Programming* (Boston: Allyn and Bacon, Inc., 1960a).

————, "Linear Programming and Management," *Business Horizons*, Vol. 3, Summer 1960b.

STRAUSS, GEORGE, and LEONARD R. SAYLES, *Personnel, The Human Problems of Management* (Englewood Cliffs, New Jersey: Prentice-Hall, Inc., 1960).

SUOJANEN, WAINO W., *The Dynamics of Management* (New York: Holt, Rinehart and Winston, 1966).

————, "Management Theory: Functional and Evolutionary," *Journal of the Academy of Management*, Vol. 6, March 1963, pp. 7-17.

SUTTON, FRANCIS X., SEYMOUR E. HARRIS, CARL KAYSEN, and JAMES TOBIN, *The American Business Creed* (Cambridge: Harvard University Press, 1956).

SWALM, RALPH O., "Utility Theory—Insights into Risk Taking," *Harvard Business Review*, Vol. 44, November-December 1966, pp. 123-138.

SWEET, FRANKLYN H., *Strategic Planning: A Conceptual Study* (Austin: Bureau of Business Research, University of Texas, 1964).

SWEEZY, ELDON E., "Technological Forecasting—Principles and Techniques," in Arthur Lesser, Jr., ed., *Decision-Making Criteria For Capital Expenditures*, Papers of the 4th Summer Symposium (Hoboken, N.J.: *The Engineering Economist*, Stevens Institute of Technology, 1966).

SWEEZY, P. M., "Professor Schumpeter's Theory of Innovation," *Review of Economic Statistics*, Vol. 25, February 1943, pp. 93-96.

TAGIURI, RENATO, "Value Orientations and the Relationship of Managers and Scientists," *Administrative Science Quarterly*, Vol. 10, June 1965, pp. 39-51.

TANNENBAUM, ROBERT, IRVING R. WESCHLER and FRED MASSARIK, *Leadership and Organization: A Behavioral Science Approach* (New York: McGraw-Hill Book Co., Inc., 1961).

TAUBE, MORTIMER, *Computers and Common Sense* (New York: Columbia University Press, 1961).

TAYLOR, FREDERICK WINSLOW, *Scientific Management* (New York: Harper and Brothers Publishers, 1947).

TEAL, G. K., "Selecting Worthwhile Research Projects," in *Achieving Full Value from R&D Dollars*, AMA Management Report No. 69 (New York: American Management Association, Inc., 1962).

TERBORGH, GEORGE, *Business Investment Policy* (Washington, D.C.: Machinery and Allied Products Institutes, 1958).

TERHORST, JERALD, "The Business Role in the Great Society," *The Reporter*, October 21, 1965.

TERRY, GEORGE R., *Principles of Management* (Homewood, Ill.: Richard D. Irwin, Inc., 1956).

TERRY, HERBERT, "Comparative Evaluation of Performance Using Multiple Criteria," *Management Science*, Vol. 39, April 1963.

THEIL, H., J. BOOT, and T. KLOEK, *Operations Research and Quantitative Economics* (New York: McGraw-Hill Book Co., Inc., 1962).

THOME, P. G., and R. G. WILLARD, "The Systems Approach, A Unified Concept of Planning," *Aerospace Management*, Vol. 1, Fall-Winter 1966, pp. 25-43.

THOMPSON, STEWART, *How Companies Plan*, Research Study 54 (New York: American Management Association, Inc., 1962).

———, *Management Creeds and Philosophies*, Research Study No. 32 (New York: American Management Association, Inc. 1958).

THOMPSON, W. W. JR., *Operations Research Techniques* (Columbus, Ohio: Charles E. Merrill Books, Inc., 1967).

THURSTON, PHILIP H., *Systems and Procedures Responsibility* (Boston, Mass.: Graduate School of Business Administration, Harvard University, 1959).

———, "Who Should Control Information Systems?" *Harvard Business Review*, Vol. 40, November-December 1962, pp. 135-139.

TIETJEN, KARL H., *Organizing the Product-Planning Function*, AMA Research Study 59 (New York: American Management Association, Inc., 1963).

TILLES, SEYMOUR, "How to Evaluate Corporate Strategy," *Harvard Business Review*, Vol. 41, July-August 1963a.

———, "The Manager's Job—A Systems Approach," *Harvard Business Review*, Vol. 41, No. 1, January-February 1963b, pp. 73-81.

———, "Strategic Planning in a Dynamic Technology: The Electronics Industry," Special Commentary, The Boston Consulting Group, Inc., mimeographed, undated.

———, "Strategic Planning in the Multi-Divisional Company," Boston, Mass., Boston Safe Deposit and Trust Company, 1964 (multilithed).

TOMB, JOHN O., "A New Way to Manage—Integrated Planning and Control," *California Management Review*, Vol. 5, Fall 1962, pp. 57-62.

TUCKER, SAMUEL A., ed., *A Modern Design for Defense Decision, A McNamara-Hitch-Enthoven Anthology* (Washington, D.C.: Industrial College of the Armed Forces, 1966).

U. S. AIR FORCE, *Communications Techniques*, Air University, Extension Course Institute, 1954.

U. S. AIR FORCE SYSTEMS COMMAND, *PERT-Time System Description Manual* (Washington, D.C., 20331: Hq. AFSC, Andrews AFB, 1963).

U. S. BUREAU OF THE BUDGET, Bulletin No. 66-3, "Planning-Programming-Budgeting," October 12, 1965.

———, *Standard Industrial Classification Manual* (Washington, D.C.: U.S. Government Printing Office, 1957).

U. S. CONGRESS, JOINT ECONOMIC COMMITTEE, *Inventory Fluctuations and Economic Stabilization*, Part IV, Supplementary Study Papers, 87th Congress, 2nd Session, 1962.

U. S. DEPARTMENT OF COMMERCE, *Technological Innovation: Its Environment and Management* (Washington, D. C.: U. S. Government Printing Office, 1967).

U. S. DEPARTMENT OF DEFENSE, War Department, *Staff Officers' Field Manual*, FM 101-5 (Washington, D.C.: U.S. Government Printing Office, 1960 edition).

U. S. Department of Defense, and National Aeronautics and Space Administration, *DoD and NASA Guide Pert Cost* (Washington, D.C.: Office of the Secretary of Defense, June 1962).

U. S. House of Representatives, *Systems Development and Management* (Part 2), Hearings Before a Subcommittee of the Committee on Government Operations, 87th Congress, 2nd Session (Washington, D.C.: U. S. Government Printing Office, 1962).

U. S. Navy, *Polaris Management, Fleet Ballistic Missile Program*, Washington, D. C., Special Projects Office, Department of the Navy, Superintendent of Documents, February 1961.

United States v. Standard Oil Co. of New Jersey, 221 U.S. 1, 1911.

Univis, *Facts about Univis* (Ft. Lauderdale, Florida: Univis, Inc., 1966).

Urban, Glen L., "Sprinter: A Tool for New Product Decision Makers," *Industrial Management Review*, Vol. 8, Spring 1967, pp. 31-42.

Usry, Milton F., *Capital-Expenditure Planning and Control*, Studies in Accounting No. 1 (Austin, Texas: Bureau of Business Research, The University of Texas, 1966).

Vaile, Roland, E. T. Grether and Reavis Cox, *Marketing in the American Economy* (New York: The Ronald Press Co., 1952).

Vajda, S., *Readings in Linear Programming* (New York: John Wiley and Sons, 1958).

Valentine, Raymond F., *Performance Objectives for Managers* (New York: American Management Association, Inc., 1966).

Vatter, William J., "Capital Budget Formulae," *California Management Review*, Vol. III, Fall 1960, pp. 52-68.

Vazsonyi, Andrew, *Scientific Programming in Business and Industry* (New York: John Wiley & Sons, Inc., 1958).

Verdoorn, P. J., "Government-Industry Planning Interrelationships," in George A. Steiner and Warren M. Cannon, eds., *Multinational Corporate Planning* (New York: Crowell-Collier and Macmillan Company, 1966).

Vickers, Sir Geoffrey, *The Art of Judgment, A Study of Policy Making* (New York: Basic Books, Inc., 1965).

Villers, Raymond, *Research and Development: Planning and Control* (New York: Financial Executives Research Foundation, Inc., 1964).

Votaw, Dow, *Modern Corporations* (Englewood Cliffs, N.J.: Prentice-Hall, Inc. 1965).

Wallenstein, Gerd D., *Fundamentals of Technical Manpower Planning*, Management Bulletin 78 (New York: American Management Association, Inc., 1966).

Walsh, Francis J., Jr., *Administration of Cost Reduction Programs* (New York: National Industrial Conference Board, Inc., 1964).

———, *Internal Auditing* (New York: National Industrial Conference Board, Inc., 1963).

Walters, J. E., *The Management of Research and Development* (Washington, D.C.: Spartan Books, 1965).

Warner, W. Lloyd, *The Corporation in the Emergent American Society* (New York: Harper & Rowe, 1962).

Warren, E. Kirby, *Long-Range Planning: The Executive Viewpoint* (Englewood Cliffs, N.J.: Prentice-Hall, Inc., 1966).

———, "Where Long-Range Planning Goes Wrong," *Management Review*, May 1962, pp. 11-12.

Waterston, Albert, *Development Planning: Lessons of Experience* (Baltimore, Md.: The Johns Hopkins Press, 1965).

WATSON, THOMAS J., JR., *A Business and Its Beliefs* (New York: McGraw-Hill Book Co., 1963).

WATTEL, HAROLD L., ed., *Network Scheduling and Control Systems CAP/PERT* (Hempstead, N.Y.: Hofstra University, 1964).

WEBER, MAX, *The Protestant Ethic and the Spirit of Capitalism, 1904,* translated by Talcott Parsons (New York: Charles Scribner and Sons, 1930).

————, *The Theory of Social and Economic Organization,* translated by A. M. Henderson and Talcott Parsons, edited by Talcott Parsons (New York and London: Oxford University Press, 1947).

WEINBERG, ROBERT S., *An Analytical Approach to Advertising Expenditures Strategy* (New York: Association of National Advertisers, Inc., 1960).

————, "Management Science and Marketing Strategy," in Wroe Alderson and Stanley J. Shapiro, *Marketing and the Computer* (Englewood Cliffs, N.J.: Prentice-Hall, Inc., 1963).

————, "The Uses and Limitations of Mathematical Models for Marketing Planning," in *An Analytical Approach to Advertising Expenditures* (New York: Association of National Advertisers, Inc., 1960).

WEINER, JACK B., "The Perilous Quest for Acquisitions," *Management Review,* Vol. 54, September 1965.

————, "What Makes a Growth Company?" *Dun's Review & Modern Industry,* Vol. 84, November 1964.

WEINGARTEN, JALLA, "The Most Dangerous Game in Marketing," *Dun's Review & Modern Industry,* Vol. 90, June 1967.

WELLINGTON, C. OLIVER, "What Is a Sound Purchase Price?" in Albert Newgarden, ed., *Corporate Mergers and Acquisitions,* AMA Management Report No. 4 (New York: American Management Association, Inc., 1958). pp. 65-72.

WELSH, GLENN A., *Budgeting: Profit-Planning and Control* (Englewood Cliffs, N.J.: Prentice Hall, Inc., 1957).

WENGERT, E. S., DALE S. HARWOOD, JR., LUCIAN MARQUIS, and KEITH GOLDHAMMER, *The Study of Administration,* (Eugene, Oregon: School of Business Administration, 1961).

WESTINGHOUSE ELECTRIC CORP., *Planning and Control of Facilities Expenditures* (Pittsburgh, Pa.: Westinghouse, 1964).

————, *Westinghouse Planning Guide* (Pittsburgh, Pa.: Westinghouse Electric Corporation, 1967).

————, *1968 Planning Procedures* (Pittsburgh, Pa.: Westinghouse Electric Corporation, June 30, 1967).

WESTON, J. FRED, *Managerial Finance* (New York: Holt, Rinehart and Winston, 1962).

————, "Norms for Debt Levels," *Journal of Finance,* Vol. IX, May 1954, pp. 124-135.

————, "Planning for Corporate Merger," *California Management Review,* Vol. V, Spring 1963.

————, editor and contributor, *Procurement and Profit Renegotiation* (Belmont, Calif.: Wadsworth Publishing Company, Inc., 1960).

————, *The Role of Mergers in the Growth of Large Firms* (Berkeley and Los Angeles: University of California Press, 1961).

————, "Towards Theories of Financial Policy," Vol. X, *The Journal of Finance,* May 1955, pp. 130-143.

WHALEN, RICHARD J., "The Unoriginal Ideas that Rebuilt Crown Cork," *Fortune,* Vol. 66, October 1962.

WHEELER, BAYARD O., "Renaissance in Business Theory," *Business Review*, Vol. XXV, February 1965, pp. 43-52.

WHITE, K. K., *Financing Company Expansion*, AMA Research Study 64 (New York: American Management Association, Inc., 1964).

WHYTE, WILLIAM H., *The Organization Man* (Garden City, New York: Doubleday Anchor, 1957).

WIERZYNSKI, GREGORY H., "G.E.'s $200-Million Ticket to France," *Fortune*, Vol. LXXV, June 1967.

WILCOX, CLAIR, *Public Policies Toward Business* (Homewood, Ill.: Richard D. Irwin, Inc., 1955.

WILLIAMS, J. D., *The Complete Strategist* (New York: McGraw-Hill Book Co., Inc. 1954).

WILLIAMS, ROBERT M., ed., *UCLA Forecast for the Nation and Southern California in 1968* (Los Angeles, Calif.: Graduate School of Business Administration, UCLA, 1967).

WILLIAMSON, HAROLD F., *Winchester: The Gun That Won The West* (New York: A. S. Barnes and Company, Inc., 1963).

WILSON, CHARLES Z., and MARCUS ALEXIS, "Basic Frameworks for Decisions," *Journal of the Academy of Management*, Vol. 5, August 1962, pp. 151-164.

WOHLSTETTER, A. J., F. S. HOFFMAN, R. J. LUTZ and H. S. ROWEN, *Selection and Use of Strategic Air Bases*, R-266 (Santa Monica, California: The RAND Corporation, April 1954).

WOLFE, HARRY DEANE, JAMES K. BROWN and G. CLARK THOMPSON, *Measuring Advertising Results*, Business Policy Study, 102 (New York: National Industrial Conference Board, Inc., 1962).

WOOLWORTH, CHESTER M., "So We Made a Better Mousetrap," *The Presidents' Forum*, Fall 1962, pp. 26-27.

YOSHINO, M. Y., "So You're Setting Up Shop in Asia!" *Columbia Journal of World Business*, Vol. II, November-December 1967, pp. 61-66.

YOUNG, STANLEY, *Management: A Systems Analysis* (Glenview, Ill.: Scott, Foresman and Company, 1966).

ZARNOWITZ, VICTOR, *An Appraisal of Short-Term Economic Forecasts* (New York: Columbia University Press, 1966).

ZEIGLER, RAYMOND J., *Business Policies and Decision-Making* (New York: Appleton-Century-Crofts, 1966).

INDEXES

Index of Persons

Ackoff, Russell L., 506
Adams, Velma A., 561
Adler, Lee, 535
Aguilar, Francis Joseph, 113, 488
Albach, Horst, 453
Albrook, Robert C., 190
Alchian, Armen A., 172
Alderman, Everett, 722
Alderson, Wroe, 343, 521, 524–25, 527, 528n, 529, 546, 546n, 550
Alexander, R. S., 521
Alexander, Tom, 352
Alexis, Marcus, 325
Allen, J. Knight, 44, 238, 462
Alsberg, Carl, 716
Andersen, Theodore A., 40, 638n, 645
Andrews, Kenneth R., 238
Anshen, Melvin, 326, 509n
Ansoff, H. Igor, 249, 448, 638n, 645, 722
Anthony, Robert N., 37, 38, 42–44, 172, 238, 662n
Argyris, Chris, 187, 294
Arnoff, E. Leonard, 555
Ash, Roy L., 71, 640
Asimow, Morris, 449
Avery, Sewell, 20
Axsmith, Douglas J., 509n

Babbage, Charles, 258, 331, 494, 688
Bach G. L., 509n
Bailey, Earl L., 557, 577
Barnard, Chester, 11, 19, 252, 257, 321, 323, 325, 328, 333, 363
Barton, Richard F., 323
Bassie, V. Lewis, 208, 210, 213
Bavelas, Alex, 135
Beauvois, John J., 695n
Beer, Stafford, 391
Beise, S. C., 91
Bell, Martin L., 524n, 524–25, 528n, 533
Bennis, Warren G., 187, 313–14, 391

Berg, Thomas L., 638n
Berle, Adolph, 173–74, 178, 312
Besse, Ralph M., 7, 26n, 94, 314
Bierman, Harold, Jr., 294, 326
Blancke, Harold, 73
Blankertz, D. F., 546
Blough, Roger, 176n, 192
Blum, E. H., 407n
Boehm, Barry W., 498
Bonaparte, Napoleon, 237
Bonini, Charles P., 326, 449
Boot, J., 456
Boulding, Kenneth, 159, 223
Bowen, Howard, 176, 326
Bower, Marvin, 25, 64, 65, 238, 719
Bowman, Donald M., 338, 509n
Brady, Rodney H., 513
Branch, Melville C., 8, 127
Brandenberg, R. G., 44, 722
Breech, Ernest R., 15, 16, 81
Bright, James R. 687, 687n, 688
Brion, John M., 528n
Brooks, John, 80
Brown, Gene, 330
Brown, James K., 15, 68, 90
Buell, Victor P., 525
Buffa, Elwood S., 383, 437, 704
Burgess, William H., 68
Burlingame, J. F., 509n
Burns, Leland S., 415–16
Bursk, Edward C., 16
Busenbury, Warren, 589
Butler, William F., 213
Buzzell, Robert D., 521, 556
Byleveld, Herbert, 179

Calderwood, James D., 207–8
Campbell, Robert Moore, 218
Cannon, Warren M., 37, 53, 109, 115, 116, 180, 192, 687, 689, 695–96, 698, 727
Carlson, Bruce, 448

Subject Index

ABOUT THE AUTHOR

GEORGE A. STEINER is Professor of Management and
Public Policy and Director of the Division of Research
in the Graduate School of Business Administration at
the University of California, Los Angeles. A frequent
consultant to private companies and United States
government agencies, Professor Steiner is co-author of
Industrial Project Management and *Multinational
Corporate Planning* (both volumes of Studies of the
Modern Corporation), as well as author of more than
45 other books and articles.

This publication under the Arkville Press imprint
was set on the Linotype in Scotch #2, with display
in Bodoni Book and Optima; presswork by Noble
Offset Printers, Inc., New York; and binding by
The Book Press Incorporated, Brattleboro, Ver-
mont. It was printed on paper supplied by The
Oxford Paper Company, New York. The Colophon
was created by Theodore Roszak.

DATE DUE		
DEC 1 5	MAR 1 9 1995	
MAR 1 1 980		
MAR 1 2 '81		
MAY '81		
JUN 9 '81		
MAY 10		
MAR 29		
APR 2 6		
APR 2 4 1987		